MAKERS OF CHRISTIAN THEOLOGY IN AMERICA

MAKERS OF CHRISTIAN THEOLOGY IN AMERICA

Edited by
Mark G. Toulouse and
James O. Duke

Abingdon Press
Nashville

MAKERS OF CHRISTIAN THEOLOGY IN AMERICA

Copyright © 1997 by Abingdon Press

This book is printed on recycled, acid-free, elemental-chlorine-free paper.

Library of Congress Cataloging-in-Publication Data

Makers of Christian theology in America / edited by Mark
   G. Toulouse and James O. Duke.
         p.   cm. — (A.R.E. membership series ; ??)
   Includes bibliographical references and index.
   ISBN 0-687-00766-6 (alk. paper)
      1. Theologians—United States—Handbooks, manuals, etc.
   2. Theology, Doctrinal—United States—History—Handbooks, manuals,
   etc.   I. Toulouse, Mark G., 1952–   . II. Duke, James O.
   III. Series.
   BT30.U6M35   1997
   230'.092'273—dc21   97-18743
                                                                            CIP

Scripture quotations are from the Authorized or King James Version of the Bible.

97 98 99 00 01 02 03 04 05 06—10 9 8 7 6 5 4 3 2 1

Manufactured in the United States of America

To
Members of the Academic Community at Brite Divinity School
Faculty, Students, and Staff
Past, Present, and Future

PREFACE

Editors of a book like this one incur many debts, for without the efforts of a great many people the result you now hold in your hand could not have been accomplished. First, a special word of appreciation is due our families; both Jeffica, an educator, and Jeanne, herself a seminary graduate, value these kinds of efforts and expect us to give our best to them. More important, perhaps, both have been productive participants in their own ways through the hours of discussion surrounding this work and their willingness to offer ideas and insights related to particular problems along the way.

Nearly two dozen scholars of American religion, obviously too many to mention by name, offered comment and criticism as we worked through the very difficult task of culling the subjects for these essays down from more than two hundred prospects to the ninety-one profiles contained in the book. Those scholars know who they are and we offer here our appreciation for their contributions to the final shaping of this volume. We owe much to the seventy-five scholars who graciously consented to write for this book and then delivered high-quality work in a timely manner. The task we undertook seemed impossibly large in the beginning, but the cooperation and hard work represented in the contributions made by these scholars transformed the task into a manageable and enjoyable undertaking.

Thanks are also due both Texas Christian University and Brite Divinity School. Texas Christian University provided a study carrel in the library, enabling one of us to hide away occasionally from those administrative tasks that could wait until later in order to work on this book. Brite Divinity School provided both of us with a summer research grant to support the final editing task. We are appreciative of the many ways Brite, led by Dean Leo Perdue, provides a context that enriches the research and teaching that goes on in this place, a context that includes state-of-the-art computers and state-of-the-art support staff. The latter refers to the excellent secretarial help we continually receive from Robin Gray and Linda Hillin, both of whom displayed a gracious spirit and commendable skill in their handling of so many phases of this two-year project. Our special thanks to Robin for the tremendous work she accomplished in taking care of the mounds of paperwork occasioned by a project of this size and scope. We are also grateful to Tom Graca, a student at Brite, who served as a research assistant at the conclusion of our efforts and who worked on an index along with a few other details related to the preparation of the final manuscript. Before we leave the subject of Brite's context, we cannot fail to mention our deep appreciation for the academic community represented within the divinity school. Both of us have worked within this lively theological community for more than eleven years, and neither of us can imagine a more enlightened or engaging place to consider the theological issues raised in a book like this one. For this reason, we have dedicated this book to the faculty, students, and staff at Brite Divinity School, past, present, and future.

CONTENTS

GENERAL INTRODUCTION

MARK G. TOULOUSE AND JAMES O. DUKE

This volume offers students of religion and other interested parties a resource for understanding the still-unfolding history of Christian theology. Nearly two millennia in the making, that history has been shaped for the last five centuries in many and various ways by theologians who, working in the territory, society, and culture of the United States of America, are typically if imprecisely referred to in shorthand as "American."

To learn of American theology is by no means to know all there is about Christian theology, which began long before European colonists first carried it with them to what they called "the new world." Christian theology flourishes among Christians around the globe. Yet it is to learn of a vital aspect of American life and thought. And the development of American theology is not merely an episode in, but is also a factor of significance for, the general development of Christian theology on "spaceship earth." The character and extent of its significance are of course open questions, at times hotly disputed. This book's aim is to orient readers to the subject matter at issue rather than to plead a case.

How best to fashion such an orientation is neither obvious nor incontestable. In keeping with its aim, this one is designed in historical-theological terms. It brings together intellectual portraits of ninety-one makers of Christian theology in America from colonial times to the mid–twentieth century and an overview of theological developments thereafter, all sketched by scholars, younger and senior, noteworthy in their fields of study. This approach seeks to capitalize on strengths of current scholarship in American religious thought in a manner helpful to those who study Christian theologians in the United States.

In such a study one walks in on a discussion already in progress among Christians. This discussion has been long, extending from one generation to another for centuries, and lively, indeed, frequently contentious. Its participants are diverse; its subject matter wide-ranging and multifaceted. Any orientation to it is necessarily selective. The selectivity of this one can be justified—or not—in terms of the general reliability, balance, fairness, and accessibility of its coverage, as judged by its usefulness to those who take such matters seriously.

Even so, some explanation of its design is in order if simply to give readers advance notice of one outcome to date of the making of Christian theology in America: to know it at all well is to realize that a phrase like "makers of Christian theology" is not as simple or as straightforward as it looks. What is actually meant by theology, when is it truly Christian, and who really makes it are among the disputed issues that go into the making of theology in America. One concern in fashioning this book has been to help show how and why this is so.

Broadly speaking, references to "makers of Christian theology" pose two distinct but interrelated difficulties. First, each word of the phrase carries an ambiguous and historically variable range of meaning. Second, American Christianity is so strikingly heterogeneous that any gains made by the effort to fix the meanings of the terms entail certain losses as well. The coping strategy followed here involves a process of weighing a variety of considerations and then making trade-offs in hopes of optimal net results.

A few of these considerations require mention. The Christianity that arrived in America was the religious faith of numerous, diverse communities. Each invariably understood itself to be Christian, belonging to the one true church of Jesus Christ, but frequently doubted the authenticity of others. Immigration patterns, internal disputes, efforts to create or re-create true Christianity, as well as racial-ethnic, social, cultural, and political differences (often termed today "nontheological" factors) spawned countless other such communities.

In addition, despite—indeed perhaps because of—the separation of church and state in the new Republic, the intermingling of pervasive national or cultural ideals and generically Christian (sometimes referred to as "Judeo-Christian") commitments has produced in and alongside communities of Christian faith what sociologists and historians term an American "civil religion." Its Christianness is now and again a matter of debate. Finally, the strain of individualism in Christianity and even more in the American ethos has led countless individuals to detach themselves from church affiliation while maintaining a faith—in God, beliefs, or values— which in their view Christians should recognize as no less truly Christian than that of the "organized churches." No one volume can represent adequately all those individuals and groups in the United States who lay claim to the name Christian.

The word "theology" is likewise complex. Its Greek root, *theos* + *logos*, has to do with speaking of—and so too giving an account of—God and things of God. Gaining currency among early Christians, the term quickly acquired various levels and shades of meaning. Even if the Christian idea of God per se might be called "theology proper," theology as a whole had to embrace the objects, the "realities," of Christian belief, hope, and love. For the vast majority of Christians coming to America, theology's primary concern was to set forth the doctrines (teachings) of the church in terms of such key headings as God, Jesus Christ, the Holy Spirit, creation, providence, human nature, sin, and salvation, the nature and purpose of the church, and eschatology ("last things," regarding the ultimate fulfillment of God's purposes). These conventional and systematic topics of the doctrinal tradition, however, might be divided and subdivided in various ways. They might also be expanded, adding, for example, discussions of theology's sources, norms, authorities, and methods, as well as conversation about church teachings with regard to morality (moral doctrine, ethics).

Accent on theology as doctrinal tradition has long been joined with a corresponding accent on theologians as "teachers of the faith" speaking to and for the church. Christian theologians are the church's theologians, members of the faith community devoted—and frequently trained and authorized—to clarify, preserve, defend, guide, and as necessary revise the teachings of the church in light of faithfulness to the will of God. Every list of theologians includes preachers, teachers, and scholars of the churches or their equivalent—sage, holy, inspiring, or otherwise gifted guides and leaders of the community. And while the theologies of these theologians are communicated in many ways, theology itself is often thought of as writings to and for the church regarding its doctrinal tradition.

From early on, however, other uses of the word "theology"—some more limited and others more expansive—can be found, even among Christians. On the one hand, the "study of theology" offered in schools or modeled on such instruction is often taken as essential for a theologian. The turn to critical thinking in science, philosophy, history, and theology beginning in the seventeenth and eighteenth centuries along with the "professionalization" of ministers and educators in the nineteenth century further contributed to defining theology in terms of critical scholarly studies. In light of such developments, theologians and theologies have become terms often applied to "specialists" regardless of church affiliation or explicit avowal of the Christian faith. This remained true even as concern arose to distinguish Christian theology from such other "fields of study" as philosophy of religion, social science, and comparative religion, the phenomenology of religion, or the history of religions.

On the other hand, there persists in American Christianity an ancient tradition that theology is in a profound sense a matter of Christian life itself. Many have argued that theology is best represented through lives formed and shared by participation in the Christian community and is exhibited as much, or even more, by feelings, attitudes, or practices as by statements of belief or learning. Inasmuch as a Christian "knowing of God and of things of God" is a practical wisdom and way of life, not to be confused with formal training, methodological rigor, or intellectual sophistication, the church's theologians are neither primarily nor necessarily those regarded as official, learned, professional, or scholarly.

These meanings of theology often significantly and harmoniously overlap. The personal diaries of colonial Puritans as well as much of nineteenth-century genteel literature, for example, bear witness to Christian convictions—typically "orthodox" convictions—with regard to God, providence, sin, salvation, faith, grace, and good works as truly as do the scholarly tomes of the church's university-trained "divines." And popular, devotional, or practical works of theology often circulate alongside and complement the more distinctively churchly, critical, academic, or specialized theological writings.

At other times, however, members of the church contest the very features so commonly assumed to distinguish "theology" as a learned profession from the popular piety of prayers, preaching, and other everyday testimonies to faith. Indeed, one dynamic in the making of theology in America is a running polemic against established theologians and their theologies. The protests are at times made that these are not truly Christian, truly churchly, or truly theological and at times made on related or equally forceful grounds such as elitism, artificiality, abstruseness, or irrelevance. Evaluating such protests is by no means an exact science: are they rhetorical strategies, unvarnished anti-intellectualism, both, or none of the above—something else again? Perhaps the most intriguing, and vexing, of cases are those of erudite, scholarly Christian theologians who publish warnings against erudition, scholarship, and even theology itself.

The term "makers" here has to do with those whose thinking and acting has been formative for the direction and shape of Christian theological history. It emphasizes activity, both in thought and in deed, representing well the activism associated with all aspects of life in the United States. The meaning of the word "makers" is bound up with perhaps the most commonplace but troublesome of conceptual tools in the historian's toolbox—the notion of influence. Estimating someone's claim to fame or blame as a maker of American theology is perhaps most readily calculated by a strictly normative definition of Christian theology. The narrower the definition, the more precise its applications. Critical historians and theologians, however, generally resort to a more broad-based, and quasi-utilitarian, quasi-statistical standard of measure, seeking out those who "influenced" most of the people most of the time. Of course, at least some other critical historians contest such estimates. Others warn that giving priority to those with "the most influence on most people most of the time" is a surefire way to discount or distort the diversity and complexity of Christian theology in America.

Each position has its point. Though "balancing" so many alternatives is out of the question, an orientation can be expected to alert readers to this built-in difficulty of the study of the history of theology. Some theologians count among the makers of American theology precisely because they were representative of numerically or culturally dominant groups of Christians. Others who gained smaller audiences, however, were nonetheless significant in forming the mosaic as a whole. Then, too, theologians famous during their lifetimes were sometimes soon forgotten and never called to mind thereafter, while others virtually ignored by contemporaries presaged later theological developments of widespread interest. Still others, denied educational opportunities, official standing, and just acclaim because of prejudice alone, are excluded from an orientation to American theology only at the price of compounding one historical injustice by another.

All things considered, then, identifying the makers of Christian theology in America is an approximation of an approximation, and bound to upset almost every reader in some way or another. Although too vast to be covered comprehensively, the diversity of Christian thought demands broad, representative treatment. Acknowledgment is due the persistence of the themes of doctrinal tradition, along with the forces and lives bent on expanding or revising the tradition, as well as writings on these topics inviting restudy (or rediscovery) and reinterpretation over time. Primary weight has been given here to these considerations, and to the figures and topics least likely to be denied recognition by scholars seeking an orientation, suitable in size and approach for general use, to the making of Christian theology in America. These are names usually included in standard courses and texts, or would be as occasion allows. At the same time, these figures are to be reckoned with even in scholarship which, re-envisioning the story of American Christianity, proposes replacing them with thinkers and thoughts

17

deemed more truly Christian, truly theological, and truly memorable. Readers will therefore find here accounts of many luminaries as well as quite a few of the subluminaries in the history of American Christianity and its study.

Even so, primary attention does not—should not—mean exclusive attention. Among the "makers" of Christian theological discussion must be included a sampling of notable dissenters, outliers, or renegades from established churches and conventional patterns of theology. To be broadly inclusive of such thinkers is neither possible nor advisable: Christians as such and Christian theologians in particular are to be distinguished from others with religious, intellectual, or cultural interests and influence. Nonetheless, this book gives the nod to a few whose dissent was very much a homegrown product of concerns arising within the churches. In the beginning, their dissent arose because of patently Christian theological sensitivities. In the end, their influence testifies to the variegated state of "church doctrine" itself. To exclude every such "contestable" name—for example, Elihu Palmer, Ralph Waldo Emerson, Margaret Fuller, Marcus Garvey, and William James—for the sake of someone's sense of definitional purity would be to ignore some of the most fateful test cases in the making of Christian theology in America.

Orientations designed along lines other than the historical-theological approach represented here are of course possible, including some which break with or cut across the key categories—traditions, churches, and denominations, doctrines of faith and morals, movements, schools, and trends of thought, and the like. Such efforts are prominent features of current scholarship, and telltale signs of creative ferment in the study of American religious thought appear in various of the essays. This book's design, however, is purposely midrange, neither macro in the sense of reframing and reordering the elements of Christian theology along extra-Christian or extra-theological lines, nor micro in the sense of dividing those elements into units particularized or refined for apt use in cutting-edge denominational, regional, or local histories. The editorial wager here is that those reexamining the history of Christian theology in America in self-consciously "revisionistic" terms will find it helpful to have at hand the resources offered here.

Like the selection process itself, decisions about the placement and length of articles reflect certain trade-offs. The portraits are set in galleries devoted to "eras" in American history—Colonial (1607–1789), National (1789–1865), Post–Civil War and New Intellectual Frontier (1866–1918), Modern (1918–1965), and Recent Times (since 1965). A division of this

18

sort is of course commonplace, and is best considered handy rather than definitive. Two points nonetheless deserve comment. The first concerns the handling of theology in the "colonial era" and in "recent times." The colonial portraits are illustrative not of the transplanting of the faith and churches of Christianity to American soil but of transitions in Christian theology which, taking root in the colonies, were points of departure and debate for theologians thereafter. Recent times are covered not by a set of portraits but in an overview by a renowned surveyor of the scene, Martin E. Marty. Second, the lives and works of some theologians span and, as it were, defy the timeline markers. In such cases, the figures are set in the era of either their first or their most notable activity.

The bottom-line judgment with regard to amount of coverage was to give every "maker" a reasonably ample showing (at least four pages) rather than merely brief mention. Most essays are vignette-sized, between six and twelve pages; a few others are somewhat longer. The space apportioned to one individual or another smacks of "favoritism," even though at least some decisions seem to be foregone conclusions—for example, is there a maker of Christian theology in America who really "merits" a few more lines of coverage than, say, Jonathan Edwards? In truth, judgments in this regard were made to ensure or balance breadth and depth of coverage rather than to signal invidious comparisons among theology's "all-stars." From an editorial viewpoint, more painful and regrettable than distributing paragraphs among these ninety-one theologians was the necessity of making some close and tough calls that exclude a number of other worthy names. It seems only fair to note that most if not all of our portraitists would have welcomed a larger canvass than that supplied them and that each pressed to say everything needful—and well—within the limited space allotted them.

These authors are notable field-specialists, expert observers of their subjects. While working independently, each has sought to comment on (1) basic biographical data regarding the life, career, and principal writings of the person; (2) the key theological issues and concerns to which the figures responded; (3) the important theological themes advanced by the figure; and (4) the thinker's impact on American theology, short-term and long-term. They have been free to deal with these matters according to their own best judgment and in their own style and voice. The result is a large, rich, and complex tapestry which, precisely because it is not altogether seamless, seems to be as honest and serviceable an orientation as possible.

THE COLONIAL ERA

(1607–1789)

INTRODUCTION

Mark G. Toulouse and James O. Duke

Colonists, mainly from western Europe, brought Christian theology to the lands of today's United States. Except for outposts of Russian Orthodoxy along the northwest Pacific coast, the theology they transplanted was as distinctly Western as they themselves were, the products of the formation and re-formation of European Christendom over many centuries. These Christians typically spoke of their faith in normative rather than strictly descriptive terms—theirs was the one true religion, the one true church, the one true theology. Religious zeal, ethnic pride, and airs of cultural superiority often intermingled. The mixture, fortified by quite this-worldly concerns, was volatile as well as potent, fueling manifold works of love for God and neighbor on the one hand and outbursts of intolerance, persecution, and warfare on the other. For the colonists' failures to distinguish these two sorts of activities clearly and consistently, Native Americans were to suffer even more than the Christians themselves.

To most of these new Americans, the word "theology" meant above all the church's doctrines (public teachings) of the Christian message. These set forth "the way, the truth, and the life" that God had made known in the law, the prophets, and finally and fully in Jesus Christ. Theologies dealt then with the content of the faith to which God called sinful humanity to affirm and to practice, the one faith pleasing to God and so too the power and hope of salvation. Theologians were those the Christian churches acknowledged as teachers of this message, and as teachers of such teachers especially.

Yet the Christianity arriving in America was manifestly diverse. This was true in the case of the late-medieval (Roman) Catholic Church. A communion of communions, it was a body united on many points, including respect for the teaching authority (magisterium) of the papacy, while embracing striking and even discordant variations of belief and practice. Its importation to the new world displays marked internal differentiations by nation (Spanish, Portuguese, French, and English) and by the character of its missionary orders (Franciscans, Dominicans, Jesuits, Recollects, Sulpicians, et al.). Protestantism was then, as it is now, a generic term for a variety of churches arising directly or indirectly from the movements of protest and renewal known as the sixteenth-century Reformation. Thus the normative claims on behalf of "the one true theology" of "the one true church" were made by and for many differing theologies of many differing churches.

The multiplicity of churches in the era of colonization is now customarily sorted into five general categories or traditions: Roman Catholic, Lutheran, Reformed, Anglican, and "Radical" (which itself encompasses strikingly varied groups). Representatives of all of them made their way to the new world. Over time each tradition contributed in its own way to the development of Christian theology in America. The coexistence and hybridization of so many types of Christianity was itself a key factor in that development. Within what would become the territorial United States, however, the colonial "makers" of Christian theology—in the term's primary sense at the time and with wide and continuous, long-term impact—emerged from the ranks of England's Reformers. Various factors apart from any judgments about the quality of their theology combined to make this so.

For Roman Catholic makers of theology per se, one is drawn to the main areas of settlement outside the territorial United States—the Spanish in Central and South America, the Portuguese in Brazil, and the French Catholics in Canada. In these areas Catholicism gained critical mass and with it social, cultural, and political as well as religious influence that had significant effects on the making of Christian theology worldwide. Bartolomé de las Casas and others of New Spain called for doctrinal revision recognizing the humanity of native Americans and exposing injustices of colonial rule. In New France, the Ursuline Marie de l'Incarnation (Marie Guyard) joined contemplative and activist strands of Catholic spirituality in ways comparable to others recognized not only as saints but as "doctors" (teachers) of the church. Here too appear noteworthy test cases of the indigenization and acculturation of theology.

Roman Catholic settlement inside the borders of today's United States was geographically vast. The rich heritage of colonial Catholic spirituality lives on in the churches, ethos, and culture of large numbers of people and many regions of the nation. Even so, these original settlements were very much frontier outposts, too small, scattered, and remote to play strong roles in doctrinal development. The relentless expansion of Protestants during the colonial era and beyond turned these outposts into virtual enclaves.

In addition, Roman Catholicism identified its theologians mainly as teachers of its teachers—bishops, leaders of religious orders, university-trained scholars. Neither secular priests, nor men and women in religious orders, nor well-informed laity were likely to claim they were theologians. Even those qualified by education or position to make such a claim were, like colonials generally, viewed with a degree of condescension if not disdain by their European peers.

To be sure, throughout this period and in some instances beyond, much the same holds for the Protestant churches from many lands planted in the "original thirteen" English colonies that formed the United States. Small in numbers and preoccupied with survival, these groups loyally sought to maintain their religious heritage, adapting their teaching of the faith as occasion required. But they were in little position to engage as equal partners in churchwide debates over theological doctrine.

In this context, the "Puritans" of New England claim a distinctive place in the making of Christian theology in America. Their theologies are of course among America's earliest—and most controversial, formative of a theological heritage praised and repudiated by large numbers throughout this nation's history. Their settlement was of a size and character such that it supported in addition to other forms of theology (e.g., devotional books, moral tracts, sermons, poetry) numerous writings similar in genre, subject matter, and often scholarly erudition to those classified as theology without qualification in the old world. Further, one finds here not merely, as in other cases, an extension of religiosity leading gradually over time to "American" reshapings of Christian theology, but the removal of a sizable portion of the personnel and resources of England's Reformed tradition to a foreign setting.

Puritan piety valued sound doctrine as well as purity of worship and morality. Its congregational polity vested teaching authority in its local-church ministers, even while it encouraged a theologically well-informed laity. Its teachers of the faith came to America's "wilderness" schooled not only in the study of scripture and Reformed theology generally but in the texts of use to Reformed thinkers in debate with other theologians. Some provision was made early on for a learned ministry in precisely this sense, with the founding of Harvard College in 1636 and the pattern of apprentice study under veteran pastors.

The term "puritanism" arose as a catchword in the long (1527–1689) and turbulent course of the Reformation in England. It came into use,

23

apparently as a term of derision, following the religious settlement under Elizabeth I for those insistent on purifying the church of worship traditions deemed remnants of Roman Catholicism. It soon expanded to cover as well associated commitments to a church purified by interpreting the doctrines of the Church of England along Reformed lines, stressing for example an inward experience of God's unmerited grace, a zeal for holy, godly living among its members, and a form or forms of church government and discipline in keeping with these aims.

Doctrinally, the movement upheld themes characteristic of the Reformed tradition which, from its sixteenth-century beginnings in Swiss cities (e.g., Ulrich Zwingli and Heinrich Bullinger in Zürich, Martin Bucer in Strasbourg and later in England, and John Calvin and Theodore Beza in Geneva) spread widely, into France, sections of Germany and Eastern Europe, the Netherlands, Scotland, and England. Given this tradition's diverse origins and outcomes, the custom of calling it "Calvinism" is more handy than precise. Yet Calvin's legacy is evident in the notable family resemblances of doctrine among the many and varied Reformed churches: the sovereignty of God, the sinful fallenness of humanity, salvation by God's grace in Christ received through faith, predestination and reprobation, obedience to God's biblical commands for Christian living, conformity in all essential matters to the faith and order of the apostolic church, and a transformist impulse to direct societies and nations as well as individuals along the paths of righteousness.

The contest for the soul—and control—of the Church of England, involving times of persecution and civil war, added churches to the Reformed family. By the mid–seventeenth century, Puritans had despaired of a reformed episcopate. But the movement embraced Presbyterians and Congregationalists, the latter subdividing into Independents or Non-separatists who remained within the Church of England in hopes of its eventual reform, and Separatists who abandoned the notion of state-connection in favor of communities of God's faithful, free of worldly attachments. Separatists, however, followed no one path. Along with separatist Congregationalists were both Particular (predestinarian) and General (nonpredestinarian) Baptists, the Society of Friends or Quakers, and countless other (most short-lived) groups of "radicals." Untold numbers gave up on organized churches and patterns of set doctrine in order to set out on personal quests for God.

Here theological biographies of four Puritan immigrants to America—John Cotton, Thomas Hooker, Anne Hutchinson, and Roger Williams—afford glimpses of commonplace themes as well as deep faultlines of instability and tension within this theological tradition. They are also the first of many offering evidence that theology is never solely religious or intellectual but inescapably bound up with social, cultural, political, economic, and various other factors.

Each figure sparked controversy. All but Cotton passed, voluntarily or involuntarily, through the Massachusetts Bay colony to other regions. Hooker's teaching in Hartford colony remained in solidarity with "the orthodox" elsewhere. Williams moved away to Providence, Rhode Island, and more radical views—becoming first a Baptist and then an avowed seeker. Puritan patriarchalism forbade considering Hutchinson a teacher of the church, though New Testament reference to Priscilla was precedent (as she reminded her opponents) for the "home school" church instruction she offered. Since she produced no theological writings, is she ipso facto no theologian? Before answering yes, consider: One of the complaints against her was that she, a woman, acted as though she were a teacher of the faith competent to challenge the teaching of the church's teachers. The conduct unbecoming one of her sex that she was charged with was the conduct of a theologian.

Cotton Mather, a truly transitional figure at the turn of the century, is, along with the several eighteenth-century theologians featured here, illustrative of tradition in transit, its survival through metamorphosis. Mather was Puritan by bloodline and conviction. Even after Anglican Britain had wrested the Bay colony from Puritan control, Mather sought to keep "the New England way" alive by memorializing its past and urging loyalists to remain steadfast. In so doing, he at times adapted the tradition to changing times, reformulating its central claims in new terms. The new terms he chose were reflective of two fast-spreading transatlantic movements, Pietism and the Enlightenment.

The eighteenth century was at once the age of reason and of pietism or evangelical revivalism. Alliances and conflicts of (by now "traditional") post-Reformation orthodoxy, pietistic fervor, and enlightened "new learning" were characteristic of the day. Theologians of the New England and mid-Atlantic colonies told of here are case studies of developments throughout the century that reshaped not only the religious life but the doctrinal tradition of Protestantism as a whole.

Enlightenment thought celebrated the light of reason. The works of "founders" of "modern" philosophy and science such as René Descartes, Francis Bacon, Isaac Newton, and John Locke offered models of critical reasoning, scientific inquiry, and advances of human knowledge that for ever-increasing numbers of people promised to dispel ignorance and superstition and set the world on the path of progress to wisdom, peaceableness, prosperity, and happiness. For church theologians, this modern thought was a two-edged sword. On the one side, it was dangerous—distrustful of authorities of the past, doggedly questioning, and proud of the "ennobling" power of human reason. Its spirit and its results challenged at many points what the church faithful had long assumed or accepted without question. On the other side, it was learning of immense appeal and practical use. And it made available new resources for showing that Christianity's God-given message, if rightly identified by careful investigation and cleansed of human errors, was intelligible and true.

Equally multifaceted, Pietism typically stressed that authentic Christianity was a religion of the heart—a passionate relationship with God, an inward experience of God's mercy toward sinners, and a commitment to devout and righteous living. Themes such as these were mainstays of Reformed theology generally and Puritanism in particular. For them, the "founder" of Pietism within German Lutheranism, Philipp Jacob Spener, and his associates tapped into not only that tradition but Christian mysticism, spirituality, and devotion as well as Luther and the scriptures. In the evangelical awakening of Great Britain, associated with the names of George Whitefield, the Countess of Huntingdon, and John and Charles Wesley, pietists undertook a renewal of Anglicanism and the (now Nonconformist) churches descended from Puritanism.

Periodic "seasons of harvest" occurred independently in America, most notably the 1734 revival in the Northampton church of Jonathan Edwards. But after George Whitefield's midcentury tours of the colonies and "the first Great Awakening," pietistic emphases on heartfelt religion, moral earnestness, and revivalism became marked features of Protestant church life. In some cases, personal experiences of rebirth, the indwelling Christ, and the outpouring of the spirit led to radical departures from orthodoxy. The failure to receive such blessings led some to despair of their salvation, or give up on religion. But to Edwards, and many others elsewhere, pietism was understood to be supportive—indeed, exemplary—of the faith taught in scripture and doctrinal tradition.

In these instances, pietistic theologies were characterized less by new doctrines than by the reworking and re-coloring of well-known themes. Old terms were spoken of in new accents: Faith is fiery feeling as well as assent to and trust in Christian truth, justification by grace through faith is a "born again" experience, sanctification is a quest for devotional and moral purity, the church is the society of those regenerated by the Spirit and disciplined in their obedience to the will of God. The creative, complex synthesis of Reformed, Pietist, and Enlightenment elements in the writings of Edwards surely goes far to account for his reputation as a theologian.

For many schooled in post-Reformation Protestant confessionalisms, however, Pietism and Enlightenment brought hard choices. Given its emphasis on experience, feeling, and moral rigor, pietistic religion was tempted to consider theological doctrine itself a secondary matter, its technicalities hardly worth disputing. Even so, dispute over the relationship of God's role and the human's role in the conversion experience was unavoidable: The debate between Whitefield the Calvinist and Wesley the Arminian in England was to be replayed over and over and in countless variations on the American scene. At the same time, Pietism raised issues of ecclesiology. Was the church on earth composed of God's saints, reborn and visibly holy, or a "mixed company" of saints and sinners alike, knit together by ties of Christian family and church worship, confession, and sacraments into an organic society?

These issues were by no means new. They appear in the New Testament itself and often thereafter in the history of theology. They were of pressing concern to Reformed theologians, and to Puritans especially. Behind these questions, and driving them to the surface first in one place and form and then again in some other, was an even more basic tension that sought release. If God's grace (gift) in Jesus Christ is truly mercy toward sinners, unmerited and unconditional, what role if any do human decisions and efforts and activities, including the work of the church itself, play in this drama of destiny—life or death, blessing or curse, salvation or damnation? Nearly all the colonial theologians covered here attempt in one way or another to answer to these questions. Their preoccupation with the questions themselves even more than their varied attempts to answer them reveals the continuity of tradition from first-generation Puritanism in America through Edwards and beyond.

The effects of Enlightenment thought on these and other doctrinal debates were not long in coming. But they were hard to measure with assurance, always still unfolding and mixed, depending on which currents of the new learning were taken into account. Perhaps the most notable effect over time was global: the terms of theological debate were modified. Although the claims and counterclaims of tradition were often restated, both were vulnerable now to challenge with respect to their historical accuracy, logical coherence, and scientific and philosophical credibility. And Enlightenment views of the perfections of nature and nature's God—lawful orderliness, benevolence, justice, harmony, and respect for human dignity, freedom, and responsibility, to name only a few—tilted the theological discussion in favor of those giving "reasonable" explanations for God's scheme of redemption.

Varied responses to the situation are on display in the theologians recounted here. In the case of Samuel Johnson, the appeal of enlightened learning in England provoked serious second thoughts about Puritanism's quarrel with Anglican tradition and as a result, a return to the doctrine and ministry of the established church. Charles Chauncy's efforts to defend "old side" Congregationalism against what he saw as individualistic and emotional disorders of revivalism were rooted in firm convictions about the rational consistency, justice, and benevolence of God's dealings with errant human creatures. Following those convictions to their "logical" conclusion, he himself was led to question the traditional Reformed doctrine of predestination.

For Samuel Hopkins and others of the "New Divinity" school, the attempt to defend the "Calvinism" of Edwardsean thought entailed re-defining—often very subtly—much of that tradition's terminology. The movement's doctrinal subtleties, however, were in alignment with a reemphasis on moral activism: love for God meant also benevolence toward all those created by God, and hence opposition to slavery. John Woolman, a Quaker, reveals the teaching of what Hopkins called "disinterested benevolence" by life-example, apart from subtleties of doctrine or even much concern for formal statements of doctrine at all. His journal is a prime example of "theology as autobiography."

John Witherspoon, passing from Scotland to Princeton College, forged an alliance between the Scottish enlightenment and Presbyterian doctrine. The dilemma of earnest Christians faced with discrepancies between God-given revealed religion and God-given reason is dramatized in the career of Elihu Palmer who, after his study of theology and a year in Presbyterian ministry, switched his allegiance from church orthodoxy to Deism, a faith in the principles of a purely natural, and rational, religion. The relationship between revelation and reason has remained a dominant theme throughout American religious history.

Thomas Hooker

(1586–1647)

Charles E. Hambrick-Stowe

The title of Puritan pastor-theologian Thomas Hooker's magnum opus, *The Application of Redemption* (posthumous, 1656), epitomizes his approach to theology. For him, as for Puritans generally, theology was soteriology—the doctrine of salvation.

Hooker is known as the founder of Hartford and the colony of Connecticut, where he settled in 1636 after three years in Massachusetts. A primary architect of New England's congregational ecclesiology, he advised the civil magistrates who composed the *Fundamental Orders of Connecticut* (1638). Although not a promoter of democracy, he implemented the theory that under God the people have the right to elect their own governors in both church and state. As the title of his huge two-volume work suggests, however, Hooker's primary concern was for the salvation of souls. Other compilations of Hooker sermons went through many London editions, including *The Soules Humiliation* (1637), *The Soules Ingrafting into Christ* (1637), *The Unbeleevers Preparing for Christ* (1638), *The Christians Two Chiefe Lessons, Viz. Selfe-Deniall, And Selfe-Tryall* (1640), and *The Paterne of Perfection* (1640). These writings focus on the spiritual mechanics by which God works in human experience to save sinners from eternal punishment and to elevate them into glory. The task of theology was to analyze and describe God's application of grace to the elect (those chosen for redemption), through the death and resurrection of the Son of God.

Hooker's salvation-centered theology was for him no mere intellectual exercise. Nor was he unique among Puritans for making the work of Christ the hallmark of his preaching. Like many other first-generation New Englanders, Hooker spoke out of the personal experience of wrestling with God and finding peace through submission, forgiveness, and the gift of grace. Biblical faith thus combined with personal experience to produce a practical theology designed for the pulpit. Theology was the handmaid of evangelism.

Thomas Hooker was born in Leicestershire, England, in 1586 during the benevolent reign of Elizabeth I. He matriculated at Queens College of Cambridge University in 1604, soon transferring to Cambridge's most zealously Puritan college, Emmanuel. At Emmanuel, worship was conducted in the "plain style," with psalm singing, extemporaneous prayer, and powerful sermons instead of the *Book of Common Prayer*'s formal liturgy. A "spiritual brotherhood" of scholars, including William Ames, whose *Medulla Theologica* (1623) influenced every New England pastor, built on the tradition of John Calvin to develop the Puritan expression of Reformed theology. Hooker earned his B.A. (1608) and M.A. (1611), teaching as a fellow from 1609 to 1618.

At Cambridge Hooker realized that an intellectual understanding of theology was inadequate for one who would preach the gospel. Anxiety and then horror for his sinfulness seized his soul. Terrified at the prospect of damnation, in humiliation before the righteousness of God, he finally knew for himself God's forgiving grace through the death of Christ and the joy of adoption into the new covenant. Other Puritans recorded similar conversions in their journals, and these became the existential basis of New England Puritan theology. Hooker's experience qualified him for his first pastoral employment, as private chaplain in a household where he counseled a prominent woman suffering from spiritual despair. Hooker not only led the woman to salvation, but married one of her attendants, Susannah Garbrand, in 1621.

After preaching for a time in London and Dedham, Hooker accepted a call as lecturer at Chelmsford in Essex. Here he appreciated the spiritual vitality of a fellowship of committed believers, which came to think of itself as "Mr. Hooker's Company," and his understanding of congregational polity began to take shape. From the Essex pulpit he expounded in a systematic way the process by which God works "the application of redemption" in the souls of sinners. Transcriptions of these sermons were published as books, without his approval, after Hooker was in New England in the mid-1630s. In 1627 Hooker wrote a preface to *The Doctrine of Faith* by his Dedham friend John Rogers in which he outlined the "order of salvation." Hooker described conversion in terms that combined psychological and biblical categories: vocation (including both eternal election and existential calling), the anguish of contrition and humiliation as "preparation" for faith, the experience of faith itself, along with the theological stages of justification, sanctification, and glorification.

Although he had powerful supporters like the Earl of Warwick, others in the Church of England identified Hooker as a troublemaking nonconformist who should be silenced. William Laud, bishop of London under Charles I, closed down Puritan lectureships and restricted the hiring of private chaplains. When Laud compelled Hooker to appear before him in 1629, Hooker used the London trip to publish *The Poor Doubting Christian Drawne Unto Christ* and to initiate plans for leaving England. The Massachusetts Bay Company urged him to join the migration to New England, but after a stint as a schoolmaster, Hooker opted for the Netherlands. His 1631 farewell sermon, *The Danger of Desertion* (1641), was a scathing indictment of Stuart England's faithlessness to God.

In Amsterdam, Hooker became embroiled in the Puritan debate over presbyterian and congregational church polity. The faction of the English Reformed church supporting Hooker's call as assistant to pastor John Paget refused to accept the authority of synods, with some tending toward congregational separatism. Hooker's *Answers to the XX Questions by John Paget* (1631) carved out the middle position known as "nonseparating congregationalism," which would come to flower in New England. Hooker believed congregations had authority to call pastors and administer church life within the context of a wider covenant with other congregations, which would meet in advisory synods as occasion required. Children of non–church members were not to be baptized, setting the church off as a communion of visible saints. After a decade of experience in New England, Hooker described this model in mature detail in *A Survey of the Summe of Church Discipline* (1648). When the Amsterdam classis barred Hooker from preaching, he became the assistant pastor of an English congregation at Delft. At this time he published *The Souls Preparation for Christ* (1632) and a preface to William Ames' *A Fresh Suit Against Ceremonies* (1633), in which Hooker rejected as unscriptural the practices of wearing the surplice, kneeling at communion, and making the sign of the cross in baptism.

Plans for Puritan colonies in New England, far from the reach of Bishop Laud (soon-to-be Archbishop of Canterbury), became compelling to Hooker. In spring 1633 he was back in England arranging passage for his family, a group of former parishioners which would become the nucleus of his congregation, and his new associate pastor Samuel Stone. Hooker—and John Cotton, who also sailed on the *Griffin*—boarded the ship in disguise to escape Laud's agents. In Massachusetts, Hooker and Stone settled with their congregation in Newtown (Cambridge), while Cotton became teacher of the Boston church.

31

Hooker soon contemplated a move west, however, complaining of the need for more land. Theological differences between Hooker and Cotton also precipitated the migration to Hartford in 1636. Cotton initiated the requirement of a "test of a relation"—oral testimony of a conversion experience—for church membership, which became standard among the New England churches. Hooker believed in the "gathered church" congregational ideal, but, arguing for "the judgment of charity," he warned against "curious inquisitions and niceties" in the admission process (*Survey of the Summe of Church Discipline*, III, 6). Hooker discerned preparatory stages of the salvation experience prior to the flowering of faith, and for him growth in grace within the church covenant after justification was as important as a decisive moment of conversion. God's work of redemption through what Puritans called the "means of grace"—the ordinances of worship, the Lord's Supper, Bible reading and meditation, family and individual prayer, and pastoral care—was a progressive process in the soul.

Hooker detected in Cotton a more stringent spirituality that emphasized the immediacy of free grace completely without human participation. For Hooker and most other New England pastors, sanctification (holiness of life) could be taken as a sign or evidence of justification. Some of Cotton's followers, especially the group that gathered at the home of radical spiritualist Anne Hutchinson, charged that this amounted to legalism or works righteousness, nothing but a covenant of works. Hooker returned to Boston to participate in the trial of Anne Hutchinson on the charge of "antinomianism." He opposed her unhinging of ethics and human participation from the work of the Holy Spirit, but also deplored the vindictive spirit of the synod that condemned the Hutchinsonians.

In Hartford Hooker preached his theology of conversion and sought to build a church and colony where godliness could flourish. Employing the logical method of Peter Ramus learned at Cambridge and a horticultural metaphor found in the Bible, he divided "the application of redemption" into two parts, preparation of the soul for salvation and the implantation (or engrafting) of the soul into Christ. The primary "means" by which God prepared the soul was not (as Hutchinson taught) the immediate work of the Holy Spirit but the Spirit working through a "plain and powerful ministry." Hooker denied that individuals could prepare themselves for salvation but insisted they were involved in the process. God was the "principal cause" turning them to Christ, and the ministry of the Word was the "instrumental cause." Through attendance at sermons and such activity as meditation on scripture, sinners would come to recognize their desperate need of salvation.

Hooker's vivid sermons were graphic in their exposure of sin and call for repentance. He identified two preparatory stages of salvation: contrition and humiliation. Contrition involved the "sight of sin," followed by "sorrow for sin." In the state of humiliation the soul then abandoned self-sufficiency and, in deep personal agony, was ready to be "plucked" from its bondage to sin and "drawn" to the Savior.

Implantation brought another two-stage process: vocation (which Hooker and the *Westminster Confession* called "effectual calling") and the actual engrafting of the soul into Christ. Divine initiative was primary, but human response was imperative. In calling the elect, God elicited disgust for sinfulness followed by attraction to the gospel. God "doth so powerfully and effectually draw the soule by this good, that it brings all the affections after it." God awakened hope, desire, love, and joy to make way in the soul for Christ. As faith was wrought in the heart, "the will saith Amen to the business" (*The Soules Vocation,* 1638, 61, 283). In the process of implantation God imputed righteousness to the soul in justification by charging the debt of the sinner to Christ, made the soul God's own in adoption, and imparted holiness through the lifelong process of sanctification. Sanctification then brought fresh experiences of what Hooker called mortification and vivification through the devotional life of meditation ("selfe-tryall"), prayer, worship, and the other "means of grace." The saint "receives a principle of life whereby he becomes active" in righteousness (*Application of Redemption,* i, 150). The image of God was thus restored in the believer. The final stage of salvation arrived only after death with the soul's glorification in heaven.

Hooker's soteriological theology not only expressed the important themes of New England Puritanism but provided a foundation for Jonathan Edwards' analysis of "religious affections" during the Great Awakening a century later. The emphasis Hooker and other early New Englanders placed on the conversion experience established patterns that would persist in the evangelicalism of nineteenth-century America.

Suggested Readings

Writings of Thomas Hooker: Sargent Bush, Jr., ed., *The Writings of Thomas Hooker: Spiritual Adventure in Two Worlds* (Madison: University of Wisconsin Press, 1980); George H. Williams et al., eds., *Thomas Hooker: Writings in England and Holland, 1626–1633* (Cambridge, Mass.: Harvard University Press, 1975).

Frank Shuffelton, *Thomas Hooker: 1586–1647* (Princeton: Princeton University Press, 1977).

John Cotton

(1584–1652)

James O. Duke

A prominent Puritan minister, John Cotton served in the Massachusetts Bay colony beginning in 1633 as an influential and at times controversial leader in theology, church life, and civil affairs. Born in Derby, England, he studied—B.A. (1602), M.A. (1606), and B.D. (1613)—at Cambridge University, first at Trinity College and then Emmanuel College. Recognition as a talented preacher-theologian began in his days as Fellow at Emmanuel (1603) and grew during two decades of service as vicar of St. Botolph's Church in Boston, Lincolnshire, until the Church of England dismissed him in 1632 for nonconformist views. By then he had long been part of English Puritanism's brain trust. Alerted that the Court of High Commission planned further action against him, Cotton fled and found refuge among compatriots in New England.

The nonconformist (Puritan) views leading to his dismissal had apparently formed in the course of his university studies. Cambridge, especially its Emmanuel College, was a center of Puritan sentiment and scholarship. Its headmaster when Cotton became a Fellow was Laurence Chaderton, a member of the delegation that presented James I and church officials with Puritan proposals for church reform at the Hampton Court Conference (1604). Cotton's conversion experience at Emmanuel was, in typically Puritan fashion, long and agonizing. Widely read in Reformed theology, both continental and English, he adopted the tradition as his own and contributed to it thereafter. The study of John Calvin's thought in particular was one of his lifelong preoccupations.

His refusal to conform to Church of England worship patterns began a few years into his ministry at Boston. Neither this decision nor his commitment to "Calvinist" theology as a whole was in his judgment a repudiation of the Church of England itself. His goal, shared by large numbers of Puritans, was to promote reform from within that church. Indeed, even after fleeing to New England and gaining renown as an advocate of congregationalist church polity, he remained a staunch opponent of separatism from the state church.

Welcomed by Massachusetts Bay leaders, Cotton began his new ministry within weeks of his arrival, this time at "new" Boston's First Church. The prestigious post made him a member of the colony's standing order of magistrates and ministers. His sermons and other writings, including some written in England but previously unpublished, appeared in print at a steady pace thereafter. The topics and genres of his publications were Puritan standard fare: doctrinally oriented, "plain style" sermons, expository commentaries on biblical books (e.g., 1 John, The Song of Songs, Ecclesiastes, the Apocalypse), treatises and studies on disputed issues, a few poems. Of these, surely the one with the largest readership was *Milk for Babes, Drawn Out of the Breasts of Both Testaments* (1646), a catechism for children in use during the remainder of the seventeenth century.

Scholars have managed to date these sources quite well. Even so, the frequent time lag between original composition and publication is one of several obstacles facing those who study his thought. There is some debate today as in his lifetime about the development and consistency of certain of his views over the course of his career. Important points, however, are readily identifiable. Attention will focus here on basics of his thought regarding salvation by grace through faith and the nature of the church.

The first question Cotton asks of children in his catechism, "What hath God done for you?" is perhaps as apt a gateway into his theology of saving grace as any. In keeping with the Reformed tradition generally, theology itself is for Cotton confessional and doxological. That is, it is public testimony to the works and promises of God made by persons grateful for all that God has done. The child who answers the question properly— "God hath made me, He keepeth me, and He can save me"—has started along the way leading to the doctrines of creation, preservation and providence, and salvation.

The doctrine of salvation was of special concern to Cotton, as to other "Calvinists." To confess, with heartfelt gratitude, that "God can save me" as one of the three remarkable things "God has done for me" was to compress in one phrase a message that took volumes of theology to set forth adequately. Anyone confessing this belief announces: humanity is in such desperate need of salvation from sin that no one and no thing except God offers even the possibility, the slightest hope, of overcoming the need. Puritan theologians like Cotton sought, then, to give "an accounting for the hope" within them (1 Pet. 3:15), ever mindful that the hope itself as well as its fulfillment were mercies God granted undeserving sinners solely out of God's sovereign good pleasure. Teachings regarding God's eternal decrees of predestination and reprobation, the sinful depravity of humanity, the limited efficacy of the atonement of Christ to those of God's own choosing, and the irresistibility of divine grace were among those emphasized in Cotton's "matured" understanding of biblical-theological doctrine.

The message packed in this catechetical phrase also gave rise to a number of vexing theological issues. Two of these sparked controversy in the Bay colony: First, are any human efforts at all involved in turning the possibility of salvation into an actuality and, second, are there any indications (visible signs) offering assurance that this turn has in fact occurred? Reformed theologians distinguished themselves from others by the firmness of their response to the first issue: salvation is God's work, and those who claim that it is due to or dependent on the efforts of sinful humans lapse into a works righteousness that robs sinners of any hope at all. But that response alone did not end the issue. Human salvation in some way involved humans—that was clear to all. The theological challenge, then, was to describe this human "involvement" without even suggesting that it rather than grace—freely given by God and unearned by humans—was the decisive factor.

Standard Puritan teaching was to urge people to take interest in those things God had appointed as the means of grace by which to bring hope of salvation to sinners, and to strive to conform their lives to God's will as set forth in the Scriptures, all the while trusting solely in God's promise of mercy in Christ. The true faith (trust in God's promise) that brings true hope in this life is as much a gift of God as is the ultimate realization of that hope in the life to come. Early in his New England ministry, and perhaps before, Cotton emphasized that neither the means of grace per se nor human efforts to take interest in them were the decisive factor in the rise of true faith. That factor was the role of the direct power of the Spirit that came—if God so willed—along with these means and human efforts. True faith is an inward spiritual union with Christ. Apart from this union, human efforts to seek conversion and strive for righteousness thereafter may be simply a temporary or sham faith. Under such preaching Cotton's church experienced an "awakening" and a marked rise in membership. And Cotton was a prime mover in leading a number of ministers to require persons seeking church membership to offer public testimony of their conversion experience.

The second—distinct but related—question of "assurance of salvation" was among those that came to the fore in the "Antinomian controversy"

(1636–38) leading to the trial of Anne Hutchinson. Antinomian means "against the law," and New England Puritans were among many who used the term often, and frequently willfully, to slander opponents as libertines. In fact, Calvinism itself spawned a "doctrinal Antinomianism" that had nothing to do with excusing immorality and everything to do with reliance on God's grace rather than human abilities and actions for salvation. Hutchinson, an admirer of Cotton's teaching in old and New England alike, complained that the colony's ministers—except Cotton—were preachers of works righteousness.

The charge had theological bite. Cotton's warnings about doing good works without the Spirit within applied both to works done in order to seek (or prepare for) conversion as well as those done after professing faith in Christ. Although Cotton's clerical colleagues firmly denied that human efforts ever obligated God to save anyone, they were willing to speak of preparatory steps in conversion and to grant (as comfort to troubled souls if nothing else) that dedication to Christ's church and righteous living might be viewed as outward signs of God's power within and hence of God's merciful disposition toward believers. Was this then what Hutchinson and perhaps Cotton too condemned as works righteousness? Cotton was, in effect, subjected to interrogation. The exchanges show how subtle the doctrinal issues and solutions to them could become. The upshot was that Cotton disclaimed antinomianism, his interrogators disclaimed works righteousness, and all avowed they had intended one another no disrespect. But Anne Hutchinson was condemned and banished.

If Cotton's views of salvation troubled Bay colony leaders, his vigorous defense of congregationalist church polity and church-state relations redeemed him in their sight. His thinking on these matters was not exceptionally original. He drew upon earlier Reformed writers, William Ames especially, as well as lessons of history learned from recent Puritan experiments in de facto congregationalism. His chief writings on the doctrine of the church include *The Keyes of the Kingdom of Heaven* (1644), *The Way of the Churches of Christ in New England* (1645), and *The Way of the Congregational Churches Cleared* (1648). The first was based on earlier work, revised and enlarged for use by the Westminster Assembly of Puritan divines in England. (Cotton, along with the other two colonists asked to join the assembly, declined the invitation.) It became a resource in the formulation of the Cambridge Platform (1648), which codified the New England church way.

Cotton emphasized the conception of a "gathered church," a congregation of believers in God's promise of mercy bound to God and one another by "covenental" ties of mutual fidelity. These communities glorify God by their worship, their celebration of Baptism and the Lord's Supper, their observance of God's commandments, their due government under pastors and elders, and their discipline of erring members—all in accord with the teachings and examples of the Scriptures. Cotton distinguished this "way" from church governance by bishops, presbyterianism, and even more sharply, separatist "independency," which he judged to be anarchy. Against Baptists, he argued that God's promise of mercy (sealed by infant baptism) embraces believers and their children, who in time and by God's grace come to own the covenant personally.

Church and state were, in Cotton's view, distinct but not separate. Each had its own duties and rights. Neither was "democratic," for once the people chose rulers, obedience to their rule was obligatory. Yet church and state were to cooperate in fashioning a "godly commonwealth" that upheld Christian faith and morality. Cotton thus defended limiting the vote and political office to church members and opposed the notion of "tolerating" religious dissenters. This stand led to extended controversy with Roger Williams, a fellow minister expelled in 1635 for questioning the purity of New England's churches and the legitimacy of its civil government. Renewing his attacks in the 1640s, Williams called Cotton's view a "bloudy tenant" (tenet). The title of Cotton's reply, *The Bloudy Tenent, Washed and Made White in the Bloud of the Lambe* (1647), indicates his line of counterargument. Although his opposition to "liberty of conscience" endeared Cotton to the Bay colony's establishment, it also contributed to the widespread tendency to equate "Puritanism" with self-righteous intolerance—an ironic result indeed in the case of a theologian of grace.

Suggested Readings

Everett Emerson, *John Cotton,* rev. ed. (Boston: Twayne Publishers, G. K. Hall & Co., 1990).

David D. Hall, ed., *The Antinomian Controversy, 1636–1638: A Documentary History,* 2nd ed. (Durham, N.C.: Duke University Press, 1990).

Larzer Ziff, *The Career of John Cotton: Puritanism and the American Experience* (Princeton: Princeton University Press, 1962).

———, ed., *John Cotton on the Churches of New England* (Cambridge, Mass.: Harvard University Press, 1968).

Roger Williams

(1603–1683)

W. Clark Gilpin

In seventeenth-century New England, Roger Williams was the foremost advocate of religious liberty and the separation of church and state. As such, he was also the earliest North American practitioner of what in the late–twentieth century would be called political theology.

Williams' theology may be called a political theology in two senses. First, his very separation of church and state demanded that he articulate principles for the proper relationship of Christianity to a political regime. In an era when most thinkers assumed that religious pluralism was one of the principal sources of social disorder and therefore favored governmentally established religious uniformity, Williams argued the opposing notion that civil harmony would only be achieved by granting liberty of conscience to differing religions. Second, his was a political theology in the sense it mounted a sustained critique of the political interests that motivated church leaders themselves. When he entitled one of his tracts "The Hireling Ministry None of Christs," he wanted to emphasize his general conviction that the force of the gospel was weakened whenever it was misemployed to sanction a particular political order.

Williams also served as a practitioner of political theology in the sense that he articulated his principles while engaged in practical political leadership and in pointed debate over specific political issues. As a leader in the founding and early governance of Rhode Island, he not only served as governor, legislator, and militia leader, but he also took two extended trips to England (1643–44 and 1651–54) in order to obtain and protect a charter for the colony. Meanwhile, his argument that the separation of church and state was the basis both for civil peace and religious freedom, enunciated in such famous tracts as *The Bloudy Tenent of Persecution* (1644), did not take the form of detached, theoretical treatises but instead appeared in polemical pamphlets on topics of public controversy.

But if the thought of Williams may be appropriately characterized by the modern term "political theology," it must be remembered that his intellectual resources were those of the seventeenth century and not the twentieth. He was an intellectual product of seventeenth-century English Puritanism. He shared the Puritan discontent with the doctrine and polity of the Church of England. He shared the Puritan hope for personal life renovated by the spirit of God and a church purified from the accumulated errors of the centuries. Indeed, his commonality with the central tradition of Puritan piety was beautifully displayed in his devotional classic, *Experiments of Spiritual Life and Health* (1652). The creativity of his thought came not from the introduction of new ideas into seventeenth-century theology but rather from the dramatically different conclusions he drew by rearranging the pivotal Puritan presuppositions about church and state.

Williams was born in London to a family of the business class; his father was a citizen of the city and member of the Merchant Tailor Company, and his mother numbered a lord mayor of London among her relatives. The intellectual facility of the young Williams attracted the attention of the famed jurist Sir Edward Coke, who arranged for his education at Charterhouse School. From there, Williams attended Pembroke College, Cambridge, and earned his B.A. in 1627, intending to enter the ministry. But his Puritan religious scruples increased, and rather than accept appointment to a parish of the Church of England, he left Cambridge in 1629 to become private chaplain to the household of a wealthy Essex Puritan, Sir William Masham. By the autumn of 1630 Williams had associated himself with the Puritan group preparing to establish a colony in New England. He arrived in Massachusetts Bay, newly married, in 1631.

By this time, Williams had moved beyond the Puritan desire to reform the Church of England from within and adopted, instead, the "Separatist" view that the established church was so corrupt that genuinely reformed congregations must have no association with it. Almost immediately this radical view of church purity embroiled Williams in debates with the ministers and magistrates of Massachusetts Bay, who denied that genuine reform required utter separation. In these debates Williams focused his attack on the state's appropriation of religious duties and symbols. He contended that magistrates had no power to coerce specifically religious practices, that the king had granted illegitimate land charters based on the false prerogative of being a "Christian prince," that civil government should not impose oaths of allegiance, and that the cross should be removed from the colonial flag.

After five years of unrelenting controversy, Williams was banished from Massachusetts and resettled in 1636 on land purchased from the Narragansett tribe and named by him Providence. Not long afterward, Williams came to espouse the still more radical ideas of the "seekers," a loose collection of the devout on the fringes of Puritanism, who believed that Christian institutions had become so thoroughly corrupted over the centuries that no valid church any longer existed and would not until new apostles arrived at the millennium and reestablished the church in its pristine form. These objections to Puritan politics and this ardent quest for the true church were gradually woven into a coherent position, and they mark the line along which Williams' thought would develop in his tracts of the 1640s and 1650s.

Although these writings dealt largely with state policy toward religion, they were primarily addressed not to magistrates and legislators but to the Puritan clergy of old and New England. Indeed, for years after his banishment, Williams maintained a respectful relationship with Massachusetts Governor John Winthrop, assisting the governor in negotiations with the Indians of New England and even joining him for a modest joint venture in the pasturage of livestock. For the ministers of the established churches, however, Williams had little patience. Beginning with his *Queries of Highest Consideration* (1644) directed at the Westminster Assembly of Divines and its proposals for reform of the English church, Williams directly challenged ministers who sought to enlist the state in the promotion of their own religious beliefs and practices. This was especially true of his decade-long controversy with the New England divine John Cotton, of which Williams' *Bloudy Tenent of Persecution* was the most notable product.

In part, the Williams-Cotton debate was a contest over issues that had led to Williams' banishment, and *The Bloudy Tenent* was largely composed of documents that had circulated in manuscript in Massachusetts Bay during Williams' residence there. But during his first trip to England (1643–44), Williams recognized that the earlier New England controversies were directly pertinent to English debate over the freedom of preaching and the responsibility of the state for religious reform. Hence, his most famous tract on religious liberty was a complex document that both justified his position against the Massachusetts ministers and employed those debates as exhortations on behalf of "soul liberty" during the English civil wars.

Williams wrote in an age of religious wars, and the book's central problem was physical violence carried out in the name of Christianity. As its title suggests, the rhetoric of *The Bloudy Tenent* was saturated with images of violence and its victims. It abounded in graphic sentences about murder, rape, the gouging of eyes, and the dashing of brains. Coerced religious uniformity had led throughout history to the spiritual murder of souls and the physical murder of dissenters who resisted the state religion in the name of conscience. Is it possible, Williams asked, to pursue religious truth without disrupting civil peace by armed combat over religious difference? This abhorrence of religiously sanctioned violence motivated his insistence on religious liberty and the separation of church and state.

Williams began his argument for what he called the wall of separation between church and state by reasserting the Puritan commonplace that the true church was composed of individuals who were spiritually reborn by an inward experience of conversion to God. For the individual, said Williams, the necessity of rebirth meant that physical birth in a nominally Christian land constituted no claim whatever to Christianity. As the title of one of his pamphlets declared, "Christenings make not Christians." For the state, it meant that no nation could present itself as a Christian populace and that no government could wrap its policies in the mantle of religion. "Christendom" was an illegitimate concept.

Williams' second conviction about the church was less typical of Puritan thought but related especially to his advocacy of religious liberty. Although he shared the Puritan hope for a truly reformed church, he did not believe that any Christian of his time knew the authentic form of the true church or had the spiritual authority to establish a church untainted by the accumulated errors of history. The pure church of earliest Christianity had been lost during subsequent centuries of corruption and would not be recovered until new apostles restored it. In the meantime, Williams, borrowing the rhetoric of Revelation, declared that humanity wandered in a spiritual "wilderness," in which the various forms of religion must be free to declare the truth as they saw it. So long as they did not disrupt the civil peace by their worship and preaching, they should be permitted the free exercise of their consciences, in the conviction that God would use the contest of religions to sift human opinion and would ultimately separate the true from the false on the Last Day.

From these two principles—that the true church was a community called by God from the wider society and that the authoritative institutional formation of this church must await the millennium—Williams argued strenuously against the Puritan idea of a "godly commonwealth," in which Christian magistrates ruled and a reformed Protestant church was the established religion of the land. The ideal of the godly commonwealth, he asserted, disastrously misinterpreted Old Testament history, because it falsely employed ancient Israel, a national state combining spiritual and civil power, as a model for modern nations. The world, he repeatedly declared, no longer contained a nation chosen by God after the manner of the ancient national church and state of Israel. Instead, since the coming of Christ, the true church consisted of gathered congregations of the spiritually reborn, drawn out from the general populace of all the nations of the world. These congregations were governed by the law of

Christ, and the authority of the modern civil commonwealth was restricted solely to protecting the bodily welfare and property of its people.

In this way, Williams emphatically opposed any form of established church, arguing not only against the Church of England in this regard but also against Puritan establishments in New England or in England during the government of Oliver Cromwell. In a recurrent analogy, Williams suggested that churches were like a guild of merchants or a college of physicians, who should be free to conduct their business as they saw fit, so long as it did not disrupt the public harmony. His scheme for handling the growing religious diversity of the seventeenth century may perhaps be delineated by distinguishing between toleration, in which an established church concedes certain rights of worship and assembly to dissenters, and religious liberty, in which no religion has a privileged status granted and maintained by the civil order.

Williams advocated a thoroughgoing extension of such liberty of conscience. Whereas most seventeenth-century English advocates of religious tolerance followed the lead of John Milton in restricting toleration to Protestants alone, Williams proposed that Roman Catholics, Jews, and Muslims should all be granted full liberty to practice their religions. Williams and his Rhode Island neighbors practiced this principle in their colonial government, and during the 1650s both Quakers and Jews found freedom to establish communities in the colony. But although he staunchly defended the civil right to liberty of conscience, Williams remained too much the "seeker" after truth to be personally tolerant of diverse beliefs, and in the 1670s he engaged in a fierce public debate with the Quakers, published under the whimsical title *George Fox Digg'd out of His Burrowes*. He did not believe that such debate within a religiously pluralistic society threatened civil peace, and he regularly advanced historical arguments to demonstrate that the true threat to civil order came from efforts to coerce religious uniformity.

In a famous letter written in 1655 to the town of Providence, Williams observed that a true picture of a commonwealth arose if one imagined that "both Papists and Protestants, Jews, and Turks, may be embarked into one ship." The diversity of religions represented on board did not affect the purpose for which the ship sailed or divert it from its destination. Although crew and passengers had liberty to practice their own particular forms of worship, it remained true that the ship's commander ought to direct its course and expect that justice, peace, and sobriety be maintained by all who sailed therein.

Did this imply that the state was purely "secular" in its nature and purposes? Williams did not think so. He distinguished sharply between religious duties on the one hand and specifically moral and civil duties on the other. Religious congregations were responsible for the former and the state for the latter. But he based these two sets of duties on a distinction between the "two tables" of the decalogue, duties owed to God and duties owed to the neighbor. Derived in this general way from the divine will as revealed in the Ten Commandments, civil duties could nonetheless be performed independently from the presence of "true religion" within the borders of a particular nation. A citizen might be a good citizen and a magistrate a good magistrate with respect to what Williams called "civil or moral goodness," without so much as having heard of Christianity. No state or governor had a religiously derived superiority.

Civil society among the Native Americans rested, he believed, on the same natural basis of morality and common purpose as that of the states of Europe. His *Key into the Language of America* (1643) was a dictionary of the native languages that included meditations on the nature of human civility, in which he regularly suggested that the New England tribes displayed more common sense of equity and morality than did the supposedly civilized Europeans.

Roger Williams thus argued that religious diversity was compatible with civil peace so long as the state did not display favoritism toward one of the religions, and he argued that public debate over religious ideas was the only humanly available means to pursue religious truth. Thus baldly stated, his views have their parallels in later American thought. Since Williams derived these principles from Puritan convictions about the particularity of revealed truth, however, his influence diminished during the eighteenth century, when political theory more often began from a general analysis of human nature and the civil import of religion was more often grounded in a natural religion shared by all. In such an environment, the practice of the old separatist and seeker might be admired, but his argumentation was dismissed as sectarian and contentious.

Suggested Readings

Writings of Roger Williams: *The Complete Writings of Roger Williams,* 7 vols. (New York: Russell and Russell, 1963); *The Correspondence of Roger Williams,* ed. Glenn W. LaFantasie, 2 vols. (Hanover, N.H.: University Press of New England, 1988).

Edwin S. Gaustad, *Liberty of Conscience: Roger Williams in America* (Grand Rapids: Wm. B. Eerdmans Publishing Co., 1991).

Edmund S. Morgan, *Roger Williams: The Church and the State* (New York: Harcourt, 1967).

Anne Hutchinson

(1591–1643)

Marilyn J. Westerkamp

Anne Hutchinson, gifted with an extraordinary mind and remarkable charisma, arrived in Massachusetts in 1634. Like many of the colonizing Puritans, she came to escape escalating persecution and to help build a new, godly country, one that would be blessed by God and serve as an example to other nations. Upon arrival, Hutchinson and her husband William joined the Boston church and established themselves among New England's leadership. The daughter of learned clergyman Francis Marbury, Anne Hutchinson had been carefully educated, and her scriptural knowledge and theological sophistication were greatly admired. At some point, she instituted private religious meetings for Boston's women, gatherings that soon included many men; at peak popularity, sixty-eight persons attended. Scarcely three years after her arrival, Hutchinson was judged a primary disturber of consensual order, leader of a large number of Bostonians who challenged the colony's social and ideological foundations. In November 1637, the colony banished her; the following March, the church of Boston excommunicated her.

The challenge represented by Hutchinson and her followers was both sociopolitical and theological. Because her followers had participated in efforts to discredit many clergy and to support the sympathetic (and obstreperous) minister John Wheelwright (Hutchinson's brother-in-law), and because she herself had spoken critically of most of the clerics, Hutchinson was accused of sedition. More important, the sacred and secular magisterium were troubled by the leadership of a woman. They accused Hutchinson of teaching men as well as women, failing to submit to her male superiors, acting the part of a husband rather than a wife, and seducing other women to follow her example. This argument involved a perception of women as intellectually and emotionally incapable of deep, complex theological study. This became especially apparent during her

45

church trial, when some predicted her theological explorations had led to heresies which would, in turn, lead to sexual misconduct.

Theologically, two issues troubled the leadership. The first involved the relationship between human endeavor and salvation. The Calvinist doctrine of predestination, espoused by Puritans, placed salvation completely in the hands of God. Individuals could have no responsibility for achieving salvation because they were powerless to effect it. Only faith in Christ could justify the innately depraved soul before God, and faith was impossible except through divine grace. Moreover, Calvinists argued, grace offered could not be refused; the saint could no more fall from heaven than the sinner could escape hell. Once grace was offered and, perforce, accepted, confirmation of justification came in the sanctification of the believer's behavior. In other words, a believer's gracious standing manifested itself in the saint's daily conduct.

Given the unconditionality of Christ's gifts of grace and faith, the Hutchinsonians (with leading cleric John Cotton) stressed the futility of human action and the passivity of believers in an absolute dependence upon God. Most New England ministers, however, found such arguments dangerous: Such attitudes led inevitably to heresy, irreligion, and anarchy. While granting the arbitrary and unconditional nature of God's actions, these ministers also understood the anxiety of believers desperate to discern some sign of their own salvation; thus preachers emphasized the hope that lay in sanctification. Many also promoted the notion that the potential saint could prepare for God's grace. Although affirming that no human effort could affect God's ultimate action, ministers encouraged believers to study scripture, attend sermons, guard their conduct, and pray so that they would be ready. Such efforts might have kept believers from feeling powerless in the face of divine majesty, but the Hutchinsonians found in preparationism hints of salvation through works. Just as the clergy decried Hutchinsonians as antinomian or anarchic, Hutchinson attacked the ministers for preaching a legalistic covenant of works.

The second issue involved Hutchinson's claim to immediate revelation. While many Puritans were inclined to reject claims to revelation as delusional or blasphemous, arguing that the age for such miraculous communication was long past, the point remained debatable. Hutchinson's claim during her trial, and testimonies to her previous prophetic declarations, precipitated a prolonged debate about the nature of revelation itself. Cotton argued that an expectation of the miraculous would represent a delusion, but any soul might have a justifiable faith in special providence. Since further discussion did not resolve this problem and threatened to raise questions about Cotton, the court avoided further discussion and banished Hutchinson for sedition.

Permitted to remain in Boston during the winter months but lodged in the home of a hostile cleric, Hutchinson was visited constantly by ministers. The declared purpose was her repentance, but the result was extensive testimony delivered at the church trial. The clergy judged Hutchinson theology heretical in several esoteric areas, most notably her views on the resurrection of the body; these questions had never before been raised. This factor was noted, and questioned, by Hutchinson as well as one accuser, magistrate Thomas Dudley. The fact that the previous issues of preparationism, free grace, and revelation were not raised indicates that the trial included the purpose to bring Cotton into clerical alignment by ignoring controversial tenets and convincing him, through these other discussions, of Hutchinson's heresy and essential sinfulness. The strategy succeeded; Cotton joined others in the condemnation and excommunication.

Later accounts, however, particularly the history written by Governor John Winthrop, would stress the threat posed by Hutchinson's claim to prophetic revelation. A charismatic woman, one whose prophetic utterances reflected her experience of communion with the divine, undermined the established secular and sacred authority. An intellectually powerful woman who criticized clergy represented a threat to order at many levels; yet during the state trial Hutchinson had successfully countered biblical arguments and still acceded to all demands that she cease public activity. But even silent, a woman claiming authority from God, authority recognized by the majority of her community, would have continued to represent a threat to the standing order. In the final analysis, although the ostensible cause for her banishment was sedition, the primary factor driving her accusers was her claims to prophetic revelation and the challenge these represented to their own magistracy and control.

Suggested Readings

Emery Battis, *Saints and Sectaries: Anne Hutchinson and the Antinomian Controversy in the Massachusetts Bay Colony* (Chapel Hill: University of North Carolina Press, 1962).

Francis J. Bremer, ed., *Anne Hutchinson: Troubler of a Puritan Zion* (Huntington, N.Y.: R. E. Krieger Publishing Co., 1981).

David D. Hall, ed., *The Antinomian Controversy, 1636–1638: A Documentary History* (Middletown, Conn.: Wesleyan University Press, 1968).

Marilyn J. Westerkamp, "Anne Hutchinson, Sectarian Mysticism, and the Puritan Order," *Church History* 59 (1990): 482-96.

Selma R. Williams, *Divine Rebel: The Life of Anne Marbury Hutchinson* (New York: Holt, Rinehart and Winston, 1981).

Cotton Mather

(1663–1728)

Winton U. Solberg

One of the outstanding Americans of his day, Cotton Mather is burdened by the handicap of a poor reputation. Scholars have contributed to the hazing of Mather, and the public harbors a stereotype of Mather as a persecutor of witches and a bigoted Puritan priest. Such an image is not only a caricature but a bad caricature of the man.

Mather descended from two of the most prominent families in New England. His grandfathers, John Cotton and Richard Mather, had been spiritual and intellectual leaders of the first generation of New England Puritans. His father, Increase, minister of North (Second) Church in Boston and president of Harvard College, became the most powerful divine in the political as well as the ecclesiastical life of Massachusetts. Increase married John Cotton's only daughter, and Cotton Mather, born in Boston on 12 February 1663, was their first child.

The boy grew up in an atmosphere of piety and intellect. His spiritual life developed with the precocity exhibited by many Puritan youths, and at an early age he became imbued with the belief he was a member of a covenanted community on which lay a divine obligation to advance the kingdom of God in America. He also became convinced he was destined for greatness.

The youth benefited from the best education then available in New England. He learned to read and write before attending school and enjoyed reading in his father's extensive library. He began his formal studies at the Boston Latin School, and in the summer of 1674 the eleven-year-old was admitted to Harvard College. Harvard's purpose was to give Christian gentlemen a liberal education, not merely to train ministers. The curriculum was designed to provide a mastery of the learned languages as well as some knowledge of classical literature and the original languages of Holy Scripture. In addition to the classics, Mather completed the circle of traditional academic studies

48

that Harvard required—logic, ethics, metaphysics, mathematics and natural philosophy, rhetoric, oratory, and divinity.

Mather exhibited a keen interest in natural philosophy, that is, science or knowledge of the physical world as distinct from the spiritual universe (metaphysics). During his student days, the Aristotelian natural philosophy that had long been taught at Harvard was being eclipsed by a new natural philosophy whose leading proponents were Bacon, Descartes, and Boyle. The natural philosophy Mather learned at Harvard was quickly outdated by the scientific revolution culminating in Newton, whose *Principia mathematica* (1687) appeared shortly after he graduated.

Always an omnivorous reader, Mather began to acquire his own library while a student at Harvard. By the end of his life his library consisted of probably four thousand volumes and was likely the largest private library in America. He kept a commonplace book, his "Quotidiana," in which he entered remarkable passages from various authors encountered in his reading, and in later years he drew from this treasury for his writings.

Mather had a speech impediment early in life, and during his first year at Harvard he began to stammer. This affliction led him to wonder whether he could continue the family tradition by entering the ministry, and for some time he laid aside thoughts about preaching and studied medicine. But he learned to overcome his speech imperfection by speaking with deliberation. By the time Mather graduated with a bachelor of arts degree in 1678, he possessed an excellent knowledge of classical languages, of classical and Christian history and literature, and of the Bible. His preparation in natural philosophy was weak, but he retained a keen interest in the physical universe. Despite a heavily mannered literary style, he was the master of his own language. He wrote clear, fluent, and graceful prose.

After leaving Harvard Mather spent seven years before settling into his life's work. He continued his studies, but the state of his soul remained a pressing concern. At the age of sixteen he experienced a religious conversion and was admitted as a member of North Church, a prestigious church and the largest in America. In 1681 he earned a master of arts degree from Harvard, and the following year he issued the first of his many publications. Meanwhile, in September 1680 he had become his father's unordained assistant at the North church. Members valued him highly and expressed an intent to call him as their pastor, but due to various vicissitudes they did not elect him to this office until 8 January 1683. Another two and a half years elapsed before, on 13 May 1685, Mather was ordained in North. He served there until his death in 1728, forty-three years later.

Mather came to his vocation at a time when New England was experiencing a spiritual crisis that had arisen over anxiety about the validity of the vision that had inspired the founding of the New Israel. While the earliest American Puritans had believed they were God's elect nation engaged in a divine mission to build a holy commonwealth, a combination of adverse circumstances led Mather's generation to question the soundness of the founders' image of their place in God's plan.

This crisis conditioned Mather's career. He had to choose between viewing Massachusetts as simply another colony in the British imperial system, a choice that spelled catastrophe for the idea of a covenanted community, or as God's elect nation still engaged in a divine mission to open the last stage in human redemption and bring a blessing upon the entire human race.

New England's time of troubles derived from a concatenation of circumstances. From 1675 to 1693 the region suffered a seemingly unprecedented series of natural disasters—war, fire, plague, severe cold, drought, sudden deaths—as well as the witchcraft mania, all of which Puritans interpreted as divine judgments. Political adversity intensified the sense of crisis. In 1684 the Crown vacated the charter of 1629 under which Massachusetts had been a self-governing Bible commonwealth, making the colony in law simply one of many in the imperial system. Not until 1691 did the king grant a new charter restoring many valued features of the earlier patent.

The Puritans also experienced a sense of religious declension. People praised the faith of the founders while denouncing their own departure from earlier standards. The jeremiad became a familiar means of analyzing the declension. Sermons and tracts observed that the colony was justly afflicted for religious laxity by natural adversities and political challenges; yet Puritans believed that the punishments visited upon them were corrective rather than vindictive. Denouncing their own apostasy while vowing to reform, Puritans were confident that God would not forsake them, because they were still a Chosen People.

These developments accompanied the advent of a new and challenging intellectual climate. When Mather was born, the medieval worldview still dominated the Western mind. It held that both nature and the supernatural were one system derived ultimately from God, who rules the physical universe by both first and secondary causes. The former were divine decrees of an inscrutable character; the latter were the regular sequences of nature that could be understood by human reason. The medieval mind believed in the supernatural and viewed the physical creation as a world of wonders, wonders that demonstrated the power of God or Satan to suspend the laws of nature. A darker feature of this mental universe manifested itself in folklore and belief in tall tales, natural phenomena (e.g., comets) as divine portents, witches, and other occult forces.

During Mather's life these age-old convictions were sharply contested by the scientific revolution that began with Copernicus in the mid–fifteenth century and culminated with Newton in the late–seventeenth century. The achievement of these years provided a new model of reality that captured the Western mind and prevailed until the twentieth century. The new view retained a conventional belief in the Christian religion while employing the experimental method, which emphasized observation and demonstration. Natural laws were part of the law of God and capable of mathematical proof. Newton, who mathematically demonstrated the revolution of the planets in their orbits, gave his name to the age.

Cotton Mather was foremost among a small group of New Englanders who remained orthodox Calvinist while adjusting to the new mentality. He did not entirely shake off ancient superstitions; as a result he acquired a reputation as a bigot and a reactionary which continues to haunt him. But in reality Mather was among the most progressive New England Puritans in responding to recent intellectual advances. He warmly embraced the new science without accepting a completely mechanistic universe.

Mather devoted his life to reinvigorating the Puritanism of the founders. He sought to redefine the nature of the holy commonwealth in light of the best thought of the age. While performing his ministerial duties—preaching, tending his flock, and publishing sermons and treatises—he also took an active part in colonial political affairs and wrote prolifically. Mather published more than 460 works during his life, mainly in history, science, and theology, and he left many thousands of pages in manuscript.

Mather's single most important publication was the *Magnalia Christi Americana: Or, The Ecclesiastical History of New England* (1702). This magnificent folio volume was a compendious history of seventeenth-century New England. The idea for the work sprang from Mather's conviction that history was one of the ways to decipher the progress of God's plan for the redemption of the race. The seven books of the *Magnalia* describe the founding of New England, its governors and ministers, Harvard College, the Congregational churches, illustrious Providences that indicated God's loving care for faithful people, and the afflictions of the churches. The bulk of the book and its richly ornamented style may seem forbidding, but the prose has admirable qualities, and despite its apparent formlessness the *Magnalia* has unity. Mather viewed the Protestant Reformation as the glorious climax of the effort to bring heaven down to earth and the New England churches as the cutting edge of the Reformation. The church history of

New England demonstrated how Christ cared for his people as they battled to advance his Kingdom. The *Magnalia Christi Americana,* which has justifiably been called one of the great works of English literature of the seventeenth century, went far to tell the story of New England to later generations.

Mather was the first American to write a book dealing with all the sciences known at the time. He welcomed the fruits of the scientific revolution, confident that to explore nature was to understand the mind of God. Two of his important literary efforts, the "Biblia Americana" and *The Christian Philosopher,* sprang from his efforts to examine the whole of scripture and the physical creation in light of the best learning of the day.

The "Biblia Americana" grew out of Mather's intense devotion to the Bible. Convinced that none of the available Bible commentaries were adequate, in 1693 he announced his intention to produce an American commentary. By laborious work he would gather the best evidence on sacred texts from learned authors, approaching scripture from every conceivable angle. He labored on his "Biblia Americana" for many years, eventually producing a manuscript of six volumes of about a thousand pages each. His massive commentary has a more settled plan than is apparent. The completed manuscript is built around the Old and New Testaments and includes essays on both testaments in the order of history. Mather attempted to reconcile the scriptural text with what he regarded as scientific fact. He worked on the manuscript until 1711 and perhaps later, but it was never published. This labor of love was monumental and unwieldy, and English authors had pre-empted the British market for such works. Mather's treatise was essentially an updating of earlier glosses, and most of his material was available elsewhere.

In abandoning the "Biblia," Mather gradually shifted his emphasis from scripture to science. In 1712 he dispatched the first of a series of letters to the Royal Society of London describing natural phenomena in America. By 1724 he had sent at least eighty-two communications discussing astronomy, geology, zoology, medicine, and related topics. Mather's "Curiosa Americana" mixed fact with fancy, and some accounts contained superstition, but he was moving from a supernatural explanation of various phenomena toward greater objectivity. An extract of the first series of the "Curiosa" was published in the *Philosophical Transactions* (1714), earning Mather election as a Fellow of the Royal Society. A year later Mather sent the manuscript of his main statement on science to London; *The Christian Philosopher: A Collection of the Best Discoveries in Nature, with Religious Improvements* appeared in 1720 (with a 1721 imprint).

This book, the first comprehensive account of all the physical and natural sciences known at the time written by an American, is important mainly for its argument in favor of the harmony between science and religion. Mather expounds this view within the larger framework of the argument from design, which holds that one may reasonably infer the existence of a purposeful Creator responsible for the creation from the evidences of order and agreement in the universe. This concept originated with pagan authors in classical antiquity and was later reinforced by Christian apologists. The design argument was deeply embedded in Western thought by the sixteenth century and reinvigorated by the scientific revolution of the early modern period. English authors elaborated the idea in terms of the new mechanical philosophy, and Mather drew heavily on these and other works.

The argument from design is a form of natural theology. Mather elaborates his thesis within the framework of the ancient metaphor of the "two books"—that God is revealed in both nature and scripture. His essays treat what is known today as astronomy, physics in the broadest sense, and the life sciences. His longest single essay is entitled "Of Man." In each essay he traces what earlier authorities had said on the subject, then recounts recent scientific advances, and finally offers a rhapsody on how science demonstrates divine governance of the physical universe. His purpose in writing was to enkindle piety. In reflecting on the religious significance of his material he asserts that the works of God exhibited in nature exemplify the power, wisdom, and benevolence of God. In closing he emphasizes the mediatorial role of Christ in the divine plan of redemption.

The Christian Philosopher found some favor in New England in the early eighteenth century, attracted a few English readers, including John Wesley, and was cited by Christian Wolff, a founder of the German Enlightenment. This book represents a departure from early New England Puritanism and is a harbinger of the Enlightenment in America. *The Christian Philosopher,* a hymn of praise to the Creator, combines theological and scientific modes of explanation to demonstrate the harmony between science and religion.

Retaining a lifelong interest in medicine, Mather wrote a lengthy manuscript on the subject which argued that there is a close correlation between spiritual health and physical well-being. This treatise, *The Angel of Bethesda,* was first published in 1972.

The author's favorite among his own books was *Bonifacius* (1710), best known as *Essays to Do Good.* The great end in life is to do good, he preached, and this little volume, which Mather published anonymously, is a record of his own attempts to do good which might serve as a model for others. In this work Mather reduced charity to a system and planted the seeds for vast schemes of benevolence. Benjamin Franklin valued the work highly and acknowledged his indebtedness to it. He stripped Mather's idea of religious raiment and introduced it into the American mainstream, where doing good continues to flourish down to the present day.

Mather's *Manuductio ad ministerium: Directions for a Candidate of the Ministry* (1726), a work on pastoral care, is a mixture of seventeenth- and eighteenth-century attitudes which reveals that the author was buffeted by the contradictory winds of doctrine. On the one hand, Mather speaks for the older Puritanism in discussing divinity or systematic theology. For example, he celebrates the works of Johann Alsted, a German Calvinistic theologian, praising Alsted's massive encyclopedia of all the sciences (4 vols., 1630) as a key to all the sciences. On the other hand, Mather reveals his indebtedness to recent thought by viewing religion more as a matter of practical conduct than of abstract contemplation of the divine. In this handbook for the composing of sermons Mather urged full acceptance of the new science while also demanding that prospective ministers view the world teleologically.

Cotton Mather looms like a mountain peak on the intellectual and theological landscape of early America. Believing he was by family inheritance destined for preeminence, he devoted his life to revitalizing the Puritanism of the founders in light of the best thought of the changing times. While serving forty-five years as pastor of North Church in Boston, he was active in the political life of the colony as well as a prolific author. Mather's most important books deal with what were the main preoccupations of the Puritan clergy: history (the *Magnalia*), science *(The Christian Philosopher)*, theology (the *Essays to Do Good*), and pastoral care (the *Manuductio*). These books, which influenced early American thought and culture, some more quickly than others, earn Cotton Mather a more favorable image than he has often been accorded, and they richly justify Mather's prominent place in American intellectual history and American literature.

Suggested Readings

Writings of Cotton Mather: *Magnalia Christi Americana. Books I and II*, ed. Kenneth B. Murdock (Cambridge, Mass.: Harvard University Press, 1977); *The Christian Philosopher*, ed. with an Introduction and Notes by Winton U. Solberg (Urbana: University of Illinois Press, 1994).

David Levin, *Cotton Mather: The Young Life of the Lord's Remembrancer, 1663–1703* (Cambridge, Mass.: Harvard University Press, 1978).

Kenneth Silverman, *The Life and Times of Cotton Mather* (New York: Harper and Row, 1984).

Jonathan Edwards

(1703–1758)

Stephen J. Stein

Jonathan Edwards, a Congregational minister in eighteenth-century New England, was a distinguished representative of the Reformed tradition. His theological ideas reflect classic concerns of Reformation theology, but they also bear his distinctive creative stamp. He is a religious figure who has attracted sustained attention from disciples, critics, historians, and scholars in a variety of fields.

Edwards came to his vocation as a minister in almost foreordained fashion. He was the only son among eleven children of Timothy and Esther (Stoddard) Edwards. Timothy Edwards was the Congregational minister in East Windsor, Connecticut. Esther was the daughter of Solomon Stoddard, a prominent clergyman in Northampton, Massachusetts. Jonathan was nurtured in the piety and culture of Puritanism, a tradition that shaped his subsequent religious outlook. He entered Yale College in 1716, received the B.A. in 1720, and studied two additional years in New Haven in preparation for the ministry. Edwards' "Diary" from these years, a set of "Resolutions" he authored, and retrospective reflections reveal a young man preoccupied with self-examination and spiritual introspection. Doubts and fears about his religious situation alternated with resolute determination to seek after righteousness and to cultivate proper attitudes and behavior. He puzzled over the state of his soul and worried because his religious experiences did not follow established Puritan patterns. In these circumstances he determined to examine closely the opinions of earlier divines concerning conversion. Early on he struck a theological note that occupied him throughout his lifetime, namely, the attempt to distinguish authentic religion from false, to discover the signs of true godliness, to describe and analyze the nature of true virtue.

Edwards' reading included authors preoccupied with the process of conversion and the practical Christian life, including works by divines such as William Ames and Thomas Shepard. These and other writers had explored the workings of grace in the hearts of saints and their subsequent lives of holiness. Two foci—formulated theologically as justification and sanctification—became the theological poles around which Edwards oriented much of his religious thought. In other words, for him theology was never merely a matter of abstraction, but always involved the application of salvation, what the Puritans called "improvement," in the life of the Christian.

Following the years of theological preparation, for a brief time in 1722–23 Edwards served a pastorate in a Presbyterian congregation in New York City. Then he returned to Yale College as a tutor for two years. He also did some supply (substitute) preaching before accepting a position as associate minister with his aging maternal grandfather, Solomon Stoddard. He was ordained into the Congregational ministry in 1727, and in that same year he married Sarah Pierpont of New Haven. Northampton became the center of Edwards' activities for nearly a quarter century. In that locale he rose to prominence as a defender of evangelical theological views.

During his years as minister of the Northampton church, a variety of factors shaped Edwards' theological ideas. For instance, he continued the vigorous, disciplined life of study he had begun years before coming to Northampton. His studies ranged widely across the Bible and biblical and religious topics, as well as other areas of knowledge, including science, philosophy, geography, and history. He recorded the fruits of these labors in private notebooks, some of which have been published posthumously while others remain in manuscript. His most significant notebooks, known as the "Theological Miscellanies," contain entries on a variety of theological concerns, from Adam's sin to "Zion" as the name of the mountain on which Israel's temple was located. Many of the entries feature traditional concerns of Puritanism, "conversion" and "covenants" being two examples. The "Miscellanies" also demonstrate the more speculative side of Edwards' theological interests. For instance, he conjectured about the nature of the future millennium.

Edwards' pastoral responsibilities were a second factor influencing his theological ideas in Northampton. He faced the weekly task of preaching two or more times and the continuing obligation of caring for the spiritual needs of his parishioners. Edwards inherited from his grandfather, who died in 1729, a parish with a tradition of evangelical activity. Stoddard had presided over five successful "harvests" during his ministry. Puritans assumed that the true Christian would experience a life-transforming conversion resulting in the fruits of visible sainthood. Edwards hoped, prayed, and worked for such awakenings in his congregation. Those hopes reached apparent fulfillment in the winter of 1734–35 when a surge of religious activity—a wave of conversions—swept through Northampton.

Edwards described that widespread religious concern in his *Narrative of Surprising Conversions* (1737). By his account a sermon he preached on "Justification by Faith Alone" had been instrumental. In it he contended that salvation of the ungodly is solely a product of faith in Christ rather than the result of any goodness, obedience, or virtue ascribable to individuals. In July 1731, he had given the Public Lecture at Boston in which he had struck the note that redemption is "entirely" dependent on the "sovereign good pleasure" or grace of God. In the *Narrative* he illustrated the theme of dependence with specific examples. In 1734 Edwards had also described the indwelling presence of God's Spirit as a divine and supernatural light filling the convert's soul which results in a sense of the excellency of divine things. The revival catapulted the town and its young minister into the limelight and created an image of Northampton as a model of religiosity.

Edwards' hopes, buoyed by the events of 1734–35, were soon dashed as the religious fervor in Northampton passed. Over the next several years he occupied himself with more normal parish activities, using the pulpit to encourage and exhort the members of his congregation. During the late 1730s he preached several sermon series giving voice to his theological concerns, none of which were published during his lifetime. In 1737–38 Edwards preached on the parable of the wise and the foolish virgins (Matt. 25:1-12), in which he examined the similarities and differences between true and false Christians, or hypocrites, and discussed the notion of "signs of grace." In the middle months of 1738 he preached on the concept of Christian charity (1 Corinthians 13), evident in disposition and action to other human beings as well as in love toward God. He explored the virtues which are the fruits of charity and the source of such love which is the Spirit of God. One commentator has described this sermon series, published posthumously as *Charity and Its Fruits* (1852), as a "phenomenology of the Christian moral life." He concluded the series on the theme of heaven as "a world of love."

Edwards sounded a similar eschatological note in a third series preached in 1739 about the work of redemption based on the biblical phrase, "and my salvation from generation to generation" (Isa. 51:8). In these sermons he examined God's redemptive activities, from the fall to the last judgment, as a means of understanding God's relationship to the world. Edwards' field of attention embraced both biblical history and events beyond revelation, including the future, or the realm of prophecy. These sermons appeared posthumously as *A History of the Work of Redemption, Con-*

taining the Outlines of a Body of Divinity, in a Method Entirely New (1774).

The fruits of Edwards' studies and theological reflections first came to public light in the 1730s in the pulpit. In the 1740s, however, he turned his energies increasingly to the writing and publication of important treatises. Events continued to have a strong impact on his intellectual agenda.

Edwards' hopes for another awakening in his congregation rose when he learned of the successes in America of the British itinerant revivalist George Whitefield. Whitefield visited Northampton in October 1740. Soon the revivals occurring throughout the American colonies—which historians have called the Great Awakening—were arousing considerable controversy. Critics and opponents, including notably Charles Chauncy in Boston, accused Whitefield and other preachers of manipulating their audiences, inciting passions, and provoking "enthusiasm"—a term of opprobrium at the time. In fact, some more radical revivalists, James Davenport as a case in point, had rejected conventional religious decorum in the name of the Spirit. Chauncy championed reason in matters of religion; Davenport embraced spiritual excess.

Much of Edwards' intellectual energy in the 1740s went into a sustained defense of the revivals and a critical examination of experiential religion. Admittedly, he himself was not above playing on the emotions of those who heard him preach, as is evident in his most famous sermon, "Sinners in the Hands of an Angry God." In it he compared the sinner's dilemma to that of a spider held over a fiery pit by only the slightest thread. Yet in his defense of evangelical religion Edwards adopted a position between Chauncy's commitment to the intellect and Davenport's to the emotions. Over several years he set forth his views on true religion in a variety of publications.

In a commencement speech at Yale College in 1741, Edwards identified negative signs or phenomena that were *not* evidence of true religion, such things as visions and extraordinary bodily effects. A year later when he published *Some Thoughts Concerning the Present Revival of Religion,* an important treatise supporting revivalism, he admitted that problems existed, but asserted nonetheless that the revivals were defensible as authentic manifestations of God's Spirit at work. Among other evidence he pointed to the resulting pattern of Christian experience that included love, joy, and peace among those being converted. But again he devoted considerable energy to showing what ought to be avoided and corrected in the revivals.

Edwards' most sustained defense of experiential religion was his *Treatise on Religious Affections* (1746). In it he defined holy affections as the essence of true religion. The "affections" were more than mere emotions, but they were also distinguishable from intellectual or notional understanding. For Edwards the affections involve the inclination of the heart and are informed by the understanding. In his treatise he described the signs of gracious affections by which true religion can be tested. Authentic piety is the product of supernatural or divine influences; it is a pure love of God unmixed with self-interest. True religion involves a new sense of the beauty of God's holiness which results in a spiritual understanding and conviction regarding the truth of the gospel. This conviction is accompanied by a sense of self-denial and an affirmation of the sovereignty and excellency of God. Conversion brings a personal transformation, a turning away from sin toward God that is evident in such virtues as meekness, love, gentleness, and charity toward others. There is a beauty in this work of God's Spirit and an enduring quality to it. Edwards concluded his discussion by stating that the chief sign of authentic religion is holy practice; this is the "business" which ought to engage the Christian. Practice must confirm profession; piety seeks expression in the Christian life. Justification or conversion (the transformation of the heart) manifests itself in sanctification, or holiness of life. The causal agent in both processes is God's Spirit.

In the following years Edwards turned his attention to several other theological topics. When the revivals dissipated again, he joined evangelicals in Scotland and elsewhere in a proposal for a concert of prayer designed to advance the church's fortunes on earth and to speed the coming of the millennium. In support of that effort he published *An Humble Attempt to Promote Explicit Agreement and Visible Union of God's People in Extraordinary Prayer* (1748). Edwards assumed that God could not reject petitions from the faithful for the pouring out of his Spirit. In these same years, he edited the journal of David Brainerd, a young missionary to the Indians who died in Edwards' home in 1747. As depicted in *The Life of David Brainerd* (1749), Brainerd was the perfect embodiment of evangelical spirituality. Edwards' account of Brainerd's life became an American spiritual classic reprinted more frequently during the nineteenth century than any other of his publications.

These times of increasing national and international reputation, ironically, witnessed growing difficulties for Edwards in his Northampton parish. After years of following the pattern of admission to the Lord's Supper established by Solomon Stoddard, Edwards changed it, insisting on a public profession by adults. As a result of his decision and because of controversy related to his pastoral style and to his family's lifestyle, open conflict erupted within the congregation. When communication broke down, Edwards attempted to persuade his opponents by publishing his views in *An Humble Inquiry into the Rules of the Word of God Concerning the Qualifications Requisite to a Compleat Standing and Full Communion in the Visible Christian Church* (1749). In it he declared that the church has the responsibility to judge adults seeking admission to the Lord's Supper or baptism for their children.

The conflict in the church led to the calling of a council comprising ministers and lay delegates in June 1750. Following a decision against him, the congregation voted overwhelmingly to dismiss Edwards. More than a year passed before Edwards resettled as an Indian missionary at the frontier outpost in Stockbridge, Massachusetts. One of the first things he did in Stockbridge was to fire off a last salvo in the communion controversy, a response to Solomon Williams' defense of Stoddardeanism. Edwards entitled his rebuttal *Misrepresentations Corrected, and Truth Vindicated* (1752).

In Stockbridge Edwards became deeply involved with the fortunes of the Indians. He criticized the policies of the commissioners responsible for the mission and suggested a variety of improvements favorable to the Housantunnock and Mohawk tribes. He preached regularly to the Indians and the personnel assigned to the outpost, often drawing on sermons delivered previously in Northampton.

In some respects the Stockbridge years were a time of astonishing productivity. His most significant publication of these years was *Freedom of the Will* (1754), a systematic attempt to counter the growth of theological ideas associated with the Enlightenment, specifically, the notions of human freedom and universal salvation traditionally associated with the Dutch theologian Jacob Arminius (1560–1609). Edwards directed his arguments against a number of contemporary authors who were attacking classic Reformed views. In this, his most intellectually demanding work, he set out to undermine the idea that the will is self-determining. He challenged the distinction drawn between natural and moral necessity and argued that no act can be independent of prior conditions. To his own satisfaction he proved the absurdity of the Arminian position and the error of self-determination, thereby vindicating the notion of God's sovereignty. In the nineteenth century much of Edwards' reputation as a philosopher rested on this treatise.

At Stockbridge Edwards turned his attention to another classic theological issue of the Reformed tradition, the doctrine of original sin. Again responding to challenges posed by the Enlightenment, he argued that the depravity of human nature can be established from both observation and experience as well as from the testimony of scripture. Human behavior universally confirms the innate tendency toward evil. He explained the imputation of Adam's sin, the mechanism by which all are tainted, as the product of God's applying his dealings with Adam to all of his posterity. Much of the treatise, *The Great Christian Doctrine of Original Sin Defended* (published posthumously, 1758), focuses on scriptural support for the doctrine.

While at Stockbridge, Edwards also worked on other theological projects which did not appear in print during his lifetime. For example, he returned to a theme which had occupied his attention through the years in his private notebooks, the end for which God created the world. In brief, Edwards declared that the ultimate objective of all God's works is the glory of God. Using the image of the sun, its light, and the reflection of that light, Edwards spoke of God's glory being communicated to the creation and reflected back by creatures to their Creator. Thus God is the alpha and the omega, the beginning and the end of creation. (In parallel, Edwards' view of the Trinity has this same reflexive quality. God the Father generates the Son, his perfect image or idea, the Logos; the Holy Spirit is the love between the Father and the Son, the infinite delight God has in himself.)

Edwards also wrote during these years a second essay on the theme of true virtue, attempting to distinguish it from claims being made for common morality by a variety of British thinkers. In his discussion Edwards compared true virtue and the morality based on the notion of a moral sense inherent in human nature. He argued for the superiority of Christian virtue, which he defined as unqualified love to God, or what might be described as love to Being in general. He did not deny the value of common morality, but asserted the superiority of beauty and truth motivated by the love of God. The former cannot escape self-love; the latter participates in pure benevolence and reflects the beauty of holiness. In 1765 Samuel Hopkins, Edwards' close friend and first biographer, published two Edwards manuscripts: *Two Dissertations, I. Concerning the End for Which God Created the World. II. The Nature of True Virtue.*

In Stockbridge Edwards also worked on other important theological projects. One drew on his sermon series dealing with the history of the work of redemption. He was reconceptualizing it as a new form of divinity in a historical mode. Over the years he had been keeping several working notebooks related to this project. They contained notes on church history, on his reading, and on scriptural exegesis. Edwards' "Notebook on the Apocalypse," a commentary on the book of Revelation, also bears on this project. He anticipated that this project would deal with all aspects of Christian the-

61

ology. He planned to cast this writing on the work of redemption in the form of a history dealing with events occurring in heaven, earth, and hell, drawing on scripture, history, and prophecy. Edwards planned another comprehensive work, which he described as a "harmony" of the Old and New Testaments. It was to embrace prophecies of the Messiah and their fulfillments, types of Christ and the antitypes to which they refer, and a discussion of the doctrinal harmony between the two testaments. This work would draw on exegetical notebooks Edwards had been compiling for several decades, including "Notes on Scripture" and the "interleaved" Bible, as well as on notebooks dealing with typology and "Harmony" itself. The "history" and the "harmony" projects both took aim at views associated with the challenge to biblical authority posed by the Enlightenment. Neither project has ever appeared in the form contemplated by Edwards.

Several of these projects came to public attention in the fall of 1757 when the trustees of the College of New Jersey (later Princeton) invited Edwards to become the college's president. In a letter to the trustees he identified some theological tasks he hoped to complete. Nevertheless, he accepted the invitation, went to New Jersey, and shortly thereafter, on 22 March 1758, died of smallpox, having submitted to an inoculation.

Edwards' theological legacy is measured in several ways. The immense body of his writings, both published and unpublished, constitutes an important unsystematic statement of Christian theology. He never completed what he once contemplated, namely, a "Rational Account of the Main Doctrines of the Christian Religion Attempted." From among disciples and colleagues of Edwards emerged an evangelical New Divinity movement that took its lead from his writings. Most notable among its early leaders were Samuel Hopkins, Joseph Bellamy, and Jonathan Edwards, Jr. These Edwardseans, and others later associated with the New England Theology, did not hesitate to refine and modify Edwards' views (and in some cases even to challenge them), but all of them stood in reverence of him and attempted to claim his mantle. Edwards' theological reputation suffered at the end of the nineteenth century, the heyday of theological liberalism in American Protestantism. In the twentieth century several neoorthodox theologians turned back to him for inspiration, including H. Richard Niebuhr. After midcentury, Yale University Press undertook the publication of *The Works of Jonathan Edwards*, a modern critical edition of his works. The renaissance of interest in Edwards shows no sign of flagging at the present time.

Suggested Readings

Writings of Jonathan Edwards: John E. Smith, Harry S. Stout, and Kenneth P. Minkema, eds., *A Jonathan Edwards Reader* (New Haven: Yale University Press, 1995).

Conrad Cherry, *The Theology of Jonathan Edwards: A Reappraisal*, 2nd ed. (Bloomington: University of Indiana Press, 1990).

M. X. Lesser, *Jonathan Edwards: A Reference Guide* (Boston: G. K. Hall, 1981); and *Jonathan Edwards: An Annotated Bibliography, 1779–1993* (Westport, Conn.: Greenwood Press, 1994).

Perry Miller, *Jonathan Edwards* (Amherst, Mass.: University of Massachusetts Press, 1981).

John E. Smith, *Jonathan Edwards: Puritan, Preacher, Philosopher* (Notre Dame: University of Notre Dame Press, 1992).

See also the introductions to the volumes of the Yale Edition of *The Works of Jonathan Edwards* (New Haven: Yale University Press, 1957–present).

Samuel Johnson

(1696–1772)

Allen Carl Guelzo

Samuel Johnson of Connecticut is a reminder of the importance of "the church question" in American Christian thought, as well as
an example of its complexity. Many of the English-speaking American
colonies were founded by religious dissenters who rejected hierarchical
government in churches, especially government by the bishops of the
Church of England. Johnson, starting from Congregationalism (the New
England system of independent congregations), moved in the opposite
direction and embraced ecclesiastical hierarchy and episcopal church government.

Johnson was born on 14 October 1696, at Guilford, Connecticut. The
congregationalism guiding Connecticut's religious life since the 1630s had
yielded to a more hierarchical form of congregationalism embodied in the
Saybrook Platform (1708), in which the government of the churches came
under the oversight of a network of Calvinistic clergy associations and
consociations. Johnson began his college studies at the Collegiate School at
Saybrook (1710), and graduated from there in 1714, just as a new library
was being assembled from the gift of Jeremiah Dummer, the colony agent
in England, and four years before the beneficence of Elihu Yale enabled the
school to be reorganized in New Haven as Yale College. Johnson briefly
taught school in Guilford, and then served as college tutor at Yale
(1716–19). Even after leaving the tutor's position, Johnson remained close
to the college by accepting the call of the Congregational parish of West
Haven and being ordained pastor there in 1720.

Johnson was particularly interested in staying close to the Dummer
books in the college library. He had begun reading "the New Learning"—
for example, Bacon, Locke, and Newton—between 1713 and 1720. His
admiration for the English origins of the New Learning tilted him toward
assimilation to English culture, especially in the form of the Church of Eng-

land. In 1719, Johnson and six Yale-connected associates (including the college rector, Timothy Cutler) embarked on a program of reading, which included the works of Richard Hooker, Thomas Fuller, John Pearson, and other Church of England apologists and theologians. Johnson became convinced that the continuing life of the church depended on a demonstrable connection of its ministry with (and therefore sanction from) the apostles. Since New England Congregationalism had shown no regard for such connections, and since the Church of England claimed an apostolic succession for its bishops, Johnson eventually concluded that he could exercise no ministry without reordination in the Church of England.

Before he could announce his intentions, the Yale trustees closed in on him, Cutler, and the other five after the September 1722 commencement proceedings, and demanded explanations. After a subsequent debate before Governor Gurdon Saltonstall on 16 October, Johnson resigned his pastorate in West Haven. In November, Johnson and Cutler left for England to offer themselves for reordination in the Church of England, and in 1723 were ordained Church of England priests in London by Bishop Thomas Green of Norwich.

Johnson returned to Connecticut shortly afterward, this time as the missionary in charge of the isolated Church of England congregation at Stratford, Connecticut. There he was responsible for the care of approximately sixty families, and had constantly to deal with savage Puritan theological criticism of the Church of England. In a series of three letters, *Letters from a Minister of the Church of England to His Dissenting Parishioners* (1733, 1734, 1737), Johnson struggled to be conciliatory to his opponents, but insisted that Congregationalism had created a serious problem for itself by mistakenly abandoning the episcopal structure of ministry for congregational independence. Johnson also vigorously defended the general "Arminian" cast of the Church of England's concept of salvation in *A Letter Concerning the Sovereignty of God, from Aristocles to Authades* (1743) and *A Letter to Mr. Dickinson in Defence of Aristocles*, both written against the Presbyterian, Jonathan Dickinson. Johnson was determined to prove that the Calvinistic doctrine of predestination, which was almost as essential to New England's theological identity as congregationalism itself, made God into an arbitrary manipulator of human free will and eliminated any sense of ethical responsibility.

Just as he had come to admire English churchmanship, so too Johnson became a disciple of English philosophy, especially that of Bishop George Berkeley, the idealist philosopher who briefly took up residence in Newport, Rhode Island (1729–31) in order to advance a plan to organize a college in Bermuda. From his reading and his personal visits with Berkeley, Johnson worked out a Berkeleyan theory of knowledge, based on the doctrine of archetypes, which he first published in *A System of Morality* (1743) and then enlarged in *Elementa philosophica* (1752). On the strength of these works, Benjamin Franklin attempted to draft Johnson for the presidency of the College of Philadelphia. But Johnson waited instead for the organization of a Church of England college, King's College in New York City, before leaving Stratford to become King's president in 1754. Unhappily, even in New York, Johnson had to fend off the efforts of hostile critics to close the college or loosen it from its Church of England moorings. He resigned in 1763, disappointed not only in the lackluster prospects of King's College, but also in his failure, ever since the 1720s, to persuade English authorities to nominate a resident bishop for the colonies to strengthen Church of England hands there. He died in Stratford on 6 January 1772.

Much of Johnson's work can be interpreted as part of an overall cultural "Anglicization" of the North American colonies in the eighteenth century, a process which came to an abrupt halt with the Revolution. But Johnson was also a self-conscious theological critic of the excessive social individualism of the congregational system. Johnson described the church as an organic society in which all individuals were ranked and related in a harmonious order, and given Christian identity by the place they occupied in the church. This criticism of the persistent individualism of American church life would be carried on in the nineteenth century by high-church-manship and the Oxford Movement in the American Episcopal Church as well as the Mercersburg Theology.

Suggested Readings

Eben Edwards Beardsley, *Life and Correspondence of Samuel Johnson* (New York: Hurd & Houghton, 1874).

Joseph Ellis, *The New England Mind in Transition: Samuel Johnson of Connecticut, 1696–1772* (New Haven: Yale University Press, 1973).

Norman Fiering, "President Samuel Johnson and the Circle of Knowledge," *The William and Mary Quarterly* 28 (1971): 199-236.

Herbert Schneider and Carol Schneider, eds., *Samuel Johnson, President of King's College: His Career and Writings*, 4 vols. (New York: Columbia University Press, 1929).

Charles Chauncy

(1705–1787)

Charles H. Lippy

Charles Chauncy, born in Boston in 1705, became the assistant to Thomas Foxcroft at Boston's First Church ("Old Brick") in 1727 after he received his M.A. from Harvard. He remained there until his death in 1787, succeeding Foxcroft as senior pastor in 1769. Chauncy's position at First Church brought prestige and prominence; his six-decade ministry drew him into the leading religious and political controversies of eighteenth-century New England.

The Great Awakening of the 1740s found the outspoken Chauncy in the role of critic. His writings challenging the revivals brought to the fore one theological tenet that would remain central to his thinking: an emphasis on the role of reason in religious experience. The Awakening promoted by the itinerant George Whitefield and by Jonathan Edwards, who became his primary theological antagonist, was suspect to Chauncy because of its emphasis on emotion. Although Chauncy did not deny that emotion was a part of authentic religion, he believed that the unbridled "enthusiasm" unleashed by the Awakening could lead the devout astray by causing them to doubt their own salvation if intense emotion did not mark their own experience. In his most famous anti-Awakening treatise, *Seasonable Thoughts on the State of Religion in New-England* (1743), a counter to Edwards' *Some Thoughts on the State of Religion in New-England*, Chauncy argued that the faithful were more likely to realize that God had brought them to salvation through regular and reasoned reliance on such means of grace as worship, scripture study, and prayer than through emotional frenzy.

Buttressing Chauncy's position was a particular understanding of religious liberty. Liberty meant the freedom to engage in the rational pursuit of religious experience. Insistence on an intense, emotional experience of conversion was nothing short of coercion that defied such liberty. Others, particularly Jonathan Mayhew and those more immediately influenced by Enlightenment religious currents, in time would develop this notion of liberty and reason more fully.

Chauncy also attacked advocates of the Awakening on the grounds that they undermined church order. The New England pattern, which Chauncy years later (in his study of patristic thought on church polity) traced to the early church fathers, was for a pastor to be called to a particular congregation and remain there until death. When evangelists such as Whitefield itinerated from place to place, preaching wherever they could gain a hearing, Chauncy felt they were directly challenging the theological integrity and pastoral ministry of the regular clergy. Should itinerancy become accepted, ecclesiastical chaos would ensue. Such chaos defied reason.

After Awakening fervor subsided in New England, Chauncy was drawn into another theological controversy. This one, relating to the doctrine of original sin, would ultimately lead him far afield from traditional Puritan thinking. Chauncy's initial intention was to write in defense of this doctrine, but the more he reasoned about it, the more he came to question its validity. For example, he found rationally repugnant the notion that infants who died would be condemned to eternal damnation because of original sin. In retrospect, Chauncy's change of mind about original sin clearly set in motion a far deeper theological shift, for Chauncy began to question the entire Calvinist scheme that revolved around ideas of predestination and damnation. Convinced his new understanding was firmly rooted in scripture, Chauncy drafted several pieces in which he argued that a benevolent Deity by definition would desire the happiness of all creation. Since ultimate happiness was rationally inconsistent with damnation, this benevolent Deity must therefore will the eternal salvation of all people.

Chauncy recognized that his new perspective could cause much theological turmoil. Hence he refrained from publishing the work he had prepared, sharing it occasionally with sympathetic friends and referring to it by the code name "the pudding." Indeed Chauncy did not release these writings until the 1780s, shortly before his death. Because of this delay in publication, traditional interpretation of Chauncy has held that these universalistic treatises represent the culmination of a lifetime of theological reflection and are directly linked to the emergence of Unitarianism in New England. While the latter point may be accurate, the former fails to recognize that universalistic thinking was central to Chauncy's thinking for thirty years. Another reason Chauncy may have refrained from publishing "the pudding" at the time he penned these works was that other controversies gaining public attention seemed more immediately threatening. One concerned a proposal to designate a Church of England bishop for the colonies. Chauncy's strident opposition had both theological and political dimensions. His own analysis of scripture and his congregationalist heritage led him to conclude that a church structure based on bishops was contrary to the Bible (as well as to reason). He feared that because bishops represented the legally established church in England, they would use the coercive power of the state to advance goals detrimental to the New England way and thereby infringe on authentic religious liberty. Then, too, in England the established church and its bishops had certain civic functions; to introduce these in the colonies would also infringe on both religious and political liberty.

Although the proposal for a colonial bishop was abandoned, Chauncy's opposition was symptomatic of a larger suspicion about British colonial policy that finally resulted in the call for American independence, a move that Chauncy wholeheartedly supported. Echoing the views of Boston's commercial elite, Chauncy endorsed independence because he believed that British policy would reduce the colonists to a position of economic slavery. Such coercion, like the religious coercion of a bishop or even the emotional coercion of Awakening enthusiasts decades earlier, was counter to reason and good order. Never well liked but generally well respected, Charles Chauncy left an enduring legacy. His challenge to religious emotionalism fostered a reliance on rational credibility, his attack on original sin helped undermine the Calvinist foundation of New England Puritan thought, and his endorsement of universalism helped pave the way for the more liberal Unitarianism of the nineteenth century.

Suggested Readings

Writings of Charles Chauncy: *Seasonable Thoughts on the State of Religion in New-England* (Boston: Rogers and Fowle, 1743); *The Mystery Hid from Ages and Generations* . (London: Printed for C. Dilly, 1784). Both volumes are available in microform in the Early American Imprint series. *Mystery Hid* has been reprinted in Religion in America series, 1 (Salem, N.H.: Ayer, 1969).

John Corrigan, *The Hidden Balance: Religion and the Social Theories of Charles Chauncy and Jonathan Mayhew* (New York: Cambridge University Press, 1987).

Edward M. Griffin, *Old Brick: Charles Chauncy of Boston, 1705–1787* (Minneapolis: University of Minnesota Press, 1980).

Charles H. Lippy, *Seasonable Revolutionary: The Mind of Charles Chauncy* (Chicago: Nelson-Hall, 1981).

Jonathan Mayhew

(1720–1766)

Charles H. Lippy

Born in 1720 on Martha's Vineyard to a family that for three generations had been missionaries to the Native Americans, Jonathan Mayhew pursued instead a career in pastoral ministry. Called to West Church in Boston in 1747, after completing his M.A. at Harvard, he remained there until his death in 1766. Mayhew was a Harvard student when the Great Awakening came to New England. At first drawn to the revivals, he came to question their value. Like other critics, he believed the revivals' emphasis on emotion both excessive and dangerous, for it challenged what became his central conviction, that true religion was based on reason and experience as well as faith. When Mayhew came to West Church, he was already known for this rationalistic approach. Influenced by the English Enlightenment, especially by thinkers like John Locke and Samuel Clarke, he is best classified as a supernatural rationalist. His position led many New England clergy to shun him; several refused to participate in his ordination and installation. He did find a friend in the older, but equally controversial Charles Chauncy.

Mayhew's views became more widely known with the 1749 publication of his sermon "The Right and Duty of Private Judgment," delivered as the Boston Thursday Lecture the previous year. He argued that initial indifference to all religious truth claims was essential, for only such neutrality would allow critical scrutiny of their foundation. Reason, given to human nature in creation, would lead individuals directly to the truth. Revelation might guide reason, but could not replace it. Individual appropriation of reason meant there could be no uniformity in religious belief. Nor was it rational to coerce persons to accept creeds or other doctrinal formulas; Christian liberty rejected all doctrinal bondage. Mayhew would in time insist that laws designed to control religious dissent were repugnant to both reason and true Christianity. Mayhew had an unbounded confidence in reason. To him, reason could not lead to error, for rational inquiry would itself expose error. The liberty of private judgment would thus automatically lead to the rejection of falsehood and expose distortions of true faith that had accrued to the Christian tradition over the centuries. Like other supernatural rationalists, Mayhew concluded that the most authentic test of religious truth came in moral behavior, for he was convinced Christianity had primarily to do with moral duties. Words or giving lip service to doctrine could deceive; actions could not.

More orthodox New England clergy were aghast at Mayhew's rationalistic approach. To them, it undermined the foundation of belief in revelation and could easily result in heresies of the worst sort. Their apprehensions mounted when Mayhew published a series of sermons in 1755 that his critics took to be an attack on the traditional understanding of the Trinity.

In these sermons, Mayhew eschewed any interest in the metaphysical nature of the Trinity, claiming he was intent on insisting there was only one God. He did challenge the orthodox, however, when he claimed that their emphasis on the Son of God eclipsed the strident monotheism he supported and therefore became a deterrent to proclaiming the Christian message to persons of other religious persuasions. Mayhew's critics felt he had denied the divinity of Christ, although he would insist in other writings he had never done so. They also argued that his position logically led to a rejection of the necessity of Christ's sacrificial death and that his emphasis on moral behavior was a thinly disguised substitution of "salvation by works" for the traditional Protestant "justification by faith." In retrospect, it is fair to say Mayhew and his detractors were using different vocabularies—his informed by supernatural rationalism, theirs by Puritan tradition—and Mayhew may not have explicated his thought systematically.

Mayhew's conviction that God and Nature had endowed humanity with rational freedom had important political consequences that were also controversial. He published a fiery sermon in 1750 on the anniversary of Charles I's death during the English Puritan Revolution in which he insisted that citizens had a right to resist and overthrow tyrannical rulers. After describing the traditional Puritan view that government was sanctioned by God to bring order to society and therefore merited the support of the people, he went on to deny that such support was absolute. Reason required obedience to government only when its authority sustained the liberty and welfare of the people, not when it abused power and became tyrannical.

Mayhew amplified that position during the crisis surrounding passage of the Stamp Act in 1765 and its repeal in 1766. In an unpublished sermon preached in August 1765, Mayhew likened British policy to slavery; the arbitrary nature of British colonial policy had replaced civil liberty with the bondage of economic slavery. Mobs attacked the homes of customs officials and burned admiralty court records the next day; popular opinion regarded Mayhew's sermon as their inspiration. His well-known sermon, "The Snare Broken," marking the repeal of the Stamp Act in 1766, echoed these sentiments. Although in this sermon Mayhew condemned mob action and asserted that the English system of government, led by a Protestant king, offered greater liberty than any other, he proclaimed that the Stamp Act taxes would have strangled the colonies economically.

For the moment, protest based on rational argument and petition had succeeded in maintaining colonial liberty. Curiously, in "The Snare Broken" Mayhew did not speak of revolution, though his exposition led in that direction. How his thought would have developed as calls for independence gained momentum remains unknown, for less than three months after preaching "The Snare Broken" Mayhew died. Jonathan Mayhew's ministerial career lasted less than two decades. Yet in that time he became one of the most influential voices in mediating the moderate supernatural rationalism of the English Enlightenment to New England. Consistent in his conviction that reason and experience must authenticate faith, he boldly called for liberty in both the religious and political arenas.

Suggested Readings

Writings of Jonathan Mayhew: *On Hearing the Word* (1755); *Seven Sermons . . . The Right and Duty of Private Judgment* (Boston: Rogers and Fowle, 1749); *The Snare Broken* (Boston: R. & S. Draper, 1766). All are available in microform in the Early American Imprints series. *Seven Sermons* has been reprinted in the Religion in America series, 1 (Salem, N.H.: Ayer, 1969).

Charles W. Akers, *Called Unto Liberty: A Life of Jonathan Mayhew, 1720–1766* (Cambridge: Harvard University Press, 1964).

John Corrigan, *The Hidden Balance: Religion and the Social Theories of Charles Chauncy and Jonathan Mayhew* (New York: Cambridge University Press, 1987).

Samuel Hopkins

(1721–1803)

Joseph Conforti

Samuel Hopkins is generally recognized as the most important Calvinist theologian in New England between Jonathan Edwards (1703–1758) and Nathaniel Taylor (1786–1858). An original thinker and engaged religious reformer, Hopkins emerged in the second half of the eighteenth century as a leader of the so-called New Divinity—a controversial school of theology that grew from the teachings of Jonathan Edwards. Many referred to the New Divinity as Hopkinsianism, testimony to Hopkins' shaping influence on the movement. During the late-eighteenth and early nineteenth centuries, the New Divinity increasingly attracted clerical and lay followers and came to dominate doctrinal writing and religious reform within New England Congregationalism. In fact, the New Divinity came to be recognized as the New England theology, the first indigenously American school of Calvinism.

Hopkins, like so many other New Divinity leaders, was a native of Connecticut. Born in Waterbury in 1721, he graduated from Yale in 1741. At his commencement Hopkins listened to Edwards defend the spiritual authenticity of the religious revivals of the early 1740s, characterized by scholars as the Great Awakening. After graduation, Hopkins studied for the ministry in Edwards' Northampton, Massachusetts, school of the prophets, a makeshift seminary where Edwards trained disciples who would continue his work of defending and explaining his brand of evangelical Calvinism.

Ordained in 1743 as the minister in a new church on the Massachusetts frontier in what was to become the town of Great Barrington, Hopkins remained an intimate of Edwards, discussing theological works in progress and formulating a doctrinal agenda that would occupy him for decades. When Edwards died unexpectedly (1758), Hopkins not only inherited many of Edwards' unpublished works; he and Joseph Bellamy, a New

Divinity disciple of Edwards from Connecticut, assumed responsibility for developing and systematizing Edwardseanism into what they described as a school of Consistent Calvinism.

Hopkins' lifelong efforts to formulate the New Divinity derived from doctrinal-philosophical arguments Edwards had presented in his great dissertation *Freedom of the Will* (1754). Edwards ingeniously reconciled divine sovereignty and determinism on the one hand with free will and moral accountability on the other. Edwards brought about this reconciliation by carefully defining natural and moral necessity.

For Edwards, natural necessity referred to physical and intellectual capacities. Individuals suffered under a necessary natural inability if they faced a physical or intellectual obstacle external to their will. A person cannot lift a thousand-pound boulder; an infant cannot solve complex mathematical problems. Such "cannots" of the natural world differed, however, from the "will not" of the moral realm. Moral necessity referred to the certainty between inclination, disposition, or motive of the will and volitions or actions. Moral necessity meant that individuals acted voluntarily, according to the disposition of their wills. Human beings were free as long as they could do as they willed, that is, as long as they could act according to the inclination of their wills. Sinners were naturally able to repent; their moral inability only amounted to the lack of an inclination to choose salvation over sin; their cannot was merely a will not.

Edwards' distinction between natural and moral necessity was critical to Hopkins' efforts to defend Calvinism against charges that it robbed individuals of their free will and thus of their moral accountability. Hopkins' New Divinity combined a traditional Calvinist stress on divine sovereignty with an Edwardsean emphasis on the voluntary character of sin and the sinner's natural ability to repent. Hopkins advanced theological interpretations that consistently attempted to reconcile determinism and moral accountability—hence, the New Divinity ministers' preferred name for their movement was Consistent Calvinism. But the consistent preaching of divine sovereignty and human moral accountability confused and antagonized theological opponents of New Divinity and has often perplexed modern students.

Consider, for example, Hopkins' controversial treatise *An Inquiry into the Promises of the Gospel* (1765). Drawing on Edwards' interpretation of natural ability and of the voluntariness of sin and virtue, Hopkins developed a doctrine of immediate conversion that seemed to diminish the importance of the means of grace—prayer, Bible reading, church attendance. Reformed theologians traditionally stressed the role of the means of

74

grace in preparing the heart for regeneration—regeneration itself being a free gift of a sovereign God. Though the means of grace could not bring about regeneration, many commonly argued that neglect of them was more sinful and displeasing to God.

Hopkins wished to continue the evangelical work of the Great Awakening. He stressed that the individual possessed the natural ability to embrace the gospel immediately. Consequently, he dismissed a gradual approach to regeneration and depreciated the moral efficacy of the means of grace and of preparation for salvation. Indeed, Hopkins argued, the awakened sinner who attended to the means of grace but remained unconverted became more guilty in God's sight. Such a morally and intellectually aware sinner possessed the natural ability to repent but continued willfully to resist the promise of salvation offered in the gospel.

Hopkins directed his evangelical theology at the large number of Congregational worshipers who led moral lives and used the means of grace but who had not experienced conversion. But he aroused the ire of moderate Calvinists in New England who advocated a church-based approach to regeneration that valued preparation, the means of grace, and a more gradual conversion process than Hopkins' immediatism. One moderate Old Calvinist, Jedidiah Mills of Stratford, Connecticut, responded to Hopkins in *An Inquiry Concerning the State of the Unregenerate Under the Gospel* (1767). Mills coined the term "New Divinity" to dismiss what he saw as Hopkins' strange doctrinal interpretations. After 1767, the theological school of Edwards' closest followers—Hopkins, Bellamy, and Jonathan Edwards, Jr.—bore the label that began as an epithet, the New Divinity.

Clerical criticism of Hopkins and other New Divinity theologians did not deter them from extending the doctrinal interpretations of Edwards' *Freedom of the Will*. Hopkins, for example, drew from Edwards while modifying the traditional reformed understanding of original sin. Reformed theologians held that God created Adam as the natural and covenantal head of humanity. On the basis of this relationship, his sin was immediately imputed to his progeny. Humans were born with a double guilt—Adam's sin and a moral corruption that was a penal consequence of that sin.

But the doctrine of immediate imputation and of hereditary sinfulness contradicted Edwards' idea that all sin was voluntary, and thus seemed to undermine the theological relationship between natural ability and moral accountability presented in *Freedom of the Will*. New Divinity theologians sought to establish a connection between Adam and his sinful posterity but in a way that protected Edwards' ideas on individual moral accountability and the voluntary nature of sin. Hopkins argued that Adam's sin was not directly imputed to his posterity; humans could not be guilty for his transgression because it was outside their natural ability. The sovereign God used Adam's sin as the occasion for constituting his posterity with a corrupt nature—a moral inability—but not as a punishment or penalty for the first sin. All sin and guilt resulted from personal and voluntary choices of the will. The divine constitution that originated with Adam, whom God designated as the head of humankind, established the certainty of sinners' choices, namely, that they would sin as Adam had. But Adam's posterity was not guilty of his sin prior to their own sinfulness. In short, God constituted Adam's descendants with a corrupt nature because of his offense, but did not judge them guilty until they voluntarily chose to sin.

Hopkins and his New Divinity colleagues adroitly reconciled natural depravity, divine sovereignty, and human accountability. But their doctrinal interpretations also continued to provoke controversy. In fact, Hopkins' New Divinity distressed some members of his own congregation. Theological opposition was one of several issues that led to Hopkins' dismissal in 1769 from his pastorate of twenty-six years in Great Barrington. A year later he was installed at the First Congregational church in Newport, Rhode Island, then a commercial and slave-trading center and the fifth largest city in the American colonies. Hopkins continued to publish works that developed New Divinity theology, and he became increasingly engaged in the antislavery movement. His famous doctrine of disinterested benevolence furnished a theological rationale for his antislavery efforts.

Hopkins explained his doctrine of disinterested benevolence in *An Inquiry into the Nature of True Holiness* (1773). The treatise was a response to criticisms of Edwards' posthumously published *Dissertation Concerning the Nature of True Virtue* (1765). Hopkins sought to improve Edwards' interpretation and thereby silence critics of New Divinity ethical theory. Edwards defined true virtue as benevolence to Being in general, which included God. Critics assailed Edwards, however, for substituting a seemingly abstract metaphysical concept (Being in general) for the biblical God. Hopkins attempted to correct Edwards by redefining Being in general as God and our neighbors, that is, God and humankind.

Hopkins also differed with Edwards on the issue of self-love. Edwards argued it was natural for an individual to love his own happiness. Self-love, then, could encourage an individual to seek salvation or eternal happiness with God. Hopkins objected that Edwards' ideas endorsed a self-centered inducement to salvation. "To give up our temporal interest, worldly interest, for the sake of eternal happiness, wholly under the influence of self-love," Hopkins wrote, "is as real an instance of selfishness as parting with all we have now, to possess, a large estate next year" (Hopkins, *True Holiness*, 70). True Christians must lose themselves in a cause higher than their own salvation—namely, in disinterested benevolence toward God and humankind.

During the American Revolution, Hopkins awakened to the injustice of slavery and increasingly saw the social implications of his doctrine of disinterested benevolence. He became one of the leaders of the Revolutionary antislavery movement. In publications such as *A Dialogue Concerning the Slavery of the Africans* (1776), Hopkins suggested that support of the antislavery cause was a form of benevolence and a sign of conversion which demonstrated whether American patriots were motivated by true virtue, that is, by disinterested love of Being in general.

Disappointed that the Revolutionary generation failed to abolish slavery, Hopkins was particularly offended that the Constitution protected the slave trade for twenty years. He increasingly thundered against the leaders of the new nation and regarded slavery as a national sin. The persistence of slavery, he feared, would bring a Providential curse on America. Hopkins' position suggests that New Divinity advocates were not celebratory nationalists who saw the millennium about to dawn in America, as is sometimes argued. Both Hopkins' doctrine of disinterested benevolence and his millennialism embraced a universal vision of Christianity.

While he labored on behalf of the antislavery cause during the Revolutionary War, Hopkins continued to write theological treatises. After a decade-long effort, he completed his most important work, *System of Doctrines Contained in Divine Revelation*, in 1793. The *System* was an eleven-hundred-page codification of the New Divinity. It attempted to systematize the work of a generation of New Divinity leaders who formulated a school of Calvinism that evolved from the writings of Edwards and that consistently reconciled divine sovereignty and human moral accountability. Hopkins' tome stands as the first comprehensive American system of Calvinist theology.

Hopkins' *System* played an important role in the transmission of the theology of the New Divinity's founders to the next generation of Consistent Calvinist theologians, missionaries, and revivalists. Hopkins remained in Newport until his death in 1803, and he witnessed the beginnings of the New Divinity's rise to a position of dominance within New England Congregationalism. The New Divinity became particularly important at Andover Seminary, America's first and the early nineteenth-century's largest postgraduate theological school, founded in 1808. Andover not only provided an institutional home for the New Divinity where the works of

Edwards, Hopkins, Bellamy, and other leaders of the New England theology were read, but it also became a center of religious reform where Hopkins' doctrine of disinterested benevolence helped inspire such causes as the foreign missionary movement.

Thus Hopkins' life and work demonstrate that the New Divinity was an original, influential, and controversial school of American Calvinism. Drawing on his mentor, Edwards, Hopkins forged a theology that blended divine sovereignty and human accountability, urged immediate repentance, and upheld a lofty standard of true virtue as self-denying, disinterested benevolence. As a result, the New Divinity promoted conversions, revivals, and religious reform and remained a vital Calvinist movement in America well into the nineteenth century.

Suggested Readings

Joseph Conforti, *Jonathan Edwards, Religious Tradition, and American Culture* (Chapel Hill: University of North Carolina Press, 1995).

————, *Samuel Hopkins and the New Divinity Movement: Calvinism, the Congregational Ministry and Reform in New England Between the Great Awakenings* (Grand Rapids: Wm. B. Eerdmans Publishing Co., 1981).

Allen C. Guelzo, *Edwards on the Will: A Century of American Theological Debate* (Middletown, Conn.: Wesleyan University Press, 1989).

John Woolman

(1720–1772)

Michael L. Birkel

John Woolman was born in 1720 in colonial New Jersey and died of smallpox while on a religious visit to England in 1772. Although perceived as talented for a mercantile career, he chose instead the humbler lot of tailor. He did so both to witness to the traditional Quaker testimony regarding a plain and simple life and to have the freedom to travel in the gospel ministry. Woolman lived through the passing of William Penn's "Holy Experiment," when Friends resigned from the Pennsylvania legislature over the issue of funding the war against the French in the 1750s. Woolman was a leader in a reform movement within the Society of Friends which called for a renewal of Friends' principles regarding peace, justice, and simplicity at a time when prosperity and war threatened their integrity.

Woolman described his own conversion experience as a conviction that the inward spiritual life and the outward exercise of true justice are inseparable. His writings, a journal, and about a dozen essays are evidence of profound thought on the nature of both inward transformation and social justice.

Slavery was an early and lifelong focus for Woolman. His *Considerations on Keeping Negroes* (Part One written in 1746 but too controversial to be published before 1754; Part Two written in 1761 and published the following year) offer his arguments against slavery, and his *Journal* shows his patient labors with slave owners to convince them that slaveholding was incompatible with the Christian gospel. Through the work of Woolman and others, Friends ultimately united against slavery in 1776 (after Woolman's death).

Antislavery efforts awakened Woolman to other issues of social justice. The same greed that expressed itself in slavery also led to ill-treatment of Native Americans and to oppression of the poor among English colonists. His "Plea for the Poor" (published 1793 but written around 1764) reminded readers that God as Creator is the owner of the world, called for a voluntary material simplification of life and a more just redistribution of goods, and gently questioned the very notion of property rights when they violate human rights. Unusual for his day, Woolman developed a theology of labor, in which he argued that God intended moderate labor for all—including domesticated animals. Failing to trust in God's providential care, people are tempted to seek security in an abundance of possessions. Unwilling to work hard to obtain them, they force others to do the work for them—hence the seed of oppression. Woolman urged his readers to ponder the model of Christ, who as divine was the possessor of all but chose to live a plain and simple life in service to the afflicted.

Central to Woolman's own development as a thinker were his own experiences among the slaves and slave keepers, Native Americans, and the poor, especially in the course of his travels in the ministry. He journeyed repeatedly to the southern colonies to witness plantation slavery firsthand. He visited a settlement of Delawares during a time of war to understand better their lives and to serve as an ambassador of peace. When traveling to England at the end of his life, he lodged in steerage with the poor sailors rather than in the cabins, seeking to understand the life of the oppressed sailors.

Through these experiences, Woolman offered profound reflections on suffering, and on the meaning of the cross. He invited his readers to exercise empathetic imagination ("near sympathy") in order to gain a sense of the condition of the oppressed. Empathetic experience of their suffering appealed to the "pure witness" of the Holy Spirit in human hearts and opened the way to interior purification: Divine love could then restrain desires for wealth and prestige. Borrowing from the apostle Paul, Woolman spoke of "the death of the carnal will." Only when purified can the mind perceive the nature of God's righteousness. This vision results in overflowing love for neighbor and commitment to labor for the elimination of human oppression. These labors include the effort to "reach the pure witness" in others, so they may begin a comparable transformation of heart.

Stated in the language of the cross (cf. Col. 1:24), Woolman's point is that the sufferings of Christ are not ended. Christ suffers with the oppressed. The seed of Christ in the heart of the oppressor also suffers because it is suppressed. To enter freely into the suffering of the oppressed, Woolman believed, was to participate in the continuing process of the redemption of the world. Although the cross opened up the possibility for redemption, a society that condones slavery and other forms of oppression is, at the social level, obviously unredeemed. Inspired by the symbolic actions of the biblical prophets, Woolman dramatized the suffering of the oppressed by walking

80

great distances to meet with slave owners, riding in steerage, refusing to pay war taxes, and paying slaves for their services when he was a guest in a slave keeper's house. Through such behavior Woolman hoped to reach the pure witness in the hearts of the oppressors, who would then cease their oppression, thereby furthering the redemption of both oppressor and oppressed.

Woolman's influence extended beyond his lifetime and beyond the Society of Friends among whom he labored almost exclusively. Later antislavery activists acknowledged their deep debt to him. Toward the end of the nineteenth century, the socialist Fabian Society of England reprinted large portions of his essay, "A Plea for the Poor."

John Woolman's life and thought continue to attract attention from later readers and writers. Proponents of simple living and ecologically based values look to him as a forerunner. Some look to him as a resource for constructing a liberation theology from the First World. Others find him helpful with regard to current questions of religious pluralism, since he speaks with genuine respect for the faith of others yet stands solidly within the particularity of the Christian tradition. And a multitude of readers continues to be moved by the gentleness and striking degree of self-honesty in his *Journal*.

Suggested Readings

Writings of John Woolman: Amelia Mott Gummere, ed., *The Journal and Essays of John Woolman* (New York: Macmillan, 1922), contains all of Woolman's essays plus many letters; Phillips P. Moulton, ed., *The Journal and Major Essays of John Woolman* (New York: Oxford University Press, 1970), is the critical edition.

Edwin H. Cady, *John Woolman* (New York: Washington Square Press, 1965).

Jack D. Marietta, *The Reformation of American Quakerism, 1748–1783* (Philadelphia: University of Pennsylvania Press, 1984).

Paul Rosenblatt, *John Woolman* (New York: Twayne Publishers, 1969).

John Witherspoon

(1723–1794)

Mark A. Noll

John Witherspoon was baptized on 10 February 1723 (his birthdate is not recorded) in the Church of Scotland parish at Gifford where his father was the minister. In 1739 he received a Master of Arts from the University of Edinburgh. Six years later, after further theological study, he took the Church of Scotland pulpit in Beith, Ayrshire. By the time he moved in 1757 to the larger, more prosperous Laigh Kirk in Paisley, he had become a figure to reckon with in Scottish church life. Witherspoon's reputation rested on his labors for the Popular party in the Church of Scotland, which throughout the eighteenth century upheld the rights of local congregations and a generally more conservative theology against the Moderates, who sought to align Scotland's hereditary Calvinism with aristocratic influence and advanced learning.

Witherspoon's best-known work was a satire entitled *Ecclesiastical Characteristics*. Other noteworthy polemics included an attack on the stage, a fast-day sermon linking religious uprightness and national prosperity, and an exhortation assaulting clerical meddling in public affairs. While he was poking fun at the Moderates, Witherspoon was also publishing constructive theological works. Major treatises on the relationship between justification and holy living (1756) and on regeneration (1764), together with printed sermons testifying to his evangelical orthodoxy, marked him as a rising theological voice.

A foray into more formal academic work—a 1753 contribution to *The Scots Magazine* that defended the reliability of physical and moral perceptions—first brought Witherspoon to the attention of Americans. So rapidly did Witherspoon's American reputation grow that, when the trustees of the College of New Jersey (later Princeton University) met in 1766 to select a new president, their choice fell on Witherspoon. After his arrival at Princeton in 1768, Witherspoon was an immediate success, not only as teacher and fund-raiser for the College of New Jersey, but as a leading figure in the Presbyterian Church and as a public spokesman for the cause of liberty. He became the central figure in the creation of the Presbyterian General Assembly in the decade after the War for Independence. To the war effort Witherspoon contributed both his forceful pen and active service. He was the only member of the clergy to sign the Declaration of Independence, and he served several terms as a New Jersey delegate to the Continental Congress.

For the history of theology, Witherspoon's importance lies in his reorientation of intellectual activity at Princeton and among colonial Presbyterians away from the pietistic idealism associated with Jonathan Edwards and New Side Presbyterian revivalism to the common-sense and scientific principles of the Scottish Enlightenment. One of his first actions as president of Princeton was to banish what he called the "immaterialism" of Bishop George Berkeley along with the theocentric ethics of Edwards, which had been a strong force at the college to that time. For his own lectures on moral philosophy and divinity, he drew heavily on the ideas of his former Moderate opponents in Scotland, especially the moral philosophy of Francis Hutcheson (1694–1746).

As Witherspoon expounded it, the philosophy of Scottish Common Sense became the foundation for useful knowledge of every sort. Common sense defended the reality of the physical world and therefore allowed a wholehearted commitment to natural philosophy (i.e., science). It defined human relationships after the model of the physical sciences and therefore demonstrated the rationality of politics. It drew an analogy between external and internal sensations and therefore facilitated a science of morals. It pictured theology as dependent upon reason and therefore paved the way for an apologetic of scientific respectability.

Where his predecessors had based true virtue on the workings of divine grace, Witherspoon was more a figure of the eighteenth century in regarding the naturally given moral capacities of humanity as the ground for ethics. Witherspoon devoted part of one chapter in his lectures on moral philosophy to showing the scientific respectability of Christian faith, and it was the predominant theme of his lectures on divinity. Those lectures assured the students that reason contains no inherent criticism of revelation and that the positive teachings of scripture reflect both sound reason and "the state of human nature." Witherspoon's remarks on divinity do include brief reflections on the standard topics in Calvinistic dogmatics, but his overriding concern is to demonstrate the reasonableness of Christianity.

By providing Princeton with a philosophical basis derived from Scottish moral philosophy and by replacing a New England tradition strongly under the influence of Edwards, Witherspoon brought Presbyterians into the mainstream of eighteenth-century theology. From the newer perspective, Witherspoon could demonstrate through reason and science the truthfulness of revelation instead of presupposing revelation as the foundation for science and reason. If his new moral philosophy lacked the cohesion of Edwards' theistic conception of the world—if for Witherspoon nature and grace, science and revelation, were beginning to go their own ways—he still was able to champion both faith and learning, divinity and science, as compatible forms of truth. The fact that Witherspoon was so manifestly a man of sincere piety and that he subscribed to the Westminster Confession of Faith made for substantial continuity with historical Calvinism. Yet underneath a common commitment to broadly Calvinistic theology, a significant move was occurring from idealism, metaphysics, and conversion to realism, ethics, and morality.

Witherspoon was a key figure for later Presbyterian theological history. His immediate successor at Princeton, Samuel Stanhope Smith, carried Enlightenment commitments even farther in the direction of a reasonable Christianity. But Witherspoon had other students, like the influential Philadelphia minister Ashbel Green, who saw him in more traditional terms. The faction under Green's leadership which ousted Smith from the College of New Jersey and founded Princeton Theological Seminary (both in 1812) made more of Witherspoon's Calvinism than of his common-sense rationality. Witherspoon's combination of commitments to the eighteenth-century Enlightenment and to historical Calvinist orthodoxy continued to shape—sometimes confusedly—American Presbyterian theology for more than a century.

Suggested Readings

Writings of John Witherspoon: Ashbel Green, ed., *The Works of the Rev. John Witherspoon,* 4 vols. (Philadelphia: William W. Woodward, 1802); Jack Scott, ed., *An Annotated Edition of Lectures on Moral Philosophy by John Witherspoon* (Newark: University of Delaware Press, 1982).

Varnum Lansing Collins, *President Witherspoon: A Biography,* 2 vols. (Princeton: Princeton University Press, 1925; repr., 2 vols. in 1, New York: Arno, 1969).

Ned C. Landsman, "Witherspoon and the Problem of Provincial Identity in Scottish Evangelical Culture," in *Scotland and America in the Age of Enlightenment,* ed. Richard B. Sher and Jeffrey R. Smitten (Edinburgh: University of Edinburgh Press, 1990), 29-45.

Mark A. Noll, *Princeton and the Republic, 1768–1822* (Princeton: Princeton University Press, 1989).

Elihu Palmer

(1764–1806)

Kerry S. Walters

Elihu Palmer, American deist, was born 7 August 1764, the eighth child of a Canterbury, Connecticut, farmer. He attended Dartmouth College, read theology in Pittsfield, Massachusetts, and served a Presbyterian congregation in Newtown, New York, for a little more than a year. His growing heterodoxy cost him his pulpit in 1789. Disgusted by what he took to be the unshakable intolerance of Christianity, he abandoned the pulpit in mid-1791 for the law. and eventually settled in Philadelphia to practice. But in 1793 he fell victim, along with his wife, to the great yellow fever epidemic. His wife died, and though Palmer survived, he was permanently blinded by his illness. Realizing a law career was impossible, he spent the rest of his life as a champion of Deism, stumping the eastern seaboard from Georgia to Maine in support of rational religion. Along the way he gave hundreds of public lectures, helped found deistic societies in New England and the Middle Atlantic states, and edited two deistic newspapers: The *Temple of Reason* (1800–1801) and the *Prospect, or View of the Moral World* (1803–1805). Palmer died of pleurisy on 7 April 1806. His second wife would have been left indigent had Thomas Paine not looked after her.

Unlike most other prominent American deists such as Benjamin Franklin, Thomas Paine, or Thomas Jefferson, Palmer's advocacy of natural religion arose squarely from within the mainstream Christianity of his day. Educated to the pulpit, Palmer knew both Christian theology and scripture well, and this expertise is reflected in his deistic writings. Moreover, his church background influenced his presentation as well as his message: Many of his contemporaries claimed that he spoke publicly on Deism with the fire of a revivalist preacher. In addition, Palmer of all the American deists dreamt of establishing deistic churches, or "temples of reason," complete with their own liturgies. In short, Palmer was a critic of Christian orthodoxy whose work arose from and frequently reflects the very tradition against which he rebelled.

Palmer's chief work is *Principles of Nature; or, a Development of the Moral Causes of Happiness and Misery Among the Human Species* (1801). Quickly becoming known as the Bible of Deism, the book offered the most systematic and radical defense of rational religion to be penned in America. Although some of its argument was derived from earlier deists, most notably John Toland (1670–1722) and Thomas Paine (1737–1809), large parts of it were genuinely original contributions to the literature of rational religion.

Like many deistic tracts of the eighteenth and early nineteenth centuries, Palmer's *Principles of Nature* is divided into two parts: a radical critique of revealed religion in general and Christianity in particular, and a defense of Deism. Palmer attacked Christianity on three counts. First, its supernaturalistic affirmation of miracles violates the immutability of natural law and runs counter to ordinary experience. Second, Christian dogmas as well as sacred scripture do violence to reason. The former defend logical absurdities such as the divine Trinity or empirical impossibilities such as the Virgin Birth, and the latter is shot through with textual inconsistencies which cast doubt on the veracity of the whole. Finally, the Christian ethos itself engenders an immorality that historically has proved antithetical to the flourishing of individuals and the progress of humanity. It preaches an unseemly humility that bruises the inherent dignity of human beings, condemns innocent persons, via the doctrine of original sin, for a primordial ancestral transgression, and it damns persons to an eternity of hell for what can only be finite sins.

Moreover, Palmer believed ecclesiastical institutions have always cooperated with political powers to subdue the general population through fear, ignorance, and superstition. The double despotism of church and state is a continuous theme throughout all of Palmer's work. At the time of his death, he was at work on the treatise *The Political World,* which systematically represented this point of view.

In place of Christianity, Palmer advocated a religion based on righteous and immortal reason. He insisted, in typical deistic fashion, that physical reality is God's true revelation, and that the same qualities of rationality and orderliness observable in nature can be attributed to the Deity. Moreover, he argued the best way to worship God is through virtuous behavior, social reform, and scientific investigation. This de-supernaturalized religion, which rejects miracles and mystery, is the only kind compatible with the dignity of both God and humans.

But the *Principles of Nature* is not simply an apology for Deism. It is also a systematic articulation of a natural morality based on the twin principles of reciprocal justice and universal benevolence, and herein lies Palmer's most original contribution. According to Palmer, revelation is not necessary as a means of discovering the nature of good and evil. Instead, the sentient nature of humanity is a sufficient foundation for defending an ethical system that requires humans to treat one another in ways that minimize suffering. Moreover, Palmer anticipates twentieth-century concerns about ethical obligations to future generations by insisting it is the responsibility of each generation to reform social institutions (such as, he tells us, slavery), which will inflict suffering on that generation's descendants.

Elihu Palmer, more than any other Enlightenment figure in America, transformed Deism into a popular movement which captured the hearts and minds of thousands of persons. He was hated and reviled during his lifetime for his espousal of radical republicanism as much as for his fiery rejection of Christianity. But one obvious result of his deistic crusade was to force Christian apologists in America to search for ways to defend their faith that would take the relentless criticisms of rational religion into account. Palmer was neither the first nor the last American to defend Deism, but in many ways, he was the best.

Suggested Readings

Roderick S. French, "Elihu Palmer, Radical Deist, Radical Republican: A Reconsideration of American Freethought," in *Studies in Eighteenth Century Culture*, 8 (University of Wisconsin Press, 1979).

Kerry S. Walters, "Elihu Palmer's Crusade for Rational Religion," *Religious Humanism* 24 (Summer 1990): 113-29.

————, *The American Deists: Voices of Reason and Dissent in the Early Republic* (Lawrence: University Press of Kansas, 1992).

————, *Elihu Palmer's Principles of Nature: Text and Commentary* (Wolfeboro, N.H.: Longwood Academic, 1990).

————, *Rational Infidels: The American Deists* (Durango, Colo.: Longwood Academic, 1992).

PERIOD 2

THE NATIONAL ERA
(1789–1865)

INTRODUCTION

Mark G. Toulouse and James O. Duke

From its founding to its Civil War, the new American nation swelled in territory and population. Waves of immigration increased its Christian diversity, which grew to span nearly the full spectrum of western Europe's churches. National independence led colonial churches toward ecclesiastical independence as well. Constitutional principles of freedom of worship and separation of church and state forced every church to compete for members, funds, and status in a free and open marketplace. Expansion to the west made those lands a mission field as daunting as it was inviting. Schisms as well as new church starts added to the multiplicity of older and in-coming immigrant churches, many of which quickly became capable of sustained organizational and theological development.

The inherited view of theology as the "true" doctrinal teaching of the "true" church remained prominent. So too did that of the theologian as a formally endorsed, and usually formally educated, teacher of the church. But these definitions could no longer be taken altogether for granted. While some might demand and many more prefer them, they were hard-pressed to police word-usage within culture at large. Other, more expansive uses of the terms became ever more common. A few of the many factors contributing to this development deserve note.

One was the emergence of the pattern of "denominationalism," an acceptance of the validity of various churches as truly Christian although separate and "denominated" by their distinctive names, polities, beliefs, and practices. The pattern formed gradually, and never without critics. The early years of the Republic were especially rife with interchurch rivalry and theological invective. As time passed, however, Protestants generally became ever more inclined to stress their similarities, to agree to disagree among themselves on other matters, and above all to join in common cause against Catholicism, radicals, infidels, skepticism, indifference, and immorality. Whether doctrinal uniformity was to be the litmus test of true Christianity was on the way to becoming a negotiable point. In any case, what were leaders of the ever-proliferating groups of Christians to be called if not theologians? They were within their own denominations teachers of the faith, even if outsiders considered their teachings theologically ill-informed, thin, or false.

In this setting, one strength of the classical definition of a theologian—its exclusivity—was at the same time its weakness. Exclusivity ran counter to the national ethos. Christians insistent on defining the true church, its true theology, and its true theologians in too narrow and partisan a manner risked appearing somewhat elitist, sectarian, and even un-American. In addition, churches dedicated to theologically learned ministers were at times forced to make exceptions and compromises. The demand constantly outpaced the supply despite the high priority given to founding new church-related schools of higher education, including theological seminaries, an innovation of the day. Meanwhile, many Christians under the influence of Pietism or the Enlightenment questioned whether the formalities of theological study and denominational endorsement were all that necessary for teaching the "simple" biblical (or rational) truths of the Christian religion.

The success of efforts to make theological education available to greater numbers and upgrade the standards for learned ministry had certain unforeseen consequences. It became ever-more obvious that theology was not church doctrine alone but also—maybe alternatively—a field of academic study. The full impact of this development made itself known only after the Civil War, for during the national era the "scholarly pastor" and "pastoral scholar" were interchangeable career options. Even so, the institutionalization of disciplinary expertise in the study of theology raised an issue still under debate: Are the "real" Christian theologians those who shape the beliefs and practices of the churches or those who shape studies relating to church beliefs and practices?

A well-informed laity was another Protestant concern, in keeping with the larger goal of advancing Christianity and civilization in the new nation. Opportunities opened up for laypersons to study theology and cognate disciplines in much the same way as learned ministers. Sharing—popularizing—the results of theological scholarship was an integral part of a pastor-scholar's responsibilities. And more and more well-educated laity proved themselves quite capable of doing precisely the same. Their presentations of the Christian message were on a par with those of ordained preachers and their teachers, sometimes more erudite than the former and more inspirational than the latter. Among them were women, excluded from seminary education and denied ordination by their churches because of gender alone.

Two broader, international, intellectual currents spreading over the American scene—Scottish Common-Sense philosophy and Romanticism—contributed something of their own to this further complication. For this reason, as well as their impact on the content and idiom of theology as a whole, each deserves at least brief comment.

The common-sense thought of the Scottish Enlightenment first becomes a noteworthy force in American theology at the end of the colonial era, with John Witherspoon. Scots and Scots-Irish immigration after the Revolution expanded its social base. It spread quickly and widely among Protestants as a defense against skepticism and authoritarianism, and from their journals, lecture halls, and school textbooks gained currency within society at large. Philosophically, common-sense thinking offered a theory of knowledge (an epistemology) affirming the reliability of sensory experiences of the external world, the scientific method of inductive reasoning as the pathway to truth, and the certainty of fundamental principles of faith and morals. It fostered in theology the continued development of various forms of "rational supernaturalism," that is, rational appeals to facts, evidences, and reliable witnesses supportive of biblical and church teachings regarding divinely revealed truth.

Romanticism was if anything even more varied—more amorphous and adaptable—than common-sense thought. It emerged in late-eighteenth-century Europe, partly a repudiation and partly an extension of the Enlightenment concept of "reason." Emphasis was placed on heights and depths of feeling, imaginative creativity, dynamic historical development, the organic relatedness of all things, the beauty of nature, and the nobility of artistic and ethical endeavor. In terms of philosophy per se, its point of departure was Kant's "Copernican revolution," which located the certainty of knowledge in the structure of consciousness itself: The "higher" role of mind (as Reason) was that of structuring the world of sensory and moral experience as a whole. Post-Kantian philosophy moved toward idealistic accounts of reality, speaking of God—the divine, the Infinite, the Absolute—as Mind or Spirit unfolding itself through the creation of the universe and achieving full self-awareness of itself over the course of history through the achievements of the human spirit.

The mix of Romantic, Kantian, and post-Kantian thought first made significant impact on Christian theology in America in the 1830s. Its effects on literature and other arts—indeed on sensibilities and the "climate of opinion" in the United States—were by then already well underway. As a philosophical-theological alternative to older confessional and scholastic theologies on the one hand and Enlightenment and common-sense rational theologies on the other, it opened up a striking new spectrum of options. Signs of its presence can be detected in speculative, mystical, and pantheistic "systems" of thought as well as in what the unwary might mistake for thoughtless, gushy sentimentalism.

The midranges of this rainbow spectrum proved most appealing and useful to church theologians. Here, amid and despite many variations can be found a new model for theology itself: religious faiths arise from profound, life-transforming experiences of the presence and power of the divine; theology arises, secondarily as it were, with human attempts to reflect upon and express such religious experiences and to communicate them to others. In the case of Christian theology specifically, this paradigm—in a phrase, theology is a reflection on and expression of religious experience—first gained currency early in the nineteenth century as "modern liberalism" with the writings of Friedrich Schleiermacher (1768–1834) in Germany and Samuel Taylor Coleridge (1772–1834) in England.

Though rival paradigms, common-sense and Romantic-Kantian thought had much the same effect in extending the meanings of the terms "theology" and "theologian"—giving rise to further extension. If theology itself is understood as either the exposition of the religious and moral principles of revealed religion (common sense) or as the vivid expression of human experiences of the divine (Romantic), the term "theologian" could no longer or so justly be defined as narrowly as before. People other than ordained ministers and theological scholars could write about Christian principles and Christian religious experiences, and did. Such writings were, to all appearances, "theological." And if the point of theology was to set forth the great truths and grand themes of the faith, there seemed no good reason to hold that this task was handled only or even best in such traditional genres of church theology as sermons, creeds and catechisms, treatises, or systems of doctrine. Other, more popular and effective forms of literature were inviting: biography and autobiography, novels and short stories, moral manifestos, poems, essays.

This exhibition of the era's makers of theology, then, expands considerably, seeking to pick up not only doctrinal developments within larger, culturally dominant churches but examples of new features and forms of Christian theologizing. These portraits are placed into six thematic groupings: New Divinity in the National Period; Emergent Mainline Alternatives to New Divinity; Revivalistic-Holiness Responses; Defining Orthodoxy; Defining Theology's Boundaries; and Concern for Ecclesiology. Certainly the portraits could be arranged in other ways. A more strictly denominational approach, for example, is always possible. This one, however, covers a broad field while highlighting trends, themes, and issues with interdenominational reach.

The theologians of later New Divinity held the continuity of tradition from Calvin to Puritanism to Edwards to Hopkins to themselves in high esteem. And indeed, in keeping with that tradition, they introduced a number of modifications and innovations that seemed to them necessary to keep the essentials of old New England's Reformed faith alive. Edwards had defended the eighteenth-century Awakening as a "surprising" work of God. Proponents of the New Divinity sought not only to defend but to prompt awakenings by "new measures" of revivalism. And while insisting that conversion was truly God's work, they insisted as well that God's work involved the efforts of zealous evangelists and earnest—willing and accountable—seekers of salvation. The moral implications of true conversion were set forth in bold relief. In the case of Lemuel Haynes, an African American Congregationalist minister, God's decree to overrule the power of sin mandated the people of God to disavow the trade and holding of slaves.

A trio of figures—Nathan Bangs, Methodist; Horace Bushnell, Congregationalist; and Francis Wayland, Baptist—pointed their churches (and others willing to give them any heed) in new directions. Each was in his own way a "progressive" within his church tradition. All three attacked New Divinity doctrine—not because they cared little about God's grace, human sin and accountability, the uniqueness of the person and work of Christ, righteous living in this world, and eternal salvation or damnation, but because they cared so much. All three were responsive to nineteenth-century developments in science, philosophy, and theology and yet discriminating in their approval of it. Their careers as well as their writings reflected adjustments and accommodations that many Protestant churches were to make to changing social and cultural conditions over the course of the century.

Early on, their progressivist views seemed daring, too daring according to many of their contemporaries. Bushnell barely avoided being convicted of heresy in a church court. By century's end, however, the vast coalition of evangelical Protestants that historians refer to by such terms as "the Protestant establishment" and "the mainline Protestant churches" held their memories in honor, calling them theological pioneers. Bangs and Wayland, both admirers of Scottish common-sense thought, had encouraged their churches to become equal partners in the continuing conversation about theology among Protestants. Bushnell—often termed a founder of liberalism and "the Schleiermacher of America"—had been among the first to guide his church into the world of Romantic sensibilities and post-Kantian ideas.

The experience of conversion to Christ, according to the theologians of revivalism, was necessary for eternal salvation. It was also necessary for the vitality of living faith here and now, redirecting believers from the path of sin to that of righteousness. Those whom God justifies (accepts) are called and empowered by God to press on toward sanctification. The theologians grouped together under the heading Revivalistic and Holiness Responses exemplify the force and effects of the emphasis on sanctification, holiness, and perfection in antebellum Protestantism. Two of them, Charles G. Finney and Harriet Beecher Stowe, came to their views from backgrounds in the New Divinity movement. Two others, Asa Mahan and Phoebe Palmer, were Methodists who revived and extended the "perfectionist" element in Wesley's thought. Samuel Schmucker, a Lutheran, sought to make room for the revivalist and activist features of American Protestantism within his church's confessional heritage.

There were of course those who took exception to the new theologies and new measures of the day on many grounds. Some were fearful that the substance of historical church doctrine and indeed the necessity of sound doctrine itself were under threat. Concerned too that post-Enlightenment trends of thought gave rise to heterodoxy, skepticism, and indifference, they warned that "winning the hearts and minds of people" by making ceaseless concessions to ever-changing times would result in a Pyrrhic victory at best. What was required, in their judgment, was a clear, firm reassertion of the enduring truths of the Christian religion—in short, a well-defined orthodoxy. Featured here are four theologians devoted to this cause: Charles Hodge and James Thornwell, both Presbyterians; Francis Kenrick, a Roman Catholic; and C. F. W. Walther, leader of the Missouri Synod Lutherans. One point worthy of note in each case is this: In the endeavor to reaffirm historical orthodoxy, they made use of varied resources of recent and contemporary vintage.

The grouping of theologians at work "defining the boundaries of Christian theology" is a sampler of New England thinkers with Unitarian connections. The connections are not altogether smooth and tight: Ralph Waldo Emerson left his Unitarian congregation in midcareer for a self-avowed "ministry at large," and Lydia Maria Child undertook a theological pilgrimage for which no church or party label is fully suited. The aim here is not in any case that of covering regional or denominational developments per se. The exhibit serves rather to highlight changing conceptions of the relationship between Christian faith and human reason.

The roots of Unitarianism stretch back long and far in history. It came to new life in Enlightenment England, and transatlantic ties if nothing else ensured its arrival in America. Yet the force with which it appeared within New England Congregationalism early in the nineteenth century was striking: the offspring of Calvinist Puritans had apparently decided to murder their parents. And indeed "Calvinist" was the one thing the Unitarians were not. Their accounts of the benevolence of God, the dignity, freedom, and moral responsibility of humanity, and the high ethical ideals embodied in the life and teachings of Jesus Christ were so contrary to "traditional" Protestantism that opponents saw there hardly anything other than willful apostasy.

Where was the boundary line of Christian theology to be drawn? The denial of the doctrine of the Trinity alone set Unitarianism out-of-bounds in the eyes of many. They did not, at least at first, view the matter that way. They claimed to be "liberal Christians" who, upholding Christianity's essentials, were doing Christianity and the whole wide world a service by overthrowing mistaken traditions about revealed religion on the basis of scripture and enlightened reason. Unlike the Deists, William Channing and Andrews Norton were rational supernaturalists, and their supernaturalism had as its focus Christian revelation. They were also, in their own way, as insistent on "orthodoxy" in the sense of Christian right-thinking and "orthopraxy" in the sense of Christian right-acting as any of their trinitarian critics.

With Ralph Waldo Emerson, Margaret Fuller, and Theodore Parker this boundary line too was tested. They made the paradigm shift from pre-Kantian conceptions of reason to a post-Kantian and Romantic conception of "transcendental" reason, and in so doing shifted attention from arguments for divine revelation to revelatory experiences of the divine. Focus on the divine in Jesus Christ led, then, to a Christian Transcendentalism. Yet "experiencing the divine" was a field of interest and exploration far more extensive than that dealt with before by Christian theologians. Must a theologian focus, and insist, on the divine in Jesus Christ alone in order to remain a "Christian" theologian? Many, Unitarians and Trinitarians alike, viewed the testing of this boundary with alarm, warning against "the latest form of infidelity," German pettifoggery, and mysticism.

The seven theologians placed together here due to their "concern for ecclesiology" are a diverse lot. The heading deserves brief explanation. These were not the only thinkers to concern themselves with the nature and purpose of the church. Virtually every theologian of the era did so: the multiplicity of Christian churches and the fluidity of church affiliation demanded no less. And of course these seven theologians were concerned about many other matters as well, and could easily be placed in other categories. Several of them—Orestes Brownson, John W. Nevin, and Philip Schaff—were representatives of distinctly post-Kantian and Romantic trends in theology. Brownson and Hecker, converts to Roman Catholicism, were as interested as Kendrick in the survival and faithfulness of Catholicism in a land under Protestant cultural domination. Nevin and Schaff, who urged Reformed Christians to recall their pre-Puritan heritage of theology and worship, played strong roles in the emergence of mainline alternatives to the New Divinity. Alexander Campbell, foremost leader of the Disciples of Christ, was—his break with home-church Presbyterianism notwithstanding—as much a biblical and post-Enlightenment empirical theologian as Hodge and Thornwell, Moses Stuart, or Andrews Norton. The "new revelation" received by Joseph Smith, founder of Mormonism (the Church of Jesus Christ of Latter-day Saints), set him on Christian theology's boundary line. Nonetheless, this set of eight portraits serves a purpose that none of the other categories fulfills as well. It illustrates the centrality of the question of the identity of the "true church" for each of these thinkers even as it calls attention to varied answers to it of important long-term significance. Considerable variety in defining the nature and purpose of the church has characterized the theological enterprise in America from this time onward.

Lemuel Haynes

(1753–1833)

John Saillant

A black Calvinist and controversialist, Lemuel Haynes explored Christian doctrine in search of ways it could be used to end slavery and improve race relations. Tutored in the 1770s and 1780s in the theology of Jonathan Edwards, Joseph Bellamy, and Samuel Hopkins, Haynes articulated a distinctive black Calvinism in sermons and essays published from 1792 to 1820; other writings from 1774 to 1833 remained unpublished until the 1980s and 1990s.

White New England Presbyterians reared Haynes almost from birth. Haynes' white mother abandoned her infant, apparently because of his close resemblance to his unnamed black father. An indentured servant until age twenty-one, the youthful Haynes gained a reputation as an inspiring lector of other men's sermons, most notably George Whitefield's. Haynes began composing his own sermons in the 1770s. After serving in the patriot militia in the War of Independence and bartering farmwork for tutoring with New Divinity ministers, Haynes was ordained a Congregational minister in 1785 and appointed minister to a frontier church in Rutland, Vermont, in 1788.

Haynes' detractors (Universalists and Christian freethinkers) branded him a "Hopkintonian"—doctrinaire and overmetaphysical. Haynes accepted the brand, referring to Hopkins' *System of Doctrines* as a definitive work. The essence of Haynes' theological writings is the application of the doctrines of Hopkins' New Divinity to the moral character of life in a society characterized by slaveholding and participation (until 1808) in the Atlantic slave trade.

Haynes began with the New Divinity doctrines that divine providence entails continued governance of all creatures, things, and acts and that even moral evil originates with God, who wills that it serve divinely ordained good. Sinning humans are selfish or self-centered, not virtuous, but God benevolently and gloriously overrules evil with good. Such doctrines led

New Divinity preachers to theorize about God's overruling of the sins of slaveholders and slave traders. The New Divinity advocates saw sin all about, but perhaps the furor over slaveholding that accompanied the republican revolution, along with Hopkins' ministry in Newport, Rhode Island, one of the prominent links in the Atlantic slave trade, made particularly striking the evident sins of the slavers. Hopkins began announcing in the 1780s that the sin in slaveholding and slave trading consisted of the forced transportation of Africans to the Americas and hence that God's overruling was the "return" of blacks to Africa. The divinely ordained good was the Christianization of Africa by pious African Americans. Many whites came to clamor for the "colonization" of blacks—their expatriation to Africa.

The divine overruling of slavery as Haynes stated it was much different from the white version. The sin in slaveholding and slave trading, he argued, consisted in usurping slaves' natural liberty and denying them an education in Christian and republican principles. God's overruling was the restoration of liberty and the extension of education to blacks, not expatriation. Haynes argued that God uses slavery as a means to increase appreciation of liberty among those who lived in a slaveholding society even if they were not slaves themselves. God sends a message to whites through the suffering of blacks, Haynes insisted. The message was to follow divine decrees as they are revealed in the divine providence of slavery. To these theological arguments, Haynes added the certitude that slavery and the slave trade were not serving as instruments for the Christianization of blacks, either in Africa or in America. Although it might seem that only a depraved Deity would ordain evils like enslavement and the slave trade, it seemed worse to Haynes to countenance the idea that the sufferings of blacks resulted from human misdeeds, with no larger significance.

Which understanding of God's overruling of the sins of slavery was truer to the Edwardsean-Hopkinsian tradition? Edwards and Hopkins argued for a "proportional" overruling: sin countered by a good that mirrored and negated the evil. For example, the Resurrection countered the Crucifixion. Did Hopkins or Haynes have a clearer understanding of the sinfulness of slavery? Was its sinfulness in essence forced transportation or the usurpation of natural liberty and the neglect of education? In the Edwardsean-Hopkinsian tradition, one's righteous deeds—the way one tries to conform to God's decrees—in this instance depends on one's understanding of the sinfulness of slavery.

Haynes also affirmed the New Divinity doctrines that all unregenerate men and women are selfish sinners, that the virtue of the regenerate is

benevolence (disinterested love of being), and that God preordains individuals to salvation or damnation. Of course, Haynes condemned slaveholding and slave trading as selfish and argued that blacks deserve the same
disinterested love as do whites. Haynes linked his military service to New
Divinity notions of virtue, and as his career matured, he gained repute as a
"preacher of the heart," one who aided in his hearers' conversion.

By 1805, Haynes was widely known in New England as a defender of
the New Divinity. His efforts earned him an invitation from Timothy
Dwight in 1814 to preach in Edwards' chapel at Yale College, the epicen-
ter of New England orthodoxy. Haynes continued to mingle black Calvinism with resistance to liberal Christianity. Certain that Calvinism implied a
critique of slavery and that blacks' best hope for dignity and equality lay in
the expansion of benevolence and the conquest of selfishness, Haynes
feared that an Arminian Christianity tolerant of differences in creed and of
the pursuit of self-interest did not bode well for American race relations.
Liberty from slavery did not entail liberal individualism for Haynes.
Although Haynes may have shared with Edwards and Hopkins an unreal-
istic estimate of the power of disinterested benevolence, his essential insight
was that a nominally free society without a strong doctrinal tradition
emphasizing social benevolence would be fearsome for blacks. Haynes
unceasingly insisted that blacks and whites are united in a providential
design that mandates disinterested benevolence.

Haynes has been the invisible man of African American theology, partly
because he affiliated with the now-distant Edwardsean tradition and partly because his critique of liberal individualism has led many to the mistak-
en belief that he was not an abolitionist. Yet he is a relevant figure to those
interested in the variations of Calvinism and those intent on calculating the
value of liberal society.

Suggested Readings

Richard Newman, ed., *Black Preacher to White America: The Collected
Writings of Lemuel Haynes, 1774–1833* (Brooklyn: Carlson Publishing,
1990).

Rita Roberts, "Patriotism and Political Criticism: The Evolution of Political Consciousness in the Mind of a Black Revolutionary Soldier," *Eighteenth-
Century Studies* 27 (1994): 569-88.

John Saillant, "'A Doctrinal Controversy Between the Hopkintonian
and the Universalistic': Religion, Race, and Ideology in Post-Revolutionary
Vermont," *Vermont History* 61 (1993): 197-216.

————, "Lemuel Haynes' Black Republicanism and the American Republican Tradition, 1775–1820," *Journal of the Early Republic* 14 (1994): 293-324.

————, "Slavery and Divine Providence in New England Calvinism: The New Divinity and a Black Protest, 1775–1805," *New England Quarterly* 68 (1995): 584-608.

Nathaniel William Taylor

(1786–1858)

Bruce M. Stephens

Nathaniel William Taylor has been hailed as the most innovative systematic theologian in nineteenth-century America. The New Haven theology of which he was the chief architect has been praised as America's one great contribution to the theological thinking of Christendom. Born in New Milford, Connecticut, to a prominent family, Taylor inherited the New England Puritanism of his father and his grandfather. He graduated in 1807 from Yale College where he fell under the formative influence of president Timothy Dwight with whom he spent an additional four years studying theology and serving as his teacher's secretary. Licensed to preach in 1810, he was called at the age of twenty-six to Center Church in New Haven, the most prestigious Congregationalist pulpit in Connecticut. A handsome, imposing, and at times overbearing and even indiscreet figure, Taylor was widely recognized as a powerful pulpit orator and a gifted thinker who combined personal piety with impressive reasoning.

In 1822 Taylor joined faculty at the newly established Yale Divinity School, where he spent the next thirty-six years systematically expounding the truths of the Christian faith to which he was persuaded all minds would yield consent through the power of reason and common sense. Truth demands the sacrifice of everything that does not hold up to free inquiry, and he urged his students to "follow the truth even if it carries you over Niagara."

Taylor applied the resources of his vigorous mind to advocating a warmer, more friendly version of Calvinism by defusing the attacks of Unitarians and Arminians against its harsher teachings on human sinfulness, divine sovereignty, and the satisfaction theory of the atonement. He drew upon the themes of human free agency, divine benevolence, and the moral government of God to ameliorate Calvinism and to present it to a nineteenth-century America which, under the influence of the Enlightenment, was ready to reexamine the relationships between the sovereignty and benevolence of God and the freedom and responsibility of moral agents.

The basic themes of Taylor's theology emerged early and remained consistent throughout his long career. Irritated by Unitarian criticism of the "moral tendency" of Orthodox doctrines, he set out to demonstrate that human beings cannot be both sinful by nature and free to sin or not. He rejected the doctrine of "natural depravity" and substituted "depravity by nature" whereby sin depends upon human choice. Sin is not the product of a sinful nature or disposition analogous to a physical trait, but it is always the result of the free choice of some object rather than God as the chief good. Human nature is simply the occasion for this preference of some private interest over God, which no one by nature is compelled to choose. But, argued Taylor, "such is their nature that they will sin and only sin in all the appropriate circumstances of their being." He argued further that there is no sin in choosing evil unless there is power to choose good, for sin is sin only if the moral agent is free to choose either good or evil. Therefore moral blame rests squarely on the shoulders of those who always possess a "power to the contrary." Sin is something human beings do, not something they are. The will has not been tainted by a sinful human nature but corrupted by the free choice of self over God.

All Calvinists agreed on the "fact" of sin, but they were far from settled concerning the mode of accounting for its origin. Taylor bristled at the Unitarian charge that Calvinists made God the author of sin by creating humankind with a sinful nature, and he struck back by arguing that human beings come into the world in such a state that without grace they will sin the first moment they become moral agents. But in turning back the Unitarian challenge, Taylor's view of human depravity simultaneously drove a wedge between liberal and conservative parties within both Congregationalism and Presbyterianism. In the ensuing debate, described by one participant as "a labyrinth where thousands have been bewildered and lost," Taylor suffered greater acrimony from his fellow Calvinists than from Unitarians. The controversy gave distinct shape to the New Haven theology and its central conviction that prior to the first act of moral agency there is nothing in human nature which can properly be called sin.

The objective then becomes to transform the choice for self and world into the choice for God. This transformation will require something that is "above nature" in the form of the gracious intervening work of the Spirit in regeneration. If human beings have such a nature that "they will sin and only sin in all the appropriate circumstances of their being," then this condition can be addressed only by the interposing and regenerating power of the Spirit. Left to its own devices the human mind can, but never will, exert its natural ability to turn from self to God in obedience. Since depravity is a moral and not a physical condition, a result of human choice and not of human nature, the work of the Spirit is directed to changing this choice from self to God in the creation of a new heart.

The sinner is active in this process of making a new heart because to bring the inherent moral powers of the sinner to life requires both human and divine agency. Armed only with the power of truth as its chief instrument, the Spirit addresses the mind and persuades it to make the intelligent choice for God over self. This shift from the choice for self to the choice for God does not often occur instantaneously, because there are preliminaries to the moment of choice during which the mind reflects upon and is moved by the truth. The "selfish principle," which deludes the sinner into thinking that the greatest happiness will come from choices centering on the self, must be displaced by choices centering on God and from which alone, according to Taylor, true happiness or "self-love" comes. This shift of priorities from self to God, from the misery of the selfish principle to the happiness of self-love, is crucial. Despite the power and persistence of the selfish principle and the almost limitless capacity for self-deception, human beings, by virtue of self-love or "the constitutional capacity for happiness," can reach higher levels of selflessness.

The drama of the self is this internal struggle between the selfish principle perverting and twisting the truth to selfish interests, and self-love or happiness, the innate capacity of the self assisted by the Spirit to transcend selfishness in the love of God. Simple moral suasion alone cannot accomplish this change, for only the work of the Spirit can create that moment when the selfish principle is "suspended" and self-love becomes the ruling principle in the soul. Taylor explored the inner world of the human heart and mind with a precision unknown in American theology since Edwards. In the logical and moral world of this New Haven divine, each sinner, assisted by the Spirit, played an active role in making the intelligent, voluntary choice in asserting the preference for God over self.

The keystone of Taylor's theology, however, is the moral government of God, the intelligent and moral universe within which the divine-human encounter is played out. He believed all past attempts at systematic theology had been "utter and complete failures" because no previous theologian had discovered and made this the central theme of theology. Making the moral government of God the interpretative principle of theology would result in "a system that contains no unanswerable objections," and it was to the task of creating this system that Taylor devoted his considerable intellectual gifts in his *Lectures on the Moral Government of God*.

For Taylor "the comprehensive theme" and final test of theology are how it addresses the government of moral beings existing under the influence of divine authority. To this end it is imperative to understand how the perfect moral government of God works to secure the highest well-being of its subjects. The "fact" of moral government then follows naturally upon the "fact" of human moral agency. Only moral agents are capable of fulfilling the law upon which the moral government of God is founded and thereby of living in happiness, or of violating the law and living in misery. The emphasis shifts therefore from human dependence on a sovereign God to human moral agents with obligations as subjects of a benevolent moral governor. There is a proper fit between moral agency and moral government because the latter works not by coercion but by the influence of divine authority through the medium of law, leading to benevolent actions which promote the well-being and prevent the misery of moral agents.

Benevolence leading to happiness and selfishness leading to misery are the two "elective preferences" of humanity; over time one or the other of these becomes a predominant, or habitual, state of mind. The law of God's moral government is designed precisely to curb selfishness and to promote benevolence as the elective preference or governing principle in moral agents. The common-sense "truth of things" is that a moral governor has the right to command and subjects have the duty to obey under the rule of law. The moral law therefore includes sanctions which are designed to draw moral beings away from selfishness and toward benevolence, thereby securing the great end of all action which is human happiness. The important point is that moral agents have not lost the power to obey the law, and Taylor was persuaded that theologians from Augustine to Edwards had been at best "but darkly wise" regarding the relation between law and the human ability to obey it.

The moral governor is related to moral agents through the sanctions of law within the moral government where God has the right to command and humans the duty to obey. The moral law is therefore both an expression of God's benevolence and a confirmation of human ability. Taylor repeatedly emphasized that legal sanctions demonstrate God's "highest approbation of obedience and his highest disapprobation of disobedience." Law is the "rule of action" within the moral government of God, and in obeying the law "all, all is action, energy—life in all its fullness of activity and strenuousness of effort." Revivalists turned to Taylor's theology for support as they set about transforming the essential truths of Calvinism to meet the conditions of post-Revolutionary America.

For Taylor the moral government of God was a system best fitted to secure the obedience and in turn the happiness of its subjects, notwith-standing the persistence of evil. Evil does not offer the slightest evidence that God is not benevolent or that the present moral system is not the best possible one. Indeed, the evil resulting from the perversion of moral agency is "incidental" to the moral government of God and in the end allows for the greatest possible good. In fact it may be impossible for God to prevent the perversion of moral agency in any greater degree than is presently done, for the simple reason that moral agents cease being moral agents the minute sin is prevented by any power or influence which destroys their moral agency. In very careful language Taylor rejected the notion that sin is "the means of the greatest good" in favor of the argument that "in the nature of things" it may be impossible for God to prevent all sin. Moral evil exists therefore not because it is the necessary means to the greatest good but because it is incidental to the best possible moral system.

It seemed inconceivable to the Dwight professor of didactic theology at Yale that Christianity had been given to the world and then left without a rational defense at this crucial juncture concerning the existence of evil. The power of reason should not be awed by the "mystery" of evil; it should be used to discover the place of evil within the rational order of God's moral government. Taylor argued that God's "inability" to prevent all evil is not a limitation of divine sovereignty but, on the contrary, another sure sign of divine benevolence, attesting that God has fitted moral agents for a moral system in which they can freely exercise the power to obey or dis-obey. Thus, even though the best moral system requires some sin, there is absolutely no evidence from scripture, reason, or common sense that God has even a slight preference for sin over holiness or for disobedience over obedience.

The administration of God's moral government requires enforcing the sanctions of law through applications of the principle of justice. Justice as an expression of divine benevolence makes pardon possible for those who have perverted moral agency and are therefore guilty. The atonement is the expedient which allows for this pardon; it is not a satisfaction for the sins of the guilty. The atonement simply renders it consistent for God to offer pardon, while simultaneously maintaining the majesty of the law and the authority of the Moral Governor. In the atonement, God as judge executes "the law of judgment" transforming it into "the law of action." The moral system is no longer one of "mere law," but is now a system of law and grace, conforming precisely to the nature of moral government. By open-ing the possibility of pardon for the guilty, the atonement does not infringe upon either the rule of law or upon human free agency, both of which are crucial to the functioning of God's moral government.

Taylor's emphasis on moral agency required a system within which moral agents have the power to choose and God has the power to influence but not to coerce them. Unlike the physical laws of nature which operate directly by coercion, the laws of moral government operate indirectly by influence or persuasion. Moral government presupposes responsible moral agents from whom God does not expect what they do not have the ability to deliver; the very nature of law requires the exercise of human ability. Obedience to the law is therefore a matter of consent, and moral government is designed to bring about this consent by persuasion and not by coercion. Taylor was persuaded that the rule of law under the moral government of God was the source not only of individual happiness and fulfillment but of social well-being and harmony as well.

This governmental version of Calvinism was reassuring to many citizens of post-Revolutionary America, who were ready for a message that centered not upon political or religious coercion but upon persuasion and an appeal to the self-determining power of the will coupled with the self-limiting power of God as moral governor. Taylor's moral governor was a constitutionally limited divine executive and his moral agents were self-determining virtuous citizens. This God and these citizens were to be united in a moral government through which both divine benevolence and human freedom would find expression. Taylor tried to persuade his critics that the theological issues which had dominated an earlier time, most notably the theme of human dependence, had yielded to an emphasis upon human moral agency. Given the prevailing state of "public opinion," his theology provided a healthy infusion of human ability into the debate.

The New Haven restatement of the themes of sin, regeneration, human ability, and moral government was not lost on revivalists looking for ways to energize the masses into being and doing good. If Nathaniel Taylor struggled to discover and to explicate the laws of moral government, his close friend Lyman Beecher worked to put these laws and this government to work ensuring the morality and perpetuity of the young republic through revivals and voluntary societies. Taylor's theology contained a very practical bent, for at its center stood the preacher seeking to persuade sinners of their duty to make a new heart. In a context where the coercive power of the state was lost to disestablishment, the persuasive power of the preacher became even more crucial now that religion was aligned with the voluntary, moral government of God and not the involuntary, immoral governments associated with human beings.

For Taylor, systematic theology, properly conceived and executed, combines the evidence of both nature and revelation to make a case that is so rational and so filled with truth that when presented to the mind it is simply irresistible. His thought reflects an unshakable confidence that the best moral system is in place and working toward a perfection in this world, which will reach its consummation in the next. Moral agents need to fall in with this system, and that is gradually occurring in the lives of individuals and in the wider social order through the rule of law and the moral government of God. This lends to Taylor's thought an abiding optimism that happiness will ultimately prevail, because the evidence from both the natural and the moral world points overwhelmingly to the benevolence of a God who does not will misery for humankind.

Throughout his career at Yale Taylor remained a preacher who taught theology, bringing "logic and tears" to the pulpit and the classroom. His love of free inquiry became a source of irritation to some and of inspiration to others, and while his opponents rejected him as apostate from Edwards, his supporters hailed him as the deliverer of Calvinism from its more objectionable aspects. Many, detractors and admirers alike, were unable to follow completely the tightly woven threads of his theological analysis, much of which was swept away by his most famous student, Horace Bushnell, who emphasized intuition over logic and symbolism over dogma.

Suggested Readings

Writings of Nathaniel W. Taylor: *Lectures on the Moral Government of God*, 2 vols. (New York: Clark, Austin and Smith, 1859); *Concio ad Clerum: A Sermon Delivered in the Chapel of Yale College* 10 September 1828 (New Haven, 1828); *Essays, Lectures, Etc. Upon Selected Topics in Revealed Theology* (New York, 1859).

Sidney Earl Mead, *Nathaniel William Taylor (1786–1858): A Connecticut Liberal* (Chicago: University of Chicago Press, 1942).

Lyman Beecher

(1775–1863)

Milton J. Coalter

Lyman Beecher popularized a pivotal shift in American Calvinist theology. As the preeminent preacher of his day, Beecher taught the sovereignty of God and the sinfulness of humanity even as he proclaimed the ability of human beings to cooperate in their own and the world's salvation. The latter message released many of his contemporaries from passively waiting on God's providential action and propelled them, instead, into actively organizing to save souls and to make the nation Christian.

Beecher contributed most to this theological transition as a polemicist and coalition builder. He attacked what he perceived as the multiple threats of Enlightenment thought, Unitarian Christianity, the Roman Catholic Church, and the barbarism of frontier life. At the same time, he organized alliances to promote revivals and to create voluntary benevolent societies and educational institutions that would instill Protestant values in American individual and corporate life.

Beecher was the son of Esther Lyman Beecher and David Beecher, a blacksmith. His mother died shortly after his premature birth on 12 October 1775, and his aunt and uncle, Catherine and Lot Benton, raised Lyman on their farm in North Guilford, Connecticut. When found unsuited for farming, Beecher was sent to study under a succession of local tutors in preparation for entering Yale in 1793.

Beecher's first impressions of Yale were unfavorable. He associated students' loose morality with the introduction of European Enlightenment ideals by Ezra Stiles, Yale's president. He also found Enlightenment Deism repugnant because it proposed a God who set creation in motion only to leave it to its own devices. Despite his later advocacy of humans' ability to alter their spiritual condition, Beecher always insisted that God is active in creation's every movement.

Stiles' unexpected death in 1795 brought Timothy Dwight to the school's presidency. Unlike Stiles, who harbored broad sympathies for learning for its own sake, Dwight addressed intellectual pursuits as a means to the higher end of bringing God's reign into human hearts. Beecher found in Dwight a mentor and a model for addressing the spiritual needs of his age. Dwight himself sparked a revival among Yale students and, in response to Enlightenment claims that reason alone could distinguish truth from superstition, attempted to provide reasonable evidence of Christianity's truth. Later, Beecher cooperated with Nathaniel Taylor, another disciple of Dwight, in trying to explain the Calvinist paradox of God's sovereignty and human free will. In the process, they would promote revivals but only by collapsing the tension between the paradox's two poles in favor of free will.

During 1797, Lyman Beecher joined the Yale Moral Society, formed under Dwight's influence to counteract swearing and gambling on campus and to promote religion through vigorous debate. This early form of voluntary society apprenticed Beecher in a new organizational structure he would later refine and seed regionally and nationally.

Beecher experienced severe spiritual struggles under Dwight's preaching at Yale. These continued until 1798 when he was baptized by Dwight and received into the College church. Beecher's conversion over a protracted period, alongside Dwight's own focus on conversion for his teaching, convinced Lyman that this experience represented the pivotal moment in the Christian life. Conversion became a primary subject for his future instruction and preaching.

In 1798, Beecher decided to pursue theological studies with Dwight. Dwight introduced Beecher to the writings of Samuel Hopkins, a disciple of Jonathan Edwards like Dwight. Hopkins had sought to explain away the appearance of divine injustice in the New England Calvinist beliefs that God is all-powerful over creation and predestines (selects) some individuals for salvation and others for damnation. He insisted that God's rule was in no way capricious since God chose to practice a loving, moral government over humanity. Humans were not sinful because they were born of the same seed as the fallen Adam. Adam was but the federal representative of his descendants. Each individual was fully capable of rendering perfect obedience to God's holy law. Yet like Adam, all would sin and were fully accountable for their own sin. Beecher would repeatedly return to Hopkins' divine moral government in order to protect God's absolute control while allowing room for human initiative.

Licensed to preach in 1798 and ordained in 1799, Beecher served congregations in East Hampton (1799–1810) and Litchfield (1810–26), Connecticut. He strove mightily, even to the point of physical exhaustion, for revival in both parishes. Yet his successes were often more pronounced in other congregations rather than his own.

In 1808 Lyman met Nathaniel Taylor. Taylor would become best known as professor of didactic theology at Yale Divinity School, an institution Beecher and Taylor helped create, and as the most representative theologian of the New Haven theology. This theology was not the exclusive creation of Taylor. As early as their first meeting, Beecher was already preaching a version of the New Haven theology, and the two men, who became intimate friends, would regularly consult with each other on theological and ecclesiastical matters.

Theologically the two churchmen were of one mind in every respect but one. The more practical Beecher was never Taylor's intellectual equal. Perhaps because of this inequality, Beecher never clearly saw that their theology significantly departed from earlier American Calvinism. He continued to use the traditional terms employed by Jonathan Edwards to describe the paradox of divine sovereignty and human free will as though the New Haven theology did not decidedly tilt the balance between the poles of that paradox in the direction of free will. In fact, the balance had shifted, for both men went beyond Edwards, Dwight, and Hopkins in suggesting that the freedom of human beings applied not simply to their ability to respond to God's call for conversion but also to their capacity to cooperate in the building of God's kingdom on earth.

Beecher's fame as a preacher spread rapidly, especially after his move to the more cosmopolitan Litchfield. His abilities to galvanize like-minded Christians in coordinated efforts to redeem society and address the church's mission drew attention to him equally as much. As early as 1806, Beecher called from the pulpit for an end to the social problem of dueling. By 1811, he had begun work on the creation of a Connecticut Bible Society. The following year, he cooperated in an endeavor that resulted in the American Board of Commissioners for Foreign Missions, the first national voluntary society to send American missionaries overseas. The same year he presented a plan to the General Association of Connecticut to combat intemperance in the use of alcoholic beverages. This plan eventually generated the formation of a national American Temperance Society whose mission and methods closely paralleled Beecher's early proposal. These and other voluntary associations like the Domestic Home Missionary Society of Connecticut or the Society for the Suppression of Vice and the Promotion of Good Morals would feel Beecher's guiding hand in their creation, and, as in the case of the American Sunday School Union, they would depend on Beecher to fuel the fires of their original visions through his sermons during their annual meetings.

More than any other member of the clergy in New England, Beecher propagated the use of voluntary benevolent societies in shaping a Christian nation. He recognized voluntary societies as a solution to the new situation of disestablishment facing churches in the early national period. Although the United States Constitution had disestablished all religious groups in 1787, certain states continued to grant special legal privileges to particular denominations. Connecticut's Congregational churches enjoyed this established status, and until their disestablishment in 1818, Beecher worked to protect their unique position. However, Beecher began his promotion of voluntary societies even before disestablishment, and he came to see these associations as the most appropriate means by which the churches could preserve the society's Christian ethos and, simultaneously, protect American democracy.

Beecher also viewed benevolent societies as ideal tools for bringing God's kingdom to America. Like Edwards before him, Beecher fervently believed that the millennial reign of Christ on earth, foretold in the book of Revelation, would come first to America. But Beecher expected Christ's rule to be a spiritual one governing people's hearts rather than the physical dominion expected by many other millennialists. The benevolent societies were to prepare the way by cleansing the culture of sins and temptations which might impair the nation's service as the vessel of Christ's final reign.

In 1819, Beecher cooperated in organizing a new journal, the *Christian Spectator,* in order to combat the temptation of Unitarianism. Beecher's open opposition to Unitarian thought evident in the journal and his leadership in Boston revivals of 1823 earned him a call to a new Hanover Street congregation in north Boston.

From his installation in 1826 until his departure from the church in 1832, Beecher successfully combated Unitarian inroads in the Boston area. At the same time, he devised a plan for itinerant clergy of established congregations among the churches of the region. This campaign generated a spiritual awakening just as reports of revivals on the frontier began to filter in.

Accounts of western revivals included troubling stories of practices not commonly pursued or condoned in New England. So in 1827 Beecher traveled with other eastern revivalists to New Lebanon, New York, where they discussed their differences with their western counterparts led by Charles Finney. This action was characteristic of Beecher's approach to many of the theological conflicts of his career. He constantly worked to

111

resolve differences among the forces promoting the kingdom of God in America.

Beecher's differences with Finney in the west and Unitarians in the east illustrate the transitional character of his theology. They also prefigure the sources of the crossfire in which he found himself during the last years of his career. Despite Beecher's protest to the contrary, his Unitarian opponents recognized certain affinities between his theological stance and their own. Beecher insisted on human ability, and his arguments seemed to suggest that God's moral government must be justified on the basis of its moral goodness rather than on that of God's sheer, arbitrary authority to rule. Consequently, Unitarians blamed Beecher's belief in God's sovereignty on his provincial origins, which, they believed, blinded him to the full implications of his views.

Western revivalists found Beecher equally stilted, but for different reasons. First, while Beecher insisted with Edwards that the Holy Spirit's actions cannot be controlled and that revivals require the Spirit's unique influence, Finney contended that God had afforded humanity all necessary means to foster revivals without special acts of the Spirit. Second, Beecher refused to equate the feelings generated by revival preaching with a true and complete new birth in Christ, while Finney focused his revivals' new measures or techniques to spark just such emotional experiences. Third, Beecher preached the sovereign providence of God's government over creation, but Finney avoided the Hopkinsian language of providence because in his view it immobilized both sinner and church with "cannot-ism"— that is, "I cannot act before God does." Finally, Beecher's interest in forging alliances for Christian reform and revival led him to moderate or delay action to eradicate certain national sins like slavery in the interest of unity. Finney's converts, in contrast, increasingly viewed slavery as so unrighteous that the issue became a litmus test for which no compromise or delay could be tolerated and by which God's friends and foes could be readily identified.

Beecher's departure from traditional New England Calvinism and his differences with western revivalists set the stage for severe controversy late in his ministry. In 1832 Beecher moved to Cincinnati to assume the presidency of newly formed Lane Seminary and the pulpit of Second Presbyterian Church. Affiliated with the Presbyterian Church in the United States of America, Lane was largely funded by Arthur Tappan, a wealthy New York businessman and a devotee of Finney and the antislavery movement. The vast majority of Lane's early student body had also been deeply influenced by Finney and were led by Timothy Weld, a firebrand for immediate emancipation.

By 1834, Beecher's brief contact with Cincinnati had proved to him that the west held great promise and peril. During a fund-raising tour through New England, he preached and lectured variations of a sermon, *A Plea for the West* (first published in 1835). His message addressed the social and spiritual challenges of the American frontier. Beecher warned that the cruel conditions of frontier survival had an uncivilizing effect upon its settlers especially since the region lay beyond the reach of organized Christian congregations. Furthermore, he noted the steady stream of new Roman Catholic immigrants finding homes in the region. Beecher believed that the Roman Catholic structure, with the pope at its head, was fundamentally despotic and, therefore, antithetical to American democracy. For Beecher, Roman Catholicism was a triple threat—political, social, and religious—to the future of the west. These threats, he held, could be met only by American Protestants supporting educational efforts like Lane Seminary as well as continuing their reformation of American life through benevolent societies. If accomplished, Beecher suggested that the kingdom of God would be initiated in the west where a new society was being born.

Beecher strove to preserve an increasingly fractious coalition of New England Congregationalists, Presbyterians, and Finney-converts to ensure this dream's fruition. However, conflict between more traditional New England Congregationalists and supporters of the New Haven theology erupted, and a conservative Calvinist seminary was created near Hartford, Connecticut. In 1837, schism also arose between New School Presbyterians, who supported voluntary societies as well as cooperation with Congregationalists, and their Old School counterparts, who opposed both. During the same period, students pressed to make Lane a bastion of anti-slavery agitation against the wishes of their school's board and president.

Beecher's willingness to compromise in order to sustain a coalition made him suspect. Thirty-eight of Lane's fifty theological students and fifty of its sixty pre-seminary students withdrew. Most of the funds for Lane promised by Tappan and former New England allies never materialized, and in 1835 Old School Presbyterian opponents brought Beecher before the Presbytery of Cincinnati on charges of heresy. Eventually acquitted of heresy, Beecher managed to rebuild Lane's student body and financial base before his retirement in 1850. He died in Boston on 9 January 1863.

Lyman Beecher's influence faded quickly following his retirement, in part because many of the changes he had initiated in American Protestantism were already moving beyond where he was willing to go. But it is also true that Beecher's power to move others was due more to the charismatic piety and dynamism of his personality than to the unique vision of the publications he left behind.

Suggested Readings

Writings of Lyman Beecher: *Autobiography, Correspondence, Etc., of Lyman Beecher, D.D.,* ed. Barbara M. Cross, 2 vols. (Cambridge: Belknap Press of Harvard University, 1961); *A Plea for the West* (New York: Arno Press, 1977).

Vincent Harding, *A Certain Magnificence: Lyman Beecher and the Transformation of American Protestantism, 1775–1863* (Brooklyn: Carlson Publishing, 1991).

Stuart C. Henry, *Unvanquished Puritan: A Portrait of Lyman Beecher* (Grand Rapids: Wm. B. Eerdmans Publishing Co., 1973).

Stephen Snyder, *Lyman Beecher and His Children: The Transformation of a Religious Tradition* (Brooklyn: Carlson Publishing, 1991).

Moses Stuart

(1780–1852)

William Baird

According to his epitaph, Moses Stuart was "the Father of Biblical Science" in America. Stuart, the son of a farmer, was born in Wilton, Connecticut. In 1799, he graduated from Yale at the head of his class. He worked for a time as a schoolteacher, but returned to Yale to study law. While serving there as a tutor, he was converted in a religious revival that swept the campus. Consequently, Stuart remained at Yale to study for the ministry under the tutelage of Timothy Dwight. In 1806, he became a minister of Center Church in New Haven.

In 1810, Stuart was called to the recently founded seminary at Andover, Massachusetts, as Professor of Sacred Literature. Two years later, he obtained a copy of J. G. Eichhorn's introduction to the Old Testament, and became convinced of the importance of German biblical scholarship. Stuart was hailed as an excellent teacher, displaying enthusiasm for his subject and concern for his students. At Andover, Stuart developed a graduate program wherein outstanding students were invited to stay beyond their seminary course for advanced instruction and experience in teaching; some were sent to Germany for additional study.

A student of Timothy Dwight, Stuart was sympathetic to the moderate Calvinism of the "New Divinity." In response to W. E. Channing's famous Baltimore ordination sermon (1819), Stuart argued that the Bible supports the doctrine of the Trinity and the divinity of Christ. Stuart opposed efforts of scientists like Yale's Benjamin Silliman to harmonize Genesis and geology. Silliman contended the seven days of creation represented eons of time; Stuart maintained they constituted ordinary, twenty-four-hour days. Stuart supported the temperance movement, and argued that the wine of the New Testament was low in alcohol. Stuart acknowledged that the Bible did not oppose slavery, although he favored its gradual elimination.

Stuart embraced a high view of biblical authority and advocated a doctrine of plenary, but not verbal, inspiration. Although he insisted that the Bible offered a consistent system of truth, he accepted a moderate view of progressive revelation, acknowledging that biblical doctrine was sometimes accommodated to the limitations of its time. Stuart's dedication to historical criticism is seen in his translation (1822) of Johann August Ernesti's *Elements of Interpretation*. He insisted the Bible was written in human language and should be understood by the same method used for other books. Opposed to allegorical interpretation, Stuart pursued the literal meaning, adopting the Reformation principle that scripture should be interpreted by scripture.

Stuart made important contributions to the study of biblical linguistics. In 1821, he published a Hebrew grammar, and later translated the important grammar of Wilhelm Gesenius. With the aid of Edward Robinson (then an advanced student, later a professor at Union Seminary, New York), Stuart translated J. G. B. Winer's grammar of New Testament Greek, and in 1834, published a grammar of his own. Stuart's handwritten Syriac grammar can be viewed in the archives of Andover Newton Theological School.

Stuart's publications dealing with the Old Testament include commentaries on Daniel, Ecclesiastes, and Proverbs as well as a book on the Old Testament canon. In the main, his conclusions were conservative. He argued, for example, that Moses had written the Pentateuch by drawing upon two traditions, E and J. Stuart also contended for the unity of Isaiah and the historical accuracy of Esther, Job, and Daniel. Stuart believed Jonah reported a factual story in which a big fish (not a whale) had swallowed the prophet—a historical account by his reckoning, confirmed by Jesus. According to Stuart, the Psalms were written by various authors, some by David.

Stuart published important commentaries on the New Testament. His two-volume work on the Epistle to the Hebrews went through seven editions in London where Stuart was hailed as a champion who could vanquish the German critics. The first volume (more than 450 pages) was devoted to critical questions, and argued at length that Paul was the author. Although his argument is generally unconvincing, Stuart dealt effectively with the problem of vocabulary. Scholars who deny Pauline authorship observe that Hebrews uses 112 words that are not found elsewhere in the New Testament. Stuart, however, counters that 1 Corinthians (which nobody questions was written by Paul) contains 230 words that appear nowhere else in the Pauline corpus. Stuart's commentary on Romans argues for the unity of the whole epistle, including chapter 16. In interpreting

Romans 5, Stuart opposed the notion that Adam's sin was imputed to all people; instead, sin is the willful act of each individual.

Stuart's two-volume commentary on Revelation can be read with profit today. To be sure, Stuart spent 140 pages in a futile effort to prove that this book was written by the same author as that of the Fourth Gospel, the apostle John. Nevertheless, Stuart made four points of enduring significance. (1) The Apocalypse must have made sense to its original readers; only a small part of the book refers to the distant future. (2) Revelation must be interpreted in terms of its literary type; it is a poetic-prophetic book like the Jewish apocalyptic writings. (3) The symbols of the Apocalypse should be interpreted generically, in terms of their general meaning, not according to particular historical data. (4) Although it must be understood in its historical setting, Revelation has a larger meaning and continuing relevance: the message of the triumph of Christian faith over the forces of evil.

Stuart made a profound contribution to theological study in America by alerting scholars to the importance of European criticism. Although his critical conclusions were conservative, Stuart promoted and mastered the historical-critical method. He recognized the importance of solid biblical interpretation for the life and ministry of the church.

Suggested Readings

Writings of Moses Stuart: *A Commentary on the Apocalypse,* 2 vols. (Andover: Allen, Morrill and Wardwell, 1845); *A Commentary on the Epistle to the Hebrews,* 2 vols. (London: John Miller, 1828).

John Herbert Giltner, *Moses Stuart: The Father of Biblical Science in America* (Atlanta: Scholars Press, 1988).

Francis Wayland

(1796–1865)

Bill J. Leonard

Baptist leader Francis Wayland was born on 11 March 1796 in New York City, three years after his parents, Francis and Sarah Moore Wayland, had emigrated from England. Wayland's father became a Baptist lay minister in 1807, serving small churches in New York state. Wayland attended Union College in Schenectady, graduating in 1813. He briefly studied medicine with two physicians in Troy, New York, but a religious awakening influenced his decision to become a Baptist minister. He also attended Andover Seminary for one year, but financial difficulties forced him to leave the school and return to Union College where he taught for four years. In 1821 he was called as pastor of the prestigious First Baptist Church, Boston. When his scholarly manner and difficulties in performing pastoral ministry created divisions in the church, Wayland returned to Union College in 1826 as professor of moral philosophy. That same year he was selected the fourth president of Brown University in Providence, Rhode Island, a position he held until 1855.

The university was in serious financial straits when Wayland arrived. He raised funds for faculty salaries, buildings, and a new library. He promoted a more rigorous curriculum and helped convince Rhode Island to begin free public primary education. Throughout his career, Wayland continued to teach and write on matters of ethics and moral philosophy. A member of the Brown class of 1834 described his method: "His definitions were clear, simple, and easily remembered. His analysis of any obscure but important part was exhaustive, omitting no essential element."

As a Baptist leader, Wayland promoted the mission enterprise through denominational societies, serving on numerous boards. As president of Brown he also maintained active membership in First Baptist Church, Providence. In 1844 he was elected president of the Triennial Convention, the denomination's national missionary organization. Francis Wayland died on 30 September 1865 in Providence.

Wayland's theological views were circulated through the publication of several books and numerous public discourses. *Elements of Moral Science* (1835) set forth his views on the nature of moral philosophy. A widely used college textbook, it dealt with theoretical and practical ethics in chapters on such topics as virtue, love for God, and personal piety. In another text, *Elements of Political Economy* (1837), he sought to articulate the "science of political economy" in terms which a lay audience could comprehend.

Wayland's theology was shaped significantly by the Baptist tradition. In works such as *Notes on the Principles and Practices of Baptist Churches* (1857), he influenced nineteenth-century Baptist theology and polity. His writings reveal his strong support for those beliefs characteristic of the Baptists. These include the necessity of conversion for every church member, immersion baptism as a sign of Christian commitment, baptism and the Lord's Supper as "ordinances" of the church, the autonomy of each local congregation, the freedom of the soul in matters of religion, and the necessity of associational relationships with Baptists of common theological sentiments. Though concerned about theological issues, Wayland urged Baptists to avoid official creeds lest such "man-made" documents undermine scripture as the sole authority for Christian faith and practice.

Theologically, Wayland was a conversionist who believed that church membership was based on the free choice of the individual believer. The church, he maintained, was a voluntary association which no one joined "unless he chooses, nor continues in it any longer than he will." This individualism affected his understanding of denominations. In the period of Baptist efforts to establish denominational connections, Wayland was particularly insistent upon the autonomy of each local congregation. He wrote that "every company of believers united together according to the laws of Christ, is wholly independent of every other; that every church is perfectly capable of self-government; and . . . no one acknowledges any higher authority, under Christ, than itself." He therefore concluded that the local nature of the church was such that it could not possibly be "represented" in larger denominational bodies. This emphasis on Baptist localism led Wayland to insist that denominational organizations should be developed only as loosely related societies composed less of official churches than of individual Christians.

In general, Wayland's theology reflects a modified Calvinism which accepted the belief that Christian missions was God's method for awakening the hearts of those elected to salvation. In *Principles and Practices of Baptist Churches*, he acknowledged that Baptists of his era had moved from a "hyper-Calvinism," which questioned the need for missionary efforts, to an emphasis on the missionary calling to carry the gospel to the entire world. In discussing the atonement of Christ he suggested that although "the way of salvation was opened to the whole race," "God, . . . in infinite mercy, has elected some to everlasting life." The table of salvation was "spread for all," but that did not "interfere in [God's] gracious purpose to save by his sovereign mercy such as he may choose." As a conversionist, Wayland was concerned that all persons might potentially be saved; yet he would not relinquish the Calvinist belief in divine election. Thus he concluded that election involved "sovereignty, but no partiality."

The ethical implications of Wayland's theology are evident in his response to the great moral issue of his day, slavery. Though not a militant abolitionist, he was an outspoken opponent of slavery. His views were expressed in a response to Southerner Richard Furman, Baptist leader and author of one of the best-known biblical defenses of slavery. In constructing his arguments, Furman appealed to certain ideas in Wayland's *Elements of Moral Science*. Wayland reacted in a series of letters which, along with Furman's responses, were published as *Domestic Slavery Considered as a Scriptural Institution*. Wayland's theological outlook led him to condemn slavery as an institution at odds with God's revealed will: It undermined the morals of master and slave alike and contradicted the basic teachings of Jesus regarding the individual's worth and liberty. As educator and theologian Francis Wayland helped shape Protestant theology and ethics in nineteenth-century America.

Suggested Readings

Writings of Francis Wayland: *Elements of Moral Science* (Boston: Gould, Kendall, Lincoln, 1841; repr. 1937); *Notes on the Principles and Practices of Baptist Churches* (New York: Sheldon, Blakeman & Co., 1857).

Francis Wayland and H. L. Wayland, eds., *A Memoir of the Life and Labors of Francis Wayland* (New York: Sheldon and Co., 1867).

William Brackney, *The Baptists* (New York: Greenwood Press, 1988).

Nathan Bangs

(1778–1862)

E. Brooks Holifield

The nineteenth-century Methodist historian Abel Stevens contended that Nathan Bangs ranked next only to Francis Asbury in influence on the Methodist Episcopal Church. He depicted him as the "representative" Methodist of the century.

This was a considerable overstatement, for Bangs had a distinctive status within a denomination suspicious of learning and theology. He represented not the typical Methodist circuit rider but the relatively small number of clerical theologians who formulated an indigenous American Methodist theological tradition. He engaged himself in every definitive theological issue in antebellum Methodism, and as early as 1829 the *Quarterly Christian Spectator* in New Haven—the journal of the Yale theologians—included his writings among the standard doctrinal works of the Methodists.

Born into an Episcopalian family of modest means in Stratford, Connecticut, Bangs, though himself lacking a formal education, learned early to imitate the self-educated Methodist circuit riders. But serious conversations with itinerant preachers during a sojourn in Canada led him to join a Methodist society, where in 1800 he underwent the experience of conversion so highly valued in the Methodist revivals. He had long been an avid reader of theology and philosophy, and at the conference in New York that ordained him in 1804, he found Bishop Asbury's preaching deficient in learning and study. After he returned from Canada to New York in 1808, he devoted himself to enhancing theological learning in Methodism.

His assignment to the John Street church in New York City in 1810 gave him a forum for defending the theology of Methodism's founder, John Wesley. In 1815 he published *The Errors of Hopkinsianism*, a critique of the Calvinist theology of Samuel Hopkins. The publisher sold 3,000 copies in six months. The following year he added *The Reformer Reformed,* a reply to his critics. These two publications foreshadowed the Methodists' frequent practice of expounding their theology through debates—about soteriology with Calvinists and Universalists, church order with Episcopalians, and polity and sacraments with Baptists.

Bangs found Calvinism lacking because its doctrine of predestination impeached the moral goodness of God and exculpated human beings of blame for their sinfulness. His Methodist alternative was to argue that since Christ died for all human beings, everyone received some of the benefits of the atonement. While insisting on original sin, even total depravity, he contended that the atonement (proleptically anticipated in an intertrinitarian covenant of redemption) provided for everyone a prevenient grace that restored to human nature the freedom—Methodists called it "gracious ability"—to repent and respond to Christ in faith. This response met the divine condition for justification (divine pardon) and new birth (regeneration or conversion). Bangs also defended, on scriptural grounds, the controversial Wesleyan doctrine of the witness of the Spirit, according to which the Holy Spirit provided an immediate, intuitive assurance of rebirth.

Bangs thought that his best-argued book was his *Examination of the Doctrine of Predestination* (1817), in which he tried to take on Jonathan Edwards by blending scriptural and theological arguments with the psychology of the Scottish Common-Sense philosophers Thomas Reid, Dugald Stewart, and Thomas Brown. His main philosophical contention was that Edwards had allowed himself to write of human motives as though they were physical causes, thereby assuming a false analogy between physical and mental acts. Bangs greatly admired the Scottish philosophy, and after becoming the head of the Methodist Book Concern in 1820 he issued an American edition of Reid's works. He also shared in his era's intense interest in ecclesiology, and his *Vindication of the Methodist Episcopacy* (1820) represented the Methodist position against the Episcopalians in the dispute over church order.

He agreed with Wesley that the Bible revealed a divine expectation— and a divine promise—that subsequent to their new birth the faithful would undergo a process of sanctification that could result in an instantaneous divine gift of perfect love for God and the neighbor. Believing that he had received this gift of entire sanctification or perfect holiness six months after his conversion, he encouraged the resurgence of interest in the doctrine of holiness within the denomination after 1830. Bangs regularly attended Phoebe Palmer's Tuesday Meeting for the Promotion of Holiness, even though he protested against her teaching that one could be assured of perfect holiness without any direct witness of the Spirit. In 1851 he published *The Necessity, Nature, and Fruits of Sanctification,* which made the familiar Methodist argument that the command in Matthew 5:48—and several other New Testament texts—for followers of Christ to "be perfect" implied a divine offer of grace sufficient to fulfill it.

He struggled incessantly to counter his denomination's populist disdain for a learned clergy. As General Book Steward, he successfully urged the church to resume the moribund *Methodist Magazine,* and in 1832 he became the editor of its successor, the *Monthly Magazine and Quarterly Review.* Eventually this magazine and the *Christian Advocate and Journal,* which Bangs founded, had a larger circulation than any other similar periodicals in the nation. As the historian of the denomination, he published a four-volume *History of the Methodist Episcopal Church* (1838–40) that both interpreted the church's growth as an example of providential agency and subtly made the case for a more learned ministry. He pushed hard for a four-year course of study for Methodist clergy, which was finally approved in 1844.

Bangs' efforts prepared the ground for a flourishing of Methodist theological writings that tried, as he had tried, to confute learned opponents while remaining accessible to the people. In this spirit, Thomas Neely Ralston of Kentucky labored to write an *Elements of Divinity* (1847) that would be so free of scholastic technicalities that it could counter the new Calvinism at Yale while remaining entirely accessible to young readers. A similar effort to reach the laity marked the *Elements of Theology* (1853) of Luther Lee, who helped form the Wesleyan Methodist Church in protest against slavery. Samuel Wakefield in Pennsylvania carried on this tradition in his *Complete System of Christian Theology* (1862), which he wrote to reach "all classes of readers, from the aged theologian to the Sabbath-school scholar" (p. 4). At the same time, polemical treatises like the *Calvinistic Controversy* (1835) of Wilbur Fisk at Wesleyan University or the *Freedom of the Will* (1864) of Daniel Whedon, the theological star of mid-century Methodism, also continued in the tradition that Bangs had inaugurated. None of his successors drew heavily on his formulations; for guidance, most looked more to Wesley's works and to the *Theological Institutes* (1823) of Richard Watson, the ablest English Methodist systematic theologian. Yet no one did more than Bangs to open the denomination in America to the proposal that serious theological reflection was a worthy endeavor.

Suggested Readings

Writings of Nathan Bangs: *The Errors of Hopkinsianism Detected and Refuted* (New York: John C. Totten, 1815); *An Examination of the Doctrine of Predestination* (New York: John C. Totten, 1817).

Leland Scott, "The Message of Early American Methodism," in *The History of American Methodism,* ed. Emory Stevens Bucke, 3 vols. (Nashville: Abingdon Press, 1964), 1:291-359.

Abel Stevens, *Life and Times of Nathan Bangs* (New York: Carlton and Porter, 1863).

Horace Bushnell

(1802–1876)

Donald A. Crosby

Horace Bushnell was a Congregational minister and theologian whose provocative preaching and writing did much to give rise to a new era of liberalism in trinitarian Protestant theology during the second half of the nineteenth century in America. Born in Bantam, Connecticut, and reared in nearby New Preston, Bushnell graduated from Yale College and Yale Divinity School. In 1833, he was ordained as minister of North Congregational Church of Hartford, Connecticut, whose congregation came to hold him in high esteem as preacher and pastor.

In 1848, he was invited to give lectures at Harvard, Andover, and Yale. Two strikingly original books (*God in Christ,* 1849, and *Christ in Theology,* 1851) resulted from these lectures and from his endeavors to clarify and defend them in response to a torrent of criticism from conservative Christians. From 1849 to 1854, Bushnell's detractors among the Congregational clergy in Connecticut tried to bring him to trial for heresy. Although they failed to win a majority of the Hartford Central Association to their cause or to shake the solid support of the North church congregation for its pastor, Bushnell barely escaped being defrocked, and the controversy surrounding him in this period set him apart from the Protestant mainstream, branding him as a dangerous radical.

His two books did indeed mark an abrupt change of direction from the Calvinism of Jonathan Edwards and his successors that had dominated the religious thought of trinitarian New England for a hundred years. Some of the rigidities of this theology—especially its doctrines of total human depravity and divine predestination—had already been softened by thinkers such as Nathaniel W. Taylor, Bushnell's theology teacher at Yale Divinity School. But Bushnell's approach to the range of issues under active debate among theologians of the day was of a different spirit and mold from that of the still regnant Edwardsean theology. He claimed to have

125

found a way to put theological discussions on a bold new footing, a way of avoiding acrimonious doctrinal battles which had created painful divisions among New England trinitarians and which seemed to preclude any hope of rapprochement between them and the Unitarians.

The principal failing of theology in New England, according to Bushnell, was a misapprehension of the nature, capacities, and limitations of language, especially religious language. From this misapprehension—which he attributed to trinitarian and Unitarian theologians alike—stemmed grave misunderstandings of the Bible and divine revelation, of differences among doctrines and creeds, of the task of systematic theology, and of specific Christian doctrines such as those of atonement, the Trinity, original sin, and the relation of human responsibility and freedom to divine grace.

Trinitarians and Unitarians alike had erred, in Bushnell's view, in assuming that all meaningful religious discourse either was, or could be rendered into, literal assertions of fact on which strict logical deductions could be based. They conceived of the Bible and revelation as consisting of such assertions, of creeds and doctrines as inferences from the assertions, and of systematic theology as a rational ordering of these assertions and inferences. All Christian doctrines, great or small, were likewise literal in their intended import, and disagreements about them were to be seen as disagreements about plain statements of fact where standard rules of logical reasoning hold sway as much as they do in mathematics or natural science.

Theologians of the day were not unaware of the pervasive presence of symbol, analogy, metaphor, figure, parable, and story in the Bible or religious language in general, but most of them believed that all such content must be rendered into literal assertions by responsible theologians and ministers in order to avoid a seductive vagueness of suggestive imagery that might easily mislead the faithful. Unitarians reasoned from this assumption that doctrines such as trinity, atonement, original sin, and the interworkings of divine grace and human free will made no literal sense in their traditional forms. Therefore these forms should either be abandoned altogether or reinterpreted into clear-cut, consistent assertions. Trinitarians tended fully to agree with the Unitarians on the necessity for rigorous logical treatment of Christian teachings and to insist that they could and should be stripped of any traces of metaphorical allusiveness or internal inconsistency, and set forth in a perspicuously literal, tightly reasoned system. Taylor, for example, confidently recommended this conception of the task of theology to Bushnell and his other students.

In sharp contrast to these views, Bushnell held that the function of religious language is not to impart literal or referential truth or to satisfy theoretical, speculative curiosity about God's inner nature, his reasons for creating the world and human beings, the ultimate explanation of evil, the precise role of human responsibility and freedom in relation to the power of God, and so on. Instead, its function is "instrumental." Religious language achieves its proper end when it has such effects as awakening human beings to the presence and power of God in the depths of their souls, stimulating development of their characters so as to bring them ever closer to their ideal nature as creatures made in the divine image, and helping them to do the work of God in the world. Bushnell meant not to deny cognitive import to religious language but rather to assert that its overriding purpose is to motivate and empower, to promote a transformative relationship of human beings with a living, loving, inwardly dwelling God.

What fitted religious language to realize this practical purpose was precisely its figurative, symbolic, paradoxical character. To purge it of this character would be to render it ineffectual. Prosaic discourse lacked the expressive, imaginative capacity required to open up the experiential dimensions of the Christian life, to create a sense of the majesty of God and the effects of God's saving work in Christ, or to begin to do justice to the awesome profundity of the Christian vision as a whole. Christians should view the Bible not as a textbook of intellectual theology but as what Bushnell in *God in Christ* called "the grand poem of salvation," a compendium of powerful metaphors, analogies, and images (e.g., a divine kingdom, altar, and sacrifice) which God had progressively built into the religious history of the Jews and then used as the symbolic framework needed to communicate the good news of Christ's coming into the world.

This interpretation of religious language led Bushnell to argue that it is a mistake to try to convert the numerous paradoxical elements of the Bible, creeds, or traditional doctrines into fully consistent statements, for that would be to fix on one aspect of their symbolic function at the expense of other essential aspects. The unresolvable tensions in the great paradoxes of Christianity—for example, nature and grace, law and gospel, the redeemed as sinners but justified, God as one and yet three, Christ as both God and human being—were indispensable to their expressive power. So vast and elusive were the depths of meaning in the Christian message that as many different angles of vision as possible were needed to gain insight into those depths. This reasoning prompted Bushnell to affirm that although every creedal and doctrinal statement in the history of Christianity probably contained some important truth, none could contain more than partial truth. Thus all of them were needed, despite their differences. Despite his fond hopes of putting theological discourse on different ground, such views gained him few allies or even sympathetic hearers among his less-enthusiastic colleagues. Only a small number of his contemporaries rallied to his defense.

Few Christian thinkers in New England at midcentury recognized or appreciated Bushnell's ideas for what they really were: a breakthrough toward a promising new outlook that historians have since come to term Protestant Liberalism. His ideas in the two books under discussion can be considered liberal in at least five important senses of that term: their downplaying of concerns about doctrinal orthodoxy in favor of religious experience and practice, their stress on the immanence of God in the human soul, their willingness to learn from many different points of view, their critique of biblical literalism and authoritarian ways of thinking, and their insistence on the crucial need to search for freshly relevant ways of understanding and applying traditional Christian teachings in a changing world.

Toward the end of the 1850s, Bushnell published *Nature and the Supernatural* (1858), a sustained argument against scientific reductionism. This book showed the strong influence of the English writer Samuel Taylor Coleridge, whose thought was itself deeply affected by that of the great German philosopher Immanuel Kant. Like Coleridge and Kant, Bushnell envisioned two fundamental aspects of the universe: The one (nature) follows strict laws of cause and effect; the other (supernature) turns on the principle of freedom. The latter—marking out the arena of divine activity in the world, human moral responsibility, and human redemption—is not a violation of the natural order of cause and effect but exists in complementary relation to it. Nature is by divine design perfectly pliable to both divine and human freedom; the natural and the supernatural together constitute "the one system of God." Bushnell objected in this book to a naturalistic origin of biological species such as that defended in the following year by Charles Darwin, contending that "successive races of living forms . . . are fresh creations, by a power out of nature and above it" and hence supernatural.

In 1859, Bushnell resigned his pastorate in the North church of Hartford on account of persistent bad health. He remained active in preaching, lecturing, and writing until his death in 1876. His books of this period include *Work and Play* (1864), *Christ and His Salvation* (1864), *The Vicarious Sacrifice* (1866), *Moral Uses of Dark Things* (1868), *Forgiveness and Law* (1874), and *Building Eras in Religion* (posthumously, 1881).

Bushnell's most enduringly influential book, *Christian Nurture*, appeared in its final form in 1861. Included in this volume were essays incorporated into an earlier one called *Discourses on Christian Nurture* (1847), as well as more recent writings. His main argument in both editions

128

was directed against the revivalist thinking pervasive in New England since the Great Awakening. According to such thinking, every true Christian must undergo a radical, sudden conversion experience without which he or she would surely be damned. Bushnell reasoned, however, that conversion could be a slow but steady process beginning in early childhood and continuing into adulthood, with no specific date when one could say one had become a Christian. This process, unfolding in the nurturing context of the Christian community, was a natural outcome of a child's baptism into that community. His view was controversial, for it seemed to many conservatives implicitly to deny the doctrine of total depravity, which for them required a decisive separation between the old life of sin and the new life of forgiveness and redemption. Noteworthy is that Bushnell's ideas, though unsettling to many, echoed those of a time before the Great Awakening—the covenantal theology of original New England Congregationalism.

Bushnell deserves to be called the founder of the new trinitarian liberalism, which came to the fore in the second half of the nineteenth century in America, even though he did not fit into that emerging tradition in all relevant respects. He opposed women's suffrage, for example, in a book entitled *Women's Suffrage: The Reform Against Nature* (1869). He did not embrace Darwinism or historical-critical biblical scholarship. Nevertheless, the openness and breadth of outlook he generally championed and exemplified helped make acceptance of these developments possible for others. Later Protestant liberals such as George Harris, Newman Smyth, Theodore Thornton Munger, Washington Gladden, and Luther A. Weigle readily acknowledged their debt to him.

Suggested Readings

Writings of Horace Bushnell: H. Shelton Smith, ed., *Horace Bushnell* (New York: Oxford University Press, 1965).

James O. Duke, *Horace Bushnell on the Vitality of Biblical Language* (Chico, Calif.: Scholars Press, 1984).

Robert L. Edwards, *Of Singular Genius, of Singular Grace: A Biography of Horace Bushnell* (Cleveland: Pilgrim Press, 1992).

David L. Smith, *Symbolism and Growth: The Religious Thought of Horace Bushnell* (Chico, Calif.: Scholars Press, 1981).

Charles G. Finney

(1792–1875)

Charles E. Hambrick-Stowe

Charles Grandison Finney was the most significant Northern revivalist in pre–Civil War America and a professor of theology at Oberlin College. From the raw materials of Calvinism he devised a thoroughly evangelical theology focused on the sinner's free choice of salvation and a life of holiness.

Finney's preaching career only began at age twenty-nine, after his dramatic conversion experience in a woods near the northern New York state village of Adams. Born in Warren, Connecticut, Finney grew up on his family's farm in Oneida County and, from age sixteen, in Jefferson County in northern New York. He attended common school and perhaps Hamilton-Oneida Academy, and as an older teen taught school in Henderson near Lake Ontario. At twenty he enrolled at Warren Academy in Connecticut, decided against going on to Yale, and taught in New Jersey from 1814 until 1818 when he returned to Jefferson County to apprentice at law. While practicing law in Adams, and directing the choir at the Presbyterian church, he began to study the Bible. Second Great Awakening revivals swept the area regularly, and it was in this context that Finney experienced his spiritual and vocational crisis in 1821.

Anguished by his sense of sinfulness, he submitted to God's righteousness, felt as if he were meeting Jesus Christ face-to-face, and received, as he put it, a mighty baptism of the Holy Ghost. Finney's rebirth, so reminiscent of conversions described in the 1600s by New England Puritans and by Jonathan Edwards in his *Life of David Brainerd* (1749), set the pattern for his evangelistic work. The Presbytery of St. Lawrence licensed Finney to preach in 1823 after a period of theological study, in lieu of seminary training, with his pastor George W. Gale. Commissioned as an evangelist by western New York's Female Missionary Society, he was ordained by the presbytery in 1824. That same year he married Lydia Root Andrews, who assisted his ministry by establishing women's prayer groups and social reform organizations.

Presbyterians more straight-laced decried Finney's manner of presenting the gospel. Like Methodists and Baptists he preached without notes, looked listeners in the eye and addressed them as "you," and called for an immediate decision for Christ. He warned of hell in vivid language and used illustrations from everyday life. Men and women responded to Finney's early preaching with extreme behavior, including weeping, crying out, falling down "in the Spirit," and emotional testimony. Finney was in full fellowship, however, with the other New School Presbyterian ministers who predominated in central New York. In late 1825, he moved to Oneida County and initiated revivals in the booming urban centers along the just-completed Erie Canal. His sermons attacked the Calvinist emphasis on God's sovereignty in the work of redemption, which he believed eliminated the possibility of human response. Sinners were advised to wait and wait and were never saved.

Finney's remarkable success in winning souls, and his theological acumen, evident at a conference of pro-revival New England Congregational and New York state Presbyterian ministers held at New Lebanon, New York, in 1827, gained Finney a national reputation. He was soon preaching for extended periods in Wilmington, Philadelphia, Rochester, and Boston. Merchant philanthropists in New York City established Finney at his own church in a renovated theater in 1832 and in the huge Broadway Tabernacle four years later. During this period outspoken New School pastors were being charged with heresy; Finney abandoned his Presbyterian affiliation and joined the more theologically flexible Congregationalists. While the Tabernacle was under construction, he also negotiated with Ohio's fledgling Oberlin Collegiate Institute about a theological professorship.

Finney and many of his New School colleagues in upstate New York developed a number of "new measures" in their evangelistic preaching in the years from 1825 to the early 1830s. Most of these were simply refinements of older pastoral methods and the introduction of Methodist and Baptist techniques. The most significant methods were house-to-house visitation, inquiry meetings following general preaching services at which anxious sinners might pray for salvation, prayer for sinners by name, testimony by both men and women in mixed congregations, tolerance of emotional excess, and the call for immediate decisions for Christ. Finney and his coworkers in the "western revivals" successfully defended such aggressive evangelism against the more moderate approach of New Englanders, led by Lyman Beecher and Asahel Nettleton, at the New Lebanon Conference. During the great Rochester revival of 1830–31, Finney introduced the "anxious seat," a section of pews reserved for those who came forward to pray for salvation, and the "protracted meeting," four-day and five-day revivals in nearby villages. He also linked spiritual rebirth to social reform while his associate Theodore Dwight Weld advanced the temperance cause (and later, antislavery).

Finney's theology gave voice to his practice. His first book, *Sermons on Various Subjects* (1835), collected his best-known work from the previous decade. His signature sermon, which exhorted, "Make you a new heart and a new spirit, for why will you die?" (Ezek. 18:31), was published as "Sinners Bound to Change Their Own Hearts." His message echoed the New Divinity of Samuel Hopkins as modified by progressive Yale professor Nathaniel William Taylor. Although direct influence is hard to trace, it is clear that New England theology was shared widely among New School Presbyterians west of the Hudson River. Finney rejected orthodox Calvinism's substitutionary theory of the atonement, espousing in its place the "governmental" and "moral influence" view by which Christ's death represented God's offer of salvation despite human sin. Redemption was not a mechanical or commercial transaction managed solely within the Godhead. Rather, Christ's death in our place satisfied the requirements of justice so that God can now offer saving grace to humanity. Each individual, although lost in sin, is still a free moral agent able to choose good or evil. Humans are culpable for their own sinfulness; Adam's fall has not removed personal responsibility. The cross makes forgiveness available to all— here Finney like the New Divinity theologians opposed traditional Calvinism's "limited atonement," which taught that Christ died only for the elect. Hence the invitation to accept God's saving grace must now be placed before every human being. Although Finney did not discourage emotionalism in worship, at the point of salvation he was a voluntarist. We are saved when our wills respond to God's gracious offer in the affirmative.

Salvation for Finney was the transformation of the will from selfishness to what he and the New England theologians called "disinterested benevolence" or selfless love. Not everyone would be saved, however, and Finney vigorously opposed Universalism. Finney also remained within the Reformed tradition, insisting that he was no Arminian or Wesleyan. He embraced, but redefined in his own terms, the doctrines of total depravity and election. Sin, he argued, is a voluntary state of mind which corrupts every corner of our lives. Finney viewed the doctrine of election as an expression of divine benevolence—God foresaw from eternity that some people could be reclaimed from sin and brought into a life of holiness. As much as he emphasized that faith is a voluntary act, Finney also insisted that no one is able to turn to Christ without God's working within by the Holy Spirit. He thus sought the same type of balance between divine initiative and human participation, through the means of grace, that had exemplified seventeenth-century Puritan spirituality.

Disinterested benevolence was the theological link between revival and the missionary-social reform impulse. Finney delivered a series of *Lectures on Revivals of Religion* (1835) in New York City in which he set forth his theology and technology of evangelism. His assertion that a revival is not a supernatural event but the result of human effort under God's influence reflected his belief that the aim of Christian evangelism was not only the salvation of individuals but the reshaping of sinful society. While Old School Presbyterians like Charles Hodge attacked Finney's free-will-oriented theology in print, anti-abolitionist mobs vandalized his church because antislavery rallies convened there. Finney preached that slavery was a horrible sin, and he denied the sacrament to slaveholders. Although warning that no reform movement should assume priority over commitment to evangelism (the fatal step taken by radical abolitionist Theodore Dwight Weld), he insisted that evangelism must always include social reform.

In 1835 the newly established Oberlin Collegiate Institute invited Finney to become professor of theology. Abolitionist students and faculty who had been expelled from Cincinnati's Lane Seminary were willing to transfer to Oberlin with Finney on the faculty. Finney moved west after stipulating that students would be admitted to the pioneering coeducational school without regard to race and that the faculty (not trustees) govern academic affairs. For a time he attempted to divide the year between teaching at Oberlin and preaching at Broadway Tabernacle, but in 1837 he resigned the New York pulpit and assumed the pastorate of Oberlin's First Church. For the next three decades Finney taught systematic and practical theology, serving as president of the College from 1851 to 1866, and frequently launched evangelistic campaigns in eastern cities during the winter months. He and his second wife, Elizabeth, embarked on two long tours of the British Isles, where his published works were widely read.

The doctrine of sanctification became the central point of Finney's theology at Oberlin. Together with president Asa Mahan and other faculty, and after reading John Wesley on "Christian Perfection," Finney adopted the language of entire sanctification, holiness, and perfectionism. His theology was driven, as always, by a practical concern. As a pastor he now saw as never before the need for spiritual growth, what some were calling a "higher Christian life," in the church after conversion. He advanced his ideas in *The Oberlin Evangelist,* with some articles collected in *Lectures to Professing Christians* (1837) and *Views of Sanctification* (1840). He published volume 1 of *Skeletons of a Course of Theological Lectures* in 1840 and volumes 2 and 3 of *Lectures on Systematic Theology* in 1846–47 (rev. ed., 1851; abr. ed., 1878).

Finney defined entire sanctification as the consecration of the believer's whole being to God. Building on his earlier understanding of free moral agency and of salvation as commitment to a life of disinterested benevolence, he embraced Jesus' injunction to "be ye perfect" (Matt. 5:48). Since God creates us as moral beings, we are capable of full obedience to God's law. Sinners who repent from sin and turn to the Savior for new life then embark on a life of holiness—defined as impartial love and unfailing desire to seek the good for others. His use of the term "perfection," tainted by the Oneida Community and other eccentric perfectionist groups, and his claim that sanctification was possible in this life brought new storms of controversy. Many New School Presbyterian and Congregationalist friends shunned him; among orthodox Calvinists Oberlin became synonymous with heresy. Although Finney shared with Methodists this fresh interest in holiness, and holiness theologian Phoebe Palmer visited him on at least one occasion, Wesleyans regarded Finney's view of sanctification as legalistic. Finney's connection of law and gospel stemmed from an essentially Reformed theological perspective in which, as in seventeenth-century Puritanism, sanctification follows justification and the Saints persevere in grace.

Finney's theological influence was manifold. His elaboration of a purposefully evangelical doctrine of the atonement, aimed at moving sinners to salvation, undergirded the revivalist tradition well into the twentieth century. His theology of postconversion experience, including such language as "entire sanctification" and "baptism of the Holy Ghost," contributed to the Holiness movement and, at the turn of the century, Pentecostalism. At the same time, Finney's linking of disinterested benevolence and social reform helped lay the foundation for the Social Gospel movement.

Suggested Readings

Writings of Charles G. Finney: *The Memoirs of Charles G. Finney,* ed. Garth M. Rosell and Richard A. G. Dupuis (Grand Rapids: Zondervan, 1989).

Charles E. Hambrick-Stowe, *Charles G. Finney and the Spirit of American Evangelicalism* (Grand Rapids: Wm. B. Eerdmans Publishing Co., 1996).

Keith J. Hardman, *Charles Grandison Finney: Revivalist and Reformer* (Syracuse: Syracuse University Press, 1987; Grand Rapids: Baker Book House, 1990).

Glenn A. Hewitt, *Regeneration and Morality: A Study of Charles Finney, Charles Hodge, John W. Nevin, and Horace Bushnell* (New York: Carlson, 1991).

Asa Mahan

(1799–1889)

Dennis M. Campbell

Asa Mahan was one of the chief exponents of the idea of Christian perfection in the nineteenth century. Although known for many other things, including persuasive preaching and especially collegiate institution building, his advocacy of Christian perfection was his chief contribution to the shaping of American theology. The doctrine of Christian perfection in theology is generally associated with Methodism. John Wesley made it a hallmark of his teaching, and it characterized much of the theological thinking of early Methodism in America. There were, however, other strains of perfectionist teaching. Asa Mahan, a Congregationalist minister, was the intellectual leader of a group known as the Oberlin perfectionists.

Born in Vernon, New York, on 9 November 1799, Asa Mahan was the son of Captain Samuel and Anna (Dana) Mahan. Early in his life, he tells us in his autobiography, he accepted the doctrines of Calvinism, which rejected any notion of human free will. By the time he was seventeen, however, he had changed his mind and come to believe that men and women have the freedom to accept or reject God, and thus have a role in their salvation and responsibility for their moral life. He would hold to this teaching throughout his life. He completed his college work at Hamilton College in Clinton, New York, in 1824. He then continued on to Andover Seminary in Massachusetts. After his graduation in 1827, he taught school and was an active participant in the revivals known as the Second Great Awakening. He married Mary H. Dix in 1828.

In 1829 the Congregationalists ordained Mahan, and he served churches in Pittsford, New York, and Cincinnati, Ohio. While he was pastor of Sixth Presbyterian Church in Cincinnati, he became a trustee of Lane Seminary, an institution founded to educate evangelical ministers in the western part of the country. His service as a Lane trustee brought him into a significant and ultimately life-shaping controversy. Seeking to keep the peace, both within the school and with its supporters, the seminary forbade its students to discuss the question of slavery. Mahan opposed the seminary policy, and when, in 1835, he became the first president of Oberlin College, approximately eighty Lane students left Cincinnati and transferred to the new institution. These moves would set important theological and institutional directions for both Mahan and Oberlin.

Under the leadership of Asa Mahan, Oberlin made significant moves to establish itself as a progressive and distinctive institution. Strongly Christian, and committed to the liberal arts and to vigorous freedom of speech, the College was the first in the nation to grant degrees to women under the same conditions as men. Moreover, from the beginning, at Asa Mahan's insistence, the institution admitted students without regard to their racial or ethnic identity. Oberlin also opened a theological college, later to be called Oberlin Seminary, to accommodate the students who transferred from Lane, and to be a center for evangelical perfectionist teaching. Mahan and his friend and colleague Charles G. Finney became widely known as leaders of "Oberlin Perfectionism."

While he was president of Oberlin, Mahan also taught philosophy and began to turn out his extensive writings in philosophy and theology. His publications in philosophy point to a keen mind and thorough understanding of the principal movements in philosophy in the nineteenth century. Although valuable at the time, it was not these works but his advocacy of Christian perfectionism that earned him a place in American theology. In 1839 he published what is probably his most important book, *Scripture Doctrine of Christian Perfection*. He aggressively argued the case that the Bible teaches that men and women can achieve perfection in holiness. Although he did not claim persons can be absolutely perfect, he did argue they can grow toward perfection. He made it clear that this perfection in holiness derives not from one's own works, but from God's grace, which is why, in principle, perfection is attainable in this life. Perfection is a gift of the Holy Spirit, and as such not to be achieved by human beings. It is, however, a gift to be sought. It requires human decision and purpose, and human beings have the capacity to make the decision to seek perfection. In his advocacy of free will, which he believed to be essential to his understanding of Christian perfection, Mahan stood in opposition to Calvinism throughout his adult life. It is possible to commit oneself wholeheartedly to Jesus Christ, to consecrate the self to be single-minded in pursuit of entire sanctification.

According to Mahan there are specific things one can do to advance in the pursuit of Christian perfection. Chief among these is the effort to build Christian character so that one seeks the higher goods of love, purity, and holiness in all things. Christian character involves training in the dispositions of the Christian life so that one's response in any given situation is purposely Christian. Critics of perfectionist teaching point to its tendency toward individualism and its possibility for pride. Mahan addressed criticism directly. He always maintained that true Christian holiness went beyond individual behavior to social ethics. His theology of Christian perfection not only contributed to, but was the foundation for, his work in opposition to slavery, his efforts on behalf of women, and his advocacy for social reform.

Mahan sought to avoid legalism and pride. The theological concept "antinomianism" refers to the idea that once one receives the gift of the Holy Spirit for entire sanctification one is incapable of sinful behavior. This thinking can lead one to self-delusory actions and to self-satisfaction. Mahan emphasized the ever-present human ability to succumb to temptation and act in sin. Thus he distinguished between the will to be perfect in holiness and one's actual behavior. The point is to seek after holiness, to will entire sanctification, but at the same time not to fool oneself into thinking that one is perfect, because only God can make such a judgment. Men and women are called always to seek to grow toward entire sanctification.

After his fifteen years of service at Oberlin, Mahan moved to Cleveland, where some associates were seeking to establish a new university. He became its president in 1850. The new institution, called Cleveland University, did not succeed, and Mahan returned to pastoral work serving churches in Jackson, Michigan, and Adrian, Michigan, from 1855 to 1860. In 1860, he became president of Adrian College for eleven years. His first wife died in 1863 and he married Mary E. Chase in 1866. When he retired, they moved to Eastbourne, Essex, England, where he continued his extensive speaking and writing. He died in Eastbourne on 4 April 1889.

Asa Mahan wrote many books and articles. In addition to his *Scripture Doctrine of Christian Perfection,* among the most important for persons interested in the development of American theology are "The Idea of Perfection" in the *Oberlin Quarterly Review* (1845); *The True Believer; His Character, Duty, and Privileges* (1847); *Out of Darkness into Light* (1876); and his own account of his life and work, *Autobiography: Intellectual, Moral, and Spiritual* (1882).

Suggested Readings

Writings of Asa Mahan: *Scripture Doctrine of Christian Perfection* (Boston: D. S. King, 1839); *Out of Darkness into Light* (New York: Willard Tract Repository, 1876); "The Idea of Perfection," *Oberlin Quarterly Review* I (1845).

Edward H. Madden and James E. Hamilton, *Freedom and Grace: The Life of Asa Mahan* (Metuchen, N.J., and London: Scarecrow Press, 1982).

Timothy L. Smith, *Revivalism and Social Reform: American Protestantism on the Eve of the Civil War* (Nashville: Abingdon Press, 1957).

Barbara Brown Zikmund, "Asa Mahan and Oberlin Perfectionism" (Ph.D. diss., Duke University, 1969).

Samuel Simon Schmucker

(1799–1873)

Jerald C. Brauer

To understand Schmucker's theology one must understand the context in which he lived and worked. His theology was a product of the effort of Lutheranism to retain its identity even while it became thoroughly at home in the American context. Lutherans were coming from Europe, primarily Germany, and found themselves in a culture dominated by English-speaking Protestant denominations. Lutherans were also heirs of a particular confessional heritage with a rich, diversified liturgical tradition and hymnody.

Revivalism dominated the American Protestant scene. Its piety shaped the theology, cult, ritual, ethics, ecclesiology, and mores of American Protestantism. At the heart of revivalism was the "new birth," considered necessary for becoming and being a Christian. Without a profound, self-conscious conversion experience, one was not and could not be a Christian. So profound was the experience that the saint could testify to the moment of rebirth. Various techniques were devised to enhance the possibility of new birth—for example, protracted meetings, emotional preaching, the anxious bench, new hymnology, extemporary prayer, and camp meetings.

Revivalism both cut across all denominationalism to encourage ecumenicity, and it split denominations, created schisms, and spawned new churches. Those churches which tended to take seriously their theological confessions and traditions found themselves, by and large, opposed to revivalism. Lutherans, in general, were among these groups. S. S. Schmucker was born and raised, devised his theology, ministered, and taught within this context. Yet as the son of a Lutheran pastor famous as a pietistic leader in revivals, Schmucker was shaped by his father's piety. At an early age he became aware of the dilemma facing the Lutheran churches.

Young Schmucker, educated by his father and friends, received a classical training at York Academy, attended the infant University of Pennsylvania, and in 1816 entered the fledgling Presbyterian Princeton Theological Seminary. Princeton probably did not do much to set his theological agenda; however, it initiated him into the center of American Protestant power, and introduced him to the very best in the English-speaking Reformed tradition. There he learned the importance of polity, and became the architect of the constitution of his General Synod when he wrote his *Formula for the Government and Discipline of the Evangelical Lutheran Church* (1823).

As a Lutheran, Schmucker resided on the periphery of American revivalism. His Princeton education brought him into its middle. Further, study at one of the centers of interdenominational ecumenical activity enabled Schmucker to meet and become lifelong friends with many of the future leaders of America's Protestant establishment—Presbyterians Charles Hodge and Robert Baird, Congregationalist William B. Sprague, and John Johns, later Episcopal bishop of Virginia. Princeton also reinforced his suspicions of Roman Catholicism and contributed to his deep-seated anti-Catholicism.

The Scottish Common-Sense philosophy taught at Princeton did not seem to influence Schmucker's theology as it did his fellow student Charles Hodge. Because of his German background, Schmucker was familiar with philosophical and theological developments in Germany far beyond those known to his student peers and even professors. Princeton did embody, however, a combination of earlier Puritan piety and contemporary revivalism which influenced Schmucker in both personal and public ethics. German pietism shared some of these characteristics, but it was neither as stringent in personal ethics nor as involved in public ethics. Schmucker's prohibitionism, extreme sabbatarianism, antislavery activism, and virulent anti-Catholicism were not products of his German Lutheran pietism.

After two full years at Princeton, Schmucker began his ministry in the Lutheran Church. He already had an agenda for his church: It needed a theological seminary to educate its ministers, a translation of one of the great Lutheran theological dogmatic systems, and an undergraduate college. Schmucker accomplished all three of these goals. In 1826, the year he founded and became the first President and Professor of Gettysburg Theological Seminary, he published an 889-page, two-volume translation of *The Handbook of Christian Dogmatics* by the Tübingen theologians G. C. Storr and C. Flatt under the title *An Elementary Course of Biblical Theology*.

Storr and "the older Tübingen school" were engaged in a form of Christian apologetics that sought to use the best in modern philosophy, particularly Immanuel Kant, to reestablish the credibility of the Christian faith in the face of rationalistic attacks. They argued that Kant's "critical philosophy" placed Christian revelation and belief beyond the pale of reason as commonly understood. Christian revelation is of such a nature that it falls outside the sphere of reason. It is not and cannot be contrary to reason. Neither irrational nor nonrational, it is arational.

Scripture is absolutely central as source and norm to elicit and validate Christian experience and belief. Sustained and critical attention must be given to scripture in order to elucidate Christian truth and doctrine. Though past theologians and confessions were not to be ignored, they were not necessary to establish the truth of Christian belief or doctrine. Schmucker chose well in calling his translation *An Elementary Course of Biblical Theology.*

This monumental task of translation forced Schmucker to a closer study of Kant, reaffirmed his biblicism, enabled him to develop and maintain a highly selective use of the Lutheran confessions, strengthened his convictions to affirm a few central or universal Christian truths, and compelled him to clarify his priorities in the Christian faith. He rearranged the entire text of Storr and Flatt and added two lengthy appendixes of his own—one on the Trinity and one on the Eucharist.

Schmucker soon discovered his translation of a great Lutheran dogmatics did not suffice for his students. He quickly decided to prepare his own text and was encouraged to do so by the General Synod of the Lutheran Church. In 1834, *Elements of Popular Theology with Special Reference to the Doctrines of the Reformation as Avowed Before the Diet of Augsburg in 1530* appeared. It went through nine editions, and hundreds of Lutheran ministerial students studied it. It was not a learned tome, but rather a popular exposition intended principally for theology students, interested laity, and pastors.

Nothing new theologically ever emerged in the text, though Schmucker worked on it over the years. He followed Storr's use of Kant and argued that there could be no conflict between reason and revelation, so that scripture remained the source and norm for Christian belief and practice. Schmucker upheld the importance and limited role of Lutheran confessions, particularly Augsburg and Luther's Catechisms, but did it only insofar as he judged them to be faithful expositions of the basic substance of Christian truth grounded in the Bible.

His flexible understanding and use of the Augsburg Confession was not shared by growing numbers of his contemporary Lutherans. Though his textbook was written in a conciliatory spirit for all Protestants, it clearly exhibited a rancor toward Roman Catholics, atheists, and Unitarians. He held firm to his idea of a few fundamental Christian beliefs shared by all Protestant Christians, who should tolerate their particular differences. His conception of Baptism and the Lord's Supper remained unchanged; he simply clarified his views by further exposition. These latter two topics as well as his view on fundamentals increasingly got him into trouble with his fellow Lutherans.

Schmucker's basic theological assumptions were grounded initially in Lutheran pietism but were reinvigorated and expanded by his contact with revivalism in America. His point of departure for all theologizing was the personal experience of conversion grounded in scripture. He believed all true Christians hold this much in common. They may differ on a number of things surrounding that experience, but never on the experience itself—a personal, existential experience of justification by faith. Whatever enhances this experience is to be affirmed; everything that frustrates it is to be avoided. Scripture alone provides the norm.

This belief, in itself, did not lead to the rejection of creeds and confessions, but it seriously questioned their role in the church. The so-called Apostolic and Nicene creeds could be affirmed as the clearest exposition of biblical truth because all Christians held them. Other confessions of faith were in his view more limited and stood under judgment of scripture, reason, and the contemporary experience of believers.

Unlike the German theologian Friedrich Schleiermacher, who insisted on the primacy of the total experience of the total Christian community, past and present, Schmucker emphasized the primacy of the current experience of the individual. Individuals must discuss and compare their experiences because ultimately current experience, in dialogue with scripture, was the basis for Christian truth. In this respect Schmucker revealed an antihistorical bias.

These views were the bases for Schmucker's ecumenical activities and writings. As early as 1838, he wrote *Fraternal Appeal to the American Churches with a Plan for Catholic Union, on Apostolic Principals*. And in 1846, he published *Overture for Christian Union, Submitted for the Consideration of the Evangelical Denominations in the United States*. A pioneer in the effort at Christian unity, Schmucker was one of the founders and leaders of the Evangelical Alliance. He wished to build unity on shared doctrine and tolerate all nonessential differences, proposing that the different churches be represented in the Alliance as churches rather than as individuals. Many of the churches did not agree with Schmucker's theological presuppositions or his plan of representation, and hence his proposals were not adopted.

Just as Schmucker's principles on ecumenicity did not succeed, neither did his proposals to his own church as outlined in the *Definite Synodical Platform* (1855). Schmucker sought a clarification of the struggle between Lutheran confessionalists and his own version of American Lutheranism. His *Definite Platform* contained nothing new in his theology; however, for the first time it put in a single public ecclesiastical document not just his

Lutheran affirmations but also his fundamental criticisms and modifications of the Lutheran confessions. Schmucker produced an "American recension" of the Augsburg Confession, which, he argued, should be adopted by the General Synod as a statement of faith for subscription by all American Lutheran ministers, a proposal with explosive repercussions.

Schmucker and his followers had been moving away from the majority of their fellow Lutherans. In the first part of the *Platform* Schmucker advanced a modified Augsburg confession in which he excised five "errors" as he called them: approval of the ceremonies of the mass; private confession and absolution; denial of the divine obligation of the Christian sabbath; baptismal regeneration; and the real presence of the body and blood of the Savior in the Eucharist. The second part of the *Platform* rejected a variety of errors in other Lutheran symbolical books.

Even Schmucker's earliest writings reveal his doubts about these doctrines, which he regarded as unscriptural and remnants of Roman Catholicism. He did not judge them to be fundamental Christian doctrines and therefore saw them as subject to removal from the confessions. He argued that the vast majority of Lutherans no longer believed or practiced them. Because of Schmucker's theological assumptions, rooted in Lutheran pietism and radicalized by American revivalism, he could not understand that the doctrines he opposed were held by many of his fellow Lutherans as central to the nature of Lutheranism. Where Schmucker wished to jettison everything connected with the old Roman Catholic mass, including all ceremonies, confessional Lutherans wanted to reject only those parts of the mass judged unscriptural and destructive of the central affirmation of justification by grace alone through faith. Where they were open to a rich liturgical heritage and traditions grounded in the ancient church year, Schmucker looked upon this openness as papist and divisive.

The five "errors" Schmucker had excised from the Augsburg Confession all involved liturgical practice. A good example is Schmucker's rejection of the Augsburg formulation of the nature and role of baptism. Lutheran confessionalists wished to affirm the Augsburg formulation because for them it demonstrated the center of their piety, namely, that before humans have done anything, God has done everything for their salvation. An infant is brought by the church, the community of Saints, to the church on command of God's Word to be baptized into the household of faith.

Lutherans believed that God's Word declared that in baptism begins a lifetime of regeneration of a child through the Word and Sacraments in the church. They were not prepared to say, as Roman Catholicism did, that there was a substance of grace infused, but they were willing to affirm that the grace of regeneration was at work, as God promised. Schmucker, however, opposed this view, maintaining instead that regeneration cannot begin until a human being is capable of expressing personal faith. Baptism is in no way related to regeneration.

For their part, Schmucker's opponents seized upon what they argued was his distortion of the Lutheran conception of the eucharist. Initially, Schmucker was prepared to permit difference of interpretation with regard to this doctrine within Lutheranism. For many years he advocated what he considered to be the true interpretation of the Eucharist, one in his view closer to Melanchthon and Calvin than to Luther and Zwingli.

His *Definite Platform,* however, dropped the article on the eucharist because he judged it theologically incorrect. This act infuriated his fellow Lutherans. To them, the Augsburg formulation was neither indifferent nor incorrect—it was the true formulation. At Marburg, Luther had fought against Zwingli for the doctrine of the real presence of the body and blood of Christ in the Lord's Supper, and accused Zwingli of having a completely different spirit. How could such a matter be indifferent? Schmucker's opponents believed he distorted the understanding of the Lord's Supper affirmed for generations by Lutherans in their various confessional books.

To the extent Schmucker's pietism was reshaped by the context of American revivalism, it was inevitable that his brand of American Lutheranism would emerge at odds with his Lutheran brethren in America. Though Schmucker sincerely believed he was a true Lutheran in a new context, he jettisoned a Lutheran understanding of the Word, Sacraments, and liturgy, and exhibited a piety at odds with the majority of Lutherans in America and Europe. However unappreciated he was in his own communion, he stood as a giant among his fellow American Protestants. He had far more constructive impact on his fellow Protestants than he did on the majority of his fellow Lutherans. He built institutions, and he shaped a portion of Lutheranism in America, but his point of view never prevailed among Lutherans generally.

Suggested Readings

P. Anstadt, *The Life and Times of Reverend S. S. Schmucker* (York, Pa.: P. Anstadt & Sons, 1896).

Virgilius Ferm, *A Crisis in American Lutheran Theology* (New York: Century Co., 1927).

Abdel Ross Wentz, *Pioneer in Christian Unity: Samuel Simon Schmucker* (Philadelphia, Pa.: Fortress Press, 1967).

Phoebe Worrall Palmer

(1807–1874)

Nancy A. Hardesty

The American "Holiness" movement is a direct outgrowth of the Tuesday Meeting for the Promotion of Holiness founded in the 1830s by Phoebe Worrall Palmer and her sister Sarah Worrall Lankford Palmer (1806–96) in the New York City home they and their husbands shared. Phoebe never thought of herself as a theologian or even had much respect for theology, but her books and teaching significantly affected American church life.

Their father, Henry Worrall, born in Yorkshire, England, had been converted under the ministry of John Wesley. After emigrating to the United States, he married American Methodist Dorothea Wade. They brought sixteen children into the world, nine of whom reached adulthood. Both Phoebe and Sarah joined the Methodist Episcopal Church as teens. In 1827, just shy of her twentieth birthday, Phoebe married a Methodist and trained physician, Walter Clarke Palmer. Sarah married architect Thomas A. Lankford in 1831.

Reared in a home with twice-daily family prayers and a high level of participation in local church activities, Phoebe was thoroughly Christian, though she never experienced "conversion." This led her to question the role of emotions in the spiritual life. The tragic deaths of three of the Palmers' first four children in the first decade of their marriage further compounded her spiritual struggle to find assurance of salvation.

Having read Wesley's *Plain Account of Christian Perfection*, Hester Ann Rogers' *Memoirs*, and *The Life of William Carvosso*, Phoebe was familiar with the notion of sanctification or "perfect love," as Wesley preferred to call it. Sarah found entire sanctification on 21 May 1835. For Phoebe the experience would not come until 26 July 1837.

In 1836, Sarah, who already led weekly prayer meetings for women at the Allen Street and Mulberry Street Methodist Episcopal churches, proposed to combine them into one meeting on Tuesday afternoons in the home the Palmers and Lankfords shared at 54 Rivington Street. Phoebe agreed. Thus, what began as an ordinary women's prayer meeting eventually became the fountainhead of Holiness teaching. When the Lankfords moved out of the city in 1840, Phoebe became its sole leader.

Interest in recovering the Wesleyan heritage of entire sanctification was widespread within the Methodist Church at this time. In 1840 the bishops urged members to "go on to perfection." Wesley had taught that entire sanctification was the culmination of a long process beginning at conversion or justification. He came to believe that some people did attain it before death, although he never claimed to have personally done so. Palmer agreed with Wesley that if God commanded Christians to be holy (see Lev. 20:7) or to be perfect (as Jesus did in Matt. 5:48), then it must be possible for people to become so, now, in the present. Both agreed that justification and sanctification are to be achieved by faith and are gifts of God's grace, not the result of human works or achievement.

In sanctification believers are enabled to keep the first and great commandment: To love God with their whole heart, soul, mind, and strength. They no longer willfully sin, though they may make errors in judgment, and they still suffer the effects of sin on their minds and bodies. For Wesley, entire sanctification may designate an instantaneous experience, but he carefully balanced this claim with an insistence that it is at once preceded and followed by gradual growth in grace. Palmer, however, following the lead of Charles G. Finney, the American revivalist who taught that religion was not something to wait for but something to do, stressed the instantaneous side of sanctification.

Palmer's 1843 classic *The Way of Holiness* begins with a question asked her by a Presbyterian minister: "Whether there is not a shorter way of getting into this way of holiness?" The response is immediate: "There is a shorter way." She amplified her teaching in several subsequent books: *Present to My Christian Friend on Entire Devotion to God* (1845); *Faith and Its Effects: or, Fragments from My Portfolio* (1848); and *Incidental Illustrations of the Economy of Salvation, Its Doctrines and Duties* (1855).

The process for Palmer involved three quick and simple steps. To describe the process she devised what has come to be called her "altar terminology." The first step was to lay one's all upon the altar, to offer to God one's possessions, children, spouse, time, talents, reputation, indeed one's entire self. This act of the will was called "entire consecration."

Step two was to have faith. From a reading of Exodus 29:37, Matthew 23:19, Romans 12:1-2, and Hebrews 13:10 (probably influenced by Adam

Clarke's commentaries), Palmer reasoned that Christ was the altar and that the altar sanctified the gift. Thus if one has completed the act of laying all upon the altar, one is entirely sanctified. Since God has promised to do it, the believer should exercise faith in that promise and claim holiness of heart and life. Where Wesley argued that the inner witness of the Holy Spirit would confirm one's sanctification, Palmer found assurance in the objective affirmation of scripture rather than subjective experience or feelings. Feelings might follow, but they were unessential.

The third step was to testify to one's experience. This was essential if one hoped to remain sanctified. Palmer identified the experience of sanctification with the baptism of the Holy Spirit and described it in Pentecostal language. Especially for women, she linked it with an enduement of power for useful service.

This led to a defense of women's preaching and teaching in *The Promise of the Father* (1859). Noting the biblical conjunction of the baptism of the Holy Spirit with power (Luke 24:49; Acts 1:4-5), she argued that Holiness is power, usually in capital letters. Though she was careful not to espouse the ordination of women or "woman's rights" in the growing secular sense, Palmer argued, with Peter and his citation of the prophet Joel (see Acts 2:17-18; Joel 2:28-29), that when people received the Holy Spirit at Pentecost, both women and men, maidservants and menservants were encouraged to prophesy. Just as Finney felt that both women and men were compelled to testify to their experience of salvation, so Palmer found women as well as men compelled to speak of their sanctification. And indeed many women witnessed to the fact that in their act of entire consecration, God called them to preach. Palmer notes the clear ministry of women in the New Testament. She quotes early church "fathers" to justify women's preaching and cites the work of early Methodist women as prime examples.

Following Adam Clarke rather than Wesley, Palmer saw entire sanctification as the beginning rather than the goal of the Christian life. She considered it essential to salvation. While Palmer's primary concern was personal holiness, she did couple it with the Wesleyan concern for social betterment. She personally worked with poor women and children at the Five Points Mission in New York City, and she encouraged other women to "usefulness" in whatever endeavors God laid on their hearts. Many women who experienced a commitment to Holiness in meetings led by the Palmers or others became active in various social reform causes.

The Palmers spent the Civil War years preaching in Great Britain (1859–63), a trip publicized in their book *Four Years in the Old World*. Upon their return to New York, Doctor Palmer gave up his medical practice so that they might hold meetings throughout New England and eastern Canada. Their involvement with Methodist camp meetings led to the formation in 1866 of the National Campmeeting Association for the Promotion of Christian Holiness, a forerunner to state Holiness associations.

Palmer's teachings were also promulgated in a periodical founded in 1839 by Timothy Merritt as the *Guide to Christian Perfection,* renamed the *Guide to Holiness* in 1846 (the word "perfection" having been brought into disrepute by the communitarian and complex marriage practices of John Humphrey Noyes). The Palmers purchased the journal in 1864 and merged it with the *Beauty of Holiness and Sabbath Miscellany.* Phoebe served as editor from 1864 to 1874; the magazine itself persevered until 1901, underwritten in later years by the Palmers' daughter, songwriter Phoebe Palmer Knapp.

Phoebe Palmer's notion of holiness as a "second work of grace" eventually spawned a group of Holiness churches including the Wesleyan Methodist Church, the Free Methodist Church, the Church of God (Anderson, Indiana), the Salvation Army, the Church of the Nazarene, and the Christian and Missionary Alliance. Her work is also foundational for those Pentecostal churches with a Wesleyan heritage, such as the Pentecostal Holiness Church, the Church of God (Cleveland, Tennessee), the Church of God in Christ, and many others.

Suggested Readings

Donald W. Dayton, *Theological Roots of Pentecostalism* (Grand Rapids: Hendrickson, 1987).

Harold E. Raser, *Phoebe Palmer: Her Life and Thought* (Lewiston, N.Y.: Edwin Mellen, 1987).

Charles Edward White, *The Beauty of Holiness: Phoebe Palmer as Theologian, Revivalist, Feminist, and Humanitarian* (Grand Rapids: Francis Asbury Press/Zondervan, 1986).

Harriet Beecher Stowe

(1811–1896)

Patricia R. Hill

Harriet Beecher Stowe was born into a singularly important religious family in nineteenth-century America. Hers was arguably the most powerful theological voice within the famous Beecher clan. Because women in the Victorian era were rarely educated as theologians, their theological work was done in genres open to female writers: fiction and poetry, travel accounts, and memoirs. Stowe used all these forms. Through her family connections she also had access to religious newspapers where she published essays and reviews that resemble more directly the writing done by ministers and scholars.

Stowe's evolving theology was informed and shaped by the collective influence of her brothers Edward, George, and Henry Ward, her sister Catharine, her husband, Calvin Stowe, and her wide reading in religious publications. She largely discarded both Calvinist theology and her father Lyman Beecher's influential reworking of it into New Divinity theology. Indeed, evidence suggests fairly conclusively that Stowe underwent a perfectionist conversion in the 1840s. In this experience the influence of Phoebe Palmer, mediated through the Holiness writings of Thomas Upham, was critical. Stowe shared Upham's fascination with Quietist mystics, especially Bishop Fénelon and Madame Guyon, who appealed, as has not been widely realized, to many Victorians. In 1850, Calvin Stowe accepted a position at Bowdoin where Upham was professor of mental and moral philosophy; the Stowes cemented a close friendship with the Uphams in the Bowdoin years, during which *Uncle Tom's Cabin* (1852) was conceived and written. Calvin Stowe, among the leading biblical scholars of his generation, introduced his wife to aspects of German Romantic theology. Her evangelical antislavery was constituted from these various elements.

Stowe's New England novels, especially *The Minister's Wooing* (1859) and *Oldtown Folks* (1869), contain her most detailed critique of Calvinist and Hopkinsian theology. She described its pernicious effects on certain

149

kinds of temperaments, and criticized its failure to embrace human emotions and its rejection of sensual, aesthetic aids to spiritual comprehension. She aligned its logic with the inexorability of natural laws. This, in her view, produced a distorted image of God. Her incarnational theology centered instead on a compassionate God who suffers with his creatures. Suffering is not to be sought, but when it comes, is to be embraced as a heavenly discipline. The heroines of her novels achieve earthly peace and joy through suffering that refines and perfects their faith.

Stowe's formulation of evangelical antislavery in *Uncle Tom's Cabin*, though it may not have literally started the big war as the apocryphal comment attributed to Abraham Lincoln suggests, profoundly altered the categories in which her contemporaries viewed the slave question. Her depiction of slavery was designed to make the reader "feel right" and consequently act to eradicate the peculiar institution. Although Stowe's version of antislavery is fundamentally religious, the holiness theology that informed her analysis translated easily into a vision, which had broad currency in the sentimental culture of Victorian America, of a purified and glorified nation. The teleology of Christian millennialism consistently shaped Stowe's understanding of national history and politics.

Theodore Hovet has demonstrated the extent to which structures of holiness theology are embedded in Stowe's antislavery novels. The second novel, *Dred* (1856), especially incorporates the call Stowe and other holiness writers made for institutional reform as Southern intransigence rigidified. Their refashioned perfectionist ideology recognized the limits of moral suasion as a method for social reform. Slavery, defined as systemic social evil, had to be destroyed before the nation could achieve its millennial destiny. Rejecting the radical nonresistance of Garrisonian abolitionism, Stowe and other moderate evangelicals articulated a rationale for engaging in political abolitionism and ultimately endorsing the violence of civil war. In theological terms that war came to be seen as atonement for national sin. The suffering the war brought was assimilated to the theology of suffering that Stowe and other holiness evangelicals had already elaborated.

Perhaps the most innovative feature of Stowe's theological reflection lies in her development of a psychology of religion that accommodated the ecclesiastical diversity of American Christianity by proposing that particular religious forms are suited to particular temperaments. Her conception of the varieties of religious temperaments prefigures some aspects of William James' typology. Religious eclecticism allowed her to embrace the liturgical practices of Episcopalianism while continuing to follow the course of holiness higher-life movements in England and the United States after the war, and simultaneously to dabble in Spiritualism. Her piety manifests a melding of traditions that parallels her formal strictures against doctrinaire privileging of sectarian forms and dogma.

Stowe's theology articulates a theory of religious aesthetics. Appalled by what she considered the aesthetic barrenness of Puritan sensibility and by the destruction of religious art during the English Reformation, she wrote an account of her triumphal European tour, *Sunny Memories of Foreign Lands* (1854), that introduced Americans to the spiritual aesthetics of Catholic art. Stowe also endorsed liturgical reforms that visually and musically enriched worship. Such aesthetic aids evoked, she argued in *The Minister's Wooing*, the emotions that were the means through which the soul was disciplined and educated as it rose to that height "where the soul knows self no more."

Union with the divine, for Stowe as for Thomas Upham, was the ultimate goal of the Christian journey. But Stowe sought to redefine the nature of divinity. In meditations on the life of Christ collected and published as *Footsteps of the Master* (1877), Stowe preferred an incarnational theology according to which God's emotional nature is revealed in Christ. Christ's passion was not, for Stowe, a mere consequence of his humanity, but a revelation of the essence of trinitarian divinity. The majestic Calvinist God of justice is thus endowed with a capacity to suffer, even in his divine nature, and to empathize with human emotions. This empathetic capacity Stowe described as a maternal or feminine aspect of God's nature. Her understanding of the incarnation attributed all that was human in Christ to Mary's nature. The miracle of incarnation was "the union of the divine nature with the nature of a pure woman. Hence there was in Jesus more of the pure feminine element than in any other man. It was the pure feminine element exalted and taken in union with divinity." The incarnation, in Stowe's dynamic theological vision, altered the character of God. Though rejecting Catholic Mariology, Stowe celebrated Mary's unique intimacy with the divine, and imagined that sympathetic union continuing in heaven. Mary thus operates to insert empathy into the divine being.

Stowe's most significant contributions to American theology all revolve around the question of emotions. A right relationship with the divine evokes "right feelings" that govern efforts to perfect society. Varieties of temperament dictate ecclesiological and devotional diversity. Human emotions are both the means through which the divine is apprehended and revelations of the analogous emotional character of the divine.

151

Suggested Readings

Marie Caskey, *Chariot of Fire: Religion and the Beecher Family* (New Haven: Yale University Press, 1978).

Joan Hedrick, *Harriet Beecher Stowe: A Life* (New York: Oxford University Press, 1994).

Theodore Hovet, "Harriet Beecher Stowe's Holiness Crusade Against Slavery" (Ph.D. diss., University of Kansas, 1970).

Thomas Jenkins, *The Character of God in America* (New York: Oxford University Press, 1996).

Charles Hodge

(1797–1878)

James H. Smylie

In 1872 Princeton Theological Seminary, American Presbyterians, and much of the Christian world celebrated the life and work of Charles Hodge. He had just completed fifty years of service as professor of theology at the seminary. During his career he had instructed approximately three thousand students, written more than five thousand pages of the *Princeton Review*, of which he was editor, and published a three-volume *Systematic Theology*, as well as biblical commentaries, sermons, treatises, devotional works, and a history of the Presbyterian denomination. Thinking of himself as an Augustinian as well as a Reformed apologist, he challenged threats to the Christian faith and life which he found in Deistic Rationalism, Romantic Idealism, and what he considered to be Darwinian Atheism. He did so with a biblically oriented Reformed Scholasticism drawing upon a Baconian-based Scottish Common-Sense philosophical method.

Hodge was born in 1797 in Philadelphia in the aftermath of the American Revolution and the yellow fever outbreak of 1795. His father, Hugh, from Irish Presbyterian stock, died shortly after Charles was born. Mary Blanchard, his mother and a well-born New Englander, took over the small family of two boys. With the help of the Hodge family, she saw that both children had a classical education along with religious training as Presbyterians who could recite the Westminster Shorter Catechism. She moved the family to Princeton where they attended the Presbyterian, though ecumenical, college. While his brother studied medicine, Charles entered the new seminary established in town when the Hodges took up residence in 1812. There the young Hodge studied with Archibald Alexander, among others, who became his spiritual and intellectual father.

Alexander, a highly intelligent Christian with a pastor's heart, arranged a course which involved biblical studies in the original languages, theological studies in Latin using Francis Turretin's massive volumes, *Institutio theologiae elencticae,* along with Christian history and pastoral studies. In conformity with the seminary's charter he also practiced arguments against Deism. In the name of reason and the scientific spirit of the age, Deists tried to redefine Christianity as a "reasonable" religion, without much of the Bible and without the trinitarianism of the Christian tradition. While Alexander attempted to imbue his students with a warm evangelical piety, he also used an inductive method in theological studies to arrive at the "facts" and a reasonable defense of the Christian faith as received from the scriptures and Christian tradition. The young Hodge absorbed this education and was ordained to the ministry in 1821 after a very brief pastoral experience. In 1822 he was called to teach at the seminary with his beloved mentor. In the same year he married Sarah Bache, a great granddaughter of Benjamin Franklin, at various times a Presbyterian turned Anglican turned Deist.

Named to the Professorship of Oriental and Biblical Literature in 1822, Hodge held the position until 1840. Feeling inadequately prepared, he traveled to New England to visit with biblical scholars there. He then spent two years (1826–28) in France and Germany. He made friends with such theologians as August Tholuck, heard Friedrich Schleiermacher and August Neander, and encountered firsthand the German "speculative spirit," à la G. W. F. Hegel. Alexander warned him to resist a "poisoned atmosphere which would lead only to skepticism, error, and even coldness." Hodge found that Schleiermacher, in his attempt to address the cultural despisers of religion, had confused the meaning of language and also the confessional content of Christianity, dissolving the Christian faith into an experience of dependence on God. During his European stay Hodge grew all the more convinced of the rightness of the Princeton approach to biblical and theological studies.

Relying on Francis Bacon (1561–1626) and later, Thomas Reid (1710–96), he held that all normal human beings are endowed by God with various faculties. These faculties permitted observations and ideas about the world on which human beings may rely. Persons needed only to gather and classify evidence and carefully generalize from these "facts." Satisfied with what he considered a scientific method of doing theology, Hodge rejected the emerging "speculative" or "mystical" methods he observed on the Continent.

Upon his return from Europe, Hodge published his first book, *A Commentary on the Epistle to the Romans* (1835). Although he recognized various forms of language in the Bible (that is, historical, poetic, and didactic literature), he seems to have been most at home with the didactic, publishing later on Ephesians and the letters to the Corinthians, which he ascribed to Paul. As an exegete, he tried to keep the larger context in focus as he set out the argument of each letter and pericope. He generally included analysis, commentary, doctrine, observations of other authors, and his own remarks. He was not as thorough in his exploration of philological insight as he was in the theological meaning of a passage.

Furthermore, according to Hodge, the ancient and Reformed creeds and confessions of the Christian community expressed the "facts" of the Bible. He was not uncritical of this heritage as he related texts to current theological criticism and discussion. He could not, however, escape completely the accusation that he already knew the conclusions on which he based his inductive study. Hodge believed that God's revelation in the Bible was made known by internal illumination of the Holy Spirit. Because of his polemic against the theological spirits of his age, which he continued to criticize, he did not always make this point of his theology clear.

In 1825, before he traveled to Europe, Hodge founded the *Biblical Repertory: A Collection of Tracts in Biblical Literature,* which became the *Biblical Repertory and Princeton Review* in 1837. He edited and was the chief contributor to its pages. The journal reviewed the literature and activities of the Christian community, especially within the Reformed family. Hodge's writings show the breadth of his interests, the sensitivity of his own faith and life, and the sharpness of his polemics against the dangers, as he perceived them, of the Christian witness. These characteristics he demonstrated in a number of conflicts with American Protestants. For example, influenced by Alexander's own experiences, Hodge expressed sympathy for some types of revivals. But he expressed his reservations and opposition to the methods and substance of the work of Charles Grandison Finney, ex-lawyer turned preacher-theologian.

One of the most popular figures of this period, and influenced by a graduate of Princeton seminary, Finney once wrote he was ashamed that anyone would subscribe to the Westminster Confession of Faith of the Presbyterian Church. Hodge was especially alarmed that the Arminianism of Finney's approach introduced a non-Reformed concept of self-determination into the revival experience. This was contrary to his emphasis on grace alone and faith alone coming down from Paul and the Reformation. In 1841, Hodge wrote a small and very popular book, *The Way of Life,* for the American Sunday School Union. In it he described the way God works through the Holy Spirit to allow the will and reason to recognize and accept divine truth as ascertained in the Bible. Hodge attempted to hold together the objective truth of Christian faith and the personal experience of that truth. Despite his writing as a theologian, according to Hodge, Finney obscured these essentials of Christian faith and life.

Hodge also expressed his concerns about the work of Mercersberg theologian John W. Nevin. In addition, he opposed New England theologians, among them Nathaniel Taylor, Edward Amasa Park, and Horace Bushnell. While Hodge approved of Nevin's attack on revival in *The Anxious Bench* (2nd ed., 1844), he was very uncomfortable with *The Mystical Presence* (1846) in which Nevin argued that Calvin taught the real spiritual presence of Christ. Taylor seemed to be undergirding with his own writings the work of persons like Finney, thus feeding modern Pelagianism and stirring the Old School–New School conflict within the Presbyterian Church at the same time. Hodge took exception to Park's "Theology of the Intellect and That of the Feelings" in *Bibliotheca Sacra* (1850), in which Park argued that one might have an erroneous intellectual idea about religion, yet find truth in one's experience. In this connection Hodge also attacked Bushnell, whose view of religious language, as expressed in *God in Christ* (1849), made it an imprecise way to communicate ultimate reality. According to Bushnell, language could only symbolize, providing momentary glimpses of ultimate truth. These arguments tended to undercut the propositional character of truth, which Hodge believed emerged from an inductive study of the Bible. Even figurative language in the Bible, Hodge argued, defined meaning and must be intelligible to the human mind.

Hodge, like other honest theologians of his time, could not legitimately avoid the topic of slavery. Following Alexander's position in an article written in 1836, Hodge held that slavery as an institution of labor was sanctioned by the "facts" of the Bible. The Christian could attack its abuses. Hodge held slaves at one time or another and treated the institution from a rather patriarchal and sentimental perspective, rather than in terms of the breeding and trading of slaves and of the harshness of the plantation system. Hodge emerged as a gradual emancipationist, and he expressed some anger over the agitation of the abolitionists. Because of his stature in the church his views were respected on this subject. Although conservative in his theology and social outlook, Hodge opposed the division of the Presbyterian Church both in 1837–38 and 1861. He did support the Union and continued to teach during the war and in its aftermath.

Hodge continued to use Turretin's *Reformed Scholasticism* as his basic theological text until the publication of his own *Systematic Theology* (1871–73) with the same number of pages found in the seventeenth-century text. This work—his crowning achievement—earned him a spot among

America's most important theologians. His volumes were erudite and well-informed. Hodge shared with his readers his accumulated knowledge covering biblical scholarship, the history of doctrine and philosophical theology, reflecting more of the Scholasticism of the early seventeenth century than an earlier Calvinism. He believed, in light of his experiences in Europe and with the New Divinity in the United States, that the "old Latin dogmatic writers" had one great merit. Although perhaps stiff, prolix, technical, intolerant, and austere, they did let the reader know what they meant. Hodge also wanted to be clear about his meaning. After his introduction on method, he divided his text into four main parts: Theology Proper, Anthropology, Soteriology, and Eschatology. Then he subdivided and sub-subdivided his presentation to cover his subject material.

In his introduction to methodology, he described what he had been practicing through the years. The Bible is not a "systematic theology" any more than nature is a system of "chemistry" or "mechanics." But the Bible contains the "truths" which the theologian must collect, authenticate, arrange, and exhibit in their internal relations to one another. Using Bacon's inductive method and adding a Common-Sense touch, Hodge concluded that ordinary and reasonable human beings would agree that the Bible is a "storehouse" of "facts" about Christian faith and life. God revealed in the Bible the meaning of revelation and the inspiration in the Bible. God used the authors of the Bible, with their own limitations, to communicate salvation knowledge. They do so in such a way that all the books are infallibly "inerrant" in what they teach, not only "in morals and religious truth," but also in statements of fact whether "scientific, historical, or geographical." Hodge utilized creeds and confessions and catechisms of the Christian and Reformed tradition as though their authors, coming later, had interpreted the "facts" of the Bible accurately.

In "Theology Proper," Hodge asserted that belief in the existence of God comes from the common sense with which God has endowed every human being. He used ontological, cosmological, teleological and moral arguments to make his case. In this connection, he condemned Darwinism as atheistic, not because of the possibility of some kind of evolutionary process, but because of Darwin's views of the struggle for existence, natural selection, and the survival of the fittest. These views denied the teleological argument, intelligent design, and a divine purpose for God's creatures and creation. He thought this point so crucial that he returned to it in a separate volume entitled *What Is Darwinism?* (1874). According to Hodge, God is sovereign, omniscient, omnipotent, and omnipresent. When he returned to the defense of the Trinity, he seemed to rely most heavily on

157

reciting the "facts" of the biblical testimony pertaining to the triune relationship, rather than the thought patterns of Hellenism. God is also a God of holiness, truth, justice, goodness, and mercy, as defined in the Westminster Shorter Catechism, which Hodge had memorized as a youth.

With regard to anthropology and soteriology, Hodge presented God as a covenant-maker in relation to human beings. He emphasized the Covenant of Works and the Covenant of Grace, reflecting his own affinity for the theology of Paul. God created all human beings in the divine image, as in the first Adam, with knowledge of God's law and with moral character. The first Adam sinned by breaking God's law. God imputed Adam's sin immediately to all Adam's descendants. The Princetonian considered this fall to have been a historical event. By holding to the idea of human beings as totally depraved, Hodge did not mean that all are equally wicked, or that anyone is as thoroughly corrupt as human beings may be, or that they were unable to do any good, judged by human standards. Human beings may contribute, for example, to civil righteousness. Rather, human beings in all acts are inclined toward self-interest contrary to the law of God, and do so sin. They are unable and unwilling to repent except under the influence of God's Holy Spirit.

Through the Covenant of Grace, and the second Adam, Christ's righteousness is immediately imputed to the believer by the unmerited grace of God and by faith alone. Hodge defined this mediatorial work of Christ in terms of vicarious satisfaction of God's justice through Christ's righteousness, death, and expiation for sin. The biblical "facts" demand as much. He also drew upon the testimony of the ancient sacrificial rites for his case. He could not accept other interpretations of the Atonement, such as the Governmental or Moral Influence views being championed by some New England theologians. While Hodge held to predestination as a Calvinist, he also taught that the atonement was efficient for all. It was, however, effective only for those who believe. Effectual grace is the work of God's Holy Spirit leading a believer to true repentance and regeneration by faith.

In the case of infants, Hodge held that all who die in infancy are saved. Hodge also held that sanctification was a work of God's Spirit which lasted until death. He thus denied tendencies toward perfectionism among some contemporary theologians such as Finney. In this process Christians are aided by God's law, about which Hodge wrote extensively in his systematics, and by the means of grace—by the Word preached, by the Sacraments of Baptism and the Lord's Supper properly administered, and by prayer.

In his treatment of eschatology, Hodge acknowledged difficulties in interpreting the "facts" of the Bible. He taught the resurrection of the body, but only in the last days when it would be united with the soul. This resurrected identity will not be flesh and blood, as Paul wrote, but will be truly adapted to the new condition for life in God's presence. Cautious about advancing details about Christ's second advent and reign, Hodge nevertheless believed the millennial reign would not begin until the last judgment and the beginning of the kingdom of God. He rejected the premillennialist speculations growing more popular in his time.

For some reason, Hodge did not include a section on ecclesiology in his *Systematic Theology*. He did write much about the church, including *The Constitutional History of the Presbyterian Church* (1840), a work supporting the Old School General Assembly over that of the New School. His *Discussions in Church Polity* (1878), collected and published posthumously, also indicate his interest in the subject. He understood the church to be the communion of all those who share in Christ's mediatorial work, and within whom the Holy Spirit dwells. This communion is essentially spiritual in nature, and thus not necessarily visible in organizational form. All professors of the faith and their children belong to the church visible where the means of grace are available. Hodge, while devoted to the system, was not a *jure divino* Presbyterian. In an address at the meeting of the Evangelical Alliance in New York in 1872, Hodge recognized the unity of all true believers, and called for a greater cooperation and union among Christians, although the visible unity of the body of Christ did not seem to be a driving force in his life.

As indicated by the honors paid him by colleagues, former students, and friends on the fiftieth anniversary of his teaching career, Charles Hodge had a widespread impact on many during his life. His influence lived on through his *Systematic Theology*, taught by his two sons, A. A. Hodge and Casper Wistar Hodge, his successors at Princeton, and through the availability and accessibility of other works such as *The Way of Life*. Professor B. B. Warfield also carried on this tradition of Reformed Scholasticism at Princeton. Although Hodge himself was an erudite man with broad contacts and interests, some of his followers could draw on his interpretations to meet what was considered the reductionism of the Modernists in religion. Some engaged in a form of Fundamentalist reductionism, defending the faith by holding "five points" as the essential and necessary articles of faith: the inerrancy of the Bible, the virgin birth, the miraculous work of Jesus, the sacrificial death of Jesus to satisfy divine justice, and Christ's bodily resurrection. In various ways Hodge defended all of these points in his theological writings.

Critics of Hodge often raise questions about his so-called scientific methodology in ascertaining the "facts" of the Bible. They also believe he was so concerned with the influence of persons like Schleiermacher on Reformed theology that he did not integrate as helpfully as he might his own sincere and deep Christian piety into his theological method and teachings. This piety was expressed not so much in his *Systematic Theology* but in *Conference Papers* (1879), talks delivered Sunday afternoons for the spiritual enrichment of the appreciative Princeton students. Charles Hodge remains one of the most important figures in the history of Christian theology, particularly within the Reformed tradition, in the United States during the nineteenth century.

Suggested Readings

Writings of Charles Hodge: *Systematic Theology* (New York: Charles Scribner's Sons, 1872–73); *The Way of Life* (Philadelphia: American Sunday School Union, 1841).

Archibald Alexander Hodge, *The Life of Charles Hodge* (New York: Charles Scribner's Sons, 1880).

Mark A. Noll, ed., *The Princeton Theology, 1812–1921: Scripture, Science, and Theological Method from Archibald Alexander to Benjamin Warfield* (Grand Rapids: Baker Book House, 1983).

John W. Stewart, "Mediating the Center: Charles Hodge on American Science, Language, Literature, and Politics," *Studies in Reformed Theology and History* 3, no. 1 (Winter 1995): 1-114.

James Henley Thornwell

(1812–1862)

E. Brooks Holifield

James Henley Thornwell, the ablest theologian of the Old South, was eulogized by the historian George Bancroft as "the most learned of the learned." Thornwell defended, with conspicuous care for logical precision, both a rigorously systematic version of Calvinist theology and the traditional institutions of southern society, including slavery. Throughout his career as a Presbyterian minister, professor, college president, and theologian at the Presbyterian Theological Seminary in Columbia, South Carolina, Thornwell promoted the orthodoxy of the Westminster Confession, which he viewed as a system that held together with the strictest logical connection. To expound the Westminster doctrines, however, Thornwell invested heavily both in the philosophy of the Scottish enlightenment and in certain theological innovations of the eighteenth century.

The death of his father, a plantation overseer in the Marlboro District of South Carolina, cast the family into poverty, but affluent neighbors in the town of Cheraw recognized Thornwell's brilliance and paid his tuition at the South Carolina College in Columbia, from which he graduated in 1831. Even as a student he admired the Westminster Confession, and in 1832 he joined the Presbyterian Church, soon deciding to enter the ministry. Two years later he traveled to Andover Seminary, which he found deficient both in its language offerings and its theology. He transferred almost immediately to Harvard, convinced that its Unitarian theology was little better than infidelity but eager to study Hebrew and German. After a year there he took a pastorate in Lancasterville, South Carolina.

By 1837, when Thornwell began to teach logic and literature at the South Carolina College, he had allied himself with the Old School Presbyterians, who resisted the theological innovations of Samuel Hopkins and Nathaniel W. Taylor which had helped create a New School faction in the church.

After voting with the 1837 General Assembly majority to extrude four New School synods, he presented to the Synod of South Carolina and Georgia a paper outlining the Old School essentials: God imputed the guilt of Adam, the federal head of humanity, to all his descendants; Jesus endured on the cross the penalty of the law and satisfied the divine justice on behalf of the elect; and no fallen sinner could become righteous apart from regeneration by the immediate and invincible agency of the Holy Spirit.

In 1840 Thornwell became the pastor of the Columbia Presbyterian Church, but the next year he returned to the college as chaplain and Professor of Sacred Literature and the Evidences of Christianity. He had already drawn public attention with tracts explaining and defending the doctrine of predestination. Now he began to produce the lectures and essays that would give him theological primacy among southern Presbyterians. The *Southern Presbyterian Review,* which he helped to found in 1847, became the main outlet for his writing. After serving as president of the college (1851–55), he became in 1856 Professor of Didactic and Polemical Theology at Columbia Seminary, where he remained until his death.

He expounded in his inaugural address a conception of theology as the science of true religion. It was a science, a *scientia,* in several senses: It was a "habitual knowledge," a knowing whose truths molded the knower's whole person; it provided as high a certainty as any other science, since all knowing had to assume unproved principles; and it arranged its truths logically and systematically. It never grasped the divine essence; it was a science of the life of God in the soul, not a science of God. But by remaining true to the biblical revelation, theologians could formulate a system of truths that produced true piety and apprehended as much of God as God wanted us to know.

The unifying principle for this theology was the doctrine of justification. How could a fallen moral creature be made just or righteous? In answering the question, the theologian assumed, Thornwell thought, three subsidiary principles: moral government, or the essential relatedness of God and humanity; the modification of moral government by a legal covenant revealed in natural religion; and its further modification by a covenant of grace revealed in supernatural religion. Thornwell's *Lectures in Theology,* begun in 1856 for his classes at Columbia, elaborated this scheme into a systematic theology designed to be consonant with scripture and with John Calvin's *Institutes of the Christian Religion.* His covenantal language reflected his extensive reading in seventeenth-century English and European theologians, especially Johannes Cocceius, Herman Witsius, Francis Turretin, and John Owen. His interest in moral government reflected his indebtedness to themes that had become prominent through the writings of such eighteenth-century theologians as Samuel Clarke and Joseph Butler, whom Thornwell admired even though he found them glaringly deficient.

For Thornwell, justification meant the imputation of Christ's righteousness to the elect. According to his covenant theology, Adam had stood in a representative federal relation to all humanity. After Adam's fall, God rightly imputed to his descendants the guilt of his sin, and their depravity was the consequence (not the cause) of the imputation. In a similar way, Christ, whose vicarious sufferings satisfied the penalties of the divine law, became the federal head of all whom God had elected for salvation. God imputed Christ's righteousness to them, and this imputed righteousness (not any inherent rightness) was the reason for their acceptance by God. Thornwell called the principle of imputation the keystone that supported the arch of the Christian system.

Convinced that these views represented the substance of the Westminster Confession and catechisms, he opposed any alternative restatement of Calvinism. Despite his liking for governmental metaphors, he disdained the governmental theory of atonement—the view that Christ died to preserve the integrity of the moral order rather than to satisfy God's wrath and justice—that he found in the thought of Samuel Hopkins and other disciples of Jonathan Edwards. He also censured the Edwardsean theologians for saying that sinners had a natural ability to repent even though they lacked the moral ability to do it without special grace. The notion of natural ability, he thought, compromised the idea of penal inability taught in the Westminster standards. He disliked their description of sin as self-love; he found the essence of sin rather in pride. And he castigated their claim that the guilt of sin came from the sinning rather than from imputation. He was even more contemptuous of Nathaniel Taylor's efforts at Yale to revise the Calvinist doctrine of original sin by relocating sinfulness in acts of the will rather than in the human nature that underlay those acts.

Even his Old School colleagues found no haven from his relentless polemic. He chided both Samuel J. Baird and Robert Breckinridge, whom he liked and admired, for failing to see that inherent depravity was the result and not the ground of the imputation of sin, though he conceded that John Calvin himself had not quite seen this point. Princeton's theologians, especially Charles Hodge, drew his scorn because they failed to accept his *jure divino* Presbyterianism: the view that the scriptures mandated the polity as well as the doctrine of the church and that only the Presbyterians had it right. Thornwell would tolerate no innovation that lacked biblical warrant, whether it be imposing restrictions on the functions of lay elders or creating denominational boards to oversee missions. The Princetonians often supported such innovations, and one motive for the founding of the *Southern Presbyterian Review* was the desire of Thornwell and his allies to "break the charm" of what he called "the Princeton ascendancy."

His scolding of fellow Presbyterians was gentle compared with his excoriation of European rationalists. Thornwell's critique of rationalism appeared most prominently in three long essays in the *Southern Presbyterian Review* (1849, 1850, 1856) on John Daniel Morell's *Philosophy of Religion,* a book imbued with German Idealism and the Romanticism of Samuel Taylor Coleridge. Thornwell grudgingly respected the Germans ("They do not rave, but reason"), but he thought that the refusal of Idealists like Hegel, Fichte, and Schelling to respect the limits of our knowledge led to a pantheism that ended logically in a nihilism that merged all differences in identity.

In a subsequent article, "Miracles" (1857), he attacked both David Hume and David Friedrich Strauss for assuming, without having demonstrated, that the seeming uniformity of experience in the modern world called into question the biblical accounts of the miraculous. To counter modern naturalism, Thornwell called for a religion of authority grounded in an infallible, verbally dictated revelation from a personal God who created a distinct world and governed it. In his essay "The Personality of God" (1861) he held that not only the biblical revelation but also the human experience of obligation presupposed belief in a superior Will. And if God was personal, revelation and miracles were to be expected.

To sustain his appraisals of rationalism, Thornwell drew on his earlier reading of both Kantian epistemology and Scottish Common-Sense philosophy. He began his study of the Scottish philosopher Dugald Stewart when he was only sixteen, and by the time he entered college he could recite passages from memory. Not until 1853 did he seriously study Kant's *Critique of Pure Reason,* but by then he had read extensively in the work of Sir William Hamilton in England, who was trying to synthesize the Scottish and Kantian philosophies. Thornwell admired Hamilton because he seemed able both to define, in Kantian fashion, the limits of human knowledge and also to confirm, in the manner of the Scots, the relative reliability of our cognitive faculties.

He revered Kant for having demolished the possibility of any "ontology of pure reason," and he accepted the Kantian idea that we could know only what was relative to our faculties. This meant that all our knowledge rested on a faith that appearances genuinely mediated the real world to us. But he argued that "laws of human belief" implicit in our cognition also compelled us to trust in our faculties as channels of reliable knowledge. The limits of our knowledge precluded a science of God; Thornwell agreed with Kant that even the existence of God could never be strictly demonstrated. But the fundamental laws of belief made it illogical for us to deny the reality of causation, and the intelligibility and moral order of the world suggested a transcendent personal Cause. Thornwell was confident that the patient accumulation of facts, in the manner outlined by Sir Francis Bacon, would evermore confirm this truth. His *Discourses on Truth* (1855), a series of lectures on moral philosophy drawing on the ethics of his beloved Aristotle, contended that the quest for truth was a moral obligation.

On that score, not only rationalists but also Catholics fell short. In a four-year debate (1841–45) with Patrick Lynch of Charleston, Thornwell argued against the authority of the apocryphal writings—the books of the Old Testament not found in the Hebrew canon—and the infallibility of the papacy. In a two-hour speech to the 1845 General Assembly, he argued against the validity of Catholic baptism, and when Charles Hodge reprimanded the assembly for accepting his argument, Thornwell published a critique of Hodge in which he maintained that the Catholic doctrine of salvation, especially its insistence that meritorious works contributed to human righteousness, denied the fundamental doctrine of the gospel. To disavow the doctrine of imputed righteousness was to fall into fatal, damnable heresy.

Thornwell's final opponents were abolitionists who described slavery as intrinsically sinful or demanded that churches exclude slaveholding members. In response to the slavery issue Thornwell expounded his doctrine of the spirituality of the church—the belief that the church, as a supernatural institution whose end was grace, redemption, and holiness, had to insulate itself from the business of the state, a natural institution whose end was justice, rights, and order. He helped to make the doctrine a commonplace of southern Protestantism. On the issue of slavery itself, Thornwell appealed to the Bible. The acceptance of slavery in both the Old and New Testaments, the epistolary exhortations to both slaves and masters, and the absence of any direct biblical condemnation meant that slavery had always had divine sanction as an economic and social institution. Thornwell conceded that the institution had its origin in the fall; he agreed that it would cease to exist at the eschatological end time. He confessed that neither southern laws nor southern masters accorded slaves the rights—to knowledge, stable families, safety, and the gospel—that should be protected among persons who were immortal spirits and fellow human beings. Though never free from assumptions of racial superiority, he deplored the "false science" that tried to define blacks and whites as different species. But he thought that the Bible had spoken, and he feared the abolitionists as infidels who would not only destroy his cherished southern society but shatter the authority of God's sacred word.

Thornwell viewed the nineteenth century as a time of great struggle, with atheists, socialists, communists, red republicans, and Jacobins on the one side, and the friends of religion, order, and regulated freedom on the other. He had no difficulty taking sides.

Suggested Readings

Writings of James Henley Thornwell: John B. Adger and John L. Giradeau, eds., *The Collected Writings of James Henley Thornwell*, 4 vols. (Richmond: Presbyterian Committee of Publication, 1871–74).

James Oscar Farmer, Jr., *The Metaphysical Confederacy: James Henley Thornwell and the Synthesis of Southern Values* (Macon, Ga.: Mercer University Press, 1986).

Eugene Genovese, "James Henley Thornwell," in *History and Politics in the Cultural War* (Columbia: University of Missouri Press, 1995).

E. Brooks Holifield, *The Gentlemen Theologians: American Theology in Southern Culture* (Durham, N.C.: Duke University Press, 1978).

B. M. Palmer, ed., *The Life and Letters of James Henley Thornwell* (Richmond: Whittet and Shepperson, 1875).

Francis P. Kenrick

(1796–1863)

Gerald P. Fogarty

K enrick was the foremost theologian among the nineteenth-century American Catholic bishops. Born in Ireland and educated for the priesthood in Rome, he was ordained for the Diocese of Bardstown, Kentucky, where he taught in the seminary. In 1829, he was a theologian at the First Provincial Council. In 1830, he was named coadjutor Bishop of Philadelphia, amid troubles with lay trustees. In 1842, he became Bishop of Philadelphia, and in 1851, Archbishop of Baltimore. His theological works included *Theologia dogmatica* (4 vols., 1839), *Theologia moralis* (3 vols., 1841–43), *The Primacy of the Apostolic See,* which went through several editions, and a multivolume revision of the translation of the English Catholic Bible (the Douay-Rheims-Challoner version, translated from the Latin Vulgate).

In his *Theologia dogmatica,* Kenrick presented a dynamic theology of tradition, which he held in common with Johann Adam Möhler, the renowned Tübingen theologian. Unlike those Catholic theologians who considered scripture and tradition as separate sources of revelation, Kenrick argued that tradition was the totality of the church's lived and living experience, including scripture. His treatment of tradition shaped the way in which he considered authority to be continued in the church. The norm for the interpretation of scripture was the consensus of the Fathers, and the norm for preserving authentic teaching was the consensus of the college of bishops under the leadership of the pope. At Vatican I (1869–70), his brother, Archbishop Peter Kenrick of St. Louis, would use this theology of collegiality to oppose the definition of papal infallibility.

In addition to his systematic work, Kenrick's translation of the Bible merits attention. Kenrick was, ironically, beginning his work on revising the translation of the Bible when he became embroiled in a dispute about the use of the Bible in public schools. Early in 1843, he had obtained permission from the Philadelphia school board to allow children to read any version of the Bible approved by their parents and not be compelled to read the King James Version, the standard Protestant translation. Anti-Catholic nativists construed this as an attempt to remove the Bible from the public schools altogether. Tension between nativists and Irish immigrants led to rioting during two periods in 1844, May 6-9 and July 5-7. Two Catholic churches were burned and several persons were killed. A grand jury blamed the May rioting on Kenrick, who, it stated, was trying to remove the Bible from public schools. Kenrick, however, made no allusion to this episode in his work on the Bible.

Like many English-speaking Catholics, Kenrick erroneously believed that in declaring the Latin Vulgate to be "authentic," the Council of Trent required that vernacular translations be made from that Latin version. Accordingly, he set about to update the language of the Douay Bible, translated from the Vulgate, which had been last revised in the 1750s. He also sought to defend the Vulgate against Protestant critics. He began by revising Genesis with the assistance of his brother, Peter, who had left Philadelphia to become coadjutor Bishop of St. Louis in 1838. In September, 1843, he wrote his brother he was convinced that the differences in the Hebrew language of the Pentateuch precluded its composition all at the same time, but he opted for a theory that, while Moses was indeed the author of the Pentateuch, he had used preexisting sources in composing the books. While Kenrick could not be considered progressive by later standards, his recognition of the problems regarding the composition of the Pentateuch might explain why, though he began with that section of the Bible, he did not publish it until 1860.

Kenrick published his version in six volumes between 1849 and 1860. The first to appear was *The Four Gospels,* translated from the Vulgate, "and diligently compared with the original Greek text." When translating the Old Testament, he would likewise compare the Vulgate with the original Hebrew text. In other words, his work was not simply a new translation of the Vulgate; he made frequent reference to the original languages. He also provided annotations taken principally from the Fathers of the church, as well as modern writers, including non-Catholics, and carefully noted where the King James version was more faithful to the original languages.

While open to Protestant scholarship, Kenrick was concerned with preserving Catholic doctrine. Thus, when he translated Matthew 1:23: "Behold a virgin will be with child . . ." he added a note that the Hebrew of Isaiah 7:14 meant a young unmarried woman, that is, a virgin. Although historical criticism was then already developing, he was frequently ambivalent in regard to certain aspects of it. On the one hand, he accepted the traditional authorship of each of the Gospels without mentioning the synoptic problem. On the other hand, he acknowledged that some scholars had challenged the authenticity of the last twelve verses of Mark.

His choice of words for his translation, however, sometimes drew upon himself Catholic criticism. The Vulgate of Matthew 3:2, for example, would best be translated "do penance," but he translated it "repent" and added a note that he was trying to bring out the need for a change of heart, the meaning of the Greek original. Bishop Ignatius Reynolds of Charleston rebuked him for deviating from the Catholic emphasis on the practice of penance. Kenrick had also explained in a note that the Greek word for "baptize" meant immersion. Martin John Spalding, Bishop of Louisville and his successor as Archbishop of Baltimore, urged him to omit the note in subsequent editions, because the Baptists were using it to criticize the Catholic practice of baptizing. Cardinal Nicholas Wiseman, Archbishop of Westminster and a specialist in oriental languages, favorably reviewed Kenrick's translation and praised his defense of the Vulgate, but then added a lengthy criticism of some of the same non-Catholic authorities Kenrick had cited.

In 1851, Kenrick published *The Acts of the Apostles, the Epistles of St. Paul, the Catholic Epistles, and the Apocalypse*. While basically conservative, he alerted his readers to some critical problems. Although he defended the Pauline authorship of Hebrews, for example, he presented all the scholarly arguments against it. He also began using the prefaces of each new volume to respond to critics of the previous one, whether in regard to his translation or his citation of non-Catholic authors. In 1857, he published *The Psalms, Books of Wisdom, and Canticle of Canticles*. Perhaps to assuage Wiseman's reservations, he dedicated this volume to the cardinal.

In 1859, Kenrick published *The Book of Job, and the Prophets*, followed in 1860 by his version of the Pentateuch, the preface to which presented his views on the relationship between science and the Bible. He acknowledged that scientific developments in the nineteenth century might force a new approach to scripture. Though making no allusion to evolution—Charles Darwin's *Origin of Species* had been published in 1859—he did discuss the geological arguments for giving an older date to the world than the Genesis account would imply. Just as he had earlier stated that the norm for the proper interpretation of the scripture was the consensus of the Fathers, now he argued that the norm for abandoning the literal interpretation of the Bible was the consensus of scientists. Not only was the science of geology unknown to the ancient world, he noted, but the Fathers of the church were also not in agreement in interpreting the Genesis account of creation as occurring over six days. What was "divinely revealed" in Genesis, he argued, was "the origin of all things from the creative act of God, and the creation of man." Later in 1860, Kenrick completed his work with the publication of the historical books, including the deuterocanonical books.

In 1858, at the Ninth Provincial Council of Baltimore, the bishops had asked Kenrick, who was presiding, to absent himself. After praising his translation, they voted to seek the support of the English hierarchy in having John Henry Newman collaborate with Kenrick on producing a single English version for use in England and the United States. Nothing, however, came of this proposal. In 1866, the bishops of the United States held the Second Plenary Council. They initially proposed adopting Kenrick's translation for the American church, but met opposition, for unknown reasons, from Archbishop Peter Kenrick. In 1884, the bishops at the Third Plenary Council again discussed adopting Kenrick's version for the American church, but merely commended it, among other versions, in their pastoral letter.

Despite the praise given to Kenrick's version, its style was frequently awkward. With its notes and its comparisons with the King James version and the original languages, it was intended more for serious students of theology than for the average lay reader. The translators who produced the "Confraternity Edition" of 1939 were aware of the Kenrick version, but it is not mentioned among the list of English versions in either *The Jerome Biblical Commentary* (1968) or *The New Jerome Biblical Commentary* (1990). His other theological insights, however, particularly on tradition and episcopal collegiality, place him firmly in the theological school that reemerged at Vatican II (1962–65).

Suggested Readings

Writings of Francis P. Kenrick: *The Four Gospels, translated from the Latin Vulgate, and diligently compared with the Greek Text, Being a Revision of the Rhemish Translation* (New York: Edward Dunigan and Brother, 1849); *The Pentateuch* (Baltimore: Kelly, Hedian & Piet, 1860).

Gerald P. Fogarty, *American Catholic Biblical Scholarship: A History from the Early Republic to Vatican II* (San Francisco: Harper & Row, 1989).

C. F. W. Walther

(1811–1887)

Robert Kolb

C. F. W. Walther was raised in a pastoral, pious family in Saxony and studied at the University of Leipzig (1829–33) during conflicts between Rationalism and the Lutheran Confessional revival movement. He followed a popular preacher, Martin Stephan, to the United States in 1839 and soon assumed leadership among immigrants who settled in Missouri. Two spells of illness (1831–32, 1840) gave him occasion to study Luther intensively and fed his hostile reaction to Rationalism and to the compromise involved in the Union of Lutheran and Reformed churches in Prussia (1817, 1830). He dedicated his life to making Luther's theology a living reality in the North American immigrant church. He had a broad command of Lutheran Orthodox thought (1580–1750), which he (somewhat critically) assessed and reproduced.

As publisher of a popular magazine, *Der Lutheraner,* he assembled disparate groups into the German Evangelical Lutheran Synod of Missouri, Ohio, and Other States (1847), serving as its president (1847–50 and 1864–78). He provided leadership through a theological periodical, *Lehre und Wehre,* and he fostered a series of "free conferences," which brought Lutherans together to seek unity through doctrinal discussions. Through Concordia Seminary, Saint Louis, which he led from 1850 to 1887, he educated hundreds of pastors, whose service in German immigrant communities gathered the largest single Protestant church among German Americans, the Missouri Synod. He wrote a number of sermon books, a pastoral theology, several works on the doctrines of church and ministry, and lectures on the proper distinction of law and gospel, published posthumously.

Crisis in his immigrant community forced him to struggle with a new formulation of the doctrines of church and pastoral ministry. He taught that the church in the proper sense is the communion of saints, the invisi-

171

ble gathering of those whom the Holy Spirit has called through the gospel. The whole church (the priesthood of all believers) possesses the power of the keys of the kingdom of God and thus forgives and retains sins through its use of God's word. It does so within the visible church, in which God establishes the local congregation as the fundamental form of the church and effects the use of God's word and the sacraments through publicly called ministers in the pastoral office. Higher levels of organization must be based on the divinely mandated congregation. Faith in Jesus Christ saves; salvation is not restricted to members of a specific church body. True believers remain in heterodox churches. However, against the background of the Prussian Union, Walther opposed all "unionism," which compromised pure doctrine. He argued that believers should strive to create a "true visible church," which confesses the truth of the scriptures purely.

Walther reacted against early historical criticism, insisting on biblical authority and verbal inspiration. The Bible contains no errors of any kind, he taught. The word of God, preached from its pages and delivered through the sacraments (Baptism and the Lord's Supper), is active and powerful in forgiving sins and bestowing new life in Christ. Walther demanded high standards of ethical performance but regarded good works as wholly without merit before God, designed only to serve the neighbor.

Influenced by Luther's *On the Bondage of the Will*, Walther led his Synod in defending the "broken" doctrine of election of the Formula of Concord (the last of the Reformation-era Lutheran confessions). This was a single predestinarian view that emphasized election as an expression of the gospel, against the synergistic (human cooperation with the Holy Spirit in conversion) position of much of later Lutheran Orthodoxy and many contemporary American Lutherans, which held that God elected those foreseen by God as the ones who would believe in Christ (election *"intuitu fide"* [in view of faith] or *"ex praevisa fide"* [on the basis of foreseen faith]). Walther taught that God's conditionless election can be known only through the means of grace.

Like every doctrine, predestination could be properly understood only within the proper distinction of law and gospel, Walther's most vital hermeneutical principle. The test of good theology lay in its application to God's people. Some resist God and need to hear law; others, broken by the law, need the restoration of the gospel. In his exposition of this key element of Luther's theology, he anticipated certain facets of the Luther Renaissance of the early twentieth century.

Walther followed the definitions of Luther and the Formula of Concord: The law reveals human sinfulness on the basis of God's commands for human living; the gospel bestows the gifts of forgiveness of sins, life, and salvation through Christ's passion, death, and resurrection, apprehended by the Holy Spirit–wrought trust in Christ. The living power of God's word makes its proper impact only when the law is proclaimed in its full severity and the gospel in its full sweetness. Thus, the law must be effectively proclaimed before the gospel can have meaning for the sinner who resists God.

Despite Pietist influences in his background, Walther opposed certain pietist practices, rejecting the use of prayer and works to struggle for the feeling of living in grace. He directed repentant sinners alone to the pardoning word of forgiveness in proclamation, absolution, and the sacraments, to Christ instead of to their own feelings. Shedding of vices, practice of virtues, contrition, and even faith itself are only God's gifts and instruments, not causes of salvation or election. He urged his students to preach faith into the hearts of parishioners by presenting the promises of the gospel rather than urging them to make the psychological effort to believe. In the proclamation of God's word, the gospel must prevail.

Though sharply criticized by other Protestants and even some Lutherans for his strict, uncompromising insistence on his understanding of Lutheran theology, his views of church polity and his understanding of the proper distinction of law and gospel widely influenced the shape of Lutheran theology in the nineteenth and twentieth centuries, within but also beyond his own church body.

Suggested Readings

Writings of C. F. W. Walther: *Selected Writings of C. F. W. Walther*, ed. August R. Suelflow, 6 vols. (Saint Louis: Concordia, 1981).

Arthur H. Drevlow, John M. Drickamer, and Glenn E. Reichwald, eds., *C. F. W. Walther: The American Luther* (Mankato, Minn.: Walther Press, 1987).

Lewis W. Spitz, Sr., *The Life of C. F. W. Walther* (Saint Louis: Concordia, 1961).

Defining the Edges of Reason and Revelation

William Ellery Channing

(1780–1842)

David M. Robinson

Wiliam Ellery Channing emerged as the theological leader of the American Unitarian movement at a period of extreme crisis and intense controversy in New England theology. The Calvinist consensus which had characterized New England theology since the arrival of Puritan settlers in the early 1600s began to give way in the late 1700s, as churches in Boston and its vicinity began to show an increasing disposition to ignore and in some instances openly attack Calvinist doctrines. Although the New England Puritans had never been free of theological controversy among themselves, the fissures that began to erupt in the late 1700s seemed serious and, to some, irreconcilable.

Proponents of more "liberal" versions of Christianity attacked Calvinism at two of its most essential and, in their view, most vulnerable points, the doctrines of innate depravity and election to grace. Controversy between the liberals and the "orthodox" (those Calvinists who had resisted the liberal critique) accelerated dramatically in the first three decades of the nineteenth century, eventually leading the liberals to form their own denomination as Unitarians. Channing largely set the tone and direction for the liberal rejection of Calvinism, and perhaps more important, helped to transform a movement based in controversy, and oriented primarily against a set of theological beliefs, into a movement that could formulate and articulate a vital and affirmative theology.

Channing was born in Newport, Rhode Island, on 7 April 1780, and educated at Harvard (A.B., 1798). After working as a tutor for a Virginia family, he returned in 1802 to Cambridge, Massachusetts, to prepare himself for the ministry, and in 1803 was called as minister to Federal Street Church in Boston, one of the officially established and supported churches of the Standing Order in New England. These churches, which had their origins in the Puritan immigration and settlement of New England, had not yet split into the liberal or Unitarian and the orthodox or Congregational wings, as would happen in the coming decades. In 1805 some of the orthodox were alarmed at the election of a liberal, Henry Ware, to the Hollis Professorship of Divinity at Harvard, believing the appointment indicated Harvard had come under the control of anti-Calvinist liberals.

The ensuing theological dispute, known as the Unitarian Controversy, marked New England religious thought for the next four decades. The orthodox responded to Ware's election by founding Andover Seminary (1808), and by more forcefully criticizing the increasing tendency to liberalism among Boston ministers. Channing's emergence as an influential theologian originated in his defense of the liberal position in several important early tracts and sermons, including *A Letter to the Rev. Samuel C. Thacher* (1815), *Unitarian Christianity* (1819), and *The Moral Argument Against Calvinism* (1820).

Channing criticized Calvinism primarily for its negative view of human nature. In the concept of innate depravity, or original sin, the Calvinists had taken the position that human nature was fundamentally flawed or corrupt, redeemable only through the grace, or undeserved favor, represented in Jesus' atonement. Closely connected with this doctrine of innate depravity was the concept of election to grace, which Channing felt undermined the sense of God's justice and benevolence. The Calvinists posited that God had foreordained those who would be elected (chosen) for salvation, and one could not therefore earn salvation or be absolutely sure that one was among those elected by God for it. Calvinists did not, of course, speak with one voice, and there were disagreements and shades of opinion and interpretation among them concerning these doctrines. Channing felt, nevertheless, that these concepts defined Calvinism, and he countered them with a theology that affirmed human potential and reestablished the benevolence of God.

Channing's theological position grew in part from one profound experience during his college years, his encounter with the concept of "disinterested benevolence" in the works of the Scottish Common-Sense philosopher-theologian Francis Hutcheson. Hutcheson believed that human moral action could not be explained by self-interest alone. Hutcheson's idea that many human actions had to be motivated by a selfless or disinterested benevolence led Channing to the belief that human nature was infused with an instinctual moral sense, which he came to understand as the presence of a divine element in the soul.

In *Unitarian Christianity* (his most important work, considered the founding document for the Unitarian denomination in America), Channing accepted the title "Unitarian" for the liberal party and explained the essential principles of the Unitarian movement. He replied to Calvinist charges that liberals were abandoning biblical truths by applying his belief in human capacity to the question of biblical interpretation. "The Bible," he stated, "is a book written for men, in the language of men, and that its meaning is to be sought in the same manner as that of other books" (*Selected Writings*, 72; hereafter cited by page number alone), that is, through the exercise of human reason. "We profess not to know a book," he said, "which requires a more frequent exercise of reason than the Bible" (73). Applying the use of reason to the Bible, Channing felt, would result in a rejection of the doctrine of the Trinity, which while "acknowledging in words, . . . subverts in effect, the unity of God" (78). Channing directly challenged proponents of the trinity "to adduce one passage in the New Testament, where the word God means three persons, where it is not limited to one person, and where, unless turned from its usual sense by the connexion, it does not mean the Father" (79).

Channing also argued that the dogma of the trinity violated the unity of Christ: "It makes Jesus Christ two beings, and thus introduces infinite confusion into our conceptions of his character" (82). This confusion about the nature of Jesus, Channing felt, reduced the significance of his suffering in the crucifixion by ascribing a divine immutability to his nature. "It is our belief, that Christ's humiliation was real and entire, that the whole Saviour, and not a part of him, suffered, that his crucifixion was a scene of deep and unmixed agony" (86). For Channing, such a view of the crucifixion heightened the significance of the love of Jesus in bearing it. Thus while continuing to believe that Jesus was a supernatural being, Channing articulated the Unitarian position "that there is one God, and that Jesus Christ is a being distinct from, and inferior to, God" (86), an Arian Christology that characterized the position of most Boston liberals at this time.

He argued in the same vein for "the moral perfection of God," taking aim at what he felt were weaknesses in the Calvinist representation of a cruel and aloof deity whose election of certain persons for salvation seemed unfairly arbitrary. Believing that such views of God undercut worshipful reverence for God, Channing declared that "we cannot bow before a being, however great and powerful, who governs tyrannically." He instead insisted that "God is infinitely good, kind, benevolent," and that reverence is founded not on God's power but on "the equity and goodness in which it is established" (87). In both *Unitarian Christianity* and *The Moral Argument Against Calvinism* Channing attacked Calvinism as a system that actually undercut the motivation for virtue. It robbed the human spirit of its aspiration toward a caring and benevolent divine parent. Its tendency was to "take from us our Father in heaven, and substitute for him a being, whom we cannot love if we would, and whom we ought not to love if we could" (88).

Moreover, Channing argued that Calvinism undercut the motivation for virtue by taking responsibility away from individuals—leading them to feel that salvation was designated for a preordained elect and thus beyond their power to achieve. Because of the Calvinist emphasis on election to grace, "a sense of the infinite importance and indispensable necessity of personal improvement is weakened, and high-sounding praises of Christ's cross seem often to be substituted for obedience to his precepts" (93). Channing held that the willed choice of the individual must be restored to a central place in theology and that the process of character building through the exercise of moral decisions was a fundamental aspect of salvation. He described his own salvation experience not as an instantaneous or sudden transformation but as a process of development that extended throughout his lifetime.

The first phase of Channing's theological development thus consisted of his defense of the liberal position and his corresponding attack on Calvinism, but as the analysis thus far has suggested, this attack was based on an underlying assumption of human spiritual capacity. In *Unitarian Christianity* he argued that "all virtue has its foundation in the moral nature of man, that is, in conscience, or his sense of duty, and in the power of forming his temper and life according to conscience" (94). The concept of human moral capacity was developed more fully in the later works *Likeness to God* (1828) and *Self-Culture* (1838), in which Channing laid out a doctrine of the culture of the soul that was enormously important to the development of Unitarianism, and its related but more radical outgrowth, the religious and literary movement called Transcendentalism.

In rejecting the Calvinist idea of election to grace, the Unitarians did not for the most part accept the Universalist position that Christ's atonement would lead to the salvation of all. Instead, they conceived life as a process of trial or probation, in which an individual's character was given the opportunity to improve through meeting challenges and overcoming obstacles to its growth. Channing understood this as a process in which the soul was cultivated and nurtured; the spiritual nature that was the inheritance of every individual must be encouraged to develop to its full potential.

Likeness to God was one of Channing's boldest statements of his belief in the spiritual potential of humanity. Preaching from Ephesians 5:1, "Be ye therefore followers of God, as dear children," he developed the idea of the shared bond between God and God's children, and stressed the necessity of enlarging and purifying that bond as the key to the spiritual life. "True religion," he declared, "consists in proposing, as our great end, a growing likeness to the Supreme Being." Yet he also insisted that the secure development of this divine nature could not be taken for granted. When human capacities "are unfolded by right and vigorous action," likeness to God is "extended and brightened." But when those capacities "lie dormant," likeness to God is "obscured," and individuals gradually lose touch with our divine nature and spiritual potential (146-47).

As Channing saw it, any connection or relationship with God was impossible without such a shared identity. "To understand a great and good being," he explained, "we must have the seeds of the same excellence" (147). The understanding and worship of God was thus dependent on the development of godlike qualities, a process in which worship manifested itself most fully in a form of imitation. Such imitation, linked to the divine qualities of justice and benevolence, required ethical practice. For Channing, worship, self-knowledge, self-culture, and ethical engagement became aspects of a seamless whole, a continuing growth of the soul toward divinity.

Channing's description of the task of the spiritual development of human nature represented a complete denial of the Calvinist idea of innate depravity, and suggests the enormous distance that had opened between the liberals and the orthodox in the two decades since the controversy had broken out over the election of Henry Ware to the Hollis Professorship at Harvard. Acknowledging that his assertion of an affinity between God and human nature would seem objectionable to some, Channing insisted that the greater danger in theology was "severing the Creator from his creatures" (153). He urged instead closer attention to what he felt were the signs of the presence and accessibility of God throughout the creation. "How much of God may be seen in the structure of a single leaf," he declared, which through its myriad connections with every part of nature, proved itself to be "a revelation of an omnipotent mind!" Such revelations of God in the smallest details of nature were also important confirmations of the presence of God in the human soul: "God delights to diffuse himself everywhere" (154).

Channing's views of the benevolence of God's nature and of humanity's sharing in it became the touchstones of Unitarian theology. Many venerated him as a prophet of liberal Christianity, and regarded him as the most authoritative voice among the Unitarians. His emphasis on the spiritual foundation of human nature and the manifestations of divinity in the natural environment would be further extended in the writings of those associated with Transcendentalism, such as Ralph Waldo Emerson, Theodore Parker, Margaret Fuller, and Henry David Thoreau. Emerson, who consulted Channing during his own training for the Unitarian ministry in the 1820s, formed his preaching on Channing's eloquent and poetic example, and emphasized the indwelling presence of divinity as one of the key themes of his thought. Margaret Fuller, the first editor of the transcendentalist journal the *Dial,* also found Channing's defense of human potential of great importance. Her book *Woman in the Nineteenth Century* (1845), one of the most important early treatises on feminism in America, applied Channing's principles of self-culture through continual intellectual and moral growth to the condition of women.

Channing's conception of the religious life as a quest for an ever-increasing likeness to God was reflected in his later address *Self-Culture* (1838). Here he compared the steady evolution of the human soul to the growth of an animal or plant, a metaphor that made each individual the gardener or cultivator of his or her own soul. Channing directed the address to a working-class audience, stressing that such a program of self-culture was possible to individuals in every economic situation. "Are labor and self-culture irreconcilable to each other?" he asked. He insisted that they were not, arguing that "the laborer, under his dust and sweat, carries the grand elements of humanity, and he may put forth its highest powers" (257, 259).

Channing's attention to the social context and political implications of his theology grew during the 1830s, as his concern with the application of the doctrine of self-culture to the working class suggests. As his theology moved toward a program of self-cultivation through an increasing imitation of the virtues of God, it emphasized the work of character-building, and the ethical and social responsibilities of the individual. Channing became particularly concerned with the social evil of slavery, entering the growing antislavery discussion with his *Slavery* (1835), an indictment of the moral evil of the system that denied dignity and freedom to persons who, equally with all others, shared in the potential divinity of human nature. Although Channing's antislavery stance was not well received by some members of his Federal Street congregation, it remained one of the dominant themes of his work in the late 1830s and early 1840s.

Because of his frail health he had adopted a somewhat aloof position with his congregation as senior minister, leaving much of the week-to-week preaching and pastoral work to his assistant Ezra Stiles Gannett. He had also become financially independent through his marriage to Ruth Gibbs, further insulating him from the necessity of tempering his views to satisfy

179

his congregation. His last work, the *Address Delivered at Lenox* (1842), was an attack on slavery delivered to commemorate the British emancipation of the slaves in the West Indies in 1834. Arguing that the slave system was a violation of human dignity perpetuated by the greed of the slaveholders, he called on the South to embark on "a settled purpose to bring slavery to an end" (296).

Channing died two months after he delivered the Lenox address on 2 October 1842, in Bennington, Vermont. His work continued to be influential in shaping Unitarianism throughout the nineteenth century; both moderates and radicals in the denomination claimed his legacy as a source of authority. His rejection of the deterministic aspects of Calvinism, his espousal of the necessity of reasoned and disciplined interpretation of the Bible, and his insistence that religion was inextricably linked with human self-development and progressive social change made him a prophet not only for Unitarianism, but for liberal Protestantism as a whole as it developed in the decades after his death.

Suggested Readings

Writings of William Ellery Channing: David Robinson, ed., *William Ellery Channing: Selected Writings* (Mahwah, N.J.: Paulist Press, 1985).

John White Chadwick, *William Ellery Channing: Minister of Religion* (Boston: Houghton Mifflin Co., 1903).

Andrew Delbanco, *William Ellery Channing: An Essay on the Liberal Spirit in America* (Cambridge: Harvard University Press, 1981).

David Robinson, "The Legacy of Channing: Culture as a Religious Category in New England Thought," *Harvard Theological Review* 74 (1981): 221-39.

Conrad Wright, *The Liberal Christians: Essays on American Unitarian History* (Boston: Beacon Press, 1970).

Lydia Maria Child

(1802–1880)

Evelyn A. Kirkley

Best-selling author, abolitionist, and theologian, Lydia Maria Francis Child was first and foremost a seeker. In her life and work, she struggled to reconcile contradictions of race, gender, and religion, and she was one of the first intellectuals to envision the United States as a "multiracial egalitarian republic" (Karcher, xv). This vision compelled her, yet remained disappointingly elusive.

Lydia Francis was born 11 February 1802 in Medford, Massachusetts, daughter of a baker who made a small fortune with the "Medford Cracker." After her mother died when she was twelve, Lydia was sent to live with relatives, and she directed her anger and grief into intellectual endeavor. Although educated at the local dame school, she loved books and became a teacher and aspired to write. In 1821 she added the name "Maria" to assert her independent identity, and in 1828 she married attorney and editor David Child; they had no children. In the 1820s, Child became a best-selling author and joined the circles of Boston's intellectual elite. In 1824 she published her first novel, *Hobomok,* an interracial romance between a Native American man and a white woman, in which she decried racial intolerance. After *Hobomok,* she wrote novels and short stories, and she edited the first national educational periodical for children. As her career in letters expanded, Child increasingly turned her attention to three issues that would occupy the remainder of her life: women, slavery, and theology.

Child was an early advocate of woman's sphere and woman's rights, and she saw no inherent conflict between the two. In 1829 she published *The Frugal Housewife,* a manual on domestic economy. In it she doled out practical advice for homemakers on a budget, from suggestions on removing spots from upholstery to delicious meals whipped up from pig's head. Child sought to elevate woman's status in the home, especially women without domestic help. She stressed the dignity of housewifery and the range of

181

skills required to do it successfully. She moved beyond domesticity in her *History of the Condition of Women, in Various Ages and Nations* (1835), a two-volume comparison of the status of women across the globe and through history. She traced women's oppression in marriage, labor, child-bearing and child-rearing, and politics, citing as well glimmers of gender equality. Yet she never explicitly advocated women's rights. Conclusions can only be indirectly drawn about her opinions on male dominance and female subordination as neither natural nor necessary. Although Child hesitated to draw ideological conclusions, she nonetheless demanded respect for women, and her work influenced her friends Sarah Grimke and Margaret Fuller and younger feminists Susan B. Anthony, Elizabeth Cady Stanton, and Matilda Joslyn Gage.

Child suffered no hesitation regarding slavery. In the 1830s, she became an advocate for the immediate emancipation of African American captives, and her uncompromising stance earned her ostracism from Boston's literary aristocracy. In 1833 she published *Appeal in Favor of That Class of Americans Called Africans,* the first fully researched and documented analysis of slavery. In it she traced the history of slavery in Greece, Rome, Africa, and South and North America. Opposing colonization to Africa and anti-miscegenation laws in the United States, she indicted the North as well as the South for racism. She declared that prejudice is contrary to the spirit of the Bible and the Declaration of Independence, that Africans are not biologically distinct, but are humans and Americans.

A landmark due to its scope and depth, the *Appeal* became required reading for agents of the American Anti-Slavery Society. However, it shocked readers used to her fiction, children's literature, and household hints. Heedless of the drastic decline in her book sales, she was one of the first women appointed to the executive committee of the American Anti-Slavery Society. Yet after a stint as editor of the *National Anti-Slavery Standard* (1841–43), she became disenchanted with tensions in the movement and withdrew from all abolitionist organizations. She remained an influential voice for emancipation, particularly in 1859–60, when John Brown's raid on Harper's Ferry spurred her to write several best-selling antislavery pamphlets.

Child struggled throughout her life for a viable religious faith. She wrote her brother at eighteen that she longed to "find some religion in which my heart and understanding could unite" (letter to Convers Francis, 31 May 1820, as quoted in Karcher, 14). She rejected the Calvinist Congregationalism of her childhood as too harsh and the Unitarianism of her brother as too cold. In 1822 she joined the Swedenborgian New Church in Boston, yet it too failed to satisfy her spiritual yearnings for beauty and truth. Her search culminated in *The Progress of Religious Ideas, Through Successive Ages* (1855), a three-volume comparison of the world's religions aimed at a popular audience. She examined Islam, Judaism, Christianity, Hinduism, Buddhism, Taoism, among others, presenting their similarities and differences without privileging Christianity.

By demonstrating religions' historical contextualization and adaptation to cultural conditions, she undermined their claims to divinely revealed truth. Child argued that religious truth is not contained in institutions and dogma, but grows within individuals and communities. She separated religion, the experience of the holy, from theology, the codification of that experience, leaving no doubt as to her disdain for the latter. Theology, declared Child, distorts religious sentiment, coerces belief, and creates idols of religious texts. She advocated religious tolerance and insisted that religions must be interpreted from their adherents' point of view. Moreover, she condemned sexual asceticism and ambiguity regarding women and slaves in the world's religions. Like her previous histories of women's status and of slavery, *Progress of Religious Ideas* is a pioneering work that anticipated later works such as James Freeman Clarke's *Ten Great Religions* (1871).

Lydia Maria Child died on 20 October 1880 and is buried in Wayland, Massachusetts. She is a significant antebellum theological figure for three reasons. First, she had a wide-ranging intellect and addressed the most pressing social and religious issues of her day. Second, she addressed a broad audience. She was more popular and better known than most "classic" contemporary theologians. Third, and most significant, she staked out radical positions on religion and theology long before they became commonplace. She was a modernist before it was hip to be modern.

Suggested Readings

Writings of Lydia Maria Child: *The Progress of Religious Ideas, Through Successive Ages*, 3 vols. (New York: C. S. Francis, 1855).

Deborah Clifford, *Crusader for Freedom: A Life of Lydia Maria Child* (Boston: Beacon Press, 1992).

Carolyn Karcher, *The First Woman of the Republic: A Cultural Biography of Lydia Maria Child* (Durham, N.C.: Duke University, 1994).

Andrews Norton

(1786–1853)

William Baird

Andrews Norton was a Unitarian theologian whose principal work was in New Testament criticism. Born in Hingham, Massachusetts, he graduated Phi Beta Kappa from Harvard at age eighteen. After a brief period of teaching at Bowdoin College, he was appointed tutor in Mathematics at Harvard in 1811.

In 1812, Norton published an essay, "A Defense of Liberal Christianity," in which he presented Christianity as a rational religion, affirming the revelation of divine truths in the Bible. Norton believed the Bible should be interpreted by the same method, the historical-critical method, used for other ancient documents. The teachings of scripture had been accommodated to the limitations of the time, and hence the Bible's abiding truths must be distinguished from temporal and local expressions.

In 1813, Harvard appointed Norton a Lecturer in Biblical Criticism and Interpretation. Named the Dexter Professor of Sacred Literature when the Divinity School was established in 1819, Norton's inaugural address advocated natural theology and a rational understanding of God. He declared that God's truth was communicated through Jesus. The New Testament, according to Norton, was of primary importance for theological study. A well-educated clergy, he believed, would benefit both church and nation. During his early years at Harvard, Norton published *A Statement for Not Believing the Doctrines of the Trinitarians* (1819). People often rejected Christianity, he stated, because they misunderstood it, and that misunderstanding was abetted by belief in the Trinity. To address this problem, Norton argued that the notion of the Trinity denied the unity of God, and that the doctrine of the two natures of Christ was self-contradictory. On the basis of biblical exegesis, Norton tried to show that the doctrine of the deity of Christ was unscriptural: Jesus did not teach that he was God, and the New Testament affirmed Jesus' humanity.

Norton's marriage in 1821 to Catherine Eliot, daughter of a prominent Boston merchant, provided him the financial resources to resign from Harvard (1830) and devote full time to research and writing. Two years earlier he had made a trip to Europe where he was scandalized by the skepticism of German biblical criticism. In response, he wrote an essay, "The Modern German School of Infidelity." Similarly dismayed by the New England transcendentalists, he reacted in "A Discourse on the Latest Form of Infidelity" by opposing in particular the Transcendentalist denial of miracles.

Norton's chief publication was *The Evidences of the Genuineness of the Gospels* (1837), an apologetic work that presents external evidence. In 1848, a second edition, enlarged to three volumes, appeared. In the work, Norton made two principal points: (1) the extant canonical Gospels were essentially the same as the original Gospels; (2) the Gospels were written by the authors to whom they had been traditionally ascribed.

First, Norton argued the gospels agreed among themselves; small variations were largely due to textual corruption. In spite of this corruption, the ancient manuscripts of the gospels were in essential harmony. Using his vivid imagination, Norton calculated that some 60,000 copies of the New Testament must have been in existence by the end of the second century—one copy for every fifty Christians, of a probable total of three million. That these copies were in harmony was evidenced, he claimed, by the essential agreement of the 670 extant manuscripts known to scholars of his time.

Second, Norton noted that church tradition had accepted the four gospels as authentic by 175 C.E. The reliability of this tradition was confirmed by Norton's belief that there was only one link in the chain between the apostles and Irenaeus (c. 180), namely, Papias of Hierapolis (c. 140). Norton also argued that the agreement among the first three gospels confirmed their authenticity. In the course of this argument, he considered the synoptic problem, the question of the interrelation of Matthew, Mark, and Luke. According to Norton, the writers of these documents did not rely on one another's gospels, a common written source, or late oral tradition. Instead, these authors, like rabbinic students, memorized what they had heard, and spent time together correcting their accounts. Norton believed all three gospels were written independently, around 60 C.E. In the second and third volumes of this work, Norton notes that the Gnostics used all four gospels, so even the heretics confirmed their authenticity.

In a later work, Norton turned to *Internal Evidences of the Genuineness of the Gospels*. Norton had written the first part of this book in 1847–48, and at his death, left an unfinished treatise as the second part. Edited and published in 1855, the book attempted, in Part I, to refute David Friedrich Strauss' notion that the gospels were largely a collection of myths. In Part II, he argued that the gospels were both internally consistent and reliable as history. According to Norton, Jesus was superior to other teachers in character, a unique person who founded a lofty moral religion. Norton believed the accounts of this exceptional life and teaching could not have been invented by the disciples; the gospels were true and authentic.

An apologetic theologian, Andrews Norton defended liberal or Unitarian thought by means of a conservative historical criticism of the New Testament. A scholar of critical skill, with command of a large body of primary and secondary sources, Norton contributed to the growing interest in biblical criticism in America. Ironically, he demonstrated that the Bible could be used in support of liberalism, while he promoted a conservative view of the Bible that continued to dominate American scholarship.

Suggested Readings

Writings of Andrews Norton: *The Evidences of the Genuineness of the Gospels,* abr. ed. (Boston: American Unitarian Association, 1873); *Internal Evidences of the Genuineness of the Gospels* (Boston: Little, Brown, and Co., 1855).

Theodore Parker

(1810–1860)

William Baird

Described as the greatest preacher of his day, Theodore Parker was an important leader of New England transcendentalism. Born in Lexington, Massachusetts, where his grandfather had fought in the historic revolutionary battle, Parker was the son of an unprosperous farmer. He began the study of Latin at age ten, and continued to display an intellectual brilliance that secured his admission to Harvard. He was denied a degree, however, since he had been unable to pay the tuition fees. In 1834, Parker entered Harvard Divinity School where he was noted for his linguistic skills, learning not only the classical and modern European languages, but also studying such esoteric tongues as Coptic and Icelandic.

After graduation in 1837, Parker became the minister of the Unitarian church at West Roxbury, Massachusetts. His liberal preaching aroused the ire of conservative Unitarians, and the Boston Association of Ministers called for his resignation. Parker, with the support of his congregation, refused. In 1843, he made a trip to Europe where he met thinkers like Thomas Carlyle in Britain and various biblical scholars in Germany, and had an audience with the pope. In 1846, Parker became the minister of the Twenty-Eighth Congregational Society of Boston, which grew to a membership of 7,000. In 1852, the Congregation moved to Boston's Music Hall in order to accommodate the crowds.

In theology, Parker was a transcendentalist. Like Emerson, he stressed personal, intuitive truth. But in contrast to Emerson's individualism, Parker affirmed the social aspects of religious thought. Where Emerson abandoned the ministry, Parker remained a minister of the Unitarian Church. He opposed, however, the Unitarianism of scholars like Andrews Norton who buttressed biblical authority with an appeal to miracles. Parker expressed his version of transcendentalism in an essay written around 1850. He described two main schools of philosophy: the sensationalist, the view that all knowledge comes by the senses, and the transcendentalist, the belief (his own) that the human mind contains a priori ideas that do not enter through the senses. Parker did not deny, however, the importance of empirical investigation and rational reflection: The truths of intuition are confirmed by truths of demonstration.

Parker's understanding of intuitive truth is illustrated by a story he related in his autobiographical reflections, written shortly before his death. At age four, while walking beside a pond on a beautiful spring day, he saw a spotted tortoise and, as he had seen other boys do, was about to strike it with a stick. Suddenly he heard an inner voice saying, "It is wrong!" When he asked his mother about the voice, she replied that some people call it conscience, but that she preferred to call it the voice of God in the soul of humans.

In 1841, Parker preached an ordination sermon in south Boston entitled, "The Transient and the Permanent in Christianity." Based on Luke 21:33 ("Heaven and earth will pass away, but my words will not pass away"), the sermon contended that some features of Christianity are merely transient. Among these are its institutional forms, rites and rituals, and rigid dogmas—like the notion of the Trinity. On the other hand, Christianity witnesses to the permanent—the life and teaching of Jesus. This eternal truth is not supported by some theory of biblical inspiration or by some christological doctrine. It is not true because Jesus taught it, it is intrinsically true—a pure, absolute religion that grows out of Jesus' oneness with God, so that he becomes a model for human emulation.

The principal summary of Parker's religious thought is found in his *Discourse of Matters Pertaining to Religion*. Based on lectures delivered in Boston in 1841, the *Discourse* was published in 1842. A fourth edition (1855) makes corrections on the basis of Parker's reading of recent German theological research. He devoted the first section to the nature of religion in general. Here Parker argued that the understanding of religion arises out of an analysis of human nature. Religion is an essential aspect of humanity; it is inborn, universal. This religious element is apparent in the human sense of dependence, and the sense of dependence implies an object, God, on which humans depend. For Parker, this religious element is the most important element of human nature.

Although the religious element is basic to all humans, Parker believed religion unfolds by evolutionary stages. In primitive cultures, it takes the form of fetishism: the worship of nature. In more advanced societies, it assumes the shape of polytheism: the worship of powers beyond nature. At its highest level, religion is expressed as monotheism, and pure monotheism, in Parker's view, is a universal religion that removes all human distinctions, requires no priesthood or intermediaries, no rigid creeds or dogmas. It does, however, affirm some basic doctrines. True monotheism, for instance, believes that humanity has evolved from a primitive state; Parker rejected the idea of a golden age followed by a fall. Monotheism also affirms the conviction that the soul of every human being is immortal. In practice, Parker's monotheistic religion opposes superstition and fanaticism, and promotes a genuine piety that functions in harmony with reason, conscience, and the human affections, promoting an authentic love of God and human persons.

The next section of the *Discourse* dealt with the doctrine of God and the idea of inspiration. Parker argued that since humans have an inborn religious faculty, they can know God. But since God can be known only by analysis of human nature, knowledge of God is always restricted by human limitations. The finite cannot fully comprehend the infinite. Human beings can only confess that God is absolute being—a being of infinite power, wisdom, justice, love, and holiness. Arguing from analogy, Parker contended that just as God is present everywhere in nature, so God is present in all people; as God supplies all the needs of nature, so God supplies the spiritual and moral needs of human beings.

Parker distinguished three views of inspiration. First, the rationalistic view claims that God can be known only by the senses. This would mean, according to Parker, that the God who is known is finite—a being grasped by finite humans, not the infinite God of true monotheism. Second, the antirationalistic or supernatural view asserts that God can only be known by special, supernatural revelation. According to Parker, this would limit God to particular times, places, and people—a denial of the universal, omnipresent, infinite God. Finally, Parker presented his own concept: the natural-religious view or spiritualism. According to this view, God is revealed as the being who supplies all the spiritual and moral wants of humanity; Parker's understanding acknowledged an inspiration that is open to all, that takes a variety of forms, that fosters human freedom.

Parker's *Discourse* also addressed Jesus and Christianity. Christian knowledge of Jesus is drawn from the four Gospels—documents written several years after the events. Moreover, the Gospel of John, in Parker's opinion, is not historical, and Matthew, Mark, and Luke are mutually contradictory. On the basis of such limited information, Parker depicted Jesus as a religious reformer who eventually broke with Judaism. Jesus was concerned not with legalistic laws and ceremonies, but with morality and matters of the spirit. To be sure, many of Jesus' ideas were mistaken; he believed in demons, a God

189

of judgment, and the imminent end of the world. Nevertheless, Jesus witnessed to the universal religious truth. This truth, Parker believed, was self-evident to the religious faculty of humans, and it needed no support from miracles or belief in Christ's divinity. Jesus proclaimed the love of God and neighbor, and practiced what he preached. He provided people the freedom to go beyond his teaching to the perfection of God.

Parker made an important contribution to American biblical studies. He appreciated the Bible as "the greatest of books," but attacked every form of biblicism. The doctrine of verbal inspiration was not supported by the biblical writers themselves, and in Parker's view, turned the Bible into an idol. Parker approved and practiced historical-critical interpretation. In a series of articles for the general reader, he wrote introductions to the Pauline epistles, affirming the necessity of understanding their historical settings. Parker translated and expanded W. M. L. de Wette's critical and historical introduction to the Old Testament and was one of the few English-speaking voices to say a good word for David Friedrich Strauss' notorious *Life of Jesus* (1835). Although critical of Strauss at points, Parker praised his learning and acute analysis, his destruction of the opposing forces of rationalism and supernaturalism.

The fourth section of Parker's *Discourse* dealt with the Bible. He decried efforts to establish the authority of scripture by ecclesiastical tradition, claims of infallibility, or arguments from miracles. According to Parker, the Bible is a human book. The Old Testament, he believed, did not prophesy Jesus. He doubted the authenticity of several books in the New Testament. In sum, Parker valued historical criticism in biblical interpretation for its ability to distinguish myth from history, fiction from fact.

Theodore Parker exercised considerable influence on his contemporaries. He lectured some eighty to one hundred times a year, speaking during his career in every northern state east of the Mississippi. He probably reached between sixty thousand and one hundred thousand listeners annually. Sometimes called the universal reformer, Parker championed virtually every social cause known to modern history. He studied the problem of class structure and poverty. He believed poverty would be eliminated only after its causes were removed. To that end, he advocated low-cost housing, cheaper food, temperance, and education. He thought the upper, mercantile class should aid the poor. He believed in universal education, supported by the state, and criticized the low wages of teachers. He was an advocate of women's rights, and opposed the ill-treatment of Native Americans. He opposed war in general and the Mexican War in particular, urging citizens to refuse to pay taxes in protest.

As early as 1841, Parker preached against slavery. He believed slaves were not treated as human beings and argued the slave states were inferior to the free states in such matters as education and literacy. He was arrested for obstructing the fugitive slave law. Parker was highly critical of the churches that failed to denounce slavery, that built expensive edifices and neglected the needs of people. A strong believer in democratic government, Parker is probably the source of the saying emphasizing government of the people, by the people, and for the people.

Frequently bothered by ill health, Parker died in Italy in 1860. He left a large legacy for American life and thought. In religion, he encouraged the move of Unitarianism toward transcendentalism. He championed the emerging and continuing tradition of religious liberalism in opposition to supernaturalism and biblicism and contributed to American religious pragmatism. Finally, he ardently believed the principles of religion should be applied to the practical problems of faith and life and so became a pioneer of religious social action.

Suggested Readings

Writings of Theodore Parker: *A Discourse of Matters Pertaining to Religion* (Boston: American Unitarian Association, 1907); *Theodore Parker: An Anthology,* ed. Henry Steele Commager (Boston: Beacon Press, 1960).

Robert C. Albrecht, *Theodore Parker* (New York: Twayne Publishers, 1971).

John Edward Dirks, *The Critical Theology of Theodore Parker* (Westport, Conn.: Greenwood Press, 1970).

Ralph Waldo Emerson

(1803–1882)

Alan D. Hodder

A sometime preacher and poet, provocative essayist and celebrated lecturer, leader, and radical spokesman for the Transcendentalist movement, Ralph Waldo Emerson exerted a broadly formative influence on the development of American religious liberalism and on American values generally. He also played a seminal role in the emergence of a distinctively American literary tradition and is increasingly viewed as a foundational figure in the development of philosophical pragmatism.

Born in 1803, in the once stolidly Puritan town of Boston, Emerson lived to witness and sometimes shape events of crucial national importance over the course of the nineteenth century. The second of four surviving sons of Ruth Haskins and William Emerson, the young Emerson represented a clerical dynasty stretching back to the mid–seventeenth century. His father, minister to the First church of Boston, had assumed the family mantle, although his advocacy of a liberal, cosmopolitan religious outlook was a far cry from the anxious Puritan faith of his forebears. When the young Emerson was eight, his father died suddenly, leaving his family in strained financial circumstances. Thereafter, the Emerson boys were raised primarily by their mother and one remarkable aunt—the charismatic Mary Moody Emerson. Self-educated, brilliant, and quixotic, Emerson's Aunt Mary was for many years his chief religious gadfly and theological mentor.

At the age of fourteen, Emerson entered Harvard College where he received training in the standard curriculum of the classics, rhetoric, history, English, and theology. Though showing some flair as a poet and essayist, Emerson compiled a modest academic record, graduating in 1821 in the middle of his class. Here, however, he first began keeping the journal which by the time of his death in 1882 amounted to scores of volumes and served, throughout his life, as a rich quarry from which to mine formulations and ideas for his mature essays, lectures, and addresses. Here too the popular young lecturer Edward Everett introduced him to the new German school of historical-critical biblical scholarship.

In 1825, after much vocational indecision, Emerson dedicated himself to the ministry and began formal study at Harvard's Divinity School. Licensed to preach the next year, he served as a part-time preacher for congregations around eastern Massachusetts until his ordination in 1829 at the historic Second church, the old church of Increase and Cotton Mather in Boston's North End. Having in the meantime married a beautiful seventeen-year-old heiress named Ellen Tucker, with whom he was fervently in love, Emerson now seemed launched on a happy and respectable career. But it was not to be: After less than two years of marriage, her lungs torn up with tuberculosis, Ellen passed away—the first in a series of tragic deaths that buffeted Emerson over the next eleven years. The next year, in protest over his church's insistence on the traditional administration of the communion rite, Emerson resigned his pastorate at the Second church and embarked on an extended journey abroad.

Emerson's mature views on the Unitarianism of his father's generation, and on Christianity in general, are best reflected in two addresses he delivered in the decade of crisis and new beginnings which followed upon his first wife's death. The first of these, "The Lord's Supper," Emerson presented to his parishioners at the Second church in the fall of 1832, to explain his reasons for stepping down. After surveying the long history of controversy surrounding the communion rite in the Western churches, Emerson devoted the bulk of his address to weighing evidence furnished by the several Gospels regarding its origins. His conclusions were, first, that Jesus never intended to establish a rite of perpetual observance, and second, that it was inappropriate to celebrate the rite as the church was then doing. Emerson's assault on the communion rite suggests the impact of German historical methods, but it was driven by his growing antipathy to the church's general adherence to what he called "formal religion"—religion, that is, in which the outer forms of religious observance are thought to eclipse its inner spirit.

In the famous address Emerson gave at the Commencement ceremonies of Harvard's Divinity School in 1838, he formulated his theological position more explicitly. Here he situated his remarks in the context of what in Unitarian denominational history has been called the "miracles" controversy. Two years previously, George Ripley, another young Unitarian minister, had publicly challenged the established Unitarian position on the biblical accounts of Jesus' miracles. Pressed on the one hand by advocates of the new biblical criticism who insisted on separating biblical history from myth (e.g., miracle stories) and attacked on the other by orthodox critics who considered Unitarian exegesis a threat to faith in supernatural revelation, Unitarian theologians had staked out a position midway between the two camps. While affirming the need for rigorous historical analysis, these theologians nonetheless insisted that the stories of Christ's miracles should not be dismissed as mythological fictions, because they provided necessary external proofs of Christ's supernatural status. Ripley criticized this preoccupation with external proofs on the grounds that it tended to undercut the priority and independence of faith in Christ.

In his "Divinity School Address," Emerson also dismissed his church's preoccupation with miracles as misguided. The word "miracle," he contended, gave the wrong impression; in such usage it was unnatural, a "Monster." His objection to the Unitarian position was not that the miracles did not happen, but rather the assumption that they were restricted to the early history of the church. In his richly evocative presentation, Emerson suggested that, on the contrary, nature itself was a continuing miracle. Although this address was designed to inspire Emerson's young listeners with this new transcendentalist vision of life, no one missed the doctrinal implications of his reverent and rhapsodic depictions of Nature.

As Emerson put it, Christianity labored under two grievous mistakes: First, it was idolatrously preoccupied with the "person" of Jesus of Nazareth, and second, it no longer appreciated that the true source of revelation was not the person of Christ but the soul itself, stronghold of the "Moral Nature"—which Emerson variously referred to as the Self, the Oversoul, or the God within. Although Emerson's view of Christ was suggested in "The Lord's Supper," here he made it explicit. Jesus was the "true man," the greatest moral exemplar and teacher in the history of the world, a veritable incarnation of the divine in humanity. But if Jesus was the son of God, so are we all children of God. Not surprisingly, Emerson's "Address" provoked an immediate cry of protest from Unitarian authorities, in particular Andrews Norton, Harvard's Professor of Biblical Literature, who lambasted Emerson for this "latest form of infidelity."

Although a belief in divine immanence had inspired some of Emerson's best sermons, it became in the months following the shock of Ellen's death in 1831 the foundation for a religious awakening. The first fruits of this awakening came with the publication of his first book, *Nature* (1836). Part sermon, part prose-poem, *Nature* represents Emerson's earliest formal attempt to put his new religious and philosophical vision into words. Although ostensibly a meditation on "Nature," the book reaches its climax in a revelation of "Spirit." Here Nature comes to be seen as the body or symbol of Spirit—God's first and veritable "book" of revelation. Though suffused with biblical tropes and images, *Nature* is not a Christian book. Rather, it is Emerson's expression of a homegrown philosophical idealism, drawing eclectically upon Stoic philosophy, Neoplatonism, natural science, mysticism, and German Romantic philosophy.

In the weeks following the publication of *Nature,* Emerson began meeting informally with several of his friends, most of them Unitarian clergymen, to discuss recent views on art, religion, and science. Proving instructive, the meetings soon attracted the notice of a wider circle of men and women who formed the nucleus of what came to be known as the Transcendentalist Movement. Although the name "transcendental" was possibly first applied by outsiders in a derogatory way (to suggest eccentricities and outlandish opinions held by the group), it derives from the critical philosophy of Kant. When Emerson looked back on the origins of the movement several years later, however, he described it as simply the most recent manifestation of a tradition of philosophical Idealism which had its origins in Plato. While transcendentalism often expressed itself in philosophical and literary forms, it originated as a religious reform movement within the Unitarian wing of the Boston churches.

Traces of New England Puritanism, Enlightenment rationalism, and of course, classical Unitarianism may be found in Emerson's thought, but the safest way to characterize transcendentalism is as an extension of European Romanticism, as it expressed itself, however belatedly, in New England in the mid-1830s. From Germany, with the work of Johann Gottfried von Herder, Johann Wolfgang Goethe, and the Idealist philosophers, Romantic ideas filtered into France and England, and later into the learned centers of the United States. The writings of Samuel Taylor Coleridge and Thomas Carlyle, in particular, served as principal conduits for the transmission of romantic ideas to America. Emerson read widely in the recent literature and philosophy from the Continent, synthesizing romantic ideas in new ways, adapting them to American purposes, and expressing them with the stamp of his own distinctive genius. Recent European discovery of the scriptures of India, Persia, and China provided a powerful catalyst for transcendentalist speculation, though in Emerson's case, the Asian texts served mainly to confirm his intuitions.

In the wake of the controversy triggered by the "Divinity School Address," Emerson withdrew from religious polemics to dedicate his energies to various writing projects. Besides his involvement with the *Dial,* the first transcendentalist literary magazine, he worked assiduously to complete two collections of essays upon which he built his subsequent reputation: *Essays: First Series,* appeared in 1841 to a generally favorable reception; *Essays: Second Series,* three years later. In these mature essays, observations about Nature continue to serve as a point of departure for what became meditations on the Self. Always guiding his observations on Nature was his search for its basic governing law, a law he variously identified as "Undulation" or "Polarity." Every structure of nature he conceived as an interplay of opposing forces—of action and reaction, centripetal and centrifugal, motion and rest. Nature, in Emerson's view, was flux not stasis— a giddy process of growth, decay, and death, best epitomized by the word "metamorphosis." But if such polarity operated at the heart of nature, this was because it was also the soul's basic law. "Undulation" in Nature is merely an expression of the perennial moral law—what Emerson typically referred to as "Compensation"—that governs the entire universe. Upon this cornerstone Emerson founded both his belief in immortality and the God within.

Appearing for the first time in 1841 was "Self-Reliance," arguably America's most famous and controversial essay. Although this essay has been variously construed as a medley of atheism and false independence, a robust declaration of democratic individualism, even a dangerous precedent for American narcissism, the "Self" Emerson described transcends the personal ego or the private self. Emerson's ruminations on the universal immanence of the moral law had convinced him that if divinity existed anywhere, it must first exist as the very ground of the human soul. To "rely" on the Self then amounts to a dependence on the God within. For this he found important corroboration from the Quaker doctrine of the inner light, and somewhat later, from his reading of the *Bhagavad Gita* and the *Upanishads.* Emerson did not believe that every impulse from within originated with God; Self-reliance depended on a careful listening and waiting, even a deliberate self-emptying, to prepare the way for divine inspiration. Citing Philippians 2:7 as his authority, Emerson noted how even Jesus' Incarnation depended upon an initial act of self-emptying or *kenosis.* To deny or empty the private self was thus to open oneself to the inspiration of the higher Self or God within.

Although continuities may be detected between Emersonian Self-reliance and Quaker piety, and even with older patterns of New England faith, Emerson's theological views represent a striking departure from tradition. Emerson was always quick to affirm his belief in the divinity of humanity and nature, but voiced doubt about doctrines which ascribed personality to God. The "Self" or divine principle in Emersonian thought was impersonal and monistic, not theistic. Also distinctive of Emersonian thought is its emphasis on becoming over being. The Self is less a fixed center than a dynamic process creating, animating, and propelling all of nature's diverse forms. Thus, Emerson exhibited marked suspicion of traditional metaphysical or theological formulations. In his essays he often adopted rhetorical strategies reminiscent of negative or apophatic theology, in recognition of his inability to represent truth in any conventionally referential manner. Everywhere the accent falls on the process of creation rather than its products or fixed formulations. Restraint, fixity, stasis—these are the villains in Emerson's thought. Good flowed from the soul's outward expansions; evil was inertia, a mere privation of good.

The publication of Emerson's first two books of essays was followed by others, including *Representative Men* (1850), *English Traits* (1856), *The Conduct of Life* (1860), and *Society and Solitude* (1870). By midcentury, Emerson had acquired the status of an American cultural icon. Through the popularization of his poems and essays, "the Sage of Concord" had become America's representative philosopher, not only in the United States but increasingly in France and England as well. By the 1870s, his annual lecture tours had taken him throughout the United States and Europe. After midcentury, Emerson's essays and addresses reflect his increasing preoccupation with politics, and with questions of ethical conduct and social relations. As the religious enthusiasm of his youth began to fade, his work showed greater concern to reconcile his faith in freedom and human possibility with the obvious limits and tragedy of human experience. Though Emerson never renounced the transcendentalist idealism of his youth, the writing of his later years indicates a deepening dialogue with skepticism and an increasing interest to place his thinking on a more pragmatist footing.

After the controversies of the 1830s, Emerson did not participate actively in the affairs of the Unitarian Church. His writings, however, helped encourage the formation of a radical wing of the denomination which led in 1867 to the founding of the Free Religious Association. Although the transcendentalist ministers and their humanistic successors remained a vocal minority in the denomination prior to the Civil War, by century's end their views had become part of a normative Unitarian outlook. Outside of his localized impact on the history of American Unitarianism, Emerson's explicit influence on Christianity in America has not been conspicuous. The reasons for this are not hard to see. After 1838 Emerson effectively divorced himself from the traditional concerns of theology and the life of the American churches. Moreover, in turning away from traditional theology, he resorted instead to the languages of philosophy and science. Most significant, his conception of Jesus as moral exemplar and his rejection of Christian theism placed him beyond the pale of the Christian churches altogether.

But this does not tell the whole story. Although Emerson has not shaped Christian thinking from within the church, his legacy has fundamentally altered the cultural landscape in which the churches have developed, if only because he has had such a massive influence upon American values generally. In philosophy, Emerson's treatment of reality as dynamic process anticipated the work of the process theologians of the twentieth century, while his emphasis on the provisional, instrumental, and emancipatory character of religious meaning prepared the ground for the fully developed pragmatism of William James, John Dewey, and later thinkers of the pragmatist school. In literary history, Emerson is commonly located at the fountainhead of the American tradition of Romantic writing, mentor and inspiration not only to such contemporaries as Henry Thoreau, Walt Whitman, and Margaret Fuller, but to prominent modern and current American writers as well. Conceived always at the crossroads of religion and literature, Emerson's writings, together with much transcendentalist work, represent a kind of literary religion, in which literary texts come to be presented and perceived as prime sources of religious meaning.

As for American religious history more generally, Emerson's legacy has been even broader but also more diffuse. In several noteworthy respects, Emersonian thought prefigured the later emergence of Protestant liberalism, and even, to a more limited degree, Protestant modernism—not least in his embrace of German philosophy, his openness to the new biblical criticism, his engagement with science and concern for social justice, and above all, in his unwavering faith in divine immanence. Transcendentalist writing has also played an important role in shaping what may be termed nature religion, an aboriginal strand of American religiosity in which nature comes to be revered as the very embodiment of the divine. Of great consequence was Emerson's pioneering role in the serious study and dissemination of Asian religious traditions. Together with Thoreau and Theodore Parker, Emerson stimulated the scholarly study of world religions in America. Emerson's interest in India and the Far East was not, however, motivated simply by antiquarian interests. Finding much to admire in Asian contemplative traditions, he set an important precedent for later American fascination with the religious traditions of the East. Finally, no account of Emerson's religious legacy would be complete without some reference to his role in preparing the ground for what has sometimes been termed "harmonial religion." Best characterized as a religious outlook in which spiritual wholeness, physical health, and even economic prosperity are seen to flow from a harmonious relationship with the divine, harmonial thought took root in America in the late–nineteenth century and has thrived ever since.

For these reasons and others, some recent religious and cultural historians have referred to Emerson as founder of the American religion. Such claims must be carefully qualified. What does it mean to speak of the American religion? In what sense might Emerson have been its founder? Moreover, since Emerson's ideas have often been the subject of distortion and even caricature, one must distinguish between what he actually wrote and the various, sometimes contradictory, ways in which his ideas have been appropriated. Nevertheless, to the extent that American religion has come increasingly to be characterized by an abiding conviction in the God within, an impatience with traditional theological and liturgical forms, an accent upon personal freedom, and a thirst for ecstatic experience, Emerson may with some justice be dubbed its founder.

Suggested Readings

Writings of Ralph Waldo Emerson: Joel Porte, ed., *Ralph Waldo Emerson: Essays and Lectures* (New York: Library of America, 1983).

William R. Hutchison, *The Transcendentalist Ministers: Church Reform in the New England Renaissance* (New Haven, Conn., and London: Yale University Press, 1959).

David Robinson, *Apostle of Culture: Emerson as Preacher and Lecturer* (Philadelphia: University of Pennsylvania Press, 1982).

Margaret Fuller

(1810–1850)

Amanda Porterfield

Margaret Fuller saw God as the divine soul expressed through the lives of men and women. She believed that Christ was an embodiment of the religious ideal of humanness to which she and other proponents of truth and holiness aspired. "I wish, I long to be human," she wrote to James Nathan in 1845, "but divinely human." In her efforts to nurture this humanity in herself and others, Fuller cultivated sincerity, self-reliance, and political and emotional freedom. Through her writings and lifestyle, she helped introduce a new paradigm of experiential religiosity that contributed to the development of American Christian liberalism. Her theological outlook anticipated existentialism in its concern for the authenticity of individual experience, liberation theology in its humanitarian concern for social justice and equality, and feminist theology in its complaint against women's oppression and devotion to women's potential.

Born in Cambridgeport, Massachusetts, in 1810 as the first of nine children, Fuller was raised a Unitarian rigorously educated by her rationalist father, Timothy, who exercised considerable influence in Massachusetts politics. Committed to a vision of the American Republic as a nation led by enlightened men and women, and to the new enthusiasm for female education sweeping the northeast, Timothy schooled Margaret in Greek, Roman, English, and French literature, biblical criticism, and the writings of Latin historians and Thomas Jefferson. Although he has often been described as domineering, and Margaret remembered her childhood as an unhappy time when she was intellectually overstimulated, emotionally deprived, and physically unhealthy, her capacity for voluminous reading and brilliant expression suggests that she provoked her father's efforts as a teacher as much as he provoked hers as a student.

Fuller contributed to the infusion of German idealism into American theology, and to the emergence of transcendentalism as an alternative to

Unitarian rationalism. Beginning in 1836, she attached herself to Ralph Waldo Emerson, and wrote him intense letters, even while visiting at his home in Concord. As a spokeswoman for the new subjective idealism associated with transcendentalism, Fuller held formal "Conversations" in which she demonstrated her own gifts of oral expression and facilitated the flow of spoken ideas among the women who joined her.

Fuller shared with Emerson a commitment to the divine soul manifesting itself in humanity, but disagreed with him about the relationship between religious and political life. He distanced himself from the fray of social agitation, while she engaged in causes and was ardent in her criticism of social inequality, especially with regard to the oppression of women. Fuller was more strident in her criticism of American culture than Emerson, believing that the high idealism embedded in the American Revolution and the founding of the Republic had been forgotten in the tawdry struggle for money and land that seemed to her to engage most of her compatriots. And Fuller also defined her distance from Emerson by arguing for the superiority of history over rhetoric and other forms of art. Although she never ceased to be moved by great works of art, she valued lived experience more highly, and believed that the ultimate purpose of art was to nurture historical experience. Emerson also lauded experience, but Fuller challenged him for confining his celebration of it to rhetoric.

Both Fuller and Emerson were founders, editors, and leading contributors to the *Dial* (1840–44), quarterly journal of theology and cultural criticism designed to disseminate the spiritual viewpoint of the transcendentalist movement. The two crossed swords over how democratically transcendentalism could be expressed, with Emerson wanting to reserve publication to a refined elite and Fuller casting a more inclusive net. She made a point of interpreting positively his negatively intended comment that she was willing to accept contributions to the *Dial* that displayed only "talent" and not "genius."

Fuller resigned as editor of the *Dial* in 1842, traveled through Ohio, Illinois, and Wisconsin in 1843, and moved to New York City in 1844, where she became a protégé and friend of Horace Greeley, who regarded her as the most intellectually gifted woman in America. As correspondent and literary critic for the *Tribune*, which Greeley edited, Fuller became the first woman journalist in the United States. She found expression for her theological and political views in the *Tribune*, and became less verbose and less self-preoccupied. Her best-known writing, *Woman in the Nineteenth Century*, published in New York in 1845, signaled her effort to establish herself in a larger, more cosmopolitan, and more political context than that of New England transcendentalism.

Although bound in some ways to the sentimental categories of her day, *Woman* articulated a set of ideas that became central to both feminist and liberal Christian theology. Fuller argued that the divine soul flowed equally through women and men, that mature individuals had qualities associated with both manhood and womanhood, and that men and women should be full and equal partners in life. But men, she claimed, exploited the natural differences between themselves and women to achieve dominance, and undermined the self-reliance of women through habitual flattery and scornful refusal to consider women equals. Men impoverished themselves as well as women by this discrimination, and forced women into the position of not being able to trust men to support their efforts to become fully human. Without denying women's domestic responsibilities, or challenging the ideal of maternal love, Fuller drew from the lives of both historical and contemporary women to argue that the natural scope of women's talents did not end there—"Let them be Sea-Captains if they will!"—and that the development of human society depended on women's liberation from narrowly defined roles and expectations.

In 1846, Fuller left New York for Europe and settled in Italy, where she became friends with the revolutionary leader Mazzini, participated in Italy's war for independence, which she compared to the American Revolution, and fell in love with the political activist Count Angelo Ossoli. She bore a son, married Angelo, and sailed for America after the Italian revolution failed. But the boat carrying the Ossoli family capsized off Fire Island in 1850. The boy's body washed ashore, but the bodies of Margaret and Angelo were never found. She was last seen standing alone beside the mast before the ship finally sank.

While her gender, along with the challenging force of her personality, caused many to ridicule her and discount her ideas, Fuller succeeded more than any other nineteenth-century American in recasting for modern usage the concerns for subjective honesty, companionate marriage, and individual responsibility for public life that characterized the New England Puritan tradition. She was similar to Anne Hutchinson in provoking discomfort through her effort to participate as a woman in the theological debates of her day, but Hutchinson has been more noticed by twentieth-century Americans, perhaps because she was less successful than Fuller in avoiding martyrdom, and perhaps because Fuller's critics were more successful in marginalizing her for posterity. But though Fuller's prescience and critical insight have often been overlooked by twentieth-century scholars and theologians, *The History of Woman Suffrage* (1881) recognized Fuller as "the precursor of the Woman's Rights agitation of the last thirty-three years." In

American theology, Fuller's ideas emerged in Elizabeth Cady Stanton's *Woman's Bible,* the writings of Matilda Joslyn Gage, and beginning in the 1960s, the works of Mary Daly and other feminist theologians.

Suggested Readings

Writings of Margaret Fuller: *Woman in the Nineteenth Century* (New York: W. W. Norton & Co., 1971 [orig. ed. 1845]); *Memoirs of Margaret Fuller Ossoli,* ed. R. W. Emerson, W. H. Channing, and J. F. Clarke, 2 vols. (Boston: Roberts Brothers, 1874).

Charles Capper, *Margaret Fuller: An American Romantic Life* (New York: Oxford University Press, 1992).

Ann Douglas, "Margaret Fuller and the Disavowal of Fiction," in *The Feminization of American Culture* (New York: Alfred A. Knopf, 1977), 313-48.

Sandra M. Gustafson, "Choosing a Medium: Margaret Fuller and the Forms of Sentiment," *American Quarterly* 47 (1995): 34-65.

THE CONCERN FOR ECCLESIOLOGY

Orestes Augustus Brownson

(1803–1876)

Arie J. Griffioen

Tracing the theological career of Orestes A. Brownson through the disorienting religious terrain of nineteenth-century America can lead one to conclude that the thought of this classic "seeker" is consistent only in the frequency of his vacillations. Affiliated with numerous Protestant groups and denominations prior to his 1844 conversion to Roman Catholicism, Brownson's thought continued to be marked by notable intellectual fluctuations until his death in 1876. Frequently reactionary and always verbose, Brownson's prolific literary output as a philosophical theologian, as well as a social reformer, journalist, and literary critic, can be as intimidating to readers today as it was so often to his contemporaries.

But the patient reader, who is advised to move through Brownson's corpus chronologically, soon recognizes Brownson's profound religious sensitivity and timely theological insights. Constantly in dialogue with current events and pivotal figures of his time, Brownson's passion for truth unfailingly led him to subject his positions to the criterion of divine revelation—however he understood it at any particular juncture of his career. The result is a fascinating theological journey that reveals as much about nineteenth-century American religion as about Brownson's own tortured soul.

Brownson was born in Stockbridge, Vermont, in 1803. Though studious and well-read, he received little formal education. From his earliest years he was exposed to various religious and cultural manifestations of New England Calvinism. His father, who died when Brownson was three, was Presbyterian, his mother a Restorationist Universalist. The aging guardian couple with whom the young Brownson lived for eight years was Congregationalist. At the age of thirteen he experienced a religious awakening through the efforts of a Methodist revivalist. In 1818 he moved west to rejoin his family at Ballston Spa, New York. Here he joined a Universalist society and was tutored by a Universalist teacher at the Ballston Academy.

After a brief hiatus with a Ballston Presbyterian congregation, Brownson returned to the Universalists in 1823 and was ordained to their ministry in 1826.

Brownson's return to the Universalists and his subsequent ordination was not so much the result of a strict adherence to the theology of its founder, John Murray, whose articulations were centrally characterized by the extension of the Calvinist doctrine of election to all humanity and a strongly experiential evangelical piety. Rather, Brownson was attracted to the work of Hosea Ballou, who, in a manner similar to the Unitarianism emerging in New England's cities, developed a more erudite theological system by applying the principles of Enlightenment rationality to the tenets of Universalism.

Brownson's earliest writings betray a rather intellectually immature and unnuanced natural theology, or rational theism. The objective truths of revelation are identified exclusively with the natural and empirical evidence for those truths; no means of active noetic (purely intellectual) appropriation of a supernatural revelation are asserted. The result is a reduction of religion to morality, to virtues practiced to bring about peace in the individual soul and the rectitude of society. Jesus is conceived as history's supreme teacher of moral truth whose mission was to reform the world through exemplary and natural means.

Brownson soon began to despair over the lack of relevance of revealed religion for his own theological thinking. Following the dictates of his reason and conscience, as well as a growing impulse toward social radicalism which alienated him from many of his fellow clergy, he resigned his ordination and in 1829 left the Universalists to affiliate with the "Free Enquirers," a utopian and agnostic movement centered in New York City and spearheaded by Frances Wright and Robert Dale Owen.

Other than his editorial work for a Workingmen's journal, little is known about Brownson's activity during this brief period. But by 1831, motivated by his study of the theology of William Ellery Channing, he had returned to Ithaca as an independent preacher and was soon ordained to the Unitarian ministry. In 1832 he accepted the position of pastor of the Unitarian Society of Walpole, New Hampshire, and in 1834 became the pastor of the First Congregational church (Unitarian) in Canton, Massachusetts, placing him in proximity to the intellectual ferment of Boston.

Channing's theology, particularly as explicated in his 1828 sermon "Likeness to God," supplied Brownson with the theological means of bringing God and humanity into closer proximity through a common predication of the attributes of freedom, goodness, and rationality. Brownson's adaptation of Benjamin Constant's religious intuitionism and Channing's lofty view of the human soul come to expression in Brownson's idea of an inner revelation testifying to God's benevolence as moral ruler of the universe, as well as the truth of Jesus' moral teachings.

Clearly a reaction to the rational objectivism of his thought as a Universalist, Brownson's new emphasis on human subjectivity, especially the idea of revelation as embodied in the subject and identified with consciousness or feelings, steered him toward the Transcendentalist movement centered in Boston around such Romantic luminaries as Ralph Waldo Emerson and Theodore Parker. Rationalism, Brownson now argued, places God at an infinite distance from the human soul; rather, God is to be found by turning within.

Though Brownson had matured beyond the barren empiricism of his earliest thought, by 1836 he began to move away from what he perceived to be the subjectivism of the transcendentalist tendency to equate revelation with the intuiting subject, which he recognized in Emerson's thought as well as his own. Through the adaptation of Victor Cousin's philosophical eclecticism, Brownson developed a synthesis of the objectivism of his first phase and the subjectivism of his second, that is, of objective reality and subjective experience. God is now asserted as objectively transcendent and independent of all persons, yet known to each through a subjective intuition (the "religious sentiment" or "reason") and confirmed by one's rationality (the "understanding"). Jesus functions as the symbolic and ideal embodiment of that religious sentiment, that is, as symbolic of the union and harmony of the divine and the human that all are called to achieve.

During this period Brownson's thought begins to flourish. Soon his influence in theology, philosophy, and sociopolitical criticism had spread among American intellectuals through his own *Boston Quarterly Review* (1838–42), later to become *Brownson's Quarterly Review* (1844–64, 1873–75). This period is also marked by the refinement of his previous synthesis through Pierre Leroux's doctrine of life by communion. This doctrine would become in Brownson's thought a foundational theological paradigm leading him to a new theological understanding of traditional Christian doctrines and propelling him into the Roman Catholic Church.

Leroux's doctrine of life by communion, as assimilated by Brownson, teaches that the true point of departure of all theology is found not in the being of either the subject or the object but in the manifestation of the being of the subject and object in communion. To be is not simply to live; rather, to live is to manifest. However, one cannot manifest oneself, cannot live, except in communion with that which is not oneself, namely, the object. Only God is self-existent (self-manifest) being. The life of each person is composed of communion with that which is not oneself, particularly God and other human persons. But one cannot commune with God directly, for finitude cannot commune directly with infinity without the mediation of an object. Humanity can only commune directly with humanity. All live in solidarity, belonging to the same body and having similar natural capacities and weaknesses.

Brownson proceeded to apply Leroux's doctrine to the theological categories of sin and grace. Throughout history, he argued, Christianity has assumed as its point of departure not a supposed divinity of humanity, as in transcendentalism, but the tragedy of human sinfulness and depravity. Sinful life results from the communion of the subject and the object. The preceding generation always supplies the sinful object of the life of the succeeding generation, the subject. The solidarity of humanity in its sinful condition can only be transcended through a supernatural influence. But as finite and natural, humanity cannot commune directly with the infinite and supernatural God. A mediator is needed, that is, a God-human who intercedes to become the object of the human race.

This is the role of Jesus, of course. More specifically, it is in the life of Jesus (not in the sense of his public ministry, but in Brownson's philosophical sense) that direct communion with God is found. God is the direct object of the life of Jesus, which becomes the real and literal object of humanity, mediating through successive generations the principle of life. In other words, Brownson's adaptation of Leroux's doctrine of life by communion provides for him an epistemological justification for the appropriation of the revelation of God as fully embodied in Jesus and mediated to humanity. Likewise, the role of Jesus shifts from that of teacher and moral exemplar to his person, considered both in its uniqueness in direct, immediate communion with God, and in its full humanity which mediates that communion to all. Christianity is the infusion of a new life into the life of humanity.

Ironically, it was Channing who pointed out to Brownson that his position opened him to the charge of Universalism by leaving the impression that salvation is automatic, resulting simply from contact with the new life infused into the human race through the mediation of Jesus. Brownson's resulting identification of specific historical and institutional means whereby one enters into communion with the mediatorial life of Jesus constitutes not only his response to Channing, but a clarification that anticipates his identification of the Roman Catholic Church as the historical continuation of the incarnation and, therefore, as the means whereby humanity is enabled to enter into Jesus' mediatorial life.

The doctrine of life by communion continued to govern, implicitly or explicitly, Brownson's theology as a Roman Catholic. For approximately the first decade the doctrine receives little elaboration, but clearly its objective side is emphasized as Brownson attempts to explain and justify his conversion through a rather scholastic apologetic for the church as the objective and exclusive means of salvation. It is not until the mid-1850s that the subjective side of the doctrine reemerges, in large part owing to his study of the Italian ontologist Vincenzo Gioberti.

Under Gioberti's influence, Brownson articulated a doctrine of creation in such a way as to assert the intuition not merely as an act of the human mind, but an ontological fact that presents God objectively as creator in every act of knowing, whether or not the person is reflectively aware of it. In effect, this philosophical assertion provides the doctrine of life by communion with an ontological basis it previously lacked. Hence the medium for communion becomes the divine creative act which establishes two orders of human existence as one dialectical whole: the order of creation as it proceeds from God as first cause and the gracious teleological order of return to God through the incarnation of Jesus.

The Christian life of communion with God is likewise dialectical. One lives in simultaneous and absolute dependence on the creative act of God for existence and on the incarnation of Jesus for redemption, but neither divine activity violates human freedom. The Christian life is always a free response to the dual activities of God that are conveyed to the individual through the church and its sacraments. Consequently, Brownson's theology as a Roman Catholic matures by focusing not only on the objective, ecclesiological side of life by communion, but also on the subjective affectivity of the Christian as free and active participation in that life.

Owing largely to the Vatican's publication of the *Syllabus of Errors*—in which Gioberti's ontologism was condemned—and perhaps to the deaths of two sons in the Civil War, an increasingly world-weary Brownson returned to a more conservative defense of the objective, ecclesiological side of his theology during the last decade of his life. Though this final period lacks significant intellectual creativity, it must be recognized as the continuing articulation of the dialectical nature of the heart of Brownson's theology: the doctrine of life by communion.

Suggested Readings

Writings of Orestes A. Brownson: Henry F. Brownson, ed., *The Works of Orestes A. Brownson*, 20 vols. (Detroit: Thorndike Nourse, 1882–87);

Patrick W. Carey, ed., *Orestes A. Brownson: Selected Writings* (Mahwah, N.J.: Paulist Press, 1991).

Leonard Gilhooly, *Contradiction and Dilemma: Orestes Brownson and the American Idea* (New York: Fordham University Press, 1972).

————, ed., *No Divided Allegiance: Essays in Brownson's Life and Thought* (New York: Fordham University Press, 1980).

Thomas R. Ryan, *Orestes A. Brownson: A Definitive Biography* (Huntington, Ind.: Our Sunday Visitor, 1976).

Joseph Smith

(1805–1844)

Jan Shipps

Joseph Smith, Jr., the founder of Mormonism, was born in 1805 into a poor and religiously unconventional Vermont family in which the father was inclined toward Deism and the mother was a Christian Primitivist. The chief sources of family income were agriculture and trading. Because making a living in New England by these means became increasingly difficult in the early nineteenth century, the Smiths moved to western New York while Joseph, Jr., was still a child. There, working at whatever came to hand to earn hard cash while also farming land that was purchased on credit, the parents and their seven children (Joseph was the third son) attempted to build up a family competency in the area around Palmyra. As a result of chicanery, the Smiths lost their farm, but they continued to live there and work the property as tenants until 1831. By that time the younger Joseph had married and established his own household.

From the time they arrived in New York through the 1820s, Joseph, Jr., worked with his father and brothers in the fields. They also worked together in other capacities. Since Joseph Smith, Sr., had enough interest in the occult to give the family a reputation for scrying (delving in magic), this could well have been a decisive factor in what happened during the younger Joseph's teenage years. Indeed, it seems entirely likely that the father encouraged his namesake in the use of a "seer stone," a sort of psychic Geiger counter to help him locate lost objects. In addition, surviving historical sources provide hints that the elder Joseph Smith was not displeased when his son's success led to his being employed in a search for buried treasure. On at least one occasion, the son was engaged as the leader of a company that dug (unsuccessfully, as it turned out) for gold, which the company's organizer believed had been buried in the region by its earlier residents.

That his parents' concern about religion was transmitted to Joseph, Jr., is evidenced by the fact that when he was only fourteen he informed family members that he had learned the true church was not then on the earth. At the time, he seems not to have made it clear to them that this information was imparted in a vision during which God and Jesus appeared to him as he prayed in a grove close to the Smith home. On the other hand, he said he gave an account of this experience to a Methodist minister. While the cleric apparently regarded what Joseph told him as little more than a youngster's delusions, events of the next few years would reveal that the adolescent Smith was preternaturally mature.

In an autobiographical account of his life published in 1838, Joseph Smith described this first vision as a manifestation which distanced him from traditional trinitarian Christianity. The sight of God and Jesus convinced him that the two personages could not be considered part of a single entity. The autobiography, which testifies to the rapidity of Smith's move into maturity as a religious figure, then recounted the spiritual events of his early adulthood. Later canonized by believers, it tells of an angel, identified as Moroni, who appeared to the future prophet in a night vision in 1823 and informed him that God had a work for him to do. During this same spiritual episode, the angel told Smith that an antique rendering of the history of former inhabitants of the Western hemisphere was buried in a hill near his family's farm. Moroni said this historical record was inscribed on thin golden plates and that it not only explained where this archaic assemblage had come from but also disclosed the "fulness of the everlasting gospel" as it had been "delivered by the Savior to the ancient inhabitants."

In his account, Smith said he unearthed the stone box that held the records on the following day. With the plates, he found a device the angel called the Urim and Thummim. It was to be used in translating the plates, but the eighteen-year-old could not undertake this task immediately. Because he was required to undergo a four-year period of purification, Joseph Smith was not allowed to take possession of the plates until 1827. By the time he was twenty-five, he had dictated a full translation of this strange metal document to Oliver Cowdery and other scribes. Some observers said he translated using the instrument found with the plates; others said he used his seer stone. While surviving accounts do not always make a distinction between these two vehicles of interpretation, the result was a text which explained itself as an abridgment and redaction of an ancient history recorded by a prophet whose name had been Mormon. Therefore, when published, Joseph Smith called the work the *Book of Mormon*.

Even as he was seeing to the coming forth and publication of this extraordinary chronicle, whose content convinced many readers that it was a supplemental work of scripture, Smith was reestablishing direct communication between divinity and humanity by becoming a prophet. Speaking for God, he announced that the ancient priesthood was restored and, through its offices, those who sincerely repented could be baptized into the restored Church of Jesus Christ, the only true church on the face of the earth. As prophet and president of this primitivist body, Smith would go on to lead what his followers understood as the "Restoration," a remarkable religious movement that over the years has grown into a tradition of considerable significance in the overall panoply of world religions.

Deriding his "gold bible," early detractors started calling the prophet's followers "Mormonites," but Smith embraced this derisive term, referring to his adherents as Mormons and to the movement as Mormonism. Revealing their close identification with Christians of the apostolic era who were called Saints and, at the same time, signaling their expectation that the end time was near, members of the restored church also called themselves "latter-day Saints." The institution they founded in 1830 was initially called the Church of Christ, but an 1838 revelation established its official name as the Church of Jesus Christ of Latter-day Saints, effectively differentiating this ecclesiastical entity from all other Christian churches. (Today the institution is often referred to as the LDS Church.)

Joseph Smith, who was known as the Mormon prophet, or simply as "the Prophet," led the movement from its beginnings until 1844 when his life was ended by an assassin's bullet. The fact that he became a victim of a paramilitary firing squad whose members regarded him and the movement he headed as a threat to the social and political, as well as religious, life of the state and nation is often recognized as an unmistakable testimony to the exceptional nature of Joseph Smith's gift as a charismatic figure. The literary critic Harold Bloom and a few others have also acknowledged his "religious genius." The significance of Smith's theological contribution is rarely credited, even though Mormonism's experiential base is, and always has been, undergirded by a distinctive belief system which rests on a theology of extraordinary complexity.

The reason Smith has been overlooked as a theological figure is obvious. Unlike those versions of Christian theology that gradually came into being as several generations of scholarly clerics worked from scripture, creedal formulations, and historical experience to devise a systematic description of the faith, and even more unlike those theologies devised by thinkers who used the tools of philosophy, reason, and logic in their efforts to describe and understand Christianity, the theology of the Latter-day Saints was, in a sense, handed down. It was delivered through found scripture and the prophetic voice, and it derives almost entirely from the years of Joseph Smith's religious leadership.

Despite the brevity of this period—it lasted only a dozen years or so—the LDS belief system was not revealed whole, complete, as it were, in every detail. As would be expected in light of the movement's embrace of an open canon and continuing revelation, requisite counterparts to being led by one who has the ability to speak for God, Mormonism's theology was introduced incrementally instead. While this historical reality does not mandate a chronological description of Joseph Smith's contribution to Christian theology, surveying the sequential introduction of its doctrinal and theological strata opens the structural components of the LDS belief system to view. Such an approach consequently discloses and clarifies much about the unusual and in some instances unique aspects of Joseph Smith's remarkable legacy. For that reason, the following précis will emphasize the concept of layering. At the same time, it will stress the critical importance of Mormonism's first prophet's role in the creation of this unique Christian tradition.

When Joseph Smith and his followers organized the church that would become known to the world as the Mormon Church, they said the true church of Christ had been removed from the earth at the time of a "Great Apostasy" that occurred at the end of the apostolic era. Under divine authority, which rested on revelation to the prophet, it was now restored. To support the claim that theirs was the only legitimate Christian institution on the face of the earth, its members pointed to three distinctive bona fides: It was led by one who was in regular communication with, and able to speak for, God; it had the ancient priesthood, recently restored through the prophetic agency of its leader; and, perhaps its greatest asset, the church had a supplementary scripture, an additional testament of Jesus Christ.

In the church's early years, the coming forth of the *Book of Mormon*, together with its strong millennialist bent, was as significant as the book's content itself, because it signaled the imminent opening of the millennium. This formidable set of claims had great appeal in the United States in the religiously unsettled situation that followed the separation of church and state and the demise of established state churches. A sound base for the Mormon movement as a millennialist form of primitivist Christianity was rapidly put into place after the church was established in 1830. Individuals, portions of families, and even whole families became members, and together with their prophet-president and his earliest followers, they turned what is best understood as the "Apostolic Restoration" into reality. This was Mormondom's first theological layer put into place.

213

In the winter of 1831, the prophet and many members of the Smith family left New York and moved to Kirtland, Ohio, where a branch of the church was prospering under the leadership of a former Campbellite minister. Considerable numbers of Smith's followers moved there as well. Other Saints moved to Independence, Missouri, the following summer, choosing this area because it had been identified by revelation as the land of Zion, the future site of a temple and the place where the Second Coming would commence. Although many converts to the new movement did not relocate immediately, two distinct Mormon enclaves were created. This pattern of settlement came in response to several revelations which forecast the congregating of believers in "one place upon the face of this land" in preparation for the great day when heaven and earth shall pass away and all things will become new.

The prophet's revelations about what became known as "the gathering" clearly reflect the Revelation of 1 John. But when a literal gathering of Saints happened in the early 1830s, it turned Mormonism toward the Pentateuch as well as the New Testament. While concepts of Zion, Israel, a covenant people, priests, and temples are integral to the *Book of Mormon* and Smith's pre-1830 revelations, what happened in post-1830 Mormonism constituted a pivotal move toward the Old Testament experience. The building of a temple, as distinguished from chapel or church, turned the hearts of these Christian children to their Hebraic fathers in a manner that gave Latter-day Saint communities a singularity that separated them from their Protestant neighbors. In Kirtland, also, the Saints started to make a clear distinction between the lesser (Aaronic, that is, Levitical) and greater (Melchizedek) priesthoods, as the perception of priesthood as a privilege of lineage took hold in Mormon minds and Mormon culture. This was and is important from the standpoint of doctrine and church organization.

Of greater theological moment, Mormons shared with all Christianity the "new covenant" and its figurative conception of Gentiles being adopted into Israel. But as they gathered from the "earth's four corners" during the 1830s, the Saints went through a transformative process that can best be described as turning the symbolic into the literal. The prophet's father was ordained as Church Patriarch in 1833 and a practice was instituted in which he gave a patriarchal blessing—an essential part of which is a declaration of lineage—to each church member. As Father Smith's ritualistic assertions of membership in the tribes of Ephraim, Manasseh, Benjamin, and others were bestowed individually, a conception of group kinship through birthright membership in Abraham's family was added to Mormonism. Before much time had passed, Saints started to believe that all who were not Mormon were Gentile. Jews and Latter-day Saints were God's only chosen people.

In sum, the literal gathering, the actual building of a temple, the distinction between the two priesthoods, and the institution of patriarchy can be descried as the "Abrahamic Restoration." Composing a second tier, this Hebraic overlay changed Mormon theology by adding to it, not by taking things away. That was made clear in the religious repercussions of the 1836 dedication of the Kirtland Temple. This landmark occasion was such a spiritual feast for those in attendance that it is sometimes called Mormonism's Pentecost. But from a theological perspective, what happened on the Sunday following is of much more enduring importance to the faith.

As recorded in Section 110 of the Doctrine and Covenants of the Church of Jesus Christ of Latter-day Saints, on that day the veil was rent allowing the prophet and the church's "First Elder," Oliver Cowdery, to see Jesus standing in the temple. They heard him say that their sins and the sins of the people were forgiven. He accepted the temple; his name would ever be there; and in the temple's sacred precincts he would manifest himself to his people. When that vision closed, a second opened in which Moses and Elijah committed to Smith and Cowdery the keys of the gathering of Israel and the gospel of Abraham. Then, in a final "great and glorious" manifestation, Elijah extended to them the keys to the dispensation of the last days, which he said were even then "at the doors." This extraordinary supernatural event tied together Mormonism's first two theological and doctrinal strata, creating a form of Hebraicized Christianity that held in tension the temple and the church.

Typical accounts of Mormonism during the 1830s are so completely centered on the experience of the Saints living in Mormon enclaves in Ohio and Missouri that the existence of Mormonism in the countryside gets lost. The prevailing picture of this period depicts a group caught up in the exhilaration of living in the presence of a prophet and the excitement of revelation rolling forth, even as members of the group lived through mistreatment and abuse from outsiders. But this experience was not universal, because being Mormon in the first few years after the church was organized was not all of a piece. To Saints living in the countryside, membership in this particular church of Christ differed from membership in other millennialist Christian churches mainly in the security afforded by the church's restorationist truth claims, in the importance accorded the *Book of Mormon* as a tangible sign of the nearness of the end time, and in preaching that encouraged church members to gather to Zion so they would be there when Christ returned. Apart from emphasis on the impending opening of the millennium, the experience of ungathered members of the church in the early days was curiously prescient of Mormonism at the end of the twentieth century when residing in enclave communities would no longer be normative for Latter-day Saints. At the same time, an examination of the LDS countryside experience supplies a clear picture of Mormonism in its original formulation by separating from the conventional picture the theological, doctrinal, and organizational enhancement that occurred in the gathering centers.

The transformation of gathered members of the church into a people whose otherness became as manifest as that of Jews or enslaved Ethiopians provides observers of the development of Mormonism with the best evidence of the impact of positioning an overlay of Hebraicism over the earliest form of this movement. For those living through it, their progression toward otherness generated an intense level of hostility against the Saints. Within a year of the temple dedication, the prophet would be driven from Ohio. Many of his adherents followed him, first to Missouri, and when opposition there turned into war, back across the Mississippi River to Illinois. Initially welcomed to the state, threats of violence soon started to separate the Saints from the surrounding populace. Yet it was in Illinois where, for the first time, what can truly be considered a Mormon kingdom came into being.

Although ever under threat of imprisonment—he had spent several months in jail—the final decade of Smith's life was spent in Missouri and in an Illinois town the Saints named Nauvoo. Much of importance occurred in the secular arena in both states, but theological developments in Nauvoo were of greater long-range significance to the tradition. There, within what seemed to him the internally secure environment of an LDS kingdom where his authority was supreme, the prophet added a final layer to the stratified configuration of Mormon theology. Through additional found texts (the books of Moses and Abraham), a sermon preached at the funeral of King Follett, and a crucial new revelation (now Section 132 in the LDS Doctrine and Covenants), the prophet appended a set of esoteric tenets—tiered heavens, proxy baptisms, celestial marriage, eternal progression toward godhood—to LDS theology. As had revelations in Kirtland, these additions would again transform Mormonism.

In particular, this final dogmatic overlay had critical implications for Mormon soteriology and worship practice. It located human life between preexistence and postexistence states and placed the ordinances of the temple—most especially the Endowment (in and through which power from on high is bestowed on participating Saints) and celestial marriage—at the very core of Mormonism. When unified with the merged gospels of Jesus

216

Christ and Abraham, these tenets set forth a plan of salvation which entails the ceaseless persistence of personality and the eternal endurance of family units. Often called "the fulness of the gospel," the final additions Joseph Smith introduced into Mormonism compose what Latter-day Saints describe as the "Restoration of All Things."

The prophet's revelation concerning the patriarchal order of marriage (i.e., celestial marriage) contained stipulations whereby men living in the dispensation in which the revelation came forth could marry into plurality in the manner of Old Testament patriarchs. Although not publicly promulgated during Smith's lifetime, this revelation was privately revealed to many leading Saints beginning in 1841. When they took the introduction of this new principle and acted on it with the same earnestness as they had acted on earlier revelations announced by the prophet, serious consequences followed. Because some of the Saints were starting to chafe under the palpable political, social, and economic ramifications of living under prophetic leadership in what the city's inhabitants regarded as God's kingdom, incipient internal opposition to Smith was already present in Nauvoo. The practice of plural (or celestial) marriage caused that opposition to break into the open and swell to such proportions that it exposed Nauvoo to external threat, which neither the prophet nor the LDS community could avoid. With the apparent complicity of the Illinois governor, Smith was murdered by disguised members of the local militia in June 1844. In order to avoid decimation at the hands of an organized mob, the Saints were forced to leave the area less than two years later.

Suggested Readings

James B. Allen and Glen M. Leonard, *The Story of the Latter-day Saints* (Salt Lake City: Deseret, 1976).

Book of Mormon: Another Testament of Jesus Christ; Doctrine and Covenants of the Church of Jesus Christ of Latter-day Saints; Pearl of Great Price, one-volume edition (Salt Lake City: Church of Jesus Christ of Latter-day Saints, 1981).

Paul M. Edwards, *Our Legacy of Faith: A Brief History of the Reorganized Church of Jesus Christ of Latter Day Saints* (Independence, Mo.: Herald Publishing House, 1991).

Encyclopedia of Mormonism, ed. Daniel H. Ludlow (New York: Macmillan, 1992). See especially essays entitled "Prophecy," "Revelation," and "Theology."

Bruce R. McConkie, *Mormon Doctrine* (Salt Lake City: Bookcraft, 1958).

Charles Porterfield Krauth

(1823–1883)

Jerald C. Brauer

Lutheranism in antebellum America was engaged in a life-and-death struggle to determine its future. In 1820 several synods came together to unite in a single cooperative body, the General Synod. Under the leadership of S. S. Schmucker, the General Synod reestablished a role for the Augsburg Confession, Lutheranism's primary confession, and required support for it as a substantially correct presentation of the fundamental doctrines of the word of God. The body then quickly established Gettysburg Theological Seminary (1826) and Gettysburg College (by 1834).

Schmucker became the leader of the movement known as American Lutheranism, which sought to strengthen a sense of identity within Lutheranism at the same time it sought to Americanize. Deeply influenced by the leading American Protestant denominations, their prevailing revivalism, and their many voluntary reform and educational societies, American Lutheranism sought to distance itself from those doctrines in the Augsburg Confession that were unpalatable to its Protestant brethren. This precipitated a deadly struggle within Lutheranism.

Charles Porterfield Krauth graduated from Gettysburg College (1839) and from Gettysburg Theological Seminary (1841), where he studied under Schmucker, T. H. Schmidt, and his father, Charles Philip Krauth. His irenic father, good friend of Schmucker, always harbored doubts about his colleague's American Lutheranism. Young Charles went through the entire Gettysburg theological system as its top student. Upon graduation he took a small country parish where, typical of that age, he pursued a rigorous course of study to build his theological acumen. He became the theological leader of Lutherans in direct opposition to Schmucker, his former mentor. Although Krauth attacked Schmucker's ideas, he retained the highest respect for Schmucker personally and never engaged in invective or *ad hominem* argumentation.

Krauth did not begin his formal teaching career until Philadelphia Lutheran Theological Seminary was founded in 1864 in opposition to Gettysburg. For twenty some years he had served in a number of pastorates, edited the magazine *Lutheran and Missionary* (1861–67), wrote copiously on leading theological issues, and delivered a number of key addresses in his synod and elsewhere.

From his earliest writings Krauth exhibited a conservative temper that questioned the radical departure of Schmucker and his fellow American Lutherans from the confessions and practices of historical Lutheranism. His editorship provided him with ample opportunity to address all the basic issues agitating Lutheranism in America. His editorials, reviews, and articles made him the most widely read Lutheran author in America. He refined and deepened his theological position in relation to concrete issues confronting his church, and revealed his depth of learning, mastery of languages, infallible logic, remarkable literary ability, and abiding sense of humor.

The central theological issue, appearing in many forms, was both historical and doctrinal. What does it mean to be Lutheran in America? Schmucker and Benjamin Kurtz led the General Synod forces as the genuine expression of Lutheranism in America, a distinctly American Lutheran church. The true mark of this Lutheranism was freedom of its members to select from the historical Lutheran confessions those doctrines which their own experience in America led them to believe were most in harmony with scripture. Its aim was for Lutheranism to resemble other evangelical Christians in America as closely as possible. Fully committed to revivalism and its practices, suspicious of all historical liturgical forms as unfit for American experience, deeply committed to all reform and other Protestant voluntary organizations, strictly sabbatarian, and vehemently anti-Catholic, American Lutheranism held to a recension of the Augsburg Confession that eliminated all doctrines that distinguished them from their fellow Protestants.

Krauth's editorship gave him a platform on which he could exhibit his theological vision of Lutheranism. He attacked American Lutheranism as an aberration. Drawing deeply from his vast knowledge of biblical materials, patristics, the great medieval theologians, Luther and the Reformers, the confessional theologians, and current theologians, he confronted American Lutheranism at every point. He was an American Lutheran, he maintained, only in the sense that he was a part of that church which happened to be in America. He was not more American because he was less Lutheran, and being less Lutheran would not make him more American.

America gives all people an opportunity to exercise religious freedom, and if they choose to exercise it in such a way that they alter, change, amend, or destroy that which connects them to Lutheranism, they should not then insist on calling themselves Lutheran. Those who exercise freedom to be what they wish have the responsibility honestly to call themselves what they actually are—and that is not Lutherans in America, but a combination of European Zwinglianism, Anabaptism, and rationalism. They may deny the defining elements of Lutheranism—adherence to the Lutheran confessions, heritage, and practices. But if they do, they are not Lutheran.

Krauth's mature theology was best expressed in the publication of his massive 840-page *Conservative Reformation and Its Theology* (1871). It received highly favorable comments from the leading scholars of his day such as John Nevin and Charles Hodge. All remarked on Krauth's extraordinary learning grounded in a mastery both of primary sources in their original languages and in the best secondary works. Though it contained some of his previous writings all were reworked and updated. His method was historical-theological. Each doctrine was subjected to disciplined exegetical, dogmatic, and confessional analysis in its historical context. The book's objective was to delineate that part of the Reformation which was conservative or Catholic over against that part which was radical.

Krauth argued that the Reformation was not primarily a radical movement but a dialectic between conservatism and progressivism. His analysis of the Reformation reminds one of Paul Tillich's point that the Reformation must be understood as the interplay between Catholic substance and the Protestant principle. How each would have understood the Protestant principle is not in all respects the same; however, as a formal structure of interpretation, they are very close. Krauth chose to emphasize the Catholic substance of the Reformation in order to combat those, particularly among the Lutherans, who denied any connection between Catholicism and Protestantism.

The conservative principle seeks to secure the present by a tenacious fidelity to the past. The progressive seeks to live in the present by constant effort, in hope, and to envision a better future. These two principles are held together and creatively interact through a third principle, the reformatory. This is not a Hegelian synthesis between the two that comes into being out of the emergence of the best in both.

Conservatism without a dimension of the progressive produces distortions such as those Krauth perceived within Roman Catholicism and Eastern Orthodoxy. Progressivism without conservatism produces radicalism, sectarianism, and revolution. The third principle, the reformatory, seeks always to harmonize the two and to critique their respective distortions. Krauth argues that these three principles, analogous to the three primary colors, are present throughout Christian history. Concrete representations of each of the three arise in history, and since each is subject to distortion, the presence of the others is necessary.

At its best, Reformation represents the conservation of the good that was and is from the past, the tradition, but at the same time has its eye on the good which is yet to come. It has a profound yet critical reverence for the past; firmly rooted in history, it realizes that there are no absolutely fresh starts. One cannot leap over history and return to "pure" apostolic, biblical times. In Krauth's eyes this was the error of Schmucker and his American Lutheran colleagues. That is why Krauth took seriously the Lutheran confessions and all of the confessions that emerged from the Reformation period, just as he took equally seriously the entire historical and theological development of the Catholic Christian community.

If Lutheranism in America successfully retained a particular identity that reflected a Catholic substance yet also a critical Protestant principle, the credit goes to Charles Porterfield Krauth more than to any other individual. Others were involved in the struggle, but he stood tall among them, particularly in the English-speaking world. Though he was famous as professor of philosophy and vice-provost of the University of Pennsylvania (1868–83), his intellectual gifts were dedicated primarily to the mastery of understanding, teaching, and writing about the special genius of the Reformation, particularly the Lutheran tradition. However, in expounding that tradition, he contributed to the self-understanding of all the related churches of the Reformation.

Suggested Readings

Writings of Charles Porterfield Krauth: Adolph Spaeth, ed., *Charles Porterfield Krauth*, 11 vols. (New York: Christian Literature Co., 1898).

Virgilius Ferm, *A Crisis in American Lutheran Theology* (New York: Century Co., 1927).

Henry E. Jacobs, *A History of the Evangelical Lutheran Church in the United States* (New York: Christian Literature Co., 1893).

Alexander Campbell

(1788–1866)

Samuel C. Pearson

Remembered today primarily as a leader of the Restoration movement in nineteenth-century America that led to a group of denominations including the Christian Church (Disciples of Christ), the Christian Churches, and the Churches of Christ, Alexander Campbell was a pastor, editor, educator, debater, Bible translator, and practical theologian whose cardinal interests included questions of biblical authority and interpretation, Christian unity, and the restoration of the patterns and beliefs of the apostolic church as a means toward achieving that unity. Campbell's father, Thomas, whose family had roots in Scotland but had long been resident in Ireland, left the Anglican Church to become a Presbyterian minister and schoolmaster. Alexander, born in 1788, joined his father's church. Yet both father and son seem to have harbored reservations regarding Presbyterian discipline and the sectarian spirit then rife within British Protestantism generally and Scottish Presbyterianism in particular. These reservations were reinforced by their association with Independents whose emphasis on congregational governance the Campbells found attractive and by their sympathy for the arguments of John Locke supporting toleration and opposing forced conformity. They were also influenced, even while lamenting the divisions within the church, by the reform programs of small groups advocating restoration of the patterns of New Testament Christianity.

When the elder Campbell left Ireland for America in 1807, Alexander was placed in charge of his school, Rich Hill Academy. The following year Alexander and other family members left Ireland to join the father, but their ship ran aground in the Hebrides compelling them to wait nearly a year in Glasgow for passage to America. Alexander Campbell reached a firm decision to enter the ministry at this time and spent the year in study at the University of Glasgow. He also became acquainted with Greville Ewing, a follower of James and Robert Haldane who advocated a simple evangelical Christianity based upon a restoration of the exact practices of primitive Christianity. By the end of his year in Scotland, Campbell's allegiance to his church, Anti-burgher Seceder Presbyterianism, became impossible to sustain. Refusing communion, he left that group as he journeyed to America in 1809.

In America Campbell learned that his father had been accepted into ministry by the Associate Synod of North America, a body representing all Seceder Presbyterians in the United States, and assigned to a parish in western Pennsylvania. There he had drifted into conflict with church officials on a variety of doctrinal issues, had been suspended from ministerial office, and had responded by organizing a group of sympathetic laypersons into a voluntary society named the Christian Association of Washington. The elder Campbell had also penned an apology and statement of principles for the Association under the title *Declaration and Address*. Alexander Campbell accepted this document as his own with its appeal for a "simple evangelical christianity, free from all mixture of human opinions and inventions" to be achieved by reliance on scripture for rule, the Holy Spirit for teacher and guide, and Christ for salvation. This plea for the restoration of primitive Christianity echoed themes present within Scottish Presbyterianism as greatly reinforced by the Campbells' contact with primitivist groups and their own experience with the sectarianism of their time. In 1811, the Association established itself as a church (Brush Run Church), chose Thomas Campbell as elder, and licensed Alexander to preach. He was ordained the following New Year's Day.

Within the first year of his ministry, Campbell came to reject both the practice of infant baptism and baptism by any mode other than immersion on the grounds that he found biblical (apostolic) warrant only for believer's baptism by immersion. Along with other members of his family and members of the Brush Run church, he then accepted immersion baptism from a Baptist minister. This act drove a further wedge between Campbell and the Presbyterians and led to a period of cooperation with the Baptists. The Brush Run church was received into the Redstone Baptist Association in 1813, but Campbell's emerging theological method, an appeal to scripture for definitive patterns of church polity and practice that might be restored in his own time coupled with a profound suspicion of formal confessions of faith, is reflected in the terms of membership. Brush Run Church joined the Association "provided always that we should be allowed to teach and preach whatever we learned from the Holy Scriptures, regardless of any human creed." This federation, always tenuous, dissolved in the years between 1830 and 1832 as Campbell and his followers, then commonly known as Reformers, left or disbanded Baptist associations or were dismissed by them and came into closer fellowship with Christian churches of the upper South led by Barton Warren Stone. From this coalition came a new denomination loosely organized and profoundly influenced by democratic social and political forces in antebellum America.

Meanwhile, Campbell had relocated from Pennsylvania to Bethany, (West) Virginia. There he ministered to a local congregation as well as to several other congregations in the region. He extended his influence through operation of a boys school and, after 1840, Bethany College. He also published a translation of the New Testament, a hymnbook, and religious journals—first the *Christian Baptist* (1823–30) and then the *Millennial Harbinger* (1830–64). The theological positions reflected in those publications were more systematically presented in *The Christian System, in Reference to the Union of Christians, and a Restoration of Primitive Christianity, as Plead in the Current Reformation* (1st ed., 1835; 2nd ed., 1839).

In *The Christian System*, Campbell enunciated a set of principles that he believed define the true church and provide a basis for Christian unity. He appealed to scripture as his final authority. In a set of rules for Bible study, Campbell demanded a historical and critical approach. Readers were urged to consider the historical circumstances of the book including order, title, author, date, and place and occasion of writing as well as the audience to whom the text was directed. They were asked to apply the same philological principles that might be applied to other literature in order to "come within the understanding distance," by which he meant approaching the Bible intent on learning the will of God. Application of these rules, Campbell believed, would lead the reader to principles of organization and patterns of worship to be regarded as normative for the church. For Campbell, such biblical Christianity would be simple and reasonable, a far cry from the complexity of both the Protestantism and the Catholicism of his day.

Though *The Christian System* is arranged in the characteristic manner of Protestant systematic theologies of the day, proceeding to address topics from the universe to the Bible, the Godhead, humanity and God's purposes for human beings, to the church, doctrines, and church discipline, Campbell focused on those themes that distinguished him and his followers from Presbyterians, Baptists, and others. He acknowledged human inheritance of a sinful nature but denied that individuals are under invincible necessity to sin. His break with strict Calvinism on this point reflected the high regard for human potential characteristic of the time as well as his own convictions regarding human responsibility and the perfectibility of society through the reformation and discipline of the mind and spirit of individuals.

He declared that faith "is the simple belief of testimony, or of the truth, and never can be more nor less than that." Thus Campbell regarded repentance as an effect of faith to be followed by baptism which he equated with immersion. Only penitent believers are subject to baptism since the institution has no abstract efficacy. He also argued that the only appropriate confession of faith is the "apostolic and divine confession" that Jesus of Nazareth is the Messiah, the Son of the Living God. He described the gift of the Holy Spirit as always following, never preceding, the individual's coming to faith and repentance and accepting baptism.

Ecclesiology is the heart of Campbell's theology, and here his advocacy of Christian union led him both to a modern understanding of denominations as representing portions of the church and to a sectarian assumption that he and his own followers, having renounced all distinctive and non-biblical elements, represented that one church of which other denominations were only imperfect reflections. Marks of this nonsectarian community include baptism of believers by immersion and weekly celebration of the Lord's Supper. He insisted that Christians must regard the church as one community though composed of many small communities. While acknowledging the biblical precedent for conferring ministerial office on specific persons as bishops, deacons, or evangelists, Campbell contended that such officers must be chosen by the whole community and that "every citizen of Christ's kingdom has . . . equal rights, privileges, and immunities." Therefore every Christian may preach, baptize, dispense the Lord's Supper, and pray for others. He alleged that matters of faith and morality should rest upon a clear biblical injunction and that other matters should be regarded as matters of expediency, though the law of love should direct all human conduct.

As Campbell gained recognition as a leader of a growing American denomination, he traveled extensively throughout the Old Northwest and the upper South and was a welcome speaker throughout the area. He frequently debated other Protestant leaders in defense of his theological position, but his most celebrated debates were with Bishop John B. Purcell of Cincinnati and with Robert Owen. As a delegate to the 1829 Virginia constitutional convention, Campbell vigorously advocated universal manhood suffrage, judicial reform, and the interests of public education. Though personally sympathetic to inclusion of gradual emancipation in the new constitution, he did not press this issue. As the Civil War approached, Campbell urged churches not to permit a person's position on slavery to become a test of fellowship, and the churches acknowledging his leadership sought to avoid schism over this issue.

As Campbell's movement and, perhaps, Campbell himself struggled with the tension between the twin goals of restoration of primitive Christianity and unity of all Christians, he transferred more and more of his millennial hope for a good society to the American nation. America reflected the unity and equality which Campbell regarded as prerequisite to this hope. The subsequent inability of American society, in which Campbell had invested so much hope, to eliminate slavery without civil war constituted a profound challenge to his democratic idealism and trust in reason and the human potential. This critical failure no less than age and declining health contributed to his withdrawal from the public arena in the last years of his life. He died at Bethany in 1866.

Campbell is the quintessential theologian of the age of Jackson. He shared both the strengths and the weaknesses of that era. His lasting influence has been primarily institutional. As the editor of the *Millennial Harbinger* for more than three decades, he was one of two or three most influential figures in the shaping of the denominations that emerged from nineteenth-century American Restorationism, sometimes termed the Stone-Campbell movement. Though he had a considerable following, his theological orientation remained grounded in an earlier pattern of Protestant rationalism even as Kantian philosophy was driving a reformulation of much American Protestant thought. Though his primary goal of transcending sectarianism in the interest of church union was attractive to those influenced by modern theological currents, his method—an appeal for the restoration of the precise patterns of church organization and worship found in scripture—was not.

Those churches shaped by Campbell's work have generally chosen to emphasize specific elements of Campbell's thought and to neglect others. More liberal followers have focused on his call for church union and embraced the ecumenical movement. Those of more conservative sympathies have concerned themselves primarily with Campbell's call for the restoration of primitive Christianity. Yet all reflect Campbell's high regard for human potential, his trust in reason to resolve religious questions, and his commitments to freedom of religion, democracy, and public education.

Suggested Readings

Writings of Alexander Campbell: *The Christian System* (Salem, N.H.: Ayer Co., 1988; repr. of the 1839 [second] ed.); Robert Richardson, *Mem-*

oirs of Alexander Campbell, 2 vols. (Nashville: Gospel Advocate Co., 1956; repr. of 1897 ed.).

Nathan O. Hatch, *The Democratization of American Christianity* (New Haven: Yale University Press, 1989).

Richard T. Hughes and C. Leonard Allen, *Illusions of Innocence: Protestant Primitivism in America, 1630–1875* (Chicago: University of Chicago Press, 1988).

Lectures in Honor of the Alexander Campbell Bicentennial, 1788–1988 (Nashville: Disciples of Christ Historical Society, 1988).

John Williamson Nevin

(1803–1886)

John B. Payne

J ohn Williamson Nevin was the chief architect of the so-called Mercersburg Theology, which championed a Christ-centered, churchly, and sacramental consciousness that sharply diverged from mainstream American Protestantism in the mid–nineteenth century. Based in the young seminary of the German Reformed Church at Mercersburg, Pennsylvania, this movement would help bring about a theological and liturgical renewal within that church which would also be felt to a lesser extent within other Protestant bodies such as the Lutheran, Episcopalian, Dutch Reformed, and Presbyterian.

Ever since the pioneering work of James H. Nichols (1961), Nevin has been recognized as one of the three or four most creative theologians in mid-nineteenth-century America. Even some of the great thinkers with whom he entered into debate testified to the acuity of his theological mind. Charles Hodge of Princeton, his erstwhile teacher and later acerbic disputant on the Eucharist, acknowledged Nevin as his most brilliant pupil. Nevin was the only critic of Bushnell's *Discourses on Christian Nurture* to whom the Hartford minister bothered to respond at length. A first-rate polemicist, Nevin disputed with a wide range of opponents within and outside his own denomination.

Nevin grasped a broader range of theological expression than probably any other American theologian. A master of the older and newer Reformed and Puritan Divinity in England and this country as well as contemporary German theology, he was also conversant with the Anglo-Catholic Oxford Movement in England, which paralleled to a certain extent his own position on the great church question of the day.

Born on 20 February 1803, Nevin grew up as the oldest of nine children on his father's farm in northern Franklin County, Pennsylvania. From his father, classically educated at Dickinson College, he absorbed a deep Scots-

Irish Presbyterian piety and learned Latin and Greek even before he entered Union College, Schenectady, New York (1817). Although reared among Scots-Irish Old School Presbyterians who were cool toward revivalism, Nevin was "converted" there at the hands of the moderate revivalist, Asahel Nettleton. Because of ill health and some discomfort with his spiritual state and vocation, Nevin was forced upon graduation to spend two years on his father's farm recuperating and consolidating his call before entering Princeton in the fall of 1823.

Nevin would come to look upon Princeton as his second home. Samuel Miller and Archibald Alexander were still in their prime, and the young Charles Hodge had just joined the faculty. There Nevin became well-grounded in the Reformed tradition even if he did not learn from his professors about that tradition's historical development. No doubt Nevin also appropriated from his professors the method of Scottish Common-Sense Realism which ruled the theological scene in America for much of the nineteenth century. This philosophy eschewed metaphysical speculation and showed a strong confidence in an empirical and logical common-sense approach to theology and scripture. Nevin would eventually adopt a more mystical, intuitive interpretation of scripture which differed sharply from common-sense reasoning.

For all their emphasis upon a logical, propositional theology based on scripture, the Reformed tradition, and common-sense philosophy, Princeton theologians did not neglect piety and the work of the Holy Spirit. Nevin reports in his autobiography that he learned from Alexander about the older seventeenth-century Puritan Divinity of Richard Baxter, John Owen, John Howe, Robert Leighton, and Henry Scougal. The "Platonizing thoughts" of the last three taught him about religion as a new life and as the "Life of God in the Soul of Man" (Scougal), a perspective which appealed to his basic mystical inclination. In 1835, for a journal he edited *(The Friend)*, he wrote a series of articles under the title "Religion as Life." Like Schleiermacher, Nevin argued that religion is more a matter of feeling than of thought or doctrine and that it involves a process of growth.

In 1830, Nevin was called to the new Western Theological Seminary in Allegheny City, a suburb of Pittsburgh. At Western (1830–40), he showed himself to be a staunch evangelical moralist, attacking—in sermons and the *Friend*—strong drink, Sabbath-breaking, fairs, the theater, and, most important, slavery. Because of his unpopular strong antislavery stance, he was forced to relinquish publication of the *Friend* after less than two years. Nevin also became embroiled in the Old School–New School conflict within the Presbyterian Church. He fully subscribed to Old School Presbyterianism, but he was not persuaded that the expulsion of four New School synods from the church at the General Assembly of 1837 was constitutional or that the Old School could claim to be the only true succession of the Presbyterian Church.

While at Western, Nevin began to study German language and literature in order to read the works of the Berlin church historian August Neander. For the first time Nevin became fascinated by the study of church history. Whereas most American Protestants, including his Princeton teachers, gave little attention to pre-Reformation church history, Nevin came more and more to appreciate the patristic and medieval periods.

Nevin's knowledge of German would be put to good use when, in 1840, he accepted a call to the German Reformed Seminary at Mercersburg (originally founded in 1825 at Carlisle). Nevin assumed the post of professor of theology alongside Friedrich Rauch, a young professor from Heidelberg, Germany, who had been a disciple of the right-wing Hegelian, Karl Daub. Rauch died within a year after Nevin's inauguration, but not before he had introduced his colleague to Hegelian ideas. At Rauch's death, Nevin assumed full responsibility for teaching at the seminary and in addition, took over Rauch's position as president of Marshall College.

In order better to acquaint himself with the German Reformed tradition and arouse a stronger historical consciousness in the denomination he had just entered, Nevin wrote a series of twenty-nine articles on the Heidelberg Catechism for the church journal, the *Weekly Messenger*. His preface to this series (1840) announced the Romantic principle of the organic development of church history, which he had learned from Neander. Reverence for the past, Nevin stated, should not negate progress, but progress should be "upwards, within the sphere of the original life of the church itself . . . not progress outwards, by which the life of the past, together with its form is renounced and 'another gospel' introduced in the room of the old." In the following years, this principle became the basis for his critical judgment of American Protestantism, which Nevin increasingly thought had lost its moorings in its Reformation roots.

Two years after Nevin's arrival at Mercersburg, an outbreak of New Measures revivalism in the local church was the occasion for the development of the Mercersburg Theology. In response to this incident, he wrote *The Anxious Bench* (1843), a pamphlet in which he decried symbol-manipulative revivalism as a form of quackery like Roman Catholic indulgences—a penitential practice playing on the fears of the people and a cheap substitute for genuine faith and repentance.

Where the "system of the anxious bench" consisted of ever-repeated conversions, Nevin emphasized, "the system of the catechism" concerned the cultivation "of the life of God in the life of the soul" through regular instruction and pastoral care. In the 1844 second edition, he argued that the anxious bench system presupposed a Pelagian individualism which understood sin as the act of a particular will (he refers here to Nathaniel Taylor's views on this subject), whereas the system of the catechism presumed sin as social, "a wrong habit of humanity itself." Likewise, according to the catechism, redemption is social before it is individual. It is rooted in Christ as the New Adam, who imparts the germ of a new humanity to his church.

Nevin's pamphlet was directed especially to the German churches, both Reformed and Lutheran, who had been swept up in the fever of Finneyite New Measures revivalism. He was intent on showing them that this brand of Christianity was not at all consonant with their Reformation confessional and catechetical foundations. It stood also in the sharpest contrast with the writings of such contemporary German theologians as H. Olshausen, August Tholuck, C. F. Sartorius, and Neander. To his growing mastery of German theology, Nevin added especially the so-called mediating theologians, such as Karl Ullmann, Isaak Dorner, and Richard Rothe, who in the wake of Hegel and Schleiermacher, sought to be true to scripture and tradition and yet attentive to the emergence of the new science and philosophy. Their goal was to steer a middle course between a rigid confessionalism and an ultrarationalism.

In the summer of 1844 at a joint convention of the Dutch Reformed and the German Reformed churches held in Harrisburg, Nevin showed the relevance, to the subject of Christian unity, of his view of the church as the "New Humanity" rooted in Christ as the second Adam. His sermon "Catholic Unity" proclaimed that the church is essentially one because it is actuated by the power of a common life rooted in Jesus Christ. Drawing on Hegelian terminology, Nevin argued that this Holy Catholic church exists now, however, more in potentiality and ideality than in actuality. While Nevin deplored that the actual church was divided, he criticized two different attitudes toward this division—one which accepted it as inevitable and placed all hope in an invisible, rather than a visible, union and the other which developed the stratagem of "a non-sect party," rejecting all denominational labels in an effort to attain Christian unity (such as John Winebrenner's "Church of God" and Alexander Campbell's "Disciples of Christ"). Christian unity was for him necessarily visible as well as invisible and a divine gift resting upon a power that precedes all contrivance and machination.

In the audience listening to Nevin's sermon was Philip Schaff, who had arrived from Germany only a month earlier. Not long after becoming Nevin's colleague at Mercersburg, Schaff wrote in his journal that to his surprise Nevin's views on the church were essentially the same as his and that "he is filled with the ideas of German theology." Schaff would lend the support of his vast erudition in church history to the emerging Mercersburg Theology. Just two and a half months after hearing Nevin's sermon, Schaff presented his own statement on the church question in his inaugural address on the theme, "The Principle of Protestantism," before the German Reformed Synod in Reading. His stress upon the medieval roots of the Reformation suggested to some in his audience a Romanist sympathy, and this impression led to charges of heresy against him at the synod meeting in York in 1845. These charges, however, were dismissed by an overwhelming vote.

Nevin defended his colleague on the synod floor as well as in his introduction to Schaff's address, which he translated for publication in 1845. His argument was that in order for Protestantism properly to counter the claims of popery and Puseyism (high-church Anglicanism), it must recognize the truth within these systems. Along Hegelian dialectical lines, the truths in the opposed systems require reconciliation—the sacramental with the spiritual, the objective with the subjective, tradition with scripture, church authority with private judgment. He agreed with Schaff that out of the present stage of Protestantism, which must be considered to be provisional, there will arise a future "evangelical catholicism." Supporting Schaff's theory of organic historical development, he maintained that, just as the papal system grew out of tendencies present in the church as early as the late second century, so Protestantism emerged out of the Middle Ages and represents the central stream of the history of the church that bears within itself likewise, evils which in time it will surmount.

In 1846, Nevin produced what must be regarded as his magnum opus, *The Mystical Presence: A Vindication of the Reformed or the Calvinistic Doctrine of the Eucharist*. In this work, Nevin made it clear that the doctrine of the Eucharist was the center of his theology as well as of his piety. As early as 1842, in an essay on the *Heidelberg Catechism,* he held that in the Lord's Supper believers experience an actual union with the life of Christ's glorified body, which is as real as the natural bond in soul and body with Adam. In *The Mystical Presence,* he greatly expanded upon this view and clearly marked it off from alternative positions—especially the low Zwinglian symbolic, memorialist understanding which reigned in nineteenth-century American Protestantism. Nevin sought to show that the

232

doctrine of the Lord's Supper as set forth by Calvin and the Reformed confessions held (1) that the sacrament does not just commemorate or represent but conveys an objective grace, and (2) that this grace consists of "the substantial life of the Saviour himself, particularly in his human nature."

Nevin entered into debate with Charles Hodge on this subject. Hodge considered the sacrificial efficacy of Christ's death as remembered in the Lord's Supper to be the dominant view of the Reformed tradition. Nevin's idea of a life-giving power received by the believer from the body of Christ, he held, was "an uncongenial foreign element" in Calvin's writings. Displaying considerable erudition, Nevin demonstrated the falsity of Hodge's interpretation of the history. Nevin argued that the notion of the sacrificial efficacy received its true significance from its connection with the idea of the "vivific power of his life." With this point he showed that the dispute with Hodge on the Lord's Supper also concerned the doctrine of Christ. Where Hodge emphasized the atonement, Nevin stressed that the atonement is grounded in the incarnation. As Dorner would correctly perceive, Nevin owed something to the Greek Fathers' emphasis upon the incarnation as the basis of a mystical salvation.

For Nevin, the doctrines of Christ and the Lord's Supper are closely connected with the doctrine of the church. Christ is the root or principle of the church. The church is the body of Christ, the medium of the "New Humanity" inaugurated by Christ. The chief means of grace mediated through the church are the sacraments of baptism and the Lord's Supper. In the Eucharist believers commune with Christ in a unique way.

Nevin saw this high doctrine of Christ and the church to be based in both the Reformation and the ancient creeds, the Apostles' Creed above all. This doctrine played an important role in his assessment of the contemporary state of Protestantism, about which he became ever more pessimistic. He characterized it as sectarian and individualistic, with no sense of history or feeling for the church and the sacraments (*Antichrist or the Spirit of Sect and Schism* [1848]; "The Sect System," *Mercersburg Review* [1849]). He applied to the current condition of the church his theory of organic historical development which insisted upon the principle of continuity throughout the history of the church. Reflecting on this principle in the essays "Early Christianity" and "Cyprian" (1851–52), Nevin sharply contrasted Protestantism in its modern "Puritan" or evangelical form with the character of the ancient church as displayed in the creeds and the writings of the church fathers. According to Irenaeus, Tertullian, and Cyprian, the church is a supranatural constitution with a somatic, not just a spiritual, unity and catholicity, which are grounded in the apostolic episcopacy centered in the church at Rome. Ministry founded on this apostolic episcopacy is thus from above, and not, as in Puritanism, from below. The sacraments are not, as in Puritanism, mere signs of an inward grace but conveyors of an objective force. The question for Nevin was how to square modern Protestantism with the Christianity of the early church. On the other hand, he was not convinced that Roman Catholicism with its heteronomous papal authority that undercut human freedom, its Mariolatry, and the dogma of the Immaculate Conception, represented a true succession of the apostolic church.

By 1851–52, Nevin was undergoing a severe theological crisis, one that was no doubt exacerbated by exhaustion due to overwork required by his multiple duties. He resigned from his chair in the seminary in 1851 and from the presidency of Marshall College in 1853. He retired to wrestle with the church question unencumbered by teaching and administrative responsibilities. He continued, however, to write articles for the *Mercersburg Review* and to serve alongside Schaff on the committee to compose a new liturgy for the German Reformed Church. Eventually, he took up teaching once again at the recently founded Franklin and Marshall College in Lancaster, Pennsylvania, and finished his career as that school's president from 1866 to 1876.

The liturgy was the Mercersburg Theology's most concrete and lasting manifestation. It was designed as christocentric, based on the Apostles' Creed, eucharistically, not homiletically focused, with the altar, not the pulpit, as the visual center. Its intent was to be objective and historical, drawing on scripture and the best of the ancient and Reformation liturgies, and yet written in a current idiom.

Although this liturgical movement stirred up considerable opposition within the German Reformed Church at large because it was regarded as too Romanist, it eventually made its way into the regular order of worship of the denomination and was adopted by many congregations. Much of the substance of the Mercersburg liturgy entered into the *Evangelical and Reformed Book of Worship,* and elements remain in the *United Church of Christ Book of Worship.* The liturgy had some influence among the Dutch Reformed and Presbyterians in Scotland and the United States.

Apart from its impact on liturgical reform, the Mercersburg Theology probably gave some impetus to the emergence of a greater historical consciousness and confessional and sacramental renewal among Lutherans. Among Episcopalians, W. P. DuBose was moved toward his churchly phase by Mercersburg themes. Its views on the Eucharist likewise played a role in the debate on that subject among Presbyterians in the South. Yet, because it was a movement within a small denomination and ran counter to the evangelical mainstream, Mercersburg Theology exercised relatively little influence on the church and theology of its own time. More recently, it has been perceived as a forerunner of twentieth-century liturgical and sacramental renewal as well as of the Faith and Order movement with its efforts at ecumenical convergence in *Baptism, Eucharist and Ministry* and *Confessing the Apostolic Faith Today.*

Suggested Readings

Writings of John W. Nevin: *The Mystical Presence and Other Writings on the Eucharist,* ed. Bard Thompson and George H. Bricker (Philadelphia: United Church Press, 1966).

Arie Griffioen and Sam Hamstra, Jr., eds., *Reformed Confessionalism in Nineteenth Century America: Essays on the Thought of John Williamson Nevin* (Lanham, Md.: Scarecrow Press, 1996).

James H. Nichols, *Romanticism in American Theology* (Chicago: University of Chicago Press, 1961).

Philip Schaff

(1819–1893)

Klaus Penzel

The life of Philip Schaff provides a window into nearly a whole century of religious developments in both the United States and western Europe. For at the very heart of his professional self-understanding was his mission as an international mediator between the churches and Christian scholars on both sides of the Atlantic. For this mission his German education and American career and the increasing ease of transatlantic commerce and communication in the second half of the nineteenth century predestined him. Indeed, Schaff was one of the first to introduce American Protestants to the creative new thought of early nineteenth-century German culture, as represented by Friedrich Schleiermacher's theology, idealistic philosophy, and the new historiography associated with such names as Johann Gottfried von Herder, Leopold von Ranke, and G. W. F. Hegel. Swiss-born and educated at the universities of Tübingen, Halle, and Berlin, he arrived in this country in 1844. He taught for the next twenty years at the Mercersburg Seminary of the German Reformed Church in Pennsylvania and then, for the last twenty-three years of his life, at New York's Union Theological Seminary. At Union, especially, he demonstrated his remarkable erudition and versatility, as he successively occupied the chairs of Theological Encyclopedia and Christian Symbolics (1870), Hebrew (1873), Biblical Literature (1874), and Church History (1887).

Schaff's German years of study left a permanent mark on his theology. An emotional conversion experience in his youth prompted the lifelong conviction that the traditional supernaturalism of Christian dogma is securely anchored in the Christian's experience of Christ's saving presence. As a student he embraced the aims of the mediating theology *(Vermittlungstheologie)*, which sought to combine the inherited orthodox Christian tradition with the new intellectual currents of German Romanticism and Idealism. Schaff's American career is in fact best characterized as that

236

of a transplanted mediating theologian. Firmly grounded in biblical faith and historical Christianity, he eagerly absorbed the romantic-idealistic philosophy of history, which combined critical attention to the historical details and a philosophical approach to history centered in "ideas" as the necessary components of historical research and ultimately viewed all history as the revelation of God.

In two early publications—*What Is Church History?* (1846) and the section "General Introduction to Church History" of his *History of the Apostolic Church* (1853)—he presented an unequaled account (and the first in English) of German Protestant historiography which culminated in the work of his great teachers, Ferdinand Christian Baur and August Neander. Since the study of the history of the universal church was the study of the church itself, he declared church history to be theologically indispensable and ecumenically inclusive. The romantic-idealistic principle of historical development made it possible for him to view the principal historical types of Christianity as necessary stages, both logically and chronologically, in the dialectical evolution of biblical truth.

At the end of his German years of study, Schaff also embraced the ecumenical program of Berlin's Lutheran high-church party for the renewal of the church. Like his German mentors, he held contemporary Protestantism to be diseased because of its one-sided emphasis on the individual's piety or reason. The proposed cure was a churchly, sacramental, and liturgical renewal that would harvest what was best in the tradition of the universal church and in due time lead to the restoration of the unity of the church by ushering in an "evangelical catholicism," the grand synthesis of Protestantism and Roman Catholicism, both leaving behind their imperfections. Schaff always believed that the "diseases" of Roman Catholicism were papal absolutism and dogmatic authoritarianism.

Schaff first sounded this clarion call for a new reformation—a reformation, moreover, that will issue from the promising ferment of American Christianity—in *The Principle of Protestantism* (1845). He advocated dialectically both the recovery of the historical foundations and Catholic traditions of the past and progress toward ecumenical goals under the guidance of God's Spirit. This characteristic dialectic distinguished Schaff's theological program from kindred movements, such as the Anglo-Catholic revival in the Church of England and the exclusive Lutheran confessionalism in Germany and the United States, as well as the eclectic approach of ecumenical programs such as Samuel S. Schmucker's *Fraternal Appeal to the American Churches* (1838). Schaff's provocative fusion of a high-church pietism and the romantic-idealistic philosophy of history was his contribution to the Mercersburg Theology.

Schaff's theological position was bound to clash with what he perceived to be the biblicism, individualism, virulent anti-Catholicism, and antihistorical mentality of antebellum evangelical Protestantism. But in the end Schaff helped further its transformation into the postbellum evangelicalism, which became increasingly "liberal" and "ecumenical." For it was increasingly informed by those new German modes of thought, especially the historical consciousness and temper of German culture, which Schaff himself had done so much to transport across the Atlantic. As he assumed the role of a leading representative of America's liberal and cooperative evangelical Protestantism during the New York years of his career, his theology evolved still further. A collection of wide-ranging essays, *Christ and Christianity* (1885), is representative of that later stage, when Schaff thought of himself as a "broad-churchman." He was now content to subdue the task of theology to the maintenance of a minimal set of orthodox doctrinal principles and to their conciliatory application, readily mitigating doctrinal differences between the churches. After all, he had always held that the spiritual reality behind theological conceptuality is primary and essential. More than ever, he distinguished himself by his ability to combine scholarship and active churchmanship. And four principal motifs—the biblical, historical, ecumenical, and apologetic—gave final form and direction to his life's work.

Eager to adapt the orthodox creeds of Calvinism to nineteenth-century evangelical sensibilities, he worked, though unsuccessfully, toward a consensus creed in the setting of the World Alliance of Reformed Churches and toward a revision of the Westminster Confession in the Presbyterian Church, which he had joined in 1870. Underlying the *Creeds of Christendom* (3 vols., 1877)—to this day an unsurpassed collection of the historic creeds—was his advocacy of a conservative creedal union which would accept all the historic creeds as complementary landmarks of the Christian faith, for creedal formulations are relative to their time and hence only partial manifestations of Christian truth. Only the Apostles' Creed he held to be permanently embedded in the foundation of the universal church. He contributed in numerous ways to the Evangelical Alliance, viewing it as the chief instrument at hand for evangelical Protestants in the quest for Christian unity. He pioneered the contemporary ecumenical concept of "conciliar fellowship," for he envisioned a visible unity, on a global scale and inclusive of Eastern Orthodoxy, Roman Catholicism, and the churches of Protestantism, where each church may continue its historical distinctiveness and tradition, though all remain open to new reformations prompted by God's Spirit.

Two early publications were representative of his mission to internationalize the theology of evangelical Protestantism: *America: A Sketch of the Political, Religious, and Social Character of the United States* (English trans., 1855), originating as a series of lectures to German audiences, and *Germany: Its Universities, Theology, and Religion* (1857). Later he edited the American adaptation of Johann Peter Lange's voluminous German Bible commentary, *A Commentary on the Holy Scriptures: Critical, Doctrinal, and Homiletical* (25 vols., 1864–80), the first comprehensive and complete English-language Bible commentary. He prepared the American edition of a storehouse of the scholarship of Germany's mediating theology, *Realencyklopädie für Theologie und Kirche*, which, after a later revision, became known as the *New Schaff-Herzog Encyclopedia of Religious Knowledge* (12 vols., 1908–14). He presided over an interdenominational committee of American scholars who cooperated with British scholars in the first official revision of the King James Version of the English Bible (1872–84).

As a biblical scholar he excelled in the minutiae of textual criticism; however, he rejected the "higher criticism" of German biblical scholarship. But even though Lange's Commentary clung tenaciously to a precritical supernaturalistic viewpoint and soon represented a superannuated position, by concentrating the attention of his many collaborators on German biblical scholarship Schaff played a strong role in the development of biblical studies in the United States.

Schaff's most widely read book, *The Person of Christ* (1865), which was a popular version of Karl Ullmann's *The Sinlessness of Christ* (English trans., 1858 and 1870), developed apologetically a Christology "from below" by attempting to demonstrate the perfection of Christ's humanity as the most persuasive argument for sustaining the traditional belief in Christ's divinity. Schaff spent the last ten years of his life bringing out the final edition of his *History of the Christian Church,* which solidified his reputation as August Neander's greatest follower. In 1888, he founded the American Society of Church History. Stimulating patristic, medieval, and Reformation studies and proposing comprehensive interpretative categories for illuminating the history and unique character of American Christianity, he left a lasting legacy as a church historian. His last address, "The Reunion of Christendom," delivered at the World's Parliament of Religions in Chicago in 1893, was a grand summary of his life's work as biblical scholar, church historian, apologist of evangelical Christianity and, most of all, ecumenical visionary and pioneer who helped to prepare the ground for the Federal Council of Churches and anticipated many of the ecumenical efforts, issues, and structures of our time.

Taken as a whole, Schaff's theological program issued from the unique confluence of German and American traditions and is best characterized as a progressive orthodoxy or liberal evangelicalism that was given special distinction by his dual vision of an "evangelical catholicism" and the "internationalization of theology."

Suggested Readings

Henry Warner Bowden, ed., *A Century of Church History: The Legacy of Philip Schaff* (Carbondale and Edwardsville: Southern Illinois University Press, 1988).

Klaus Penzel, ed., *Philip Schaff: Historian and Ambassador of the Universal Church—Selected Writings* (Macon, Ga.: Mercer University Press, 1991).

David S. Schaff, *The Life of Philip Schaff, in Part Autobiographical* (New York: Charles Scribner, 1897).

George H. Shriver, Jr., *Philip Schaff: Christian Scholar and Ecumenical Prophet* (Macon, Ga.: Mercer University Press, 1987).

Isaac Hecker

(1819–1888)

R. Scott Appleby

Born in New York City to German immigrants, Isaac Hecker was by turns a restless soul, a spiritual pilgrim, the founder of a religious community, a mystic, a theologian and philosopher of history, and a visionary whose contested intellectual legacy sparked a major controversy in the Roman Catholic Church. In life he was best known as the founder of the Congregation of the Missionary Priests of St. Paul the Apostle, the first United States Roman Catholic male religious order. In death Hecker became the inspiration for a generation of French and American priests whose celebration of church-state separation, religious liberty, and other tenets of modern American republicanism provoked the papal condemnation of "Americanism" (a.k.a. "Heckerism") in 1899.

Baptized a Lutheran, Hecker as a child was introduced to the Wesleyan perfectionist movement by his mother, a devout Methodist. Many years later, however, he claimed he was raised "with no positive religion at all." After a brief stint attending public school and several years working at his brothers' bakery, Hecker left home at the age of twenty-two to join the Transcendentalist utopian community at New England's Brook Farm. He made this monumental decision after experiencing what historian David J. O'Brien calls "perhaps the central moment" of his life, a dramatic religious conversion which Hecker later described as an angelic visitation. The experience convinced him of a special calling, an impression of Hecker shared by Orestes A. Brownson, the famous Boston editor and reformer, who was also in the midst of a spiritual journey characterized by a rejection of Protestant religiosity. Brownson and Hecker, who formed a lifelong association, were received into the Catholic Church the same year, 1844. Where Brownson remained a layman, Hecker was ordained to the priesthood in 1849.

Influenced by post-Kantian Idealism and the current of Romanticism flowing through American religion, Hecker was convinced that America's political and cultural values, including religious liberty, had prepared the way for a new age of the Holy Spirit. Thus he founded the Paulists in 1858 as an innovative Catholic missionary society which eschewed religious vows and devoted itself to the evangelization and conversion of non-Catholics in the United States (rather than to the sacramental and catechetical needs of hundreds of thousands of newly arrived Catholic immigrants). Yet Hecker himself conducted parish missions to Catholics throughout the country after 1858, and his Paulist colleagues soon found it necessary to focus their pastoral attentions on Catholic immigrants. Hecker also served as a theological consultant to Archbishop Martin John Spalding at the Second Plenary Council of Baltimore (1866) and the First Vatican Council (1869–70). As leader of the Paulists he published the *Catholic World,* a journal of religious thought and opinion, and established the Catholic Publication Society to distribute low-cost apologetical and spiritual tracts.

In his principal writings Hecker crafted a new presentation of Catholicism directed to middle-class and upper-class Americans. In *Questions of the Soul* (1855), *Aspirations of Nature* (1857), and a series of significant essays (anthologized as *The Church and the Age,* 1887), he presented the church's sacramental and spiritual tradition as the objective correlate to the subjective search for meaning characteristic of most American lives.

Questions of the Soul established Hecker as a nationally prominent spokesman for the burgeoning Roman Catholic Church. The treatise began by noting how the American character—liberated from the prejudices of the past and freed to follow reason, trust intuition, and accept the guidance of "the affections of the heart"—reflected the deepest truths about human nature. Hecker then attempted to demonstrate his central thesis: Catholicism, because it possessed the ultimate wisdom about human nature, was the true destiny of the United States as a religious society. From his own religious past Hecker retrieved the language of the American "seeker" and transformed it into a Catholic prayer. Replacing Emersonian "self-reliance" with "the humility to obey," and "self-culture" with self-denial and surrender to God, Hecker portrayed Catholicism as the fulfillment of the highest American ideals and the one cultural force capable of genuine transcendence.

Embracing Catholicism's comprehensive soteriology (plan of redemption) and organic social vision, Hecker rejected Protestantism as theologically inadequate to the spiritual needs of the United States. In most of his preaching and writing Hecker, unlike Brownson, avoided polemics, preferring to emphasize the common ground shared by Catholics and Protestants; in his diary, however, he portrayed Protestantism as a moribund, irrelevant, and erroneous religion of "individualism and antagonistic selfishness."

Yet Hecker was also uneasy with the theocratic ambitions of Catholic triumphalists who yearned for a restoration of the church's privileged position in the state. To him, a "Catholic America" meant something far more extraordinary: a providential era in which the Holy Spirit would lead all Americans, Catholics and non-Catholics alike, to an orderly consensus and a universal brotherhood based on an interior experience of the Holy Spirit. This interior experience, Hecker taught, confirmed the same message of natural rights and natural laws proclaimed by the church and in historical events. America's religious pluralism was a temporary necessity; eventually, he wrote in *Aspirations of Nature,* the country of the future would require a common faith to express its common experience of God and realize its true promise.

In other words, Hecker's vision was universalist and eschatological rather than merely political or religious. The advent of a truly Catholic America would reveal the underlying spiritual unity between the "externals" of the Catholic faith—its sacraments, hierarchy, and institutions—and the immediate presence of the Holy Spirit in each individual soul. Ironically, however, Hecker was less concerned with externals than with reaching out to the elite unchurched Yankees, to other "earnest seekers," and to individual middle-class Catholics. In regulating the spiritual discipline of the Paulists, he discarded many of the traditional rules and observances of religious orders and encouraged his followers to be attentive to the mainstream of American cultural and social life.

Hecker's expectation of a millennial harvest of American souls for a renewed and spiritualized Catholicism seemed utopian in the context of the ecclesial politics of his era. Far from embracing the modern world, the church was retreating into a fortress mentality and strengthening its exclusivist institutional boundaries. In 1870, after the First Vatican Council defined the doctrine of papal infallibility, Hecker attempted to put the best possible face on the decision, interpreting it as the necessary means of securing the external forms of the faith and thereby making way for a new age of the Spirit and freedom of conscience in individual lives. Privately, however, Hecker was depressed by Vatican I and the triumph of ultramontanism (papal autocracy) it represented; afterward, he took an extended convalescence in Europe, effectively ignoring his responsibilities as religious superior of the Paulist community in the United States.

A complex, brilliant, isolated, and ultimately misunderstood man who kept his own counsel, Hecker was an unlikely founder of a religious order much less of an international reform movement. His experiences of mystical prayer, coupled with long episodes of introspection and inattention to organizational matters, suited his temperament but detached him from the pressing demands of religious leadership. In the hands of devoted but less-talented Paulists such as Augustine Hewit, Hecker's second-in-command, and Walter Elliott, his official biographer, the delicate and finely interwoven elements of Hecker's thought unraveled; the founder's nuanced liberalism became a crude Americanism and a triumphalist Catholicism.

Indeed, it was the French translation of Elliott's biography, *The Life of Father Hecker* (1891), which extended and slightly distorted Hecker's legacy. Lacking formal training in systematic theology and philosophy, Hecker never really devised a consistent theology of the Holy Spirit. This left Hecker vulnerable, posthumously, to the French conservative Charles Maignen's charges that he embraced Illuminism (the direct revelation from God to the individual soul) and a "Protestant emphasis on freedom." No one familiar with Hecker's own ideas, rather than those of his Americanist interpreters Archbishop John Ireland and Father Felix Klein, would have suggested that "Heckerism" involved denigration of the sacramental mediation of the church, the supernatural virtues, or the contemplative life. Nonetheless, these were among the most serious charges made in *Testem benevolentiae* (1899), Pope Leo XIII's condemnation of ideas attributed to Hecker and clustered under the label "Americanism."

Hecker has been claimed as a prophet of the type of modern Catholicism affirmed in the Second Vatican Council (1962–65), but it is more accurate to say that he was the first prominent Roman Catholic thinker to develop and popularize a providential view of the United States. The continuing debate over how the Catholic Church should respond to America's special place in salvation history is perhaps Isaac Hecker's most enduring legacy.

Suggested Readings

Writings of Isaac Hecker: *The Church and the Age* (New York: Catholic Publication Society, 1887).

Walter Elliott, *The Life of Father Hecker* (New York: Arno Press, 1972; repr. of original ed.).

David J. O'Brien, *Isaac Hecker: An American Catholic* (Mahwah, N.J.: Paulist Press, 1992).

William Portier, *Isaac Hecker and the First Vatican Council* (Lewiston, N.Y.: Edwin Mellen, 1985).

POST–CIVIL WAR AND NEW INTELLECTUAL FRONTIER

(1866–1918)

INTRODUCTION

Mark G. Toulouse and James O. Duke

American historians still have difficulty reviewing the ebb and flow of American life without breaking it in some significant way at the Civil War. Of course, it is not true that the fateful event made all things new. Continuities existed in matters economic, political, and religious, as postwar leaders in all these areas tried to pick up the pieces of their lives and rally their constituencies to carry on as before. Yet the devastation and divisions caused by the war combined with other strong forces, cultural and intellectual, to challenge the status quo in ways impossible to imagine just a decade or so earlier. Christian theology, pressed into service by all parties involved in or affected by the conflict, certainly was not immune to the forces swirling around it afterward.

The context for theology had changed dramatically. Even before the war, hopes for an evangelical empire crashed headlong into the reality of sectional schisms among its three chief denominational representatives (Baptists, Methodists, and Presbyterians). The holy war of words waged by religious leaders on both sides was not easily forgotten once the passion of battle had passed. During the era of Reconstruction, Northern leaders intensified feelings of hurt among Southern whites as they pressed their agendas on the churches with little willingness to heed the voices of "defeated foes." Regionalized forms of church life maintained hard lines and although divided and disheartened, the churches remained energetic enough to find new ways to fight.

If coping with their own divisions was not challenge enough, evangelicals faced still tougher challenges from other postwar developments. African American Christians enjoyed new freedoms but suffered new racist indignities. The mixed situation translated quickly into a vital and independent theology, addressing the needs of the people in the pew. The rise of a politically active church helped blacks in the struggle to survive in a segregationist age and to challenge the theological dogma of white supremacy.

Immigration added to the stress experienced by white American Protestants. Some twenty-five million immigrants arrived between 1865 and 1915, and vast numbers of them were Catholics who hailed from eastern and southern Europe. New Englanders learned the meaning of diversity and did not like it much, forming anti-immigration associations to stave it off. At the same time, migration at home moved westward. The once-dominant Protestant churches rededicated themselves to Christianization and civilization, which they viewed more or less as synonymous tasks. Native Americans were displaced; railroads, industries, cities, and churches were built, and fifteen new states were formed before 1912.

Rapid urbanization and industrialization caught the churches off guard, comfortable as they had been with rural and small-town surroundings. In the early years, they had little to offer other than knee-jerk responses to the explosive growth of the cities. In his best-selling book *Our Country,* Josiah Strong, Congregational minister and leading social critic, could list seven perils of the city, the majority of them linked in one way or another to Catholicism. The increasing concentration of wealth produced an underclass of exploited laborers overwhelmed by sheer poverty and despairing of ever finding a better life. Some preachers emphasized the opportunities for success, promising truly hard-working Christians "acres of diamonds," as one popular preacher of the period put it. At times others set forth warnings and proposals about the "right" relationship of theology and society. Still others preached a message envisioning the end times, when the problems of the world would be no more. Late in the century, violent struggles between labor and capital symbolized the deep problems etched into the social structure by the inequitable distribution of national wealth.

Tripling its population by the turn of the century, and bolstered by popular theological links between American goodness and divine mandate (manifest destiny), the nation flexed its muscle as a world power for the first time in 1898, acquiring the Philippines in its first imperial venture as a colonial power. The size of the world was shrinking even as the power of a few wealthy nations was increasing. As America's economic influence reached into new corners of the world, the church tagged along with the gospel. Earnest missionary efforts covered the globe, and as the churches encountered non-Christian religions face-to-face, they gradually developed new theological understandings of faith, church, and mission. Near the end of the century, 1893, the World Parliament of Religions brought together in one city, Chicago, representatives of nearly every great world religion. In light of such experiences, American Protestants tempered denominational pride with ecumenically shared commitment, working cooperatively in spite of their divisions by forming cooperative bodies such as the Federal Council of Churches of Christ in America (1908) and participating in an ecumenical missionary movement.

These post–Civil War developments certainly provided a strikingly different context for theological work in America. Perhaps, however, the most important forces operating on American theology during these days were those stemming from intellectual, rather than merely cultural, developments. An ideological polarity (science vs. religion) found its way into the swirling mix of cultural polarities (rich-poor, North-South, East-West, black-white, Protestant-Catholic, rural urban, citizen-immigrant). These were years of open and sustained confrontation between scientific inquiry and long-standing religious worldviews. New trends in inquiry—experience-based "developmental" accounts in natural science, philosophy, and the emerging social sciences—stressed that everything changes, even "changeless" religious truth.

Theology prior to the Civil War rested primarily in the hands of ordained ministers, who moved freely from pulpit to seminary rostrum to teach the basic religious-moral truths of the Bible. Few made a career of theological scholarship. Fewer still doubted the biblical story of creation. Those who did were easily written off as tainted by currents of "modern" skepticism or infidelity prized by European rationalists, especially in Germany's universities. Darwin's groundbreaking work on evolution challenged Christian theories of creation and human origin, and its origin in England and accessibility in English made it a book that was not easily ignored. Theology now had to deal with the findings of science more seriously than ever before. For many religious Americans, the situation seemed to pose an either-or: either science or faith. Protestant appeals to the literal meaning of the Bible, once mounted against fallible churchly traditions, were redirected toward the "pretensions" of scientific thinking. Other minister-theologians, however, interpreted the new context as an opportunity to redefine the task and results of theology itself; they devoted themselves to bridging the gap between scientific reason and Christian revelation, seeking to adapt the methods or ideas of science, development, and progress into their theological reflection.

The emergence of the new scientific disciplines transformed university life in America. Previously religious educational institutions, the ivy league schools for example, confined the study of religion to one department even as they expanded their curriculum to include anthropology, psychology, and sociology—all disciplines providing scientific answers to questions previously handled by religion alone. Public (and hence "secular") universities spread, and there "theological" questions and answers could be safely ignored in formal instruction as matters of uninformed opinion or personal feeling. The study of history, including religious history, became more a scientific endeavor than a religious one. Before long, the scientific study of religion itself, complete with accompanying critical and comparative studies of the relationship of Christianity to other world religions, posed a new threat to the comfort levels of Christians everywhere.

The study of the Bible became the new frontline in what seemed to many to be the "warfare" between science and religion. With the credibility of theology at stake, some theologians began to transform the theological enterprise by incorporating aspects of the scientific methodology. Questions about the reliability and authority of the Bible, typically blunted in years past by accusing questioners of skepticism or unbelief and overcome by fresh appeals to the excellencies of the Bible itself, could no longer be handled so readily. Textual ("lower") criticism had long had a place in American biblical studies, but historical or "higher" criticism went far beyond seeking the original, and presumably authoritative, wording of the texts. The higher critics asked the same, broadly framed questions relating to the authorship, dating, composition, cultural backgrounds, and accuracy of the biblical texts as historians asked of other bodies of literature.

In the midst of these changes, theology emerged as a much more highly specialized field of scholarship encompassing a much more highly diversified collection of scholarly disciplines. Although there were minister-theologians, scholarly popularizers of theology, and unscholarly theologians in abundance, defining a "true theologian" became increasingly difficult and controversial. Some with reputations as the most learned in the study of the Christian religion were suspected (and on occasion, formally charged) by church people of being neither truly Christian nor truly religious. In other cases, those esteemed as church leaders and loyalists were scorned by some as unschooled if not hopelessly ignorant with regard to the "serious" study of theology.

The development of divinity schools and seminaries fitfully followed two lines, those friendly to the scientific turns in theology, and those mightily opposed to them. Increasing numbers of American theologians studied abroad and brought back the scientific, "liberal" perspectives they found there. This new theology, as it came to be called, helped to tear the fabric of evangelical Protestantism into opposing camps, liberal and conservative, with considerable variety characterizing all sides of the resulting debates.

Women found the new developments in theology somewhat liberating. Some of the most "liberal" churches started to relax their restrictions against women's leadership; some of the most "conservative," such as the Holiness and Pentecostal movements, acknowledged that spiritual gifts were not gender-specific. A few women became founders of religious movements reflective of Christian impulses but distinctly new by comparison with established churches.

Our makers of theology during this period represent most of these unfolding trends. After the Civil War, African Americans—former slaves as well as free blacks—emerged as powerful theological voices both within predominantly white denominations and apart from those structures in the black churches. The Christian theology they set forth was by no means monolithic, but it was shaped nonetheless by a common conviction that true Christian faith could uncover and nourish a sense of God-given worthiness among a people oppressed by the ruling powers of this world and provide them spiritual resources for their continuing struggle for liberation.

Frederick Douglass, born a slave, found from scripture in his own way, as Nat Turner did in his, a condemnation of servitude and a calling to new life. Escaping to freedom, he was in some ways a syncretist in matters religious, committed to a biblical vision of shalom and salvation and for that very reason appreciative of the "amazing grace" coming by way of his companions in slavery and critical of much of the so-called Christianity proclaimed by complacent whites. His sermons, addresses, and writings—especially his journal—illustrated the autobiographical style of theology prevalent among African Americans: One's theological witness to God is made as much, indeed more, by a life struggling to express God's justice against the enormous odds of oppression than by abstract arguments about abstract ideas. Alexander Crummell represented a theology of discontent as a black leader in the white-dominated Protestant Episcopal Church. Fueled by the liberal tendencies to have faith in progress, Crummell urged blacks toward the development of self-love and inner character, believing these to be essential elements in the fight to defeat racism and prejudice. Bishop Henry McNeal Turner expressed his leadership in black theology through a deep commitment to the African American church, the African Methodist Episcopal Church particularly. Rejecting the Eurocentric American patterns of theology and setting the precedent for black theology to come, he challenged the assumption of a white God among whites or any other Christians by theologizing about a black God.

During these years, a substantial number of white theologians devoted their lives to mediating the conflicts so evident in postwar American life. Among these early mediating theologians of faith and culture, Henry Boynton Smith stands out as one of the first of America's Evangelical Protestants to study in Germany. His experience helped him to provide leadership in shifting American theology away from the ideas associated with Scottish Common-Sense Realism toward those represented by contemporary European thought. This shift included a new christocentric focus, as opposed to the classically theocentric one, and a movement away from the all-controlling debate between divine sovereignty and human agency. As ministers, one in the evangelical mainstream and the other in the Unitarian Church, Henry Ward Beecher and James Freeman Clarke sought in their own ways to mediate the tension Christians experienced as they struggled to relate faith in God to the awesome changes in their cultural and intellectual landscape.

The appearance of the social sciences had a profound effect on the development of theological themes in this period. Representing a very early form of "scientific modernism" in their approach to theological issues, some thinkers heartily embraced the new scientific disciplines born during these years. Theology witnessed, for example, the start of a new pragmatic school, embodied particularly in the work of William James and Josiah Royce. The age of conflict between science and religion produced great anxieties. Both of these men, while affirming the eternal connectedness between science and religion, illustrated a theological shift away from creeds toward an empirical and psychological study of the pragmatic benefits of human religious experience, both individual (James) and communal (Royce). Borden Parker Bowne, Mary Baker Eddy, and Rufus Jones, though vastly different in the conclusions they reached, wove together, in their own significant ways, themes from Christian faith with various elements borrowed from the emerging social sciences.

More distinctly evangelical and church-oriented in their approaches to the integration of science and religion than the early modernists, but committed to the endeavor nonetheless, a number of theologians created a new stripe of evangelical, or churchly, liberalism. The first woman ordained by mainstream Protestantism, Antoinette Brown Blackwell, a liberal spirit moving more and more in the direction of Unitarianism, wrote prolifically on metaphysical themes connecting Christian faith and the latest scientific theories. Standing in the middle of the storm over biblical authority, William Porcher DuBose and Charles Augustus Briggs combined a passion for evangelical faith with foundational theological work in biblical studies growing out of the latest methods of scientific inquiry. The shift in America to German theological influences is obviously central to their work; Briggs spent three years studying in Germany.

Sharing their approach to the Bible, but working primarily in theology, pastor-theologians Newman Smyth and William Newton Clarke set forth the earliest and most complete systematic expressions of evangelical liberalism (Clarke's book passed through some twenty editions by the end of the period). Smyth arrived in Germany to study just as Briggs was completing his work there. The careers of both Briggs and Clarke serve well as symbolic of the transition affecting the writing of theology during this period: the shift from primarily the work of pastor-theologians to that of full-time academic and professional theologians, as evidenced by most of the theological writing in the next generation.

Finally, there were still other evangelicals who concentrated their theological efforts on the ethical issues affecting their time. The activities of Methodist Frances Elizabeth Willard illustrate how some forms of conservative evangelical theology found active expression in various reform movements of this period and were transformed in the process. She worked tirelessly on behalf of temperance and the equality of women, often fighting her own denomination's social conservatism on the latter issue. Both Washington Gladden and Walter Rauschenbusch are more representative of the heart of evangelical liberalism as they addressed social questions. Gladden developed a popularized version of the Social Gospel from his firsthand pastoral experience in dealing with the problems of the poor, prayed for one day of the week and preyed upon the other six. Rauschenbusch, German trained as a theologian and church historian, systematized the Social Gospel by combining concern for individual salvation with an equal desire to seek social salvation. As in the case of many other theologians of this period, Gladden and Rauschenbusch were mediating theologians who sought to bridge the gap between church and culture, between theology and the social sciences, between personal religion and social responsibility, between the theology of their own generation and the theology of the next.

The conservative response to the cultural and intellectual developments after the Civil War varied considerably, as is evident in the different theological approaches of Edgar Young Mullins and Benjamin B. Warfield. Uncomfortable with the Calvinist themes found in much of Southern Baptist life, Mullins modeled an experiential approach to theology, heavily influenced by Schleiermacher's emphasis on Christian experience in defining the meaning and claims of the Christian faith. Though influenced as well by the burgeoning studies in the psychology of religion, Mullins

251

remained passionately critical of the move to replace the supernatural assumptions of Christian faith with the natural assumptions of science. Science had its place in its own sphere but it must not tread on Christian ground.

Warfield, on the other hand, worked hard to keep the Calvinist fires burning in conservative circles. Also very active in the biblical debates of his time, Warfield's critical and extensive defense of the inerrancy of the biblical "autographs" played a role in the heresy trial of Charles A. Briggs and served the next generation of fundamentalism in its battles with modernism. In this age of science, heavily dependent on European research and scholarship, Warfield held out for the old-line alliance of Reformed orthodoxy and Scottish common-sense realism. Like Mullins, Warfield was critical of naturalistic presuppositions; unlike Mullins', his system made room for the evolutionary hypothesis. He also criticized the period's general reliance upon religious experience as a source for theological reflection, something well represented in Mullins' own theology.

Other Christian groups during this period formed their theology by emphasizing millennial themes and dissenting from more conventional conservative involvements. The anxiety created by this age filled with conflict and polarities caused many Christians to long for the end of history itself. One particularly strong current in the conservative stream is represented in the dispensational theology of Cyrus I. Scofield. His influence flowed across denominational lines and affected many Christians in denominations where some fairly strong liberal currents existed as well.

New millennial Christian movements gathered on fertile ground near these more-traditional apocalyptic waters. The theological creativity of Ellen Gould Harmon White resolved the cognitive dissonance associated with the Millerite disappointment to form the Seventh Day Adventist Church. Meanwhile, Charles Taze Russell rejected both higher criticism and Calvinism. After an encounter with Adventism, he developed a complex interpretation of prophetic passages to herald the second coming of Christ and the soon-to-come end of the world. Thus, Jehovah's Witnesses were born. Mormonism, born a generation earlier as a millennialist form of primitivist Christianity, had now to deal with the problems of a second generation. As modern theological insights appeared, the movement spawned many Mormonisms, illustrating that even the most tightly knit of Christian groups were not immune to the challenges posed by the new social and intellectual frontier.

Frederick Augustus Douglass

(1818–1895)

Will Coleman

If one's theological perspective can be traced in one's story, Frederick Augustus Douglass is an exemplary model of how theology and autobiography are interconnected. Like Augustine of Hippo, Douglass understood that his faith journey was directed by the hands of a force greater than himself. Like Athanasius, another North African, Douglass fled into exile several times to avoid persecution within a nation baptized in the civil religion of Christendom but without the moral will to ensure freedom with equality for its citizens. Above all, like Moses, Douglass became a representative of a people who struggled to overcome slavery and gain self-respect. In the several autobiographies of his eventful life, Douglass fashioned a narrative which claims a sense of God, self, and peoplehood within the context of slavery, freedom, and the struggle for equality.

Frederick Augustus Bailey was born a slave on a Talbot County, Maryland, plantation in February 1818. Years later, while escaping from slavery, he changed his surname to Douglass. This date of birth was discovered after his death. Like most slaves, he did not know his exact age. Searching without success for his birth date, he finally concluded the year to have been 1817. For him, knowledge of one's birth date constituted knowledge of self. Although he failed to discover his exact date of birth, and therefore, this sense of self, he nevertheless created a place for himself in the broader context of American history vis-à-vis its racial attitudes and practices toward African Americans.

Bailey's first master owned more than 500 slaves, including Douglass' grandmother and mother. He viewed his grandmother, Betsy Bailey, who reared him until he was sold into slavery, as a "priestess." Harriet Bailey, his mother, was only vaguely known to him. She had been sold to another owner and, able to visit her son only four or five times, died before he was nine. The identity of his father, who was white, was never made known to him.

In 1826, Bailey was sent to Baltimore. This was an important event in his life: He felt "chosen" by Providence. He grew confident that God's hand was upon his life and he was being selected for something better than chattel slavery. For a while this was verified. In the home of Hugh and Sophia Auld he was treated like a human being instead of property. Mistress Sophia began teaching him at age ten how to read and write. The instruction lasted about a year until Hugh objected that education would arouse other desires within Bailey, including that for freedom. He was correct; Bailey had already discovered the power found in the gift of words. He secured a copy of Webster's speller, mastered the alphabet, and by age twelve he could read. After purchasing a copy of the *Columbian Orator* he was on his way to becoming an orator himself.

Early on, Bailey noted how prayer and singing provided insight into the dehumanization of slaves and their desire for liberation. In 1831 he was converted at a prayer meeting. Already he had been influenced by a Reverend Hanson, a white Methodist. A black man, Charles Johnson, taught him the importance of prayer in preparing for conversion. But it was "Uncle" Lawson, a pious slave, who became his mentor and spiritual father. Lawson not only reinforced the fourteen-year-old's appreciation for the hand of God directing his life but gave him an experientially based theological framework for understanding the difference between the Christianity professed by most southern whites and that practiced by "the poor" like Uncle Lawson.

That sense was soon tested. A year after his conversion, at age fifteen, Bailey was sent to Edward Covey, a well-known slave breaker who humiliated Bailey with hard labor and severe beatings until finally, in desperation, he fought back and to his surprise Covey backed off. One additional note is that Bailey possessed a good luck charm for protection against Covey. This item had been given to him by another slave, Sandy Jenkins, the "root doctor," a practitioner of African American folk magic. Although Bailey ascribed his success to the use of his own willpower against that of Covey's, Jenkins was quick to remind him that hoodoo also had a hand in the matter. The incident illustrates the attraction toward syncretism in slave religion.

Like many other slaves, Bailey had heard of Nat Turner, the charismatic African American Baptist preacher in Virginia and leader of a rebellion against white oppression. Inspired by his interpretation of biblical passages, Turner had seen visions of judgment and justice rendered against white slaveholders. Turner believed God was calling him to lead an army against these evildoers and to free enslaved African Americans. Fifty-seven men, women, and children died in the rebellion. Turner was captured, hanged, and flayed, and throughout the South a ban was placed on all meetings by slaves (including praying and preaching) without white supervision. No doubt inspired by Turner and his own hard-earned ability to read, Bailey formed a secret school along with several other slaves. Together, they made plans to escape, but were betrayed in their effort. The local whites demanded that they be lynched. Instead, Thomas Auld sent him to work at a Baltimore shipyard. In time (1831), it became his port of entry into freedom. In 1838 he married a freedwoman, Anna Murray, after she helped him escape slavery from Delaware to Philadelphia.

In order to avoid capture as a fugitive slave, Frederick Augustus Bailey changed his surname to Douglass (after a character in Walter Scott's *Lady of the Lake*). From Philadelphia he went to New Bedford, Massachusetts. There he associated with Quakers and their "antislavery church," known for their nonviolent resistance to the institution of slavery and their involvement in the development of the underground railroad. Douglass befriended William Lloyd Garrison, an abolitionist, member of the American Anti-Slavery Society, and editor of the *Liberator,* the premier abolitionist newsletter of the day. Joining the Society's speakers circuit at twenty-four, Douglass became a symbol of the horrors of slavery and model of the cultured humanity that freedom could eventually bring to a former slave. He also gained firsthand experience of prejudice and discrimination during his travels in the North. People who were initially amazed by his ability to speak became disturbed by his eloquence, wishing him to speak in the stereotyped dialect of a "darkie" rather than with his distinctive diction. Even some of his white colleagues encouraged him to leave the thinking to them. Insult was added to injury when his former slave status was challenged altogether. In 1845, he published his first autobiography. Despite risk of capture, he used real names and places in order to substantiate his story. He now understood that his testimony had to be shared in his own words and style as a witness to his God-given responsibility to discover his own voice.

That same year, the Antislavery Society sponsored Douglass to undertake a speaking tour in Britain. He was amazed by the "absence of prejudice." In his speeches he waged war against American hypocrisy. Newspapers in the United States responded by labeling him an extremist. His British friends purchased his freedom from Thomas Auld for 150 English pounds. After two years of exile, he returned to the States as a freedman and with his family moved to Rochester, New York. Inspired, he started his own paper, the *North Star,* in Boston with funds raised by

British friends. Garrison opposed this idea, and hence Douglass began to move away from Garrison and the "antislavery church" in order to reshape the discussion about slavery and express his own, more radical position. Moral suasion was, in his view, only one method for securing freedom and respectful citizenry. Force and resistance were other options. Two points of tension led to a break between Douglass and Garrison in 1849: the use of the Constitution to fight slavery and the leadership of the antislavery movement itself. While Garrison believed that the Constitution supported slavery, Douglass held that its principles should be used to tear down the institution. In addition, Douglass increasingly felt that the antislavery movement should be led by blacks, with a black voice—in other words, blacks should be at the forefront of their own struggle for freedom.

Events surrounding the national debate of 1850 over the admission of new states as free or slaveholding states and passage of the "Fugitive Slave Act" put all African Americans at risk of enslavement or recapture. In response, Douglass encouraged self-defense in order to ensure black freedom. Like Harriet Tubman, "the black Moses," he also became personally active in the underground railroad. In a historic speech of 1852 (which he insisted on delivering on the 5th instead of the 4th of July), Douglass attacked the nation's hypocrisy and barbarism with respect to liberty, equality, and African Americans. The 1857 Dred Scott Decision, which denied that blacks had any civil rights that whites should honor, confirmed his burning critique of the popular understanding of citizenry, liberty, and equality. Douglass again called on blacks to respond with moral, and if necessary, physical resistance. Where Sojourner Truth, another great African American abolitionist, was committed to the Quaker strategy of nonviolence, Douglass had concluded that liberation from oppressors who called themselves Christians could not be achieved solely through rhetoric: Faith in God and armed resistance had to be an option for blacks, especially in the wake of white repression.

In the early fall of 1859, Douglass met secretly with John Brown, a radical white millennialist who believed himself called by God to participate in the black liberation struggle. Douglass discouraged Brown from undertaking his ill-fated attack on Harpers Ferry. But Brown proceeded with his plan, and was captured and executed. Implicated in the plot in a letter written by Brown, Douglass fled, first to Canada and then England. Returning after the death of his second daughter, he was granted amnesty.

Although Abraham Lincoln is often seen as the Negro's friend, Douglass viewed him in biblical terms as a man much like Pharaoh. Lincoln contended that whites and blacks were completely different, and his original preference was to ship blacks back to Africa. He became engaged in the politics of emancipation only reluctantly after 1860. Douglass opposed this idea strongly; he wanted black freedom to take place within the so-called Promised Land, not through removal from it. African Americans had every right to be here as did their white counterparts, and with God's help, they were going to fight for it. Consequently, Douglass welcomed the coming of the Civil War and the 1862 announcement of the Emancipation Proclamation.

Another issue of the day was the participation of blacks in the Union army. Although many whites opposed this idea, Douglass insisted on it, convinced that blacks could not win respect without active participation in this apocalyptic confrontation. Thus the #54 Massachusetts all-black infantry was formed. Douglass' own sons volunteered. Of the 179,000 black soldiers who fought in the war, 38,000 died.

In 1865, slavery was officially abolished by the 13th Amendment. Douglass, then forty-eight (forty-seven) years old, delivered a speech advocating the enfranchisement of blacks in former slave states. He sensed that freedom for four million people without respect would be worse for them than slavery had been. Douglass was not shortsighted in his assessment of coming events, but visionary. "Black Codes" were established prohibiting blacks from owning either land or arms, rights fundamental to European American life. Unpaid "slave labor" was reinstitutionalized. At the same time, Douglass' former ally, Garrison, dismantled his antislavery machinery, and many white women disapproved of black suffrage, feeling that it was their turn now that blacks had gained freedom. Douglass had joined the women's suffrage movement as early as 1848 and remained one of its strongest male supporters until his death. Hence he tried to maintain a dual emphasis strategically, and continued working to strengthen the cause for the black vote. By 1866, President Andrew Johnson had begun the Reconstruction of the South. Douglass' Republican allies in Congress led the struggle for passage of the 15th Amendment (1870), which granted blacks the right to vote. Ironically, duly elected black congressmen were not welcomed in the halls of the Capitol and were often ridiculed by their so-called political allies.

As white terrorism emerged and spread throughout the South, not even African Americans in the North escaped the wave of racism. Douglass' own home in Rochester, New York, was burned to the ground in 1872, an example of what he called the "Ku Klux Spirit." Demoralized, he moved his family to Washington, D.C., where he campaigned for President Ulysses Grant's re-election. He was further disturbed by "Blue and Gray" reunions among white veterans, which in his view symbolized not racial reconciliation, but discrimination. The fact his own sons were unable to get jobs as skilled publishers was a reflection of the broader national context. Douglass' hopes for racial harmony and mutual respect remained unfulfilled.

During the nation's 1876 centennial, Douglass spoke at the "Freedom Monument" event in honor of Lincoln. Drawing on his own experience, he called Lincoln a great man who nevertheless was the white man's president. Lincoln's perception of the image of God, he said, had been very limited where blacks were concerned: They were an entirely different species from whites and undeserving of equal rights in this nation. His first order of business had been to preserve the union, not to free the slaves.

In 1878 Douglass and his family moved into a new, spacious house called "Cedar Hill" in Anacostia, just across the river from Washington, D.C. There he received many dignitaries. President Rutherford B. Hayes appointed him to the position of United States Marshal. As a representative of his people, Douglass associated his own honor with that of his people.

The withdrawal of federal troops from the south reignited a new wave of persecution against blacks. Fifty thousand "Exodusers" moved north in order to escape the vengeance of their white adversaries. Douglass tried to discourage blacks from migrating, urging them to remain on the battlefront of their hard-earned freedom, resist oppression, and demand respect. He paid a cost for this position, as many blacks felt that he was out of touch with their persecution and anguish. Douglass was a staunch believer in the race and saw himself as an example of what could be achieved through persistent willpower and determination. To many, his own resolve and political savvy had earned him the title "sage of Anacostia." In a changing social climate, however, his wisdom was doubted by those who were experiencing the contemporary form of white racism most directly.

Anna Douglass, his wife of forty-four years, died in 1882. After two years of mourning, he married Helen Pitts, a white suffrage leader and graduate of Mount Holyoke Seminary. This union created both public criticism and internal family tensions. In addition to racial differences, Helen was twenty years younger than Douglass. Nevertheless, he was determined that theirs would be a happy marriage. They traveled to Europe and North Africa. In 1889 he was chosen as the United States minister to Haiti, but resigned after only two years, over American policy regarding Haiti.

In 1890 Douglass returned to the battlefront for African American liberation by joining Ida B. Wells in the antilynching movement. The 1890s were a decade of lynching throughout the South, and "Jim Crow" practices (radical segregation of the races) were strictly enforced. Douglass did not hesitate to speak out against the hypocrisy of so-called enlightened and Christian white Southerners. Though his strength was waning as he aged, he continually appealed to blacks to maintain hope in adversity. A firm believer in the inevitability of racial equality, he challenged the popular rhetoric of the day by calling racism and its eradication a national problem, not a Negro one. Until the very end, he advocated freedom and equality for all people. He died in the same month of his birth, 20 February 1895, after attending a women's rights meeting.

Frederick Augustus Douglass was one like Moses in responding to a call to speak out against oppression and injustice. Along with Sojourner Truth and Harriet Tubman, he emerged as a prophet and leader from among one of the most oppressed people in Western history. His own theological perspective was informed by his strong sense that God directed his path from slavery to freedom. But he was not content to secure his freedom alone; he became a writer and spokesperson for an entire race within a nation that resented their presence as much as it needed their labor. He was a political agitator who, never satisfied with half-way measures, demanded the total liberation of African Americans. He was a visionary who early on perceived the relationship between racial and gender oppression and equality. He was a millennialist who believed that the end of slavery was near and must be fought for so that a new kingdom could emerge. Even in times of apparent defeat, he was an optimist who felt hope could overcome despair as long as one continued to struggle for one's God-given rights to freedom and dignity. For him, nothing worthwhile could exist without struggle. Finally, he was a prophet of agitation because he believed that God was on the side of those who took an interest in their own liberation along with that of all people.

Suggested Readings

Writings of Frederick Douglass: *Narrative of the Life of Frederick Douglass, An American Slave, Written by Himself* (New York: Signet, 1968; repr. of 1845 ed.); *My Bondage and My Freedom* (New York: Dover, 1969; repr. of 1855 ed.).

Philip Fortner, ed., *The Life and Writings of Frederick Douglass,* 4 vols. (New York: International Publishers, 1975).

———, ed., *The Life and Writings of Frederick Douglass: Supplementary Volumes, 1844–1860* (New York: International Publishers, 1975).

William S. McFreely, *Frederick Douglass* (New York and London: W. W. Norton & Co., 1991).

Alexander Crummell

(1819–1898)

Susie C. Stanley

Alexander Crummell, a theologian concerned with ethical issues, was born a free black in New York. Contrary to Frederick Douglass, whose experience as a slave shaped his perception of race relations, Crummell's encounters with antebellum prejudice as a free black had the most profound influence on him. His theology of discontent resulted from this context. He endured discriminatory treatment as an adolescent while traveling to Noyes Academy in 1835. Founded by abolitionists, the school welcomed blacks, but neighbors soon expressed their opposition by closing it. Crummell subsequently attended Oneida Institute for three years. As a young adult, Crummell received permission to prepare for the priesthood in the Protestant Episcopal Church. General Theological Seminary, however, denied him admittance because he was black, so he studied informally at Yale. While at New Haven, he organized black members of a local parish into a separate congregation. This was likely his first expression of separatism, but it was separatism within white-controlled Episcopalianism rather than affiliation with one of the independent Methodist denominations organized by blacks. Despite his separatist inclinations and the prejudice he experienced within his denomination, Crummell could never bring himself to join the black Methodists. He strongly opposed their pietism and decried emotionalism in religious expression. He further maintained that conversion alone was insufficient to ensure one's salvation; good works also were a contributing factor.

Ordained in 1844, Crummell, during the next year, became rector of a black church in New York. He and his family traveled to England in 1848 to raise money for his congregation. He lectured on abolitionist topics, favoring immediate emancipation of the slaves in the United States and initially opposing colonization efforts. He also attended Queens College, Cambridge, studied the classics, and earned a B.A. in 1853.

Rather than return to the United States, Crummell and his family sailed to Liberia where he became a citizen and vowed that Liberia would be his lifetime home. Having changed his position on colonization, Crummell became a strong advocate of black nationalism. A lecture trip to the United States in 1861–62 included pro-colonization speeches at a time when most earlier supporters had abandoned this policy. While in Liberia, he was an Episcopal missionary, public moralist, and educator, serving as principal of several schools and a professor at Liberia College. He encouraged ecclesiastical separatism within the Episcopal Church in Liberia by organizing other black priests to press for an independent black diocese. Infighting ultimately doomed the project.

Standing in the forefront of the African civilizationism movement, Crummell believed that prejudice would diminish as blacks became civilized. Colonization provided the opportunity to build a superior civilization. While the primary responsibility of the missionary was to spread Christianity, the secondary objective was to introduce native Africans to civilization. Believing that native African civilization was inferior, Crummell's goal was to imitate English civilization. He believed in eventual superiority with the assistance of divine Providence and quoted Psalm 68:31 ("Ethiopia shall soon stretch out her hands unto God") to bolster his position. Crummell's black chauvinism resurfaced in Marcus Garvey's philosophy. Crummell's confidence in progress, revealed in his promotion of "Ethiopianism," reflected an optimism fueled by his theological historicism.

Crummell returned to the United States in 1872, abandoning his commitment to colonization. He pastored in Washington, D.C., founding St. Luke's parish in 1879 and serving this black congregation until his retirement in 1894. Crummell maintained that the development of character was the primary factor in eliminating prejudice. Rather than pursuing agitation, blacks must assume responsibility for fostering character among themselves. Perhaps his Arminianism influenced his position that blacks should take responsibility for ending racism. Crummell appropriated components of Anglican Bishop Joseph Butler's moral theology into his own. Rather than simply adopt an individualist, aristocratic ethic of conscience which supported the status quo, however, Crummell reshaped it into a collaborative and democratic ethic which became a theoretical justification for opposing racism. Where Butler's concept of self-love related to individual salvation, Crummell affirmed a this-worldly emphasis in which self-love became a means of contributing to the "uplift of the race."

Crummell argued that instead of trying to transcend their blackness (which he considered impossible in American society), blacks should celebrate their race and work together in black associations to foster racial pride. This separatist position contrasted with the assimilationism of Frederick Douglass and shares common ground with some forms of the black separatism that arose in response to the civil rights movement a century later. Efforts to deny one's race constituted heresy, according to Crummell, as did opposition to black associations. Following Crummell's death, Marcus Garvey also promoted self-help, calling it Negro Improvement.

There were significant areas of agreement and disagreement between Crummell and his contemporary, Booker T. Washington. Both preached self-help under the guidance of an elite group of blacks. They differed, however, on the composition of this group. For Crummell, the elite was to consist of philosophers; for Washington, of businessmen. Both considered education a key to liberation. But while Washington was content to demand industrial education, Crummell promoted classical education as well. Crummell's separatism also clashed with Washington's accommodationist approach. One of the motives for founding the American Negro Academy in 1897 was to counteract the popularity of Washington's Tuskegee Institute. The Academy, limited to forty men, had the objective of civilizing the Negro race. Crummell's agenda directly influenced W. E. B. DuBois' concept of a "talented tenth," which had the same goal. While his views on colonization changed over time, Crummell's commitment to the building of character never wavered.

Suggested Readings

Writings of Alexander Crummell: in addition to numerous articles, three volumes of sermons: *The Future of Africa* (New York: Charles Scribner, 1862); *The Greatness of Christ* (New York: T. Whittaker, 1882); *Africa and America* (Springfield, Mass.: Willey & Co., 1891); *Destiny and Race: Selected Writings, 1840–1898,* ed. Wilson Jeremiah Moses (Amherst: University of Massachusetts Press, 1992).

Wilson Jeremiah Moses, *Alexander Crummell: A Study of Civilization and Discontent* (New York: Oxford University, 1989).

J. R. Oldfield, *Alexander Crummell and the Creation of an African-American Church in Liberia* (Lewiston, N.Y.: Edwin Mellen, 1990).

Henry McNeal Turner

(1834–1915)

Darryl M. Trimiew

In early May 1915, in Atlanta, Georgia, twenty-five thousand people gathered to view the body of Bishop Henry McNeal Turner. Who was this man that generated such veneration? Clearly he must have been a charismatic leader. Of him, W. E. B. DuBois wrote in *Crisis* (July 1915): "[He] was the last of his clan: mighty men, physically and mentally, men who started at the bottom and hammered their way to the top by sheer brute strength; they were the spiritual progeny of African chieftains and they built the African church in America."

Perhaps Turner was indeed a descendant of African nobility, for he was born free on 1 February 1834 in Newberry Courthouse, South Carolina, a slaveholding state, to free parents, Sarah Greer Turner and Hardy Turner. Sarah's mother, Hannah Greer, who helped raise Henry, maintained that her husband, David Greer, had been the son of an African king. Turner certainly acted as if this family history was true and carried himself with royal dignity.

Yet the veneration he received was due not to his lineage but to his deeds and his words. During the years of his ministry, his church—the African Methodist Episcopal Church, a northern denomination—attained national and international influence, and this achievement must be attributed, to some extent, to the tireless work of Turner. Still, to explain how he helped shape the American theological landscape, we must turn from his ecclesiastical endeavors to his theological contributions.

Although Turner was not a systematic theologian, his work was nevertheless profoundly influential as a forerunner to what is now known as black theology. Just as John the Baptist prepared the way for Jesus, so too, long before James Cone, J. DeOtis Roberts, Martin Luther King, Jr., Malcolm X, or even Marcus Garvey, Turner boldly relativized the white supremacist color scheme of Western Christianity's anthropomorphic image of God. Claiming the right to engage in theological reflection in 1898, Turner wrote in *Voice of Missions,* "We have as much right biblically and otherwise to believe that God is a Negro, as you buckra, or white people have to believe that God is a fine looking, symmetrical and ornamented white man." In making this claim, Turner scandalized African American and European American churches alike. The comfortable theological, cultural, and ideological hegemonies of the religious establishment were rocked by this first salvo of religious and theological pluralism: a portent of things to come.

In most respects, Turner's theology was not innovative. Like most Methodists, Turner did not have many ideas that were fundamentally different from foundational, standard Wesleyan theology, except, of course, on the issue of race. What was important about Turner's theology was its inherent revelatory qualities, its disclosive powers. Turner disclosed that the normative theological agenda of America—that this country was divinely created and ordained for the sole use of European colonists, who alone were made in God's image—was no more than a projection of "the new Israelites." Neither they, European American colonists, nor their putative "hewers of wood and drawers of water," namely African American slaves, would thereafter be able to embrace without question the theological dominance of the color scheme of the "white" church.

Turner's remark also discloses the tendency for Christian communities to regard themselves as created in the "image of God." Turner correctly understood that every human community must, if it is to be healthy, have and communicate a healthy self-image. Historically speaking, Christians of European descent, worshipers of an incarnate God who also became an active human, ministered in the New World with an image of God that was the spiritualized ideal of their paradigmatic role models, that is, white males. Turner objected to this approach because he understood that such claims about God were not declarations by whites for whites but by whites for all humanity. In other words, one particular Christian community attempted uncritically to impose its own norm upon all Christians. Turner unceasingly resisted this act of theological imperialism because he was determined to create some theological space within which African Americans, as a community of faith, could determine who God was and how God should be represented to themselves and others.

By his own creative theological imaging, Turner demonstrated his commitment to helping his community define not only who God was but also who they were as a people worthy of respect. His representation that God is black was not to establish a theory about the being of God, but it did declare and enhance an unambiguous self-love movement for and among blacks. Thus Turner's greatest contribution to theology resulted from his exposure of the Eurocentric nature of American Christianity's self-definition. Turner's work allows us to see the development of theology as a process inextricably bound to forces and constraints of ideology.

Yet no discussion of Turner's theology would be complete without an examination of his understanding of God's preeminent project for the Americans of his era. As an heir to the "back to Africa movement" of Alexander Crummell and a precursor to the pan-African philosophy of Marcus Garvey, Turner became the most dominant apostle of African American emigration to Africa. He took several trips to Africa and assisted in the establishment of churches there. Further, he held forth, until his death, the theological necessity of that return for at least some of the African American community. Turner's demand for a return to Africa was central, not peripheral, to his overall goal of liberation for African Americans and central as well to his understanding of the mission of the church as the obedient servant of God.

As time passed and the memory of slavery receded in the minds of Americans, Turner's emigration plan continuously lost ground to other nativist approaches for African American self-improvement from a variety of leaders, including such notables as Booker T. Washington and Francis K. Grimke. This determination by African Americans to stay in America and fight for their civil and political rights has proved to be the final approach and cannot be interpreted as anything other than at least a partial rejection of Turner's legacy. That Turner was incorrect in his assessment of the will of God in this respect is irrelevant to the underlying thrust of his total endeavor: to instill in the African American masses a sense of identification with Christianity, Africa, self-respect, and missionary zeal. This potent fusion of disparate values worked, as it did years later for Marcus Garvey, to create and nurture racial pride and powers of resistance in the African American community, even though neither Garvey nor Turner incited the actual emigration of very many people.

Turner's embrace of Africa and the notion of "blackness" was invaluable to a people who had just escaped from slavery and were constantly bombarded with religious and political propaganda castigating the continent of Africa, its culture and the physical appearance of its residents and diaspora. Turner's rejection of Eurocentric American theological standards, and especially the doctrine of America's "manifest destiny," acted as a prophetic judgment against the nation. In consonance with his criticism of the color scheme of America, Turner also called into question the reigning ideological translations of the Bible, the sacred text. In 1895 Turner took notice of the work of Elizabeth Cady Stanton, an early feminist, who, along with others, had retranslated the Bible from a feminist perspective. Turner approved of this attitude and the intent of feminist work.

The insight Turner obtained from the work of Stanton led him to reject standardized versions of biblical texts and call for the development of translations sensitive to the needs of the African American community. This radical demand set him apart from his contemporaries. Turner's recognition that knowledge about God and the worshiping community's representation of God need not be uniform was a great contribution to the development of modern theological pluralism. His work was especially appropriate because of its timeliness. Turner wrote in the late–nineteenth century and in the early twentieth century—an era in which European American theologians were busily promulgating theologies that justified popular myths of African American inferiority, legitimating the oppression of Jim Crow.

In a world that did not respect African Americans, Turner demanded respect, for himself and others. Perhaps it was this majestic, assertive, invigorating spirit that engendered the reverence of the masses during his life and at his death and produced the grief-stricken crowds in Atlanta. Though DuBois was correct in calling Turner the last of his "clan," his strength and wisdom survived him and served as a foundation for black theology advocates and independent-minded clergy. This forceful call for liberation and respect is the lasting legacy of Bishop Henry McNeal Turner.

Suggested Readings

Writings of Henry McNeal Turner: *Emigration of the Colored People of the United States: Is It Expedient? If So, Where To?* Prepared by Request for the Colored National Conference to meet in Nashville, Tennessee, 6 May 1879; repr. in *Respect Black: The Writings and Speeches of Henry McNeal Turner,* ed. Edwin S. Redkey (New York: Arno Press, 1971).

Stephen W. Angell, *Bishop Henry McNeal Turner and African American Religion in the South* (Knoxville: University of Tennessee Press, 1992).

Darryl M. Trimiew, *Voices of the Silenced: The Responsible Self in a Marginalized Community* (Cleveland: Pilgrim Press, 1993).

Henry Boynton Smith

(1815–1877)

Albert H. Freundt, Jr.

Henry B. Smith was recognized as one of the foremost Presbyterian theologians in America in the nineteenth century. Born 21 November 1815, in Portland, Maine, he was raised a Unitarian. In a revival in Bowdoin College, Brunswick, Maine, during his senior year he was converted to an intensely personal and Christ-centered form of evangelical Christianity which led him to reject Unitarianism. He began theological studies at Andover Seminary in 1834, but withdrew because of sickness brought on by too much work and too severe self-discipline. In 1835 he began studies at Bangor Theological Seminary, but poor health once again required him to drop out.

After a year of studying German and teaching Greek at Bowdoin, Smith sailed for Europe in 1837, the first of several trips there. He spent the winter in Paris, attending lectures, studying on his own, and recuperating. In 1838 he was at the University of Halle, where he was much influenced by August Tholuck, who befriended him. In 1839 he moved to Berlin, where he sat under J. A. Neander and E. W. Hengstenberg, and was influenced by Hegel and Leopold von Ranke. He was thus one of the first Americans to have the benefit of graduate study in Germany.

Smith saw the central idea of Christianity as the mediation of Christ and made this the ruling principle of his theology, life, and work. When he was only twenty-one he had written, "My object is to make and harmonize a system which shall make Christ the central point of all important religious truth and doctrine." This goal was reinforced by his study in Germany. He returned home in 1840 with his orthodox faith intact and with a firsthand knowledge and respect for German scholarship. His acquaintance with German thought and historical criticism put him in a position to make a contribution to American intellectual life that few others at the time could make.

Bad health continued to plague him. He taught at Bowdoin for a while. He taught Hebrew at Andover (1845–47) during his pastorate of the Congregational church at West Amesbury, Massachusetts (1843–47). From 1847 to 1850 he taught philosophy at Amherst College and had a number of articles published.

In 1850 he joined the New School Presbyterian denomination and was made church history professor at Union Seminary, New York. In 1855, after a year or two in which he also taught systematic theology, he was transferred to the chair of theology. Presbyterians soon recognized Smith as the leading theologian of his denomination. He also served as the first chairman of the American executive committee of the Evangelical Alliance, and his reputation helped to bring intellectual credibility to his seminary. His *History of the Church of Christ in Chronological Tables* was published in 1859. Translations of German works, including his revisions of Gieseler's textbook on church history (1855–79) and Hagenbach's on the history of doctrine (1861–62), helped introduce Americans to the evangelical scholarship of Europe. He edited the *New York Evangelist,* and from 1859 until his death, coedited the *American Theological Review* and its successors, the *American Presbyterian and Theological Review* and the *Presbyterian Quarterly and Princeton Review.* Through his writing he exercised an even wider influence than through his teaching.

Smith understood systematic theology as "the combined result of philosophy and faith, and its highest office, to present both in their most intimate conjunction and inherent harmony." He had a unique ability to draw upon the theological and philosophical resources of his age and to put them to the service of christocentric piety and orthodox apologetics.

Smith had found in the evangelical philosophy and theology of Germany a Christ-centered piety that mediated between orthodox confessionalism and a radical rationalism. The advocates of this point of view combined their biblical faith with the idea of an inner principle expressing itself in historical development. For Smith this principle was "incarnation in order to redemption." In his lectures on theology he stated:

> We cannot reduce the principle to a single word: "Incarnation" or "Redemption"; we must take both. Incarnation does not of itself involve redemption, and redemption without the incarnation would not be Christianity. Moreover the two are related as ground and consequence, means or measure, and result. Hence the full idea of the Christological principle of theology is that of INCARNATION IN ORDER TO REDEMPTION.

Placing great emphasis on the history of doctrine and the idea of historical progress, he believed that a system of theology was needed that would strive to mediate between the conflicting parties of the times.

Even though he was an heir to the theology of Jonathan Edwards and of the more conservative Edwardseans, Smith was preeminently a mediating theologian, seeking the reconciliation of differences. He mediated between New England theology and the best of contemporary German thought, and between the extremes of New School and of Old School Presbyterian positions. He sought to reconcile the theology of the Edwardeans with that of the whole Reformed tradition as well as the contemporary evangelical theology and piety he had learned in Germany. He demonstrated that he loved truth more than he hated error and, in his critical reviews, he showed he could see and appreciate the measure of truth which belonged to views from which he differed. He chose to understand rather than to refute, to create bridges between positions wherever possible.

He expanded the concerns of theology from that of the Edwardseans to that of the whole Reformed tradition. Prepared to update traditional forms of Reformed theology, he found help in the christocentric theology of Germany. His hope was to conserve the best of the tradition and progress beyond current conflicts to a new and better synthesis. Unfortunately Smith did not live to elaborate his theological system. His last years were a constant struggle with illness. He retired in 1874 and was made professor emeritus, but when his health permitted he lectured at the seminary on apologetics. He continued to write articles and to edit the *Review*. His chief works were not published until after his death (7 February 1877). *Faith and Philosophy* (1877) was a collection of his essays and reviews. His *Lectures on Apologetics* (1881), *Introduction to Christian Theology* (1883), and *System of Christian Theology* (1884) were compiled from his lecture notes.

Smith brought new perspectives to bear on American Calvinism. He helped to promote a shift in philosophy in America from Scottish to German ideas, and from a theocentric to a christocentric theology. He marks a shift from preoccupation with divine sovereignty and human agency to a grand Christ-centered vision of history leading to the ultimate victory of Christ's kingdom. He saw the drama of redemption by Christ at the center of Christian history, Christ's mediation as the central principle of his theology, and the doctrine of Christ as the central doctrine that illumines and makes intelligible all other doctrines. History was, for him, the record of the progress of the kingdom of God.

In the reunion of the Presbyterian Church, Smith found an opportunity to apply his mediating principles to a practical situation. He was moderator of the New School Presbyterian Assembly (1863) and the most powerful influence in their reunion with the Old School (1869). His orthodox view of the inspiration and infallibility of scripture and his respect for the whole Reformed tradition made him a conservative influence in New School Presbyterianism. During the years of their separation from the Old School, the New School Presbyterian denomination became more decidedly orthodox, and much of the effort to reunite was due to the influence of Smith's teaching and writing. He took the ground out from under Old School opponents, including Charles Hodge, by advocating reunion on the doctrinal basis of the Westminster Standards, "interpreted in their legitimate grammatical and historic sense, in the spirit of the original Adopting Act, and as 'containing the system of doctrine taught in the scriptures.'" Regarding the Westminster Confession and Catechisms, Smith stated, "All that we can do is to accept them in their essential and necessary articles with a recognition of possible, though guarded diversities of explanation, the system and doctrines remaining in their integrity."

Smith was an accomplished scholar as a philosopher as well as a theologian, and a man of profound learning as well as personal winsomeness. He inspired students with devotion to Christ, to the scriptures, and to evangelical Christianity, and acquainted them with a vast fund of knowledge and made historical method and reality integral to theologizing and the theological curriculum. His familiarity with philosophy and theology, the Reformed tradition, and the intellectual currents of his age, his reconciling spirit, and his endeavor to encourage independent thought in his students made his influence both broadening and exciting.

Suggested Readings

D. G. Hart, "Divided Between Heart and Mind: the Critical Period for Protestant Thought in America," *Journal of Ecclesiastical History* 38 (1987): 254-70.

Bruce Kuklick, *Churchmen and Philosophers* (New Haven: Yale University Press, 1985).

Richard A. Muller, "Henry Boynton Smith: Christocentric Theologian," *Journal of Presbyterian History* 61 (1983): 429-44.

Lewis F. Stearns, *Henry Boynton Smith* (Boston and New York: Houghton, Mifflin and Co., 1892).

Henry Ward Beecher

(1813–1887)

Diane Apostolos-Cappadona

The fourth son of Lyman Beecher and Roxana Foote, Henry Ward Beecher was born on 24 June 1813 in Litchfield, Connecticut. Although raised in a religious household, Beecher only realized religious certitude, a "conversion," on that "blessed May morning" of 1837. This ecstatic personal experience brought an intoxicating sense of God loving humanity despite sinfulness; thereby, love replaced duty and justice. This visceral personal experience fused with the emerging Christian Romanticism to shape Beecher's religious life and his preaching. His theological transformation affirmed the principles of Christian Romanticism: the centrality of God's love, faith in a merciful God, a christocentric theology grounded in the revelation of a personal Christ, the intuitive nature of Christianity, an appeal to experience, a stress on human consciousness, and the centrality of the family and education as spiritual vehicles.

Beecher was licensed by the Cincinnati Presbytery for his first parish at the Presbyterian church in Lawrenceberg, Indiana, in 1837. He began his lifelong association as a newspaper columnist, which provided him with a regular audience larger than any single congregation. Ordained by the New School Presbytery of Cincinnati in 1838, he began an eight-year tenure at Second Presbyterian Church of Indianapolis, a New School congregation, where Beecher emphasized church membership, Temperance and Sunday School societies, and revivals. A period of intense self-scrutiny resulted in his own development as one of the most gifted preachers of American Protestantism. Beecher pursued a careful study of Jonathan Edwards' sermons and the Apostles' evangelical methods in the book of Acts. Successful preaching effected moral change in the hearts of the audience, and a good sermon's religious lesson corresponded to a current social concern. Beecher had a remarkable capacity for interpreting religious ideas and synthesizing these with the societal changes confronting his congregation. He

271

espoused Christian Romanticism's confidence in a spiritual domesticity characterized by the idealization of childhood, the primary role of the mother, and the family as the ideal Christian environment.

During his forty-year service as minister of Plymouth Church in Brooklyn, both Beecher and his congregation paralleled the theological and social transformation of American culture. Beecher revealed an interest in all theological questions, moral concerns, practical applications of religious values, and moral and political reforms. He preached twice every Sunday to overflow crowds, and his popular public lectures were presented in cities and towns throughout America. His popularity was such that when Plymouth Church burned in January 1849, a new structure was built to accommodate 2,500 persons. The oratorical skills displayed in his five speeches in England in 1863 converted public sentiment against slavery and to support for the North.

During this time, Beecher contributed regularly to the *New York Independent, New York Ledger,* and *Christian Union.* Literary scholars acknowledge Beecher's editorials as among the finest in the history of the American press. His principal writings include *Star Papers, or Experiences of Art and Nature* (1855); *Freedom and War* (1863); *Norwood: A Tale of New England Life* (1867); *Evolution and Religion* (1885); and *Life of Jesus Christ* (1891). Beecher's texts were replete with pressing public questions and an advocacy for reforms. Although not an original thinker, he was well schooled in human interests and gifted in his ability to grasp fundamental principles and facts, and to clarify issues. Throughout his ministry, Beecher advocated God's love, the joyous glory of the Christian life, and the humanity of Jesus. This Jesus was a moral teacher and humane redeemer, not a judge. Beecher's empathy with the struggles of the human heart, and his application of fundamental moral truths to existential situations fulfilled the religious needs of his congregation. During his lengthy career, he championed abolition, women's suffrage, free trade, and evolution, among other reform causes.

In the 1870s, Beecher's popularity suffered from the "Tilton Affair." Members of Plymouth Church, Theodore and Josephine Tilton were befriended by the Beechers. Despite the minister's influence, Tilton's radical ideas on marriage and religion led to his removal as Assistant Editor of the *Independent.* Following a series of miscues, Tilton charged impropriety between his wife and Beecher. Despite all efforts at discretion, a succession of public denials and accusations culminated in Tilton's formal legal complaint demanding $100,000 in damages. The sensational six-month trial ended in a hung jury in 1875; the Council of Congregational churches found

Beecher "not guilty" of improprieties in 1876. His public position recovered, Beecher continued his career as a minister, public speaker, and writer until his death on 8 March 1887.

As the embodiment of middle-class values, Henry Ward Beecher provided leadership during that theological and cultural shift of antebellum America away from traditional Calvinism toward Christian Romanticism. His talented perceptions of majority sentiments and shifting opinions propelled his name to the forefront of every prominent social and political issue from abolition to industrial reform. His confidence in the fundamental American values of freedom and progress combined with a commitment to the New Theology, so that he advocated the adaptation of Christian theology to contemporary culture. Beecher responded to both the changing intellectual and theological currents, and to the new social and cultural patterns of both antebellum and reconstructionist America. In this he presaged both the best and the worst in evangelical preaching from Billy Sunday to Norman Vincent Peale and Billy Graham, as well as to the televangelists. His application of theology to current cultural and social issues was a preamble to Paul Tillich's method of correlation and H. Richard Niebuhr's ethics of *Christ and Culture*.

Suggested Readings

Writings of Henry Ward Beecher: *Lectures to Young Men on Various Important Subjects (1844)* (Ann Arbor, Mich.: University Microfilms, American Culture Series, 1978); *Yale Lectures on Preaching* (Tustin, Calif.: American Reprint Service, 1985).

Mary Caskey, *Chariot of Fire: Religion and the Beecher Family* (New Haven: Yale University Press, 1978).

Clifford E. Clark, *Henry Ward Beecher: Spokesman for a Middle-Class America* (Chicago: University of Illinois Press, 1978).

William G. McLoughlin, *The Meaning of Henry Ward Beecher: An Essay on the Shifting Values of Mid-Victorian America, 1840–1870* (New York: Alfred A. Knopf, 1970).

James Freeman Clarke

(1810–1888)

David M. Robinson

James Freeman Clarke's development as a minister and theologian is in many ways synonymous with the emergence and institutional growth of the Unitarian denomination in America. His work encompassed a direct involvement with the Unitarian expansion in the Midwest, a consistent effort to integrate the perspective of Emerson and the Transcendentalist movement into the institutional life of the Unitarian denomination, and the cultivation of a broader understanding of world religions. Clarke's work as a church reformer and institution builder and his persuasive articulation of liberal theological principles accord him a place of leadership in the evolution of liberal Protestantism in America.

Clarke was born on 4 April 1810 in Hanover, New Hampshire, and raised in Newton, Massachusetts, where he was in close contact with his step-grandfather, James Freeman (1787–1835), minister of King's Chapel in Boston, and an important early spokesman for Unitarianism in Massachusetts. Clarke graduated from Harvard College (1829) and Harvard Divinity School (1833) during a period in which Harvard had become the center for theological liberalism, and an important training ground for the Unitarian ministry. He subscribed to the theological premises of William Ellery Channing and other Unitarian leaders, who had rejected Calvinist doctrines of innate depravity and election to grace, and affirmed human spiritual capacity and a life dedicated to self-culture and spiritual growth. Clarke also formed early friendships with Margaret Fuller (1810–50) and Frederic Henry Hedge (1805–90), sharing with them an intense interest in German literature and philosophy and a predisposition to a renewed idealism in theology and philosophy that came to be known in the late 1830s as Transcendentalism.

After completing his ministerial studies Clarke took a pastorate in Louisville, Kentucky, in 1833, hoping to help establish a Unitarian presence in the newly developing regions of the Ohio Valley. Although he found the work there difficult and eventually returned to Boston, he established and edited the *Western Messenger,* a periodical that became associated with Transcendentalism through its defense of Emerson and its publication of his work and that of others who shared his views. Although some Unitarian leaders viewed Emerson and his followers as a danger to the theological integrity and institutional stability of the church, Clarke, like Hedge, remained committed to Emerson's concept of the intuitive basis of religious truth and a sense of individual religious self-determination that flowed from it. Moreover, both Clarke and Hedge remained committed to the church as a necessary and viable institution within which religious experience and moral commitment could be cultivated.

Clarke's marriage in 1839 to Anna Huidekoper provided him a degree of financial independence, and he returned to Boston to establish the Church of the Disciples in 1841. There he enjoyed a more vital intellectual atmosphere, closer contact with the leadership and the mainstream of the Unitarian movement, and freedom to experiment in his style of ministerial leadership and church organization. Over the next half-century Clarke gained increasing influence among Boston Unitarian circles as a man open to new and progressive theological views but also committed to the stability and open inclusiveness of the church. Clarke and Hedge advocated a "Broad Church" position in Unitarianism in which a noncreedal inclusiveness and an emphasis on ecclesiastical history, Christian ethics, and progressive social action kept the church open to a wide spectrum of theological opinion. In nineteenth-century Unitarianism that spectrum ranged from traditional Christian theism to Emersonian intuitive idealism to radical forms of scientific and empirical theology.

Though Clarke sympathized with Emerson and counted himself among the transcendentalists, thus positioning himself on the progressive and experimental wing of the denomination in philosophical opinion, in the 1860s he supported the efforts of Henry Whitney Bellows (1814–82) to establish the National Conference of Unitarian churches in an effort to bring more organizational coherence to Unitarianism, and he resisted the impulse among some of Bellows opponents who formed the Free Religious Association to move outside the Unitarian denomination. In the later phase of his career, Clarke effectively articulated some of the key theological concerns and assumptions of nineteenth-century liberal religion, notably in his essay "The Five Points of Calvinism and the Five Points of the New Theology," included in *Vexed Questions in Theology* (1886).

Rejecting the five points of Calvinism, "Absolute Decrees, Atonement by

Christ for the Elect Only, Original Sin, Effectual Calling, and the Persever-
ance of Saints" (*Vexed Questions,* 9), Clarke instead proposed "five points
of the coming theology" (10), which came to be a generally accepted sum-
mation of the Unitarian outlook in the late-nineteenth and early twentieth
centuries. Clarke proposed "the Fatherhood of God" (10) as the first point,
stressing the parental attributes of wise guidance and caring justice as
essential to a view of God. Clarke added "the Brotherhood of Man" (11)
and "the Leadership of Jesus" (12) to the doctrines of the new theology,
stressing a sense of humane service and ethical engagement as exemplified
in Jesus as the most essential elements of Christianity. His choice of words
pointedly deemphasized the importance of belief in the supernatural nature
of Jesus, and he warned against too great a reliance on fixed creedal statements in theology, contrasting them with a more open and activist dedication to the ethos of Jesus.

The final points of Clarke's new theology were "Salvation by Character"
(14) and "the Continuity of Human Development in All Worlds, or the
Progress of Mankind Onward and Upward Forever" (15-16). With these
propositions, Clarke emphasized the ethical focus of liberal theology,
recovering and reemphasizing the centrality of "works" to the concept of
salvation. He also sounded the note of optimism and faith in human
progress that was a hallmark of the liberal theological outlook at the turn
of the century. Clarke urged his readers to discover their own distinctive
natures, which had a divine origin. This act of self-discovery would bring
the deep satisfaction of a self-fulfillment that was part of the natural order,
but it was far more significant than a narrow program of self-indulgence or
self-aggrandizement. The fulfillment that Clarke advocated was bounded
by the conviction that service to others was a crucial element of self-fulfillment, and his admonition to discover one's particular nature carried with
it the responsibility for an unremitting development and expansion of one's
potential being. Clarke offered a message that was affirming and supportive, but also demanding.

Clarke also made an important contribution to the growing interest in
world religions among nineteenth-century Unitarians. Both Emerson and
Henry David Thoreau had been strongly impressed earlier in the century
by the translation and publication of the scriptures of the Eastern religions,
finding in them important confirmation for their own sense that Christianity was one of many expressions of the human religious impulse. Clarke's
Ten Great Religions (1871), revised and republished in a number of editions in the later 1800s, offered a consideration of both ancient and modern religions of the world in relation to Christianity. Clarke surveyed the

historical development and key doctrinal emphases of the world's religions, but remained anchored in his Christian perspective, seeing Christianity finally as a vehicle through which the most important emphases of all religions could be merged. Clarke thus argued for the evolution of Christianity into a universal religion that would subsume the others, but his sympathetic interest in the variety of the world's religions was a contribution to a more general growth in American Protestantism's sensitivity to the importance of non-Christian religious traditions.

Clarke remained the minister at the Church of the Disciples in Boston until his death in 1888, continuing as an active and significant denominational leader. His stance of inclusiveness and noncreedal openness to new and varied perspectives in theology made him an important influence for stability in Unitarianism during a period in which the denomination struggled with schism between the radicals of the Free Religion movement and those led by Bellows who were engaged in augmenting and consolidating institutional strength. Clarke's theological influence and reputation rest on his widely sympathetic and inclusive outlook, combined with his ability to integrate and articulate new religious ideas into the rapidly evolving perspective of nineteenth-century liberalism.

Suggested Readings

Writings of James Freeman Clarke: *Self-Culture: Physical, Intellectual, Moral, and Spiritual* (Boston: Houghton Mifflin, 1880); *Ten Great Religions: An Essay in Comparative Theology* (Boston: Houghton Mifflin, 1871); *Vexed Questions in Theology: A Series of Essays* (Boston: George H. Ellis, 1886).

Arthur S. Bolster, *James Freeman Clarke: Disciple to Advancing Truth* (Boston: Beacon Press, 1954).

Robert D. Habich, *Transcendentalism and the Western Messenger: A History of the Magazine and Its Contributors, 1835–1841* (Rutherford, N.J.: Fairleigh Dickinson University Press, 1985).

David Robinson, *The Unitarians and the Universalists* (Westport, Conn.: Greenwood Press, 1985).

Arthur Versluis, *American Transcendentalism and Asian Religions* (New York: Oxford University Press, 1993).

Daniel Denison Whedon

(1808–1885)

Dennis M. Campbell

Daniel Denison Whedon was among the most significant Methodist theologians of nineteenth-century North America. His work on freedom of the will contributed to the development of an indigenous Wesleyan theology. Its appeal to human experience changed the course of Methodist thought, and set a trajectory giving Methodist theology a distinctive philosophical method that would characterize work in this tradition for decades into the twentieth century.

Born 20 March 1808 in Onondaga, New York, Daniel D. Whedon was the son of Daniel and Clarissa (Root) Whedon, and a descendant of Thomas Whedon, who came to New Haven from England in 1657, and later lived in Branford, Connecticut. He graduated from Hamilton College in Clinton, New York, in 1828, and then studied law in Rochester, New York. While there he was converted under the preaching of Charles G. Finney and joined the Methodist Episcopal Church. Whedon, a gifted student and communicator, took up teaching in 1830 when he was invited to serve as an instructor of Greek and Mental Philosophy at the Oneida Conference Seminary in Cazenovia, New York. In 1832, he returned to Hamilton for one year as a tutor.

Wesleyan University in Middletown, Connecticut, a school of the Methodist Episcopal Church, appointed him Professor of Ancient Languages and Literature in 1833. During his time at Wesleyan, the Methodist Episcopal Church was embroiled in controversy over slavery. LaRoy Sunderland, and four other radical abolitionists, issued an "Appeal" to the New England and New Hampshire Annual Conferences in 1835 calling for immediate abolition. Whedon, along with other moderates, feared that such an absolute stand might split the church. He drafted "A Counter Appeal" signed by eight prominent Methodist leaders, including Wilbur Fisk, who was the first president of Wesleyan, and Abel Stevens, a

Methodist historian. This position sought a middle ground between the radical abolitionists and the slaveholders, arguing that slaveholding was not necessarily sinful, but that no expansion of slavery should be permitted.

On 15 July 1840 Whedon married Eliza Ann Searles of White Plains, New York. In the course of their marriage they would be the parents of five children. After ten years at Wesleyan, Whedon was ordained deacon and then elder in the Methodist Episcopal Church, and was appointed pastor in Pittsfield, Massachusetts, where he served for a year before being moved to the church in Rensselaerville, New York. Evidently he was not a person whose disposition was easily suited to pastoral ministry, however, and he welcomed election as Professor of Rhetoric, Logic, and History at the University of Michigan in 1845. While at Michigan he became involved, once again, in controversy over slavery. His vocal opposition to its expansion, and his political activity, resulted in his termination in 1853, when he returned to the pastorate in Jamaica, New York. He opened a school in Ravenswood, New York, but it was not successful.

Whedon's most significant service came after the General Conference of the Methodist Episcopal Church elected him editor of the *Methodist Quarterly Review* in 1856. A substantial quarterly publication, the *Review* carried articles on theological issues and important intellectual developments in American culture. The journal possessed great influence, and, as editor, Whedon exercised formidable leadership in Methodism. At a time when the church had no general boards or agencies, and no national bureaucratic structures, editors and publishers served as connectional officers. In shaping the editorial direction of the journal, he set the agenda for discussion of theological trends in both North America and Europe. Whedon served as editor for twenty-eight years, being elected each quadrennium by subsequent General Conferences. He was awarded two honorary degrees, the D.D. by Emory and Henry College, and the LL.D. by Wesleyan University, in recognition of his service to the church.

After the initiation of his service as editor of the *Methodist Quarterly Review,* his published work began to appear. In 1856 he published a collection of his *Public Addresses.* He was well known among church members for his biblical commentaries. He published *Commentary on Matthew and Mark* in 1860, the five-volume *Commentary on the New Testament* between 1860 and 1875, and the seven-volume *Commentary on the Old Testament* between 1880 and 1886. These commentaries were used by preachers and laypersons for sermon preparation, Bible studies, and personal devotion. There are three published works of importance to scholars and persons interested in the development of American theology. These are his article "Doctrines of Methodism" published in *Bibliotheca Sacra* in 1862, his book *Freedom of the Will,* published in 1864, and a posthumous collection of writings published in 1887 entitled *Essays, Reviews, and Discourses.*

Until well into the nineteenth century, theology in North America was dominated by Calvinist thought. The Reformed tradition shaped most early educational institutions and provided much of the intellectual leadership for the new nation. Many Americans regarded Methodists as uneducated revivalists. Their theological foundations were provided by John Wesley, the Anglican founder of Methodism, and his immediate English successors John Fletcher, Adam Clarke, and Richard Watson. Nathan Bangs, the most important early American Methodist theologian, continued Wesleyan themes and sought to emphasize points of difference with the dominant Calvinism.

One of the central issues had to do with the nature of the human condition in regard to human agency and free will. To what extent does a person have freedom to choose, and therefore, responsibility for moral choice and action? Perhaps the most important American theologian, Jonathan Edwards, set forth an uncompromising theological position which emphasized God's sovereignty to such a degree that men and women were seen to be unable to control their own destinies. Debates about human nature and freedom of the will were central to American theology in the first half of the nineteenth century. This issue came to occupy Daniel Whedon's attention. It is the topic which shaped his principal book and for which he is most remembered.

Whedon argued that the reality of human freedom was the chief point of difference between Calvinism and Arminianism. The term "Arminian theology" came to be used popularly to describe Wesleyan Methodist theology. While Wesleyan theology is richer and more complex, Arminianism was a shorthand description of a tradition that emphasizes the reality of human free agency graciously given by God. Whedon put great weight on human capability. He argued that experience demonstrates that persons do have freedom to choose one or another path. Moreover it was obvious to him that logic, as well as experience, required this view. A person cannot be blamed for what he or she cannot help. Responsibility demonstrates and demands free will. If we are to hold persons responsible for their actions, then we must understand that they were able to choose to engage in those actions.

Theologically, Daniel Whedon referred to John Wesley, but was more dependent on the work of John Fletcher, who advanced Wesley's discussion of the morally responsible Christian life. He attended less to the scriptures, and more to the experience of Christian men and women. It is clear that Whedon understood the reality of human freedom as a gracious gift from God. Human freedom is not something that men and women have achieved; it is what they have been given. This gift is the result of the atonement of Jesus Christ on the cross. The work of Jesus Christ has made human freedom a reality. In turn, men and women are held responsible for the way in which they choose to live their lives. God calls, and gives the power to respond, but human beings may choose to respond or reject God, by the grace of Jesus Christ. Whedon deals with the full range of Methodist doctrines: divine sovereignty, foreknowledge, sin, redemption, justification by faith, regeneration, witness of the Spirit, and entire sanctification. In doing so, however, his dominant interest is to advance the argument that God's grace has given men and women the freedom to respond positively to this path of salvation.

Whedon's work emphasized human agency and experience. Methodist theology helped to shape, and no doubt was shaped by, dominant themes in American culture. Whedon reasserted the basic continuity between Wesleyan theology and American democratic liberalism, which lifted up, in theory, the freedom of the individual, the dignity of every person, and the capacity of persons to shape their own lives as well as the life of the community. Methodist thinking, in this sense, was compatible with the experience of nineteenth-century Americans, and this no doubt contributed to the phenomenal growth of Methodism in the course of the century.

The enduring significance of Daniel Whedon's work may have to do more with what it occasioned than with the specific claims made for freedom of the will. His work represented an important step in the development of an indigenous Wesleyan theology. His interests attended to the prevailing intellectual currents of mid-nineteenth-century America. His arguments were less biblical and more philosophical. They appealed to human experience and built a philosophical case for the necessity of human freedom, which in turn becomes a starting point for theological reflection. The move toward a philosophical foundation for theology began to characterize theology in the Wesleyan tradition. After his death in Atlantic City, New Jersey, in 1885, Whedon's successors built on his theological approach and method.

Later Methodist theologians increasingly took philosophy as a starting point for theology. The most distinctive American Methodist theology came to be known as Boston Personalism. Based at Boston University School of Theology, Personalism was thoroughly philosophical in its method and treatment. Personalism was certainly not a direct outgrowth of Whedon's work, but Whedon's move toward an indigenous Wesleyan theology based, in part, on human experience, opened the door to other and further developments along these lines. Subsequent Methodist work in process philosophy and process theology can also be seen in this light.

Suggested Readings

Writings of Daniel D. Whedon: *Freedom of the Will* (New York: Carlton and Porter, 1864); *Essays, Reviews, and Discourses* (New York: Phillips and Hunt, 1887).

Dennis M. Campbell, *Authority and the Renewal of American Theology* (Philadelphia: Pilgrim Press, 1976).

Thomas A. Langford, *Practical Divinity: Theology in the Wesleyan Tradition* (Nashville: Abingdon Press, 1983).

Frederick A. Norwood, *The Story of American Methodism* (Nashville/New York: Abingdon Press, 1974).

William James

(1842–1910)

Donald A. Crosby

Although known primarily as a psychologist and philosopher, William James devoted much attention in his extensive writings to religious phenomena and theological issues. The sparkling originality of his work in all its dimensions, psychological and philosophical as well as religious, exerted important influence on the development of liberal, empiricist, and process forms of Christian theology in America. This influence was no doubt enhanced by James' inimitable style, direct and down-to-earth in its focus on the concreteness of experience and compellingly lyrical in its beautifully crafted sentences and pervasive use of vivid illustration and imagery.

Born in New York City, James was one of five children. His father was a theologian strongly influenced by the ideas of Emanuel Swedenborg. One of his three brothers, Henry, became a prolific and renowned novelist. William thought at first that he wanted to be a painter but eventually decided on a scientific course of study and in 1869 earned an M.D. degree at Harvard University. In 1873 James accepted a position teaching anatomy and physiology at Harvard. He soon moved into psychology and established the first laboratory for physiological psychology in the United States. In 1878 he contracted to write a book based on his psychology lectures. The book finally appeared in two volumes under the title *Principles of Psychology* (1890) and quickly made James famous throughout the world.

James began teaching philosophy at Harvard in 1879, and the *Principles* is a fascinating exhibition of the interplay of his psychological and philosophical interests. His subsequent writings in philosophy built upon themes first ventured in the *Principles*, most notably a functional, nonsubstantialist concept of the self which viewed it as an ever-changing and yet continuous stream of thoughts and feelings; an emphasis on the fundamental role of activity and purpose in the self's development, as over against the then regnant Associationist psychology; an insistence on experience as the basis

283

of all reliable knowledge that was sharply critical of the atomistic nominalism of traditional British Empiricism and of that tradition's tendency to downplay or ignore the crucial role in experience of such non-sensuous factors as emotion, evaluation, recollection, anticipation, effort, and aim; and a constant reminder of the selective, partial, and even distorting character of conceptual interpretations of the overbrimming fullness of experience. These were also to be important orientations or themes in James' later deliberations about religion and theology.

His next important publication was *The Will to Believe and Other Essays in Popular Philosophy* (1897). Two essays in this collection, the title essay and one entitled "The Sentiment of Rationality," defended the proposition that it was rational to accept beliefs for which there was no compelling theoretical evidence for or against, so long as these beliefs, held as hypotheses to be continually tested in experience and for their coherence with other important beliefs, gave promise of energizing and enriching human life. It would in fact be irrational to refuse to repose initial faith in momentous beliefs such as those that ascribe moral and religious meanings to the universe, or to fail to give those beliefs a fair trial in everyday life. Some beliefs, James insisted, can only be verified or falsified in a wholly engaged, active way that requires firm commitment to their truth. The option of suspending judgment about all theoretically uncertain beliefs, recommended by James' contemporary, the English agnostic and anti-religious philosopher William Clifford, would admittedly guard against falling into error and was appropriate in some circumstances. But James observed that this option also foreclosed the possibility of confirming beliefs that could only be assessed by trusting them and putting them into practice. In fact, some beliefs are even made true in this way; they "cannot become true till our faith has made them so." He used the example of a climber in the Alps whose only route of escape from a bad situation is a terrible leap. The climber's hope and confidence help to make true the proposition that he is capable of leaping the chasm.

These two essays enlarged upon a basic point of view to which James had come during a severe emotional crisis in 1869–70. His strong emphasis on the active role of the self in the *Principles* also reflected lessons he had learned from this experience. Having completed his medical training, James was depressed by the Newtonian science of his day, in which an iron law of causal necessity was assumed to reign, leaving no place for human freedom or responsibility. He was strongly tempted to suicide. But he found his way out by reading *Essais de critique générale* (4 vols., 1854–64) by Charles Renouvier. This author convinced him that causal determinism cannot be proved any more than can belief in freedom, and that he should abstain from idle, brooding speculations and act as if he were free, thus avowing a world congenial to moral striving and the importance of individual effort.

James turned his attention to the psychology of religion in *The Varieties of Religious Experience* (1902). Six themes of this complex and enlightening book are especially worthy of note. The first is its preoccupation with concrete religious experiences rather than with the intellectual content of religious traditions or their institutional histories and forms. A study of particular religious persons and of the specific details of their experiences was the necessary starting point and basis, James believed, for the psychology of religion and for any general inferences to be drawn in philosophy and theology about the nature of religion or the truth of religious claims. Accordingly, *Varieties* is packed with vivid firsthand reports of religious experiences and James' detailed discussions of those experiences.

Second, James stressed the importance of the distinction between descriptions and evaluations of religious phenomena, insisting that careful description is prior to and distinct from evaluation. He reserved his own general evaluations of religion for the end of the volume, once the voluminous descriptive data had been organized and presented.

Third, he offered three main criteria for assessing the truth and value of religious claims: immediate luminousness, philosophical reasonableness, and moral helpfulness. The third criterion shows the close connection James perceived between religion and morality. It is also consonant with the thesis of the two essays just discussed. In the first lecture of *Varieties* James contended that the religious life must be judged "by its results exclusively," not by its origins; and in chapters on saintliness he explored the idea that we can look to the life of the saint as the foremost exemplar and confirmation of the practical fruits of religious experience.

Fourth, he paid considerable attention to the topic of religious conversion and speculated that conversion experiences could be accounted for, at least in part, by incursions of the subconscious aspect of the self into its conscious part. Fifth, he devised typologies and descriptions of "healthy-minded" and "morbid-minded" (or "sick-souled") religious persons, and of "once-born" and "twice-born" kinds of religious personality. These distinctions are illuminating, and they have had much influence in the study of religion. Finally, James argued at the end of *Varieties* that religious experience should be regarded with the utmost seriousness, and that it gave significant evidence of the existence of a "More" of the same quality as the individual self but operative in the universe outside the self, "of an ideal power with which we feel ourselves in connection," and of the opportunity of experiencing "union with *something* larger than ourselves" in which

285

we can "find our greatest peace." He added that this "More" might need to be conceived in polytheistic rather than theistic terms, or as limited rather than absolute in character, and that there were no guarantees, the universe being the diverse, open, and contingent system that it is, of the world being wholly saved.

The term with which James' philosophical outlook is most commonly associated was the title of his next important publication after *Varieties*. In 1907, *Pragmatism: A New Name for Some Old Ways of Thinking* appeared. This was also the year of James' resignation from his position as Professor of Philosophy at Harvard (he had been appointed to that position in 1885, but between 1889 and 1897 his title was Professor of Psychology). He continued to lecture and write, and in 1909 a sequel to *Pragmatism* was published in which he responded to critics of the earlier volume. The new book's title was *The Meaning of Truth*. James consistently acknowledged indebtedness for his discovery of pragmatism to a fellow member of the Metaphysical Club in Cambridge, Charles Sanders Peirce. He also traced its roots to English and Scottish empiricists such as John Locke, George Berkeley, David Hume, Thomas Brown, Dugald Stewart, and James and John Stuart Mill.

In *Pragmatism* and *The Meaning of Truth* James defended the notion that an alleged difference that made no difference in practice was no real difference. And only those beliefs that were allowed to function as hypotheses testable by future experiences, and that were supported by the future experiences they predicted, could be said to be true. Moreover, all putative truths were fallible and must continually be brought to the test of experience. Truth or knowledge was acquired by determining and following out the consequences of a belief, through whatever intermediate experiences were required, to the terminus of that belief, which was its predicted effects. When that terminus was reached and the predicted experiences attained, then the belief in question had been verified. If that terminus could not be reached, then the belief in question was falsified.

To gain further insight into how James understood pragmatism and how he applied it to religious questions, we can consider his discussion in *Pragmatism* of "materialism" and "spiritualism" (which he equated with theism). For materialists of his day, James noted, everything about nature could be explained by blind laws of physics. Hence, nature's ultimate destiny and its "higher" aspects, such as minds and their achievements, were entirely run by and reducible to its "lower," purely physical, aspects. In contrast, "spiritualism" was the belief that the world is "guided, not by its lower, but by its higher element," meaning "that mind not only witnesses and records things, but also operates them." He contended that if one were to take a merely *retrospective* view, no important differences could be discerned between the two worldviews. That is, the present state of the world would remain the same by either interpretation of its origin and nature, just as the intrinsic quality of a play would be the same when the curtain was run down upon it, regardless of whether we attributed its authorship to a genius or a common hack. Since we had here a putative difference that really made no difference in experience, the meanings of the seemingly different views were for all practical purposes indistinguishable, and the question of their relative truth or falsity was moot.

James observed that the situation became altogether different when conceived in terms of a *prospective* analysis of implications of the two worldviews for the future. Here was a difference that made a significant difference, one that could be tested for its truth by projected future experiences. Darwinian materialism's denial of design in nature, for example, gave no reason to expect betterment of the world; chance evolutionary changes and blind causal laws were without purpose or direction. Theistic faith in design, on the other hand, was "a term of *promise*," enabling us to act upon the supposition of a "seeing force" that guided things toward a better future. With its belief in the inexorable rule of entropy, materialism also pointed to the ultimate dissolution of the universe and all its attainments. Spiritualism, by contrast, implied moral hope, confidence in a moral order that was not merely transitory but eternal. A spiritual worldview thus made a sizable difference in the outlook of humans on the future and its importance for their moral beliefs and strivings.

When viewed with an eye to the future not the past, the issue between materialism and spiritualism was a genuine issue whose truth or falsity could be pragmatically adjudicated. James' basic point in this discussion, as in all his writings on philosophical, religious, and moral themes, was that the fundamental meaning of a worldview hung on its implications for the practical needs, concerns, and experiences of the life that lay ahead. And a significant test of the claim of a worldview to truth was whether it empowered humans to live with an active confidence that could itself contribute to a better world, or left them with an attitude of resignation and despair that doomed in advance the prospect of bringing about such a world. Worldviews were not true or false in some absolute, antecedent manner; they were made true or false only by our acting upon them. Of course, we could not make them true just by willing them to be so. James allowed for the possibility that theistic faith might be falsified by stubborn experiences that continued to frustrate it and call it into question, just as it might be confirmed and supported by future experiences. To return to his example of the climber in the Alps, the climber might fail to leap the chasm despite all his grit and determination. James also noted that such faith would need to "run the gauntlet of all our other truths. It is on trial by them and they on trial by it."

In *A Pluralistic Universe* (1909), James weighed the relative cases of materialism, absolute idealism, and traditional theism, and proposed in their place his own hypothesis of a finite deity operating within a pluralistic world. Materialism, he argued, accorded no significant place to mind and its accomplishments, thus alienating human beings from the basic character of the universe. Traditional theism gave no plausible account of why a God who was all-powerful, complete in himself, and radically distinct from the world would have any need for activities of humans in that world. The absolute idealism of thinkers like F. H. Bradley in England and James' colleague at Harvard, Josiah Royce, asserted a much more intimate relation between God and the world than traditional theism did, but its "one substance" metaphysical monism could not adequately account for the diversity of beings in the world, for change, for chance, for human freedom, or for the existence of evil.

For James, only the hypothesis of a pluralistic world, with God viewed as a supreme but not all-powerful one among the many, could allow for greatest intimacy of relation between God and the world while preserving the integrity and enduring importance of individual things. In such a world, the fulfillment of God's purposes depended on the contributions of others, just as their greater well-being depended on him. Evil, in this scenario, need not be attributed to God but to contingencies of an imperfect, still-unfolding world, including misuses of human freedom. There was admitted hazard and uncertainty in such an outlook, for the highest values were dynamically in the making rather than eternally realized in an all-sufficient God, and there could be no absolute guarantee of the future attainment of these values. But the pluralistic hypothesis also conferred abiding value and meaning on human life, for it meant that human beings could be regarded as partners with God in the struggle for a better world.

William James died on 26 August 1910, in Chocorua, New Hampshire, shortly after returning from a European trip with his wife, Alice. The last of his most important works, *Essays in Radical Empiricism,* was published posthumously in 1912, as edited by Ralph Barton Perry. Here James sought to show that distinctions between selves and their objects were functional and variable, and were not distinctions between different substantive entities. He also discussed his pragmatic method at length, attacked the absolute idealism of F. H. Bradley and the atomistic empiricism of David Hume, and argued for a processive, pluralistic metaphysics. Finally, he explored the idea of "pure experience" as the basis for conceptualizations of the world. All that was finally real and significant, according to James, could be found within the teeming flux and diversity of pure experience—a notion with affinities to the central idea of *durée* (duration) in the writings of a French philosopher who greatly influenced him, Henri Bergson. One of the chapters of *A Pluralistic Universe* is a highly appreciative interpretation of Bergson's thought.

James' writings influenced philosophers as diverse in outlook as John Dewey, Edmund Husserl, Alfred North Whitehead, and Ludwig Wittgenstein—philosophers who have had their own significant impacts on theological thought in America. His focus on concrete experience as the basis of all reliable knowledge, including religious knowledge; his emphasis on a depth and richness of experience that includes but also extends beyond ordinary sensate experience; his intensive study of religious experiences; and his pragmatism helped to give rise to an empirical brand of theology in American religious liberalism that had its principal location at the University of Chicago Divinity School and was championed there in various ways by theologians such as Bernard Loomer, Shailer Mathews, Bernard Meland, and Henry Nelson Wieman. James' ideas have also figured prominently in versions of religious empiricism developed by thinkers such as William Dean, Nancy Frankenberry, and John E. Smith. With views that closely resemble and that probably substantively influenced such aspects of Whitehead's philosophy as the latter's concepts of experience in general, of religious experience in particular, and of God, James was an important precursor of process theology in America, as represented by the philosophical theologians Charles Hartshorne, John B. Cobb, Jr., and Daniel Day Williams. Wieman and Loomer can also be included in this group.

Suggested Readings

Writings of William James: Frederick Burkhardt, general editor, *The Works of William James* (Cambridge: Harvard University Press, 1975).

Bennett Ramsey, *Submitting to Freedom: The Religious Vision of William James* (New York and Oxford: Oxford University Press, 1993).

Charlene Haddock Seigfried, *William James' Radical Reconstruction of Philosophy* (Albany: State University of New York Press, 1990).

Robert J. Vanden Burgt, *The Religious Philosophy of William James* (Chicago: Nelson Hall, 1981).

Josiah Royce

(1855–1916)

John K. Roth

Shortly before he died in Cambridge, Massachusetts, on 14 September 1916, Josiah Royce summarized how his philosophical and religious interests had originated. He recalled that his early home was Grass Valley, a California mining town only a few years older than Royce himself, who was born there on 20 November 1855. Although he heard his elders describe the place as new, the young Royce noticed abandoned mines, rotting structures, and graves. They all looked old. The land's majesty, moreover, was anything but recent. Ages were in it. Royce explained that these experiences made him wonder not only about his particular California locale but also about how things were related and why.

Some of Royce's early writings—including an 1887 novel called *The Feud of Oakfield Creek*—would focus on California, but his sense of wonder led to many other destinations as well. He came to see that experience is fundamentally relational and social. Only because existence is structured that way can it also be individual and personal. But how did those connections work? Why was life like that? Such questions took Royce on a journey that made him one of the most respected philosophers and religious thinkers of his day. Nevertheless, in the middle decades of the twentieth century, his thought went out of style. Too religious to suit the tastes of skeptical philosophers, Royce's views were also too philosophical to satisfy the dominant religious trends. As the twenty-first century approaches, however, interest in many of Royce's insights has been rekindled because his philosophy concentrates on the idea of community.

Royce's philosophy and religious thought stressed that human beings are not isolated individuals. Instead, Royce argued, persons are essentially relational beings, and the quality of our lives depends on the nature of the community life that we establish and sustain. In Royce's mind, these ideas were closely related to two others: interpretation and loyalty. Few, if any, American thinkers have probed the significance of the concepts of personhood, community, interpretation, and loyalty more deeply than Royce did.

Except for two summers and some other short visits, Royce left California for good in 1882, when he went to Harvard University as a sabbatical replacement for the philosopher-psychologist William James. Prior to 1882, Royce had studied at the University of California. After graduating in 1875, he spent a year in Germany and then continued his philosophical inquiry at Johns Hopkins University. There he met James and received his Ph.D. Although Royce and James had profound philosophical differences, they were lifelong friends. Largely through James' influence, Harvard called Royce from his teaching position at the University of California. At first, Royce's Harvard appointment was only for a single year, but well received, he was soon offered a permanent position. For the rest of his life, Royce made Harvard his academic home.

Royce published his first important book, *The Religious Aspect of Philosophy*, in 1885. It was followed by a series of influential writings. The most important include *The World and the Individual* (two vols., published in 1899 and 1901), *The Philosophy of Loyalty* (1908), *The Sources of Religious Insight* (1912), and *The Problem of Christianity* (1913). In these works, Royce developed, amplified, and refined his systematic philosophy and religious thought. Influenced by German thinkers such as Immanuel Kant and G. W. F. Hegel, his outlook was a form of absolute idealism.

Royce's absolute idealism grew from his fascination with the permanent possibility of error in human judgment. Royce argued that we could really be mistaken (as we surely are on occasion) only if there is an Absolute Mind that grasps and assesses all experience wholly and completely so that an error is truly known, and thereby constituted as such, when we judge incorrectly. Royce contended, moreover, that such knowledge is possible only if all realities are expressions or signs of the Absolute Mind, which thus must be regarded as the Absolute Will and Interpreter as well. Otherwise, Royce asserted, a dualistic gap between knower and known could intrude to block the very unity required to guarantee that truth can be distinguished from falsity.

As Royce explored these ideas, his absolute idealism was amplified by at least three other basic themes. (1) Human awareness is incomplete, human judgment is fallible, but our reasoning power is still sufficient to discern the basic structures of reality. It is even possible to devise a philosophical system that describes, clarifies, and proves the existence of these structures for us. (2) Royce's Absolute or God manifests itself in, but is not simply identifiable with, a vastly rich temporal universe of real individual beings, who are organically and socially related. In particular, human life is a manifestation of the Absolute. Through God's will, awareness, and interpretation, all of these manifestations are unified and known as a fully good and meaningful totality. (3) Persons are centers of purpose and striving; therefore, human life involves suffering and a struggle with evil. Although suffering, tragedy, and loss pervade human experience, Royce affirmed that in facing those obstacles courageously, in achieving success wherever one can, and in recognizing that one's relationship with God ultimately entails the overcoming of every evil, one can experience positive meaning and joy. Each person is an essential component in the universal community willed and known by God. In that community, salvation can be found as evil is transcended and death is overcome.

Royce's idealism was not an isolated perspective in the philosophical and theological world of his time. To the contrary, it was a version of one of the dominant trends in much of Western Europe and the United States in the last half of the nineteenth century and into the early years of the twentieth century. Nevertheless, while Royce represented the mainstream, he also lived when philosophical and religious currents were shifting. Increasingly, both the content and the strength of absolute idealism's claims were criticized for not being sufficiently empirical and for failing to do justice to human freedom and its moral struggles. Royce was taken to task especially by his friend William James, who argued that Royce's God entailed a theological determinism in which human lives are complete before they are actually lived. Even worse, said James, Royce's philosophy made inescapable the evil that people do and the suffering they experience.

Royce replied to these charges as follows: God's eternal knowledge is not a temporal foreknowing that eliminates freedom. God knows free human acts as free, but God's knowing neither determines nor causes them. As for evil and suffering, they are necessary conditions for the absolute goodness and perfection of existence as a whole, because that goodness and perfection require the overcoming of evil. Yet no particular instance of evil and suffering is necessary. In human experience, such particularities are the result of free human actions for which men and women are responsible. God's reality, however, guarantees what human power cannot—namely, that every instance of evil and suffering will be overcome so that the salvation of all existence is secured.

In the late–twentieth century, Royce's metaphysical system seems as problematic as it was hopeful, but the analyses he developed while focusing explicitly on the predicaments of human existence stand the test of time much better. It is in these areas that renewed interest in Royce's work has focused. Royce stressed, for example, that social relationships are fundamental. It makes no sense to speak of individuals apart from them. All of the purposes and goals that we human beings pursue thrust us into interaction with other persons and with nature. If we strip away these relationships, the self that remains is a bare abstraction and not anything that can be identified with a particular living person. Persons are real. Individuals exist. But they are inseparable from social relationships that make selfhood possible.

According to Royce, a human self is a temporal process of experiencing, willing, and choosing. But persons do not experience, will, and choose in identical ways, because each self is a particular center of purpose and striving. Each person embodies perspectives, goals, needs, and projects that find expression in and through the social settings in which one's life unfolds. The world in which we live is shared, because it is relational and social through and through, but the world shared is also interpreted by each of us as experience develops and indeed as our senses of selfhood are affected in the process. Just as social relations are fundamental and selfhood is never divorced from purpose and striving, so experience, selfhood, and the world itself are inseparable from interpretation that reflects the particularity of our times, places, and perspectives.

In Royce's view, we become persons by acting, by pursuing interests, by striving for the achievement of goals. But the self will be either fragmented or unified in direct proportion to one's success in finding and actualizing a life pattern that can be consistently and harmoniously pursued through time. Among other things, such a pattern entails a chance for the discovery, expression, and cultivation of talents and abilities and a recognition of the fact that no action or event occurs in a vacuum. The actions of one affect the many. One person's well-being is vitally linked to the well-being of other people and to the conservation of the natural environment that sustains human life.

Royce believed that loyalty—the dedicated and thoroughgoing commitment to a cause—is a basic ingredient in selfhood. But he also recognized that many causes are destructive and that much loyalty is misguided and misplaced. He urged, therefore, an ethical principle that supported his belief that the quality of individual lives depends on the quality of the communities in which they exist. Royce's principle was that our fundamental moral responsibility ought to be that of being loyal to loyalty.

This principle points toward a community where all individuals are free, where they use their abilities and cultivate their interests, and where all of these persons and factors encourage and support one another. As Royce

293

interpreted loyalty to loyalty, he stressed the importance of giving ourselves to the goals that do the most to build the spirit of service that is necessary for improving life together. To be loyal to loyalty is to be dedicated to defending the rights of every person and to strive for the conditions of justice that best nurture the development and exercise of these rights. Loyalty to loyalty also entails the will to resist conditions—blindness, selfishness, powerlessness, and power abuse, for example—that undermine, ignore, or waste those opportunities. As Royce understood it, loyalty to loyalty aims toward human freedom and dignity.

For Royce, a person's life never finds completion in time. Our hopes get dashed; our causes are often lost. There is always something fragmented and broken about us. Royce's absolute idealism, however, did not leave matters there. Fragmentation was not the end; brokenness was not the last word. Royce thought that human selves were the expression of the Absolute Self in whom we live and move and have our being. Our striving and interpreting are manifestations of a God who wills and interprets and knows in ways that redeem all things and make them whole and well. In that sense, reality itself is truly a community.

Twentieth-century history makes Royce's metaphysical vision much less certain than he took it to be. Just for that reason, however, his insights about selfhood, community, interpretation, and loyalty remain timely and significant. Comprehending how individual well-being depends on sound understandings of community, interpretation, and loyalty is not likely to lead to a reaffirmation of Royce's absolute idealism. Nevertheless, that comprehension remains important. Mending the world's fragmentation and brokenness depends on it.

Suggested Readings

Writings of Josiah Royce: *The Philosophy of Loyalty* (Nashville: Vanderbilt University Press, 1995; repr. of 1908 ed.).

John Clendening, *The Life and Thought of Josiah Royce* (Madison: University of Wisconsin Press, 1985).

John K. Roth, ed., *The Philosophy of Josiah Royce* (Indianapolis: Hackett Publishing Co., 1982).

Borden Parker Bowne

(1847–1910)

Russell E. Richey

One of six children, Bowne was born on 14 January 1847 in Leonardville, New Jersey, to Margaret (Parker) and Joseph Bowne. The Bowne family was of Puritan stock, William and Anne having come with the first generation of Puritans to settle Salem. The family had relocated to New Jersey where Bowne's father was a farmer and justice of the peace. The home was devoutly Methodist (his father was also a local preacher) and strongly oriented to that tradition's ethics, including antislavery and temperance.

Bowne early took an interest in books and ideas. Educated at Pennington Seminary, he then attended the University of the City of New York, graduating Phi Beta Kappa and valedictorian in 1871. He excelled in school, producing while in college an essay on Herbert Spencer that was later published. From the same institution he received the A.M. in 1876. In the interim he studied from 1873 to 1875 in Halle, Göttingen, and Paris. While studying in Europe, Bowne came under the influence of Rudolf Hermann Lotze and Hermann Ulrici through whom he came to terms with the various nineteenth-century philosophical traditions. He would thereafter show decided affinities with Immanuel Kant, G. W. Leibniz, and Bishop Berkeley and engage other thinkers appreciatively but critically.

Bowne taught school after college briefly and also served as pastor in Whitestone, New York, Methodist Episcopal Church (1872–73). There he met and married Kate Morrison. After his return from study abroad, he became assistant editor of the *Independent,* an important, serious, widely read religious journal, and then assistant professor of modern languages in his alma mater. In 1876 Boston University called him to the chair of philosophy and to head that department, a position he held for thirty-five years. He served as dean of the Graduate School of Arts and Sciences from 1888 to 1910.

As a philosopher and shaper of the tradition of philosophy at Boston University, Bowne wove strands of idealism, neo-Kantianism, biblical criticism, Romanticism, and rationalism with those from his heritage (Methodism's moralism, high valuation of freedom, insistence on individual responsibility, optimism of grace, hope for perfection) into a distinctive modernist Methodist metaphysic. Known as personal idealism, personalism, or transcendental empiricism, this Boston philosophy had a strong influence on Methodism nationally through Bowne and three generations of his successors: first, through Albert C. Knudson, Edgar S. Brightman, Francis J. McConnell, George Albert Coe, and Ralph T. Flewelling; second, through Walter E. Muelder, Georgia Harkness, L. Harold DeWolf, Paul Deats, John Lavely, S. Paul Schilling, and Peter Bertocci; and third, through numerous others, but including Martin Luther King, Jr.—to constitute a significant contribution to American philosophy. The tradition was focused at Boston University. However, that school trained, both in its divinity and doctoral programs, a significant portion of northern Methodism's ecclesiastical and academic leadership. Bowne also shaped that church's thought and ethic through numerous influential books, essays in important journals, and articles in various papers.

Bowne sought a recasting of Wesleyan theology that would respond to materialism and secularism, be credible in a scientific and humanistic world, hold together monist and pluralist perspectives, function with both idealist and empiricist agendas, and synthesize philosophically the major fields of knowledge. Key to this apologetic was a metaphysic that conceived of personality as ultimate and an epistemology he eventually termed transcendental empiricism. Personhood or personalism he thought the key to the nature of reality and to the order of the world. The individual who experiences that order and interprets the world is a cognitive, indivisible, self-conscious unity existent through successive experiences, a substantial self. True and full personhood is found in God, a nature revealed in Jesus Christ, a reality in which alone freedom, identity, and unity are realized. Human fulfillment comes from partaking of and realizing the potential of personhood, also made possible through Christ and God's grace.

Knowledge of self, of nature, and of God was possible because ultimate reality itself is personal and the individual knower can turn to and depend on this cosmic Person. Clues to the existence of the cosmic Person, God, can be discerned in the mind's dependence on notions of space, time, continuity, and causation—categories not finally inherent in the phenomenal world. But Bowne does not establish proofs for the existence of God and for gaining access to God solely through the senses and the intellect—

working from the world of nature to God. He rejects both that line of argumentation and the premises—materialist, naturalistic, or monist—under which such proofs might be mounted. Nevertheless, the world has a Creator and behind it lies the Creator's active, purposeful willing.

God, moreover, is not absent, "Deist-like," but is engaged with creation. Indeed, Bowne makes the immanence of God a primary theme. God, the cosmic Intelligence, guides, orders, and directs nature, does so constantly and effectively not once for all, and does so in and through all of nature—both personal and nonpersonal. In the world God acts in a willful fashion. So also acts humanity, individuals each possessed with his or her own freedom. The interplay of such complex willing and of the dynamics and inertias of the natural world meant that the world was not readily understood in relation to the divine Will. Divine causation, miracles, and evil remained puzzles or problems. What Bowne did affirm is that God is One, absolute, and infinite. In this affirmation of God, in this will to believe, Bowne was a kindred spirit to William James, though they were apparently not always close and proceeded in different fashions to clarity.

Though Bowne did not aspire to a rationalistic or naturalistic proof of God and though he presumed that revelation and faith finally convinced the believer of God's existence, presence, and purposes and though he asserted that atheism was every bit as much a hypothesis as theism, Bowne did make use of cumulative and teleological arguments and certainly insisted on the importance and necessity of philosophical reflection about God.

It was philosophy's task to detail and develop theistic belief. He argued strenuously—and against Herbert Spencer—for an intelligent Designer over a mechanistic universe whose only patterns derived accidentally through evolution. In knowing this Intelligence, persons do proceed analogically, he conceded, drawing inferences from experience and certainly from human self-experience. Also philosophy had—as Kant had insisted—the resources of human morality and religion, the noumenal, with which to work. Developing these, Bowne gave personalistic force to classic Christian affirmations about God:

—to the unity of God in terms of which the unity of the human person and the reliability of human knowledge could be justified;

—to the unchangeability of God, contrasted but keyed to human experience of time;

—to the omnipresence of God, a point developed in relation to God's active role in nature;

—to the eternity of God, placing God beyond those determinants (time, space, causality, continuity) that God creates and maintains;

—to the omniscience of God, putting God beyond the limits with which finite minds operate and in awareness of all that is open to human action and thought but not necessarily engaged in foreknowing or certainly predetermining;

—to the omnipotence of God, affirming that God is not limited by God's own nature and certainly not by the nature that God has created;

—to God as creator, insisting however that to so claim is not to render God abstract or to confuse God with nature or to lose the mysterious, holy, personal nature of God.

God is for Bowne, of course, good, which is not to deny the existence of evil, or to assign it to God, or to use it to infringe the divine majesty, or to expect that human expectation of the universe exhausts what can be said about the nature of God.

Inherent in such a theodicy and in Bowne's notion of personhood—human and divine—was a high emphasis on willing and freedom. Human freedom and responsibility were axioms in Bowne's Wesleyan heritage. However, seen against the evolution of Methodist thought, Bowne's argument for free will represents an outworking and departure from classical Arminian notions. Bowne's argument for free will did not premise human freedom with the Wesleyan insistence on prevenient grace. Instead, he explored notions of free will in the context of epistemology and morality. Bowne considered the free personal will essential to there being any reliable truth and duty. From this flowed an ethic, which in Kantian fashion, put a premium on autonomy, on altruism, on the value of persons, on practical reason, and on living according to moral principle.

Bowne's epistemology also reflected that of Kant. Accepting the distinction between noumenal and phenomenal, Bowne operated with an epistemic dualism and was highly critical of monisms of whatever character. The individual in knowing apprehended the phenomenal world, organizing and interpreting a reality mediated through the senses. While the knower must remain alert to possibilities for misperceiving or misconceiving what is known, Bowne believed that the categories for knowledge reliably derived from the active engagement of the mind with the world and that the patterns of reflection—logic in particular—built up coherences, categories, intuitively and sensorily derived, that could be depended on. Bowne stressed the active rather than the passive character of the person's knowing and gave knowing, in distinction to Kant, a purposive dimension.

Immanental and optimistic, personalism valued freedom and morality; sought to balance the rational, volitional, and emotional; took religious experience seriously, expecting religious commitment to express itself in life (ethics); accented the individual but also the relationship of persons, one to another and all to God; and strove to integrate the various kinds of knowledge. In certain areas traditional, in others avant garde, Bowne's immanental theological formulations, his reworking of Christian doctrines, his opposition to intolerance, anti-intellectualism, and fundamentalism, and his support of biblical criticism earned him critics. One of them, George A. Cooke, charged Bowne with heresy, resulting in Bowne's trial by the New York East Conference (MEC) in 1904. Cooke alleged that Bowne taught doctrines of the Trinity, miracles, inspiration, atonement, and redemption contrary to the Methodist Articles of Religion and established doctrinal standards. A distinguished "Select" committee headed by Frank Mason North heard the case, questioned Bowne, deliberated in all some sixteen hours, and voted unanimously to reject the charges.

Termed Methodism's "Last Heresy Trial," it vindicated personalism and discredited the opposition. The trial embittered Bowne toward theological reactionaries. He received warmer reaction from other quarters, including that accorded him in China and Japan on a world tour that he made in 1905 and 1906. The Imperial Educational Society of Japan made him an honorary member. Ohio Wesleyan and New York University also recognized him with honorary degrees. Bowne died on 1 April 1910, in Boston.

Suggested Readings

Writings of Borden P. Bowne: *The Atonement* (Cincinnati, 1900); *The Christian Life* (Cincinnati, 1899); *The Christian Revelation* (Cincinnati, 1898); *The Essence of Religion* (Boston: Houghton, Mifflin, 1910); *The Good* (New York, 1895); *The Immanence of God* (Boston: Houghton, Mifflin, 1905); *Introduction to Psychological Theory* (New York: Harper, 1887, [1886?]); *Kant and Spencer; A Critical Exposition* (Boston: Houghton, Mifflin, 1912); *A Man's View of Woman Suffrage* (n.p., 1910); *Metaphysics* (New York: Harper & Brothers, 1882); *Personalism* (Boston: Houghton, Mifflin, 1908); *Philosophy of Christian Science* (New York: [1908?]); *The Philosophy of Herbert Spencer* (New York: Nelson & Phillips, 1874); *Philosophy of Theism* (New York: Harper, [1887?]); *The Principles of Ethics* (New York: Harper, 1893, [1892?]); *Studies in Christianity* (Boston, 1909); *Studies in Theism* (New York: Phillips & Hunt, 1879); *Theism: Comprising the Deems Lectures for 1902* (New York: American Book Co., 1902); *Theory of Thought and Knowledge* (New York: Harper, 1897).

Paul Deats and Carol Robb, eds., *The Boston Personalist Tradition in Philosophy, Social Ethics, and Theology* (Macon: Mercer University Press, 1986).

Thomas A. Langford, *Practical Divinity: Theology in the Wesleyan Tradition* (Nashville: Abingdon Press, 1983), 119-24.

Francis J. McConnell, *Borden Parker Bowne: His Life and His Philosophy* (New York: Abingdon, 1929).

Charles B. Pyle, *The Philosophy of Borden Parker Bowne* (Columbus: S. F. Harriman, 1910).

Harmon L. Smith, "Borden Parker Bowne: Heresy at Boston," in *American Religious Heretics,* ed. George H. Shriver (Nashville/New York: Abingdon Press, 1966), 148-87.

Mary Baker Eddy

(1821–1910)

Amanda Porterfield

Mary Baker Eddy espoused a radically idealistic form of Christian thought; she believed that Love was a Divine principle and that nothing else finally existed. She tied this idealism firmly to Christian theology, arguing that the New Testament revealed that Christ was Love and that Love triumphed over evil, death, and the illusion of material reality. Emphasizing the rational coherence and empirical validity of her theology, Eddy argued that assent to Christ was not a matter of embracing anything mysterious or nonrational but of recognizing that Christ was a Principle with universally explanatory power. Thus Jesus and others who understood Christ were Scientists who possessed the Truth about the ultimate nature of reality. This Truth empowered its knowers to dispel error, including illusions about the existence of disease, and the suffering those illusions caused.

In its concern for healing, Christian Science had a strong pragmatic aspect that balanced and justified its radical idealism. Eddy believed that the healings Jesus performed were the visible signs of his knowledge of Christ, and hence were the key to understanding the nature of Christ and the true meaning of the New Testament. Because of her attention to religious knowledge and its visible expression, Eddy's conception of Christian practice centered on healing rather than on any form of liturgy.

Eddy dated her discovery of Christian Science to her recovery from a fall on the ice in Lynn, Massachusetts, in 1866, when she was forty-five years old and married to Daniel Patterson, an itinerant dentist. A sufferer from chronic illnesses, Mary Baker Patterson was a patient and disciple of Phineas P. Quimby, a clockmaker, daguerreotypist, and healer in Portland, Maine, who used mental influence to treat disease. Quimby died sixteen days before Patterson's fall, and only three months after the death of her father, Mark Baker. Bereft of her mentor and her father, and emotionally estranged from her husband, the bedridden Patterson experienced the presence of Christ while meditating on the New Testament stories of Jesus' healings. Believing herself to have been healed by the power of Christ, she rose from her bed three days after her fall. In 1870, she began instructing students in the principles of Science and in the practice of healing without medicine. In 1873 she divorced Patterson, and four years later married one of her practitioners, Gilbert Eddy.

Mary Baker Eddy founded the Massachusetts Metaphysical College in Boston in 1881, and served as its sole faculty member until its closing in 1889. The college enrolled hundreds of students in short courses focusing on Eddy's theology and its application in treating disease without medicine and enabling painless childbirth. In an effort to consolidate her work and maintain the authority of her teaching over the work of her followers, Eddy established the Church of Christ, Scientist, and laid the cornerstone for First Church in Boston in 1884. As a religious organization, the church was geographically far-reaching and financially successful; by 1906 there were 682 branch churches, all debt-free, with 40,011 members in towns and cities across the United States. Church organization was highly centralized, with each branch church directly responsible to the Mother church in Boston. Eddy's authority was so firmly institutionalized that after her death in 1910, the church continued to flourish under the guidance of a Board of Directors, and no other leader emerged to assume or recast her mantle.

The singular quality of Eddy's authority within Christian Science is partly the result of belief in her role as the modern successor of Jesus. Although the exact nature of the relationship between Jesus and Eddy was a subject of dispute during Eddy's life, and continued to provoke controversy after her death, both she and her disciples emphasized her similarity to Jesus during the years she was building a following and establishing her church. They compared his resurrection to her rising from bed three days after her debilitating fall, and represented her special religious status by the reverential term Mother. But late in her life, Eddy rejected the name Mother and forbade comparisons between herself and Jesus. Various factors seem to have contributed to her decision to downplay her personal charisma, including her commitment to the consistent elaboration of her theology, which stressed Principle and muted personality.

Other factors, including hostile criticism of the imperious aspects of her personality by former students and skeptical outsiders, and her own desire to prevent any of her disciples from usurping or inheriting her authority, led Eddy to designate her principal writing, *Science and Health with Key to the Scriptures,* as her only legitimate successor. But belief in Eddy's authority as a latter-day Jesus persisted and proved difficult to expunge. As late as the 1930s and 40s, the church considered publishing Bliss Knapp's *Destiny of the Mother Church,* which presented Eddy as an "incarnation of truth" comparable to Jesus. The church decided against publishing the book in 1948 on the grounds that its claim was heretical because Eddy had forbidden comparisons between herself and Jesus, but reversed its decision in 1991 after Knapp's wife and sister made a $50 million bequest contingent on the church's publication of the book.

Eddy's theological writings include *Unity of Good* (1887), *Miscellaneous Writings* (1896), *Christian Science versus Pantheism* (1898), and most important, the authoritative text of Christian Science, *Science and Health.* Eddy published the first edition of this text in 1875, and revised it four times, in one case with the help of a Unitarian minister, James Henry Wiggin. The final edition of 1906, *Science and Health with Key to the Scriptures,* remains the centerpiece of Christian Science life, along with the New Testament. Distancing itself from literal interpretations of the Bible, this text defines Christian doctrine in symbolic terms, and interprets the central elements of Christianity in terms of mental experience. Thus *Science and Health* describes prayer as loving and truthful desire, atonement and eucharist as the meeting of individual mind with Christ, and marriage as the companionship of masculine and feminine qualities. The text distinguishes Christian Science from spiritualism, contrasting the explanatory power of Christian Science with spiritualism's appeal to mysterious phenomena, and the idealism of Christian Science and its rejection of materialism with the spiritualist belief that human beings have an immortal material form that can be conjured up after death.

Science and Health explains the apparent existence of material reality as a consequence of erroneous belief—material reality and its various manifestations seem to be real when individuals believe in their existence. Even though they lose their hold on individual minds when seen in the true light of Christ, erroneous beliefs in material reality and disease can be intensely painful and debilitating. The suffering caused by disease and materialism epitomizes mortal life, Eddy believed, and Christian Science treated that suffering.

Eddy's belief in Animal Magnetism also receives attention in *Science and Health,* although its place in the text diminishes over the course of five editions, and occupies only a brief chapter in the final edition. In that chapter, Eddy identified Animal Magnetism with mesmerism, which she associated with the work of the eighteenth-century Austrian physician, Franz Anton Mesmer. Mesmer's treatment of disease presumed belief in an intangible magnetic fluid that emanated from individuals and could exert force on objects at a distance. In some of his treatments, Mesmer assembled patients around a vat of diluted sulfuric acid, and had them grasp iron bars or hold hands in his efforts to direct and magnify the effect of positive mental influence traveling through this magnetic fluid. Banned from Austria for practicing magic, Mesmer continued his work in Paris until forced to flee during the French Revolution. Historians have credited him with the modern discovery of hypnotic influence and with pioneering efforts to understand that phenomenon in scientific terms. Mesmer's efforts to develop a scientific method for treating mental illness without medicine provided a point of departure from which both Christian Science and various forms of psychotherapy eventually grew, although in both cases belief in a magnetic fluid that conveyed mental influence was repudiated.

Eddy's mentor Phineas P. Quimby began practicing a form of mesmerism after attending lectures and demonstrations in 1838 by the Frenchman Charles Poyen, who used hypnotic suggestion to control the behavior of his subjects. Building on the "electrical psychology" he learned from Poyen, Quimby employed a young clairvoyant, Lucius Burkmar, to diagnose illness and prescribe remedies. But when Quimby learned he could lead Burkmar to suggest alternative remedies that were equally effective but less expensive, he concluded that the illnesses Burkmar diagnosed were caused by his patients' beliefs about their illnesses and that these beliefs, rather than the illnesses they caused, should be treated directly. Quimby accordingly dispensed with Burkmar's services, and began talking his patients out of negative ideas about their illnesses and into positive ideas about health. Although he still utilized the mesmerist technique of scalp manipulation because his patients demanded it, he no longer believed that the sessions served actually to transmit electrical fluid but that they contributed to his patients' belief in the effectiveness of his treatments.

The question of Eddy's indebtedness to Quimby has occasioned much controversy, especially among Eddy's critics, who claimed that she represented his ideas as her own. Eddy revered Quimby during his lifetime, but later distanced her ideas from his. In response to complaints about her failure to acknowledge her indebtedness, Eddy later maintained that Quimby had borrowed from her, not the reverse. She never fully acknowledged that her own theology emerged out of the context of her enthusiasm for Quimby or that his thinking departed from mesmerism's belief in electrical fluid. Quimby's ideas did in fact play a crucial role in the development of her theology. His practice of healing by suggestion inspired her investment in the mental science of healing. And his interpretation of Christianity as a science of healing led to her concept of Christ as the principle of Truth that banished all disease-causing thought. But Eddy was more saturated with the language of the New Testament than Quimby, and theology was her primary mode of expression. Where Quimby made the mental treatment of suffering his chief and overarching end, such treatment was not an end in itself for Eddy, but a visible sign of what she understood to be the true meaning of Christ revealed in the New Testament.

Eddy asserted her identity as a Christian thinker over against mesmerism, often referring to it as Animal Magnetism, and accused Quimby of not distancing himself sufficiently from that belief system or its practice. She became increasingly persuaded that mesmerism was a powerful and ubiquitous source of negative mental influence. Eddy rejected the materialist aspects of mesmerist theory even more firmly than Quimby, but she was convinced that negative beliefs were extremely powerful, and that some of her students betrayed her, and even attempted to injure or kill her by thinking about her maliciously. She regarded these individuals, and all other specialists in mental influence who were invested in the existence of material reality, disease, and death, as subtle practitioners of mesmerism. Though Quimby himself was not overtly malicious, Eddy faulted him for not resisting the malice of materialism strenuously enough.

Some critics have missed both the coherence of Eddy's thought and the depth of her commitment to Christianity, and dismissed her writings as the illogical effusions of an infirm, hysterical woman who could not face reality or tolerate any will other than her own. But her theology is actually quite coherent and more fairly understood as a remarkably creative if unschooled form of American Protestant thought. She lacked all but the rudiments of a formal education, and became acquainted with philosophical idealism not through any systematic study but only through popular literature and conversation, especially with her brother, who studied metaphysics at Dartmouth. But as her correspondence with Bronson Alcott in the 1870s reveals, there are profound similarities between her thought and the ideas of New England Transcendentalists, some of whom also denied the independent reality of the material world and viewed this world as a manifestation of Spirit. While transcendentalism was on the wane in America after the Civil War, Eddy persisted in carrying forward a radical and popular variant of its commitments to the ultimate reality of Spirit, and to the authority of Spirit's revelation to individual mind. If she rode against the increasingly popular currents of social Darwinism, which emphasized the material and social progress of human civilization, she rode with the tide of enthusiasms for scientific discovery and principle, mental and physical health, and psychosomatic treatments which were also growing in popularity in late-nineteenth-century America. Moreover, her idealistic interpretation of the New Testament left her completely unencumbered by the anxieties about scientific and literary criticism of the Bible that plagued many of her contemporaries.

Eddy's thought anticipated certain reformist agendas in American health care, such as natural childbirth and mental strategies for achieving wellness and freedom from pain, and paralleled efforts to establish psychotherapy as a scientifically legitimate treatment for psychosomatic illness. But however farsighted Eddy was in her belief in the power of mental influence, her gender and lack of formal education excluded her from discussions with contemporaries who participated in the professionalization of science in late-nineteenth-century America. Her Divine Science developed outside the main currents of scholarly thought, largely sidestepped the intellectual challenges of secularization, and addressed an overwhelmingly female constituency. The lack of serious attention her theology has received in academic circles is partly due to the profound division between the male-dominated, increasingly professionalized culture of academic life and the female-dominated culture of piety characteristic of religious life and thought in America from the Civil War into the 1960s.

Since then, theologies outside the mainstream have received more attention. Yet while Christian Science has generated some interest among intellectual historians, it has gained little attention from theologians. In recent years, feminist theologians have celebrated the achievements of religious women of the past who have been insufficiently appreciated, but have not found Eddy's thought attractive or useful, perhaps because of its denial of the positive spiritual significance of the natural world, which feminist theologians often consider the locus of spiritual beneficence and women's authority. At the same time, membership within Christian Science has declined, and the church has been beset by serious financial troubles and internal divisions. In the absence of any revitalization movement within Christian Science, and in the face of today's celebration of the spiritual dimensions of the natural world, the theology of Mary Baker Eddy has lost some of its popular appeal.

Suggested Readings

Writings of Mary Baker Eddy: *Science and Health with Key to the Scriptures* (Boston: First Church of Christ, Scientist, 1906).

Edwin Franden Dakin, *Mrs. Eddy: The Biography of a Virginal Mind* (New York: Charles Scribner's Sons, 1929).

Stephen Gottschalk, *The Emergence of Christian Science in American Religious Life* (Berkeley: University of California Press, 1975).

Stuart E. Knee, *Christian Science in the Age of Mary Baker Eddy* (Westport, Conn.: Greenwood Press, 1994).

Robert Peel, *Christian Science: Its Encounter with American Culture* (New York: Henry Holt and Co., 1958).

Julius Silberger, Jr., *Mary Baker Eddy: An Interpretive Biography of the Founder of Christian Science* (Boston: Little, Brown and Co., 1980).

Rufus Matthew Jones

(1863–1948)

Kerry S. Walters

Rufus Matthew Jones, Quaker philosopher, historian, and theologian, was born 25 January 1863 in South China, Maine, and died 16 June 1948 in Haverford, Pennsylvania. Educated at Haverford College, Heidelberg University, the University of Pennsylvania, and Harvard, Jones taught at a Quaker school and seminary before beginning a forty-one-year career (1893–1934) as philosophy professor at Haverford College. A recorded minister in the Society of Friends from 1890 until his death, he edited the *Friends' Review* (later the *American Friend*) from 1893 to 1912 and helped found (1917) the American Friends Service Committee, serving as its first chair. Jones published sixty books (including four volumes of memoirs) and thousands of articles, ranging from the scholarly to the popularly devotional. He was also in great demand as a lecturer. At the time of his death, his contribution to letters had earned him more than a dozen honorary degrees as well as scores of other awards. The London *Times* referred to him as "the greatest spiritual philosopher living in America since William James."

Generally speaking, Jones' work can be divided into two groups: his historical studies of Quakerism and western mysticism, and his theological-philosophical works. In the former (e.g., *Studies in Mystical Religion*, 1909; *The Quakers in the American Colonies*, 1911; *Spiritual Reformers in the Sixteenth and Seventeenth Centuries*, 1914; *The Later Periods of Quakerism*, 1921; and *New Studies in Mystical Religion*, 1927), he argued for an interpretation of the Quaker tradition as well as late medieval and Reformation theology that stressed the mystical element. Although his historical studies remain classics, Jones has sometimes been accused of overplaying the mystical at the expense of the doctrinal, especially in his accounts of Quakerism. In his more theological-philosophical works (e.g., *Social Law in the Spiritual World*, 1904; *The Inner Life*, 1916; *Pathways to the Reality of God,* 1931; *Spirit in Man,* 1941; and *A Call to What Is Vital,* 1948), he defended his own religious worldview, which itself is deeply mystical.

Jones' religious thought intimately reflects the Quaker heritage he loved. Although rich and multifeatured, his religious writings revolve around three related themes: the presence of the divine in humans, the unity of existence, and a mysticism of affirmation.

In keeping with his Quaker background, Jones argued that the human being contains within itself a spark of the divine, and, consequently, the most immediate path to God consists in plumbing the depths of one's own soul. He most often referred to this indwelling Presence as "the Beyond that is Within," "Divine Spirit," "the Spirit of Truth," or following Emerson, "the Over-World." But it obviously corresponds to the traditional Quaker notion of "Christ Within," although Jones himself rarely used the phrase.

A corollary of Jones' belief in the indwelling presence is his emphasis that immediate intuition of God is indeed attainable, since there is no radical separation between humans and the divine. Jones, no irrationalist, acknowledged that it is entirely possible for human reason to think its way to some understanding of God, but he was suspicious of theological speculation that assumed a wide gulf between God and humans. Indeed, such speculation, he argued, could impose artificial barriers even when its intentions were otherwise. For him, God and humans belong together, but are frequently rent apart by "arid and artificial" metaphysical schemes: far better, then, to hearken to the "Inner Light" than to abstractions of school theology in the search for God. In this regard, Jones is again loyal to his Quaker roots. He also echoes Ralph Waldo Emerson's argument that "self-reliance" naturally follows from the presence of the divine within humans.

Jones' refusal to separate the divine from the human points to the second characteristic of his religious thought, its metaphysical monism. Reality cannot be divided into the natural and the supernatural. Instead, just as divine and mortal reality intersect in the human soul, so physical and nonphysical reality intersect in the world. Put another way, what we take to be the natural realm is actually infused with the divine presence. We discover God in exploring the depths of our personal being, but we can also encounter traces of the divine by looking beyond the physical qualities of the world. Jones was in complete sympathy with Goethe's remark at the end of *Faust* that everything which is transient is but a symbol for an underlying and durable reality. For him, temporal dimensions are only aspects of the eternity which penetrates every moment.

Perhaps the most intriguing aspect of Jones' religious thought is his view of mysticism. His interest was more than merely academic; Jones himself believed he had experienced no fewer than three distinct mystical experiences, and made it clear he considered them the spiritual foundations of all his explicitly religious writings.

What Jones means by mysticism is not entirely clear; several definitions of it can be found throughout his works. But the one most in keeping with the wider tenor of his thought appears in his 1934 memoir *The Trail of Life in the Middle Years*. There he defined mysticism's essential characteristic as "the attainment of a personal conviction by an individual that the human spirit and the divine Spirit have met, have found each other, and are in mutual and reciprocal correspondence as spirit with Spirit." This notion of correspondence between spirit and Spirit is essential to Jones' account, and separates his mysticism of "affirmation" from the apophatic, or negative, mystical tradition. In apophatic mysticism, the goal is to eliminate the self or ego through a regimen of spiritual exercises until it no longer remains, thereby creating a void, as it were, into which God flows. For Jones, however, this sort of mystical union leaves the individual with "empty hands." In aiming for an ecstatic leave-taking of self-awareness, it destroys the possibility of human awareness of God because it transcends consciousness, dissolving the knowing subject into a blank, abstract nothingness.

In opposition, Jones argued that the human encounter with the divine does not negate what is finite so much as bring it to spiritual fruition. In the mystical experience of God, the individual is affirmed in his or her finitude as a child of God. But in its affirmation of human finitude, Jones' notion of mysticism also points to the potential within humans for growing into an increasingly intimate relationship with God. Jones understood the life of Jesus as an illustration of this sort of mystical union. For all these reasons, Jones' affirmative mysticism aligns more with the biblical than the Platonic tradition.

Jones' favorite passage of scripture—quoted again and again in his writings—is "the spirit of man is the candle of the LORD" (Prov. 20:27). Jones' interpretation is that the human spirit can be lighted by Spirit and thereby become a vehicle of revelation as well as growth in the divine presence. But such a possibility does not come about from unilateral movements on the part either of God or of humans. Instead, it involves a "mutual and reciprocal correspondence," in which the individual gradually climbs the "Jacob's Ladder" of the soul to find a "communion with the Beyond Within," and God, through grace, offers illumination. There is, so to speak, a mutually sought embrace that characterizes affirmative mysticism. As

Jones says, there is a double act in which the Above reaches downward and the below reaches upward. This notion of "mutual and reciprocal correspondence," so central to Jones' view of mysticism, he derived from Clement of Alexandria's notion of human response to God as one of the lover searching for the beloved.

Although not widely read today, Rufus Jones was immensely influential during his lifetime. His devotional works were eagerly snapped up by the general reading public, and his more erudite tomes on the history of western mysticism are still staples of college and university libraries. It is arguable that no Quaker since George Fox had done as much as Jones to awaken people to the spiritual life.

Suggested Reading

Writings of Rufus M. Jones: Harry Emerson Fosdick, ed., *Rufus Jones Speaks to Our Time: An Anthology* (New York: Macmillan, 1951).

Antoinette Brown Blackwell

(1825–1921)

Janet Nelson

Antoinette Louisa Brown Blackwell was a nineteenth-century preacher, public lecturer, moral reformer, women's rights activist, theologian, philosopher, poet, and novelist. Blackwell herself considered the ministry to be her primary vocation, and she is recognized as the first American woman ordained by a large Protestant denomination. Her theological project can be characterized as one of engagement and reconciliation with other strands of nineteenth-century social, moral, and scientific thought. Specifically, she sought to prove that the Christian faith was compatible with the full equality of women, and in her later, more philosophical writings, she attempted to reconcile religion with science, particularly the new theories of evolution developed by Charles Darwin and Herbert Spencer.

Born into a liberal orthodox family in Henrietta, New York, Blackwell felt the call of her vocation early in life. She became a member of the local Congregationalist church when not yet nine years old, and in her youth declared her intention to pursue a then unprecedented career for women— ordination as a minister. She was one of the first American women to receive a college education, completing the Literary Curriculum at Oberlin, designed for the more limited educational training deemed appropriate for women. She then applied and was reluctantly granted permission to attend graduate classes in the Theological Department, but not permitted to enroll officially in the program. While Oberlin offered the only coeducational and interracial education in the country, and professed a liberal theology under the leadership of Charles Finney and Asa Mahan, it maintained a conservative position on women taking an active public or professional role. Blackwell wrote a paper entitled "Exegesis of 1 Corinthians, XIV, 34, 35; and 1 Timothy, II, 11, 12" on the biblical injunctions that women are to keep silence in church and are not to teach or "usurp authority over the man." In the paper, she presented an interpretation that supported the full and equal participation of women in the church, including the ministry. Despite its favorable reception, evidenced by its publication in the *Oberlin Quarterly Review*, Blackwell was refused a degree and ordination upon completion of three years of theological study. Years later, Oberlin would recognize her academic achievements, granting her an honorary A.M. (1878) and an honorary D.D. (1908).

Blackwell became a popular independent speaker on the lyceum circuit, speaking out on abolition, temperance, and women's rights, and guest preaching at the request of individual liberal churches. At the suggestion of her college friend Lucy Stone, Blackwell became a regular speaker at Women's Rights conventions, assuming the responsibility of providing a theological defense to the movement's many clerical opponents. "That which is right is right eternally, both for men and for women. Where God has granted ability to act in any direction, he has given the right to act," she proclaimed at the convention held in Cleveland in 1853, echoing her predecessor, Sarah Grimke (Hardesty, 65). She was, however, something of an anomaly to many of her activist colleagues who rejected her religious framework as essentially antithetical to women's rights and did not support her ministerial aspirations. When Blackwell proposed a resolution that the Bible upholds woman's social, moral, and religious equality, she was going against the increasingly secular orientation of the movement, and her resolution was tabled at conventions in 1852 and 1853.

Blackwell realized her lifelong goal in 1853 when she was ordained to the ministry of the Congregationalist church in the small village of East Butler, New York. Though initially delighted with her new pastoral duties, doubts soon arose. Blackwell found herself deeply troubled by the orthodox Calvinist doctrine on infant damnation, and more generally with orthodoxy's view of a harsh and punishing God, at odds with her own liberal belief in a merciful, loving Divinity. For the first time, her deeply felt religious faith failed her, and her spiritual crisis led to a breakdown in her physical and mental health. After only a year, she resigned her post in East Butler. Eventually she would be attracted to Unitarianism, whose liberal views and emphasis on rationality and free will would provide her with a more congenial theological framework. She was ordained a Unitarian minister in 1878. Though continuing to preach throughout her life, she would never again occupy a permanent pulpit.

After marriage in 1856 to Samuel Blackwell, and the birth of five children who lived to adulthood, Blackwell turned her attention to the study of science and philosophy, particularly metaphysics. In her subsequent published works, *Studies in General Science* (1869), *The Physical Basis of*

Immortality (1876), *The Philosophy of Individuality* (1893), *The Making of the Universe* (1914), and *The Social Side of Mind and Action* (1915), she attempted to reconcile the new scientific theories with her religious beliefs. While accepting the theories of evolution developed by Darwin and Spencer, she drew from them very different social, moral, and religious implications. Blackwell argued that the existence of a benevolent God, the immortality of the soul, and the essential harmony, unity, and cooperation of life are all revealed through natural laws perceptible to all human beings. Humanity is progressively evolving toward a more just, more perfect society. Much the same way she had earlier criticized traditional religious views on the subordination of women, Blackwell now challenged the new "scientific" authority that upheld woman's natural inferiority, by arguing that women were equal to but distinct from men in *The Sexes Throughout Nature* (1875). Although her work was generally favorably received, it rested on assumptions which could not then, or now, be scientifically proved. Her moral and theological arguments consisted primarily of metaphors and analogies drawn to scientific theories.

Blackwell's place in history rests on being "the [woman] pioneer who first opened the door of the American pulpit, having borne her cross, if cross it were, and wearing her crown now" (Cazden, 243). Fittingly, Blackwell was named Minister Emeritus in 1908 at the Unitarian church she had helped to found in 1903, and lived to cast her first vote in the election of 1920, at the age of ninety-five.

Suggested Readings

Writings of Antoinette Brown Blackwell: *The Sexes Throughout Nature* (New York: G. P. Putnam's Sons, 1875).

Elizabeth Cazden, *Antoinette Brown Blackwell: A Biography* (Old Westbury, N.Y.: Feminist Press, 1983).

Nancy A. Hardesty, *Women Called to Witness: Evangelical Feminism in the Nineteenth Century* (Nashville: Abingdon Press, 1984).

Carol Lesser and Marlene Deahl Merrill, eds., *Friends and Sisters: Letters Between Lucy Stone and Antoinette Brown Blackwell* (Urbana and Chicago: University of Illinois Press, 1987).

Alice S. Rossi, ed., *The Feminist Papers: From Adams to deBeauvoir* (Boston: Northeastern University Press, 1973).

William Porcher DuBose

(1836–1918)

Donald S. Armentrout

William Porcher DuBose's ancestors were Norman French Huguenots who settled in South Carolina in 1686. Most of the Huguenots of the South Carolina Low Country were generally absorbed by the Church of England. At a temporary home in Winnsboro, thirty miles north of Columbia, William Porcher was born on 11 April 1836, the son of Theodore Samuel Marion and his first cousin, Jane (Porcher) DuBose, and soon after he was baptized in the courthouse by an Episcopal priest who served the people of Winnsboro from his parish in Columbia.

When William was eight years old, the family moved to a plantation called "Roseland," three miles from Winnsboro, so the DuBose boys could attend Zion College in that town. Here William did well in all his subjects except mathematics, and because of that deficiency his father decided to delay his entrance into the University of Virginia and sent him to the South Carolina military college, The Citadel, in Charleston. DuBose entered in 1851, and completed his studies in 1855, with first honors. In 1854, while at The Citadel, he had a "conversion experience." After a long march and attending a "roaring farce" of a play, DuBose and two other cadets spent the night in a hotel. That night, as the others slept, DuBose got up to pray. While he was praying a light shone about him, a presence filled the room, and "an ineffable joy and peace" took possession of him.

Although it was not the custom of the time to be confirmed and become communicants of the Episcopal Church, DuBose was confirmed at St. Michael's Church, Charleston, in November 1854. It seems that about this time he began thinking seriously of entering the ministry. In October 1856, DuBose left for the University of Virginia at Charlottesville, and in 1859 he received an M.A. degree.

In October 1859, he entered the theological seminary of the Protestant Episcopal Church in the diocese of South Carolina at Camden, which had

315

just opened on New Year's day of 1859. He was called away from the seminary by the Civil War in his middle or second year in 1861. During the war he was wounded three times and was once taken prisoner. Ordained deacon on 13 December 1863, at Grace Church, Camden, he returned to his Confederate troops at Greeneville, Tennessee, as a chaplain. After the war, he and his wife, the former Anne Barnwell Peronneau, whom he married in 1863, returned to South Carolina, and DuBose became the rector of St. John's, Fairfield, which included St. John's, Winnsboro, and St. Stephen's, Ridgeway. He was ordained priest on 9 September 1866, and two years later became the rector of Trinity Church, Abbeville. In 1871, he was elected Chaplain of the new University of the South at Sewanee, Tennessee.

From that year until his death on 18 August 1918, DuBose worked in the University of the South in a variety of positions, as chaplain (1871–83) and teacher in the College of Arts and Sciences (1871–93). In the Theological Department, which he founded, he served as Professor of Systematic Divinity and Exegesis (1872–75); Professor of Exegesis and Homiletics (1876–79); Professor of New Testament Language and Interpretation (1878–1907); and Professor of Old Testament Language and Interpretation (1872–1907). In 1893–94, he provided administrative leadership as Acting Dean and from 1895 to 1908 as the second Dean of the Theological Department. That department, now called the School of Theology, was—it was said—for years the elongated shadow of DuBose.

Primarily a biblical exegete and teacher of the New Testament, DuBose wrote five of his six principal books as studies of the New Testament. The *Soteriology of the New Testament* (1892) offered a New Testament theology stressing the person and work of Jesus Christ. *The Gospel in the Gospels* (1906) studied the Synoptic Gospels and stressed the humanity of Jesus Christ. *The Gospel According to St. Paul* (1907), primarily a study of Romans, emphasized the doctrine of justification by grace through faith. *High Priesthood and Sacrifice* (1908) examined the book of Hebrews and claimed that Jesus Christ is the great high priest because of his death. *The Reason of Life* (1911) considered the Johannine literature and emphasized the incarnation of God's reason in Jesus Christ.

The scriptures, especially the New Testament, were the primary source for DuBose's theology. He not only accepted the scriptures as "the tribunal of final resort for determining what Christianity is," but he accepted the insights of higher criticism and rejected any form of biblical literalism. He insisted that truths expressed in the scriptures in the objective form of history may be truths independently of the literal truth of the history. It is not necessary to believe the story of the Garden and the Fall to be historical fact in order to find in the story the most effective account of spiritual truths and realities. One does not have to take the story literally in order to understand that human beings are by nature sinful and unclean. He also rejected the idea that the Bible gives us propositional theology. He insisted that the New Testament no more gives us doctrine than nature gives us science. The New Testament presents the facts but not the theory—the matter of Christian doctrine, but not finished doctrine or doctrines of the whole matter of Christianity.

DuBose insisted that the Bible must be understood in terms of both its humanity and its divinity. The chief issue in Christian thought is the coexistence and union in one of the two elements of the divine and the human. This problem met us first in the mystery of the person of Jesus Christ. "To hold the very Godhead and the very Manhood in the unity of the one personality, and to hold each as in nowise to deny or impair the other, even by remote consequence, was no easy task; yet it was accomplished by the church in the first great period of its doctrinal history." DuBose argued that the Bible must be understood in this christological context, clearly articulated by the Council of Chalcedon (451 C.E.), that Jesus Christ is one person in two natures, and that the Bible is both human and divine.

DuBose noted that some people treat the Bible as completely divine, stressing the theory of a literal mechanical inspiration. Others treat it as completely human. He rejected the first position as a hermeneutical Docetism (the denial that Christ is human), and the second as a hermeneutical Ebionism (the denial that Christ is divine).

DuBose's point was that the truth of Christianity does not need external props, whether of a mechanical infallibility of scripture or of the absolute authority of an infallible pope. His entire understanding of the authority of scripture is summarized in this one sentence: "I believe that the scriptures are scripture because they are true, and not true because they are scripture."

DuBose taught that to understand scripture one must know the mind of the church. A person cannot interpret scripture apart from the mind of the church, which originally produced it. The mind of the church was most fully expressed by the first seven ecumenical councils of the church. This argument is found in his other principal book, *The Ecumenical Councils* (1896). He believed the councils must be studied over and over again, because through them the church had defined the person of Jesus Christ. The councils articulated the doctrines of the trinitarian God and the person of Christ. They were the beginning of theological reflection, not the end.

For DuBose theology was Christology. Jesus Christ is fully God; Jesus

Christ is the perfect expression of God so far as God is revealed at all. Jesus Christ is the "raying forth" of God's otherwise invisible glory; he is the "outward impress of God's secret substance." Jesus Christ was to him not a name, not a memory or tradition, not an idea or sentiment, not a personification, but a living and personal reality, presence, and power. "He is God for me, to me, in me, and myself in God." To the question, What of God can we see and know in Jesus Christ? DuBose answered, all of God that is communicable to us or receivable by us. DuBose insisted that he could doubt, he could at times disbelieve, God anywhere, everywhere except in Jesus Christ. Furthermore, Jesus Christ is God's final revelation; he is the final and complete word of God to humanity.

The love of God has been expressed fully in Jesus Christ. So far as our knowledge and experience can go, nowhere else in all God's universe, in all God's infinite and manifold activities, is God so God as in the person and work of Jesus Christ. This divine love is not any property of God but it is actually God's nature, and that love was raised to its highest power in the incarnation and in the cross. The manger and the cross are God at God's best.

For DuBose the incarnation continues in the church. The church is the true continuation of Christ and the proper body of his incarnation. Consequently the church is Jesus Christ himself, and relation to it is relation to him. Within the church, the sacraments of Baptism and Eucharist unite the believer to Christ. Baptism is admission into Christ's death and resurrection, and the Eucharist is continued participation in that death and resurrection.

William Porcher DuBose is the most significant theologian in the history of the Episcopal Church. He has had an influence on numerous English theologians, but until recently has been neglected by most Americans. Several collections of some of his writings have been issued, and his work is now being more widely read.

Suggested Readings

Writings of William Porcher DuBose: Jon Alexander, ed., *William Porcher DuBose: Selected Writings* (New York: Paulist Press, 1988); Donald S. Armentrout, ed., *A DuBose Reader: Selections from the Writings of William Porcher DuBose* (Sewanee, Tenn.: University of the South, 1984).

Charles Augustus Briggs

(1841–1913)

Richard L. Christensen

A scholar of great breadth of learning in history, theology, and biblical languages, Charles Augustus Briggs combined an evangelical piety with the insights of modern historical methods of interpretation in an attempt to discern the truth of the faith for his day. Although he is best known as the center of a stormy controversy over biblical authority which resulted in a heresy trial, Briggs' great passion was the cause of church unity. That passion undergirded all his scholarly work.

After an evangelical conversion at the University of Virginia in 1858, Briggs joined the Presbyterian Church, then in 1861 entered Union Theological Seminary in New York. After two years there, he had to abandon his studies temporarily to manage the family barrel business during the Civil War. But in 1866, bearing a letter of introduction from the respected church historian Philip Schaff, the young man went to begin study in Berlin accompanied by his new bride, Julia Valentine Briggs. For the next three years, he studied scripture and theology with such prominent European figures as biblical scholar Ernst Hengstenberg and theologian Isaak Dorner. Dorner communicated to the American student a mediating theology which sought a middle way between a rigid Lutheran confessionalism and a shallow Protestant liberalism. Briggs returned home to take a Presbyterian pulpit in Roselle, New Jersey, but soon afterward began teaching at Union Theological Seminary in New York, where he would spend the rest of his life as a faculty member.

From his study with Dorner, Briggs learned the theological principle of unity in diversity. Just as the three persons of the Trinity were an organic unity, Dorner declared, the best works of the triune God were diverse, but unified. This principle of unity in diversity showed itself in the study of the Bible, where Briggs sought to use the latest historical methods to demonstrate the basic unity of the Bible's message. This concept of unity in diver-

319

sity enabled Briggs to view the various Christian denominations as branches from the same root rather than as adversaries. He came to believe that a critical analysis of the message of the Bible, together with investigation of the historical development of the use of the Bible in doctrine, could bring the church to an expression of faith which could speak to contemporary society. The method required both the serious study of history and the serious study of the Bible. The influence of Dorner showed itself in Briggs' later concern for revision of church confessions, writing of church history, and efforts for church unity.

The use of modern critical methods of Bible study eventually brought Briggs into conflict with the stalwart defenders of Presbyterian orthodoxy at Princeton Seminary, Archibald Hodge and Benjamin Warfield. In a series of articles in the *Presbyterian Review* beginning in 1881, Briggs and his opponents laid out the battle lines over biblical criticism, which proved to be the seeds of the fundamentalist-modernist controversy of the twentieth century. Hodge and Warfield fired the first shot as they put forward the view that the inspiration of the scriptures extended to the very words themselves. Assurance of truth involved a rational certainty concerning the written words of scripture. The Bible, they claimed, was an "errorless record" of the message God wished to communicate to human beings. The scriptures were considered revelation both in their substance and their form. The words of the Bible were objective grounds of faith, and their reliability would be threatened if a single error were found.

In response, Briggs distinguished his opponents' doctrine of inspiration from that found in the historic creeds and confessions. He rejected the theory of inerrant verbal inspiration on the grounds that neither the scriptures nor the historic creeds sanctioned it. Quoting the Reformed confessions of the sixteenth century, he noted that the scriptures were considered authoritative, not merely by consent of the church but by the inward testimony of the Holy Spirit in one's heart. He pointed out that both Luther and Calvin acknowledged errors in the text but were not dismayed by them. The false mechanical theory of the Princeton men would mean that one had confused the news of grace with divine grace itself. Briggs accused the conservatives of driving a wedge between the human element in the scriptures and the inspiration of the scriptures, thus resulting in a reliance solely upon the external authority of the words of scripture and a neglect of the internal testimony of the Holy Spirit. For the conservatives, the thoughts and the words of scripture could not be separated, while for Briggs, the substance alone was infallible. Critical study of the words could help to reconcile the diverse portions of the Bible into a higher unity.

His concern for church unity moved Briggs to participate in the fledgling World Alliance of Reformed Churches and to suggest a model for federation of the Reformed churches in the United States. His critical studies led him to the conclusion that theology and doctrine underwent development over time. No ecclesiology or system of doctrine could be viewed as complete or final. Such a stance prompted his entry into the Presbyterian debate over revision of the Westminster Confession in the late 1880s, a debate he viewed as one small step in the drive toward a larger church unity.

His efforts for the revision cause brought Briggs into conflict with more conservative elements in the Presbyterian Church. In the fall of 1889, seeking to strike a telling blow for both creed revision and his vision of church unity, Briggs published a sharp attack on the conservatives—*Whither? A Theological Question for the Times.* He accused them of substituting a rigid "orthodoxism," as he called it, for the historical faith expressed in the Westminster Confession. He accused Hodge, Warfield, and others of a rigidity of understanding that caused disunity in the church. True orthodoxy recognizes the development of the church and its doctrine in history, moving forward to take in all truth. The conservatives, Briggs proclaimed, had made the Westminster Confession their bedrock principle and interpreted scripture through the lens of the Confession rather than the reverse. This actually denied the Westminster Confession itself and denied the Reformation principle of *sola scriptura.*

Whither? also made it abundantly clear that the great vision for the unity of the universal church took precedence over all other concerns. In a rather remarkable declaration for its time, Briggs argued that the rigidity of orthodoxism prevented Christians from recognizing the essential unity between Protestants and Roman Catholics. He went beyond previous calls for Protestant cooperation by envisioning an alliance with Roman Catholicism and "all other branches of Christendom." These two great streams of the historical church would be reconciled into something "higher and better," Briggs believed, with the continued progress of the church in the work of historical scholarship. Theological progress, he said, is not in the direction of simplicity, but of variety and complexity. All the churches should strive to incorporate all their disparate truths into one, larger, comprehensive truth of Christ. Briggs held strongly to the conviction that modern critical scholarship could provide a powerful impetus toward the reunion of the churches precisely by uncovering the relative historical circumstances that had led to the creeds and confessions that modern Christians viewed as divinely inspired.

Briggs foresaw great changes ahead for the whole Christian church. Believing denominationalism to be the great curse and great hindrance of the church, he described three factors which would work together to bring about its demise. The rise of liberty of conscience out of the Reformation, the consequent variety of faith expressions, and the spirit of free inquiry in biblical and historical matters would result, he concluded, in the decay of denominationalism. The open debate and conflict arising from freedom of conscience and critical scholarship would eventually result in a convergence of views and the consolidation of the churches. Holding an organic, developmental view of history, Briggs promoted the idea that continuing progress in the development of doctrine had a necessary place in the life of the church. Toleration and the interchange of various points of view would be necessary for the continuing movement of the church toward real unity. The work of critical scholarship would uncover what Briggs called the "genuine achievement" of each church tradition, and each of these would contribute to a comprehensive understanding of the church.

For Briggs' conservative adversaries in the Presbyterian Church, his views of development and convergence of doctrine were incomprehensible. In their view, truth was explicit in the scriptures. No higher form of truth could be arrived at over time—it had simply been given once and served for all time. Briggs' view of pluralism and movement in theology seemed too loose an understanding of the faith and finally an abandonment of the central claims of the Bible.

The controversy over Briggs' views on historical criticism of the Bible eventually resulted in a heresy trial. Appointed to the newly established Edward Robinson chair of Biblical Theology at Union Seminary, Briggs presented an inaugural address in January 1891 which had two main purposes. In his concern for the sources of church authority and the uses and misuses of the scriptures, he sought, first, to set forth his views on the authority and inspiration of the scriptures in opposition to his conservative opponents. His second—and for him more important—purpose was to reconcile various historical views of religious authority for the sake of church unity. This underlying irenic purpose, however, was obscured by his polemical and defiant tone of delivery. Briggs argued that God spoke through three sources of authority: the Bible, the church, and Reason. By "Reason" he meant both intellectual and emotional experience. These three, he declared, are complementary, not contradictory.

Reaction to his address came swiftly. Because he had failed to state his conviction that the Bible functioned as supreme authority, Briggs' enemies accused him of abandoning the centrality of the Bible. A series of heresy trials resulted in a conservative General Assembly suspending him from the ministry in 1893.

In 1899, Charles Briggs became ordained in the Episcopal Church and continued his work on church unity from that setting. In the last decade of his life, he met with Roman Catholic leaders and scholars, championing a reconciliation between Protestantism and Rome remarkable for its time. He also participated in efforts to defend liberal Catholic scholars from Vatican censure.

His significance in the making of theology in North America lies in his clear statement of the historical-critical view of biblical inspiration and his opposition to verbal inerrancy, thus providing the backdrop for the fundamentalist-modernist controversies which came to the fore in the 1920s. But significant, too, though less recognized, was his vision of the unity of the church. He had a great confidence that the fact of development in history made possible the actual unity of the church. Unity could be achieved, Briggs believed, because the various streams of Christianity each incarnated some elements of the truth of faith. The movement of history tended toward a reconciliation and convergence of these streams. Briggs intended the historical-critical method of biblical study to enable church bodies to recognize their catholicity, break down the walls of denominationalism, and thus foster the unity of the whole church. Through his biblical study, his attempts to reconcile various views of church authority, and his emphasis on the ancient church confessions as foundational, Charles Briggs foreshadowed in his work much of the ecumenical activity of the twentieth century, such as the discussions of the Faith and Order Movement, the Consultation on Church Union, and the increasing cooperation of Protestant and Roman Catholic scholars.

Suggested Readings

Writings of Charles A. Briggs: *Biblical Study: Its Principles, Methods, and History* (New York: Charles Scribner, 1883); *Church Unity: Studies of Its Most Important Problems* (New York: Charles Scribner, 1909).

Richard L. Christensen, *The Ecumenical Orthodoxy of Charles Augustus Briggs* (Lewiston, N.Y.: Edwin Mellen, 1995).

Mark Massa, *Charles Augustus Briggs and the Crisis of Historical Criticism* (Minneapolis: Fortress Press, 1990).

George Shriver, *American Religious Heretics: Formal and Informal Trials* (Nashville/New York: Abingdon Press, 1966).

William Newton Clarke

(1841–1912)

Claude L. Howe, Jr.

The last decade of the nineteenth century was a critical time of transition for American religion in general and American theology in particular. The New England Theology ("New Divinity") had provided the dominant theological outlook for Protestant thinkers, uniting Calvinism and revivalism into a coherent system of thought, but differing views of the Bible and universe as well as radical social demands of an industrial society were challenging its effectiveness and acceptance. Traditional Calvinism and pietistic Arminianism survived in confessional denominations and evangelical pulpits, but the search for a new theology accelerated as the new century approached.

Theological liberalism emerged as a progressive response to changing intellectual trends and cultural needs. By 1890 liberal theologians had accepted the evolutionary hypothesis with its implications as well as the higher critical approach to interpreting the Bible. Many traditional concepts such as endless future punishment or original sin or the person and work of Christ were reinterpreted, and personal religious experience transcended the authority of Bible or church or creed.

William Newton Clarke published *An Outline of Christian Theology* in 1898, providing a systematic exposition of classical theological categories from a modern perspective. God, Humanity, Sin, Christ, the Holy Spirit, "the Divine Life in Man," and Things to Come were interpreted with a full awareness and acceptance of recent historical and scientific developments and with a place of primacy reserved for Christian experience. Twenty editions of this work had been published by 1914, and Clarke is remembered as the first systematic theologian of theological liberalism in America.

Born on 2 December 1841, at Cazenovia, New York, Clarke was the second son of Baptist pastor William Clarke and Urania Miner. In this devout home and at a local Methodist secondary school (Oneida Conference Seminary), the young man imbibed an evangelical pietism that led to his conversion and pursued a scholastic interest in languages, studying Latin, Greek, and German. In 1858, Clarke enrolled at Madison University (later Colgate) in Hamilton, New York, receiving the A.B. degree three years later. Some of his classmates then entered the Union Army, but the recent graduate was not physically strong and had chosen the Baptist ministry for his vocation. He continued his academic studies at the Hamilton Theological Seminary, from which he graduated in 1863.

Impressed more in seminary by the pastoral and exegetical approach of Hezekiah Harvey than the philosophical and critical outlook of Ebenezer Dodge, who had studied in Germany under August Tholuck and Isaak August Dorner, Clarke accepted his first pastorate at Keene, New Hampshire. Here he continued diligent study of the Greek New Testament and performed his pastoral duties faithfully until May 1869, when he became pastor of the First Baptist church of Newton Center, Massachusetts. Emily A. Smith became his bride in September, and the couple remained in the pastorate for eleven years. Clarke then moved to the Olivet Baptist church in Montreal, Quebec, until 1883 when he became professor of New Testament interpretation at the Baptist Theological School in Toronto. After four years there, Clarke returned to the pastorate, accepting the church in Hamilton, New York, the home of Colgate University where he had been educated. When president and theology professor Ebenezer Dodge died January 1890, the university asked Clarke, his pastor, to teach his classes. After a few months, Clarke resigned from the church and became the J. J. Joslin Professor of Christian Theology at Colgate University.

While in Montreal, Clarke received an invitation from President Alvah Hovey of Newton Theological Institution to write the *Commentary on the Gospel of Mark* for *An American Commentary on the New Testament*. This work was published in 1881 after Hovey deleted a few comments on the inspiration of scripture and added an additional view of chapter 13, which had been interpreted as referring to the fall of Jerusalem, not the return of Christ. Clarke's other chief works were primarily theological; those written after his *Outline* include *Can I Believe in God the Father?* (1899), *What Shall We Think of Christianity?* (1899), *A Study of Christian Missions* (1900), *The Use of the Scriptures in Theology* (1905), *Sixty Years with the Bible* (1909), *The Christian Doctrine of God* (1909), and *The Ideal of Jesus* (1911). Some of these works were based on lectures at such prestigious institutions as Harvard, Johns Hopkins, and Yale. Clarke's accomplishments were recognized by honorary doctorates from Yale (1900), the University of Chicago (1901), and Columbia University (1910).

Clarke should be viewed not as a creative, original thinker but as a perceptive Christian preacher and teacher who responded to contemporary developments and needs openly and confidently. His theological system was basically a traditional orthodoxy, modified by current views of the Bible and universe and reinterpreted in light of Christian experience. Distinctly an evangelical liberal rather than a scientific modernist, his views would be neither conservative enough for fundamentalists nor liberal enough for the modernists in the controversies that erupted in the decade following his death.

Clarke's insistence that Christian theology must be altogether Christian ensured that his theological outlook would be centered in Christ. His point of departure, however, was not so much the person or work of Christ as the character of God revealed by Christ. The conviction that God was and always had been such a being as Christ revealed dominated his theology and gave it an ethical consistency which was perhaps the most unique element of his thought.

Clarke interpreted God as the personal Spirit, perfectly good, who creates, sustains, and orders all in holy love. There is no tension between God's holiness and love, for love desires to impart good, and holiness shows what is good and how it should be imparted. The time, method, and process of creation are proper subjects of scientific investigation, but the theologian insists that God is creator by whatever means. The God revealed in Christ is also a purposeful God, indwelling creation and directing the process in holy love toward God's divine objectives. Seeking to avoid pantheism and Deism, Clarke described the relation of God and the universe as the immanence of the transcendent God.

The sources of theology are manifold, Clarke maintained, and may be found anywhere—science, history, philosophy, other religions, nature, and human nature. Since humans bear God's image, to know them is in part to know God. Recent study of the universe has brought an enlarged conception of God and God's method of working, while study of humans in biology, physiology, psychology, history, and other sciences also contributes to theology. The calmness and confidence with which Clarke received modern knowledge accounts in part for the cordial reception of his views by many contemporaries.

Although theology utilizes other sources, the primary source is Christian revelation, found chiefly in scripture. But revelation comes first in experience as God's self-disclosure and then as written record. Matters of date or authorship or interpretation are proper subjects of investigation, and not all portions of scripture are equally informative or acceptable. Humans, not writings, are inspired, and the authority of scripture rests upon the truth it conveys. Clarke approved of the historical-critical approach in interpreting scripture, asserting that it had unified and Christianized his Bible, but in reality his perspective complemented more than duplicated this approach. Christian theologians, he said, should receive and utilize the Christian element in scripture. By this he meant not so much the words or teachings or personality of Jesus as such, but the whole contribution that he made to religious thought and experience concerning God or God's relation to humans. This element could be identified not by its label or locality but by its nature and quality. Thus it could be found progressively in the Old Testament but supremely in the New and uniquely in Christ, who reveals the character of God.

The liberal theologian focused on the personal and practical aspects of theology, avoiding for the most part abstract or metaphysical discussions. God appears as Father, Son, and Spirit, which Clarke described as triunity rather than trinity, with stress on the unity of being and purpose. Christ is human and divine, revealing what God is and what humans should be, while the Holy Spirit is God in humanity. Sin is taken seriously, arising from both the animal nature and spiritual nature, and humans are free and responsible, bearing God's image.

Clarke never doubted that Christianity is the only true religion, superior to and worthy of displacing all others. His interest was not in ecclesiastical organizations but in Christian people responding in Christ to the purposes of God, though he welcomed a growing unity and cooperation among Christian groups on a voluntary basis. His task as theologian was to set forth significant teachings of the Christian faith in a systematic but unscholastic manner for his own generation, confident that following generations would have the same task to perform in light of their own experiences. His writing and teaching encouraged many Christians who felt with Harry Emerson Fosdick that they must have a new theology to adjust to new thought patterns while conserving essential Christian convictions and practices revealed by God in Christ through the Holy Spirit.

Suggested Readings

Emily A. Clark, ed., *William Newton Clarke: A Biography* (New York: Charles Scribner's Sons, 1916).

Claude L. Howe, Jr., *The Theology of William Newton Clarke* (New York: Arno Press, 1980).

Newman Smyth

(1843–1925)

John L. Farthing

In the crucial decades just before and after the turn of the twentieth century, Newman Smyth became an influential advocate for a "modernist" perspective seeking to mediate between traditional faith and contemporary culture. His theology offers a classic statement of "evangelical liberalism" in its most articulate, persuasive form.

Smyth's studies at Andover Theological Seminary (class of 1867) left him dissatisfied with "orthodoxy"; rather than "circling the wagons" to defend orthodoxy against the corrosive tendencies of enlightened criticism, Smyth looked for common ground between religion and science. Continuing his studies in Berlin and Halle (1869–70), he found in August Tholuck and Isaak Dorner a theological reconstruction in which religious commitment makes common cause with modern science and philosophy. His studies in Germany introduced him to the critical view of scripture, which he heartily embraced and transmitted to his American readers. Unlike those who feared literary-historical criticism would reduce Holy Scripture to a collection of merely human documents, Smyth argued that the historical character of revelation itself requires the critical approach: The only kind of faith threatened by historical criticism, he suggested, is a bibliolatry that makes scripture itself the object of faith.

The influence of German thought in shaping Smyth's vision is most apparent in his relation to the theology of Friedrich Schleiermacher (1768–1834). Smyth adopted Schleiermacher's view of religion as a realm of intuition and feeling. "Experience" and "consciousness" play a role in Smyth's theology that suggests a profound continuity with Schleiermacher's emphasis on "feeling" *(Gefühl)*. At the same time, Schleiermacher's appeal to "the cultured despisers of religion" found repeated echoes in Smyth's natural theology.

A key to understanding Smyth's theology is to recognize he was a pastor-

328

theologian, serving from 1882 until his death in 1925 as pastor (or pastor emeritus) of Center Church in New Haven, Connecticut. Neither Smyth nor his parishioners could ignore the currents of intellectual criticism emanating from Yale University. Permeating Smyth's writings is a pastoral concern for sincere believers who know enough about the implications of modern science to question whether Christianity is compatible with what biologists, physicists, and other scientists have discovered about the nature of the world. In the late–nineteenth century, reason (the critical spirit) was often set against faith (traditional theism). Smyth sought to bridge this gap. He sought to reassure perplexed believers by showing that the insights of biblical religion are compatible with modern science and philosophy; the two realms, he argued, constitute an organic harmony. Smyth intended to preserve the core of historical Christianity, while expressing its central ideas in a language and conceptuality that made sense to people whose mentality and sensibility were being shaped by a scientific view of the world.

Equally at home in the pastor's study and in the biology laboratory, Smyth saw no conflict between the truth proclaimed from the pulpit and the best results of scientific research. He hoped to span the chasm between religion and science by linking a deeply personal piety with a rigorous intellectual honesty; his was an ecumenical Protestantism that combined American empiricism, pragmatism, and optimism with a social conscience and a deeply pastoral sensitivity.

Although Smyth's temperament was generous and inclusive, his theology aroused fierce opposition among defenders of orthodoxy. Two aspects of his theology proved controversial. First, Smyth rejected the belief that those who never hear the gospel will be damned. He argued instead for a "future probation." Everyone will have the opportunity to receive the salvation Christ offers. His critics feared this view might undermine the urgency of the missionary enterprise.

Conservatives were also troubled by Smyth's claim that religious ideas are subject to the historical conditioning that shapes other aspects of culture. Although his adversaries feared that such a view might reduce Christianity to a mere product of human culture, Smyth's "historicism" rested on a thoroughly biblical sense of God's presence within the ambiguities of the historical process. The God of the Bible, he argued, is profoundly immanent in nature and history; this same God is revealed in the processes of our own culture, including scientific research. For humans—temporal beings, immersed in historical processes of change and growth—a static deposit of changeless truth would be no revelation at all. Hence the discovery that evolution can be seen within biblical revelation itself is neither distressing nor scandalous. Far from threatening authentic faith, evolution provides the key to understanding God's way of working for the salvation of the world.

Smyth's thought tended toward integration and synthesis. His approach was radically relational and systemic. Reality, he insisted, is not a series of discrete, unrelated spheres of existence. The world is a single organism. Everything is what it is through its relatedness to all other realities. This perspective led Smyth to reject American individualism; in the 1880s he became an early proponent of "the Social Gospel," grounding his social critique not just in the imperatives of the Sermon on the Mount but in a conception of the world rooted in scientific observation and analysis.

A sense of the interrelatedness of all things was not just a facet of his religious idealism; it was a view of reality made possible by recent advances in the natural sciences. The vast diversity of things observed and described by modern science betrays an underlying organic harmony. Smyth saw in the universe a multiplicity of forms within which a single Energy is moving the world toward its teleological fulfillment. This intelligent, creative Energy Smyth identified with the Judeo-Christian God. Teleological tendencies identified by evolutionary science suggested to Smyth something akin to the creative process of a purposeful Intelligence rather than the mindless operation of impersonal, mechanical laws. The trajectory of the evolutionary process is toward the emergence of mental, affective, and spiritual life.

Even apart from the biblical revelation, Smyth thought it was clear that the final truth of existence is the supreme value of personal and social life. Not things but persons are of ultimate importance. Smyth's "personal realism" envisions a synergy between God and the world: God takes the initiative, to which the world responds. Repudiating the determinism of Calvinist orthodoxy, Smyth emphasized the moral freedom underlying the dignity and responsibility of human beings who are not God's puppets but God's coworkers.

This view of the human situation is one expression of Smyth's optimism. In evolution he saw evidence of a progressive tendency in cosmic and human history. He was confident, moreover, that reality is trustworthy and knowable; he saw no reason to doubt the possibility of coming to a knowledge of what is true and real in the life of the world. Faith, in Smyth's view, is not an alternative to knowledge; it is a way of knowing. In this perspective there is no place for nihilism or cynicism or epistemological despair.

While stressing the importance of subjective consciousness, Smyth remained confident that what takes place in the life of faith is a form of genuine knowledge, based not on an infallible book or pope but on the realities grasped in an act of human intuition informed by the data of experience. He intended to proceed scientifically—that is, empirically and inductively. He proposed an empirical theology open to all the facts. In contrast to the siege mentality of some conservatives, Smyth's theology radiated confidence and serenity. He was confident that all truth is a revelation of God. Faith, therefore, cannot be threatened by an openness to truth that comes from a "secular" source; faith in God—whose name is Truth—can only be deepened by an honest confrontation with the facts.

This spirit of openness can also be seen in Smyth's involvement in the nascent ecumenical movement. Smyth believed that every theological formulation remains partial; he left no place for the dogmatism that keeps Christians alienated from one another. His longing for harmony, coupled with his optimism about the possibilities of redemption within history, encouraged him to dream of "a grander Catholicism" in which the Protestant principle and the Catholic substance would come together in a mutually enriching synthesis.

Although he rejected a dogmatism content to repeat and defend formulas inherited from the past, the orthodox ("evangelical") strain in Smyth's thought is unmistakable. Jesus as the Christ retained a revelatory and normative significance. Smyth's perspective was thoroughly christocentric; he believed that the Incarnation reveals the law governing cosmic evolution. What Jesus reveals is not an utterly new beginning but a consummation of the continuing incarnation of God in the history of the cosmos. God is present in Jesus, but in a way that is prototypical and exemplary rather than unique and irrepeatable. The decisive revelation in Jesus lies in what he revealed about the possibilities open to all of creation.

Subsequent history called into question the liberal optimism that pervaded Smyth's view of God, humanity, and the world. The reality of evil turned out to be more recalcitrant than Smyth supposed. For thoughtful Christians during the generation leading up to 1914, however, Smyth's apologetics provided resources for optimism and self-confidence in an intellectual climate in which it was not at all clear that Western humanity could find a way to embrace both the heritage of faith and the promise of modernity.

Newman Smyth was a pivotal figure in the attempt to forge a symbiotic relationship between Christianity and the kind of culture that has emerged in Europe and North America since the Enlightenment. Today his optimism about human nature and historical progress may seem tragically naive. Yet his sense of the continuity between the natural and the supernatural, his way of viewing scripture and tradition as resources rather than authorities, and his determined openness to the modern world may prove instructive for a continuing dialogue in the postmodern context.

Suggested Readings

Writings of Newman Smyth: *Old Faiths in New Light,* rev. ed. (New York: Charles Scribner's Sons, 1887); *Christian Ethics,* 3rd ed. (Edinburgh: T. & T. Clark, 1892); *Recollections and Reflections* (New York: Charles Scribner's Sons, 1926).

John L. Farthing, "Ecumenical Hermeneutics: Newman Smyth and the Bible," *American Journal of Theology and Philosophy* 11 (1990): 215-32.

Bryan Glenn Gentle, "The Natural Theology of Newman Smyth" (Ph.D. dissertation; Ann Arbor: University Microfilms International, 1976).

Frances E. Willard

(1839–1898)

Nancy A. Hardesty

Temperance leader and woman's rights activist Frances Elizabeth Caroline Willard was not so much a professional theologian as a crusader for social justice. Her theology found expression more in her activities than in theoretical writings or scholarly lectures. Born 28 September 1839 in Churchville, New York, she moved at age two with her parents Josiah Flint Willard and Mary Thompson Hill Willard to Oberlin, Ohio. Both parents wished to study at Oberlin College under the progressive leadership of President Asa Mahan and revivalist-turned-theology-professor Charles Grandison Finney. In this hotbed of social reform, young Frances learned to read from *The Slave's Friend* and heard students such as Lucy Stone practice the rhetoric of abolition and woman's rights. After five years, the family of five migrated again to Janesville, Wisconsin. There the family embraced Methodism.

"Frank" (as she was known throughout her life) and her younger sister Mary attended Milwaukee Female College in 1857, and then the whole family moved to Evanston, Illinois, so the girls could enroll at the Methodists' new North Western Female College, from which Frances graduated in 1859. After teaching for several terms and taking a grand tour of Europe and the Middle East, Willard became president in 1870 of Evanston College for Ladies, which merged with Northwestern University after the Chicago fire of 1871 made fund-raising difficult.

The "temperance crusade" began in Ohio during the winter of 1873–74 and spread across the country. Evanston women soon organized a temperance society. Willard became its president. At a statewide convention (October 1874) Willard was elected secretary. She served as a delegate to the November convention in Cleveland, Ohio, that formed the national Woman's Christian Temperance Union, and she was chosen its corresponding secretary.

Willard had found her vehicle, but her vision was always broader than alcohol issues. Her early involvement in women's education led to a commitment to the advancement of women in all areas. By 1876 she was committed to woman's suffrage, a position many considered much too radical. In 1877 she resigned her post with the Chicago Union and joined evangelist D. L. Moody as his director of women's meetings. She spoke every afternoon on a biblical text and even preached one Sunday at Moody's request. While with Moody in Boston, she met musician Anna Gordon, who became her lifelong secretary and companion.

She returned to the W.C.T.U. full-time in 1879 when she was elected national president. Within two years, she had convinced the membership that suffrage as an instrument of "Home Protection" was a reasonable strategy and goal. Within a decade she quadrupled the membership of the W.C.T.U., making it the country's largest women's organization. In 1891 she became founding president of the World's W.C.T.U. She led both groups until her death on 17 February 1898.

Frances Willard's theology and social activism reflect her lifelong commitment to her beloved Methodist Episcopal Church. She became a member of Evanston First Methodist after her conversion experience during a bout with typhoid fever in 1859. Her journals as a young woman reveal a very sincere, if conventionally Victorian, faith. In the centennial year of American Methodism, 1866, she raised money for Barbara Heck Hall at Evanston's Garrett Biblical Institute. She was influenced by the Holiness preaching of Phoebe Palmer, who visited Evanston in 1866. Methodist women provided the base for the W.C.T.U., and Methodist churches most often served as their meeting places.

Like Wesley's, Willard's theology was orthodox and pragmatic. Her goal was the "Christianizing" of society, though she more often phrased it in terms of making the whole world more "homelike," governed by "mother love." Despite the Victorian rhetoric, Willard's views reflect the changes in the mainline Protestantism of her day. By the 1870s she was having doubts about the "literal" interpretation of scripture—especially as those interpretations were used to keep women in submission. Her constant travel and contact with all sorts of women gave her a wider ecumenical view. Willard even reached out to the Roman Catholics of the Total Abstinence Society. They warmly received her, but many W.C.T.U. members voiced the anti-Catholic and anti-immigrant sentiments of their day.

Her work with the Prohibition and Populist political parties and with the Knights of Labor put her in touch with Jewish women, for whom she expressed admiration. As the Union reached around the world, her respect for Oriental religions grew and she explored theosophy, intrigued by the work of Annie Besant. Mourning the death of several family members, including her beloved mother, Mary, in the 1890s she explored spiritualism. In her autobiography *Glimpses of Fifty Years,* she speaks of finding great good in all religions.

Like Wesley, Willard advocated a social Christianity. She called it her "do-everything" policy. The Union promoted women's education, prison reform, safe housing for young working women, day nurseries and medical dispensaries for children of the poor, raising the age of consent, prevention of sexual abuse and the exploitation of women and children, among other causes. In her later years, Willard was attracted to Christian Socialism. She frequently contributed articles to W. D. P. Bliss' magazine *Dawn* and was friendly with the British Fabians Beatrice and Sidney Webb.

Although Willard's commitment to Methodism was steadfast and she was revered as its most renowned laywoman, the church was not kind to her. When she became president of the W.C.T.U. in 1879, she suggested that members bring greetings to other prominent organizations, especially religious denominations—a common practice. However, a resolution to allow her to speak at the 1880 General Conference was met with hours of acrimonious debate. Although the vote eventually favored her speaking, opponents maneuvered to adjourn the meeting for the day. Rather than risk further embarrassment, she simply wrote a gracious note to be read to the Conference and left. Eight years later she returned as one of five women elected as delegates from across the country. Again there was lengthy debate, and the women were refused recognition.

Delivering her presidential address to the W.C.T.U. later in 1888 from the same platform, Willard threatened to withdraw from the Methodist Episcopal Church and to found her own denomination in which women would be treated as equals. But she never did. That same year she published *Woman in the Pulpit,* defending women in ministry. She herself felt called to ordination and viewed her work as that of an evangelist. She noted the selectivity with which scripture is often applied. Women were denied ordination and a voice in church politics on the basis of two texts, Willard noted, but nineteenth-century American Methodists did not argue that scriptures had been violated when their patriot parents rebelled against England or when northern Methodist abolitionists encouraged slaves to disobey their masters. The W.C.T.U. always honored women ministers from all denominations, asking them to speak and pray from the Union's own platforms and placing them in local pulpits during annual conventions.

In many ways Frances Willard epitomizes nineteenth-century American Protestant Christianity and mirrors its movement. Despite the church's faults, of which she was painfully aware, Willard continued to see it as a force for social good.

Suggested Readings

Writings of Frances E. Willard: Carolyn De Swarte Gifford, *Writing Out My Heart: Selections from the Journals of Frances E. Willard, 1855–96* (Urbana: University of Illinois Press, 1995).

Ruth Bordin, *Frances Willard: A Biography* (Chapel Hill: University of North Carolina Press, 1986).

Nancy A. Hardesty, *Women Called to Witness: Evangelical Feminism in the Nineteenth Century* (Nashville: Abingdon Press, 1984).

Washington Gladden

(1836–1918)

John Newton Hewitt

Washington Gladden served one of the longest and most distinguished pastoral ministries in American history. His career as a Congregationalist minister spanned the period from the Civil War to the First World War, a time of enormous social transformation. Gladden is remembered today for his pioneering contribution to the Social Gospel and his bold stands in the interests of democracy, social justice, and religious freedom. His autobiography, *Recollections* (1909), is one of the richest accounts ever written of church life in the Victorian era.

Born in 1836 at Pottsgrove, Pennsylvania, Gladden was raised in the pietistic home of a Methodist lay preacher. After his father's death (1841), he was sent to live on an uncle's farm near Owego, in western New York, a region so noted for its religious revivals that it became known as the "Burned-over District." Gladden attended Presbyterian and Baptist meetings during these formative years, and received a good elementary education. While apprenticed to the Owego *Gazette,* his moral sensitivities were aroused by the public debates surrounding slavery. When the minister of his Presbyterian church was fired for taking a stand with abolitionists, Gladden spent a couple of years of disillusioned "church-neglect," eventually finding a new lease on spiritual life with the Congregationalists, who seemed to strike an appropriate ethical note.

Gladden prepared for the ministry at the Owego Academy (1855) and Williams College, Massachusetts (1856–59). At Williams he came under the progressive theological influences of Mark Hopkins and John Bascom. Ordained by the Congregationalists in 1860, Gladden served pastorates in Brooklyn (1860–61) and Morrisania, New York (1861–66). At Morrisania he studied the writings of Horace Bushnell and the New Theology. These readings had a decisive impact on his theological orientation. When called to the pastorate at North Adams, Massachusetts, in 1866, Gladden insisted on having Bushnell preach at his installation—a gesture of support for his embattled mentor, whose liberal views on the atonement had been bitterly attacked by theological conservatives.

Earlier than most of his contemporaries, Gladden saw how important the changing social and industrial circumstances were to the presentation of the gospel. He addressed many of these topics in his early sermons. While in North Adams, he called for a society in which all men and women were truly equal. Later, while serving at the North Congregational church in Springfield, Massachusetts (1875–82), Gladden began to face up to economic issues and workers' rights. His popular series of lectures dealing directly with the application of Christian principles to the socioeconomic sphere were subsequently published in *Working People and Their Employers* (1885).

Gladden's most fruitful period came during his long ministry at First Congregational Church, in Columbus, Ohio (1882–1914). He counseled the striking Hocking Valley coal miners, and his sermons on just worker-management relations became the basis for his book *Applied Christianity* (1886). Gladden believed that a Christian social doctrine which emphasized an ethos of democracy, fellowship, and "the society of the Golden Rule," provided the key to reintegrating mass industrial society. Theologically, this was the ethos of the kingdom of God, and it became for Gladden the primary motif of applied Christianity.

He continued to develop this theme in several later works, *Tools and the Man: Property and Industry Under the Christian Law* (1893), *Ruling Ideas of the Present Age* (1895), a critique of individualist socioeconomic theories, and *Social Facts and Forces* (1897), his most important contribution to the emerging discipline of sociology. *Social Salvation* (1902) was a series of important lectures delivered at Yale in which Gladden addressed civic education and reform, and the "redemption of the city."

The specific role the church played in society as a voluntary association formed a second element in Gladden's democratic social vision. In *The Cosmopolis City Club* (1893), Gladden wrote a fictional account of the formation of a voluntary society to instigate civic reforms. This inspired quite a number of philanthropic civic clubs to be formed in leading cities, with church groups providing a large portion of the membership. In *The Church and the Kingdom* (1894), Gladden clarified his ecclesiology, maintaining that the kingdom includes the church but the church does not include the kingdom.

Democratic society (a social organism) is one body with many members (voluntary associations), and for the social organism the coordinating "life-force" is the life which is in Christ. The church's task is to stimulate the Christianization of society through participation in philanthropic social action. Gladden outlined these specific responsibilities in *The Christian Pastor and the Working Church* (1898). He also believed that individual churches needed to form ecumenical municipal federations of churches for the coordination of social reform (*Federation for Service*, 1914). Gladden had already paid a price for his ecumenism: in 1893 an offer of the Presidency of Ohio State University was withdrawn following his attack on anti-Catholic organizations and his defense of Catholics' right to freedom of religion. It was some compensation that he was elected Moderator of the National Council of Congregational Churches in 1904.

As well as believing the church should play a direct role in social organization, Gladden advocated a theology compatible with the best of modern scholarship. Where other clergy might have disguised their modernist theological persuasions in the pulpit, Gladden sought to popularize biblical criticism in *Who Wrote the Bible?* (1891), and tackle head-on doctrinal questions raised by modern reason in such books as *How Much Is Left of the Old Doctrines?* (1889) and *Present Day Theology* (1913). Gladden remained passionate in his belief that one of the virtues of modern theology was that it demystified the essential Christian truths, thus exposing Christianity's democratic core.

At the time of his death in 1918, Gladden's hopes in the inevitable progress of the kingdom of God had been severely shaken by the devastation of the First World War. He was astute enough to understand that this would undermine much of the optimistic vision of the Social Gospel. But he never lost faith in Christ whom he continued to serve. Of course this theology was bound to the culture of the late–nineteenth century, shaped as it was by the implicit belief in progress consistent with that age. Yet Washington Gladden has secured a deserved place in the history of American theology, leaving a legacy of some 38 books, manuscripts of more than 1,500 sermons, more than a hundred articles and pamphlets, and several popular hymns. Nobody of his generation did more to popularize liberal theology and social Christianity. Gladden was the preeminent Congregationalist of his day, but loyalty to his denomination in no way compromised his commitment to ecumenism. It is perhaps fitting then that a Baptist theologian and church historian, Walter Rauschenbusch, should sum up his impact in a letter to Gladden soon after they met in 1908: "To me you are one of the veterans who made it easier for us of the next generation to see our way and to get a hearing."

Suggested Readings

Writings of Washington Gladden: *Recollections* (Boston: Houghton, Mifflin and Co., 1909); *Social Salvation* (Boston: Houghton, Mifflin and Co., 1902); *Tools and the Man: Property and Industry Under the Christian Law* (Westport, Conn.: Hyperion Press, 1975); the following are reprinted editions: *Applied Christianity: Moral Aspects of Social Questions* (Salem, N.H.: Ayer Co., 1977); *Who Wrote the Bible? A Book for the People* (Salem, N.H.: Ayer Co., 1977).

Jacob Henry Dorn, *Washington Gladden: Prophet of the Social Gospel* (Columbus: Ohio State University, 1967).

Richard D. Knudten, *The Systematic Thought of Washington Gladden* (New York: Humanities Press, 1968).

Walter Rauschenbusch

(1861–1918)

Robert T. Handy

Pastor of an urban congregation for eleven years and seminary professor for twenty-one, Walter Rauschenbusch never claimed to be a systematic or doctrinal theologian. But he struggled with theological issues throughout his career, and made lasting contributions to the theological thought of the twentieth century. Born in Rochester, New York, on 4 October 1861, the son of (Karl) August and Caroline (Rhomp) Rauschenbusch, Walter grew up in a pietistic German Baptist tradition. His father was a professor in the German Department of Rochester Theological Seminary. But because August wanted his son and two older daughters to know the many Rauschenbusch relatives and traditions in his native Germany, in 1865 he sent his family there, where Walter's early education flourished for four years, and then continued at both private and public schools in Rochester. During his senior year in high school he had an evangelical conversion experience, was baptized, and soon felt a call to ministry.

He returned to Germany to study for four years at the Evangelical Gymnasium at Gütersloh. Back home in 1883, he combined a senior year at the University of Rochester with a first year at the seminary. The liberal tendencies of such thinkers as Friedrich Schleiermacher, Albrecht Ritschl, Julius Wellhausen, and Adolf Harnack influenced his theological reflections. Graduating in 1886, he accepted a call to the Second German Baptist church in New York, very near Hell's Kitchen, one of the worst sections of Manhattan. He was immediately confronted with the haunting problems of many of his parishioners, working-class persons with minimal incomes and irregular employment, forced into poor housing. The realities of the social evils of the period quickly caught his attention. He met several pioneers of the Social Gospel, supporting reformer Henry George's 1886 campaign for mayor, making friends with economist Richard T. Ely, and writing articles on social issues. He deplored the gap between Christian efforts for social reform and secular approaches by socialists, labor leaders, and others.

As pastor, he won the affections of his people, and raised funds for a new, larger building on 43rd Street; it was dedicated in 1890. But later that year increasing deafness, first noticed five years earlier, led him to submit his resignation. The congregation responded by offering him sabbatical leave. A grateful Rauschenbusch sailed for Europe in 1891, using the time to seek restoration of his hearing and to continue his search for a distinctively Christian uniting of personal and social religion. The first quest failed: The hearing impairment was found to be incurable.

His second quest, however, to find links between piety and social reform, was significantly advanced. In England, he deepened his knowledge of the Fabian socialists with their attention to gradualist, educational, and legislative approaches to extending freedom into economic life. He observed how poverty was fought by various religious, social, and labor movements, and read widely in reformist and socialist literature. The bulk of his nine months abroad was spent in Germany, where he focused his studies on the New Testament and sociology. He wrote a lengthy manuscript with the working title "Revolutionary Christianity," suggesting not recourse to violence, but an emphasis on evolutionary change and the renewal of both individual and societal life. Unpublished during his lifetime, the preparation of the manuscript proved to mark a turning point in his life. (It was finally printed in 1968, after Max Stackhouse discovered the scattered original chapters among Rauschenbusch's papers, and carefully edited and introduced it with the title *The Righteousness of the Kingdom*.)

Resuming his pastorate, Rauschenbusch used the manuscript in preparing many addresses and articles. The theological concerns that he was to explore for the rest of his life had taken clear shape. He had matured at a time when critical-historical approaches to an understanding of human affairs, religions, and institutions were steadily gaining ground in Western education. Historical method applied to the scriptures strengthened a principle of authority for his theological views. He came to the firm belief that the work of scholars versed in critical methods did provide reliable clues for understanding the Bible in ways previously impossible. Not only did the new approach clarify for him the Old Testament, notably the writings of the Hebrew prophets, but also the New, most importantly with respect to the life and teachings of Jesus Christ. He was confident that the very personality of Jesus could now be felt with fresh power as biblical passages were interpreted anew.

Rauschenbusch was convinced that a close approximation of Jesus' true greatness could be grasped better through the slower methods of historical study than through the assertions of theological dogmas about the person of Christ. In his many addresses and writings, he relied on the authority of Jesus, the word made flesh, as the one close to God and able to make God known to humans. He was convinced that the fullness of divine revelation was manifest in Jesus Christ, the focus of authority for Christian life, thought, theology, and ethics. Rauschenbusch could be critical of any theological position that did not accept the authority of Jesus clearly, including those close to his own views. Though often classed as a theological liberal, he found that any party line could distort the gospel, noting in 1891 that the average religious liberal could destroy a nation's reverence for the Bible.

Relying on the authority of Christ, Rauschenbusch found confirmation for a strong theological position he had long held. From the time of his conversion to his death, he continued to be concerned with the evangelical message of personal salvation. Aware of the depths of human sin rooted in selfishness and rebellion against God, he always emphasized the importance of personal commitment for salvation. He never minimized the need for evangelism; a conference at Northfield with the famous revivalist Dwight L. Moody in 1888 was an important milestone in his life. In later years he teamed up with Ira D. Sankey to prepare hymnals in German that included gospel songs. On his deathbed he affirmed the importance of personal religion, and believed his public work had been a form of evangelism. If a theological label is needed for him, "evangelical liberal" may be the best.

Rauschenbusch coupled an emphasis on individual salvation with a concern for social salvation, a stance quite new on the American scene where individualism had long been largely unchallenged. For him, the salvation of society had been central in Jesus' ministry, for his purpose was not only to make God known and loved, but also to found a new society on earth, for which he provided the basic principles of conduct. Rauschenbusch declared that the great task of his epoch was recasting social institutions. He returned often to the theme that Christianity offers to the individual victory over sin and death, and to humankind a vastly improved, ennobled, and redeemed social life. Throughout his career, in his writings and actions, he kept pointing to practical reforms that individuals, associations, and religious institutions could undertake to help in the work of social salvation. He saw the Social Gospel as the old message of salvation enlarged, intensified—and socialized. The doctrine of social salvation, he affirmed, offered biblical and theological bases for Christians to become involved in transforming the society in which they lived.

What brought together and held in creative tension the old and the new in Rauschenbusch's theological thought was Jesus' teaching about the kingdom of God. This came to him as a new revelation in 1891 when he was delving into New Testament interpretation at a time when many biblical, historical, and theological scholars were pointing to the centrality of the kingdom of God, especially in the Synoptic Gospels. Though details of the new vision that became the focal point of his theology and practice were to change somewhat, his conviction that the kingdom or reign of God is the first and most essential dogma of the Christian faith never wavered. It deeply influenced his personal religious life as well as his public teaching that the powers of the Kingdom can well up in the individual soul and provide a starting point for commitment to social justice as the kingdom summons all to play a role in transforming the world into a reign of righteousness.

Rauschenbusch never belittled the immense importance of the Christian churches, but sharply criticized their tendencies through much of church history to put themselves rather than the kingdom of God first. As he saw it, churches are working organizations to evangelize, to create the Christian life in individuals, to serve the kingdom in their outreach in society, and to call attention to wrong and suffering in the interests of justice. If they neglected these responsibilities, they ceased to follow Jesus, the initiator of the kingdom of which God was the creator. Rauschenbusch clearly favored church patterns that had risen after the Reformation and especially as part of the Calvinist and free church movements, with a continuing interest in Anabaptist history. He respected and served the churches as fellowships for worship and service, but his passion was for the kingdom, the very marrow of the gospel.

After that crucial year in which his life and thought found a new direction, he returned to his pastorate, but his preaching and activities changed as he increasingly focused on the doctrine of the kingdom. He soon began to describe himself as a Christian socialist: for him, a mild, nonviolent, evolutionary, largely nonpolitical, and moralized version of socialism. In 1893 he participated in the first of some twenty annual meetings of the Brotherhood of the Kingdom, a group of Baptist and other ministers and laity who were troubled by rampant socioeconomic evils and were actively interested in labor and reform movements. He exchanged and tested ideas and suggestions for religious social thought and reform tactics in this and other gatherings and groups engaged in the work of Christian social reform. In that same year he married German-born schoolteacher Pauline Rother, who proved to be a loving and loyal helpmate; five children were born of the union.

When an invitation came in 1897 to teach in the German Department in Rochester Theological Seminary, he responded favorably. His deafness had become a hindrance in the pastorate, and he welcomed the challenge of helping to educate ministers. In 1902 he was promoted to professor of church history in the English Department, finally finding the opportunity to get back to work on the manuscript of 1891. But he soon found that the consuming doctrine of the kingdom had opened many new windows for him, and he wrote a significant new book, *Christianity and the Social Crisis* (1907), his first in English, though he had written or edited several in German. In the book, he thought he had spoken so strongly on controversial themes that his seminary position might be threatened, for he had advocated serious Christian attention to socialism as one of the great elemental forces of human history despite its limitations, and sharply criticized capitalism for its excessive competitiveness and tendency to concentrate wealth among a few.

To his surprise, the book immediately caught wide public attention. He had mastered a lucid, effective style, and was thoroughly committed to the positions he advocated. It came at a time when the so-called muckrakers had exposed the depths of the social problems, strife between workers and employers had highlighted them, and the progressive movement for change was rising in public prominence. His insights were presented in powerful, often dramatic fashion. His abilities as historian, interpreter of the Bible, and social and ethical thinker along with his practical reform experience and his personally profound Christian commitment combined to bring him wide following and fame. They also put him in great demand as speaker and writer, and soon he was recognized in North America and beyond as a very prominent leader in Christian social thought. His seminary teaching schedule was rearranged so he could continue his research, accept some of the many invitations heaped upon him, and continue to write books, articles, and pamphlets.

Three years later appeared his favorite among his own books, *For God and the People: Prayers of the Social Awakening* (1910), which like all of his books in English was reprinted many times and translated into other languages. He had written most of the prayers, illustrating the linking of deeply devotional and earnestly social themes. Two years later appeared his most programmatic volume, *Christianizing the Social Order* (1912), which drew on various social reformist writings of the period. Like the political parties being strongly influenced by the progressive spirit, he was optimistic about the future. America was still broadly considered to be a Christian (predominantly Protestant) nation, but he considered its social order to be semi-Christian. He was hopeful it could still be made more fully Christian.

By "Christianizing" he meant bringing society into harmony with the ethical and moral convictions identified with Jesus Christ. He explained that many who were not Christians might consent that in Jesus humanity has reached one of its highest points, declaring that Christianizing means humanizing in the highest sense. He made the excessive claim that four basic

345

aspects of the social order had undergone constitutional changes that brought them into the work of advancing Christianization: family, church, education, and even politics, the latter largely through the spread of democracy. But he found that the economic system was fundamentally unchristian, and he highlighted many practical suggestions for reform. In his longest and most technical book, however, he did not neglect to include a chapter on personal religion, concluding that it was primarily concerned for the kingdom of God and the salvation of human beings.

The outbreak of World War I in 1914 saddened him greatly, for he had close family ties on both sides, and was inclined toward pacifism. Because the United States did not enter the war until April 1917, at first he urged that neutrality be strictly defined, and felt the lash of criticism for his stand. He suffered the suspicion often accorded those of German background, though his love for democracy never wavered. In his next book, *The Social Principles of Jesus* (1916), he returned to one of his favorite themes. *Social Principles* was a basic handbook for college and other voluntary and study groups, in which he selected biblical passages accompanied with commentaries as he sought to draw younger persons to understand Jesus' teachings and their significance for social reform, in and among nations.

His last book, *A Theology for the Social Gospel*, was not cast in the familiar form of systematic theologies but offered a challenge to theologians and others to take seriously the burgeoning movements for Christian social thought and action. His aim was to provide intellectual bases for the Social Gospel and contribute to theology's ability to deal with continuing changes in church and culture. More than half the book dealt with three doctrines so important in his theology—sin, salvation, and the kingdom of God—but with fresh insights and nuances. He had long been aware of the universal human tendency to sin, that ethically humans sag downward by nature. His awareness of the social aspects of sin had been sharpened by the war. Defining sin as sensuousness, selfishness, and godlessness, he chose to put particular weight on the second, for it emphasized sin's ethical and social aspects. He pointed out that people rarely sin against God alone.

Though Rauschenbusch knew that many modern theologians did not take the doctrine of original sin seriously, he defended it as one of the few efforts of individualistic theology to gain a solidaristic view. He went on to detail how sin is transmitted not only biologically but through social forces and traditions. He described what he dramatically called the super-personal forces of evil, and traced the lineaments of the social idealizations of evil, which added up to a formidable kingdom of evil. Before discussing social salvation and the role of the churches in it, once again he emphasized the basic importance of the salvation of the individual. A chapter on the kingdom of God brought to a thoughtful climax his years of probing that doctrine. He declared that the kingdom was divine in its origin, progress, and consummation. Initiated by Christ, it is a miraculous and continuous revelation of God's power, righteousness, and love.

The remainder of the book commented on contributions the Social Gospel had to offer to the doctrines of God, the Holy Spirit and inspiration, prophecy, baptism and the Lord's supper, eschatology, and atonement. He was to be much criticized for saying that Jesus democratized the conception of God. He did dwell on God's immanence and presence in human affairs, but did not neglect references to God's transcendence. He had long wrestled seriously with eschatological concepts, carefully distinguishing between prophecy and apocalypticism. He interpreted Jesus as emphasizing the former, opting for the gradual growth of the kingdom, always both present and future. He curtly dismissed the writings of those European theologians whom he found to be overemphasizing the eschatological elements in Jesus' teaching because of their kinship and sympathy with the bourgeois classes.

Not long after the publication of his final book, Rauschenbusch had to give up teaching, and died of cancer in his native city 25 July 1918. His voice and pen were stilled, but his important books, various anthologies of his writings, and articles and books about him have continued to be published throughout the twentieth century. His life and ideas have long continued to exert an influence in theological and ethical thought and action, notably through the Niebuhr brothers and Martin Luther King, Jr., but through many others as well. Controversial in his lifetime, he has remained so; his contributions have been criticized by some of those who have taken him seriously, and sharply rejected by others. In many ways he was a man of his time, deeply involved in its struggles, influenced by its dominant cultures and theologies, even as he sought to reform them. He continues to have relevance for those of later generations.

Suggested Readings

Writings of Walter Rauschenbusch: *A Theology for the Social Gospel* (New York: Macmillan, 1917); *The Righteousness of the Kingdom,* ed. Max L. Stackhouse (Nashville/New York: Abingdon Press, 1968); Winthrop S. Hudson, ed., *Walter Rauschenbusch: Selected Writings* (New York: Paulist Press, 1984).

Paul M. Minus, *Walter Rauschenbusch: American Reformer* (New York: Macmillan, 1988).

Edgar Young Mullins

(1860–1928)

E. Glenn Hinson

E. Y. Mullins exerted a seminal influence in restating theology for Baptists as President of the Southern Baptist Theological Seminary (1899–1928), the Southern Baptist Convention (1921–24), and the Baptist World Alliance (1923–28). Sensitive to both Baptist opportunities and problems of identity in the early twentieth century, he reshaped the ponderous Calvinism of James P. Boyce, his predecessor as President of Southern Seminary, by way of an emphasis on religious experience and revelation as it reached its culmination in Jesus Christ and put forth a fresh understanding of the Baptist tradition.

Mullins' theology was shaped by a number of influences: the conservative Baptist theology of his father, his conversion experience, and his theological training at Southern Seminary; studies in philosophy and psychology of religion, especially the personalism of Borden Parker Bowne and Hermann Lotze and the psychology of religion of William James; the experiential theology of Friedrich Schleiermacher (notwithstanding strong critical comments about Schleiermacher's pantheism, definition of religion as feeling of absolute dependence, and view of the person of Christ), Lewis French Stearns of Bangor Theological Seminary, and Frank Hugh Foster of Pacific Theological Seminary in Berkeley, California; and Mullins' own environment with its concern for the individual, freedom, democracy, optimism, and pragmatism.

Born in Franklin County, Mississippi, 5 January 1860, and reared in Corsicana, Texas, where his family moved when he was eight, Mullins was educated at Texas Agricultural and Mechanical College (1879 graduation) and the Southern Baptist Theological Seminary (B.D. 1885). After fourteen years' service as a pastor in Harrodsburg, Kentucky, in Baltimore, Maryland, and in Newton Center, Massachusetts, interrupted by a brief stint as Associate Secretary of the Foreign Mission Board of the Southern Baptist

Convention in 1895, he spent the remainder of his career as President of the Southern Baptist Theological Seminary in Louisville, Kentucky.

As Professor of Theology as well as President of Southern Seminary and influential leader not only among Southern Baptists but among Baptists around the world, Mullins spread his attention over three broad areas of interest: systematic theology, Christian apologetics, and the Baptist tradition. Assuming the chair of theology held by Boyce's successor F. H. Kerfoot, he gradually phased out Latin readings of Anselm and Francis Turretin in advanced theology as the course evolved into biblical theology. In 1917 he replaced Boyce's *Abstract of Systematic Theology* in the edition revised by Kerfoot with his own *Christian Religion in Its Doctrinal Expression*. Whereas Boyce owed much to Charles Hodge and Francis Turretin and shared their staunch Calvinism, Mullins sought to wed the facts of historical revelation of God in Jesus Christ with what he called "the facts of Christian experience."

Mullins probably made his most original contribution to apologetics, in employing Christian experience as a strong bulwark for the claims of the Christian faith, but his reinterpretation of the Baptist tradition has exerted the widest and most lasting impact among Baptists everywhere. Where earlier Baptists had sustained their tradition—baptism by immersion, believers' baptism, and congregational polity—on the basis of scriptures, Mullins identified "the competency of the soul in religion under God" as the distinctive historical principle from which Baptists can draw "axioms" definitive of the tradition.

In *The Christian Religion in Its Doctrinal Expression* Mullins brought his experiential approach to bear on all points conventionally touched on in systematic theologies. Authority rests on revelation as it has reached its supreme expression in Jesus Christ. For revelation, however, Christians depend on the scriptures as the authoritative source of information regarding the revelation of God in Christ, and they are final in all matters of faith and practice.

In line with this understanding of revelation, Mullins began his theological construction with Christology rather than theology. On the basis of experience of the redeeming activity of Christ, the believer declares the person of Christ to be divine. Mullins disputed the Chalcedonian doctrine of two natures and leaned toward Monophysitism (a single, divine nature) as expressing best the impression Christ made on early Christians. On the basis of Christ's preexistence, he also questioned kenotic theories which distinguished attributes before and during the incarnation. Christ retained all divine attributes in the incarnation but under the restraints of a human life. Mullins rejected all theories of Christ which diminished his divine nature. Although the New Testament does not use the word, Mullins concluded that it taught a doctrine of the Trinity.

Mullins contended that the purpose of creation can be inferred from redemption. God created in order to produce a kingdom in which God's own image would be reflected. Humankind is the end of creation, the connecting link between physical and spiritual. Providence is God's direction of the universe toward its goal. Mullins here denied both continuous creation and the Deist understanding. God has created and preserved the world and is continually directing it, though respecting human freedom in the process. Christians should not hesitate to accept the miraculous or believe in the efficacy of prayer.

Mullins attributed sin to the rupture of a personal relationship between humankind and God, a result of human free choice. He rejected both Calvin's idea of Adam as the official covenant head of the human race and Augustine's assertion that all humankind were seminally present in Adam. In his doctrine of the atonement he found fault with most of the traditional atonement theories in the tradition. Though seeing some truth in each, he preferred exposition of New Testament teaching wherein Christ's atonement entailed identification with the human race, a life of obedience to God, and subjection to the operation of the law of sin and death. Christ did for sinful human beings what they could not do for themselves. Mullins championed a doctrine of universal atonement against Calvin's limited atonement, and denied that God's election takes away human free will. Divine sovereignty and human free will remain paradoxical, with God respecting God's own self-limitations. The key point is that God takes initiative in salvation, and seeks to save as many as will respond in freedom to that initiative.

The Christian life, Mullins believed, begins in the work of the Holy Spirit in repentance and faith—the germinal grace from which spring all other graces: regeneration (change in moral and spiritual disposition), justification (God's declaration of forgiveness in light of the work of Christ), adoption, and union with Christ (the most central and vital truth of the Christian life). The Christian life continues in sanctification (setting apart for service and inner transformation). Mullins warned here against extremes of Calvinist emphasis on divine direction to the exclusion of human response and of Arminian emphasis on free will. God constrains and guides, but does not coerce.

In his understanding of eschatology Mullins acknowledged the figurative nature of New Testament references but committed himself to the historical realization of various eschatological events. The key resided, he believed, in resurrection. He sought to reconcile statements of realized and futuristic eschatology. He made room for an intermediate, disembodied state, but believed in the Second Coming of Christ as a future event. The resurrection of the body is a vital element of Christian hope, but the resurrected body, as 1 Corinthians 15 makes clear, will differ greatly from the present one. Mullins assumed both continuous and final judgment. Heaven, he thought, is a place and not merely an inward state.

In his apologetic theology, Mullins departed from traditional efforts to establish the truth of Christianity by proof based on miracles and sought to meet objections to evangelical Christianity by using the principles its critics employed. He was especially critical of those who adopted the presuppositions of modern science and thought and who then sought to reclaim only as much of traditional faith as could be reconciled with those assumptions. In his view the main issue was the supernaturalism of Christian faith versus the naturalism of modern physical science, modern rational philosophy, historical criticism, and comparative religion. Science and religion had a right to pursue their methods in their separate spheres, but when science invaded the religious sphere it lost its authority. In earlier years Mullins regarded evolution as properly descriptive of the orderly progression in the history of nature; later, in the midst of the evolution controversy in the Southern Baptist Convention, he rejected it altogether. At the same time, however, he resisted inclusion of judgments on scientific matters in confessional statements and opposed legislation against evolution or any other scientific theory.

Modern philosophies—agnosticism, pantheism, materialism, idealism, critical monism, pluralism, and even personalism and pragmatism—fail if they exclude supernatural reality. Historical criticism is acceptable if employed in a truly scientific way, but modernists rejected every aspect of supernaturalism in scriptures because of their naturalistic presuppositions. Comparative religion, too, was guided by naturalistic presuppositions, which led to overemphasis on the impact of environment on Christian origins.

Mullins argued for theism as the strongest of all worldviews on the grounds that it affirmed the highest principle known in human experience, namely, the principle of personality. Historical criticism properly used sustains that Jesus Christ is the divinely appointed Savior and Redeemer. Even unbelievers acknowledge the moral grandeur of Christ, whose appearance cannot be explained by natural evolution. Arguing from Christian experience, he insisted that moral, religious, and intellectual results prove the truth of Christian claims.

Regarding the Baptist tradition, Mullins thought Baptists had made their point about baptism by immersion, believers' baptism, and congregational polity and needed to restate their fundamental principles. From the distinctive historical principle of "soul competency" he deduced seven "axioms": (1) the theological—the right of a holy and loving God to be sovereign; (2) the religious—the equal right of all persons to direct access to God; (3) the ecclesiastical—the right of all believers to equal privileges in the church; (4) the moral—the necessity of freedom for the soul to be responsible; (5) the religio-civic—a free church in a free State; (6) the social—"Love your neighbor as yourself"; and (7) the civic—the sovereignty of the state residing in its citizens. Mullins believed the "axioms" would apply to the support of institutions, voluntary cooperation beyond the local level, cooperation between religious bodies rather than union, and contributions to democratic ideals of American civilization and to world progress.

On the basis of these principles, he also criticized both Roman Catholicism and historical Protestantism. Roman Catholicism, he charged, was founded on the principle of the incompetency of the soul in religion. This led it into errors regarding the nature of religious and ecclesiastical authority, interpretation of scriptures, the power of the priesthood, and the necessity of the sacraments. Historical Protestantism, combining the Roman Catholic principle of soul incompetency with the spiritually authentic principle of soul competency, failed to carry out consistently the inner logic of its own movement. It thus erred regarding infant baptism, sacramentalism, centralized church governments, and union of church and state.

E. Y. Mullins' restatement of theology affected Baptist thinking in his day profoundly but probably did not reach far beyond Baptist circles. As Professor of Theology at the Southern Baptist Theological Seminary, he shaped the thinking of leading Baptist ministers throughout the South. Of greatest lasting impact were his reshaping of Calvinist theology to sustain more forcefully the evangelistic and missionary endeavors of the Southern Baptist Convention and his restatement of Baptist principles. Election as President of the Southern Baptist Convention from 1921 to 1924 placed Mullins in a critical position of leadership during the evolution controversy. In that role he prevented the introduction of an anti-evolutionary statement into the 1925 Baptist Faith and Message, the first doctrinal statement adopted by the Convention. From the formation of the Baptist World Alliance in 1905, Mullins generated excitement among Baptists around the world with his calls for restatement of Christian theology, apologetics, and Baptist principles. His service as President of the Alliance from 1923 until his death in 1928 deepened and broadened the impact of his thought.

One cannot locate today any significant contemporary theologian outside Baptist circles who would reflect the influence of Mullins. His restatement of theology, however, has continued to influence Southern Baptist life and thought. W. T. Conner carried on in the tradition of Mullins' biblical-experiential theology at Southwestern Baptist Theological Seminary. The axioms of religion have undergone several revisions, most recently by Herschel H. Hobbs, Oklahoma pastor and denominational leader who served as President of the Southern Baptist Convention and headed the committee which revised *The Baptist Faith and Message* in 1962–63. Hobbs, a prolific author, fits the Mullins mold.

Curiously, Mullins' restatement of theology is at the center of the controversy in the Southern Baptist Convention today. At least one group of those who now control the leadership of the Convention seek to restore the Calvinism of James P. Boyce to a dominant position in Southern Baptist seminaries, either reinterpreting Mullins or shunting him aside altogether. Moderates, by contrast, continue to cite Mullins as the chief interpreter of Baptist thought.

Suggested Readings

Writings of Edgar Young Mullins: *The Axioms of Religion: A New Interpretation of the Baptist Faith* (Philadelphia: Judson Press, 1908); *The Christian Religion in Its Doctrinal Expression* (Philadelphia: Judson Press, 1917); *Christianity at the Cross Roads* (Nashville: Sunday School Board of the Southern Baptist Convention, 1924); *Why Is Christianity True?* (Chicago: Christian Culture Press, 1905).

Bill Clark Thomas, "Edgar Young Mullins: A Baptist Exponent of Theological Restatement" (Th.D. diss., Louisville: Southern Baptist Theological Seminary, 1963).

Benjamin Breckinridge Warfield

(1851–1921)

W. Andrew Hoffecker

Benjamin Breckinridge Warfield refined the carefully reasoned teachings of Calvinistic Princeton theology in the tumultuous generations leading up to World War I. As theological diversity and inclusivism were growing among American denominations, he labored mightily to maintain the Princeton traditions started by Archibald Alexander, the founder of the seminary and progenitor of both its theology and piety, the influential Old School theology of Charles Hodge, its most famous theologian, and the call of Archibald Alexander Hodge to base American culture upon Christian foundations.

Raised in a wealthy Virginian family, Warfield received private schooling and entered Princeton College in 1868. His early academic interests included mathematics and natural science, which flowered under the instruction of President James McCosh. After graduating from Princeton with highest honors in 1871, he studied abroad. While in Europe he surprised his family by announcing his intention to enter the ministry. He enrolled at Princeton Seminary and learned his theology under the elder Hodge. Following his marriage in 1876 he spent another year studying theology in Europe. Upon his return, he served as assistant pastor in Baltimore for a year and then began his teaching career in New Testament at Western Seminary in Allegheny, Pennsylvania. When A. A. Hodge died in 1887, Warfield changed fields by succeeding him as Professor of Didactic and Polemic Theology at Princeton.

He differed from his Princeton predecessors by his lack of active involvement in the political and practical battles of the Presbyterian Church in the U.S.A. By temperament aloof and austere, Warfield isolated himself from public life to devote many years caring for his invalid wife. But his demeanor and social remoteness permitted a prodigious writing career. Besides monographs and several collections of sermons, his comprehensive scholarly articles and book reviews (alone numbering almost 800) fill more than ten volumes.

Arguably the most gifted theologian of his time and perhaps the most wide-ranging in his interests, Warfield marshaled his talents to conserve Reformed orthodoxy. A gadfly both to liberals who sought to keep American theology in step with new ideas emanating from Europe and to conservatives who developed innovations in revivalism and practical theology, he measured all ideas against the standards of traditional Calvinism. Like many liberals he brought a high level of critical scholarship to theology, but he rejected their radical conclusions. Like many conservatives he shared a passion for theological battle, but he was more open to higher criticism.

Warfield's most important theological contribution began prior to his arrival at Princeton when he coauthored "Inspiration" with A. A. Hodge in *Presbyterian Review* (1881). In it and more than forty subsequent articles, Warfield articulated what fundamentalists, as affirmed in their controversy during the 1920s with modernists, and many of today's evangelicals maintain is the correct understanding of the nature of scripture. He insisted that the Bible is in its entirety the Word of God. Given (but not dictated) by the Holy Spirit through the instrumentality of human authors, its inspiration extends to all its parts, including the words themselves. Thus the Bible is entirely trustworthy, and its original documents, the autographs, are inerrant. Warfield argued his case exegetically by painstaking analysis of biblical texts, historically by exposing scholars who had defended similar views in previous eras, and apologetically by refuting critical attacks on biblical authority and harmonizing problem texts.

Historical theologians debate whether Warfield's view of inspiration represents an innovation in Reformed thinking. Some allege that the Warfield-Hodge view is a definite hardening in the conservative position in response to the number and ferocity of liberal attacks in the late–nineteenth century. Defenders respond that belief in inerrancy in the autographs enjoyed the support of not only most American theologians prior to 1880 but also of a wide spectrum of believers throughout church history. Warfield's emphasis upon this consensus enabled followers to establish two high-water marks of conservatism in the Presbyterian Church by adopting the Portland Deliverance (1892) and the Five Point Deliverance (1910). The former required ministers to subscribe to inerrancy on pain of dismissal. It figured prominently in the heresy trials of Charles A. Briggs (1893), Henry Preserved Smith (1894), and Arthur C. McGiffert (1900). The Five Point Deliverance delayed efforts to make the church more inclusive in theology by requiring ministers to subscribe to doctrines similar to fundamentalism's five points (one of which was inerrancy).

Princeton's distinctive theological method, with its dependence on Scottish Common-Sense Realism, also reached its highest development in Warfield's writings. In an age captivated by Newtonian science, he followed the tradition of his predecessors by adopting an apologetic based on rational and empirical evidences to authenticate biblical religion, and a distinctive theological method to construct an unassailable theology. Both approaches presupposed that God constituted the mind, of believers and nonbelievers alike, so that they could apprehend reality objectively. Just as scientists arrive at natural laws by an inductive investigation of physical reality, so theologians construct doctrinal systems by gathering and arranging the facts of scripture.

Confronted with increasing skepticism toward religion in the secular culture and a pervasive subjectivism in theological and apologetic method, Warfield believed Christianity's mission in the modern era consisted in nothing less than to "reason its way to its dominion." Apologetics is a preparatory science to demonstrate the authenticity and veracity of the Bible through evidences. Critics object that Warfield naively assumed, as did his fellow Princetonians, that a common-sense, religious appeal to natural and supernatural evidences could lead unbelievers to the knowledge of God. They insist that such epistemological optimism contradicts the Reformed view of human depravity, which states that sin not only corrupts the heart but also darkens the mind, severely undercutting people's ability to examine a rational appeal to external evidences. Defenders respond that he stressed that the Holy Spirit must enlighten non-Christians so that they can comprehend God's truth. In addition, Warfield also wrote movingly of the internal power of the written word, which immediately convinces the reader of its divinity.

Not all of Warfield's Calvinist contemporaries adopted his evidentialist apologetic. Dutch theologians Abraham Kuyper and Herman Bavinck, for example, argued that an antithesis existed between modern thought and the gospel. Since only redeemed minds use reason properly, rather than appealing to rational proofs, the task of the apologist consists in arguing *out of* the scriptures rather than *to* the Bible. This debate over the nature of facts, the proper use of reason and the Bible, and the possibility of neutrality continues today among evidentialists and presuppositionalists.

Warfield claimed that he and his predecessors simply reiterated the theological views of Augustine, Calvin, and the Puritan divines. Warfield lauded Calvinism as being the highest expression of theism, the most pure manifestation of religion, and the essence of evangelicalism. In an age that cut its teeth on American democratic ideals and belief in human progress, Warfield reminded theological progressives, who had jettisoned Calvinism, that true

356

progress is made only as one penetrates the difficult doctrines of the faith. He never tired of defending election and original sin. An advocate of a strict confessionalism, he refused to serve on a committee to revise the Westminster Confession. And though the traditional Reformed emphasis on reforming cultural life was not an emphasis in his writings, he did discuss this theme. He touted Calvin's contributions to America's free institutions while lamenting that American Christianity had lost its leaven. Writing self-consciously as a Southerner, he chastised the church for countenancing racial segregation and deplored the lack of public policies to advance the cause of blacks.

During the years from 1880 to 1920 hardly a new theological perspective, foreign or domestic, escaped Warfield's attention. His trenchant critique of the naturalistic worldview that liberals employed to reinterpret traditional Christian teaching was not widely appreciated in his own era. Warfield shrewdly defended Christianity's supernaturalism by pointing out that liberals' denial of biblical miracles and reinterpretation of traditional doctrines rested more on antisupernaturalist presuppositions they brought to the passages rather than any compelling arguments derived from the Bible itself. Rather than expositing Christianity, liberals radically reshaped it to fit their own philosophies. In the process they redefined human nature as good and devalued the person and atonement of Christ.

In an age preoccupied with religious experience, Warfield insisted that religious devotion to God be based on sound biblical theology. In Sunday afternoon conference addresses at Princeton, Warfield and other professors addressed matters of piety. He pleaded with seminarians to integrate zeal for God with their academic work and to enhance their private religious lives with corporate worship. Not surprisingly, he rejected Friedrich Schleiermacher's interpretation of religion as the feeling of absolute dependence on God, in favor of Augustine's view of religious experience. Because of their brevity, many of Warfield's statements on devotion give the appearance of being an afterthought of his rational analysis of a biblical text or doctrine. Despite an intellectual cast in his writings, however, Warfield demanded that Christian experience and Christian theology never be separated. As an antidote to both lack of theological correctness and coldness of heart, Warfield devised a trinity composed of an authoritative scripture, a renewed intellect, and an obedient heart, the three sides of the "triangle of truth."

But liberals were not alone in making subjectivist errors, and Warfield, despite agreement with conservatives on other doctrinal essentials, chided members of the Holiness movement for their innovative methods in practi-

357

cal theology, particularly the doctrine of sanctification. He criticized the Oberlin Theology of Charles G. Finney and other forms of perfectionism for relinquishing God's sovereign grace in salvation and accepting the Pentecostal interpretation of the baptism of the Holy Spirit as normative in the Christian life. Despite the numerical success of many evangelists resulting from their combination of theological innovations with pragmatic revival methods, Warfield warned that their techniques rested on the Arminian view of human ability to choose to be saved. He rejected Pentecostal reports of revelatory experiences and miracles as counterfeit because they compromised the original apostolic office and the apostles' message recorded in scripture. He preferred Jonathan Edwards' conceptions of religious experience and revivalism because they manifested a Calvinist theological foundation.

In his most positive reaction to modern thought Warfield interacted with Darwin's teaching on evolution. Unlike later fundamentalists, who tend to reject evolution completely because they believe it contradicts the biblical creation account, the Princetonians carefully examined Darwin's teachings. None of them rejected evolution cavalierly.

Despite being by his own confession a "Darwinian of the purest water" as a result of his undergraduate education, Warfield distinguished between central and peripheral issues in evaluating Darwin and his science. Fascinated with Darwin's declining interest in aesthetic and religious matters, Warfield wrote sympathetically of Darwin's early religious interests; yet he lamented the spiritual atrophy that enveloped his later life.

Warfield went so far as to argue that evolution, correctly understood, was compatible with Calvin's teaching on Genesis 1. Calvin strictly reserved the term "creation" for God's initial creative act *ex nihilo*. In all his subsequent activity God merely modified what he had initially created. God providentially directed through secondary means all changes in his original creation. Calvin thus taught a "pure evolutionism" in which God's providence alone developed all things by modifying the original "indigested mass." As a creationist (as opposed to traducianists, who believed that people inherited both body and soul from their parents), Calvin believed the only exception to God's providential developing of the created order was creating every human soul out of nothing. Even though Warfield agreed with Calvin that evolution occurred under the control of divine providence, he warned that a naturalistic understanding of the concept would have negative impacts on the wider culture.

Warfield's death in February 1921 marked the passing of an era. Although his followers at Princeton attempted to sustain his Calvinist perspective, the reorganization of the seminary's board in 1929 led it to adopt a more inclusive theological stance. As a result, J. Gresham Machen led a contingent to withdraw and form Westminster Seminary in Philadelphia with the express purpose of maintaining Warfield's Old Princeton theology. While continuing to espouse much of Warfield's views—a high level of scholarship, a staunch commitment to biblical inerrancy, advocacy of consistent Calvinism, and a piety rooted in biblical theology—Westminster ironically modified his apologetics by adopting the presuppositionalism of Cornelius Van Til.

Suggested Readings

Writings of Benjamin B. Warfield: *The Works of Benjamin B. Warfield*, 10 vols. (Grand Rapids: Baker Book House, 1991); John E. Meeter, ed., *Selected Shorter Writings of Benjamin B. Warfield*, 2 vols. (Nutley, N.J.: Presbyterian and Reformed Pub. Co., 1970–73).

W. Andrew Hoffecker, *The Princeton Piety* (Nutley, N.J.: Presbyterian Reformed Pub. Co., 1981).

John E. Meeter and Roger Nicole, *A Bibliography of Benjamin Breckinridge Warfield 1851–1921* (Nutley, N.J.: Presbyterian and Reformed Pub. Co., 1974).

Mark A. Noll, ed., *The Princeton Theology, 1812–1921* (Grand Rapids: Baker Book House, 1983).

Cyrus Ingerson Scofield

(1843–1921)

Curtis W. Whiteman

Cyrus Ingerson Scofield was born on 19 August 1843 to Elias and Abigail. Elias moved the family from near Clinton, Michigan, to Lebanon, Tennessee, where Cyrus was raised in the Episcopal Church and began preparation for college. When the Civil War broke out he enlisted in the 7th Regiment of Tennessee Infantry (1861). Requesting a discharge from Confederate Secretary of War, George Randolph, Scofield gained release from duty following the battle of Antietam (1862). Moving to Saint Louis, he prepared for the legal profession and married Leontine Cerre (1866) in a civil ceremony. Late in the decade the couple relocated to Atchison, Kansas, where Cyrus was admitted to the Kansas bar (1869) and became actively involved in politics, serving in the Lower House of the Kansas Legislature (1871) and as the appointed United States District Attorney for Kansas (1873). For reasons not entirely clear, Scofield soon resigned and returned to Saint Louis without his wife and two daughters. Cyrus and Cerre eventually divorced (1883).

Confronted by Tom McPheeters, an ardent personal evangelist, Scofield experienced conversion, becoming a born-again Christian. He came under the tutelage of James H. Brookes, pastor of Walnut Street Presbyterian Church. Brookes, who was theologically influenced by the dispensational teachings of Plymouth Brethren leader John Nelson Darby, played an influential role in establishing a series of Bible and Prophetic conferences (beginning 1875), which shaped the dispensational premillennial theology of American fundamentalism. A zealous convert, Scofield participated in the Saint Louis evangelistic campaign of Dwight L. Moody (1879–80), joined the Pilgrim Congregational church (1880), and became acting secretary of the local YMCA (1880).

Licensed to preach by the Saint Louis Association of the Congregational Church, Scofield moved to Dallas (1882) to pastor First Congregational

Church. In his ordinational examination, he emphasized a literal interpretation of scripture and the personal premillennial second coming of Jesus Christ. The church grew steadily to a membership of eight hundred. He married Hettie Van Wark (1884), a parishioner in his congregation. Scofield also worked as denominational superintendent for mission in the Southwest and created a comprehensive Bible correspondence course (taken over by Moody Bible Institute in 1914). He published *Rightly Dividing the Word of Truth* (1888), a defense of dispensational premillennialism, which propelled him to the status of a leading figure in American fundamentalism.

Scofield left Dallas (1895) to pastor Trinitarian Congregational Church in East Northfield, Massachusetts. Although not a close associate of D. L. Moody, Scofield did preach Moody's funeral sermon and assumed the presidency of the Northfield Bible Training School. More important was Scofield's announcement of his intent (1901) to construct a reference Bible based on the dispensational premillennial theology developed through the Bible and Prophetic conferences begun by Brookes. To pursue the project Scofield returned to the Dallas church (1903) but soon left to devote full-time effort to the reference Bible.

The pinnacle of Scofield's career as a biblical and theological scholar was the publication of *The Scofield Reference Bible, King James Version,* by Oxford University Press in 1909 (expanded 1917). He used the dispensational premillennial scheme as the framework for referencing the text of scripture. The underlying principle of Scofield's system was that one could determine the progressive and consistent revelation of God through the infallible, inerrant, and literal message of the Bible.

Scofield defined a dispensation as "a period of time during which man is tested in respect of obedience to some specific revelation of the will of God." Seven dispensations were delineated in the biblical text. In the dispensation of innocence (Gen. 1:28–3:13), the Edenic Covenant, God required a simple test of humankind, warning of the consequence of disobedience. Eve failed the test through pride, while Adam was deliberately disobedient, and both were removed from the Garden of Eden. The dispensation of conscience (Gen. 3:23–7:23) required that people do good and abstain from evil according to what their consciences dictated. The record of the good (Abel, Enoch, and Noah), and the evil (Cain), run throughout this dispensation. Humankind, by and large, failed the test and endured the resultant judgment where all persons perished save Noah and his family. The dispensation of human government (Gen. 8:20–11:9) began with the Noachic covenant. Humankind was entrusted with governing the world on behalf of God (stewardship) but the Babel episode (Gen. 11:1-9) exemplified the irresponsibility of people in relation to God's commands and expectations.

The dispensation of promise (Gen. 12:1–Exod. 19:8) was specifically Jewish in intention, requiring the faith of the Israelites in God's promises to Abraham. At this juncture the work of God with Jews and Gentiles moves in separate but parallel directions. The dispensation of law (Exod. 19:8–Matt. 27:35) also applied to Israel, requiring her obedience to the laws given by God to the nation in the Mosaic covenant. During this period, Gentiles continued to live under the dispensation of human government. The dispensation of grace (Matt. 27:35; John 1:14, 17), the sixth dispensation, began with the incarnation, death, and resurrection of Jesus Christ. This period, also termed the age of the church (Acts 1), extends to all people and requires faith in Christ's work of atonement. At the conclusion of the current dispensation will come the pretribulation rapture of the church, the great tribulation and the literal historical second coming of Jesus Christ to establish the millennial kingdom, which is the seventh dispensation, the fullness of times (Eph. 1:10; Dan. 9:20-27; Rev. 20, 21). During this period, God's plan for Jews, Gentiles, and the church will be brought to fulfillment.

By 1920 the seven dispensational eons defined and organized by Scofield had become the standard theological framework for American fundamentalism. The *Scofield Reference Bible* was rapidly accepted as the norm for the explication of dispensational premillennial theology, and continues today as a primary source and support of fundamentalist thought.

Following publication of his reference Bible, Scofield became a popular speaker at Bible conferences throughout the country. He and his family moved from Dallas to the New York City area. In 1914 Scofield was influential in founding the Philadelphia School of the Bible, and in 1917 published an expanded notes version of the reference Bible. Having withdrawn from the public arena because of increasingly poor health, Cyrus Ingerson Scofield died on 24 July 1921.

Suggested Readings

J. M. Canfield, *The Incredible Scofield and His Book* (Vallecito, Calif.: Ross House Books, 1988).

George M. Marsden, *Fundamentalism and American Culture* (Oxford: Oxford University Press, 1980).

C. G. Trumbull, *The Life Story of C. I. Scofield* (New York: Oxford University Press, 1920).

Ellen G. H. White

(1827–1915)

Ruth Alden Doan

Born outside Gorham, Maine, on 26 November 1827, Ellen Gould Harmon (later White) grew up under the influences of New England farm and town life, Methodism, and Millerite Adventism. Scholars uniformly point to a tragic accident in her childhood as a turning point: on her way home from school one day, another child threw a rock that hit her in the face. Ellen remained unconscious for three weeks, had trouble breathing for some years, and remained permanently disfigured. Kept out of school by her injury, she educated herself independently. Her formative religious experiences came within the fold of the Millerite movement, which centered on a prediction that Christ would come in 1843 (later revised to 1844). Under Millerite preaching, Ellen experienced a dramatic conversion and also received the first of many visions. Among the Millerites, too, Ellen found her husband, James White. The Whites had four sons, two of whom lived to adulthood and to work within the Seventh-day Adventist Church. James White would share leadership in the church with Ellen White until his death in 1881.

After the Millerites' Great Disappointment of October 1844 (Christ did not return), White sought an explanation and a direction as did others in the movement. Aided by visions, she began to devise a coherent interpretation, not only of the Disappointment itself, but of the course of history, the nature of God, and the end of humankind. She gathered followers around such special emphases as the Saturday Sabbath, and her movement took organizational form by 1863. For the rest of her life, White acted as leader of the Seventh-day Adventist Church. She elaborated the church's message and helped to carry it throughout the world, including extended trips to Europe (1885–87) and to Australia and New Zealand (1891–1900). When White died in 1915, her church counted more than 130,000 members on several continents.

Her many publications included *A Sketch of the Christian Experience and Views of Ellen G. White*, *Testimonies for the Church* (7 vols.), and *Spiritual Gifts* (4 vols.), which included the first version of her landmark work *The Great Controversy Between Christ and Satan*. She also wrote numerous articles for church periodicals. White oversaw the rapid building of institutions under the auspices of the church, especially an extensive network of hospitals and educational institutions. Not a systematic theologian, White shaped and led a popular religious movement; her theological writings aimed largely toward defining that movement, giving guidance to her followers, and answering her detractors.

White's theology emerged out of her participation in a millennial movement, and her eschatology takes a central role in her thought. Her historicist stance threw the fulfillment of the majority of biblical prophecies into the past. Like a number of nineteenth-century interpreters, she saw the French Revolution as a significant event in a cosmic sense. On events in her own lifetime, and on events to come, she differed sharply from the majority of her contemporaries. First, as a former Millerite, she sought to put the experiences of those watchers for the end into a meaningful scheme. White followed the interpretation of Millerite Hiram Edson, who asserted that although the Millerites were mistaken in expecting the return of Christ to earth in 1843 or 1844, they were not mistaken in their chronology. Edson and White and their followers said that an event of significance had, indeed, taken place in 1844, but that event had taken place in the heavenly realm.

In that year, Jesus Christ had moved from the first apartment of the heavenly sanctuary to the second apartment, the holy of holies. That movement also represented a development in the scheme of judgment. A number of former Millerites asserted that the door of mercy was shut in 1844—those who had not joined the true followers of Christ by that date would no longer have an opportunity to do so. White acceded to that view in the 1840s, although she later repudiated the so-called Shut Door theory, following an interpretation devised by her husband that said that the movement to the holy of holies introduced the investigative judgment, a period during which all those who claimed to side with the righteous would come up for a final assessment before Jesus and the angelic host.

The interim period of the investigative judgment, according to White, also would see the reception of the three angels' messages announced in Revelation. The first angel's message, White believed, was the Millerite message. The second angel's message called the faithful to come out of Babylon—to recognize the fallen nature of the world and the church in its union with the world—and to join with true believers. The third angel's message required believers to separate from those who did not follow the commandments; specifically, White urged that this message insisted on the seventh-day Sabbath and condemned efforts to pass Sunday laws in many states in the late–nineteenth century.

After the third angel's message, according to White's interpretation of prophecy, Jesus would leave the Sanctuary and prepare to descend to earth. At the Second Coming, the righteous, both dead and living, would rise up out of a world destined to become home to Satan and the evil angels for a thousand years. The final battle at the end of that thousand years, said White, would lead to the final triumph of Christ and to Satan's own recognition of the justice of God. In interpretations that deviated from those of many of her contemporaries, White went on to predict the destruction of the wicked—annihilation rather than consignment to hell—and the burning of the earth. Thus White offered an interpretation of the course of earthly and cosmic history, which inspired in her followers a sense of impending crisis that lent urgency to their everyday belief and action as well as a specific picture of the future that reinforced her teachings on the nature of humankind, the requirements of faith, and the purpose of earthly existence.

White's theology, then, began with prophecy. She looked upon the Bible as an authoritative but not inerrant work. Those who wrote the scriptures were inspired by God, but, according to White, inadequacies of language crept into the texts. Officially, White's visions took second place to the scriptures; the visions clarified the Bible but did not displace it. Even in White's own writings, however, the line between support for scripture and addition to scripture blurred. White's visions numbered perhaps 2,000 in her lifetime. Subjects of the visions ranged from the personal—touching on the specific sins of church leaders—to the theological. Among the most important were an 1847 vision confirming the seventh-day Sabbath, a series in 1848 laying the foundation for the Seventh-day Adventist faith, and the first vision on health reform in 1863 at Otsego, Michigan.

As emphasis on the seventh-day Sabbath might imply, the Adventist movement originally placed a strong emphasis on following the law. In the earlier decades of her leadership, White joined her husband and others in implying that salvation came through adherence to the law. After her husband's death, however, White came to question that stance. At a crucial General Conference held in Minneapolis in 1888, White publicly embraced a shift toward emphasis on justification by faith. Adventists continued to debate the relationship between adherence to the law and justification by faith thereafter, however.

After 1888, White herself gave more attention to the concept of sanctification. Although she had once favored the notion of a second blessing, a dramatic experience of perfection, she followed her contemporaries and, perhaps, the demands of her role in Adventism toward a concept of gradually developing holiness. She urged her followers to understand that they must be cleansed through a continuous process. Indeed, her new notion of holiness was tied to her millennialism in that she saw the gradual sanctification of individuals as preparation for the advent to come. If she did not finally clarify whether this meant that the millennium was ultimately contingent upon the spiritual progress of individuals, this would only signify that she was again more concerned with inspiration and persuasion than with theological distinctions.

White's notion of the purification of the individual reached beyond the spiritual realm. Inspired by visions, White emphasized health reform as a path to greater spirituality as well as a means to a better physical life. She urged her followers to forgo meat—at first because it would arouse the passions, and later because of morality and hygiene—and she often added butter, eggs, and cheese to the same category. She also stressed the importance of avoiding tea, coffee, tobacco, and alcohol. Simultaneously, White supported the movement of the church into building health-related associations and institutions. Health reform was less a theological issue for White, however, than an assertion of the special identity of Adventists. At most, White's ideas on health paralleled and supported her ideas about the need to cleanse the individual before the arrival of the millennium and her focus on transcending the dualities of material-spiritual and body-spirit.

During her life, White did not carry broad influence in larger theological debates or developments. Indeed, much of the influence of White and the Adventists of the nineteenth century was negative: Contemporaries avoided ideas specifically because they were associated with Adventism. Thus, the Millerites inspired suspicions about premillennialism, the theory of the investigative judgment led some to reassert that judgment was complete at death, and annihilationism drove others to reject any modifications to their views of the afterlife. Insofar as her ideas matched those of broader popular movements, as did her ideas on holiness and on health reform, she acted as a participant more than as a leader of those trends.

After her death, White's importance lay primarily within her own church and not beyond it. Adventists tended to elevate White's own stature in the twentieth century, essentially raising her visions to the same level as scripture and sometimes using acceptance of and adherence to her visions as tests of faith. Perhaps ironically, insistence on the literal authority of White went along with a tendency among Adventists to share many of the perspectives of Fundamentalism. Just as Adventist leaders asserted White's authority against such questioners as John Harvey Kellogg, they also increasingly shifted toward an acceptance of the Bible's literal authority—the inerrancy of White paralleled the inerrancy of scripture. By the later twentieth century, criticism of White's ideas on sanctification and questioning of the nature of White's visions had emerged and propelled theological debates within Adventism. Whether her ideas would reach beyond the group that she had nurtured remained an open question at the end of the century.

Suggested Readings

Writings of Ellen G. White: *Life Sketches of Ellen G. White* (Mountain View, Calif.: Review and Herald Publishing House, 1915); *The Great Controversy Between Christ and Satan* (Boise, Idaho: Pacific Press Publishing, 1888; repr. 1950).

"Ellen Gould (Harmon) White," in *Seventh-day Adventist Encyclopedia,* ed. Don F. Neufeld (Washington: Review and Herald Publishing Association, 1976).

Gary Land, ed., *Adventism in America* (Grand Rapids: Wm. B. Eerdmans Publishing Co., 1986).

Ronald L. Numbers, *Prophetess of Health: Ellen G. White and the Origins of Seventh-day Adventist Health Reform,* rev. ed. (Knoxville: University of Tennessee Press, 1992).

Charles Taze Russell

(1852–1916)

Ronald B. Flowers

Charles Taze Russell, born in 1852 in Pittsburgh, Pennsylvania, was the founder of the group called, after 1931, the Jehovah's Witnesses. That the group was earlier known as "Bible Students" discloses that Russell's theology was Bible-centered, although he did not employ a literalistic interpretation. He readily accepted the value of text criticism, then called lower criticism. He believed this method of scholarship gave the interpreter an accurate text of the Bible, as close as possible to what the authors actually wrote. Though Russell's method of interpretation was complex, he dismissed the historical-critical method (higher criticism) being developed at the time. Instead, he interpreted the legal and historical parts of the Bible literally, while interpreting the poetic, and especially the prophetic, parts allegorically and typologically. In other words, Russell read the prophetic passages by understanding one thing (the type) as a prefiguring of a subsequent thing (the antitype). As Russell tried to make biblical passages relevant to the nineteenth and twentieth centuries, he interpreted postbiblical events as the antitypes of biblical types.

Russell's personal religious history was convoluted. In turns he was a Presbyterian, a Congregationalist (with thoughts of becoming a minister), and a skeptic. In 1869, he encountered the Adventist movement, with its emphasis on the imminent second coming of Christ, an idea he found so captivating it dominated the rest of his life. He gathered others around him who were also interested in studying the Bible for insights about the second coming. This community became the core of the Zion's Watch Tower Tract Society, incorporated in 1884.

Russell focused his theology on the chronology of the Bible and how it pointed to the second coming of Christ. Of staggering complexity, his theology utilized the "prophetic" books of Daniel and Revelation by claiming the days mentioned in those books actually refer to years (see Num.

14:33-34, Ezek. 4:1-8, esp. v. 6). In his system, through a complex mathematical maneuvering of the numbers, the 1,260 days of Revelation 12:6 (which corresponds to the "three and one-half times" of Dan. 7:25 and Rev. 12:14), the 1,290 days and 1,335 days of Daniel 12:11 and 12 respectively, and the 2,300 days of Daniel 8:14 all refer to years of 360 days each. Russell's millennial scheme also emphasized the biblical notions of Jewish jubilee years and the "times of the Gentiles." In the Jewish system, a jubilee year began after 49 (7 x 7) regular years for a total of 50 years (Lev. 25:10). Russell saw this as a type of the antitype Jubilee Year, which would begin the Millennium. The "Gentile times" was a period in which the Jewish nation was in disfavor with God (Luke 21:24).

Russell used these concepts and others to calculate some significant dates in the divine plan of the ages. For example, he believed that the last Jubilee (the type) was in 625 B.C.E. Because each cycle of Jubilee years was 50 years, in the "antitypical" fulfillment of the Jubilee, he multiplied cycles of Jubilee years, 50 x 50 = 2,500. Thus he said that the 2,500 years of Jubilee ended in 1874, the beginning of 1,000 years of Jubilee, or the Millennium (the antitype). He argued that 1874 marked the Second Coming of Christ. Obviously, that had not been observed. But Russell was convinced that the Greek word *parousia* could be translated by the English word "presence" (rather than relying on the traditional word "coming"). Consequently, he concluded that Jesus had invisibly begun his presence on earth in 1874. In his view, Bible chronology showed that Jesus had been baptized in the autumn of 29 C.E.; he interpreted this event as the "type" for the beginning of his invisible presence in 1874 (antitype). Three and one-half years later (33 C.E.) he rode into Jerusalem as King, a "type" of his assuming power as Heavenly King in the spring of 1878 (the antitype). So, Russell believed the kingdom of Heaven was established in 1878 (1874 + 3.5).

Russell believed the "times of the Gentiles" would end in 1914. He arrived at this date by determining that the Gentile times began when the Babylonians captured Judah (606 B.C.E., by his calculation) and took Jews into Exile. Since Daniel 4:10-17 states that "seven times" shall pass over Nebuchadnezzar (the Babylonian King), Russell applied his understanding that the "seven times" of Daniel equaled 2,520 years (7 x 360 = 2,520). The passage of 2,520 years from the year 606 B.C.E. indicated that the times of the Gentiles (Luke 21:24) would end in 1914.

Russell seemed to believe true Christians would be taken to heaven in 1914. Simultaneously, earthly institutions would be broken apart and God would substitute theocratic rule on earth for current political governments. The kingdom of God on earth (begun in heaven in 1878) would begin. As early as 1907, Russell began to prepare his followers for the possibility that these things would not happen in 1914. He acknowledged that he would be sorely disappointed if his prediction did not come true, but if it did not, it would mean only that one string on his theological harp would be broken; the harp, however, could still play the beautiful music of truth. On 2 October 1914, Russell announced that the Gentile times had ended, even though there had been no visible signs of the events just mentioned. Still convinced of the truth of his prophecy, he died on 31 October 1916.

Russell was a prolific writer. His principal writings were *The Object and Manner of Our Lord's Return* (1877), *Food for Thinking Christians* (1881), and *The Millennial Dawn* (6 vols., 1886–1904, renamed *Studies in the Scriptures* after 1904). In 1879, he began a monthly magazine (semimonthly beginning in 1892), *Zion's Watch Tower and Herald of Christ's Presence*.

Russell rejected the Calvinism of his youth, and also rejected any theological notion connected with predestination. On the basis of passages such as 1 Timothy 2:5, Hebrews 2:9, and 1 John 2:2, he believed in the substitutionary atonement of Christ for all humanity. But Russell was not a universalist: all would be ransomed, but not all would be saved. The ransom gave all the chance of a final choice of whether or not to live under God's laws. The opportunity for that final choice would occur during the millennium.

Although Russell affirmed the divinity of Jesus, he rejected both the concept of the Trinity and the idea that Jesus was somehow coequal and coeternal with God. Like the fourth-century Arians, he believed the doctrine of the Trinity was imported from paganism. The classical doctrine of the Trinity, he wrote, conveyed incorrect views of God, Jesus, and the Holy Spirit. The true Christian must reject it.

Jesus was not equal to God (John 14:28, 1 Cor. 15:28); he was a creation of God (Rev. 3:14, Col. 1:15), a separate person from God (John 8:17-18), illustrated by the fact that Jesus prayed to God (Matt. 26:39). Jesus was not God the Son, though he was the Son of God. According to Russell's theological understanding, the Holy Spirit is not a person at all, but rather is the active force of God. In the Bible, the Spirit is never given a personal name. And the Bible says that persons can be "filled" with the Spirit (not possible if the Spirit is a person). Consequently, the Spirit must be a powerful force that emanates from God to accomplish the divine will in the world.

Russell also chastised traditional Christianity for being wrong about both the nature of human beings and the question of eternal punishment.

On the former, he marshaled biblical arguments against the idea of an immortal soul. Humans do not *possess* a soul, which somehow has an independent existence, but they *are* souls (Gen. 2:7; 1 Cor. 15:45). When a person dies, the soul dies (Ezek. 18:20). Russell believed the Bible denies the immortality of the soul. Traditional Christianity's affirmation of it simply illustrated once again the strength of paganism's influence on Christianity. Eternal life for the righteous is a gift from God, not something inherent in the life of the soul.

For Russell, it followed that there is no hell. He could not believe a loving God would assign people to an eternal, burning torment. Neither did he believe the Bible supported the idea. The words *sheol* in the Old Testament and *hades* in the New actually referred to the tomb, death. Hell is synonymous with death. All humans experience it, but all humans are also ransomed from it by the sacrifice of Christ and given a final chance to accept or reject God's will. Russell interpreted *gehenna* to mean "the second death," or utter destruction. Those who reject, during the millennium, the opportunity to know God's truth will be eternally annihilated (Heb. 6:4-6, 10:26-29, Rev. 2:8).

What of the righteous who choose God's way? Russell believed a small number (the "little flock" of Luke 12:32) would spend eternity with Christ in heaven and the remainder (the "great multitude" of Rev. 7:9-17) would spend eternity on paradise earth (Rev. 5:9-10, 21:1; Matt. 5:5, 6:10). The number of the little flock who would spend eternity in heaven was 144,000 (Rev. 7:4, 14:1-3). Obviously, more than that would be true followers of God. After the little flock had received their reward, the remainder of the righteous would live on earth restored to Eden-like purity (which is the reason Russell did not predict the end of the physical world in 1914).

Finally, Russell believed the churches of Christendom were wrong, that collectively they constituted the "Great Babylon" of Revelation 17:5, from which the righteous must come out (Rev. 18:4). This judgment he based on their holding doctrines contrary to those described here, which he believed were firmly based on a careful reading of the Bible. Needless to say, Protestants and Catholics did not much appreciate Russell or his followers.

Most of these ideas were not original with Russell; he derived them from a variety of sources. He did pull them together into a coherent whole, convincing enough people of their veracity for a movement to result. However, over the years the Jehovah's Witnesses have changed or abandoned many of his concepts, and most members now are unaware of either Russell or his influence on the movement. The movement stopped publishing his books in 1927 and ceased circulating them in 1932.

Suggested Readings

Writings of Charles T. Russell: *Studies in the Scriptures,* 6 vols. (Allegheny, Pa.: Watch Tower Bible and Tract Society, 1886–1904).

Jehovah's Witnesses: Proclaimers of God's Kingdom (Brooklyn: Watch Tower Bible and Tract Society of New York, 1993).

M. James Penton, *Apocalypse Delayed: The Story of Jehovah's Witnesses* (Toronto: University of Toronto Press, 1985).

Alan Rogerson, *Millions Now Living Will Never Die: A Study of Jehovah's Witnesses* (London: Constable and Co., 1969).

Mormonism After the Death of Joseph Smith

Jan Shipps

Particular precursors anticipated the developments that, taken together, constitute Mormonism's three distinct layers of theology and doctrine. First, in place before the organization of the church, the *Book of Mormon* and restoration of the priesthood provided a launching pad for the movement. Second, a hearty response to revelations calling for the gathering that would bring believers together to create a Latter-day Saint culture as well as religious organization came before and probably stimulated the Hebraicizing of Mormonism, of which the building of the first Mormon temple was a part. Third, the dedication of the Kirtland Temple and the subsequent literal (definitely not merely figurative) organization of the kingdom of God were antecedent to the introduction of the esoteric doctrines that the Latter-day Saints refer to as the gospel's "fullness." Considering Mormon theology from a historically stratified perspective is helpful because it illuminates what often appears cryptic and enigmatic. In addition, this approach helps to account for the high rate of falling away that occurred during the prophet's lifetime and to explain the virtual atomization of the movement that occurred after his death.

Even though the addition of new layers of theology and doctrine changed Mormonism in radical ways, many of the movement's adherents, first in Kirtland and Missouri and later in Nauvoo, welcomed the revelation of new tenets, readily assimilating them into the faith. General acceptance of the concept of continuing revelation notwithstanding, each time a new stratum of theology and doctrine was imposed on existing belief and practice, a substantial number of Smith's followers were disturbed enough to leave. Those who rejected new dogma were generally branded as apostate (or worse). Yet persuasive evidence suggests that, in cases too numerous to count, the problem was that the ones who left were so thoroughly committed to the form of Mormonism to which they had been converted that they regarded the new revelations as false prophecy.

Some fell away when it became clear that there was more to Mormonism than the truth of the *Book of Mormon* and the restoration of the priesthood and the church. Others later rejected the form of Mormonism that existed after revelation made it clear that the restored church was a family church, one that included membership in the family of Abraham and, in addition, was led by an elect family (the Smiths). Numerically, the greatest repudiation of new revelation may have come with the addition of the final theological and doctrinal layer, which transformed the movement into what those who were faithful to the end of Joseph Smith's life and beyond believed to be "the restoration of all things." A leading reason for defection at this point was the advent of the actual practice of plural marriage.

Despite their having been troubled by the various theological, doctrinal, and organizational additions and perhaps by the lengthening distance between themselves and other Christians, what happened to Joseph Smith's followers after 1844 makes it obvious that many of them had only been kept within the fold by the prophet's charismatic leadership. Following his death, the movement's heterogeneity spawned many Mormonisms. Although most failed, all are significant because the combined histories of groups that trace their origins to Joseph Smith reveal common agreement about the *Book of Mormon* being ancient scripture. Their histories also indicate an impressive level of acceptance of the legitimacy of the claim that the church organized in 1830 by Smith and his followers was truly the restored Church of Jesus Christ. The issues dividing them can usually be related to acceptance or rejection of restorations subsequent to the initial apostolic restoration. This is especially important in understanding what divided the two largest and best-known of the movement's surviving institutional manifestations.

The Church of Jesus Christ of Latter-day Saints headquartered in Salt Lake City, Utah, has nearly ten million members. The Church of Jesus Christ (RLDS) headquartered in Independence, Missouri, has far fewer, only a bit more than 250,000 at last count. Despite the discrepancy in size, these two institutions are equally important to an adequate understanding of Mormon theology because they reflect the Mormonism that existed at separate stages of the movement's theological, doctrinal, and organizational existence.

Joseph Smith's mother, his brother William, and his first wife, Emma, remained in the Midwest after the prophet's murder. In 1860, as soon as Joseph Smith III was willing to take the lead, a substantial group of the prophet's followers reestablished the church. In doing so, they put forth the original claims of the restored Church of Christ, including the assertion that their leader, the eldest son of the first Mormon prophet, was also a prophet. From that point until 1996, the prophet-president of the "Reorganization," as this group called itself, was always a direct descendant of Joseph Smith. Thus it was a family church in a literal sense. For many years, its members also held on to the concept of birthright membership in the family of Abraham. This situates the RLDS church precisely at the center of Mormonism as it existed after its first two doctrinal and theological strata were in place. Its location there is affirmed by the fact that from its beginnings, the identity of this Latter Day Saint church was framed in light of its downright repudiation of the theological additions that the prophet put in place in Nauvoo. This repudiation disavowed celestial marriage altogether; although Emma Smith knew better, members of the Reorganization believed that the practice had been initiated by Brigham Young. It also rejected the whole complex of dogma that derives from the idea of the restoration of ancient temple ordinances that make possible the immutability of the family unit and eternal progression toward godhood.

The Saints who followed Brigham Young west created the Church of Jesus Christ of Latter-day Saints. After they reached the Valley of the Great Salt Lake, they re-created Nauvoo Mormonism not simply in all its theological, doctrinal, and organizational fullness, but with its various elements on or very near the surface. In view of their geographical isolation, they were able to create a realm "in the tops of the mountains" that was politically and economically organized as the Kingdom of God. Plural marriage was not merely accepted there; it was celebrated as evidence of a new patriarchal order of the ages. Although they did not repudiate Jackson County, Missouri, as the site of Zion, for all practical purposes, the Latter-day Saints turned the intermountain west into Israel. Where its citizens regarded Brigham Young as a prophet, his chief theological assertion—that Adam and God were one and the same—has been pushed to the margins as theological speculation. Instead, Young's turning Joseph Smith's prophetic vision into reality is accounted his greatest religious achievement.

Young's accomplishment went unappreciated by the nation's political and economic leaders, who regarded it in secular terms. At the same time, the nation's churches, viewing this western Zion in religious terms, condemned Mormons as heretics. Consequently, the U.S. Congress, representing the overwhelmingly non-Mormon portion of the population, moved slowly but deliberately to frustrate the LDS enterprise. The outcome was that, after almost fifty years of being in the world, the Saints dismantled their earthly kingdom in order to save their cultural integrity. Then, in order to save their temples, and hence their distinctive form of Christianity, they relinquished the practice of plural marriage. The implications of what they had done were not immediately clear, but these moves gradually led to a transformation of Utah Mormonism, the most complex form of the faith.

The esoterica introduced into the LDS belief system in Nauvoo has not been abandoned, but it is no longer open to view. Bundled into a set of sacred tenets, much as software programs are bundled into packages, this theological layer is now mainly discernible in the concept of the Saints as a "temple-going people." Yet the removal from view of this crowning stratum of LDS belief did not turn Utah Mormonism into a movement somewhat comparable to the Reorganization, even in the eyes of those outside the faith. Saints held on to the concept of the gathering for a very long time. While church leaders announced that Zion is where the people of God are and started discouraging emigration of Saints to the area of the West known as the Mormon culture region in 1921, new converts continued to regard Utah and its environs as Zion and continued to settle there. The western Mormon enclave lived on, and does so today.

Now, however, the membership of the church has expanded so exponentially that gathering all the Latter-day Saints in the West would be impossible. One result of this growth is that living in LDS cultural enclaves is no longer the norm. Members live across the nation, and today more Saints live outside than inside the United States. The practical effect of this shift is colossal, but so are its religious implications.

As members of the church flowed into Kirtland from all directions, their response to revelation made way for the creation of such a sense of specialness that the Saints came to regard themselves as birthright members of Abraham's family. New revelation has not suspended this concept. But as the church itself is moving out to the four corners of the earth with a newly universalized message made possible by a 1978 revelation that extended the privileges of the LDS priesthood to all worthy males, including African Americans, there are indications that figurative membership in Abraham's family may once again be gaining as much importance as literal membership. As more and more Saints are "adopted into Israel," the LDS church is reminding everyone—its own birthright members, new converts, and the world—of the importance of Christ, the Atonement, and its own rootedness in Mormonism's bedrock, the Church of Christ. It is not renouncing its endowment of idiosyncrasy that being a temple-going people implies, and it is in no way disavowing the peculiarity given to it by the revelations that turned the faith into a form of Hebraicized Christianity. But just as the Reorganization has been doing for generations, the Church of Jesus Christ of Latter-day Saints is presenting itself first and foremost as Christ's restored church.

Lest it appear that the wheel has come full circle, that the Saints are back where they started, neither the Reorganized Church of Jesus Christ of Latter-day Saints (RLDS) nor the Church of Jesus Christ of Latter-day Saints is precisely the same church that was organized by the Mormon prophet and his followers in 1830. None of the several sectarian Mormon institutions fill the bill either. The foundational elements of Mormonism (the *Book of Mormon*, priesthood restoration, and the restored church) have remained firmly in place across the tradition, but revelation received after 1830 wrought changes throughout the movement. A dramatic recent example is a 1994 revelation to the sitting president of the RLDS church. By designating as its new president a man who is not a direct descendant of Joseph Smith, this revelation severed the lineage link that historically signaled connection between the RLDS church and Mormonism's founding prophet. The result is likely to be as dramatic in the life of the Reorganization as the 1890 Manifesto was in the life of the LDS church. But the RLDS church may well weather the change, for Saints of all stripes share a legacy of continuing revelation. Receipt of, and the necessity of assimilating to, new doctrinal tenets is a part of being Mormon.

When revelation alters faith, the results often generate dissent. In some instances, dissenters who question the legitimacy of new revelation lead to schism which, in turn, can lead to the development of new forms of Mormonism. This is a process that started happening in Mormonism during the 1830s. It continues today as groups of Utah Saints refuse to believe that the 1890 Manifesto ending the practice of plural marriage was a revelation and as members of the Reorganization refuse to accept the 1985 revelation that extended priesthood ordination to women. Both dissenting groups are creating new forms of Mormonism. Such organizational volatility is eloquent testimony both to the health of the tradition and the complexity of the theology which was revealed through the agency of Joseph Smith, the Mormon prophet.

Suggested Readings

James B. Allen and Glen M. Leonard, *The Story of the Latter-day Saints* (Salt Lake City: Deseret, 1976).

Book of Mormon: Another Testament of Jesus Christ; Doctrine and Covenants of the Church of Jesus Christ of Latter-day Saints; Pearl of Great Price, 1-vol. ed. (Salt Lake City: Church of Jesus Christ of Latter-day Saints, 1981).

Paul M. Edwards, *Our Legacy of Faith: A Brief History of the Reorganized Church of Jesus Christ of Latter Day Saints* (Independence, Mo.: Herald Publishing House, 1991).

Encyclopedia of Mormonism, ed. Daniel H. Ludlow (New York: Macmillan, 1992); see esp. essays entitled "Prophecy," "Revelation," and "Theology."

Bruce R. McConkie, *Mormon Doctrine* (Salt Lake City: Bookcraft, 1958).

THE MODERN ERA

(1918–1965)

INTRODUCTION

Mark G. Toulouse and James O. Duke

As the twentieth century unfolded, the United States came to occupy a position of unquestioned world power. Its new status signified not only military might but increasing prosperity based on the growth of its population, its cities, its industries and commerce, its educational and cultural institutions. Pride in "the American way of life" ran strong in the nation. Despite times of distress—two world wars, the depression, cold war rivalry, and a nuclear arms race—there remained widespread confidence in America's capacity to rebound and meet any challenge with success. Yet Americans had paid a high price for such oft-praised gains. A sense of aloofness and safety from problems of the world was no longer an option. Lessons about the interconnectedness of nations had to be learned by trial and error. World leadership in politics and economics brought with it responsibilities, and vulnerability. Difficulties arising in some remote corner of the world could trigger a chain of events with massive effects at home.

In the main, the national view defined America as a nation called to be a force for good in the world, defending and promoting the principles of democracy, Western civilization, and religious (Bible-based if not specifically Christian) morality. But defining what it meant to be a force for good in specific cases was often a matter of controversy, religious as well as political. Were stability, peace, prosperity, and progress more likely achieved by restraint and compromise at the risk of appeasement, or by steadfast, even violent resistance at the risk of loss of life? In this situation, Christians might either deal with such issues directly (as many did, coming down on one side or the other)—or define the faith in terms other than these "social" and "political" considerations.

What at one moment seemed a clear line of demarcation along these lines was at other times overwhelmed by events. The sinking of the *Lusitania*,

Nazi action after Munich, and the attack on Pearl Harbor, for example, turned many Christian pacifists into warhawks, and the Marshall plan for rebuilding Western Europe seemed as benevolent as it was militarily advisable. But world affairs were only on occasion apparently clear-cut. Being a "force for the good" routinely involved alliances and strategies of dubious morality. America's self-image as a righteous nation was by no means universally shared. Even those inclined to pass off anti-Americanism as ideological animus had to reckon with the "Ugly American" image as depicted in the 1958 novel of that name (by William J. Lederer and Eugene Burdick). Questions about the church's social witness in national and international affairs were addressed by nearly every theologian of the modern era represented here.

Churches, like the nation itself, stepped up their international commitments. The end of the First World War brought renewed enthusiasm for foreign missions. Increased American influence on the world scene meant more open doors for the missionary enterprise. As they moved into the twentieth century, America's Protestants especially geared up to meet the opportunity and the need, dedicating themselves anew to worldwide evangelization. Expecting to change the world, they found themselves caught up in a process of change. Many advocates of world missions seeking to love and care for those in sin and life-misery gained firsthand experience of points that new social scientific inquiry set down as data and theory. Conversion to Christ was not by itself the solution to the problems that beset non-Christians. Westerners trying to preach Christ alone according to scripture alone were as likely to preach Western culture as well or instead. Having come to people in areas of the world where Christianity was unknown because Christ called them to be loving and caring, how could they disdain, indeed condemn, loving and caring elements of the non-Christian religious traditions they encountered, or overlook the unloving, uncaring elements of the Western Christianity they imported to foreign parts?

Interest in historical, comparative, and philosophical studies of world religions increased markedly. As early as 1932, a "Layman's Foreign Missions Inquiry," chaired by Harvard philosopher William Hocking, concluded that social service, rather than evangelistic witness, should drive the missionary enterprise. Did this mean that being Christian no longer mattered at all? Not many in church missions would or could say no. Yet once posed so starkly, the question forced divisions among Christians—once united on missions, whether "liberal" or "conservative" at home. The unifying trends of the earlier missionary movement gave way to discord and fragmentation.

The wealth of the nation, growing along with its international status, was also a strong influence on the making of Christian theology, with mixed results. Being American had its blessings, that is, its economic benefits. But Christians were at odds with one another about how to interpret the well-being of the nation in theological terms. Even as they debated the matter, they perceived within their own churches and society at large various signs that their efforts might have little if any impact on the wider social scene. What had been a historic combat against skepticism, infidelity, and indifference became, from the "roaring twenties" on, a more diffuse concern over the "secularization" of American culture. Secularization took so many forms that even the attempts of churches and church movements to oppose it were subject to criticism as compromising, ineffectual, or counterproductive. Thus to some the Social Gospel seemed more social—and hence "secular"—than gospel, while to others, appeals to the "ol' time religion" of individualist conversion and morality seemed at best tacit endorsements of the "secular" status quo.

Meanwhile, ministries like those of Norman Vincent Peale and Bishop Fulton J. Sheen—the former of Methodist background, the latter Roman Catholic—stressed better living, health, and happiness through religion. In both cases the messages of self-help with Christ's advice were amplified by new electronic media, radio and television. Radio's power as a medium of communication had already been demonstrated in earlier decades by the success of Aimee Semple McPherson's advocacy of help—though not through self-help but by the Pentecostal outpouring of the Holy Spirit in response to human neediness. The rapid growth of "secular" psychology as a social science and a helping profession was at once a challenge and an opportunity to Christians seeking to understand the dynamics of sin, guilt, anxiety, conversion, salvation, hope, and human well-being. Along with exploratory studies of the relationship between psychology and theology came a new emphasis on pastoral care and counseling in Christian ministry.

The diversity of Christian, indeed religious, thought in America was surely evident to anyone with eyes to see during this era. But its acknowledgment—marked by the rhetorical turn from reference to "diversity" as the proper descriptor to that of "pluralism"—came fitfully and only within limits until a later date. Sociologically speaking, Protestants generally, and those among them willing to accept (qualifications or misgivings notwithstanding) the values of "Christianity and American culture" in particular, held dominance. That dominance was, in many respects, as illusory as it was real, however. Protestants differed in their views of Christianity and American culture. Catholicism had continued its growth throughout this period. As early as the 1920s, its number had more than doubled that of the two largest American Protestant groups combined. Although Al Smith, the first Catholic presidential candidate, failed in his 1928 run against Herbert Hoover, the race was competitive. Various attempts to secure WASP power, including restrictions on immigration and periodic resurgences of the Ku Klux Klan, ultimately failed. In the context of its times, the election of John F. Kennedy as president ratified that Catholics were true Americans and that other true Americans held no grudges against Catholics. Vatican II reassured many Protestants that fears of a Roman Catholic president were unfounded. Among Roman Catholics, the national election and the church Council proved to be historic turning points.

By this date, Jewish sociologist of religion Will Herberg had chronicled the beginning of "pluralism" in his 1955 book, *Protestant-Catholic-Jew*. Those of all three faiths shared a set of core (Bible-based) values. In America, a "land of opportunity," because of those values as well as talent and persistence, members of those faiths had proved themselves worthy of the acceptance and respect of all. African Americans renewed their struggle for just such acceptance and respect during this decade. Their requests and then brave protests demanding equal rights, justice, and full citizenship were to become inspirations and models for similar movements in coming years.

During the post–World War II decade of the 1950s, revival of religious interest spread over the American scene. Church membership rose across the denominational spectrum, and beyond. Church building, membership rolls, and religious book sales boomed. Congress added the words "under God" to the pledge of allegiance in 1954. So sweeping was this revival that its character and significance cannot yet be fully defined with assurance. It was, according to one's viewpoint, either the best or the worst of religiosity in America. For example, simultaneously it heralded the heyday of so-called mainline or liberal Protestantism, the rise of neo-evangelical Protestantism as symbolized by Billy Graham, and the finest hour or the last gasp of "traditionalist" Roman Catholicism. The high point of Christian influence on national life, and, in some cases, the triumph of American civil religion reduced the religious faiths to voluntary societies for the promotion of "the American way" on the premise that having some faith (no matter what it might be) is good for every American and good Americans are good for the world. Theologies—critical and uncritical, sophisticated and naive, Christian, semi-, quasi-, or anti-Christian, as well as non-Christian—found market niches. By the end of the era, secularity itself was transformed into a new form of cultural religiosity, dutifully described, analyzed, and evaluated by sociologists of religion and theologians alike.

This volume has noted various and changing conceptions of theologians and their theologies. Their effects persist in the modern era, some gaining or regaining new strength, others undergoing redefinition or more or less fading from common use. The growth of theology as an academic discipline and research specialty, emerging after the Civil War, gained in prominence. Field-expertise in the several (and expanding number of) theological disciplines made theologians "scholars" in much the same sense as their peers in the arts and sciences of "the academy." Accorded high respect for their learning by Christians generally, these theologians were also routinely chided for their "ivory tower intellectualism." Among some "conservative" churches, refusing to have or heed theologians of this sort was a source of some pride.

Amid praise for and misgivings about "scholarly" theologians and their theologies, an equally striking transformation taking place was not very often discussed. The view—and role—of the minister as pastor-theologian (represented so well in earlier pages of this book) was in decline. Of the theologians covered in this section, Martin Luther King is the lone pastoral theologian, earning his Ph.D. before going to leadership in the church and the nation. He is, however, joined here by a few others working outside the academy: Marcus Garvey, Dorothy Day, and Thomas Merton. Three of the four names on this short list call attention to the fact that the established theologians in higher education throughout the period remained mostly white and male. Georgia Harkness was one of the more notable exceptions, the diversity of the academy finally beginning in earnest during the 1960s. The days of easy transition from pulpit to lectern were passing. Reinhold Niebuhr's move from the pastorate to Union Theological Seminary in 1928 might be considered symbolic of this turn of affairs: The move could still be made, but not readily or well—except by a pastor-theologian with gifts akin to those of Reinhold Niebuhr.

In most cases, Protestants expected their ministers to have theological training, but not actually to be theologians—that is, theologians in the same sense as the teacher-scholars who had trained them. Pastors in the modern period became known more for their preaching or their skills in other "practical" tasks rather than for their theologizing. And, as the period progressed, theology became less important as a component of preaching and other practical tasks than it once had been. By the mid-1960s the gap separating award-winning scholarly, churchly, and popular theology (and for Protestants the gap between the people in the pew on the one side and their ordained church leaders and theological scholars on the other) had grown menacingly large. A number of the theologians featured here attest, either by their own words or those of their interpreters, how difficult it had become to identify who is and is not "really" a Christian theologian. In ordinary conversation and in the media, various (now narrow, now expansive or even vague) references to Christian theologians could routinely pass without comment—everyone knew what was meant. Yet by the mid-1960s, it was fast becoming ever more obvious to increasing numbers of Christian theologians that how to define the task of Christian theology was itself a theological question.

The essays here also illustrate how the American response to the modern age took many forms. The two main liberal responses early on in the era are represented by the evangelical liberalism of William Adams Brown and the scientific modernism of Shailer Mathews. Brown, in the tradition of Charles A. Briggs, Newman Smyth, and William Newton Clarke, modeled a christocentric form of liberalism. His modern confidence in historical and human progress, together with his desire to build the kingdom of God on earth, powered his involvement in the early ecumenical movement. Shailer Mathews embraced modernity more fully. He worked to translate Christian faith into categories compatible with evolutionary social theory, sociological analysis, historical and literary approaches to the Bible, and the pragmatic effectiveness of religion to meet human need. The advocacy of Mathews, and others like him, for a modernist version of Christianity responsive to developments within culture triggered a fundamentalist counteroffensive.

J. Gresham Machen provided the most scholarly and articulate voice among the fundamentalists of this time period. His intellectual plea for fundamentalism, anchored in older Princeton orthodoxy, proved more durable than the populist ramblings of William Jennings Bryan during the 1925 Scopes Trial in Dayton, Tennessee. One of the few fundamentalists with educational experience in Germany, Machen utilized his firsthand acquaintance with German liberalism in a self-defined crusade to protect American Christianity from theological modernism, which he considered a complete abandonment of the truths of the Christian faith. Heavily invested in the battles between modernist and fundamentalist forces within the Presbyterian Church during the 1920s, Machen's body of theological work clearly represented the forceful nature of early American fundamentalism. Francis Schaeffer, a student of Machen's shortly before his death, perfected Machen's tendencies toward separatism and also provided theological foundations for the religious right beginning in the 1970s.

The "classical liberalism" of Brown, Mathews, and other theologians of the early twentieth century, in both Europe and America, occasioned another response that came to be known as neoorthodox, dialectical, or neo-Reformation theology. Theologians like Karl Barth and Emil Brunner on the continent, and Reinhold Niebuhr in America (in the name of "Christian realism"), challenged the confident connection liberalism had made between Christianity and culture. These thinkers emphasized instead the great gulf between the transcendence of the God of the Bible and culturally conditioned definitions of who God is. H. Richard Niebuhr and Paul Tillich also took a dialectical approach to theological themes and issues, differing from classical neoorthodoxy perhaps most in their resolve to explore the paradoxical relationships of Christianity and culture in extensive detail. They stressed both God's judgment and God's grace, highlighting both the divine condemnation of the human tendency to save oneself and their absolute confidence in God's gracious intent to redeem the human situation.

This current of thought—in neoorthodox, dialectical, realistic forms—all but defied neat and tidy categorization in terms familiar to American Christians, theologians included. The new movement looked suspiciously fundamentalist to liberals and suspiciously liberal to the fundamentalists. Accustomed to debating one another, liberals and fundamentalists were hard-pressed to figure out how anyone could possibly find fault with both of their positions at one and the same time. Highly critical of the liberals for accommodating the Gospel to sociocultural values, the Niebuhr brothers still somehow managed, each in his own distinctive manner, to prize critical social-scientific inquiry and activities on behalf of social justice. Having asserted the "Protestant principle" that the transcendence of God relativizes any and every human undertaking, including everything that the church undertakes, Tillich proceeded to devise a "theology of correlation" between Christianity and culture.

Liberalism, fundamentalism, and neoorthodoxy were not the only theological options through the 1940s. The personalist philosophy of Borden Parker Bowne found theological expression during this period in Albert C. Knudson, who used it to criticize these other options. His emphasis on human personality, freedom, and self-consciousness was elaborated by others into a foundation for social activism. Georgia Harkness mixed personalism with the critical realism of Reinhold Niebuhr, combining her theological concerns with an activist social conscience. Dorothy Day found herself influenced by the personalism of Peter Maurin calling for individual self-sacrifice for the good of others in the manner of Christ.

Marcus Garvey, W. E. B. DuBois, and Martin Luther King, Jr., struggled, taking differing routes, to proclaim good news of dignity and hope to African Americans, drawing on the black experience in America throughout history. Garvey emphasized black nationalism and self-reliance. DuBois pioneered in historical and sociological studies by his analyses of the divided black self (attempting to be both African and American). Martin Luther King, Jr., represented the quintessential model of how biblical themes, civil religious themes, African American piety, personalism, and social activism combined as he emphasized the God-given worth of the human personality and the responsibility of all Christians to work toward social justice.

Most Christian liberals remained self-consciously Christian even though they fully embraced scientific methodology. But there were some thinkers whose work moved them beyond merely Christian liberalism. Following the pragmatism of William James, John Dewey emphasized the practical consequences resulting from beliefs. He left the church and developed a form of religious naturalism or humanism in which human experience and scientific method provided the only authorities for human knowledge. Dewey's work supports the hypothesis that most movements in American philosophy have been implicitly religious in character, and as such have held special appeal to those seeking to support or reform Christian theology in America. Surveys of the theology in this era customarily describe the trends and options not in terms of confessional or denominational ties but in terms of the type of philosophical or social-scientific resources that are put to use. Henry N. Wieman, for example, followed Dewey in both his pragmatism and his empiricism. He counted himself a theistic naturalist who found God's presence in the creative activity of finite human beings. Pragmatism also exerted an influence on D. C. Macintosh, who argued for the reasonableness of belief in God on the basis of the kind of life such a belief makes possible. Charles Hartshorne's empirical process theology most clearly illustrates the trend of more recent American thought to emphasize becoming rather than being.

Having followed the liberal strands through this period, it is time to step back for a moment and pick up another counter-movement in American theology. The neo-evangelical movement arose in response both to fundamentalism's inability to maintain an intellectually credible witness and neoorthodoxy's display of many liberal leanings. The foundations of neo-evangelicalism were laid by the written work of two theologians. Edward J. Carnell continued the Calvinist and Reformed strands of orthodoxy found in the earlier theology of Machen, while criticizing him for being a separatist. Carl F. H. Henry called fundamentalism back to an awareness of social issues while he offered an orthodox combination of faith and reason that always placed the latter in service to the former. Both Carnell and Henry stressed evangelical alliances and helped to establish Fuller Theological Seminary. Billy Graham's break with fundamentalism and his links to Wheaton College and Fuller helped the new movement gain a broad popular base.

Theological representatives of Eastern Orthodoxy must be included in this collection of essays. This tradition has roots in America dating to Russian Orthodox settlements of the late–eighteenth century in Alaska and the Pacific Northwest. Yet its significant growth in membership took place within the modern era, and by the middle of the twentieth century the Orthodox churches and their theologians had gained a secure place as dialogue partners with America's other Christian theologians. Largely due to the work of Georges Florovsky and John Meyendorff, the Orthodox church has maintained a significant presence in the ecumenical movement. These Orthodox theologians stressed patristic theology, a strongly christocentric focus, and a belief in the centrality of the eucharist, all of which have demonstrated their value in offering a theological critique of Western temptations to count too highly such concepts as self-determination and self-sufficiency.

Developments in American Catholicism during this period are clearly reflected in the writings of Thomas Merton and John Courtney Murray. The best-selling status of Thomas Merton emerged from a theological combination of syncretistic themes and styles unusual in American life at the time. He represents as well a different stripe of theologian. In some ways, his theological value emerges—like that of Frederick Douglass—in the midst of his life-story, a journey of faith narrated by autobiographical reflection, rather than in studies of doctrines per se or methodological approaches to the study of theology. John Courtney Murray's work marks the juncture where American Catholics fully embraced the American democratic social experiment without compromising Catholic theological distinctiveness. His writings provided key building blocks forming the theological foundation for the Roman Catholic Church's engagement with the ecumenical church in America, and for its mature appreciation of the meaning of religious pluralism. This latter development is particularly appropriate since the most significant characteristic of American religion by the mid-1960s was a growing realization that no Christian group would be able any longer to avoid either the reality of religious pluralism or its implications for the future of American theology.

William Adams Brown

(1865–1943)

William H. Berger

Presbyterian minister, ecumenical pioneer, and leader in theological change in America, William Adams Brown was born 29 December 1865, in New York City. After study at Yale University and Union Theological Seminary in New York, Brown studied with Adolf von Harnack, the renowned church historian. Subsequently, Brown returned to Union Theological Seminary where he served as professor of systematic theology from 1895 to 1930. Unwilling to use the traditional theology textbooks of his day, he put his lectures into book form. His *Christian Theology in Outline* (1906) became a standard theology text in the first half of the twentieth century.

Brown described his own theology as a "new theology." The new theology was "modern," in its desire to interpret the faith for the "modern" scientific age, especially in terms of social service and historical progress. It was "liberal" in its desire for freedom of thought and in its acceptance of diverse theological opinions. At the same time, Brown insisted that his new theology did not involve a new faith, or new gospel. The constant for all theology was the historical personality of Christ and the fact of Christian experience throughout history. Hence, Brown's theology could also be termed "evangelical" or "christocentric liberalism."

For Brown, theology was not a set of organized propositions based on biblical teaching, as in traditional Protestant theology. Rather, theology was the product of experience, expressed in thought forms appropriate to a particular time. The task of theology was to interpret in ever new theological forms the constant experience of the gospel, to understand Christ not only in the terms of traditional Christian beliefs, but in relation to the ideas of the time. The common ground between the new theology and that of the past was the common experience of the gospel of Christ.

However, Brown's understanding of the gospel differed significantly from much traditional Protestant thought. In 1902, Brown wrote *The Essence of Christianity: A Study in the History of Definition,* in which he defined the essential gospel as moral and ethical, rather than doctrinal. The person of Christ could be discovered only through a critical reconstruction of the Gospels, which, following Harnack, cleared away the "mists of dogma and of tradition" surrounding the historical Jesus. For Brown, the essential gospel centered in service to the world through the building up of a cooperative society based on the principles of love and sacrifice, a society called the kingdom of God. These principles were embodied in the life and death of Jesus Christ. This practical and nondoctrinal gospel was the basis for all Christian theology.

Brown defined the central methodological principle of the new theology in "The Old Theology and the New" (1911). The new theology, according to Brown, no longer held to a sharp distinction between the supernatural and the natural, as had the old theology. For the new theology, God was not considered distinct from the universe but was found within the course of human history and, especially, human progress. Christ was seen not so much as a supernatural figure, but as the highest expression of the divine purpose in human life. The kingdom of God was not an otherworldly realm, but the progressive realization of the principles of Christ in human history. The church existed not as a society of saved persons distinct from the world, but as a society dedicated to the larger task of building the kingdom of God in the world. Finally, Brown viewed the Bible not so much as a divinely inspired book, isolated from other books, but as a record of religious experiences to be understood within their historical contexts. Brown's article on new theology embroiled him in theological controversy in the Presbyterian Church between 1910 and 1915. Thus, while active in the home mission work of his church during that period, he began to devote most of his church service to the larger interdenominational and worldwide ecumenical organizations.

In 1917 he moved to the forefront of interdenominational leadership when he began his service as Secretary of the General War-Time Commission of the Churches during World War I, the Protestant interdenominational cooperative agency for national wartime service. On the world ecumenical scene, he was instrumental in the Life and Work Movement, which sought to join the churches in cooperative social action. He chaired the Programme Committee for the first Life and Work Conference in 1925, served as president of the Universal Christian Council for Life and Work in 1933, and was one of the presiding officers at the Oxford Conference on Church, Community, and State in 1937.

Related to his interdenominational and ecumenical involvements, one theological theme appeared frequently in Brown's writings and set him apart from many of his theological counterparts: his theology of the church. For all liberal theologians, the kingdom of God was an all-encompassing social concept, and the church was subordinate to the kingdom. This kingdom Brown defined as a society organized around the principles of love and mutual service, progressively realized in human history. Brown refused to draw any sharp line between the church and the world, and refused to confine salvation, or spiritual life, or supernatural activity within the church. The world rather than the church was the primary arena of divine activity.

However, due to Brown's labors through the ecumenical organizations, and in part due to the failures after the First World War in attaining the larger goal of a cooperative society, the church began to assume a larger role in his thinking. In *The Church Catholic and Protestant: A Study of Differences That Matter* (1935), Brown demonstrated his growing belief that the organized church held a unique role with respect to divine activity in the world, going so far as to say that the organized church was the normal agent for divine activity in the world. The kingdom of God was still the ultimate ideal of an international cooperative society, but Brown defined the church as the first expression of that society. For the church to accomplish that role in society, however, it would need to overcome its divisions.

To that end, Brown considered himself a mediating theologian, whose task was that of uniting theological differences around a common theological center. On the one hand, he believed the theological task was to reach the modern listener, to whom certain traditional Christian beliefs were no longer acceptable, and to present those permanent elements of the Christian faith in a form that would appeal to those who had broken with the past. On the other hand, the theological task was to engender sympathy for the new theology on the part of those who held traditional beliefs, showing the new theology's ties with the past, and demonstrating that both old and new theologies grew out of similar religious experiences.

The new theology provided a means by which the practical essence of the Christian faith could be defined, and theological differences sympathetically understood. Likewise, the twentieth-century ecumenical and interdenominational organizations, such as the General War-Time Commission and the Life and Work Movement, represented for Brown an effort to unite Christians and churches in accomplishing a common practical goal in society, despite their theological differences. Brown's ideal of church unity culminated in the formation of the World Council of Churches. After 1935 Brown had served as a member of the continuation committees of both the Life and Work movement, and the Faith and Order Movement, which were devoted to facilitating organizational and doctrinal unity among the churches. Serving as a liaison between the two, he was a primary instigator in bringing these main streams of the twentieth-century ecumenical movement together to form the World Council of Churches, for which he served on the planning committee. Brown described the Council in a book written shortly before his death, *The New Order in the Church* (1943). Uniting churches on a christocentric basis, allowing for theological diversity in an atmosphere of mutual respect, and maintaining a concern with transforming the social order, the World Council of Churches represented for Brown, in some measure, that new order of organized church life appropriate to the new theology.

Brown died on 15 December 1943. By the middle of the twentieth century the new theology, with its belief in the possibilities of establishing the kingdom of God on earth, and its blurred distinction between the supernatural and natural, had faded from the theological scene. The first two Assemblies of the World Council of Churches in 1948 and 1954, under the influence of a new generation of theologians including Karl Barth and Reinhold Niebuhr, rejected many of the themes of the new theology. At the same time the Council, along with other interdenominational and ecumenical organizations Brown helped bring into existence, operated very much on patterns set out by the new theology. In large measure these organizations have ensured the continued influence of his theological thinking.

Suggested Readings

Writings of William Adams Brown: *The Church Catholic and Protestant: A Study in Differences That Matter* (New York: Charles Scribner's Sons, 1935); *Modern Theology and the Preaching of the Gospel* (New York: Charles Scribner's Sons, 1914); "The Old Theology and the New," *Harvard Theological Review* 4 (1911): 1-24.

Kenneth Cauthen, *The Impact of American Religious Liberalism* (New York: Harper & Row, 1962).

Shailer Mathews

(1863–1941)

W. Creighton Peden

Shailer Mathews was born in Portland, Maine, on 26 May 1863. Jonathan Mathews, his father, was a storeowner and Baptist deacon. Through his mother, Sophia Lucinda, Mathews was descended from several generations of teachers and ministers. He was reared in a middle-class Victorian evangelical family. In working for his father, Mathews developed a lifelong progressive Republican concern for the problem of justice in the workplace.

In 1880 Mathews entered Colby College, where he came under the influence of Albion W. Small and the German historical economic school, which stressed that economic organization is not based on a rigid law of nature but a social construct. This economic perspective provided Mathews with a sociological and theoretical perspective for understanding social change. His studies at Colby also exposed Mathews to the theory of evolution, later foundational for his intellectual explorations. From Colby, Mathews went to Newton Theological Institute (1884–87), where he became interested in historical study as a means of understanding and evaluating Christian doctrine. Upon graduation, he decided on a career in education instead of ordained ministry. He returned to Colby to teach in 1887 until he entered the University of Berlin in 1890. In Berlin he was influenced by Adolf Wagner toward a reformist, instead of revolutionist, understanding of effective social change and in general further mastered the rigorous critical-historical methodology which served as the foundation for his social process theology.

In 1894, Mathews became professor of New Testament history and interpretation at the Divinity School of the new University of Chicago. In 1906, he shifted to the chair of historical and comparative theology and also served as Dean of the Divinity School from 1908 until his retirement in 1933. During his Chicago years, he lectured widely and often to both ecclesiastical and academic audiences, and served in editorial roles in *Chris-*

tendom, Biblical World, World Today, and *Woman's Citizen's Library.* He also served as president of the Northern Baptist Convention, the Church Federation of Chicago, the Federal Council of Churches, and the Church Peace Union, and as director of religious work for Chautauqua. In his magisterial survey of American religious history, Sidney Ahlstrom notes that Mathews was one of the foundational thinkers of the American Social Gospel movement, even more influential at the time than Walter Rauschenbusch.

Mathews undertook a program of theological reconstruction that moved beyond European liberal theology toward a theological foundation for Christian social reform. Based on his continuing involvement in political and progressive reforms, he stressed the need for a measured process of progressivism instead of a revolutionary approach in social reform, which is illustrated in *The French Revolution* (1901). In this work he strongly relied on the developing field of social psychology for understanding the revolutionary approach. Mathews also applied the social psychological perspective on revolution to his interpretation of Jesus' messianic role in *The Social Teaching of Jesus* (1897; revised as *Jesus on Social Institutions,* 1928) and *The Messianic Hope in the New Testament* (1905). In *The Messianic Hope,* Mathews focused on the importance of a future-oriented (eschatological) understanding of the kingdom of God, taking into account the current discussion in German biblical scholarship, especially the work of Johannes Weiss on Jesus' proclamation of the Kingdom.

Mathews contended that the contemporary world confronted the most extraordinary intellectual transition since the early church had come under the influence of Neoplatonic philosophy. This intellectual change was captured by the metaphor of "evolution" as the symbol of the new perspective of reality. In attempting to understand the role of religion in this process of intellectual and social change, Mathews asked, "What is religion?" and answered by claiming it is a series of historical, social experiments based on human needs. The social acts are human attempts to ward off danger by trying to relate and adjust to a superhuman force within the cosmic process. For Mathews, a religious faith is either consistent or inconsistent with one's social reality, and this reality therefore must serve as the basis for a true conceptual understanding of God. As his perspective became increasingly evolutionary, he defined religion as a process of adjustment to the personality-producing activities of the cosmos. Although Mathews continued to emphasize the social acts of religion, he placed them in a wider context than the immediate environment of the individual of the group, namely, the environment of cosmic mystery.

Mathews affirmed a functional criterion for determining the value,

393

meaningfulness, or truth of religion based on the sociohistorical method, which he developed with his Chicago colleague Shirley Jackson Case. This method required viewing Christian doctrines as both a function of and creative response to the dominant social mind of any given historical period. Mathews argued that the constant element of evolving religion resides in the attitudes and convictions held rather than in the doctrines presented. These attitudes and convictions enable the individual and the group to relate themselves to those activities meeting their needs. When religion is conceived as a way of meeting human needs, the crucial issue is not truth but pragmatic efficiency. Religion is to be evaluated on the basis of the efficiency of its patterns in integrating human life with those elements of the known universe capable of satisfying personal needs.

Mathews applied his theory of religion to the crisis facing humanity before and after World War I. Prior to the war he applied sociological analysis to this crisis in an attempt to reconstruct theology as the basis for Christian social reform. This analysis is evident in *The Church and the Changing Order* (1907), *The Gospel and Modern Man* (1910), and *The Making of To-morrow: Interpretations of the World To-day* (1913). During this period Mathews took a pacifist position. But when the United States entered the war he supported the Allied cause "to make the world safe for democracy," as seen in *The Spiritual Interpretation of History* (1916). In *Patriotism and Religion* (1918), he identified the spirit of democracy with both the kingdom of God and creative religious thinking. Mathews increasingly stressed democracy as the ideal for creative social evolution—an approach also evident in George Birney Smith and Edward Scribner Ames. The evolution of society is influenced by human creativity. For religion to perform its role, a theology is required which enables a community of consciousness or social mind to form around democratic ideals.

Mathews came to understand the Christian religion as "loyalty to Jesus." By this he meant that Christians were those who fostered the attitudes and convictions of this tradition rather than relying on doctrines, dogmas, or literature. Progress in the Christian religion depends on its ability to grow and meet the needs of succeeding generations by developing more adequate theological-ethical metaphors for the emerging social mind of any period. Mathews argued, in "Theology and the Social Mind" (1915), that Christian attitudes and convictions must be reconstructed within a theology relevant to the emerging community consciousness evident in the creative scientific-democratic social process.

Mathews' study of the doctrine of God illustrates this reconstructed theology, as seen in *The Spiritual Interpretation of History* and "The Deity of

Christ and Social Reconstruction" (1920). The emergence of bourgeois capitalism, science, and democracy required a more creative view of God than was possible under the monarchical metaphor of early Christianity. The new metaphor for God devised by Mathews focused on personality as the most important feature of existence. God is creatively understood as those personality-evolving and personally responsive elements of our cosmic environment with which humans are organically related. Mathews was always careful to assert that the God of his concept is not limited to the conceptual activities under consideration. Rather, God expresses and furthers the relation between existing things. Mathews contended that the objective reality of the cosmic activities, which he designated as God, can be proved on the evidence provided by human observation. In general, Mathews asserted that his concept of God can stand the test of experimental validation just as well as any of the ideas evaluated by science.

In *The Faith of Modernism* (1924), Mathews offered his strongest postwar argument for employing the sociohistorical method in order to understand and express essential Christian beliefs in terms of the creative social mind of his day. He understood this social mind as seeking not only to expand scientific knowledge of nature but to extend liberty and justice to all. For Mathews the modernist Christian supported freedom of thought which incorporated scientific research in order to think religiously. The modernist also employed the method of historical and literary science in the study of the Bible to enable evangelical Christianity to meet the world's spiritual, moral, and social needs. Mathews understood the theological task of modernism to be an extension of the continuous historical process in which Christianity had evolved—a historical process of being loyal to Jesus.

In his earlier writings, Mathews focused on an interactive process between eternal Christian truths and changing culture. In later writings, however, the emphasis is on the metaphor "loyalty to Jesus." Being loyal to Jesus describes the historical process of the development of Christianity by which the values and ideals held by the individual and the community are transformed through believing that Jesus is the savior. In *The Faith of Modernism*, Mathews described modernism as a process which understands the continuous development of Christianity as keeping in tension essential Christian values-attitudes and changing culture. This creative process combines an effort to keep in tension eternal Christian convictions with the understanding that there are no constant factors in developing Christianity. In taking this position, Mathews attempted to separate himself from that form of liberalism which in his judgment sacrificed the constants within the Christian tradition by placing undue emphasis on the adaptive cultural process.

For Mathews, it is always necessary to keep in mind the reciprocal relationship between the development of Christianity and the evolution of culture. Mathews' sociohistorical method focused on a process of mutual interchange in which Christianity influences and is influenced by changing culture. However, in *Creative Christianity* (1935), Mathews modified his view of the process of mutual interchange between developing Christianity and culture. This later sociohistorical understanding presented Christianity more as responsive to rather than initiatory of cultural evolution. In taking this position, Mathews, sensitive to the inhumanity demonstrated in the war, was separating himself from nineteenth-century liberalism and its view of progress.

The primary interpreters of Mathews, and of other leading voices from the Chicago School and the Social Gospel tradition, have been fundamentalists and neoorthodox thinkers (especially Reinhold and H. Richard Niebuhr). Mathews was constantly under attack by fundamentalists, whom he claimed in his autobiographical essay ("Theology as Group Belief," 163-93) considered him part of an unholy trinity, along with the pope and the devil. The general line of neoorthodox attack stated that Mathews uncritically accepted the late-nineteenth-century understanding of the inevitability of progress, and offered a simplistic account of social reform based on a sentimental view of Christian love, ignoring the hard realities of power and justice. According to the two Niebuhrs, the basic problem was that Mathews and his associates did not believe in sin, and as a result, were inevitably tied to an inadequate view of social reform. Having a false understanding of human nature, Mathews and the tradition he represented sought to bring to reality the kingdom of God by appealing to a sentimental view of humanity's higher self. W. A. Visser 't Hooft added the charge that these thinkers failed to take seriously enough the transcendence of God. In essence, the complaint was that Mathews was one of the "culture Protestants"—thinkers who identified the kingdom of God with the development of culture.

This neoorthodox interpretation of Mathews failed to take into account the development of his thought and his differences with German liberalism. On the one hand, Mathews began his theological reconstruction from an evolutionary perspective. On the other hand, he grounded his theology in an evangelical understanding of the teachings of Jesus and by 1905 had rejected a social interpretation of the kingdom of God. Numerous scholars have pointed out the deficiencies of the neoorthodox reading of Mathews and the need for a more careful textual investigation of his thought within its historical context. John Bennett, for example, established that neoorthodox thinkers, including the Niebuhrs, were strongly influenced by these so-called culture Protestants. William Lindsey has forcefully argued that Mathews' position regarding social change can be best described as reflecting a realism in harmony with the views of neoorthodox theology.

The contributions of Shailer Mathews and the early Chicago School have received in recent years a more appreciative interpretation from American theological thinkers more in tune with the concerns of classical American philosophy. This appreciative study is evident in the work of the scholars of the Highlands Institute for American Religious Thought and the *American Journal of Theology and Philosophy*, whose emphasis includes "themes of relevance to the 'Chicago School' of theology." William Dean has demonstrated how Mathews' sociohistorical method responded to William James' and John Dewey's historicist challenge to theology, and Delwin Brown has indicated how this method, used by Mathews and the early Chicago School, anticipated the new historicism of the last decades of the twentieth century.

Philosophers and theologians influenced by evolutionary, pragmatic, and relational thought continue to find their orientations enriched by an appropriation of the sociohistorical method. Mathews' thematic focus on the kingdom of God and social reform has re-emerged in recent liberation theology, as well as in the U. S. Catholic bishops' concern for economic and social justice. The attempts of Mathews to democratize Christianity by making current religious scholarship available to the laity and establish the reciprocal relationship between evolving Christianity and culture can also serve as a model for the role of public theology in American religious thought. Further, Mathews contributes to our continuing appreciation of historical traditions and the place of religion in social reform. His sociological, scientific, democratic, and pragmatic methodological approach and his emphasis on public theology may someday help, as Mathews himself intended, to liberate American religious thought from those forces which seek to limit Christianity to a prescientific and precritical fundamentalism.

Suggested Readings

Writings by Shailer Mathews: *The Social Teachings of Jesus* (New York: Macmillan, 1897); *The Messianic Hope in the New Testament* (Chicago: University of Chicago, 1905); *The Faith of Modernism* (New York: Macmillan, 1924; repr., New York: AMS, 1970).

William D. Lindsey, *Shailer Mathews' Lives of Jesus: The Search for a*

Theological Foundation for the Social Gospel (Albany: State University of New York Press, 1997).

Shailer Mathews, "Theology as Group Belief," in Virgilius Ture Anselm Ferm, ed., *Contemporary American Theology:* Theological Autobiographies, 2nd Series, vol. 2 (New York: Roundtable Press, 1933), 163-93.

W. Creighton Peden and Jerome A. Stone, eds., *The Chicago School of Theology—Pioneers in Religious Inquiry,* vol. 1: *The Early Chicago School, Shailer Mathews* (Lewiston, N.Y.: Edwin Mellen, 1997), 119-86.

J. Gresham Machen

(1881–1937)

Bradley J. Longfield

J. Gresham Machen was born on 28 July 1881 in Baltimore, Maryland, to Arthur Webster Machen, an attorney, and Mary Gresham, a writer. Raised in an affluent, cultured, Old School Southern Presbyterian home, he attended a private school and early memorized the Westminster Catechism. Machen studied classics at Johns Hopkins University, graduating as valedictorian in 1901, and continued his education at Princeton University and Princeton Theological Seminary where he concentrated in New Testament studies. In 1905 he traveled to Germany to study for a year at Marburg and Göttingen.

While in Germany Machen endured a profound religious crisis sparked especially by the differences between the liberal theology of the Marburg theologian Wilhelm Herrmann and the conservative Presbyterian orthodoxy of Machen's boyhood. Despite misgivings, he returned to Princeton Seminary in 1906 as an instructor in New Testament where he eventually became a devout defender of the Old School Calvinism that dominated Princeton. He was ordained to the Presbyterian ministry in 1914 and promoted to Assistant Professor of New Testament in 1915. In the course of his career Machen wrote two significant studies of the New Testament, *The Origin of Paul's Religion* (1921), in which he argued that Paul's religion was grounded on the redeeming work of Jesus, and *The Virgin Birth of Christ* (1930), in which Machen contended for the historicity of the virgin birth. He also wrote a very popular introduction to biblical Greek.

Machen is best known for his role as a leader of the militant conservatives in the fundamentalist-modernist controversies in the Presbyterian Church in the U.S.A. in the 1920s and 1930s. As tensions between liberal and traditionalist Presbyterians mounted in the wake of World War I, Machen sought to defend the church from the advances of theological modernism. In a landmark volume, *Christianity and Liberalism* (1923),

399

Machen outlined the differences between traditional Protestantism and liberalism in order to demonstrate that liberalism or modernism was a completely different religion from Christianity.

He opened by setting the controversy between conservatives and liberals squarely within its historical context. Intellectual, social, and economic changes of the foregoing century, he argued, while bringing material advance, challenged traditional Christianity and impoverished spiritual and cultural life. Key in this was the advent of naturalistic materialism and the consequent rise of liberal theology. In an effort to accommodate the faith to modern ideas and ideals, Machen insisted, liberalism had simply abandoned Christianity.

While liberalism departed from historical Christianity on every essential doctrine, Machen argued, the most significant difference between Christianity and liberalism concerned the importance of doctrine itself. Traditional Christianity was rooted in doctrine, but liberalism, having accepted the claims of historicism, understood doctrines to be merely tentative expressions of Christian experience.

Christianity emphasized the sovereignty and transcendence of God, Machen averred, but liberalism stressed God's immanence in history and humanity. This led inevitably to an optimistic view of humanity for liberals that, contrary to historical Protestantism, abandoned any view of human sinfulness and therefore any real need for grace and forgiveness.

Christianity and liberalism likewise parted ways on their understandings of Christian authority. Traditional Protestantism had understood the Bible, God's inspired and inerrant word, to be the final authority for Christianity, but liberalism looked to Christian consciousness or Christian experience as the foundation for the Christian life. While not wanting to deny the importance of Christian experience, Machen insisted that though experience confirmed, it could never replace, the scriptural witness as the ultimate authority for Christian faith and practice. From the very early church forward, Machen argued, Christianity had insisted that Jesus was the Savior and object of faith, but liberals looked to Jesus merely as an example for faith and rejected the miracles, virgin birth, bodily resurrection, and deity of Christ. That is, Machen insisted, liberals abandoned the supernaturalism of the Bible for a naturalistic view of the world and therefore abandoned historical Christianity.

Finally, in opposition to the traditional Christian belief that salvation is rooted in the vicarious atonement of Christ and that believers are justified by faith, liberalism looked for salvation through obedience to the commands of Christ. Liberalism, Machen argued, was a faith in the imperative mood, based in ethics, while Christianity began with an indicative, the proclamation of what God had done in Jesus Christ.

Not all liberals, Machen conceded, held all of the views he considered. Nevertheless, liberalism needed to be examined by its logical implications rather than by its extant manifestations. Given the naturalistic presuppositions of liberal religion, he argued, liberalism inevitably tended toward paganism.

Inasmuch as liberalism and Christianity were two distinct religions, Machen concluded, liberals ought, in all honesty, to withdraw from Christian churches. But, he allowed, if liberals gained control of the evangelical churches, conservatives would have to withdraw. Above all, evangelicals, in the face of an increasingly assertive liberalism, needed to fight for the faith.

In the years following the publication of *Christianity and Liberalism* Machen followed his own advice. In the mid-1920s he unsuccessfully opposed efforts in the Presbyterian Church to broaden the doctrinal boundaries of the church, and in 1929, when the administration of Princeton Seminary was reorganized to allow for greater theological diversity at the school, Machen resigned his position and led in founding Westminster Theological Seminary in Philadelphia. In 1933, convinced that the Board of Foreign Missions of the Presbyterian Church tolerated liberals, Machen founded the Independent Board for Presbyterian Foreign Missions, which ultimately resulted in his suspension from the ministry in 1936. That year he led in the formation of the Presbyterian Church of America (later the Orthodox Presbyterian Church). He died 1 January 1937, in Bismarck, North Dakota, while fostering support for his fledgling denomination.

Machen stands as one of the leading scholarly spokesmen of the classic fundamentalist movement. His work not only helped to galvanize fundamentalism in the 1920s but influenced many of the leaders of later evangelicalism and fundamentalism in America. Additionally, he served as an example for the intellectual renewal of the evangelical movement in the mid–twentieth century. Many of Machen's books remain in print and continue to be widely read, especially among evangelicals.

Suggested Readings

Writings of J. Gresham Machen: *Christianity and Liberalism* (Grand Rapids: Wm. B. Eerdmans Publishing Co., 1985; repr. of 1923 ed.).

D. G. Hart, *Defending the Faith: J. Gresham Machen and the Crisis of*

Conservative Protestantism in Modern America (Baltimore: Johns Hopkins University Press, 1994).

Bradley J. Longfield, *The Presbyterian Controversy: Fundamentalists, Modernists, and Moderates* (New York: Oxford University Press, 1991).

George M. Marsden, *Understanding Evangelicalism and Fundamentalism* (Grand Rapids: Wm. B. Eerdmans Publishing Co., 1991).

Francis Schaeffer

(1912–1984)

Jack Rogers

Francis Schaeffer retained an early American Puritan-Enlightenment worldview and brought it into the twentieth century in a rigid and separatist form. Born in 1912, Schaeffer was raised during a period of turmoil in the Presbyterian Church and American culture. In 1935 he entered Westminster Seminary in Philadelphia. The next year its founder, J. Gresham Machen, defrocked by the Presbyterian Church in the U.S.A. for setting up the Independent Board of Presbyterian Foreign Missions, began a new denomination, the Orthodox Presbyterian Church. Schaeffer followed some of Machen's former allies, who separated to maintain premillennialism and abstinence from alcohol. This group formed the more conservative Bible Presbyterian Church and Faith Seminary, where Schaeffer finished his formal education. Years later Schaeffer led a dissident faction, which founded the Reformed Presbyterian Church Evangelical Synod and Covenant Seminary in Saint Louis. That seminary advertises a Francis Schaeffer Institute.

Schaeffer was little known outside conservative religious circles in the United States until 11 January 1960, when *Time* ran a story on him entitled "Mission to the Intellectuals." The "intellectuals" were American college-age young people tramping through Europe trying to find themselves. The *Time* writer's daughter had landed at L'Abri (French for "the shelter"), a study and communal living center in Huemoz, Switzerland, operated as an independent faith mission by Francis Schaeffer and his wife, Edith. The mixture of work, prayer, relaxation, and continuous discussion with Francis combined to form a homelike atmosphere in which the *Time* writer's daughter and others came to a fresh Christian commitment.

The form in which Schaeffer presented the Christian message was what he called the method of antithesis. Its basic style and content he had imbibed at Westminster Seminary in 1935. Machen had taught that Christianity and liberalism were two different and opposed religions. Cornelius

Van Til, who had left the Princeton Seminary faculty with Machen in 1929, taught Schaeffer apologetics, how to defend the Christian faith. Van Til's method was to presume the Christian system of thought (in its Old Princeton form developed by the Hodges and Warfield) and then to show the inadequacy of his opponent's presuppositions.

Schaeffer developed his distinctive form of presentation in conversation with people. He would ask foundational questions about life and reality. Then he would challenge his listeners' presumably relativistic presuppositions and offer biblical absolutes which answered all questions about the nature of the universe, the meaning of life, and its cultural manifestations in philosophy, theology, art, music, and history. Schaeffer's conversations and lectures developed into a trilogy of books which formed the hub from which his other works extended: *God Who Is There, Escape from Reason,* and, *He Is There and He Is Not Silent.* For many evangelicals Schaeffer's books provided their first encouragement to wrestle with philosophical questions and modern culture.

Schaeffer practiced a pre-evangelism he called "taking the roof off." The apologist's job was to expose the tension between a person's non-Christian assumptions and the real external world. He did this, not by careful study of nature or culture, but by citing the Bible, which gave inerrant propositional truth about everything it touched including the cosmos and human history. One of Schaeffer's chief philosophical enemies was G. W. F. Hegel, who asserted that truth came in synthesis, rather than in the antithesis of absolutes versus relativism. The other was Søren Kierkegaard, whom Schaeffer accused of advocating an irrational leap of faith which led to despair. Schaeffer's rationalism made him dismissive of neoorthodoxy, which he charged with "mental gymnastics" and "black magic in logic." When Karl Barth once replied to a paper Schaeffer sent him, Schaeffer referred to Barth's theology as "insanity." Although Schaeffer wrote eloquently of the need for Christians to exhibit love for one another and their neighbors, he was from the beginning to the end of his career a separatist who refused to cooperate with anyone who did not hold his views.

In the early 1980s Schaeffer became a "guru" of the New Religious-Political Right. His *Christian Manifesto* was much praised during the Reagan administration. He became a guest at dinner parties of Republican members of Congress, and his books were discussed by Senate wives in their weekly Bible study. At Schaeffer's death in 1984, President Reagan proclaimed him "one of the greatest Christian thinkers of our century." Schaeffer's twenty-two books have sold more than three million copies. His five-volume complete works, subtitled *A Christian Worldview,* have gone through multiple printings.

His influence continues through movements he encouraged. *Christianity Today*, as recently as 1995, identified Schaeffer as the chief architect of both the Pro-Life Movement and the New Religious-Political Right. His views were promoted through expensive coffee-table books, professionally produced film series, and national lecture tours in the 1970s. Schaeffer popularized the views of Reconstructionism. This movement asserts that the Old Testament law should be applied in minute detail as working social policy in the United States. Schaeffer and Reconstructionism have been foundational to the thinking of New Right figures such as Jerry Falwell and Pat Robertson.

How do we account for Schaeffer's influence? People who feel that the world is awash in a sea of relativism want simple, absolute answers. Schaeffer gave those answers in the guise of European scholarship.

Schaeffer was not a scholar. His self-designation was that of an evangelist. He presented the simple gospel of Jesus Christ, in his L'Abri days, in patient, empathetic conversation. As he became a media figure, he fell prey to the pretensions of his publicists who proclaimed him a "theologian and philosopher," the "foremost evangelical thinker of our day." Positively, Schaeffer invited evangelicals, raised in an anti-intellectual atmosphere, to think. For many, he was the starting point for an intellectual pilgrimage which took them far beyond him. Negatively, those who became encapsulated in his system took on another form of anti-intellectualism. Those who have politicized his absolutes now present oversimplified solutions to the complex problems of American life.

Suggested Readings

Writings of Francis Schaeffer: *How Should We Then Live? The Rise and Decline of Western Thought and Culture* (Old Tappan, N.J.: Fleming H. Revell, 1976); *Whatever Happened to the Human Race?* (Old Tappan, N.J.: Fleming H. Revell, 1979).

Thomas V. Morris, *Francis Schaeffer's Apologetics* (Chicago: Moody Press, 1976).

Ronald W. Ruegsegger, ed., *Reflections on Francis Schaeffer* (Grand Rapids: Zondervan, 1986).

H. Richard Niebuhr

(1894–1962)

C. David Grant

Helmut Richard Niebuhr was a very influential mid-twentieth-century Christian ethicist and theologian. Brother to Reinhold, another very important ethicist and theologian, H. Richard taught at Yale Divinity School from 1931 to his death in 1962. He published six influential books during his lifetime: *The Social Sources of Denominationalism* (1929), *The Kingdom of God in America* (1937), *The Meaning of Revelation* (1941), *Christ and Culture* (1951), *The Purpose of the Church and Its Ministry* (1956), and *Radical Monotheism and Western Culture* (1960). Evidence of his continuing influence in theology can be seen in the posthumous publication of several important essays as well as three books— *The Responsible Self* (1963), *Faith on Earth* (1989), and *Theology, History, and Culture* (1996). His influence on theology remains great, due to his many students who have become leading theologians and ethicists today.

Helmut, the name he used until the 1920s, was the youngest son of Gustav and Lydia Niebuhr. His father, a German immigrant, was a minister in the German Evangelical Synod of North America and served pastorates in Missouri and Illinois during Helmut's childhood. Like his older brother Reinhold, Helmut went off to Elmhurst College and then Eden Seminary to prepare for ministry in the German Evangelical Synod of North America. (After World War I the denomination dropped the word *German,* becoming simply the Evangelical Synod of North America.) After serving as a pastor for two years, he was called to the faculty of Eden Seminary, where he taught from 1919–22. He entered Yale Divinity School in 1922 and completed both a B.D. and a Ph.D. by 1924. He then returned to Illinois to serve as President of Elmhurst College, but resigned three years later to return to the faculty of Eden Seminary. The reputation he earned because of *The Social Sources of Denominationalism* resulted in his appointment in 1931 to the faculty of Yale Divinity School, where he remained until his death.

Three key themes are focal points in Niebuhr's thought: the relativity of human life and thought, the absoluteness of God, and the structure of human faith. His work defines and sorts out the various relations and tensions among these key themes.

The Relativity of Human Life and Thought. In the Preface to *The Meaning of Revelation,* Niebuhr described his approach to theology as an attempt to combine the interests of Ernst Troeltsch (1865–1923) and Karl Barth (1886–1968). Troeltsch was a German theologian and historian who wrote extensively about the problem of historicism. Troeltsch's own study of the stream of Christian history led him to conclude that our knowledge of values and religious realities is not absolute but develops within human history. As such, even the most deeply held religious beliefs are subject to the changing sociological conditions and cultural ways of thinking prevalent in any given historical community.

Niebuhr's 1924 doctoral thesis at Yale had been about Troeltsch, and historicism was clearly on his mind as he prepared his first book for publication. *The Social Sources of Denominationalism* appeared in 1929. In it he argued that denominational differences among Christian churches in the United States were due more to economic, cultural, and ethnic differences than to differences in theology and doctrine. He went so far as to call denominationalism the "unacknowledged hypocrisy" of the church. He would later modify this negative attitude toward denominationalism, but his own activity in the Evangelical church during the late 1920s mirrored his theoretical view: he became chair of his denomination's Committee on Relations with Other Churches and advocated union with two other prominent German immigrant denominations, the Reformed Church and the United Brethren. But the 1929 Plan of Union was rejected and Niebuhr withdrew from involvement in his denomination's merger attempts after 1930 (Diefenthaler, 17-18).

Niebuhr's mature reflections on the nature of historicism and human relativity can be found in *The Meaning of Revelation* (1941). He argued that human life is fundamentally historical, and hence all of our knowing, feeling, and acting takes place in particular historical situations. As such, we cannot transcend our historical and social location: We are in history, he says, "as the fish is in water" (48). What we see is always seen from our point of view, and there is no transcendent point of view available to humans. All human endeavors are historically relative and it is idolatrous for us to think otherwise. Niebuhr was careful, however, not to draw a skeptical conclusion from his relativism. If our knowledge is always limited and partial, then one might conclude that we cannot know the universal. But Niebuhr refused to go down this path. Instead, he argued that our historically relative knowledge is knowledge of the universal from our own point of view. To understand God, the Christian community must understand God from its point of view, and he undertook to analyze the "patterns of interpretation" that emerge from within the point of view of Christian faith in God.

As a corollary to this historical relativism, Niebuhr adopted a confessional method in theology. The theologian confesses his or her standpoint, then explicates what the world and God look like from that point of view. Such a method is "objectively relativistic" since it proceeds "with confidence in the independent reality of what is seen, though recognizing that its assertions about that reality are meaningful only to those who look upon it from the same standpoint" (*Meaning of Revelation,* 22).

The Absoluteness of God. If the thought of Troeltsch was the root of Niebuhr's reflections on human relativity, then certainly the thought of Barth played a role in shaping the second principal theme in Niebuhr's thought, the absoluteness of God. Because of his affinity with Barth's view of God's sovereignty, Niebuhr is often classified with his brother Reinhold as an American neoorthodox theologian. But H. Richard's view of God's sovereignty was quite distinct from Barth's.

For Barth, God's sovereignty was primarily expressed in God's otherness. God's transcendent separation from creation provided the key to understanding God's reality. Niebuhr, however, saw God's sovereignty in God's absolute presence in creation. Everything with which we have to do as humans is of God; God is everywhere present. All that befalls us, for Niebuhr, is to be understood as being from God. Thus God's sovereignty is to be understood as that absolute reality up against which we find ourselves as finite human beings.

This is a consistent theme throughout Niebuhr's work from the 1930s until his death. In his only published dispute with Reinhold, H. Richard wrote two articles for the *Christian Century* in 1932. Japan had recently invaded China. Reinhold joined with those Christians who thought that some form of coercion against Japan should be used. H. Richard instead counseled that nothing be done, because God is sovereign and is acting in history. "This God of things as they are is inevitable and quite merciless. His mercy lies beyond, not this side of, judgment" (*Christian Century* 49 [1932]: 379). When Reinhold accused H. Richard of "identif[ying] everything that is occurring in history . . . with the counsels of God" (416), Richard replied with a clear statement of his own view: "God, I believe, is always in history; he is the structure in things" (447). God's absoluteness is thus to be seen in God's determining character as present in our experienced world, not in the otherness of a God who is fundamentally apart and separate from the world.

In the 1940s, Niebuhr continued exploring this line of thought that sees God as the reality that determines our existence. In a 1943 article in the Methodist Student Movement's magazine *Motive,* he identified God with "the nature of things," "the secret of existence by which all things come into being, are what they are, and pass away," and "the great abyss into which all things plunge and as the great source from whence they all come" ("The Nature and Existence of God: A Protestant's View," *Motive* 4 [Dec. 1943]: 45). Christians learn to call this abyss and source "God," but it is a reality everyone comes up against in life. That Niebuhr included this 1943 essay with only minor changes in *Radical Monotheism and Western Culture,* published in 1960, shows that this deterministic view of God continued to be a central focus of his theological reflections.

It is in light of the absoluteness of God and the relativity of all human thought that Niebuhr's work as a Christian ethicist can best be seen. Niebuhr's approach was not that of setting forth ethical laws or propositions to be followed and obeyed. In fact, his writings contain few instances in which he directly reflected on what Christians ought to do in particular moral situations. What he did do was set out the context for individual Christians to make their own decisions. That context is the sovereignty of God seen as the determining character of all reality. Niebuhr's most famous and memorable ethical principle was his admonition, "God is acting in all actions upon you. So respond to all actions upon you as to respond to his action" (*The Responsible Self,* 126). The Christian is to see all that befalls her as being the result of God's action. The task she then has is to make a "fitting" response to God's action. But what is fitting in one situation may well not be fitting in another. Discerning the fitting response is the task of the responder to God's action. Thus he calls his ethical theory "responsibility ethics."

The Structure of Human Faith. The absoluteness of God and the relativity of humanity: How do these two seemingly incompatible foci come together? Niebuhr's understanding of faith provides the connective tissue. Niebuhr explicated his understanding of faith in two works, *Radical Monotheism and Western Culture* (1960) and *Faith on Earth* (posthumously, 1989). The latter work was actually the foundation on which the argument in *Radical Monotheism* was based. *Faith on Earth* presented Niebuhr's view of faith as an essential characteristic of human life. All human relations are built on the personal attitude of faith: We trust our companions and are loyal to them. These relations of trust and loyalty for Niebuhr are value relations. Trust is the response we make to our sense that we are valued by the companion; loyalty is the response we make to the companion's value. All knowing, believing, and acting involve these two dimensions.

But faith entails more than the two dimensions of trust and loyalty. When I trust in and am loyal to a companion, a third reality is involved in that faith relation. When, for instance, I have faith in my companion in the university and she in me, there is a third reality to which her and my trust and loyalty implicitly refer, the pursuit of truth. Or when two soldiers must keep faith with each other on the front line of battle, trusting in each other and being loyal to each other, there is a third reality to which their faith refers: the faith in the patrol of which they are a part. But then their faith in the patrol involves a faith in the larger grouping of the troop or company of which that patrol is a part, and so on. Finally they reach the reality of the nation that sent them into battle, or the cause of freedom for which they fight. Thus, human faith between companions always for Niebuhr pointed to a third reality beyond the companions in relation. The basic structure of faith is therefore always triadic.

Faith becomes religious when one cannot appeal to a higher valued reality beyond the third component of the triads of faith. In the foregoing example, if the soldiers finally ended the nested triads by appealing to the nation as the final value behind which they could not go, then the nation would become their center of value. For Niebuhr, *God* is another name for *center of value*.

In *Radical Monotheism and Western Culture* Niebuhr suggested that our religious faiths are basically of three types. Polytheism is the situation when we have multiple centers of value, each independent of the others. We live in some situations with our nation as our center of value; in another situation money becomes our center; in yet another situation we seek pleasure as our center. Without anything to tie these together we live fragmented lives, chasing after one god, then another. Often this fragmentation leads us to place one of these centers of value as primary over all others. Doing so, we become henotheists. We have a single center of value, a single god, but we choose a finite reality. Nationalism, naturalism, and humanism are examples of such henotheistic faiths.

Henotheism and polytheism, for Niebuhr, ultimately fail as adequate forms of religious faith. Polytheism leaves us torn between competing centers of value, and henotheism, because its god is a finite reality, cannot guarantee for us any meaning beyond its particular limited center. We are thus driven beyond all the relative centers to a faith that finally takes as its companion the entire universe of being and sees its center of value as being precisely in the transcendent Absolute that is the source and ground of all being. Such a faith Niebuhr called radical monotheism. For radically monotheistic faith, the ultimate center of value is God, who values all of being as good. To trust and be loyal to the God of radical monotheism is to place oneself in companionship to universal being and to see oneself in relation to all that is, inclusive even of what from other centers of value might be judged to be bad.

To see God as "the Circumambient Being" for whom whatever is, is good, is to trust in and be loyal to being itself. But this is not our natural attitude to the universe. Universal faith first manifests itself, according to Niebuhr, as broken faith: We meet reality as that which tries to thwart our efforts, as that which destroys our values, as that which brings us all to naught. God as Universal Being first meets us as our enemy. We come to distrust reality; we are prone to be disloyal to it; we flee to the small gods, to the security of our henotheistic faiths. But in Christian faith, broken faith is restored to wholeness. Christians come to see the all-determining reality that they face, no longer as enemy but as friend. They learn to call that reality "Father." Christians remain relative and limited, but through radically monotheistic faith they come to see all of their limited and relative actions in light of their faith in the Absolute that stands behind every finite, relative being.

For Niebuhr, it is Jesus Christ who makes possible this transition from distrust of being to trust of being. How this happens, Niebuhr said, cannot be fully explained. Christians can only confess that it has happened for them through Jesus Christ, who meets them in Christian communities. But Niebuhr's radically monotheistic Christian faith prevented him from centering God's reality in Jesus. He was critical of Karl Barth's theology for this reason. As we have seen, Niebuhr found Barth's emphasis on the sovereignty of God very appealing as he struggled to emphasize God's absoluteness. But he parted company with Barth's extreme Christocentrism: Niebuhr thought that Christians must employ other symbols and metaphors to understand their faith in God and God's relation to them. But what every Christian finally must confess in his or her personal faith is that "the movement beyond resignation to reconciliation is the movement inaugurated and maintained in Christians by Jesus Christ" (*Responsible Self,* 177). Whether there are other ways that humans come to trust in and be loyal to being, is not a question that Niebuhr explored. He was willing to stop with his confessional method, saying, This is how

I see things from my point of view, though surely others have other points of view. But all our points of view are greatly relativized in the face of the absolute. No better summary of Niebuhr's overall theological approach can be found than this: "None is absolute save God and . . . the absolutizing of anything finite is ruinous to the finite itself" (*Radical Monotheism,* 113).

Suggested Readings

Writings of H. Richard Niebuhr: *The Meaning of Revelation* (New York: Macmillan, 1941); *Radical Monotheism and Western Culture* (New York: Harper, 1960); *Faith on Earth: An Inquiry into the Structure of Human Faith* (New Haven: Yale University Press, 1989); *The Responsible Self: An Essay in Christian Moral Philosophy* (New York: Harper & Row, 1963).

Jon Diefenthaler, *H. Richard Niebuhr: A Lifetime of Reflections on the Church and the World* (Macon, Ga.: Mercer University Press, 1986).

Reinhold Niebuhr

(1892–1971)

Robin W. Lovin

Reinhold Niebuhr was an important figure in Protestant social ethics during the middle decades of the twentieth century. The son of a German American pastor, Niebuhr was born near Saint Louis in 1892 and grew to maturity in Lincoln, Illinois. Following theological study at Yale, he became a pastor in Detroit, where he learned firsthand the problems of labor unrest and race relations that strained growing cities in the years after World War I. By the late 1920s, he had achieved a national reputation as a preacher, writer, and political activist, and in 1928, he joined the faculty of Union Theological Seminary in New York.

Niebuhr's first influential work was *Moral Man and Immoral Society,* published in 1932. Niebuhr insisted that power and self-interest are part of every human activity, including the pursuit of justice. His reservations about religious idealism drew sharp criticism from theologians who were accustomed to preaching the transforming power of love as a solution to the problems of industrial society. For those who were sobered by the experiences of World War I and the global economic crisis which followed, Niebuhr's analysis suggested more effective ways to deal with political and social problems, and he quickly became the chief spokesperson for a way of thinking that called itself "Christian Realism."

The Christian Realist, Niebuhr explained, does not deny the claims of love and justice, but recognizes that self-interest will keep people from acting to change their society unless they are also constrained by power. The constraint need not be violent, but even nonviolent resistance is an exercise of power. The nonviolent resister rejects violence, but cannot reject power. Toward the end of *Moral Man and Immoral Society,* Niebuhr set out the implications of this view for those who hoped for changes in race prejudice and discrimination: justice would come only when the demand for justice was joined with an effective use of power. Decades later, Niebuhr's assess-

413

ment would prove an important starting point for Martin Luther King, Jr., and his nonviolent civil rights movement.

Despite Niebuhr's criticism of the sentimentality and utopianism of earlier Christian thought, his convictions at the time he wrote *Moral Man and Immoral Society* were socialist and pacifist. Many of his critics then and later argued that he had abandoned the traditional sources of Christian ethics for radical social views grounded in social theory, not theology. His warnings in *Moral Man and Immoral Society* that we must view the moral claims of the powerful with skepticism and beware of religious fanaticism among the powerless seemed to some to confirm the suspicion that he found nothing of moral or social relevance in the content of Christian belief.

Niebuhr was certainly concerned with the relationships between economic activity, social position, and religious belief. Like his brother, H. Richard Niebuhr, who was by this time teaching theology at Yale, Reinhold Niebuhr understood that what a denomination or religious group believes to be true is the result of a complex interaction between doctrinal traditions and social experience. H. Richard Niebuhr was controversial in his own way for a book he published in 1929 titled *The Social Sources of Denominationalism*. From our perspective, some decades later, *The Social Sources* and *Moral Man and Immoral Society* appear as groundbreaking efforts to arrive at a realistic understanding of how people live out their religious beliefs, contrasted with a more traditional, systematic exposition of what those beliefs are. Neither brother, however, regarded the content of religious beliefs as irrelevant.

In *An Interpretation of Christian Ethics* (1935), Reinhold Niebuhr gave a more balanced view of the relationship between theology and social theory. Christian faith, with its acceptance of sin and tragedy, provides an important alternative to the optimistic, results-oriented values of modern culture, which expects endless, steady progress. The problem is not with Christian beliefs, Niebuhr argued, but with the Christian churches, which have lost their distinctive understanding of human limitations and possibilities just at the point where the culture most needs it.

Christianity offers a distinctive view of the human condition, which is also the best guide for human conduct. This conviction provides the structure for Niebuhr's greatest work, *The Nature and Destiny of Man*. First published in 1941, the book began a few years earlier as the Gifford Lectures, delivered in two series in 1939 at the University of Edinburgh. In the anxious months prior to World War II, Niebuhr's affirmation of the Christian conception of human nature seemed to provide a reason for the risks and sacrifices that lay ahead. By the time he began the second series, on human destiny, the European war had already begun.

The Nature and Destiny of Man weighed the Christian understanding of human experience against the leading Western alternatives, both classical and modern. "Man has always been his own most vexing problem," Niebuhr began. We are aware of our capacity for greatness and self-sacrifice for a higher cause, and we also know the brutality and selfishness with which we pursue even our trivial interests. We do not know what to make of ourselves, what to expect of our neighbors, or how to guide our own choices in the light of these ambiguous possibilities. The biblical view of human nature does not dissolve these ambiguities, but it enables us to make sense of them, and to establish realistic expectations of ourselves and others.

Niebuhr attempted to show that the Bible is the best practical guide to human expectations of politics and social life. That is not quite the same thing as attempting to prove what the Bible says is true. The biblical view makes claims about human destiny that will only be fulfilled beyond history. As long as we remain in history, we cannot prove these claims are true, and our acceptance of what the Bible says about human destiny will require a measure of faith. But we can undertake a limited, practical validation of the biblical claims by showing that when we use the biblical understanding of our humanity as a guide to life, we will live better than we could by reliance on the classical view, or on the many versions of the modern alternative.

Classical Western thought, beginning with the Greeks, understood human beings primarily as intellect or reason, capable of grasping universal truths, but also tragically subjected to the limitations of the senses and the fragility of the body. Modern theories, from Renaissance humanism through the Enlightenment and Marxism, emphasize human freedom and power over nature, remaking reality according to our own needs and goals. The biblical view differs from both of these. Our capacity for the universal, according to the biblical view, lies less in our reason than in our imaginative grasp of God's presence in the world of God's creation. Our embodiment, therefore, is not a tragic source of limitation, but the starting point for true freedom. We are never simply trapped within our natural starting point as the Greek philosophers feared, but neither can we free ourselves from it as completely as the various forms of modern thought have hoped. Despite the powers of science and technology, our mortality and fragility persist, as inescapable as the ancients believed they were. Despite our ability to imagine universal peace and harmony, self-interest

415

leads us to reject the greater good in favor of short-term personal satisfactions.

Neither Marxist nor market utopias have been able to eliminate the pursuit of individual gain at the expense of the common good. The biblical understanding of human nature raises no such false hopes. By rejecting the more flattering accounts of our possibilities, it opens our eyes to the modest, but real prospects for improvement actually there. Yet the biblical view also warns us that even these limited achievements are fragile and temporary. The sources of self-interest do not lie in the external forms of society, which might be changed by more effective politics or more efficient technology. They lie deep within ourselves, and though we can keep them in check, we cannot eliminate these sources of self-interest without destroying our own humanity.

The Bible, of course, does not consist chiefly of discourses on human nature such as we might find in the writings of a modern philosopher. The Bible presents narratives of human origins and human history that say we are both created in God's image and creatures with limits like the rest of God's creation. In these biblical myths, we find the true measure of our humanity. By calling these accounts "myths," Niebuhr did not, of course, mean that the Bible consists of stories that are not literally true. His point was rather that the difficult, complex, and ambiguous truths about our lives can be better expressed in these narrative forms than in the rigid either-or of a reasoned treatise on human nature. Scripture gives us an imaginative grasp of a truth that eludes reason. That, Niebuhr believed, is why the Christian tradition has always stressed memory and imagination alongside the Greek view of reason as the defining feature of human nature.

Those who share the biblical understanding will know, even if they cannot fully articulate it, that human beings are created for freedom, in the image of God. Human beings are also capable of aggressive self-assertion or passive submission to others, actions which deny God's image in others and in themselves. Christian Realists, therefore, maintain carefully balanced expectations, both in their personal lives and in politics, because they understand that the freedom that is part of God's image can easily become an instrument of domination. We are apt to use our dreams as a means of subordinating other people to our will. We are apt to allow the dreams of others to become our idols, sacrificing our freedom to their purposes and subjecting ourselves to their judgments. Niebuhr wrote frequently about how these things happen in politics, and in the 1940s he saw both Hitler's National Socialism and Stalin's Soviet Communism as political evils that grew from mistaken estimates of human powers and limitations. Part of the enduring value of *The Nature and Destiny of Man,* however, is that Niebuhr understood that these dynamics are pervasive in human life. Marriage and family relationships, relationships in the workplace, and loyalties in domestic politics can be understood in these terms, no less than the international politics of imperialism and revolution that dominated the news as Niebuhr prepared his Gifford Lectures.

Niebuhr suggested that these pervasive attempts either to deny the limits of our creaturely finitude or to evade the possibilities of creation in God's image are what the biblical view means by sin. The concept of sin, so foreign to the modern, optimistic assessments of human nature, led to frequent misunderstandings of Niebuhr's work by critics who assumed that his purpose, like some latter-day revivalist, was to castigate a whole variety of political and social purposes as sinful and to leave his readers with an impression of human nature as irremediably evil.

The point in *The Nature and Destiny of Man,* however, is quite different. "Sin" referred not primarily to the array of individual choices and behaviors that Niebuhr denounced, but to the denial of our finitude and our possibilities that all of those individual sins have as a common characteristic. Neither is our human nature, both as image of God and as creature, evil in itself. In contrast to the classical view, and to some ways of reading the biblical tradition, we are not evil because we are confined to a limited and perishable body, nor because our knowledge and power are less than God's. Sin originates in the anxiety our finitude provokes. It is because we fear that vulnerability that we set ourselves up to dominate others, or devote ourselves to the idols that others set up for us. All such denials are ultimately futile, of course. We remain as finite and vulnerable as ever, though we can diminish our own lives and wreak great destruction upon others before the illusion plays itself out.

The solution to this human problem is not a more effective measure of protection against our finitude. Thinking in those terms merely leads to more inventive forms of sin. The solution is to accept the vulnerability and ambiguity that goes with being created in God's image and being God's creature. The solution lies in perfect trust in God, who sets the terms of our life, rather than in a mistrustful effort to hold the course of our life entirely within our own power. For Niebuhr, the significance of Jesus in the biblical understanding of human nature is that Jesus perfectly exemplifies this trust in God that displaces our sinful denials of our human condition. The basic goodness of this combination of freedom and finitude which is human being is revealed in Jesus, and the source of evil in our human denials of it becomes apparent, too. Much of the second half of *The Nature and Destiny of Man* is devoted to understanding the meaning within human history of this revelation that the anxieties of human finitude are ultimately overcome. Niebuhr explored this theme not only within the narratives of Jesus' life and teaching, but also within the prophetic and messianic expectations of the Hebrew Scriptures. The theology of *The Nature and Destiny of Man* continued to provide a framework for Niebuhr's interpretation of events through the rest of his career. Explicitly theological themes, however, have less prominence in his later works, as he devoted more time to the exploration of the traditions of Western politics and ethics and the interpretation of current events.

The developments in Niebuhr's own thought and the momentous changes in the world required a new statement of political principles. By the time the United States entered World War II, Niebuhr was clearly no longer a pacifist, and he had reluctantly broken with the Socialists to support Roosevelt's New Deal in 1936. In 1944, he published *The Children of Light and the Children of Darkness,* for which he provided the subtitle, "A Vindication of Democracy and a Critique of Its Traditional Defense." His case for democratic government and its values did not rely on optimistic estimates of human capacity for self-government, but on a realistic assessment that those who are given great power over human affairs need to be checked by a countervailing power that is widely dispersed among the people. Niebuhr summarized the book's argument in one of his most famous aphorisms: "Man's capacity for justice makes democracy possible; but man's inclination to injustice makes democracy necessary" (*The Children of Light and the Children of Darkness*, xiii).

As United States foreign policy settled into wary internationalism and vigilant anti-Communism after World War II, Niebuhr's unsentimental view of the realities of international politics became a powerful influence on policymakers and diplomats. During these years the preacher and professor at Union Theological Seminary became one of America's leading public figures, sought after for speeches and interviews, and featured on the cover of *Time* magazine.

Early in 1952, Niebuhr, then just short of sixty years old, suffered a stroke which left him partly incapacitated and greatly reduced the travel, speaking, and political activism that had accompanied his heavy load of teaching and writing. Nevertheless, even this reduced output was quite large compared with that of his colleagues in the church and the academy, and he remained a leading figure in American intellectual and religious life, insisting on both the possibilities and the limits of human creativity and commenting incisively on the events of the day. After his illness and before his official retirement in 1960, another whole generation of students at Union Theological Seminary had the benefit of his lectures on Christian ethics.

Reinhold Niebuhr died in 1971. Criticism of his work during the last years of his life and shortly after his death suggested that he might be seen chiefly as a man of his own time, with little influence in the quite different political and religious world that followed. His global vision was shaped by the cold war, a conflict that was changing even during the last years of his life, and that ended decisively two decades later. On the American scene, Niebuhr had been overtaken by the momentum of the civil rights movement after 1954, and some African American critics took note of his political caution, rather than his underlying commitment to racial justice. Women found his work too centered on the masculine world of power politics, alert to forms of sin that result from aggressive self-interest, and strangely silent on those that result from passivity and weakness.

All of these limitations are present in Niebuhr's work, but as it becomes possible to view his writings from a more objective distance and to focus on the underlying convictions of Christian Realism, rather than on his occasional judgments about specific events, his importance for the future of Christian theology becomes apparent. His emphasis on the realities of power served at the beginning of his career to correct the optimistic assumptions of American culture at the beginning of the twentieth century. The realistic assessment that weighs both human possibility and human sin may serve the future as an example of nuanced and balanced application of theological tradition to the understanding of contemporary society. In a time that seems dominated by a sense of failure and a fear of human limits, authentic Christian Realism may require more appreciation of real human possibilities that Niebuhr's own writings usually revealed. His insistence that we deal with ourselves both as God's creatures and as created in God's image will, however, continue to provide a standard for Christian social ethics.

Suggested Readings

Writings of Reinhold Niebuhr: *Moral Man and Immoral Society* (New York: Charles Scribner's Sons, 1960); *The Nature and Destiny of Man,* 2 vols. (New York: Charles Scribner's Sons, 1964); *The Children of Light and the Children of Darkness* (New York: Charles Scribner's Sons, 1972).

Robin W. Lovin, *Reinhold Niebuhr and Christian Realism* (Cambridge: Cambridge University Press, 1995).

Paul Tillich

(1886–1965)

John Dillenberger

Born in 1886, Paul Tillich was the son of a Lutheran pastor in the Starzeddel, a village then part of Germany and now of Poland. He received a Doctor of Philosophy degree from the University of Breslau (1910) and a Licentiate in Theology from the University of Halle (1911). In 1912 he was ordained in the Evangelical Church of the Prussian Union, Berlin. From 1914 to 1918, he was a chaplain in the German army, mainly in the midst of the intense battles on the western front. Afterward he served as a lecturer at the University of Berlin (1919–24), as a member of the theological faculty of the University of Marburg (1924–25), and as a professor of philosophy at the Dresden Institute of Technology (1925–29) together with an adjunct appointment in theology at the University of Leipzig. He was dismissed from his post as professor of philosophy at the University of Frankfurt by the Nazis in 1933, and in that year he emigrated to the United States. Throughout this period, he had been active in the religious socialist movements in Germany and was a pioneering figure in the development of a theology of culture. His first public lecture (1919) was "The Idea of a Theology of Culture."

Upon his arrival in New York City under the auspices of faculty members at Columbia University and Union Theological Seminary, Tillich started a new career. For the next twenty-two years he taught at Union, where he became Professor of Philosophical Theology. In his early days in New York, he helped organize and lead a self-help group for refugees, and joined the Theological Discussion Group that usually met in Washington, D.C., and the Philosophy Club at Columbia University. Retiring from Union in 1955, he went first to Harvard Divinity School as University Professor and thereafter, from 1962 to his death in 1965, to the Divinity School of the University of Chicago as the Nuveen Professor of Theology.

When Tillich came to the United States, his thought was known only by those who read German theology and philosophy. The first translation of one of his German works had appeared as *The Religious Situation* only the year before. Although Tillich had read English texts in Germany, now at the age of forty-seven, he had to learn to speak and think in English. His article, "The Two Types of the Philosophy of Religion" (1946) was the first he wrote in English which was then translated into German. This transition with respect to language, masked by the Germanisms in his speech, meant that German no longer provided the single or even the predominant structure for his thinking and writing. Bilingual to the end, his work in the United States soon took on the coloration of that English-speaking country.

Nevertheless, the theological, political, and cultural patterns of the German situation, intertwined as they were, shaped his work in the United States. Like Karl Barth, Tillich believed that the gospel had been buried in the dominant, culturally conditioned, liberal Christianity of the time. But the two responded to this challenge in diametrically opposed ways. Barth entered into what he called the strange new world of the Bible, one in which the revelatory dynamics of faith made present in Jesus Christ a God whose "wholly other" character shattered every apparent affinity between the human and the divine. To Barth, the biblical God brought judgment and promise to the world, and obedience to this God meant opposing those who identified any historical development—whether benign or evil like the Nazi movement—with the kingdom of God. Theology must take its cue strictly from scripture. Questions of philosophy, culture, and the political order belonged to the human but not the theological domain.

For Tillich, however, the language of the human domain embraces the language of both faith and culture. The problem facing theology is solved not by retreating into scripture but by recovering the depth dimensions of human life for the sake of theology itself. This recovery requires the study of culture generally and the entire history of philosophy in particular. Of Tillich's wide-ranging philosophical study, two things must be said. First, he did not identify himself with any particular philosopher or philosophical tradition. Second, the insights he drew from philosophers were those they suggested to him, and these did not necessarily correspond to what the philosopher directly said or intended. Tillich entered into the historical and contemporary conversation in order to give an account of the range of perceptions that compose the human drama. Only such a fully orbed humanity, with its grandeur and estrangement, is the soil in which the riches of God's relation to creation and the human condition can be perceived and articulated.

That is the setting in which Tillich lectured in systematics at Union and began writing the systematic theology which he early on resolved to write. Volume I, "Reason and Revelation" and "Being and God," appeared in 1951, toward the end of his time at Union; volume II, on "Existence and the Christ," in 1957, while he was at Harvard; and volume III, "Life and the Spirit and History and the Kingdom of God," in 1963, when he was at Chicago's Divinity School.

The five main divisions of his system disclose a method of correlation, in which a polar concept, such as reason, is neither opposed to nor subsumed under revelation. The relation, however, assumes the givenness of reason and revelation as entities in their own right. Philosophy is the domain of human thought and imagination. Reason, a broad cultural, philosophical concept, is a main avenue for understanding being, existence, and life, which, taken together, pose the basic question or questions of humanity to which God, Christ, and Spirit are the answer. At its core, theology has to do with the delineation of having been grasped by the reality of Jesus as the Christ, the manifestation of the New Being. For Tillich, this reality could not be expressed by retreating to biblical language but only by explicating the interrelation of the biblical message (as distinct from biblical words) with manifestations of culture and imagination. Hence, for Tillich there is never an either-or or a both-and, but always a dialectical, sometimes para-doxical relation in which questions require new answers, and in which answers are themselves affected by the questions.

The body of the system is Being and God, Existence and the Christ, and Life and the Spirit—a kind of trinitarian core. Reason and Revelation is a methodological foreword. Its contents could be incorporated into the three middle sections but are separated as a kind of introduction in a time when readers want to have methodological questions first, even though method is subservient to or the product of affirmation. History and the kingdom of God deals with how the gospel in relation to culture is both set out for us to see and to live in. These materials too could therefore have been set with-in the three center sections.

In Tillich's view, this approach has two merits. First, it makes clear that theology is not an enterprise in which one must move from certain prem-ises to conclusions. One can enter the enterprise at any point and then move in the circle which is theology. System is the fullness that results from reflecting out from the point of entry. It differs, then, from a *Summa*, designed to cover everything, and from monographs on particular subjects, either as a chosen limit or as a substitute for the whole.

Second, a system (as Tillich conceived it) builds into itself a reminder that no theology is final. Theology is open to continual modification in response to new perceptions arising out of cultural manifestations and new light from the gospel itself—both, of course, in an indeterminate but dialectical relation with each other. Situations in which faith is unacceptable to culture or a culture is unacceptable to faith require new departures which avoid a doctrinaire culture or an orthodox theology. In short, over against Barth, Tillich believed that an authentic theology required a dialectical engagement with culture, for "religion is the substance of culture, culture is the form of religion."

A systematic approach was one of the dominant forms of theology from the 1940s into the 1960s. The works of Tillich—indeed theologies generally—were read in universities and theological schools, and at the height of his prominence, his sermonic writings touched a wide range of public figures and intellectuals. Even then, however, no theologies were cast exactly in the Tillichian mold, although the number of those influenced by Tillich's thought in various ways was legion. Since the 1960s, interest in systematic theologies has declined, and the goal of theological system-building itself has largely given way to other approaches, typically less expansive and more particularized. The result is that Tillich's theology, like that of most of his contemporaries, has moved from center stage to become the backdrop of current discussion. Yet a number of motifs in his thought continue to receive attention. Of these, several should be noted.

The concept of *kairos*—a moment in which the eternal breaks into history giving rise to new creations—first became important to Tillich at the end of World War I. He believed that with Germany's defeat, new opportunities were ahead and the time was ripe for new creations to emerge. This did not happen, the kairos concept was sometimes used by his opponents, and although initially optimistic after World War I, Tillich became pessimistic about the future in the immediate aftermath of World War II. Yet the concept remained a part of his thinking. As a frame in which to see past historical events, kairos was a fruitful concept, but there were no criteria for predicting or anticipating moments of kairos in the future.

The terms "autonomy," "heteronomy," and "theonomy" can be seen in a similar frame of reference. They are particularly illumining in viewing past historical periods, distinguishing when a culture lives out of its given self, an imposed law of the self, or a self-transcending self. The categories are lenses of recognition, but cultures have no way to decide to move from one to the other. They happen or do not happen.

So it is with the place of symbol in society and religion. Unlike signs, symbols cannot be made but emerge within human cultures. Humans participate through symbols in realities of which they are a part, in which they are caught up, and which they cannot control. Thus the study of its symbols discloses much about a religion or a culture. Tillich also points out a negative side of symbols, which can be called the demonic—a situation in which alleged good or even downright evil becomes destructively operative beyond all decisions humans make.

In sum, these concepts—kairos; autonomy, heteronomy, theonomy; symbol; the demonic—represent angles of vision about what is deeply embedded in society, but about which humans have little control, a kind of destiny in which human decisions are so surrounded by facets of being that outcomes cannot be counted on. Inescapable realities such as these define human estrangement, theologically known as sin. For Tillich, as for Luther, there is no step from one to the other, only glimpses and intimations of grace and a faith by which one lives in hope beyond hope, in accepting that one has been accepted.

For Tillich, faith is not guaranteed by but can be said to be grounded in God as being itself. Being itself in Tillich's sense means that which gives reality and power of being to all there is, that without which being would not be. Only such a concept of God keeps God from being understood as one being among others, perhaps the greatest in a pantheon. At once the power and presence of being, God is that which is beyond universal and particularity—the ground of both yet also a reality concretely present. Only such a God is truly God, the God beyond all gods. Only such a God is the unconditioned, and as such that which can be the basis of humanity's ultimate concern. This daring concept, found already in Tillich's early writings, has been the most troubling for many readers of Tillich.

Tillich's concept of salvation as a restoration to psychic health, sometimes attended by physical health as well, has received positive attention. In Tillich's career, this topic came to its fullest development in the first two decades in America, when he entered into dialogue with psychologists such as Karen Horney and Rollo May. Indeed, Tillich's new learning in the United States came less from reading and study, as was the case in his training in Germany, than from conversations with philosophers, scientists, social scientists, and other intellectuals.

Tillich's formulation, Jesus as the Christ, reflects his conviction that historical events are too unsure to be the basis of faith. For Tillich, to be grasped by the reality of the Christ delineated in scripture is the basis of faith. Hence, even if it were discovered that a person by the name of Jesus did not exist, someone existed of whom it was believed that he was the Christ. This conviction, influenced by his teacher, Martin Kaehler, led Tillich to develop a position that is not based on historical research into the life of

Jesus. It was also his answer to the various dead ends of the quest for the historical Jesus, and would undoubtedly be his answer to current interest in "new quests." For Tillich, biblical documents provide the reality of the Christ by which we may be grasped. Only the Jesus who is the Christ is worthy of faith. Hence, both a Jesus who is not the Christ and one whose life in history is depicted as though God were stalking the earth are equally rejected. What is required is a reading of scripture in which Jesus and the tradition cannot be separated.

Already in 1937, Tillich had published an essay, "The End of the Protestant Era?" (reprinted in *The Protestant Era,* 1948). Here he distinguished between what he called "the Protestant principle" and "Catholic substance." The former involves the prophetic notion of a critical understanding of all forms of religion as finite, while the latter maintains the foundations of the church intact, particularly with respect to the sacraments. In retrospect, the distinction is no longer as pronounced as it once was. Indeed, the two were not that separate in Tillich's own life. Still, the question for Tillich was, could a Protestantism constituted on such a self-critical principle survive and was a church claiming exemption from the Protestant principle of self-criticism worthy of survival.

Toward the end of his life, Tillich became interested not only in the Protestant-Catholic issue, but in coming to terms with other religious traditions as well. Although he had always considered Christianity the religion most capable of joining together all the threads of diverse religious perception, he became so involved in understanding Buddhism that had he lived to write other works, his theology might have undergone significant changes. Hints of that future are evident in his last public lecture, "The Significance of the History of Religions for the Systematic Theologian."

Finally, the visual arts played a strong role in Tillich's life and thought. In the midst of lulls in the terrors of his life in the trenches of World War I, Tillich found solace in viewing and studying reproductions of works of art in the journals accessible to him, many works which he himself had never seen. Botticelli's *Madonna and Child with Singing Angels* was one such painting, for when he first saw it, he found himself (as he records the event) in a state approaching ecstasy. In its beauty, he saw Beauty itself and the divine source of all things manifested. The event affected his whole life. But that Renaissance painting, with its beauty combining peace and sorrow in harmony, was quite unlike the fissures and depths of expressionistic art which, for him, became the clue to all art. The visual arts, Tillich held, laid bare the form and style of a culture with immediacy.

Already in *The Religious Situation* he had indicated that there was more sacredness in a still life by Cezanne or a tree by van Gogh than in a painting of Jesus by Uhde, or for American eyes, a painting by Warner Sallman. Hence, the form and style of a period may be more religious than the subject matter of religion itself. One may argue with his judgment that Picasso's *Guernica* is the best example of a Protestant painting, that Grünewald's *Crucifixion* in the Isenheim altarpiece is the greatest German painting ever executed, or that the *Resurrection* in that altarpiece is the best of that subject, with its transformation of the finite into the infinite. But they indicate his immersion in the world of art. Tillich wrote more than thirty articles on art and architecture and, in his German period, personally knew many prominent artists and architects of his time. While in America, he had fewer contacts with artists, but spoke widely on art and religion in leading American museums. His diaries disclose that while on trips, he always found time to see works of art. His living example is mainly responsible for the number of programs in religion and the arts that have emerged in theological education.

Tillich was both a philosopher attuned to culture and a theologian. Dedicated to both, he believed one could not be one without being the other, that the two reached out to each other. Yet he also insisted on maintaining the distinction between the two, for their very interrelation depended on the difference. Questions and answers are different, but need each other.

It was precisely the breadth of his agenda for theology and life that influenced and still influences those who read him. But this breadth makes it difficult for those who have been under his tutelage to say precisely what it is that has been learned. It is not so much the content as it is the scope of the approach that makes life forever different.

Suggested Readings

Writings of Paul Tillich: *On Art and Architecture* (New York: Crossroad, 1989); *The Courage to Be* (New Haven: Yale University Press, 1952); *Systematic Theology,* 3 vols. (Chicago: University of Chicago Press, 1951–63).

Wilhelm Pauck and Marion Pauck, *Paul Tillich: His Life and Thought* (New York: Harper & Row, 1989).

Albert Cornelius Knudson

(1873–1953)

Rebekah Miles

Albert Knudson was the first theologian of Boston personalism, an idealist philosophy stressing "personality" as the key for understanding God and humanity. As professor and dean of Boston University's School of Theology, Knudson championed personalism as an alternative to the "irrationality" of fundamentalist and neoorthodox theologies and to the "superficiality" of some liberal theologies (particularly Henry Nelson Wieman's naturalism).

Many personalist assumptions were familiar from Knudson's boyhood in Methodist parsonages of Minnesota. Boston personalism, developed by Methodists, echoed the Wesleyan themes of human freedom, God's goodness, and the cooperative relationship between God and humans. Knudson's parents, both Norwegian immigrants, trained their nine children not only in Methodist doctrine but also in Methodist piety, its emphasis on holiness of life and heart.

On receiving his undergraduate degree in 1893, Knudson left Minnesota to prepare for the Methodist ministry at Boston University. There he met Borden Parker Bowne, the leading philosopher of personalism. Bowne's comprehensive philosophy transformed Knudson so dramatically that he later described the experience as almost redemptive. As a doctoral student, Knudson resolved to continue Bowne's work by devising a systematic theology of personalism.

Knudson followed the call to systematic theology by a circuitous route. In his first seven years of teaching, Knudson served on the faculty of three institutions where he taught almost everything but theology. His subjects included church history, Bible, philosophy, sociology, and economics. (He later quipped that at Baker University he held "not a chair but a whole settee.") In 1905 he was invited to Boston University to teach Old Testament, replacing a professor who had been "fired" by Methodist bishops for his critical, scientific biblical studies. (This controversy was not unusual; Bowne had been tried and acquitted for heresy the year before.) Only in 1921, when Knudson became Professor of Systematic Theology, did he turn to his vocation as theologian.

Knudson's theology is best seen in five of his dozen books. In *The Philosophy of Personalism* (1927), Knudson traced the history of personalist themes through Western philosophy and Christian theology. He argued that personalism makes sense of human experience and solves perennial philosophical problems. Knudson's systematic theology is found in *The Doctrine of God* (1930) and *The Doctrine of Redemption* (1933). In *The Principles of Christian Ethics* (1943), he devised a personalist moral theology and addressed specific issues including war, family, and economic justice. In *Basic Issues in Christian Thought* (1950), the best introduction to his theology, Knudson summarized his position, criticized other current theological options (neoorthodoxy and naturalism), and trumpeted personalism as the preferred alternative to solve both current and ancient dilemmas.

For Knudson, human experience, including reason, is an appropriate source for theology because humans reflect the Creator in whose image they are made. Human experience grounds theological, philosophical, and ethical reflection. The key element of this experience is "personality."

For idealist personalists like Knudson, his mentor Bowne, and his colleague Edgar Brightman, only personality is ultimately real. (In contrast, realist personalists like Georgia Harkness and D. C. Macintosh insisted that the natural world also has reality.) For Knudson, the objects and creatures that humans assume to be real are simply expressions of the activity of God, the divine personality. Unlike the rest of creation, humans, created in the image of God, are personal and thus real. Human personality, characterized primarily by freedom but also by self-consciousness, the power for knowledge, and the capacity for social relationships, imperfectly mirrors the personality of its Creator. The human capacity for social relationship, for example, is seen in the divine personality as it creates humans for relationship and through Christ restores them to relationship. This restoration in Christ is necessary because of human sin.

Human freedom, the central characteristic of personality and the image of God, is also the source of sin. Though God, who is wholly good, creates humans free so they can choose the good, humans misuse freedom, turning away from trust in God and their true natures. Knudson refused to make God the cause of sin or evil, insisting on the perfection and goodness of divine personality. In contrast, his colleague Brightman turned to the concept of divine finitude to explain evil in creation and human life.

Though Knudson rejected the doctrine of inherited original sin, he insisted that the misuse of freedom is a universal human problem. Though God does not cause sin, God does effect the solution in Christ. Jesus, a human who fully depended on God and interacted with the Spirit, had a unique "God-consciousness." Rejecting substitutionary or ransom theories of the atonement, Knudson insisted that Christ's life and death, especially his love, reveal God's personality and provide a model for human personality. Through the example of Christ, the human personality can come to trust in God and to use its freedom not for sin but for cooperation with God. By this divine-human interaction, humans can grow in grace, coming to love self, God, and others more fully, and thereby move toward Christian perfection, the fulfillment of human personality.

Knudson's immediate legacy was impressive. As Methodist leader elected to several General Conferences, Knudson promoted the Methodist union of 1939. As teacher he shaped generations of pastors and professors. As scholar he developed the implications of personalism for systematic theology. As dean he defined the personalist vision of the School of Theology. Knudson ensured the dominance of personalism within Boston University but not beyond it. He argued that personalism solved ancient problems in philosophy and theology; few theologians of the last decades have agreed. Perhaps the most enduring legacy of the personalists is not the comprehensive philosophy they developed but the social change they inspired through later personalists like civil rights leader Martin Luther King, Jr.

Suggested Readings

Writings of Albert Knudson: *Basic Issues in Christian Thought* (Nashville/New York: Abingdon-Cokesbury Press, 1950); *The Doctrine of God* (Nashville: Cokesbury Press, 1930); *The Doctrine of Redemption* (Nashville: Cokesbury Press, 1933); *The Philosophy of Personalism* (Boston: Boston University Press, 1927); *The Principles of Christian Ethics* (Nashville/New York: Abingdon-Cokesbury Press, 1943).

Georgia Elma Harkness

(1891–1974)

Rebekah Miles

Georgia Harkness, a self-described "chastened liberal" and "theistic realist," attempted to synthesize main streams of midcentury American theology. Her theology distinctively blended evangelical Methodist, personalist, liberal, and realist themes. Widely known as a popularizer of theology for laypeople, Harkness wrote thirty-six books and hundreds of articles on Christian theology and life. She is often remembered as a pioneer among women in theology. Christened the "famed woman theologian" by *Time* magazine, Harkness was the first woman admitted to the American Theological Society and the first to hold an important seminary position in theology.

Harkness' Methodist roots are evident in her theology. Among the fourth generation to live on her family's farm near Harkness, New York, her childhood centered on the Harkness Methodist Episcopal Church. She and her three siblings were steeped in the piety of devout parents. Harkness, like many other young Methodists, experienced evangelical conversion. (She later wrote that over several years of her childhood she was converted at the winter revivals only to backslide during the summers just in time to be converted again at the next winter revival.) Central to her later theological development were the Methodist themes of human freedom, the universality of grace, personal and social holiness, and human cooperation with divine grace. Though she questioned the Methodist doctrine of entire perfection, she continued to emphasize salvation as a process of growth toward Christian maturity.

As an undergraduate at Cornell and a graduate student in religious education at Boston University, Harkness was influenced by the Social Gospel movement. *The Church and the Immigrant* (1921), a revision of her master's thesis, reveals strong Social Gospel commitments and assumptions. The movement's emphasis on human cooperation with God to bring about more just social conditions and the partial realization of the kingdom of God was in continuity with Methodist concerns for social holiness and its insistence on divine-human cooperation. Though the mature Harkness was less certain about the direct relationship between human efforts and the coming of God's kingdom, she continued to emphasize social justice as a theologian and activist.

Harkness' inheritance from Methodism and the Social Gospel movement was given a comprehensive philosophical framework through her doctoral work in philosophy at Boston University, where she studied with leading personalists Albert Knudson and Edgar Brightman. Boston personalism insisted that "personality" was key for understanding reality. Human personality, especially its freedom and relationality, pointed to the divine personality in whose image it was created. Harkness' early work, particularly her exploration of the philosophy of religion in *Conflicts in Religious Thought* (1929), revealed a deep indebtedness to Knudson and Brightman. She rejected their idealism, however, insisting that not only personality, but also the material world was real. In spite of growing differences, Harkness' later theology maintained an enduring focus on personality.

In the late 1920s and 1930s, while teaching at Elmira College (1922–37) and Mount Holyoke (1937–39), Harkness' thought shifted. She moved away from philosophy and toward theology, drew more heavily on scripture, and emphasized human sin, redemption in Christ, personal holiness, and the mission of the church. Several forces prompted the change. The deaths of her devout parents and her growing involvement in the church recalled her to the evangelical emphases of Methodism. Harkness' participation at ecumenical conferences in Madras and Oxford renewed her concern for the universal church and its mission. The transition was also spurred by a move to theology after fifteen years teaching philosophy.

Finally, her liberal optimism, like that of many others, was tempered by economic depression, increasing political tensions in Europe, and the influence of theological realism. Her encounters with the realists increased when she was invited in 1935 to join the Fellowship of Younger Theologians whose previously all-male membership included Reinhold and H. Richard Niebuhr. Although critical of some realists for caricaturing liberalism and devaluing human experience as a source for theology, she also saw them as an important corrective to liberal excess. Calling herself a liberal evangelical and a theistic realist, Harkness developed her mature theology out of a modified personalist framework and in response to these other diverse theological movements. The *Recovery of Ideals* (1937), an exploration of the moral crisis in American life, was an early attempt at

431

such a synthesis. The majority of her works, undertaken while a professor of theology at Garrett Biblical Institute (1939–50) and the Pacific School of Religion (1950–61), furthered this synthetic theology through the examination of classical theological categories and questions. *Understanding the Christian Faith* (1947) summarized Harkness' developing theology. *Christian Ethics* (1957) carried out the implications for moral theology. *Divine Providence* (1960), representative of Harkness' mature thought, traced God's activity in creation and redemption.

For Harkness, a primary source for theology is nature, particularly human nature. Humans can see God not only in scripture but also in the orderliness of creation. The gradual progress of biological and social history evidences God's purposeful care in continuing creation. The personality of humans, created in God's image, draws them toward and gives them clues about God. Human personality, characterized by freedom, relationality, feelings of moral obligation, religious awe, and the capacity to reflect on the past and hope for the future, is the source of both human greatness and destruction.

Humans are not only free and self-conscious as personality; they are also bound to nature. Out of the crucial tension between nature and spirit, humans can imagine new possibilities and transform nature. When guided by God, the transformation may be a part of continuing creation. The tension is also the source of universal human sin. Because of freedom, humans can turn away from God and toward the self, distorting their personality and social relationships. True freedom and just social relationship are made possible only through God's redemption, which draws humans back into greater fullness of personality. Even so, human sin is never fully overcome.

God works to redeem humans through creation, Christ, and the Holy Spirit. Food, work, rest in nature, relationships with family and friends, are all creation-centered avenues of redemption. For the early Harkness, Christ redeems through his example. Through his life and death, Christ showed the self-giving love that is central to divine personality and the ideal for human life. In her later work, Harkness also insisted that in Christ God gave Godself for human salvation, mysteriously unleashing a power to overcome sin and death. Through trust in Christ, this power can deliver individuals from sin and begin the transformation of human life.

For Harkness and many other Methodists, salvation continues by the work of the Spirit in cooperation with believers, allowing them to grow in love and to form more loving societies. Throughout Harkness' career she insisted that the kingdom of God begins both in the hearts of believers and also in their cooperative work with God to improve social conditions. In her later work Harkness also emphasized the limits of human cooperation. Only God can bring the initial human steps to fruition in the Kingdom. Humans cannot know with certainty what aspects of their work are a part of God's continuing creation; nor can they ever achieve perfection. In the face of suffering, failings, and pretense, humans must simply live in love and responsibility, trusting in God's providential care and ultimate victory.

In 1974, the day after proofreading the final manuscript of *Understanding the Kingdom of God*, Harkness died unexpectedly. Her eulogizers praised Harkness as a pioneer theologian and activist. As a public theologian, she was a critic of racism, sexism, and discrimination against homosexuals, a proponent of economic justice from the depression and New Deal through the prosperity of the 1950s and 1960s, an opponent of American internment of Japanese Americans during World War II, and a pacifist, speaking out against World War II, Korea, and Vietnam. She opened doors for women in ministry and academy through her teaching and example. She was influential in the decision of the Methodist church to give full clergy rights to women. (Though she was ordained in 1938, full clergy membership was denied her as a woman.) As a writer and scholar Harkness attempted to bridge both the differences among theological positions as well as the distance between academic and lay theology. Perhaps the neglect of her theology since her death can be traced to this role as bridge. Because she wrote theology for laypeople, she was taken less seriously by academic theologians. Because she did not fit neatly into any of the camps, she did not have the full loyalty of any one group. Harkness' work, which has gained more attention recently with the centennial of her birth and the renewed interest in naturalist-realist theologies, distinctively embodies the tensions of midcentury American theology.

Suggested Readings

Writings of Georgia Harkness: *Christian Ethics* (Nashville/New York: Abingdon Press, 1957); *Conflicts in Religious Thought* (New York: Harper, 1929); *The Recovery of Ideals* (New York: Scribner, 1937); *Understanding the Christian Faith* (Nashville/New York: Abingdon-Cokesbury Press, 1947).

Keller, Rosemary Skinner, *Georgia Harkness: For Such a Time as This* (Nashville: Abingdon Press, 1992).

Dorothy M. Day

(1897–1980)

Patricia McNeal

Dorothy M. Day was a journalist, pacifist, and cofounder of the Catholic Worker movement. She was born in Brooklyn Heights, New York, 8 November 1897, the daughter of John I. Day, a sportswriter. Essentially a conservative, John Day often laced his writings about racing and racetracks with strongly moral quotations from the Bible and Shakespeare. The Days were not churchgoers but had austere Scots-Irish Presbyterian roots and Dorothy found the coldness of the family life unsatisfying.

Though not a churchgoer, Dorothy Day revealed a religious sensibility in her youth when in her writings she mentioned books or singular episodes of her early encounters with religion. Dorothy wrote of attendance at church with a neighborhood friend, of her joy when she heard her brothers singing in the choir of a small Episcopal church, of the arrival of a Christian Science practitioner who tried to help her mother become a believer to relieve her intractable headaches, and of an adolescent friend who quoted the Bible and sang beautiful hymns. Dorothy also mentioned that the writings of Augustine influenced her greatly during her adolescence.

Unable to embrace her parents, Day began to embrace the poor and the oppressed. As a young girl, she moved with her family to Chicago and began reading writers like Carl Sandburg, Jack London, and Upton Sinclair. She also began to forsake Lake Michigan and lovely unspoiled parks for the West Side with its poor immigrant families, all worse off than she, and in their own way fascinating to a growing woman of her background—she romanticized Chicago's slums and carried this vision with her to college.

Initially unaffected by World War I, she entered the University of Illinois at Urbana on a scholarship, which she supplemented by caring for children and doing housework. During her two years at college, formal academic disciplines did not capture her interest; she missed classes and disdained the customary patterns of college social mixing. She read everything by

Dostoyevsky, who impressed her profoundly, along with the works of Gorky, Prince Kropotkin, and Leo Tolstoy, and she became preoccupied with poverty, misery, and the class war, eventually joining the campus socialist club. As she put it, "I was in love with the masses."

Leaving college in 1916 because of academic dissatisfaction and financial need, Day moved with her family to New York, where her father had taken a job on the *Telegraph*. She went to work as a reporter and columnist on the socialist *Call*. Her father's disapproval led her to rent a room on Cherry Street, in the slums of the lower East Side, and never again did she live with her family.

On her own at nineteen, Day spent the next two years in the tumult of Greenwich Village life. While on the job at the *Call*, she reported on and often participated in strikes, picket lines, peace meetings, and antiwar demonstrations. She also joined the Industrial Workers of the World, because she shared its anarchistic verve and distrust of Marx. In 1917, Day left the *Call* and went to work for the Anti-Conscription League before joining the staff of the radical *Masses*. She left Greenwich Village early in 1918 to begin nurse's training at King's County Hospital in Brooklyn, after deciding that the choice was not contrary to her pacifist principles. In her autobiography, *The Long Loneliness,* Day reflected on her pacifism during World War I and cryptically wrote, "I was a pacifist in what I considered an imperialist war though not pacifist as a revolutionist."

During these years Day did have brief moments when she experienced religion. In 1917, she joined sixty other women to protest the treatment of imprisoned suffragists. Though as a radical Day never intended to vote, she and others were arrested for their demonstration of support, and when they refused bail they were sentenced to thirty days in the Occoquain Prison. While in jail, an attendant brought her a Bible, and she read it. The Psalms comforted her, yet she decided the comfort received from religion was a sign of weakness. Many mornings, after staying up all night with Village friends, she attended early morning Mass at Saint Joseph's Church on Sixth Avenue. At King's County Hospital she attended Sunday Mass regularly. Despite these religious experiences, Day can best be seen as a traditional American-born radical who reflected a strong but nondoctrinaire dissent against the corporate capitalist state that existed in the United States.

While at the hospital Day fell in love with Lionel Moise, a former *Kansas City Star* reporter and moved in with him shortly after the November 1918 Armistice. The war had ceased but Day's personal struggle had just begun. She spent the next seven years of her life pursuing unsuccessful and often tragic personal relationships that ended in suicide attempts, an abortion, a marriage, and a divorce. Unlike Augustine, Day tried to keep these seven years of her life hidden and never spoke of them. They were very significant years because they exhibited the power of her emotional life and her capacity to love another human being. The best account of these years is an autobiographical novel she wrote and published in 1923. Though not very successful, the publisher, A. & C. Boni, sold it to Hollywood on the strength of the name, *The Eleventh Virgin*. For her novel Day received a payment of $2,500, which she used to buy a cottage on the shore of Raritan Bay, Staten Island. A few months later she began to live with Forster Battingham, a young biology instructor. She continued to view herself as a writer. Within a year, Bell Syndicate bought her second novel, *What Price Love?* for newspaper serialization.

On 3 March 1927 Dorothy Day gave birth to her daughter Tamar. She was happy, though Tamar's father was not. Battingham wondered what point there was in bringing another person into a world of hopelessness and injustice. In *The Long Loneliness,* Day tells how the birth of her child compelled her to become a Catholic:

> No human creature could receive or contain so vast a flood of love and joy as I felt after the birth of my child. With this came the need to worship and adore. I had heard many say they wanted to worship God in their own way and did not need a church in which to praise Him. . . . But my very experience as a radical, my whole make-up, led me to want to associate myself with others, with the masses, in praising and adoring God. Without even looking into the claims of the Catholic church, I was willing to admit that for me she was the one true church.

This choice meant that Day would have to leave her mate, who was deeply irreligious and found all that he needed in nature. Her choice of Catholicism also meant parting with her lifelong radical friends. In some aspects, Day's choice is not entirely incomprehensible. She ultimately seemed to be searching for something her past experiences had not satisfied. Her conversion signified a belief in a deeper reality, a belief so strong she was willing to leave all for it. What had led to this conversion is not clear. During her pregnancy Day did pray more; she resumed keeping a diary; she reread the writings of Augustine; she read the lives of the Saints and identified with Teresa of Avila and Therese of Lisieux.

Day had her daughter Tamar Teresa baptized and then months later, on 28 December 1927, entered the Catholic church and was baptized in the church of Our Lady, Holy Christians, in Totenville, Staten Island. The action was almost wholly mechanical after all the agony she had undergone in leaving Forster Battingham. There was no consolation for her. For the next five years, Day raised her daughter and explored her faith. During this time she worked at a variety of jobs and traveled to Hollywood, Mexico City, and Florida, but always returned to New York. While on a writing assignment to cover the Washington hunger march, she noted the complete absence of the church's presence on behalf of the poor and knew that somewhere the faith she had embraced had been turned aside from its true historic mission. She was aware of a frequent dichotomy between the doctrinal ideals of Catholicism and their implementation by church members, and in her autobiography she wrote that she "loved the church for Christ made visible. Not for itself, because it was so often a scandal to me."

After the hunger march, Day went to the National Shrine at the Catholic University and prayed "with tears and with anguish, that some way would open up for me to use what talents I possessed for my fellow workers, for the poor." As she knelt there she realized that "after three years of Catholicism my only contact with active Catholics had been through articles I had written for one of the Catholic magazines. Those contacts had been brief, casual. I still did not personally know one Catholic layman." She had made sacrifices to convert to Catholicism, but she knew she also had much within herself to bring to the church: her love of the masses, her pacifism, even her anarchism, but especially her desire to love God. Soon she found her role in the church. Day wrote, "When I returned to New York [December 1933], I found Peter Maurin—Peter, the French peasant, whose spirit and ideas will dominate . . . the rest of my life."

Maurin was born in France in 1877. He joined the Christian Brothers, a religious community of men, only to leave to join Le Sillon, a lay movement whose goal was to Christianize modern democracy. To escape the draft in France, he emigrated to Canada in 1909. As a teacher, a social observer, and a man who not only worked with the poor but had been one of them, he devised from these experiences his philosophy of Catholic radicalism which he brought to Dorothy Day in 1933. Day contended Maurin spent his first few months "indoctrinating" her.

Maurin believed that "the most traditional Catholicism was of supreme social relevance to modern humanity, and that it was only necessary to 'blow the dynamite' of that ancient church to set the whole world afire." His vision rejected the liberal myths of nation state, technology, and progress. Instead, Maurin drew extensively on the central teaching of orthodox Catholicism and posited the Garden of Eden, the Fall, the light of the Beatitudes, the darkness of oblivion, sacred community, and sinful alienation as central to his social vision. Thus, Maurin's radical ideal was rooted not in the material world but in the realm of the spirit. His goals would be achieved at the end of time—with the second coming of Christ.

Besides this eschatological view of history, the other distinctive feature Maurin presented to Dorothy Day was personalism. This concept of personalism involved suffering and even tragedy. It basically meant that individuals would reenact in their own lives the mystery of the crucifixion of Christ. Maurin saw personalism expressed in individuals who embraced voluntary poverty and at the cost of personal sacrifice performed the works of mercy proclaimed in the Beatitudes. Individuals, he believed, should daily practice the corporal works of feeding the hungry, clothing the naked, and sheltering the shelterless.

Personalism rather than political analysis appealed greatly to Day. She had been attracted in vain to political groups such as Socialists and the Industrial Workers of the World in hopes of finding solutions to the plight of the poor. In Christian personalism the solutions rested with the individual and were not dependent on historical circumstances. Victory also was ensured because of a power beyond history—Christ. It would be Day's activism combined with Christian personalism that would keep the Catholic Worker movement embroiled in the messy affairs of society rather than only writing or talking about them.

Maurin never ceased to point out what he believed to be the greatest enemies to attaining the Catholic Worker ideal in contemporary America—nationalism and capitalism. Maurin did not believe there was anything new in his analysis of these twin enemies, but he did believe his solution was new. He presented Day with a Catholic Worker ideal that was a viable alternative to the American way of life.

The twin enemies of nationalism and capitalism led Day to apply to herself the term "Catholic anarchist." She did this during the 1930s when the authority of the federal government had become almost sacred to millions of people, who perceived the New Deal to be the one and only hope for solving society's ills. Day's anarchism, on the other hand, meant increased responsibility of one person for another, of the individual to the community along with a much lessened sense of obligation to or dependence on the "distant and centralized state." Her personalism combined with her love of the masses was reflected most keenly in her sense of solidarity. This led her to embrace the theological teaching of the "Mystical Body of Christ." She wrote, "That very sense of solidarity made me gradually understand the doctrine of the Mystical Body of Christ whereby we are the members one of another."

Maurin had no blueprint for decentralizing and simplifying American society. At best, all he could offer were a few religious guidelines. Yet these guidelines were all Day needed to begin her work. According to William Miller, a historian whom Day selected to be her biographer, "What Peter Maurin did for Dorothy was to reorient her vision from the object to the subject, from collectivism to Christian personalism. He also provided her with something she had not had—an understanding of the meaning of the church and her position in it."

Day believed the Catholic Worker ideal was a positive Christian alternative that should be made available to every individual who desired it. For this to occur, it was first necessary to present the ideal to others. Day's first effort was what she knew how to do best—start a newspaper. She entitled it the *Catholic Worker* to announce a Catholic presence and concern for the poor and oppressed. Day also witnessed daily to this concern by embracing voluntary poverty and establishing a house of hospitality on Mott Street in New York City. The house of hospitality, by providing food, clothing, and shelter to the poor and oppressed, would ensure a daily, living example of the works of mercy proclaimed in the Beatitudes. Later, Day began a farm commune in Easton, Pennsylvania.

As the Catholic Worker movement spread beyond New York, the concept of a newspaper, a house of hospitality, and a fascination with the simplicity of the rural life continued to define the Catholic Worker movement. Day had successfully made Maurin's ideas a concrete reality. As a convert to Catholicism, Day also made a unique contribution to the history of American Catholicism, for the Catholic Worker movement founded in 1933 in New York City was fundamentally a movement of Catholic laypeople.

Dorothy Day's most unique contribution to Catholicism was her proclamation of Catholic pacifism as the ideal response to war. The Catholic Worker was the first Catholic group in American history to claim such a position. After World War II, Robert Ludlow, who edited the *Catholic Worker*, and Ammon Hennacy, who brought an activist dimension to the movement, helped integrate nonviolence into the pacifist position and encouraged lay initiative in changing the social order through direct actions on behalf of peace and social justice. Day and the Catholic Worker movement were committed to pacifism and nonviolence; they were the heart of the American Catholic peace movement during the Vietnam War, assisting in the formation of other groups such as the American Pax Association, the Catholic Peace Fellowship, and Pax Christi USA. As a result, the Roman Catholic Church's official teaching on war and peace issues changed from its normative position of the just war concept to the inclusion of pacifism as a valid option for Catholics to embrace.

Day's proclamation of pacifism led her to leave the *Catholic Worker* in 1943. She had become involved in the Lacouture retreat movement, and under the spiritual direction of John Hugo her faith deepened as she tried to live a more perfect Christian life. In an attempt to evaluate her life, she removed herself from responsibility for the movement and removed her name from the masthead of the paper. World War II brought death and destruction to large areas of the globe and desolation to Dorothy Day. Her Catholic pacifist stance had exacted a great toll on the movement, reducing the number of houses of hospitality from 32 to 16, and the circulation of the newspaper from 130,000 copies to 50,500 copies. The flow of invitations to speak at parishes, schools, and seminaries around the country had ended. Even Peter Maurin had said that "perhaps silence would be better for a time than to continue our opposition to war." The demands of peacemaking on Day were as great as the demands of war. Whatever doubt may have arisen concerning her life at the *Catholic Worker* before her sabbatical, she was back with the movement in six months, never to leave again until her death.

On the issue of pacifism as in everything she did, Day never attempted to provide a theological explanation. One reason was that she did not consider herself qualified to offer detailed theological rationales for her actions. Rather, she acted out of convictions that never wavered: love of the masses, pacifism, and even anarchism. She combined these convictions with a faith in God, a loyalty to the Catholic church, an embrace of the gospel message, and a love that knew no limits.

Dorothy Day died on 29 November 1980. The movement she founded did not cease with her death, however. It flourishes today with Houses of Hospitality in the United States of America, Canada, England, Germany, and the Netherlands. The New York City house continues to publish the *Catholic Worker* at a penny a copy. In death Day continues to inspire many people because of her unselfish love of the poor and the oppressed. Indeed, many Catholics pray that the church will one day proclaim her a saint.

Suggested Readings

Writings of Dorothy Day: *From Union Square to Rome* (Silver Spring, Md.: Presentation of the Faith Press, 1939); *Houses of Hospitality* (New York: Sheed & Ward, 1939); *The Long Loneliness* (New York: Harper, 1952); *Loaves and Fishes* (New York: Harper & Row, 1963).

Dwight Macdonald, "The Foolish Things of the World—I and II," *New Yorker* 27 (4 October 1952), and 27 (11 October 1952).

Patricia McNeal, *Harder Than War: Catholic Peacemaking in Twentieth-Century America* (New Brunswick, N.J.: Rutgers University Press, 1992).

William D. Miller, *Dorothy Day: A Biography* (New York: Harper & Row, 1982).

Marcus Moziah Garvey

(1887–1940)

Mark A. Lomax

Born in St. Ann's Bay, Jamaica, on 17 August 1887, Marcus Moziah Garvey became one of Africa's greatest sons. The youngest of eleven children born to his parents, Garvey possessed an irrepressible passion for his people. Between his teen years and his midtwenties Garvey traveled throughout Jamaica, Central and South America, and Europe. Everywhere he went, the apparent degradation of people of African descent appalled him. By age eighteen, he had already immersed himself in politics. He spoke out on behalf of the working poor both in Jamaica and in Costa Rica, and participated in workers' strikes for fair treatment and higher wages. A printer by trade, he often wrote articles and edited newspapers that stirred up unrest among the masses. Such experiences were mere preparation for his life's destiny.

After an unsuccessful attempt to establish the Universal Negro Improvement and Conservation Association and African Communities League on the island of Jamaica in 1914, Garvey moved to the United States in 1916. He had planned to stay only five months to raise money for his organization, but was so warmly received that he decided to stay.

In Garvey's view, the institutional church, including the black church, had failed people of African descent. The church encouraged Africans around the world to look beyond their sufferings on earth and concentrate on the promise of peace in heaven. Believing this message to be detrimental to the welfare of African people, Garvey preached a gospel of black nationalism, race pride, and self-reliance, and tailored the theology of the church to suit these objectives.

Garvey established the first chapter of the Universal Negro Improvement Association in Harlem, New York, in 1917. The general purposes of the organization were to improve the condition of African people around the world, establish a central nation for people of African descent, and teach

African people the mysteries of economic development. At its peak, the Association (UNIA) boasted six million members worldwide. Its assets included grocery stores, restaurants, elementary schools, a college, and a steamship company called the "Black Star Line." UNIA's motto was "One God, One Aim, One Destiny." The business enterprises, the motto, and the organizational structure of the UNIA were designed to promote Garvey's black nationalist agenda.

Though not a religious organization as such, the UNIA's chapter meetings resembled worship services in the black church. Members said prayers and sang hymns. Speakers often chose religious themes to exhort UNIA's members to stay the course to African unity. And many people considered the African Orthodox Church (AOC), led by bishop George Alexander McGuire, as the religious wing of the UNIA. The organization's battle cry was "Africa for the Africans." The deepest desire and greatest hope of its members was the redemption of Africa. Those members who were not inspired by dreams of repatriating to the Motherland were moved by visions of doing business with those who did. The person who inspired such hope, whom many called "Moses" and others exalted to a place next to the Creator, Son, and Holy Spirit, was Marcus Moziah Garvey.

The God Garvey worshiped and served, was the same God to whom the other great reformers of the Christian faith—Luther, Calvin, and Zwingli—prayed. Garvey believed God was, and is, the Creator and Sustainer of the cosmos, the Almighty and Everlasting Spirit who was one substance and three persons. Garvey's God was also different from that of the other great reformers of the Christian faith. Garvey's God was black.

Though astute enough to know that God has no color, Garvey realized most human beings think in images. Just as white people conceived of God as white, and yellow people had the idea of a yellow God, so Garvey believed Africans should possess the idea of a black God. He thought that African people should see God through their own eyes. Through this reasoning, Garvey concluded that the God of African people was the God of Ethiopia, the Everlasting, the Almighty, One God of all time.

God, to Garvey, was principally the God of peace and love, but also a Warrior Lord—a bold sovereign who did not hesitate to defend the heavenly Kingdom against Lucifer's challenge to God's power. Indeed, Garvey envisioned God as conscripting all of the angels, archangels, cherubim, and seraphim of heaven to defeat the overzealous and prideful Lucifer. Garvey reasoned that sovereigns of the great nations of the earth, including African nations, should defend the rights of their citizens and the boundaries of their lands as aggressively as God did heaven's.

Garvey believed in a God who was both transcendent and immanent: transcendent in the sense that no human being or spirit occupied a level equal to God's; immanent in the sense that God sustained and governed the universe. God worked through spiritual means in the world. Garvey's emphasis on self-reliance meant that women and men could not depend on God to do for them what they could do for themselves. Though God sometimes intervened in the affairs of humankind, God rarely interfered with human relationships. Garvey taught that God gave human beings all they needed to survive. It was up to them to work out the details of their survival.

During a religious ceremony in 1924 at the International Convention of the Negro Peoples of the World, Garvey and the members of UNIA canonized Jesus the Christ as a "Black man of Sorrows" and the Virgin Mary as a "Black Madonna." God the Holy Spirit, though without physical form, bore the semblance of African humanity. Jesus the Christ was a man of reddish-brown color who had been falsely accused, arrested, persecuted, and crucified without due process of law. To these views, Garvey attached a radical gospel of moral and spiritual revolution hoping to emancipate his beleaguered people from the vice grip of Roman imperialism.

Although most "mainstream" civil and ecclesiastical leaders, black and white, characterized Garvey as a buffoon, the members and friends of the UNIA were inspired by his conception of the Godhead. They saw the similarity between Jesus, the black Messiah and redeemer of the world during the first century, and Garvey himself, the black Messiah and redeemer of Africa during the twentieth century. They dreamed that African people would rise from the dust of worldwide oppression and humiliation. They worked diligently to make their dream a reality.

In practically every large city of the country and a few rural areas and small towns, Garveyites started businesses, established institutes, and diligently spread the good news of Garvey's program. These efforts were not limited to the United States. Poor, oppressed people of color in the West Indies, Central and South America, and Africa were inspired by Garvey as well. His deepest hope was for African people to experience a cultural, spiritual, and economic resurrection. He wanted his people to walk in a new moral, physical, and intellectual consciousness so they could compete with the powers represented by the greatest European nations on earth.

A student of the Bible, though he rarely interpreted it literally, Garvey thought the Bible revealed an aspect of God's nature, character, and person. He did not believe a single book could contain all that humanity could know about God. The Bible offered one way of looking at God. Other great religious traditions, he believed, revealed God as well. But Garvey took the Bible seriously and often used biblical stories to promote the interests of the UNIA. In his Christmas sermon of 1921, he reminded the congregants that Jesus with his parents had fled into Africa when running from Herod and that an African, Simon of Cyrene, had carried his cross. His Easter Sunday sermon of 1922 was entitled "The Resurrection of the Negro." In addition, Garvey sometimes compared the suffering and persecution of Jesus to his own.

Perhaps the most important category in Garvey's theology, considering the condition of African people around the world during his lifetime, was his anthropology. He believed the UNIA could not successfully accomplish its objectives if he failed to instill racial pride in African peoples. The primary obstacle to the progress of Africans was their failure to believe that God had as much investment in them as in any other people. Time and again he insisted that Africans were created in the image and likeness of God just like all other people. The African lacked nothing in the intelligence and ability given to other human beings. He frequently reached back to ancient history and exhorted his followers to understand that Africa was the cradle of humanity; that Africans built the first modern civilizations in Egypt and northeast Africa; that Africa left the world the legacy of science, art, architecture, philosophy, and religion.

Garvey used his anthropology to instill race pride in African people around the world. He detested the sight of African people playing subservient roles to European people and firmly believed that no person deserved to be treated as a lord or master by another person. God alone was Lord and Master of all people. Although Garvey's parents raised him in the Methodist church, and as an adult he converted to Catholicism, he welcomed people of other faith traditions to the UNIA. Though the vast majority of UNIA members were Christians, some were Muslims, others were members of the black Hebrew Israelite community, and still others had no religious affiliation at all.

Garvey embodied a bold, progressive vision for African people and, in spite of his detractors, was no buffoon. His radical brand of black nationalism insulted many African American leaders who, during the World War I era, were trying to chart a course leading to integration and full assimilation into the American mainstream. Leaders of African nations who were largely dependent on the good graces of European colonialists to sustain their economies feared that open affiliation with Garvey would be a tactical error. Though in the southern United States and in many places in colonial Africa there were strict prohibitions against Garveyism, his message heartened the masses of poor people of African descent who heard it.

Today, students of African American history know Garvey as a great leader and social prophet who fought tirelessly for the liberation of his people. In the West Indies the popular reggae singer Bob Marley revived his legacy in the memory of Afro-Jamaicans. People of African descent in North America often invoke Garvey's name with a long list of other great ancestors of African American people. Yet many people do not know his theology or the exact nature of the vision and accomplishments of the UNIA.

Garvey redefined Christian theology to promote African liberation. For him, African liberation was holistic, embracing the physical, spiritual, economic, political, social, and moral realms of human experience. Though the black church has historically been forced to address the broader issues of black life, it is, relatively speaking, just beginning to warm up to the idea of a Christ of color. To date, however, there is no broadscale movement in the black church toward embracing a black Godhead.

Suggested Readings

Amy Jacques Garvey, ed., *The Philosophy and Opinions of Marcus Garvey: Or, Africa for the Africans* (Dover: Majority Press, 1986).

Tony Martin, *Race First: The Ideological and Organizational Struggles of Marcus Garvey and the Universal Negro Improvement Association* (Dover: Majority Press, 1976).

Judith Stein, *The World of Marcus Garvey: Race and Class in Modern Society* (Baton Rouge and London: Louisiana State University Press, 1986).

William Edward Burghardt DuBois

(1868–1963)

James H. Cone

William Edward Burghardt DuBois is the preeminent African American intellectual in U.S. history. He was born in Great Barrington, Massachusetts, 23 February 1868, three years after the Civil War, and died in Accra, Ghana, 27 August 1963, one day before the March on Washington. The War and the March marked not only the span of DuBois' life, but crisis moments in the history of the black struggle for justice, whose philosophy and goals in the twentieth century were primarily defined by DuBois' work.

W. E. B. DuBois began his college education at Fisk University (1885–88) and then went to Harvard where he became the first African American to receive a Ph.D. (1895), after a two-year study at the University of Berlin in Germany. His doctoral dissertation, "The Suppression of the African Slave Trade," was published as the first volume in the Harvard Historical Studies (1896).

DuBois is best known as a social activist, the leader of the opposition to the accommodation philosophy of Booker T. Washington, and one of the founders of the NAACP (1909), whose official organ, the *Crisis,* he edited for twenty-four years (1910–34). DuBois, however, was also a great scholar. His writings influenced every area of black intellectual endeavor, including politics, sociology, history, economics, international affairs, literature, black studies, and religion. He has been correctly called a "Renaissance man," because no area of humanity escaped his vast intellectual outreach and concern, especially the political and economic rights and the cultural and religious achievements of people of African descent. He taught classics at Wilberforce University (1894–96) and history, economics, and sociology at Atlanta University (1897–1910, 1934–44), and wrote nineteen books and hundreds of essays—all of which focused on the life and thought of black people in the United States, Africa, and throughout the world.

DuBois is widely regarded as the "Father of Pan-Africanism." One cannot begin to understand black thinking on any subject without engaging the thought of DuBois.

DuBois' contribution to black religious thought is found in three areas: (1) a penetrating analysis of the origin and meaning of black religion; (2) a persuasive critique of the ethical failings of white Christianity; and (3) pioneering historical and sociological studies of black churches.

Scholars of black religion are greatly influenced by DuBois' profound analysis of the divided black self—the struggle to be both African and American. "One ever feels his twoness," DuBois wrote in his classic text, *The Souls of Black Folk* (1903), "an American, a Negro; two souls, two thoughts, two unreconciled strivings, two warring ideals in one dark body whose dogged strength alone keeps it from being torn asunder."

Nowhere is this "double-consciousness" more evident than in the beliefs and practices of black religion. A syncretistic faith, black religion is an adaptation and mingling of both the primitive religions of the African forests and the white Baptist and Methodist faiths in the American South. DuBois first encountered black religion in the raw at a revival meeting in the hills of Tennessee. It was an "awful" experience, a scene of expressive human emotions such as DuBois had never seen before. He called it "a pythian madness, a demonic possession, that lent terrible reality to song and word." This captivating description contains DuBois' widely quoted characteristics of slave religion—"the Preacher, the Music, and the Frenzy." They are heartfelt expressions of black people's spiritual strivings, their struggle to reconcile the faith of their African fathers and mothers and the Christian religion of white slave masters.

"The Preacher is the most unique personality developed by the Negro on the American soil," DuBois wrote. "A leader, a politician, an orator, a boss, an intriguer, an idealist—all of these he is, and ever, too, the center of a group of men, now twenty, now a thousand in number." The spirituals are called "sorrow songs," "the rhythmic cry of the slave," which "tell of death and suffering and unvoiced longing toward a truer world, of misty wanderings and hidden ways." Though "distinctly sorrowful," they are also songs of hope and resistance—profound expressions of "faith in the ultimate justice of things." The most striking manifestation of black faith is "the Frenzy or the Shouting, when the Spirit of the Lord passed by, and, seizing the devotee, made mad with supernatural joy." The frenzy is the visible manifestation of God's uplifting presence, the devotee's public testimony that he or she is in communion with the Lord. "It varied in expression from the silent rapt countenance or the low murmur and moan to the mad abandon of physical fervor,—stamping, shrieking, and shouting, the rushing to and fro and wild waving of arms, the weeping and laughing, the vision and the trance."

The second area of DuBois' contribution to black religious thought is his scathing critique of white Christianity. It laid the foundation for the later attack on white religion and theology in black liberation theology. DuBois defined the value of white churches not by their "supernatural significance" or their erudite theology, but by their ethical practice, that is, whether they followed the "Golden Rule" by treating blacks as they themselves wanted to be treated. In his most famous prediction, DuBois said, "The problem of the twentieth century is the problem of the color-line." This problem is also the ethical test which white churches failed miserably. They supported the slave trade, defended American slavery, and are themselves communities of racial prejudice. According to DuBois, the moral failure of white churches negated their Christian identity. If Jesus, "the greatest of religious rebels," came to America, he would identify with blacks and others of "low degree" and would "put down the mighty from their seats."

The third area of DuBois' contribution is his historical and sociological studies of "The Negro Church" in *The Philadelphia Negro* (1899) and *The Atlanta University Publications* (no. 8, 1903). These volumes and other essays on black religion are still vital resources for students of black religion. DuBois was ambivalent about black churches. On the one hand, he recognized them as the social center of black life and the most distinctive expression of African culture. He also praised the black church as a center of social uplift and for being a democratic community where the mass of the membership participates in the governing power of the denomination.

On the other hand, DuBois recognized the cultural and moral dilemma of black churches, especially their struggle to cope with the double life of African Americans in the ever-changing "worlds within and without the Veil of Color." Double life creates a spiritual and ethical schizophrenia, giving rise to conflicting "streams of thought and ethical strivings." Accordingly DuBois did not view the black church as a source of inner spiritual freedom or as an effective agent of political liberation. Its theology was too childish and its leaders too political and ignorant to cope with the problem of race in the modern world. (DuBois put his faith in the "Talented Tenth"—the "exceptional men" of the race.) Yet, DuBois had an enormous influence on later religion-based leaders. That influence consisted of his profound analysis of the traditions of integrationism and separatism, embraced respectively by Martin Luther King, Jr., and Malcolm X, and further developed by black and womanist theologians.

Suggested Readings

Writings of W. E. B. DuBois: *The Souls of Black Folk* (New York: Fawcett Publications, 1961); *The Autobiography of W. E. B. DuBois: A Soliloquy on Viewing My Life from the Last Decade of Its First Century* (New York: International Publishers, 1968); *W. E. B. DuBois: A Reader,* ed. David E. Lewis (New York: Henry Holt & Co., 1995).

David L. Lewis, *W. E. B. DuBois: Biography of a Race, 1868–1919* (New York: Henry Holt & Co., 1993).

Manning Marable, *W. E. B. DuBois: Black Radical Democrat* (Boston: Twayne Publishers, 1986).

Martin Luther King, Jr.

(1929–1968)

James H. Cone

Martin Luther King, Jr., was born in Atlanta, Georgia, 15 January 1929, and was assassinated in Memphis, Tennessee, 4 April 1968. In that short span of thirty-nine years, he became not only America's most influential preacher, but also one of the nation's most important theologians. King proclaimed and interpreted the meaning of the Christian faith for American life in sermons, essays, and books with such spiritual power and rational clarity that few people remained unmoved by his proclamation and unpersuaded by the logic of his argument.

As preacher and theologian, King revolutionized American thinking on religion, politics, and race. Before King, segregation was a way of life in America, widely accepted and openly practiced even in the churches. Few white Christians, even among preachers and theologians, regarded racial discrimination as a moral evil that radically contradicted the gospel of Jesus. But after people heard King's sermons and read his reflections on God's meaning for America and humanity, segregation for most became politically unacceptable and morally repugnant.

The prophetic and rational power of Martin King's sermons and theological discourse revealed not only his righteous condemnation of racism, but also his angry denunciation of poverty and war. When King spoke, America listened. He pricked the nation's conscience, making Americans uncomfortable practicing segregation, tolerating poverty, and supporting war. While most theologians spoke only to one another and to their students, King spoke to the nation and the world. Even King's enemies had to acknowledge the truth of his moral and theological claims. President Ronald Reagan and a mostly conservative United States Congress, after much prodding from the American public, elevated King to the status of a national symbol, 20 January 1986, making his birthday a national holiday—a distinction no other theologian or religious leader holds.

Martin King was a reluctant theologian. He viewed his vocation primarily as a preacher in the black Baptist tradition of his father, Martin Luther King, Sr., and his maternal grandfather, Alfred Daniel Williams. Both were leading community advocates of racial justice while serving as pastors of Ebenezer Baptist Church in Atlanta, which Martin Jr. joined at the age of five. King's understanding of the Christian faith was strongly influenced by the profound spirituality of his parents and the evangelical faith of the black church community of Ebenezer and elsewhere.

King's faith was also influenced by his educational experience at Morehouse College, especially the weekly Tuesday addresses of Benjamin E. Mays, its president, and the theological reflections of George D. Kelsey, one of its prominent teachers in religion. Outspoken opponents of segregation, Mays and Kelsey stimulated King intellectually and spiritually. They modeled a rational way of thinking about God that engaged the disciplines of philosophy, sociology, and the sciences, but did not negate the faith of Ebenezer, which was highly emotional and seemingly irrational and dependent upon biblical literalism. They convinced King there was no irreconcilable conflict between scientific thinking and theological discourse, faith in God and the fight for social justice. Convinced he could bridge the apparent gap between the Christian faith and the modern world and fulfill his calling to serve humanity in the black church, King decided to become a minister during the summer of 1947.

At Ebenezer and Morehouse, Martin King was taught he was a person with dignity and worth, even though society treated blacks as second-class citizens. The knowledge that he was somebody empowered King to believe he was as important in God's eyes as any white person. "God is no respecter of persons," preachers and teachers proclaimed often from the pulpit at Ebenezer and in the chapel and lecture halls at Morehouse. "Out of one blood God created all that dwell on the face of the earth." King internalized the faith of the black church, especially its emphasis on the dignity that God bestows upon all people at the moment of their creation. The God-given worth of human personality became the foundation of King's theology as he later developed it in graduate school and articulated it with great passion in the context of the civil rights movement.

King moved to Crozer Theological Seminary in 1948 and later to Boston University School of Theology where he received the Ph.D. in systematic theology in 1955. In these liberal Northern schools he acquired additional philosophical and theological tools for articulating his belief about God and human dignity. Like most graduate students, King was attracted to the thinking of his teachers, who were leading advocates of theological liberalism and sharp critics of the neoorthodox theology of Karl Barth and his followers. The personalistic philosophy of Edgar S. Brightman and its theological articulation by L. Harold DeWolf provided King a broader intellectual basis for belief in a personal God, the inherent worth of the human person, and the Christian duty to engage in social justice ministry.

King's theological perspective came to maturity during his intense involvement in the civil rights movement. Theology is the critical side of faith. It is faith examining itself, seeking to understand God's meaning in a world where belief is deeply problematical. King's theological explorations in graduate school were largely abstract and did not seriously engage the core of his personal faith or force him to think deeply about the challenges of the faith in a world full of black pain and suffering. When King became a key participant in the civil rights movement, however, both his faith and his theology were tested again and again by daily threats of violence and the enormous task of telling the religious meaning of the black struggle for justice to the nation and the world.

The threats against King's life had a profound effect on his faith and theology. These began shortly after he assumed the leadership of the Montgomery bus boycott and continued throughout his life. The most unsettling threat occurred 27 January 1956. "Nigger," said the voice on the telephone, "we're tired of you and your mess now, and if you are not out of this town in three days, we're going to blow your brains out and blow up your house." Although it was normal for King to receive about forty hate-calls daily, this particular one rocked him, undermining his moral courage. This moment of crisis forced King to make real the faith he had accepted as a child at Ebenezer and to make sense out of the theology he had learned in graduate school. It was a time for prayer, a time to reach out to the God that his mother and father told him about. As he prayed for strength and courage to do the right thing, he heard a voice which commanded him to stand up for righteousness, justice, and truth, "and lo, I will be with you always." King interpreted this experience as a direct encounter with God, assuring him that he was not alone in the fight for justice. It was a spiritual and a theological turning point in his life. Fear left him. An inner calm relaxed him and focused his spirit and thoughts on the God who promised to be present with him in the "storms of life." From that moment on, as he faced daily the prospects of death, King never wavered in his commitment to justice and his determination to make Americans understand that racism is a violation against God and humanity that cannot be tolerated.

King's understanding of the Christian faith, therefore, was derived from three main sources: (1) the African American church community; (2) his graduate school studies in theology; and (3) his ministry as civil rights activist. These sources gave him the raw materials for creating a prophetic and liberating theology. This theology was not academic. It was a deeply spiritual theology, publicly accessible and politically engaged, carved out of his practice of nonviolence and his intellectual effort to make intelligible to the American people the reasons why they should join black people in the defense of their humanity.

King's theology focused on three themes—justice, love, and hope—that he viewed as interconnected. His understanding of each was derived mainly from the Bible and the black religious experience.

Justice. No theme was more important for King's theology than the justice of God. Justice is often a prominent theme in the religious and political thinking of people who are slaves. Israelites were slaves in ancient Egypt, and blacks were slaves in modern America. Thus both Jews and blacks spoke of God as the liberator of slaves, the protector of the weak, and defender of the poor, the One who punishes the wrongdoers for their evil deeds. These biblical and black ideas of God resonated with King, who moved back and forth between them as he reflected on what justice meant for America in the second half of the twentieth century.

The absence of racial justice in America launched King into his civil rights ministry, forcing him to become the public theologian-philosopher of the black freedom movement. When the people of Montgomery asked him to be their leader, he could not say no. God, he believed, was speaking to him through the people, calling on him to fulfill his promise to serve humanity. In King's view, one cannot claim to be God's servant while remaining unconcerned about the establishment of justice for one's brothers and sisters. The gospel demanded political involvement in the national life of the nation, taking sides with those most oppressed.

King spoke of injustice in concrete terms: racism, poverty, and war. He called these the three great evils of our time. He focused first on racism, blatantly displayed in legal segregation in the South and deeply embedded in the fabric of American culture. He called racism America's chief moral dilemma, a cancer in the body politic and in the body of Christ. He criticized the churches not only for often supporting segregation in society, but for practicing it in their own congregations. The eleven o'clock worship is America's most segregated hour, King lamented, and the Sunday school the most segregated school of the week. This was a flagrant violation of the churches' theology of reconciliation. King aroused the moral conscience of the churches and thereby transformed their understanding of the Christian faith. He showed that the Christian faith could be validated only through the practice of justice.

King recognized that injustice was connected with poverty—an evil that incorporates racism but not exclusively defined by it. Like racism, poverty is global, but unlike racism, it embraces all races, nations, and cultures. Nothing angered King more than the great economic gap between the rich and the poor in America and around the world. He was appalled that America stored surplus food while people were starving in this land and in Africa, Asia, and Latin America. "I know where we can store that food," King often said. "In the wrinkled stomachs of the world's poor." In his sermons and writings, King reflected on God's judgment against the rich and the powerful. He preached often about Jesus' parable of the rich man, commonly called "Dives," and the poor man, Lazarus (Luke 16:19-31). Dives went to hell, King said, because he failed to bridge the gap separating him from Lazarus. King contended that America was going to hell, too, unless the nation used its material resources to eliminate poverty and thereby enhance the quality of life for the poor here and abroad. Poverty is a deadly sin, a flagrant violation of the righteousness of God. "The judgment of God is on America," King proclaimed repeatedly in sermons and lectures.

When King wrote theology to save America from the injustices of racism and poverty, government officials were often offended by his harsh words. But they could tolerate that offense more than his condemnation of America's involvement in the Vietnam War. At first, King wanted to believe that what America was doing in Vietnam was just and right. Thus he was slow to take a stand, disturbed but remaining silent, as he focused his ministry on ending racism and poverty at home. But the time came when he believed that "silence is betrayal." He knew that he would be severely criticized as a traitor to his country and to black people's struggle for justice.

While government officials and mainline civil rights leaders denied any connection between the fight for justice at home and the search for peace abroad, King strongly disagreed. King's bottom line was theological. The Vietnamese are God's children whose lives are just as sacred as Americans, and hence America has no right whatsoever to kill them. The more King critically examined America's conduct in Vietnam, the more evil he saw in it. Like a biblical prophet standing before the people of Israel, King stood before the people of this nation (Riverside Church, New York, 4 April 1967) and declared America to be "the greatest purveyor of violence in the world today." In the name of God, King urged the nation's leaders to stop the madness.

Love. The theme of justice in King's theology is connected with his well-known and dominant principle of love. Although his ministry began with an accent on justice, King soon connected it with love, which he interpreted as the only way to achieve justice. Love was the dominant theme in Gandhi's philosophy, liberal Protestant theology, and the black religious tradition—

all of which influenced King. But it was the biblical tradition, especially the story of Jesus' life with the poor and his death on the cross, that defined love's central meaning for King. Jesus' cross was the ultimate expression of God's love for humanity. In this event, God redeemed humanity and granted salvation to all. It is because of the saving power of Jesus' cross, his willingness to forgive his enemies, that King came to believe that suffering is redemptive. "To be a Christian," King said, "one must take up his cross with all its difficulties and agonizing and tension-packed content, and carry it until that very cross leaves its mark upon us and redeems us to that more excellent way which comes only through suffering."

King turned to Gandhi's idea of nonviolence (Satyagraha) for a political expression of his theological understanding of love. Interpreting the Montgomery bus boycott, King said: "Christ furnished the spirit and motivation, while Gandhi furnished the method." King urged blacks to love whites, to be nonviolent in their struggle, so that they could achieve not only justice but even more important, the transformation of the heart of the oppressor and thereby generate the spirit of forgiveness and reconciliation among white and black Americans. Unjust suffering, he contended, is redemptive, both for the white oppressor and oppressed blacks. "To suffer in a righteous cause is to grow to our full humanity's stature."

King's idealism contrasted sharply with the "Christian realism" advocated in the day, most notably by Reinhold Niebuhr. For Niebuhr, love was an ideal which justice could only approximate. King turned Niebuhr upside down, asserting that love is not (as Niebuhr thought) an "impossible possibility," but the only way to achieve justice. King identified love with nonviolence and insisted it was the Christian way to heal the racial divide.

It is not easy for the oppressed to love their oppressors, to turn the other cheek as Jesus commanded in the Sermon on the Mount. Many blacks had deep political and theological reservations about following King down the nonviolent road. Black nationalist Malcolm X initially considered King a traitor for suggesting such an outrageous idea: Nonviolence merely disarmed blacks and invited whites to commit brutality against them. Malcolm supported what King said about justice—that blacks should demand respect as human beings—but could never quite reconcile himself with King's method of achieving it. King's call for African Americans to love their white oppressors, Malcolm contended, was too heavy a psychological burden for oppressed people to bear. "Love yourself!" Malcolm retorted. Yet King could not reconcile himself with violence or even self-defense in public demonstrations. Both violence and self-defense beget violence and destroy community, but love and nonviolence beget forgiveness and reconcile enemies.

Hope. The third element in King's triad of virtues was hope, the belief that God's purpose for humanity could not be destroyed by the forces of evil. Hope is always easy when historical evidence shows that events are leading toward justice. Indeed, it is often hard to separate hope from optimism when one believes in the liberal idea of the goodness of humanity and the inevitable progress of history toward a good society. As a student of liberalism and a strong advocate of integration, King held fast to these beliefs. Victories in Montgomery and Birmingham, the sit-ins and Freedom Rides, and the impressive gathering of blacks, whites, and other Americans at the Great March on Washington deepened King's belief that Americans of all colors and religious persuasions would soon create a society free of racism, poverty, and war.

But King's optimism was shattered in the riot-torn cities of America and on the battlefields of Vietnam. Racism, poverty, and war were not passing away but actually becoming more pervasive. The moral conscience of whites, which King thought would be transformed through nonviolent love, seemed immune to transformation. Many white liberals who supported him during his fight against segregation in the South vigorously opposed him in his fight for justice in Chicago, Cleveland, and other northern cities. King became deeply pessimistic about the prospects of justice in America. He found himself alone and depressed as liberal whites in government, churches, labor, and business turned away from him. Even African Americans, especially the young militants in the Black Power movement, ridiculed King's idea of nonviolence and love. Using Malcolm X's language, they advocated achieving justice "by any means necessary."

Despite several attacks from leaders in white and black communities, King held fast to his faith that God's justice for America is coming, and evil cannot stop it. Justice is coming through love just as Jesus' resurrection came through the cross. Thus hope, for King, became radically *theological,* that is, focused exclusively on God, who raised Jesus from the dead. No matter what evil people did or how successful they were in doing it, King continued to preach that the universe was on the side of justice and thus God's purpose for humanity will become a reality in the world. King was killed in Memphis while marching with garbage workers, bearing witness that the eternal will of God is embodied in the demands of the poor for justice.

King's theological legacy in the African American community is great and obvious. He radicalized conservative black churches, making the struggle for justice an essential element in their understanding of the Christian faith. Without his ministry black liberation and womanist theologies would be unthinkable. King's legacy, however, is much broader and deeper than the African American churches and black and womanist theologies. It can

456

be argued that liberation theologians in the Third World were deeply influenced by King's linking of the practice of justice with the identity of the Christian faith. He was doing liberation theology before the phrase was coined by black and Latin American theologians during the second half of the 1960s.

It is revealing, however, that King's legacy in the white communities of America and Europe is to be found less in the discourse of professional theologians, most of whom ignore him, than among the people of America and of the world. No other theologian's reflection on America has touched as many lives as his. He transformed how the world thinks about justice, love, and hope in regard to race, poverty, and war. His name symbolizes freedom not only in the African American community but among diverse groups of people in America and throughout the world. He deepened our understanding of humanity and of God.

Jonathan Edwards and Reinhold Niebuhr are often referred to as America's greatest theologians. In terms of the impact of their writings on professional theological discourse in America, they hardly have any competitors. But when theological greatness is measured by moral intelligence and commitment, Edwards and Niebuhr do not even belong in the same room with King. In times of slavery and segregation, both Edwards and Niebuhr virtually ignored moral issues related to racism, America's original and most persistent evil. They spoke mainly to and for the dominant white community and overlooked blacks and other people of color. King, however, spoke to and for all justice-seeking people in America and around the world. His legacy is global, affecting people's struggles for justice in China, Philippines, Eastern Europe, Africa, and Latin America. Among American theologians, there is hardly anyone as influential and courageous as King. He was America's moral conscience. Martin King sacrificed his life, not just for blacks but for the "least of these" everywhere, no matter their color or religion or nationality.

Suggested Readings

Writings of Martin Luther King, Jr.: *Where Do We Go From Here: Chaos or Community?* (Boston: Beacon Press, 1967); *A Testament of Hope: The Essential Writings of Martin Luther King, Jr.*, ed. James M. Washington (San Francisco: Harper, 1986).

James H. Cone, *Martin and Malcolm and America: A Dream or A Nightmare* (Maryknoll, N.Y.: Orbis Books, 1991).

David J. Garrow, *Bearing the Cross: Martin Luther King, Jr., and the Southern Christian Leadership Conference* (New York: Morrow, 1986).

John Dewey

(1859–1952)

Steven C. Rockefeller

Well known as a pragmatist philosopher, progressive educator, and social reformer, John Dewey was also a liberal religious thinker. Throughout his career he endeavored to overcome the split between religious faith and science and to integrate fully religious life and everyday life in modern culture. His mature philosophy combines naturalistic humanism with a religious faith in the democratic way of life, piety toward nature, and a mystical sense of belonging to the larger universe. His collected works fill thirty-seven volumes, and few philosophers have had such a wide influence on their times.

Dewey was born and raised in Burlington, Vermont, in a middle-class family. Throughout his youth he was an active member of the Congregational Church. At the University of Vermont he was drawn to the study of philosophy and went on to earn a Ph.D. in philosophy at Johns Hopkins University. There he fell under the spell of Hegelian idealism with its grand vision of the world as an organic unity evolving under the governance of God, the immanent divine mind and absolute ideal. G. W. F. Hegel's philosophy was the most ambitious and influential of the early-nineteenth-century liberal efforts to reconcile Christianity and modern culture. From 1884 to 1894, young Dewey taught at the University of Michigan. During this period he remained engaged in the life of the Congregational Church and constructed his own neo-Hegelian philosophy and liberal understanding of Christianity.

In the mid-1890s he moved to the University of Chicago (1894–1904). There he established an experimental school for children and soon became a national leader of the progressive education movement. The transformation of society, he argued, can best be achieved by beginning with the transformation of the school. During the Chicago years Dewey abandoned his neo-Hegelian idealism and all traditional forms of Christian theology, terminated his membership in the church, and embraced a new form of empirical naturalism and humanism. Dewey's new philosophical outlook was fully developed in the course of his career at Columbia University in New York City (1904–39). As an empirical naturalist, he relied on experience and the experimental method of science as the sole authority in matters of knowledge. Emphasizing this approach, he maintained that there is one world, the evolving world of nature, of which humanity is an interdependent part. His evolutionary naturalism anticipates the kind of ecological worldview that would be embraced by many philosophers and ecotheologians during the final decades of the twentieth century. Dewey was a humanist in the sense that he centered his attention on the problems of people and maintained a basic faith in the capacity of human beings to deal with the challenges of life.

Fundamental to his new naturalistic humanism was the distinctively American philosophical outlook known as pragmatism, initially developed by Charles Saunders Peirce and William James. Dewey rapidly emerged as the leading champion of the movement. As a pragmatist (or instrumentalist) he argued that the meaning of ideas and beliefs is to be found in their practical consequences. He viewed ideas as guides to action and sought a more effective integration of thought and action in practical life. He was especially interested to show how the experimental method of science could be employed as a method of cooperative social problem solving. He also endeavored to devise an experimental method of moral valuation that would overcome the troublesome split between science and morals in modern culture. His professional career coincided with the period of the emergence of the social sciences, and he believed that the new social and moral sciences, or what he called social intelligence, would do for the cause of social progress what the physical sciences had done for industrial progress.

As a political and social activist Dewey was a tireless defender of freedom and human rights, and he helped found the American Civil Liberties Union, the NAACP, The American Association of University Professors, and the New School for Social Research. An outspoken supporter of the labor movement and the women's movement, Dewey also became a leader in the post–World War I movement to outlaw war internationally. Between 1919 and 1930, he traveled extensively overseas, spreading his social philosophy and theory of education in China, Japan, Mexico, South Africa, the Soviet Union, and Turkey.

In order to understand Dewey's religious outlook, it is necessary to explore further his early life and thought. During his adolescence Dewey underwent a fairly severe emotional crisis. It involved feeling painfully troubled by a sense of divisions and separations instilled in him by the religious worldview pervading the Vermont culture in which he was raised—the dualisms of God and nature, self and world, spirit and flesh, the perfection of Christ and the sinfulness of humanity. This crisis filled him with an intense emotional craving for unification that profoundly influenced his philosophical and religious thinking. It explains his lifelong concern to break down all dualisms, including the separation of the divine and the human, the ideal and the real, the spiritual and the material, the individual and the community, and ultimate meaning and everyday life. His life's work as a philosopher, including his religious thought, can be understood as a quest for the ideal and for unification of the ideal and the real.

Another important factor in the development of Dewey's religious thinking concerns the way he came to identify the religious life with the democratic way of life and the scientific search for truth. He first made these connections during his neo-Hegelian period in the 1880s and 1890s. This time in American history witnessed the emergence of the labor union, settlement house, and Social Gospel movements as well as the Populist Party and the Progressive Movement. Deeply influenced by these forces, Dewey sought to integrate the Christian religious life with the struggle for progressive social change. Neo-Hegelian philosophers like young Dewey understood God to be immanent in history as the spirit of freedom and authentic community. In his early thought Dewey, therefore, concluded that the individual finds liberation from sin and guilt, the peace and joy of unity with God, and ultimate meaning not by abandoning the world or by trying to live in the past, but by identifying his or her self with the shared life of the community, which is the life of God, and by striving to actualize the ideal. In this way he unified the sacred and the secular, religious life and everyday life.

Dewey further argued that being a Christian in modern America meant commitment to the democratic ideal—to the democratic way of living and working together. He identified Christian ethics with the ethics of democracy, contending that the democratic ideal and the supreme ethical ideal are one. In early writings he associated the democratic ideal with the kingdom of God. Democracy meant for Dewey much more than a theory of government. He conceived of it as a personal way of individual life involving values and attitudes that should shape human conduct in all the relations of life—in the family, school, church, and workplace as well as politics. It is a vision of the ideal of community life perfected and the essence of the practical meaning of Christianity.

The attitudes and values Dewey associated with the democratic ideal include respect for the absolute worth of the individual and opportunity for all to develop their distinctive capacities. He urged faith in the potentialities of human nature and in the capacity of all persons for self-government if proper conditions for education are provided. In his view, a democracy seeks to develop autonomous creative individuals, but it also demands of all a high degree of social responsibility. Dewey rejected the idea of an atomistic and self-centered individualism, teaching instead that the individual and the community are interdependent. The self finds fulfillment in and through relationship and participation in the community life. He put special emphasis on sympathy as an essential democratic virtue and taught the practice of tolerance, amicable cooperation, and nonviolence. He opposed all attitudes that cause discrimination against people on the basis of gender, race, religion, class, or ethnic origin and promoted free communication and the sharing of experience across all social boundaries.

As a young philosopher Dewey also closely associated both Christianity and democracy with the experimental method of inquiry and the cooperative scientific search for truth. Democracy, which is opposed to authoritarian and dogmatic approaches to the truth, relies on experience and the experimental method in resolving social and moral conflicts. Regarding Christianity, Dewey asserted that God and the truth are one and that historically Christianity has been centrally concerned with the revelation of truth. He further reasoned that living Christianity in the modern world is to be identified with the continuing discovery, communication, and embodiment in human society of liberating truth, which is made possible by democracy and the experimental method. Democracy and experimentalism are in this view the leading forces for the social liberation and spiritual unification of humanity. With these liberal thoughts in mind, Dewey's Christian faith was gradually transformed into a faith in the democratic way of life and social intelligence. His work as a pragmatist clarified his understanding of the experimental method and deepened his faith in experience and intelligence.

When in the 1890s Dewey abandoned his neo-Hegelian idea of God and the church, he retained a deep interest in religious experience and maintained what he described as a religious faith in democracy and intelligence. His new naturalistic humanism was a form of religious humanism. Throughout his life he held the conviction that a person who followed the democratic way of life would find the meaning and the fulfillment he had formerly associated with the Christian way of life and relationship to God. His mature empirical and naturalistic understanding of religious experience and faith is set forth in *The Quest for Certainty* (1929) and *A Common Faith* (1934).

In *A Common Faith* Dewey tried to distinguish religion from what he called the religious quality of experience. He used the noun "religion" as a strictly collective term that refers to the many institutional religions with their diverse creeds and rituals. The religious quality of experience, he explained, is not necessarily connected to any religion, and he wanted to emancipate the religious from religion. He also wanted to free it from connection with the supernatural. The religious quality of experience may be fully explained by reference to natural conditions and causes. In addition, religious experience is not to be conceived as a special kind of experience separate from aesthetic, scientific, moral, or political experience or companionship and friendship. It is not the result of interaction with some distinctly religious object like a supernatural deity.

Dewey explained that many different kinds of natural human experience may have a religious "effect" or "force" that gives to a person's experience a distinctly religious quality. Experiences with a religious effect are those which precipitate a unification of self and of self and world, awakening a sense of inner peace and harmony with the world. Experience acquires a religious quality when the self achieves a deep enduring adjustment in life, involving a sense of the meaning and value of existence that can carry one through times of loss and tragedy. The kind of profound unification of self and adjustment that Dewey associated with religious experience involves a person's whole being.

A religious unification of the self may come about in a wide variety of ways according to Dewey. He found from his own life experience that certain passages of poetry, sustained philosophical reflection, and devotion to a cause may all have a religious effect. Many different things may acquire religious meaning and value in the life of different people. The search for knowledge, the struggle for justice, dedication to creative art work, human friendship, and relations with nature may each have a unifying effect, transforming the quality of a person's experience. In all of this one finds Dewey, like Martin Buber, trying to identify the realm of religious experience with the everyday world of natural relations with persons, nature, and the ideals that inspire creative work and moral commitment.

Dewey believed the most fundamental source of a deep enduring adjustment is a religious faith, which he defined as a commitment of the whole self to a unified inclusive vision of the ideal. In other words, a religious faith is a unifying moral faith. A moral faith involves being possessed in the deeper center of the self by an imaginative vision of the ideal, and it becomes religious in character when the object of faith is a comprehensive ideal that can unify the self as well as self and world.

When religious faith is understood in this fashion, there can be no basic conflict between science and faith. Religious faith leaves to science the business of establishing matters of fact. It is committed unalterably only to the value of discovering the ideal possibilities of existence and working to actualize the ideal. It is concerned with creation of a future, not with propositions about the past. Dewey explains that authentic ideals are real possibilities of nature projected as desirable goals by the idealizing imagination, and in this sense there is continuity between the real and the ideal in nature. Scientific inquiry may cause adjustments in some aspects of the vision of the ideal. However, science cannot alter humanity's capacity to devote itself to the quest for the ideal.

What attracted most attention in *A Common Faith* was Dewey's proposal for an empirical and naturalistic understanding of God or the divine. Dewey did not insist on the use of God language, but he argued that it could have social and religious value for many people and he wanted to clarify how a religious humanist might use it. First, Dewey identified God with the inclusive ideal, that is, the object of a religious moral faith. Second, he argued that an empirical concept of God should include all those conditions and processes in nature, the self, and society which contribute to the uniting of the ideal and the real. Dewey noted that God has historically been associated with the ideal and with those forces that work for the good in history. However, he was careful to point out that as an empirical naturalist he does not mean to suggest that God is a being, a unified reality, or transcendent. The natural and social forces that constitute God are all part of the one world of nature, and they are unified only in the imaginative vision of people and through human effort. Dewey proposed using God language simply as a kind of poetic language designed to inspire commitment to the ideal and to focus energy.

In developing his understanding of a religious attitude toward life, Dewey also argued that a vital religious faith, which is concerned with realizing the ideal possibilities of life, should include an attitude of piety toward nature. As an evolutionary naturalist Dewey had a keen sense of the interdependence of humanity and nature. He wanted to avoid the two extremes of a romantic idealization of nature and a defiant atheism that views nature as indifferent or hostile to humanity. His middle way involved an attitude of heartfelt respect for nature. It recognized that although nature includes imperfections and obstacles to human well-being, it is also the source of all ideal possibilities and of the quest for the ideal as well as the locus of all realizations of the ideal. In the struggle to unify the ideal and the real, Dewey urged humanity to see itself as a cooperating part of a larger whole. Reflecting the influence of poets such as William Wordsworth and Walt Whitman, Dewey's natural piety was deepened over the years by emotional intuitions and intense aesthetic experiences of a mystical nature. These experiences instilled in him a profound sense of belonging to the larger universe including feelings of cosmic trust and inner peace.

Dewey entitled his lectures on religious experience *A Common Faith* because his objective was to make explicit what he understood to be the basic elements of the common faith of men and women throughout history in all cultures with a highly developed moral consciousness. His argument was that the essence of a vital religious faith has always been a concern to envision the ideal possibilities of life and to actualize the ideal. Ideals have often been projected onto a transcendent God for safekeeping, but ideals have their actual origin in the world of relations between people and with nature, and it is in this world they must be realized if they are to be secure. Each generation bears responsibility for conserving, expanding, and transmitting the heritage of values it has received so that future generations receive this heritage more securely established and widely shared. This for Dewey is the essence of the religious attitude and faith he worked to promote. It is all one with what he meant by a faith in the democratic way of life and social intelligence. Dewey believed that such a faith coupled with respect for nature was the only hope for freedom, justice, peace, and global community in a multicultural world. Furthermore, his experience had taught him that those who commit themselves wholeheartedly to this way of life will find their lives sustained and elevated by the natural grace that is the religious quality of experience.

The publication of Dewey's religious views in the 1930s sparked lively debate among philosophers and theologians. Conservative religious thinkers rejected Dewey's thinking as secularism and atheism. Reinhold Niebuhr criticized him for not dealing adequately with the problem of evil and for putting too much faith in social intelligence. Some naturalistic humanists strongly objected to his use of God language as inappropriate and confusing. Some liberal theologians, such as Henry Nelson Wieman, were enthusiastic about Dewey's naturalistic approach to an understanding of God, although Wieman urged Dewey to attribute a unity to the being of God that Dewey denied.

At the end of the twentieth century a strong revival of interest in Dewey's philosophy and democratic faith is underway. Wherever men and women are drawn to religious humanism and naturalism in their quest for freedom and community, pursuing a middle way between a supernatural theism and a despairing atheism, Dewey's thought offers insight and inspiration.

Suggested Readings

Writings of John Dewey: *A Common Faith,* in *John Dewey: The Later Works, 1925–1953* (Carbondale: Southern Illinois University Press, 1986), vol. 9, 1-58.

Steven C. Rockefeller, *John Dewey: Religious Faith and Democratic Humanism* (New York: Columbia University Press, 1991).

Robert B. Westbrook, *John Dewey and American Democracy* (Ithaca, N.Y.: Cornell University Press, 1991).

Henry Nelson Wieman

(1884–1975)

Tyron Inbody

Henry Nelson Wieman was the premier empirical philosopher of religion and theologian in the United States between the mid-1920s and the late-1960s. His most important work was done at the Divinity School of the University of Chicago from 1927 to 1946. Wieman's naturalistic theism flowed against the tide of a renewed supernaturalism in Europe and the United States following World War I. He was simultaneously a principal representative of American liberalism in his effort to locate theology within an empirical-naturalistic perspective and a theocentric critic of liberalism in his rejection of its prevailing subjectivism and humanism. Consequently, Wieman represented the epitome of modernism with his method of locating and interpreting theological beliefs within a naturalistic view of reality and an empirical-scientific method, and served as a forerunner of postmodernism in his effort to interpret religious life, practice, and commitment beyond subjectivism and moralism.

Born in Rich Hill, Missouri, in 1884 to a Presbyterian parsonage family, Wieman was raised in a pious but nondogmatic atmosphere. After a few years there and in Kansas, the family moved to the lower San Joaquin Valley of California when Henry was nine. He spent one year at Occidental College and then completed his undergraduate studies at Park College in Missouri (1907), where in his senior year he had an ecstatic experience which refocused his life work from journalism to religious inquiry. Unable to attend Union Theological Seminary in New York because of family needs in California, he attended San Francisco Theological Seminary, and upon graduation (B.D., 1910) won a year's scholarship to study at Jena and Heidelberg with Rudolf Eucken, Wilhelm Windelband, and Ernst Troeltsch.

Although he had no interest in devoting his life to professional ministry, he was ordained and spent two and a half years as a pastor in Missouri and California. He then went to Harvard for two years of doctoral study under

466

W. E. Hocking and Ralph Barton Perry, graduating (1917) with the dissertation "The Organization of Interests." After teaching philosophy at Occidental College (1917–27), he moved to the University of Chicago Divinity School, where he became the leading religious naturalist and empiricist of his era. Upon retirement he spent several years as visiting professor in various institutions, and then established a second career at Southern Illinois University (1956–66). Wieman died of Parkinson's disease in Grinnell, Iowa, at the age of ninety-one.

Numerous thinkers influenced Wieman's thought. Although Calvinism as a system of thought (Charles Hodge) remained thoroughly alien to him, he was deeply influenced by Calvinist sensibilities on such matters as the primacy of faith, the otherness of God, God's omnipresent initiative, and the need for transforming grace which works beyond human effort. In college he was introduced to Immanuel Kant, G. W. Leibniz, G. W. F. Hegel, and Josiah Royce, and during his pastorates was influenced by Henri Bergson's notions of intuition and creativity. Hocking's idea of God and Perry's theory of value were the principal influences at Harvard. Thereafter, George Herbert Mead, Wyndham Lewis, and Morris Cohen influenced him, but he especially studied the works of A. N. Whitehead and John Dewey, the former an influence in the twenties and thirties, the latter shaping his mature empiricism and pragmatism.

Wieman's thought was shaped by at least three theological issues: the vitality of the practical religious life, correct religious beliefs in a scientific age, and the reformation of Christian doctrine. His foremost concern was with what theologians call soteriology. Wieman was trying to find an interpretation of religion most practically useful in dealing with the issues determining human destiny for good or for ill. His intellectual life focused on one single problem: What operates in human life with a character and power such that it will transform human beings as they cannot transform themselves, saving them from evil and leading them to the best that human life can reach, providing they meet the required conditions? Nothing is more important than discerning the true nature of what creates the good of life and therefore commands the self-giving of faith.

His interest in religion, therefore, was not descriptive but normative. Religious inquiry is a search not for what people actually do commit themselves to but for what they rightfully should. Religious faith is not the act of believing doctrines, regardless of their source, but an act of giving oneself to the creative source of human good once one has reliable knowledge about the nature of that reality. His concern for truth was driven first and foremost by his conviction that anything short of truth will lead to suicide if not corrected. His prophetic and Calvinistic search for an objectivity, ultimacy, and singleness which transcends any kind of idolatry put him in close sympathy with the early-twentieth-century Barthian revolution against the humanism of much liberal religious thought.

Wieman was concerned about the truth of religious belief in an age of science. As a philosopher of religion he sought a clarity and certainty of belief that was characteristic of the modernist project—a search above all for the sake of religious living, but also for objective certainty in a period of the supremacy of scientific method and truth. If, as he believed, traditional religious beliefs about the existence of a supernatural divine being are false, then the methods and criteria of science should be used to determine what in fact works in human life with truly sustaining and saving power.

Finally, Wieman wanted to reform the beliefs of the Christian church. He distinguished between the actual content of religious beliefs and practices and the formal, clarifying concepts of religion. The former, though primary, will be confused, blundering, and false until clarified by the philosopher of religion. Although he did not separate them, there is a seeming dichotomy between human beings in the act of worship and human beings in the act of inquiry. We have no right to believe anything beyond the evidence. The religious inquirer, therefore, is a critic and corrector of belief. The task of the philosopher of religion is not to defend cherished beliefs or win the cultured despisers to faith but to test and determine the truth in matters of religious belief. Thus Wieman was equally critical of orthodoxy, neoorthodoxy, and liberalism insofar as they held to cherished beliefs instead of seeking the truth.

Wieman, though known as a philosopher of religion, was nevertheless a theologian. There were a number of theological themes Wieman explored throughout his career: the nature of religious faith, religious liberalism, theological naturalism, empirical method in theology, theory of value, and God.

Religious faith is a commitment to the true nature of that reality to which we should give ourselves without reservation. The problem of living is not being religious; the problem is to commit oneself with completeness to what truly is the source of all human good, and to get knowledge of its nature and its demands so that we can intelligently avoid disloyalty to it and provide the conditions it requires. Wieman's primary focus is not the experience of the holy or a supernatural being but the experience of rebirth, which points not to a transcendent realm but manifests a creativity operating in the human mind and in interpersonal relations. The correct understanding of God is important because when the error is an error of ultimate faith, thus misdirecting the use of our power, self-destruction is sure to follow sooner or later. Ultimately for Wieman faith both precedes and judges the life of reason, however much one insists upon the need to employ critical reason to clarify and discipline the act of faith.

Wieman was a theological liberal in the sense that he was a religious seeker who would not deliberately hold any religious belief on the ground of the authority of tradition; religious beliefs must be supported by rational consistency on the one hand and observed events on the other. At the same time he moved far from the liberalism of his day, which preached and put faith in religion, religious values, and religious experience. His thought was a reform within liberalism, the relinquishment of the Kantian rationale for religion as ethics, and a recovery of a more concrete, empirical note, intending to restore the objective reference within religious experience.

Wieman was a naturalist both in his metaphysics and his epistemology. Naturalism is a metaphysics of events—the affirmation that all causal efficacy is rooted in temporal and spatial events—and an epistemology that demands some observed order of events as an indispensable part of the evidence for any proposition held to be true. Although a metaphysical naturalist, his naturalism was based not on a dogmatic metaphysical claim about nature (there is only one story not two to reality), but on an epistemological approach which, looking at observable events and qualities and structured relationships, claimed this realm to be the limit of human knowledge. The source of human good which should command religious faith must be either identical with or necessarily connected with some order of events actually going on in life, in society, in history—hence, a process. His is a religious naturalism in the sense that the reality to which the religious commitment is made is interpreted as an order of actual, temporal, spatial, material events. What distinguished his naturalism from other naturalisms, apart from his religious commitments, had to do with the metaphysical status of qualities, which will be discussed below.

Wieman, as a product of his time, believed that the empirical method the sciences had developed and perfected for dealing with the facts of experience provided a kind of certainty which religious people could ill afford not to appropriate for the sake of religion. Evidence according to naturalists has two parts: logical consistency (noncontradiction) between propositions held to be true, and conformity between any proposition held to be true and some observed order of events which exemplifies directly or indirectly what the proposition affirms. Wieman is most consistently a naturalistic empiricist in his characterization of concrete reality as creative process, the living situation taken in its concrete wholeness as event.

He set forth his empirical method in his first two books, where he stated that the knowledge of God must be ultimately subjected to scientific method, the method by which truth and error are discriminated and knowledge verified. The error of a proposition can be corrected and its truth tested only by checking it against some observed order of events. Although one cannot correct error or discover truth merely by observation of events—because reason, imagination, intuition, sensitivity, and other factors must come into action in the religious search, after the right kind of proposition (theory) has been brought forth in the imagination through this complex process—the final testing of it must always be some order of events directly or indirectly observed. Truth consists of concepts put into the form of beliefs which can be verified by way of experimental operations of observed events. As he moved from his earlier interest in Whitehead's speculative metaphysics toward more empirical and observational thinking, he became more pragmatic in his claim that ideas are not disclosures of the inner being or the ultimate nature of reality but are instrumentally useful in adjusting to the environment, a point anticipating the late-twentieth-century idea that reason is an interpretation of the environment and not a picturing of reality.

In his early books Wieman used the term "mysticism" to describe the kind of experience he appealed to for religious knowledge. For him, however, mysticism referred simply to a certain way of experiencing the world of empirical fact, namely, the immediate awareness of the fullness of some concrete experience. He became fearful that such a term would degenerate into sentimentality and vagueness, the opposite of the empirical method. Thus, the way to proceed was to narrow the search to what can be empirically known with clarity and certainty. That search focused on the interpretation of value which can be experimentally determined and delineated. The interpretation of value, he believed, is the one line of inquiry that, when followed far enough, leads directly to the goal of religious faith. This goal can be understood in two different senses, either as the highest ideal good yet to be achieved in the realm of possibility (humanism) or as the creative source of all good rooted in existence (religious naturalism).

Wieman's procedure was to explore the nature of value so far as it can be found in the process of events, then trace that process to its source. Qualities and experienced events are identical. Value is defined as qualitative meaning, the connection between events whereby present happenings enable the person to feel not only the intrinsic quality to the event itself but also the qualities of many other events related to them, which is the only intrinsic good. Although values have to do with qualities, they are not merely subjective. Qualities are "out there" in the world, as objective and existential as matter or energy or anything else. They are no more "in the mind" than the earth or sea or sky is "in the mind" of one who experiences them. Everything we experience in the world is determined by its relation to many other strands of existence, all mutually determining one another. Event is quality, quality is event, and event-quality is the ultimate ontological reality. Wieman explored for its theological significance the process that creates value in the local situation, in the life of the individual, society, and history. The source, the genesis, of qualitative meaning is the creative event, the empirical location of the meaning of God.

Wieman defined God in terms of concrete experience and offered a naturalistic interpretation of God's reality. Any interpretation of God not derived from and identified with a process of existence can be nothing more than an ungrounded construction of the imagination. Likewise, ideal possibilities are fantasies unless they can be derived from some process of existence. Therefore, all attempts to begin with ideal possibilities, the cosmic whole of things, revelation, or any other transcendental realm as though it were the realm of the divine, is doomed to failure. God can be found only in existence. "Whatever else the word God may mean, it is a term used to designate that Something upon which human life is most dependent for its security, welfare and increasing abundance. That there is such a Something cannot be doubted. The mere fact that human life happens, and continues to happen, proves that this Something, however unknown, does certainly exist." The divine is an immanent and finite creativity at work within the evolving universe. God is that feature of our total environment which most vitally affects the continuance and welfare of human life. "God is this most subtle and intimate complexity of environmental nature which yields the greatest good when right adjustment is made."

The character of events that distinguishes God from human and every other kind of reality is a kind of creativity. In his earlier writings, the naturalistic equivalent to the idea of God is the "progressive integration" or "creative" or "progressive synthesis" at work throughout the universe. Later, Wieman focused his naturalistic definition of God more in terms of the "creative event" or "creative interchange" between humans. He moved from God as Whitehead's principle of concretion, which provides order to the creative activity throughout the evolving universe and wholeness in human beings, to defining God empirically in human relationships, what transforms human beings within the natural world.

His later concept narrows even more, from creativity in human psychology to the way creativity works in human communication, culminating in the fourfold creative event which distinguishes God. Creative transformation consists of increasing (1) the range and diversity of what the person can know, (2) the ability to understand appreciatively other persons and peoples, (3) the freedom of the person in the sense of one's ability to absorb any cause acting upon oneself, and (4) the capacity of the person to integrate a great diversity of experiences.

One must, therefore, emphasize the instrumental character of his concept of God. God is the movement, not the mover—a claim analogous to the statement that gravity is not an occult force that moves objects but an observable behavior between events. God is not the product of speculative metaphysics but is the name for the behavior of the universe that is creative. God empirically described is the form (structure, character) of actual events which distinguishes the source of all human good so far as this source cooperates in a way qualitatively different from human operations and produces values more important for human existence and human improvement than those humans can produce on their own initiative. Thus Wieman distinguishes between the created good and the creative good, between what is created and what creates.

Wieman was so preoccupied with and emphatic about the objective reality of God that Charles Clayton Morrison, editor of the *Christian Century,* referred to him in the thirties as "the American Barth." Yet his naturalistic concept of God caused him to deny that God is personal (traditional theism), that there is a final causality (teleology), and that there is any cosmic conservation of value (as in Charles Hartshorne and Schubert Ogden).

Wieman's influence in his times is apparent in his inclusion in *The Library of Living Theology* (vol. 4: *The Empirical Theology of Henry Nelson Wieman* [1963]), and in his sustained conversations with such religious thinkers as John Dewey, D. C. Macintosh, Max Otto, Robert Calhoun, Walter Marshall Horton, Bernard Meland, Bernard Loomer, and Daniel Day Williams. Wieman's version of empiricism and pragmatism, however, was submerged by existentialism and the analytic movement in philosophy and theology in the 1950s, by Barth's neosupernaturalism, and by Hartshorne's process rationalism when he came to the University of Chicago. Although in contemporary postmodern philosophy of religion and theology many doubt the objective reality of the structure Wieman claimed to find in experience, his influence is still felt today in such theologians as John Cobb, for whom the idea of creative transformation stands at the center of his thought, and Gordon Kaufman's version of naturalism. One can see the direct influence of Wieman on the philosophy of religion in the work of current writers for whom the divine signifies something more than human ideals and aspirations.

472

Suggested Readings

Writings of Henry Nelson Wieman: *Religious Experience and the Scientific Method* (New York: Macmillan, 1926); *The Source of Human Good* (Chicago: University of Chicago Press, 1946); *Intellectual Foundation of Faith* (New York: Philosophical Library, 1961).

Nancy Frankenberry, *Religion and Radical Empiricism* (Albany: State University of New York Press, 1987).

Marvin Shaw, *Nature's Grace: Essays in H. N. Wieman's Finite Theism* (New York: P. Lang, 1995).

Douglas Clyde Macintosh

(1877–1948)

S. Mark Heim

D. C. Macintosh figures prominently in the history of liberal Protestant thought in North America, as one of the leading philosophical theologians of his time. He taught for thirty years at Yale Divinity School, influencing a generation of Protestant thinkers who passed through his classroom, including Reinhold and H. Richard Niebuhr. He developed a distinctive vision of empirical theology, contrasting with the better-known empirical theologies that emanated from the University of Chicago.

In Europe, Schleiermacher's theology grew from the seeds of pietism and rationalism. Macintosh's career illustrates that a similar hybrid grew and flourished independently on American soil. In his evangelical environment doctrinal orthodoxy was presumed, but emphasis fell powerfully on the need for an experience of conversion and transformation to confirm personally these beliefs. The primary impetus to Macintosh's theological liberalism was a confidence that this process could be reversed: Empirical study of religious experience could reconstruct and verify the essentials of Christian faith.

Born in rural Ontario, Canada, Macintosh came from an evangelical Baptist background, leavened with a strong Wesleyan family connection. It is instructive that Macintosh himself recounted two conversion experiences. One, at age ten, he soon after regarded as the product of emotional manipulation. At age fourteen, however, he underwent a profound conversion which satisfied even his strong intellectual cautions and issued in a firm commitment to conform his life to that decision. The continuing reality of this personal faith remained the unshakable reference point for Macintosh's thought, a fact confirmed in his last but perhaps least-known book, *Personal Religion* (1942).

There was a six-year hiatus between Macintosh's high school graduation and his entrance to university. During this time, he worked on his family farm and then taught in one-room schools as well as pastoring a small church. The period from completion of high school through his study at McMaster University and his doctoral work at the University of Chicago was marked by a restless intellectual search for a solid philosophical basis for religious faith. At various times Macintosh entertained radical readings of many traditional theological propositions, but always in search of a certain intellectual foundation for the cognitive validity of religious experience. Themes characteristic of his later work already appear: a focus on religious epistemology, a desire to root theology in empirical facts, an interest in moral values as integral to faith. In his writing, Macintosh devoted much care and space to cataloging philosophical options and suboptions. His books were popular for use as textbooks as much as for their exposition of his views. The encyclopedic format sometimes obscured the fact that this was in large measure the history of a journey: Macintosh had adopted many of these major philosophical stopping points at some stage during his personal search.

He early determined that the essence of Christian evangelical faith could and must stand on grounds other than an appeal to authority, scriptural or ecclesial. Philosophy became his passion, and epistemology his primary theme. Through it he sought for that sure foundation upon which religion could claim its own core of knowledge, knowledge as valid as that in any other area of human life.

His original evangelical context was steeped in a Scottish common-sense realist approach to questions of religious knowledge. During his college days, partly under the influence of the work of William James, he moved briefly toward an agnostic empiricism. What followed was a migration via Kant to speculative idealism. Macintosh arrived at Chicago as a Hegelian of sorts, seeing absolute idealism as the surest ground for theism. He was not converted to the instrumentalist pragmatism of his Chicago philosophy teachers, nor to the radical empiricism of his theological mentor there, George Burman Foster. But he came to share their criticism of idealism, concluding that an idealistic absolute was no adequate substitute for the ordinary believer's empirical insistence on a living God. If idealism ensured God's reality only by collapsing it into the reality of shared human values, Macintosh found a similar failing in radical empiricism, with its agnosticism whether experience had any referent but further experience. His dissertation, "The Revolt Against Metaphysics in Theology," argued that this revolt was mistaken, that theology must seek to connect both experience and values to a metaphysical source. A key article, "Representational Pragmatism" (1912), reflects this emphasis: he agreed with pragmatism to test religious faith by its effective fulfillment of real human need, but he insisted that this usefulness must be taken as verification of the metaphysical reality of the religious object.

Macintosh noted that his studies in a rather traditionalist university had inclined him toward a more radical, empiricist outlook. But doctoral studies at Chicago where such an outlook was standard evoked from him a reaction in favor of a renewed tradition, a "modern evangelicalism." The tension between the two emphases marked the rest of his career. He sought a philosophical perspective that would balance "fundamental religion" (devotion to ideals) and "experimental religion" (dependence on divine reality). God could be defined either as that in which we must believe in order to live the noblest and fullest life or as the reality which produces in us certain predictable effects when we attune ourselves to it. God can be a hypothesis which becomes reasonable because of its effect on our life, including our cognitive life. God can be a fact of our experience, an ensured if highly austere fact we seek to clothe with fuller and richer qualities. Macintosh argued that both are valid cognitive paths, and he developed both in his arguments for the truth of Christian faith.

In 1909 Macintosh took a position at Yale Divinity School, where he would teach and live the rest of his life. With the publication of his first influential work, *The Problem of Knowledge* (1915), his philosophical position had reached a settled form, substantially identical to that extended much later in *The Problem of Religious Knowledge* (1940). The two stand as bookends to his philosophical career. He called his position critical monistic realism: "realism" because he objected to any epistemology that denied independent reality to the objects of knowledge; "monistic" because he insisted that some features of this independent reality are in fact immediately grasped in our perception; "critical" because he denied we have any unmediated perceptions and therefore must distinguish in experience what is accurate and what attaches to our projections. The constant feature in Macintosh's religious epistemology was an insistence that faith be rooted in reliable knowledge of God—not knowledge of our idea of God, not knowledge of "divine" values, not knowledge of the usefulness of acting as if there were a God. This conviction seems to have influenced many of his students who went on to a neoorthodox perspective. Despite Macintosh's consistent emphasis on religious experience, he regarded religious experience always as a medium, never as itself the substance of faith.

After serving as a chaplain and YMCA worker in World War I, Macintosh returned to Yale. His war experience and later reflections on it would lead to a decision that made him famous far outside the academic world:

his application for United States citizenship was rejected because he declined to promise unequivocally to bear arms in future conflicts, reserving the right to judge the morality of each instance. The case attracted wide attention and was carried to the Supreme Court, which in 1931 confirmed his exclusion from citizenship. That precedent was eventually overturned, but too late to affect Macintosh.

He published *Theology as an Empirical Science* (1919), followed in 1926 by *The Reasonableness of Christianity*. The first attempted to specify—to the point of equationlike formulas—what dependable results could be expected when humans adopted the "right religious adjustment." The adjustment he described was plainly a generalized pattern drawn from evangelical Protestant piety. Relations between individuals and God were qualitative and imprecise, but still experimentally testable and quantifiable in broad terms. Theology was a science based on the testing of religious hypotheses in experience. Macintosh emphasized that the data of this science could only be gathered by acting on the religious hypothesis, by behaving in prayer and morality as if the divine reality were dependable so as to see what effect followed. He was much criticized for abandoning Christian tradition, particularly in regard to Christology. In principle, Macintosh did not regard the historicity of Jesus as a necessary presupposition of Christian faith. How could a mere change in historical opinion make one cease to be a Christian, he asked, if Christianity were a living fact of one's own religious experience? In practice, he was fully confident that Jesus was the supreme embodiment of right religious adjustment to God and so could rightly occupy the central place in Christian experience.

Macintosh was clear that theology as an empirical science could establish only a rather generic core of truth, which it was appropriate to fill out with biblical faith beyond what could be empirically verified. This was central to Macintosh's extended arguments with Henry Nelson Wieman and John Dewey. He objected that they were mistaken to limit themselves to the impoverished conception of deity that could be philosophically confirmed. *Reasonableness,* rather than adopt the empirical strategy of confirming that a dependable divine factor exists to which humans can adjust and then supplementing this empirical theology with speculation, instead begins with a rather full definition of what God is and proceeds to argue for the reasonableness of this postulate on the basis of the life which it makes possible. Macintosh called this an argument from moral optimism, which paralleled rather than opposed the empirical approach.

At the end of his career, Macintosh viewed the rise of neoorthodoxy with some dismay. After the brothers Niebuhr offered critical contributions to a

Festschrift for their old teacher, Macintosh engaged them in an intense series of articles that outlined certain ironic features of his liberalism and their renewed orthodoxy. The brothers attacked Macintosh for excessive optimism about human moral values as an index to the divine and criticized him for watering down theological truths to philosophical generalities in search of an illusory certainty. But Macintosh chided the Niebuhrs for undermining Christian convictions by defending traditionalist doctrines only as vehicles for psychological and social insight, "mythical" truth, while surrendering all metaphysical claims. If "liberalism" was an invidious label, Macintosh maintained it applied to the neoorthodox more than to him.

The relative obscurity which claimed his thought after his death (1948) stemmed partly from its complexity, but partly from its mediating character. It served many as a bridge, few as a home. Acknowledged as a great teacher, Macintosh had no direct disciples. His philosophical rigor helped keep alive the hope for an intellectual brief for the core of Christian orthodoxy, a hope which was most dramatically fulfilled in the next generation by those who made the case in a very different, more existential manner. His influence lived on in those like his successor at Yale, Julian Hartt, who continued to grapple with an empirical approach to theology. So long as that great strand of American thought that runs from Jonathan Edwards to William James and John Dewey continues to be a source of renewed theological reflection, Macintosh's work will merit rediscovery for its shrewd insights into that tradition and for the breadth of his own version of it.

Suggested Readings

Writings of D. C. Macintosh: "Toward a New Untraditional Orthodoxy," in *Contemporary American Theology: Theological Autobiographies*, vol. 1, ed. Vergilius Ferm (New York: Round Table Press, 1932); *Theology as an Empirical Science* (New York: Macmillan, 1919); *The Problem of Religious Knowledge* (New York: Harper & Brothers, 1940).

S. Mark Heim, "The Path of a Liberal Pilgrim: A Theological Biography of Douglas Clyde Macintosh" [Parts I and II], *American Baptist Quarterly* 2 (1983): 236-55, and 4 (1985): 300-320.

Preston Warren, *Out of the Wilderness: Douglas Clyde Macintosh's Journeys Through the Grounds and Claims of Modern Thought* (New York: P. Lang, 1989).

Charles Hartshorne

(1897–)

Delores J. Rogers

Charles Hartshorne belongs to that wing of the American Empirical Movement which concentrates on the rational and necessary structures making possible any or every empirical or concrete situation. Necessary structures are not to be confused with the natural laws which apply only to this world. A world different from ours could have a different pattern or set of laws. Necessary structures refer to structures necessary if there is to be any—not just this particular—contingent universe. According to Hartshorne, the proper sphere of metaphysics is that of ascertaining what are the necessary structures supporting continuity and change in any possible world. While it is not necessary that any particular concrete event be part of any and every particular universe, it is necessary that every conceivable universe have both abstract and consequent (concrete) aspects.

Hartshorne was born into a well-to-do family with strong liberal leanings. His grandfather had been a Quaker and his father, Francis, received both his B.A. and M.A. from Haverford College, a Quaker institution. Francis became an Episcopal priest and Charles grew up listening to the sensible, rational sermons of a kindly nonfundamentalist interpreter of the Christian tradition. His mother Marguerite's sane and unselfish outlook on life also influenced him.

These family influences were important to the kind of philosopher-theologian Hartshorne became. A home where a kindly, cultivated, religious rationality reigned would not be fertile ground for the radical angst central to existentialist theologians on the continent. Though the novelty of Hartshorne's vision cannot be explained by his background, it is surely no accident that he has spent so much of his adult life trying to explicate in a sane and rational fashion the meaning of God. Growing up, as he did, in the relative peace and security of a Pennsylvania parsonage, Hartshorne's exposition never conveys the emotionally shattering experiences which seemed to shape much of continental theology.

It is only fair to add, however, that even a casual reader of Hartshorne's works can see that the "Consequent Nature of God" in his thought is an original attempt to put into reasoned language the poetic mythology of the passion of Christ. If the Christian tradition is clear and true to itself when it affirms that the figure of Jesus teaches something about God, then something like Hartshorne's "Consequent Nature" is almost demanded. The "Consequent Nature" is an attempt to come to terms with the God who is with humankind in its sufferings and, of course, in its everydayness and its moments of joy as well.

As a young student at Yeates, a small private school, Hartshorne was attracted to the study of nature. From Yeates, Hartshorne went to Haverford College. From both his father and his elementary school teachers, Hartshorne grew up accepting the idea that evolution was God's way of working in the world. On the other hand, until 1918, Hartshorne accepted in an uncritical fashion that the world was composed of a dualism of inanimate nature and mind. While working as an orderly in France at the end of his second year at Haverford, he sat and surveyed the countryside. As he looked out at the scene in front of him, the influence of the romantic poets, especially Wordsworth, and the philosophy of Emerson coalesced. Nature, as Hartshorne understood it at that moment, is constituted by feelings. Nature is not lifeless matter; at its most elementary level, nature is composed of sentient processes. As a young instructor at Harvard, where he had finished his undergraduate work and earned an M.A. and a Ph.D., Hartshorne found this view of nature confirmed by Charles Peirce and Alfred North Whitehead.

Following Whitehead's lead, Hartshorne made plain that this idea does not mean that trees and rocks are feeling subjects or that they think. Rocks and trees do not have feelings, but the individual units of rocks or trees have feeling or sentience, admittedly of a very low level. The rocks and trees are democratic societies, because feeling can be attributed to the individual units making up the rock or the tree but not to the tree or rock as a unit. Personal societies, however, have a dominant strand which influences the rest of the members of the society. This dominant strand at its most advanced is properly referred to as mind. Human beings are personal ordered societies. The dominant strand within a personal society receives its genetic character or distinctiveness from the way in which each member of the dominant strand remembers or prehends (to remember or perceive) their common past.

The realization that all of reality is sentient and at its more advanced level mental or rational (panpsychism) is basic to Hartshorne's thought. He also derived from Whitehead the basic notion of asymmetrical relations. The full impact of this notion hit him during his teaching career at the University of Chicago (1928–55): The present can inherit characteristics from the past, but can in no way re-create or change the past. The past is given. Although one can reassess one's relation to the past, the past itself—however adequately or inadequately perceived or remembered—cannot be changed. Simply stated, A can influence its descendant B, but B can in no way influence its predecessor A. The continuity and determinate character of our world are dependent on asymmetrical relations. Freedom and change are due in part from the way in which the already-determined past is assimilated in order to make concrete or actual a new possibility.

At the University of Chicago, and especially after receiving a dual appointment in the Divinity School and the philosophy department, Hartshorne began to influence a whole new generation of theologians, including John Cobb and Schubert Ogden. His influence on Process Theology continued during his years at Emory (1955–62) and the University of Texas, and continues even today.

For Hartshorne, the fact that the world exhibits rational continuity is one reason for asserting there must be "Someone" who has set the basic structure of our world. Hartshorne heard Martin Heidegger lecture in Germany, but the American was never able to appreciate the basic metaphysical question asked by the German philosopher. Hartshorne denies that Heidegger's question, Why is there "Something" rather than "Nothing"? is meaningful. For Hartshorne, one can question why this contingent actuality rather than that contingent actuality, but one cannot seriously ask why something is as opposed to why nothing. "Nothingness" is basically a nonsensical concept, since the world is filled with somethings. One, however, can ask what kind of necessary being is needed for there to be somethings and a world of structure and freedom.

Hartshorne argues for the existence of God on the basis of rational design and contingency. He also revives the ontological argument of Anselm. His reasons for reviving the argument begin with the intuitive belief that there is something rather than nothing, and that this something is basically mental (panpsychism). He further believes the human mind can know the structure necessary for any contingent world. For Hartshorne, what Anselm had overlooked was that God necessarily has a primordial and a consequent nature. For Hartshorne, the God known by rational thought is both perfectly abstract and perfectly relative.

This organizing mind, or God, is both the basis of all other sentient entities and itself a person. As person, God contains all other sentient actualities in itself as a human body contains individual cells. The world is God's body. On this last point Hartshorne seems to be in general agreement with Bradley and other Absolute Idealists. He parts company with them by insisting that the individual cells determine their own actualization. Freedom is a real constituent factor in the universe and each actual entity is self-created. God's organizing structure and the relevant past entities provide the material which each actual entity prehends in a unique way in its becoming.

Hartshorne understands Becoming, as opposed to Being, to be the fundamental metaphysical reality. God's concrete or consequent nature is the prior reality; God's primordial nature is an abstraction from that concrete reality. For thinkers who hold to the priority of being, a being (or substance) is that substratum that endures through time with changing accidents. For process thinkers who hold to the priority of becoming, the enduring character of existents is caused by the fact that each unit of experience is prehended by a following unit. A chain of events through time linked together by the form of prehension called memory, and exhibiting markedly persisting characteristics, is a person. A human being is a person and God is a person. They differ in that a human being is a chain of a limited number of prehensions of the past. In God's consequent nature or aspect, God prehends (preserves in memory) the entirety of all past entities. The character of a person, whether a finite person or God, arises from the abstracting from a personal chain of events of the prominent characteristics of that chain.

Classical theism thought of God as the prime exemplar of being. The neoclassical theism espoused by Hartshorne understands God as the prime exemplar of becoming. Classical theism held that God was perfect substance and could not possibly change. This gave a certain security to the religious person who could trust a perfect and enduring God, but this notion of perfection also left classical theism with the puzzle of how it was possible for God to be affected by human beings. If God was affected, this would mean change and if God were perfect—so ran the logic—God could not possibly change. Some thought to overcome this difficulty by defining God's omniscience in such a way as to include knowledge of future events. Thus in God's perfect foreknowledge God was already affected by all future contingent events. For Hartshorne this leads to the only possible conclusion, that is, that future events are predetermined. For Hartshorne, if God from all eternity knows in advance what will happen, then there can be no real freedom in the universe. History and the empirical universe become a sham.

Hartshorne also rejects the classical doctrine of omnipotence. If God has all the power, then human beings have no power to choose. Human responsibility has no meaning. Whatever choices human beings may seem to make are not real choices, because only God has the power to determine what will happen. Religion may consider a God of unsurpassing power important, but a God with all the power in the universe leaves no room for free actions by other entities and thus undermines the moral sense necessary for religions. Augustine's doctrine of grace as well as Calvin's predestination are examples of reasoning from omnipotence. For Hartshorne, neoclassical theism addresses the issue of human freedom and God's knowledge and power in a way that is satisfactory to religion in the notion of dual transcendence. God is both absolute and relative in ways that are unsurpassable by any other entity.

Hartshorne uses his concept of dual transcendence to revise the notion of omnipotence. Hartshorne envisions God, as absolute, as having all the power necessary to hold any possible universe together. Nothing can surpass God in power. Perfect power means that God has all the power necessary for the preservation of our world but does not deny that other beings also have power. Human decision and moral responsibility are thus possible. Furthermore the doctrine of dual transcendence means that God is the only person absolutely affected by the freedom of others. God both suffers and enjoys all the decisions of others. As absolute, God envisions all possibilities. In God's consequent or concrete nature, God perfectly prehends all actuality resulting from creaturely decision. Omniscience in this formula comes to mean that at any given time, God absolutely knows all actualities and all potentiality. As primordial or abstract, God knows perfectly all that could be known at any given moment. In God's consequent state, or concrete actuality, God's knowledge continues to increase as new entities are actualized. The world is social and bound together by the love of God, who both sets the conditions for finite existence and freedom and accepts as an eternal part of God the results of that freedom.

Suggested Readings

Writings of Charles Hartshorne: *Man's Vision of God and the Logic of Theism* (Hamden, Conn.: Archon Books, 1964; repr. of 1941 ed.); *The Logic of Perfection and Other Essays in Neoclassic Metaphysics* (La Salle, Ill.: Open Court, 1962); *Anselm's Discovery* (La Salle, Ill.: Open Court, 1965); *Creative Synthesis and Philosophic Method* (London: S.C.M. Press, and La Salle, Ill.: Open Court, 1970); *Wisdom as Moderation: a Philosophy of the Middle Way* (Albany: State University of New York Press, 1984).

Edward J. Carnell

(1919–1967)

George M. Marsden

Edward J. Carnell was one of the bright intellectual stars of the "new evangelical" movement in the two decades following World War II. Carnell's most important contributions to theology are found in a series of volumes on apologetics. For a brief time, one of the leading spokespersons for evangelicals in American ecumenical circles, he was known for his frank criticisms of some leading figures in mainline Protestantism. He also became known for some sharp critiques of fundamentalism.

The loyal but always ambivalent son of a Baptist fundamentalist pastor, Carnell is a classic example of someone who wrestled throughout his career with the intellectual implications of his fundamentalist heritage. His interest in intellectual matters was first stimulated at Wheaton College in Illinois under the tutelage of Gordon Haddon Clark. A conservative Calvinist philosopher, Clark emphasized the intellectual integrity and rational defensibility of traditional Protestant teaching. Clark encouraged Carnell to study at Westminster Theological Seminary in Philadelphia, where Carnell worked principally with the Dutch-American Calvinist apologist Cornelius Van Til and the Scottish systematic theologian John Murray. These influences left a distinctly Reformed stamp on his theology, although Carnell always remained a Baptist whose loyalties favored a more broadly Reformed interdenominational evangelical coalition, rather than any strictly defined orthodoxy.

Graduating from Westminster in 1944, Carnell determined to understand firsthand the modern threats to such conservative theology by entering the Th.D. program at Harvard Divinity School. There he wrote his dissertation "The Concept of Dialectic in the Theology of Reinhold Niebuhr," receiving his degree in 1948. In the meantime he had simultaneously undertaken Ph.D. work in philosophy at Boston University, where he worked with the noted philosophical personalist, Edgar Sheffield Brightman and wrote his dissertation "The Problem of Verification in Søren

Kierkegaard" (1949). At Harvard and Boston University Carnell considered he had shown that Reformed or Calvinist orthodoxy could be successfully defended against the best in modern thought. During this time (when he was also pastoring a small church or teaching part-time or full-time at Gordon College) he also wrote his first book, *An Introduction to Christian Apologetics* (1948). This volume received a much acclaimed $5,000 (a good year's salary) "Evangelical Book Award" from the publisher, William B. Eerdmans Publishing Company.

This remarkable set of achievements before he was thirty years old catapulted him into the forefront of the nascent movement to transform "fundamentalism" back into "evangelicalism." In 1949 Carnell joined the recently founded Fuller Theological Seminary in California where he was formally allied with Carl F. H. Henry and Harold J. Ockenga, two other leaders of what for a time became known as the "new evangelicalism." One goal of the movement, especially as Carnell understood it, was to bring fundamentalism back into the traditions of classical Augustinian orthodoxy. Carnell saw his own mission as being especially to lead the movement back into intellectual respectability and apologetic feasibility.

Carnell's prominence in the movement was enhanced when in 1954 at age thirty-five he became president of Fuller Theological Seminary. Fuller Seminary had emerged as a leading intellectual center for the new evangelical movement. Several of its faculty had close ties with Billy Graham, thus giving the movement a substantial popular base and lending plausibility to its leaders' declarations that they might even spark a Christian renewal of the nation. To build a broad base for such a revival, Graham found it necessary by 1956 to break with the narrowly separatist aspects of his fundamentalist roots. Carnell's intellectual contributions should be viewed in this context of the new evangelicals' larger hopes to transform the culture. Like Graham, Carnell hoped to help turn the nation around by effectively presenting essential gospel teachings, while jettisoning what he considered the counterproductive peculiarities of fundamentalism.

Carnell's most significant theological contributions are found in four books on apologetics published between 1948 and 1960. In these there is a definite progression in his thought, although the four are also complementary. Each developed more or less the same general argument, that traditional Christianity provides the hypothesis or worldview that is most consistent both in its own internal logic and in its correspondence to our actual experience. In *An Introduction to Christian Apologetics*, he followed roughly the path of his early mentor, Gordon Clark, in emphasizing the "systematic consistency" of Christianity, particularly with respect to the inescapable law of noncontradiction. Christianity best explains the place of humans in the cosmos. For instance, the hypothesis that humans and the universe were created as the Bible claims, despite problems in its empirical verification, explains far more than does its opposite. It explains how there can be apparent order in the universe, despite its extreme diversity. It also explains how there can be meaning in human hopes and aspirations, despite human finitude. Thus Christianity provides the most satisfactory response to the human "soul-sorrow" that arises from the disparity between human aspirations and limitations.

In *A Philosophy of the Christian Religion* (1952), Carnell broadened his argument for the superiority of Christianity by emphasizing the human need for values to live by. People must, of course, test purported revelations to ensure they are not inconsistent with rationality or empirical criteria, but reasons of the heart will play a large role in recognizing the authenticity of God's claims. Carnell showed the emptiness and the weaknesses of various values or ideals that humans may live by: pleasure, economic security, science, intellect, humanism, and various inadequate religious ideals, such as commitments to gods that cannot forgive, to a God who forgives everything, or to an institutional church (Roman Catholicism). By contrast, the biblical revelation of a just but loving God who makes it possible for humans to love others provides the most complete set of values to live by.

Carnell's most ambitious and original work was *Christian Commitment* (1957). Once again he sought to find authentication of traditional Christian revelation in universal human experiences that it best explains. This time the common ground was found in the innate human sense of justice or injustice. Carnell provided many illustrations of this sense, from trivial examples of resentment when someone cuts in line ahead of others, to the agony of recognizing the predicament of human helplessness. The Christian worldview, recorded in the Bible, reveals that God is not only a righteous judge who will avenge us, but also a loving savior who will forgive the injustices that we commit.

In *The Kingdom of Love and the Pride of Life*, Carnell found a point of contact in another universal human trait, the need to be loved. His point of departure was modern psychotherapy, which depicts so much of human anxiety in terms of frustrations or distortions of early childhood needs for love. Once again, God's revelation in Christ proves to be the most consistent and fulfilling response to this need. Christ tells us to come to him "as little children" and offers us the acceptance that we so often see thwarted in human relationship. Love, he concluded, is the center of the Christian gospel and should likewise be at the center of apologetics.

Carnell's other most important publication and the one he probably became the best known for was *The Case for Orthodox Theology* (1959). This volume was part of a three-part series presenting the case for liberal theology (L. Harold DeWolf), neoorthodoxy (William Hordern), and conservative Protestantism. That Carnell was asked to write the latter of these volumes (published by a mainline Protestant press) was a sign of the prestige he had attained as a spokesperson for the evangelical cause. He was frequently asked to be the conservative Protestant representative in forums and debates. Carnell's "orthodoxy" meant essentially an American evangelical version of the Reformed theological heritage. He defined his position over against the liberal and neoorthodox options especially by emphasizing that he spoke for "that branch of Christendom which limits the ground of religious authority to the Bible."

The conservative Reformed and formerly fundamentalist heritages with which Carnell identified had adopted biblical "inerrancy" as a fundamental test of the faith. Carnell himself was instrumental in making this standard a part of the required faculty creed in his early days at Fuller Theological Seminary. Also in his critical theological studies growing out of his two doctoral dissertations, published as *The Theology of Reinhold Niebuhr* (1951) and *The Burden of Søren Kierkegaard* (1965), he emphasized the failure of those figures to face up to the objective claims of Christian revelation. In *The Case for Orthodox Theology*, however, he made a point of noting that not all orthodox evangelicals held to the inerrancy of the minute detail of scripture and also suggested ways that more latitude could be built into understanding what sorts of interpretations were entailed by an affirmation of the doctrine of "inerrancy."

More alarming, however, to many of his conservative evangelical allies was that his strongest polemics were not against neoorthodoxy or liberal theology, but against fundamentalism. Carnell polemicized against the "cultic mentality" of fundamentalism. Particularly he singled out J. Gresham Machen (1881–1937), one of the leading forebears of the intellectual dimensions of the new evangelical movement as being unduly dogmatic, combative, and separatist. Carnell's stance fit with the emerging evangelical movement's repudiation of ecclesiastical separatism, marked particularly by Billy Graham's break with fundamentalism. But in the highly charged atmosphere left in the wake of Graham's break, the sharpness of Carnell's tone brought critiques even from some of his friends.

The strain of a seminary presidency, an unabated writing schedule, continued teaching, and controversy was beginning to take its toll. Added to these were deep personal anxieties reflected in some of the insights in his later apologetic books, but which Carnell was increasingly unable to escape. In

1959 he resigned from the presidency of Fuller. In 1961, he suffered a severe psychological collapse. He received a lengthy series of shock treatments, but continued to be plagued by periodic depression. In his later years he continued to write and to teach at Fuller, but he had become a shadow of his former self. He died of an overdose of sleeping pills in a hotel in Oakland, California, where he was scheduled to address a Catholic ecumenical workshop. The coroner declared the death "undetermined whether accidental or suicidal." He was survived by his wife, Shirley (Rowe), and two children.

Carnell's greatest long-term influence probably came from his teaching. A superb lecturer, he inspired a generation of Fuller Seminary students and others to intellectually vigorous and emotionally sensitive expositions of the Christian faith. His writings seem to have had less lasting direct influence. One of his anxieties at the height of his career was that his books, despite their acclaim in some evangelical circles, were not having the watershed impact he had hoped they would. Despite the apparent influences of his apologetic insights in some later evangelical writers, his own works soon dropped largely out of sight. His conservatism with respect to scripture cut him off from most ecumenical circles, and his antifundamentalism cut him off from some conservatives. Others among his more progressive evangelical admirers soon moved beyond him. Furthermore, Carnell's work showed little explicit grounding in any identifiable historical tradition of Christian apologetics. As a spokesperson for a sort of evangelicalism that was attempting to reform the fundamentalist heritage, he set out almost as though he were a man without immediate roots to create a Christian apologetic de novo. His career, however, proved too short for him to create a new school of thought.

Suggested Readings

In addition to Carnell's chief works, already cited, see his collected essays: *The Case for Biblical Christianity*, ed. Ronald N. Nash (Grand Rapids: Wm. B. Eerdmans Publishing Co., 1969).

Gordon R. Lewis, *Testing Christianity's Truth Claims: Approaches to Christian Apologetics* (Chicago: Moody Press, 1976).

Rudolph Nelson, *The Making and Unmaking of an Evangelical Mind: The Case of Edward Carnell* (Cambridge: Cambridge University Press, 1987).

John A. Sims, *Edward John Carnell: Defender of the Faith* (Washington, D.C.: University Press of America, 1979).

Kenneth W. M. Wozniak, *Ethics in the Thought of Edward J. Carnell* (Washington, D.C.: University Press of America, 1983).

Carl F. H. Henry

(1913–)

Roger E. Olson

On 14 February 1977, *Time* magazine declared Carl F. H. Henry "the leading theologian of the nation's growing Evangelical flank." Most observers of postfundamentalist, conservative Evangelicalism (that form of conservative Protestant Christianity strongly distinguishing itself from Fundamentalism) would agree that Henry ranks as its most influential thinker between World War II and the end of the twentieth century. When *Time* featured him in its "Religion" section in 1977, Henry was writing his seven-volume magnum opus *God, Revelation, and Authority* *(Word)*.

According to his autobiography *Confessions of a Theologian* (1986), Carl Ferdinand Howard Henry was born to immigrant German parents in New York City on 22 January 1913. Like most Evangelicals, he traces the beginning of his Christian life to a second birth (Henry is unashamedly a "born again Christian") or "great awakening" on 10 June 1933.

After his conversion, Henry attended Wheaton College in Wheaton, Illinois—a veritable "Mecca" for evangelical Christians wishing to gain higher education apart from the stifling atmosphere of extreme right-wing Fundamentalism or the secular influences of liberal colleges and universities. While studying philosophy at Wheaton, Henry came under the influence of Gordon Clark, a leading conservative Protestant thinker who emphasized reason over emotion and taught that only orthodox Christianity provides a completely coherent world and life philosophy.

Henry graduated from Northern Baptist Seminary in Chicago, entered into ministry with the Northern Baptist Convention (later renamed the American Baptist Churches in the U.S.A.), and eventually earned a Ph.D. from the University of Boston. His mentor there was philosopher of religion Edgar Sheffield Brightman. Throughout the 1940s Henry flew back and forth between Pasadena, California, where he helped found Fuller Theological Seminary, and the Boston area where he taught at Gordon College while working on his doctoral degree. Through these travels and activities, Henry gradually became the center of a growing cohort of conservative Protestant scholars who were dissatisfied with the narrowness and anti-intellectualism of much Fundamentalism and wished for a new identity. This core group, with Henry at its center, founded the Evangelical Theological Society which eschewed literalistic, anti-intellectual Fundamentalism while affirming the inerrancy of the Bible.

Henry's first notable book, *The Uneasy Conscience of Modern Fundamentalism*, appeared in 1947. It symbolized a decisive break between the newer evangelical theology of Henry and his friends and the older Fundamentalism, which continued to exist in increasingly separatistic isolation from the rest of the Christian world.

Throughout his career Henry's main message to both liberals and conservatives in theology has been "Strictly avoid subjectivism!" Everywhere he looked Henry saw modern theology falling into irrelevance due to an overwhelming infection by the viruses of existentialism, privatized religion, emotionalism, and irrationalism. Early in his career Henry criticized Fundamentalism for detaching itself from culture and intellectual endeavors and retreating into a subculture of its own making, thus abdicating influence for good in the wider world. In the middle of his career Henry criticized neoorthodoxy (e.g., Barth, Brunner, Niebuhr) for adopting existentialism as a basis for theological reflection. Henry has consistently, and harshly, objected to liberal theology's "maximal acknowledgment of the claims of modernity" as a form of religious syncretism. Late in his life Henry has turned his harshest attacks against fellow Evangelicals whom he sees as abandoning the only possible safeguard against Christian retreat from objective truth—the full verbal inspiration and inerrancy of Holy Scripture.

Henry's main theological contribution has been as a critical theologian. He has never been particularly interested in theological innovation or even new construction. He has seen himself as a "voice in the wilderness" of modern and postmodern subjectivism, irrationalism, and relativism who cries out for a return to the foundations of authentic Christianity. The first and most basic foundation of all, according to Henry, is the proper relationship between faith and reason. When that is abandoned or distorted— as Henry is convinced has happened in most modern theology—the slide down the slippery slope to irrationality and irrelevance (of Christianity to culture at large) is inevitable.

According to Henry, the only valid approach to religious epistemology, and thus to theological method, is rational presuppositionalism. Every belief system, he argues, begins with certain unprovable but self-evident axioms or presuppositions (what early church father Origen called "first principles"). These exist at the foundations of every science or discipline as well. They are inescapable. However, Henry avers, that does not make them irrational. Rationality itself depends on one such basic law: the law of noncontradiction. This is the most basic, universal canon of all reasonable investigation, argument, and discourse and when abandoned or ignored its absence inevitably leads to cognitive nihilism.

A second axiom or law is closely related to the first and comes into play when evaluating complex systems of belief such as ideologies, worldviews, and systems of theology (whether Christian or not). It is the test of coherence. Insofar as a belief system contains contradictions, it must be judged flawed if not absolutely and utterly false.

These tests, Henry believes, provide the Archimedean standpoint for judging all systems of truth claims, and he takes it as self-evident that there can be only one comprehensive system of truth. If the true system is comprehensive, then every false system must be incoherent (that is, contain contradictions). Any two truly comprehensive systems of truth would be identical and therefore there can be only one.

According to Henry, then, rational presuppositionalism begins with these universal assumptions, without which there could be no testing of truth claims, and proceeds to analyze and evaluate all existing systems of truth. All such systems accept certain basic truths—first principles—on faith. Christianity is no exception. But faith alone cannot justify or falsify systems of belief. That is reason's role and it uses the tools of the laws of logic here mentioned. Henry is confident that, in the end, Christianity turns out to be true not because faith says so but because its belief system (orthodox Protestant Christian theism) provides the most coherent, comprehensive, and self-consistent account of reality which also has greater power to explain human experience than any alternative worldview.

The false alternatives Henry criticizes are (among others) naturalism and its offspring secular humanism, paganism (e.g., polytheism), monism (including pantheism), and liberal Protestant Christianity. Henry dismisses existentialism and neoorthodoxy (among other worldviews and theologies) as irrational and therefore unintelligible because they reject the basic canons and norms of reasonable discourse.

Henry reserves some of his most severe criticisms for alternative basic epistemological methods used by some fellow evangelical apologists and theologians—especially "evidentialism." Evidentialists believe it is possible to confirm the truth of orthodox, Protestant Christianity by means of empirical and historical verification, but Henry accuses them of settling for merely probable truth on shaky epistemological grounds and of making the authority of divine revelation dependent on nonrevelational evidences and arguments which does it a serious disservice. Of course, evangelical evidentialists offer two rebuttals: First, the same argument can be turned on Henry and other evangelical rationalists in that they make the authority of divine revelation dependent on logical laws not derived solely from revelation itself, and second, "rational presuppositionalism" is merely a sophisticated version of fideism and therefore subject to the same objections Henry levels against religious irrationalism.

When Henry turns from general religious epistemology to theological method in particular, he labels his preferred approach "evangelical theistic presuppositionalism" and treats it as the only proper extension of rational presuppositionalism into Christian systematic theology. According to Henry, orthodox Christianity is a rational system of cognitive truth, which begins with two axioms which are believed by faith and justified rationally. The first is the "ontological axiom" affirming the existence of the living, personal, transcendent-immanent God, and the second is the "epistemological axiom" affirming divine revelation in the form of cognitive-propositional truth claims. On these twin pillars rests the entire superstructure of Christian belief, and insofar as either or both of them are compromised, Henry avers, the entire superstructure is in danger of collapsing into unintelligibility and irrelevance.

Henry is primarily concerned to explicate, defend, and use the second axiom—the Bible as God's self-revelation through a coherent set of propositional truth claims. In *God, Revelation, and Authority* he uses this axiom as the touchstone for evaluating all religious truth claims and finds many, if not most, wanting. According to Henry, all the diseases and dysfunctions of modern theology—from Fundamentalism to Deconstructionism—could be healed by restoring the Bible and the proper functioning of human reason to their appropriate roles. Although he does not consider biblical inerrancy absolutely necessary for evangelical belief, Henry does argue vehemently that it is required for consistent evangelical belief in the full authority of scripture. He is quite willing, however, to qualify the "inerrancy" of the Bible in many ways that Fundamentalists would eschew and more liberal theologians (and some progressive Evangelicals) would consider excellent examples of the proverbial "death by a thousand qualifications."

Carl F. H. Henry's influence on post–World War II conservative Protestant theology in North America can hardly be overestimated. For many

Evangelicals he is the paragon of the postfundamentalist evangelical thinker. He has earned almost universal (if somewhat grudging) respect from liberal theologians, and even many Fundamentalists would like to claim him as one of their own. If there is any one group of thinkers with whom Henry stands in greatest tension it is younger, progressive Evangelicals who wish to push the boundaries of traditional conservative theology by flirting with postmodernity. In the twilight of his stellar career of evangelical consensus-building, Henry feels that the evangelical tent may be stretching too far in attempting to include too many diverse modes of thought. And he warns that by departing from solid agreement on propositional revelation through a rationally intelligible, verbally inspired, inerrant scripture, Evangelicals may be giving up their historic opportunity to restore authentic Christianity in the modern world.

Suggested Readings

Writings of Carl F. H. Henry: *Confessions of a Theologian* (Waco, Tex.: Word, 1986); *God, Revelation, and Authority*, 6 vols. (Waco, Tex.: Word, 1976–84); *Toward a Recovery of Christian Belief: The Rutherford Lectures* (Wheaton, Ill.: Crossway Books, 1990).

Georges Florovsky

(1893–1979)

John H. Erickson

The external circumstances of the life of Georges Florovsky reflect the turbulence but also the intellectual excitement of the Russian emigration. Born in Russia of a well-educated clergy family, he was educated at the Odessa University and taught philosophy there until 1920, when he fled the Russian Revolution. He sought refuge first in Sofia, Bulgaria, and then Prague, Czechoslovakia, where in 1922 he married Xenia Ivanovna, beloved companion for the next fifty-five years of his life. Florovsky supported himself by teaching subjects ranging from the philosophy of law to literature, but like so many other displaced members of the intelligentsia he devoted the greater part of his mental and emotional energy to issues relating to Russia's spiritual destiny. And like others of the "Eurasian" movement, with which he was associated for a time, he understood the Russian Revolution to be the expression of a wider crisis of Western culture.

In a series of critiques of Russian intellectual history, he sought to demonstrate how the "cunning of reason" had enticed the pre-Revolutionary Russian intelligentsia into uncritical acceptance of diverse naturalistic and deterministic ideologies subversive of human freedom. In conceiving history as an inevitable natural, organismic "development," Florovsky argued, not only Marxist materialism and other forms of utopianism but German-Russian idealism, and other more benign ideologies as well, ultimately dehumanize men and women by depriving them of the necessity to choose and act, the possibility to create. The only way out of this impasse is through the religious experience of faith, the experience of true freedom, which gives meaning to the spiritual choices, for good or ill, of each human person and makes history a "creative exploit," an "ascetic achievement" *(podvig)*, a series of miraculous encounters of unique and irreplaceable human beings with God.

In 1926 Florovsky was invited to teach patristics at the recently found-ed St. Sergius Theological Academy in Paris, where his colleagues included Nicholas Berdyaev, Sergius Bulgakov, and other leading intellectuals who had returned to the church during the "Russian religious renaissance" of the early twentieth century. These were fruitful but not always tranquil years. Florovsky was relatively uninterested in the social issues which pre-occupied many of his older colleagues. He had little sympathy for what he regarded as esoteric and dogmatically amorphous speculation, including Bulgakov's "sophiology," which gave perfected creation a quasipersonal reality (Sophia) within the inner being of God. He viewed with distrust the neo-Slavophiles' preoccupation with the "Russian soul" and its alleged innate religiosity. Instead, in his *Eastern Fathers of the IVth Century* (1931) and *Byzantine Fathers of the V-VIIIth Centuries* (1933), he drew attention to the continuing relevance of the Orthodox church's patristic heritage, calling for a "neo-patristic synthesis." And in his magnum opus in the field of intellectual history, *The Ways of Russian Theology* (1937), he exposed the many false turns, enticements, and "pseudo-morphoses" which Rus-sian theology had experienced, most often due to various Western influ-ences (scholasticism, pietism, deism, idealism), precisely because of the absence in Russia of critical theological reflection grounded in Christian revelation but articulated in response to the fundamental questions posed by philosophy.

It is easy to misunderstand the thrust of Florovsky's thought at this point. A work with few heroes, *The Ways* is indeed a devastating critique of much of Russian "high" theology, particularly—though by no means exclusively—as it developed in the wake of Peter the Great's massive pro-gram of westernization. But the "neo-patristic synthesis," which Florovsky held up as an alternative, was not mere archeologism, a return to an "uncorrupted" eastern past. Florovsky did not have in mind—and certain-ly never attempted to write—a systematic theology assembled out of proof-texts from the ancient fathers of the church. For Florovsky, the fathers—particularly those of the Greek East of the fourth through the eighth centuries—wrestled successfully with basic issues which confront Christian theology in every age. For example, ancient Greek thought, like much of modern philosophy, was inclined to impersonal naturalism and determinism, which ultimately deprived the world's time and matter—and hence personal human existence—of any meaning or metaphysical content.

By contrast, the "Christian Hellenism" of the Greek fathers, by fully assimilating the biblical understanding of creation and eschatological judg-ment, restored the phenomenal world (including human persons, invested as they are not only with immortal souls but also with material bodies) to its true dignity. According to the "Christian philosophy of creation," a subject Florovsky returned to repeatedly, God freely created an "other," contingent but also free, and infinitely loved. In this as in so many other ways, Florovsky maintained, the church fathers transformed Hellenism from within, adapting it fully to biblical revelation. Their achievement therefore remains even today a trustworthy paradigm for the Christian theologian.

During the 1930s Florovsky became increasingly involved in ecumenical activities, initially in the Orthodox-Anglican Fellowship of St. Alban and St. Sergius and then also in the Faith and Order Movement. At the 1937 Edinburgh Conference on Faith and Order, Florovsky emerged as a principal spokesman for Orthodoxy and was appointed to the Committee of Fourteen, which was to be responsible for organizing the World Council of Churches. A busy schedule of academic conferences and ecumenical gatherings took Florovsky away from Paris frequently, and the outbreak of World War II found him and Xenia Ivanovna stranded in Yugoslavia. As the war ended and communism advanced in Eastern Europe, they were virtually trapped in Czechoslovakia, gaining permission to leave only after the intervention of prominent English and American friends.

Back in Paris, Florovsky found the atmosphere at St. Sergius even less congenial than before the war, and in 1948 he moved to America to become dean and professor of dogmatics and patristics at St. Vladimir's Seminary, then housed in borrowed quarters in New York City. During his six years at St. Vladimir's, Florovsky raised academic standards and gave the seminary a pan-Orthodox and ecumenical orientation, but as he himself admitted, he had little talent for administration or diplomacy. Relieved of his position at St. Vladimir's, he was appointed lecturer and then professor of Eastern Church History at Harvard Divinity School in 1956, and following his retirement from Harvard in 1964, he became a visiting professor in the departments of Slavic Studies and of Religion at Princeton University.

During these American years, Florovsky continued his ecumenical involvements, serving as a member of the Central Committee and the Executive Committee of the World Council of Churches until 1962 and as a member of the Faith and Order Commission into the 1970s. In addition, the academic world brought him into close contact particularly with the leading Protestant theologians of his time. All this gave him a new forum for presenting Orthodox theology—and very often for critiquing Western theology. In addition, his experiences aided him in the development and restatement of themes he had articulated earlier within the more circumscribed world of the Russian emigration. In richly allusive articles, lectures, sermons, and other occasional presentations, Florovsky touched one way or another on most aspects of theology, but he did not devote equal energy and attention to them. Compared with other leading Orthodox theologians, he was relatively uninterested in triadology (trinitarian theology) and pneumatology. Not even the much-vexed problem of the procession of the Holy Spirit (the Filioque issue), which for centuries has divided East and West, elicited his sustained attention. On the other hand, he returned again and again to Christology and the work of Christ, together with the closely related subjects of Mariology and ecclesiology.

It is hardly surprising that Florovsky, as an Orthodox theologian, should defend the ancient formula of the Council of Chalcedon (A.D. 451) according to which Christ is one person in two natures, without confusion, without change, without division, without separation. This formula excludes monophysitism (as well as some expressions of Protestant neoorthodoxy), which in concentrating on the divine would reduce the human to insignificance. It also excludes Nestorianism (as well as much of liberal Protestantism), which would separate the two natures in order to concentrate on the human, on the historical figure of the man Jesus. But, insists Florovsky, here drawing attention to the further precisions devised by Eastern theology following Chalcedon, the relationship of the divine and the human in Jesus Christ is "asymmetrical." The correct answer to the question "what is Jesus Christ?" is indeed "both God and man," but the correct answer to the question "who is Jesus Christ?" can only be "the second person of the Trinity." In Christ there is no separate human hypostasis (person). The unique subject for the entire work of redemption, the one who was incarnate of the Virgin Mary, the one who died on the cross and rose from the dead, is none other than God's only Son and Word.

As in Christology, so too in redemption and the spirituality that flows from it, the relationship between God and humanity, the Creator and the creature, is asymmetrical. In the theosis (deification, divinization) to which human beings are called, there is no confusion of the divine and the human, no absorption or transmutation of the human into the divine. Creaturely human beings retain their distinct nature, bearing the precious burden of freedom given to them in love by their Creator. But this is not a message of human self-sufficiency. Human nature is distinct from the divine, but it is not meant to be divided or separated from it but rather penetrated by its saving energy and power. And requisite for this is free human response to God's gift, freely offered in love.

Here, according to Florovsky, lies the significance of Mary. She is neither the great exception among human beings scarred by original sin (as the

Roman Catholic dogma of the immaculate conception might tend to suggest) nor simply the culmination of Old Testamental preparation for Christ, the chosen vessel for God's ultimate identification with humankind. She is the great example of the free human person. Her assent to God's will expressed at the Magnificat was the freedom of obedience, but still true freedom. It was human freedom as it is meant to be: the freedom of love and adoration, of humility and trust, and of cooperation *(synergia)* with God's saving plan.

For the christocentric Florovsky, ecclesiology was above all an aspect of Christology. In the church, Christ's body, his work of re-creation, sanctification, and transfiguration continues; the theosis of humankind is accomplished; salvation is perfected. In it, Christ meets us not as isolated individuals but in our mutual catholicity, as persons in communion—above all in the eucharist—with Christ and with one another. And Florovsky was serenely confident in Orthodoxy's claim to be this church, the one church, the true church. In his ecumenical activity he was vigorously opposed to any ecclesiological relativism or indifferentism; for example, he was a chief proponent of the "Toronto Declaration" (1950) on the ecclesiological significance of the World Council of Churches, according to which membership does not imply that each church regards the other members as churches in the true and full sense of the word. But as Florovsky also was quick to point out, "the true church is not yet the perfect church" ("Confessional Loyalty in the Ecumenical Movement," *The Student World* 43 [1950]: 204). Orthodoxy's claims must be understood in an inclusive rather than an exclusive sense, for the church's charismatic limits do not exactly coincide with its institutional limits. It is for the Lord of the harvest to make the final determination as to the limits of Christ's church on the last day, when the building up of his Body will be complete.

In the course of a long scholarly career stretching from Odessa to the ivied halls of Harvard and Princeton, Georges Florovsky lived in many worlds and worked in many fields. (It is interesting to note that one of his first published articles was on the mechanism of reflex salivary secretion!) In America his immediate influence would appear to be at least as great among Slavicists as among theologians. Among the Orthodox, his greatest contribution to date would appear to be the impulse he gave for rediscovery of their patristic heritage. The coherence and consistency of his thought have not yet been fully appreciated. In the coming decades, however, as his works begin to circulate more widely, especially in his native Russia, Florovsky's theology may have an even greater impact on younger generations of theologians than it did even in his own day.

Suggested Readings

Writings of Georges Vasilievich Florovsky: *The Collected Works of Georges Florovsky* (Belmont, Mass.: Nordland; Vaduz, Liechtenstein: Buchvertriebanstalt, 1972ff.).

Andrew Blane, ed., *Georges Florovsky: Russian Intellectual and Orthodox Churchman* (Crestwood, N.Y.: St. Vladimir's Seminary Press, 1993); see esp. Mark Raeff, "Enticements and Rifts: Georges Florovsky as Russian Intellectual Historian," and George H. Williams, "The Neo-Patristic Synthesis of Georges Florovsky," as well as the biographical sketch and complete bibliography of Florovsky's publications.

John Meyendorff

(1926–1992)

John H. Erickson

Son of Russian emigré parents of aristocratic Baltic German origin, John Meyendorff was born and educated in France, completing his theological studies at the Orthodox academy of St. Sergius in Paris in 1949 and his doctorate at the Sorbonne in 1958, the year also of his ordination to the priesthood. In 1959 two publications established his reputation as a leading Byzantinist and patristics scholar: his critical edition of the *Triads in Defense of the Holy Hesychasts* of St. Gregory Palamas, the fourteenth-century Byzantine proponent of perpetual internalized "prayer of the heart" or hesychasm, and his *Introduction to the Study of Gregory Palamas*. These were pioneering works. Palamas had earlier been known and studied within Orthodox circles, but his *Triads* and other chief treatises were unpublished, and the few Western scholars who had presented him to a wider audience tended to regard his theology and the spirituality behind it as confused and aberrant.

Those raised on the scholastic manual theology of pre–Vatican II Catholicism saw Palamas' distinction between God's essence and "energies" as compromising the principle of divine simplicity. Those who, in line with so much of medieval and Reformation theology, interpreted salvation chiefly in terms of vicarious atonement found talk of *theosis* (divinization, deification) unfamiliar at best and looked askance at monastic claims to mystical vision of the divine light through contemplative prayer. Meyendorff's great achievement in this and subsequent works was to demonstrate the consistency and full continuity of Palamas' theology with the spirituality of the Greek fathers of antiquity and with the classic expression of the Christian faith they articulated.

As Meyendorff insisted, for Palamas—and the Orthodox Christian tradition as a whole—God is indeed transcendent in essence, but cannot be limited by such philosophical categories. As the living, personal God of

Christian revelation, God is also willingly immanent in God's "energies." In Christ, the Word of God incarnate and made truly human, humanity is penetrated by divine energy, filled by grace with divine life. In Christ, that life of communion with God for which human beings were created in the beginning is restored. Seen in this perspective, "knowledge of God" is not an intellectual experience of the mind alone, as some currents in Christian spirituality under the influence of Greek philosophy would have it. Rather, as in the Bible, it involves the whole human being, both body and soul. In prayer (most notably in the psychosomatic form practiced by the hesychasts) and in service, in the sacraments, and indeed in the entire life of the church as a community, human beings are called to participation in divine life, to "know" God through communion.

In 1959, the year of his emergence as an important scholar, Meyendorff emigrated to the United States with his wife and young children to join the faculty of St. Vladimir's Orthodox Theological Seminary, then in New York City, later in Crestwood, New York. Soon he also became a Senior Fellow at Dumbarton Oaks, Harvard University's Byzantine research center in Washington, D.C., and beginning in 1967 he served as Professor of Byzantine History at Fordham University. In 1984 he became Dean of St. Vladimir's, a position he held until his retirement less than a month before his untimely and unexpected death from pancreatic cancer. Like his predecessors in that position, Georges Florovsky (1893–1979) and Alexander Schmemann (1921–83), Meyendorff was instrumental in bringing the intellectual and cultural tradition of Russian emigré theology to American Orthodoxy as well as to the wider Christian community.

In America, through numerous books and articles, Meyendorff continued to explore patristic and Byzantine theology with the scholarly precision of the historian. Though he dealt with virtually all the classic issues in theology (creation, anthropology, Christology, pneumatology, triadology, etc.), he wrote no systematic treatise, the closest being his study of *Byzantine Theology: Historical Trends and Doctrinal Themes* (1974). Like many Orthodox theologians through the centuries, Meyendorff feared systematization's ineluctable tendency to force theology into conceptual categories foreign to its very nature. For him this did not imply lack of concern for the true content of the faith or disinterest in precise theological definitions; he repeatedly called attention to the Christian East's efforts to find words "adequate to God" and appropriate for expressing religious truths. But, as he also insisted, the same Christian East acknowledged the incapacity of conceptual language to express the whole truth, precisely because the whole truth was accessible only in personal encounter and living communion with God, whose self-revelation to humankind is accomplished in the person of God's Son, Jesus Christ. If specific "doctrinal themes" in Orthodox theology can be identified and explored systematically, this is only because the great Saints and fathers of the church have borne witness to the same truth, as experienced above all in the sacramental life of the church.

Meyendorff always sought to be holistic in his presentation of Orthodox theology, maintaining a balance between "institution" and "event," Christology and pneumatology, office and charism. Still, he was relatively uninterested in certain subjects. For example, he had little taste for what he called "esoteric mysticism," that is, presentations which stressed the more exotic aspects of the Christian East. On the other hand, he repeatedly drew attention to certain issues which he regarded as particularly significant for Christians today. Committed to church as well as scholarly endeavors, he was actively involved in the mundane realities of Orthodox church life both in America and abroad. In the face of jurisdictional fragmentation along ethnic lines in America and inter-Orthodox rivalry on the global level, Meyendorff called for a recovery of sound ecclesiological principles. With his colleague at St. Vladimir's, Alexander Schmemann, he helped popularize the "eucharistic ecclesiology" of Nicholas Afanasiev, their teacher at St. Sergius, which stressed the eucharistic nature of the church and the eucharistic basis for its unity and structures: When all the faithful in a given place, regardless of class or economic or ethnic particularities, gather together under the bishop's presidency to become one body of Christ in the eucharist, there is the church in all its fullness—one, holy, catholic, and apostolic—not just a part of the church. This emphasis on the centrality of the eucharist for all aspects of church life was to have a transforming effect on Orthodoxy in America down to the parish level.

As a member of the Central Committee of the World Council of Churches and moderator of its Faith and Order Commission (1967–76), Meyendorff was also a leading representative for Orthodoxy within the ecumenical movement. Decrying its perceived tendencies toward secularism and relativism, he insisted that church unity and responsible Christian witness to the world are impossible without reference to sound theology, and that sound theology is impossible without reference to tradition. But as he repeatedly pointed out, tradition is not the same as traditionalism, mere repetition of inherited formulas. By relying on internal and experiential criteria rather than on external authority, Meyendorff argued, the Orthodox East has been able to maintain a "living tradition" capable of addressing new challenges precisely because it has been faithful to the fullness of truth revealed once for all in Jesus Christ, truth which by its very nature is inexhaustible.

Meyendorff also saw in the theocentric anthropology of the Orthodox East a healthy antidote to the prevailing Western illusions of human autonomy, self-determination, and self-sufficiency. Created in the image and likeness of God for a life of communion with God, human beings are not the products and hapless prisoners of impersonal natural forces. Just as the trinitarian life of God is a life of perfect personal openness, of mutual indwelling of the three divine hypostases, so also true human life is a life of personal openness, to God and to one's fellow creatures, in love that transcends the limits of nature.

In the last years of his life, Meyendorff turned ever more to the study of church history. In *Byzantium and the Rise of Russia* (1980), he called attention to the role of hesychasm as a unifying cultural movement in late-medieval Eastern Europe, and in *Imperial Unity and Christian Divisions: The Church 450–680 A.D.* (1989), he examined the forces, both spiritual and institutional, which held diversity in unity in the centuries preceding the schism of East and West. Yet as he insisted, the study of church history would be a meaningless academic exercise if it did not include the search for consistent and permanent ecclesiological principles. What impressed him most, whether in Christian antiquity or in late-medieval Orthodoxy, was the extent to which unity of faith and church order was maintained without recourse to a uniform and juridically binding administrative system. Certainly for John Meyendorff, commitment to apostolic truth as experienced within the sacramental life of the church was the only viable basis for Christian unity. The church's institutional expressions might reflect this truth and help to safeguard it, but they did not in themselves offer any infallible guarantee.

Suggested Readings

Writings of John Meyendorff: *Byzantine Theology: Historical Trends and Doctrinal Themes,* 2nd ed. (New York: Fordham University Press, 1979); *Christ in Eastern Christian Thought,* 2nd English ed. (Crestwood, N.Y.: St. Vladimir's Seminary Press, 1975); *Imperial Unity and Christian Divisions: The Church 450–680 A.D.* (Crestwood, N.Y.: St. Vladimir's Seminary Press, 1989); *Living Tradition* (Crestwood, N.Y.: St. Vladimir's Seminary Press, 1978).

Dimitri Obolensky, "John Meyendorff (1926–92)," *Sobornost* 15 (1993): 44-51.

Thomas Merton

(1915–1968)

Lawrence S. Cunningham

On 10 December 1968, Thomas Merton died in Bangkok, Thailand, after leading a conference for a group of Christian contemplatives. It was twenty-seven years to the day from his entrance into Our Lady of Gethsemani Abbey in Nelson County, Kentucky, as a postulant for the Order of Cistercians of the Strict Observance, known more informally as the Trappists. The personal journey that brought Merton first to the monastery in Kentucky and finally to the Far East can be reconstructed from a series of autobiographical works beginning with his accounts of his early premonastic life (*The Secular Journal,* 1959) and his conversion and early monastic life (*The Seven Storey Mountain,* 1948) through his several published monastic journals and a short account of his hermitage living (*The Day of a Stranger,* 1982), and on to the *Asian Journal* (1973). Supplementing these works are his letters, which now number five volumes, and the publication of his personal journals, continuing since 1995.

Merton was born on 31 January 1915 in Prades, France, to an expatriate father, Owen Merton, who had left his native New Zealand to pursue a career in painting. Merton's mother, Ruth Jenkins Merton, was an American of Quaker background. In 1921 Merton lost his mother to cancer, and Owen, true to his wandering nature, took his son to Bermuda and New York before again settling in France and placing Thomas in a French boarding school. In 1928 the father, to improve sales of his artistic work, moved to England, and the following year Thomas was enrolled in Oakham, an English public school. Owen's death in 1931 left Thomas (and his younger brother, Jean Paul, who was killed in World War II) orphaned while still in their teens.

Awarded a scholarship at Clare College of the University of Cambridge, Merton matriculated there in 1933. In 1934 he left Cambridge and England rather abruptly and somewhat mysteriously. (The best guess is that

504

the cause was an unplanned pregnancy of a young woman.) He entered Columbia University in New York (his maternal grandparents lived on Long Island), remaining there until 1939 having earned a bachelor and master's degree. During his days at Columbia Merton went through some experiences crucial for his future. Through a series of encounters with the Catholic literary and theological tradition, prompted by his studies in English literature, and the reading of Christian devotional works like Augustine's *Confessions* and *The Imitation of Christ,* Merton took instructions and was baptized a Catholic on 16 November 1938. The following two years saw him complete his M.A.; make an abortive attempt to join the Franciscans; teach at Saint Bonaventure's University in upstate New York; and work as a volunteer in a Catholic Friendship House in Harlem.

After an Easter retreat at the Kentucky monastery, Merton decided to enter the Trappists' order. By early 1942 he had received the habit of a Trappist novice and was given the religious name of Louis. Although he published his *Thirty Poems* (1944), Merton had no firm intention to continue his writing for a general public. At his abbot's urgings, however, he wrote an account of his Christian conversion. Published in 1948 (a year after he had taken solemn vows and a year before his ordination to the priesthood) under the title *The Seven Storey Mountain,* the book became a national bestseller. It gained 600,000 in hardcover sales in the United States within a year, was translated into a number of languages, and still sells briskly nearly fifty years after its first printing. This autobiographical study evidently touched a deep nerve in postwar American culture hungering, as it was, for some sense of religious rootedness after the horrors of the war.

Seven Storey Mountain would make Merton a celebrity not only in the world of Catholic America but on a larger scene as well. Over the next twenty years he wrote an astonishing number of books (about fifty titles), pamphlets, essays, reviews, and poems on a wide variety of subjects: from contemplative and monastic studies to essays on everything from social justice to art and literature. A prolific correspondent (the five volumes in print do not account for all of his letters), Merton was also a steady translator of poetry, especially Latin American poets. He did all this while observing the full monastic horarium, which ran from two o'clock in the morning until shortly after sundown, as well as serving important offices in the monastic community (e.g., master of scholastics, novice master). After a long debate within the order, Merton was allowed to retire to a hermitage for a period of time each day beginning in 1960; in 1965 he resigned as novice master and lived permanently in the hermitage until his fateful Asian trip, which would be the final great event of his life.

Anyone who wishes to synthesize his thought is faced with an overwhelming problem: Merton was neither a systematic thinker nor easily categorized as a theologian, philosopher, literary critic, poet, social commentator, or "spiritual writer." He did a little of all of those things but none in any sustained fashion. He wrote some books out of pure obedience and others out of pure love. In the late 1960s he even made a kind of "fever chart" of his works and graphed them on a scale ranging from "awful" to "good." The former were the pious potboilers, the latter his more experimental essays. He saw in his own life changes and growth. In the 1960s he could satirize the Merton of *Seven Storey Mountain* as a pious icon for parochial schoolchildren or a pseudo-prophetic figure stalking away from urban life with copies of John of the Cross and the book of Revelation in his hands.

Close readers of Merton have also seen significant shifts in his thinking. The early Merton was highly critical of the secular world, austere in his style of life, and preoccupied with perfection and personal spiritual growth. In an early essay he argued that to be a true contemplative one had to leave poetry behind. His strictures against the "world" could be strident. He was very much influenced by a then-frequent Catholic tendency to place a wide gulf between nature and grace. Only as he matured did he see how limited and cramped his outlook had been in the first flush of his monastic experience.

In the 1950s his attitude shifted. He recognized himself more in solidarity with the larger Christian world in particular and the suffering world in general. From this time on he produced essays and poems on peace, racial justice, dialogue with East and West, ecumenism, and interreligious dialogue. His thinking on this whole range of issues would anticipate, in many ways, developments coming to fruition only after the Second Vatican Council.

The bibliography of works dedicated to Merton's thought is enormous, but none of the studies is bold enough to argue that it has completely synthesized his thought or even constructed a theoretical framework to account for the parameters of his vision. Nonetheless, it is possible to set out the main areas where his thought and writings have been most influential and so to give some small indication of why most of his books remain in print and why he still has a strong impact on such a wide variety of persons.

First, more than any other person in modern times, Merton set forth in a fresh and compelling manner some of the wisdom contained in the seventeen-hundred-year tradition of Christian monasticism. Indeed, if one does not understand Merton as a monk, one simply does not understand him. To a postwar America in the 1940s and 1950s, his writings were strong medicine for people who had been nourished on the upbeat piety of such media figures as Norman Vincent Peale or Bishop Fulton J. Sheen. Merton focused attention on such traditional monastic topics as the value of silence, the need for purity of heart, simplicity in life, the recovery of the Word of God as a central resource for prayer, the value of penance and self-denial, and the possibility of a contemplative awareness of God who is at the center and heart of all things. In books like *Thoughts in Solitude* (1958) and his classic *New Seeds of Contemplation* (1962) as well as his translation of some of the sayings of the early desert monks (*The Wisdom of the Desert* [1960]), he brought to a large and appreciative audience a strain of spirituality that had hitherto been almost always found only in the cloister. Americans had a large appetite for this kind of spirituality as a counterpoint to the upbeat, brick-and-mortar variety of Catholicism found in the postwar period in the United States.

Of all the monastic subjects Merton treated, contemplation was the one to which he turned time and again. For Merton, contemplation was, as he said variously in *New Seeds of Contemplation,* "pure and virginal knowledge" or a "deep awareness of the source" or "knowledge too deep for words or images." It was nothing esoteric or even "mystical." It was, rather, the cultivation of that sense of God as the ground and foundation that is beneath and under everything we are and everything we know. It is the kind of knowledge one comes to in the depth of prayer when one is alert and watchful. It is the same kind of knowledge that comes from a profound appreciation of nature, an authentic encounter with the Word of God, and compassion for other people. Merton's contemplative vision possessed roots in John of the Cross, the Cloud Author, and earlier monastic writers who traced their lineage back to Pseudo-Dionysius and Gregory of Nyssa.

It is against the background of Merton's commitment to the contemplative life that one must assess his interest in Eastern forms of religious discipline, especially Zen Buddhism. Merton's attraction to Zen was partially aesthetic: How could a Cistercian, imbued with a tradition demanding simplicity and austerity in art and architecture, not be impressed with a tradition which pared things down to essentials and argued that the mindful act of calligraphy or making tea or arranging a flower or shooting an arrow could be a means of contemplative awareness?

Beyond the aesthetic element, however, was the Zen emphasis on enlightenment coming from a monastic regimen of disciplined practice.

Although Merton was most fascinated by the Zen tradition, he read widely in Hinduism and in the Sufi mystics of Islam as well. With no illusions about the dangers of a facile syncretism, he nonetheless felt that the contemplative tradition in the various religions of the world should be approached with respect and with a willingness to learn. The entire purpose of his fateful Asian journey was an attempt, as he said, to be in touch with the great contemplative traditions of the East. He was convinced that authentic interreligious dialogue could fruitfully begin at the level of contemplative experience.

Like all true contemplatives, Merton sought unity over separateness. In the 1950s he read deeply in the literature of Eastern Orthodoxy because he wanted to overcome in his own heart the divisions of East and West. He found the sophianic elements of Eastern spirituality congenial to his own view that the Spirit of God dwelled in the very fabric of human reality. That conviction led him to correspond with Boris Pasternak, in whose writings he saw deep spirituality reflecting the "Hidden Christ" of Orthodox piety.

In the same period, largely under the influence of his then-novice Ernesto Cardenal (later Minister of Culture in the Sandinista government of Nicaragua), Merton corresponded with—and read deeply in—a number of poets from Central and Latin America. He translated their works and wrote on their poetics. Again, he felt that he could build in his own life a kind of "bridge" between North and South America. Although he wrote little on Latin America from an explicitly technical theological angle, one reads his correspondence with these writers and his own reflections as a kind of anticipation of the liberation theology which would become so noteworthy in the 1970s.

As Merton's self-understanding of monasticism grew, it became apparent to him that like all monks he needed to understand his relationship to the large world outside the monastery. He was deeply suspicious of the notion that monks were surrogates who did penance for those who sinned, or who prayed in order to "make up" for those who were too busy to pray. He most decidedly did not think that the monastic life was, as it were, the spiritual engine room of the church. For Merton, the monastic life was one way of being a Christian; a way that emphasized the living out of certain New Testament values: the voluntary embrace of poverty; the following of the Christ who prayed and lived in the desert; the need for purity of heart; celibate living as a sign of the coming Kingdom. A collection of his essays on the monastic life (*Contemplation in a World of Action*, 1971) reveals the range of his thought, both historical and reflective, as he attempted to understand the contemplative life against the culture of his own day.

When challenged by activist friends in the 1960s to leave the monastery for the life of an "activist," he resisted the temptation. His desire was to make his own life a sign of the great struggles for racial justice and against war and the arms race. He once wrote that he wanted his life to be both a great *no* to injustice, torture, judicial murder, and war, just as he wanted his life to be a great *yes* to all that was human, beautiful, fulfilling, and oriented to God. He felt that an eremitical life of simplicity and nonviolence was a kind of prophetic protest against all that was wrong with the contemporary world.

His writings on behalf of peace and social justice distressed his monastic superiors, who thought it unseemly for a cloistered contemplative to write on such matters. Forbidden for a time to publish in these areas, Merton, a very obedient monk, quit publishing on social questions. But he also did a very Mertonian thing: He wrote long letters (more like essays) to friends, mimeographed them as copies for others, and distributed them through a network of activists and admirers. He called them, with a tad of gallows humor, the "Cold War Letters." Many of these letters (some really essay-length) would see light in various collections of his essays.

The last decade of Merton's life was one of incredible productivity amid some personal turmoil as he moved from his life in community to the hermitage which had been built on the extensive grounds of the abbey. He worked on translations, composed experimental poetry, produced books, and for one year (1967) edited a "little magazine" called "Monk's Pond." Was there any center to this frantic activity and from where might it have come? The answer to that question is the closest we will get to understanding the degree to which he had a "program" or anything approximating a coherent theological worldview. The answer to that question will also answer another question: Why, so many years after his death, and with some of his writing having a somewhat dated sound to it, is Merton still so popular, read by so many, and the object of such interest?

The short answer is that Merton was a theologian in the sense in which the word was used in the patristic period, especially by monastic writers. He was certainly not a theologian in the professional sense of the term. However, the older understanding of the word "theologian" was succinctly stated by the old fourth-century monastic writer, Evagrius of Pontus: "The one who truly prays is a theologian; a theologian truly prays." Merton was a person of deep prayer who also had (and cultivated) the gift for language. What stands behind his writing is nearly three decades of psalmody, reflective readings of the scriptures, and the quiet prayer of the contemplative. Merton wrote, in short, out of spiritual experience. He possessed a deep center in his life from which he felt free to radiate out to everything he saw as either hinting at the gospel or helping him to be more faithful to the faith he had embraced while a young man.

One of the early desert fathers said that the monk, like the seraphim and cherubim, should be "all eye." Merton, in relating to the world around him, tried to be just that. He insisted one could find in beauty the presence of God (a belief due probably from his youthful study of the poet Gerard Manley Hopkins) just as he believed that monastic retirement from the world *(anachoresis)* did not mean indifference to the world. He responded to his own tradition, the insights of other traditions, and the actual exigencies of his own time as a monk committed to the contemplative life.

Readers of Merton tend to fall into two large groups even though the groupings tend to overlap. There are, first, the readers of his more autobiographical writings who are attracted to the story of his Christian pilgrimage. They tend to find in Merton a reasonable account of how one rather deracinated intellectual was able to come to faith and then grow into that faith in newer and deeper ways. Second, there is another large body of readers who find some of his books like *Thoughts in Solitude, New Seeds of Contemplation,* and *Mystics and Zen Masters* (1967) "classics" of spiritual literature, which encourage them in their own prayer life. In both instances Merton appeals to large numbers of people who are not Roman Catholic or even Christian by reason of his capacious nonjudgmental cast of mind, his passion for social justice, and his profound sense of the reality of God.

One does not read Thomas Merton for technical theology. Indeed, he himself wrote only one such book early in his monastic life: *The Ascent to Truth* (1950) on Carmelite mysticism from the perspective of scholastic theology. In his introduction to the French translation of the work, Merton admitted that it was not the kind of book a monk ought to have written. Academic theology was simply not his metier.

It is probably Merton's life as revealed in his writings that will be his most lasting legacy. Much of his writing was autobiographical (although he was very circumspect about revealing everything about himself), with a particular focus on how he made sense of his life as a Christian and, more especially, as a monk. Hence it may well be his life that teaches us the most and, in the process, may make him a paradigmatic figure for our time. This is not to say that everyone is called to be a monk (although large numbers were so inspired by his writings in the 1950s), but that everyone is called to face the challenges of belief, the issues of integrity, the need for purity of heart, and strategies for listening and responding to God in a culture which

510

is massively indifferent to the presence of the divine. Merton did that with a goodly degree of openness and equanimity. Whether writing about a non-believer like Albert Camus or Shaker arts or the early desert monastics, he always kept that open eye for the hints of the transcendent.

In the final analysis the best angle from which to see Thomas Merton is to call him (as one of his monk confreres so named him) a "spiritual master." From that perspective, Merton finds his place today among those who have a keen interest in the now-emerging field of spirituality. His life and writings have as their ultimate focus the relationship of the human to the divine as something not to be only thought of but to be embraced and experienced. Every relationship is many-faceted, complex, ambiguous at times, and alternately deeply satisfying and fraught with uncertainty. All of those characteristics show up in the wide range of Merton's published works since he well knew, as he once wrote of the prophet Jonah, that he traveled in "the belly of a paradox."

Suggested Readings

Writings of Thomas Merton: *The Seven Storey Mountain* (New York: Harcourt Brace, 1948); *New Seeds of Contemplation* (New York: New Directions, 1962); *Mystics and Zen Masters* (New York: New Directions, 1967); *Thomas Merton Spiritual Master: The Essential Writings*, ed. Lawrence S. Cunningham (Mahwah, N.J.: Paulist Press, 1992).

Michael Mott, *The Seven Mountains of Thomas Merton* (Boston: Houghton Mifflin Co., 1984).

John Courtney Murray

(1904–1967)

Dennis P. McCann

American Catholic theologians generally agree with Charles E. Curran's view that John Courtney Murray is "the most outstanding Catholic theologian in the United States in this century." Others have written more and weightier books than Murray did, and Murray died before either the impact of Latin American liberation theology or the religious convulsions triggered by Vatican II (1962–65) had shifted the terrain upon which American Catholic theologians do their thinking. But Murray's critical reflections on the Roman Catholic Church's traditional posture on church-state relations made it possible for American Catholics to become full partners in this nation's continuing experiment in democracy. His life-work characteristically culminates, not in a personal statement but in an ecclesial directive, Vatican II's celebrated final document, *Dignitatis Humanae* (The Declaration on Religious Freedom, 1965), which acknowledged religious freedom or freedom of conscience as the linchpin of Catholic social teaching on human rights.

Unlike other prominent Christian theologians of his generation—the Niebuhrs and Tillich are the most obvious examples—the details of Murray's personal biography seem largely irrelevant for understanding his theology. But, however opaque, his resume does reveal some of its salient features. Murray was a New Yorker. He was a lifer among the Jesuits, having joined the community at the tender age of sixteen upon his graduation from Xavier High School. The steppingstones in his career are precisely what one would expect of a Jesuit blessed with exceptional academic promise: B.A. and M.A. in philosophy from Weston College, a stint of high school teaching in the Philippines, theological studies at Woodstock College, graduate studies in systematic theology at the Gregorianum in Rome culminating in an S.T.D. in 1937, and then appointment to the posts he was to hold until his death in 1967—member of the pontifical faculty of theol-

512

ogy at Woodstock from 1937 on, and editor-in-chief of *Theological Studies,* beginning in 1941. The resume suggests a talented insider, a Jesuit version of William L. Whyte's "organization man" who, despite whatever setbacks, remains unfailingly loyal to the company.

The list of Murray's publications confirms the impression of high intelligence in service to the church, but it does not account for the extraordinary impact his personality had upon his colleagues and students. For many Murray epitomizes the best that the pre–Vatican II Catholic seminary system had to offer. An exclusively male domain, the seminary inculcated passionate loyalty to the church and selfless detachment from everything else, tempered by an unfeigned respect for learning and a capacity for irony carefully honed on the absurdities of ecclesiastical life. James Hennessey's description of Murray effectively places him in the fading memories of his students: "An olympian and urbane man, generally thought of as aloof—his friends attributed it to shyness—formidable in debate and equipped with a sesquipedalian vocabulary and a dry sense of humor, Murray was a giant . . . " (Hennessey, "Murray, John Courtney [1904–1967]").

The brief sketches published some time after Murray's death by colleagues who worked closely with him—the editor at Sheed and Ward, Philip Scharper, who pulled together some of Murray's most accessible and provocative essays into the celebrated *We Hold These Truths* (1960), and Monsignor George G. Higgins, who lived with Murray in Rome during the Council—convey the same awed affection, but they diverge in their perceptions of his personal situation. Dwelling mostly on the theological controversies of the 1950s which forcibly silenced Murray for a time, Scharper compares Murray to James Fenimore Cooper's Natty Bumppo—the hero of the Leatherstocking novels—whom D. H. Lawrence canonized as "the essential American soul—isolate, almost selfless, stoic, and enduring." Scharper accuses the American Jesuits of failing to rally to Murray's defense when the Vatican ordered him to cease publication on church-state relations. "He had gone out on a limb, and while none of his brothers handed him a sharp saw, at best they kept moving beneath him with a fireman's net. He had waged his theological battle alone, and he was alone in what he called his 'defeat'" (Scharper, "John Courtney Murray").

The comparison with Bumppo, however bizarre, suggests a larger agenda than simply shaming Jesuits, as if that were even possible. Like many of Murray's admirers today, Scharper wants to place Murray's work at the center of the question of American Catholic identity. Is it possible to be, in Scharper's words, "both a Catholic and an American without denying or at least diminishing one of the dual loyalties"? This question seems pointless only until you start to think seriously about it. A meaningful answer depends on coming to terms with our collective moral scruples about what it means to be an American, as well as the exquisitely particular anxieties that, even today, vex the consciences of educated Catholics. D. H. Lawrence's comment on Natty Bumppo is a highly tendentious, if not downright flattering, reading of the American experience; for Scharper, however, it allows Catholics to embrace the question at the center of Murray's work without succumbing, either in fact or in appearance, to the imperialism so often identified with either Roman Catholicism or the United States of America.

Higgins' portrait of Murray is far more straightforward, though hardly less illuminating. It stems from a later period when Murray had been rehabilitated by Francis Cardinal Spellman, the Archbishop of New York, and established in Rome as a Conciliar peritus. Enjoying a succès d'estime reminiscent, perhaps, of Thomas Jefferson's sojourn in Paris, Higgins' Murray bears little resemblance to Natty Bumppo. Though still "too much of a gentleman and by temperament too courteous and reserved to take the floor away from more boisterous conversationalists," Murray is at the center of the intellectual life of the American Catholic clergy holed up at the Casa Villanova. Higgins specifically denies that Murray was less well regarded by the U.S. bishops than by the progressive Europeans, whose thinking dominated the Council. "Murray, far from being ostracized by the American bishops, was, if anything, lionized by them" (Higgins, "Some Personal Reflections"). But here, too, a larger agenda is at stake. The *Declaration on Religious Freedom* was seen—then, as now—as a vindication of the distinctive experience of the Catholic church in the United States. Murray had become a hero to the American bishops, and frequently a spokesman for them, because he had managed to translate their pastoral experience as full partners in what Martin Marty has called "the public church" into a theological discourse—still literally, in Latin—that the rest of the Catholic hierarchy now regarded as opportune and persuasive.

Murray remains something of an enigma, precisely because both portraits are true, and not just sequentially. Murray is both an American original and a Catholic apologist whose works substantially define the framework in which public policy questions are addressed by the American Catholic church today. As scholars working on Murray's legacy have shown, the most fruitful way to understand that framework is developmentally or, if you will, praxeologically. Murray's point of departure for becoming his denomination's finest public theologian was the controversy over the limits to "intercreedal cooperation" that had resurfaced in the early 1940s. How was it possible for Catholics to collaborate in public life with non-Catholics, given the chasm that everyone sensed separated this particular faith tradition from all other forms of American Christianity?

There was less than the normal amount of theological shadowboxing at stake in this question, for the controversy occurred at a time when the social reforms mandated by the New Deal and the imminent prospect of U.S. involvement in World War II were demonstrating both the need for and the efficacy of an ecumenical approach to public policy questions. The most authoritative Catholic voice in public affairs at the time was the National Catholic Welfare Conference (NCWC), which had inherited the style of ecumenical coalition-building forged, without benefit of significant theological reflection, in the crucible of World War I. Murray's theological argument in behalf of intercreedal cooperation, then, was a defense of the policies already established by custom in the NCWC. But it raised the ire of Catholic purists, who feared that such easy familiarity with non-Catholics would lead many to slide down the slippery slope of "indifferentism."

The theological gauntlet, fairly or no, had now been thrown down by Murray's opponents. "Indifferentism," in their view, was the besetting sin of liberal Protestants. It is what provoked the ire of educated Catholics when later they were to contemplate the seemingly innocuous slogans of Eisenhower-era social harmony, like the Advertising Council's "Attend the church of your choice." Murray had to devise his theological argument in a church that still paid more than lip service to the idea that "outside the Church there is no Salvation," and that this same church, in theory, could and should exercise a privileged position in public life. In short, the issues upon which Murray made his theological reputation—the validity of religious pluralism, freedom of conscience, and the nature of church-state relations in a democracy—were forced upon him by circumstances, and not the other way around.

The centerpiece of Murray's theological perspective is his deepening philosophical and theological insights into the natural law tradition. Seeking to establish the continuity between his own thinking and the broad outlines of papal social teaching, Murray dutifully assented to Pope Leo XIII's canonization of Thomistic Scholasticism as the *philosophia perennis* that defined human reason, and therefore what is reasonable, in Catholic apologetics. At the same time, however, he tried to show how some of Leo's own specific inferences from the natural law—notably, his conception of church-state relations, including especially the church's duty to support governments whose policies promoted distinctively Catholic moral principles—were obsolete, and thus no longer binding upon Catholics.

Murray thus parted company with previous American Catholic apologists—notably, John A. Ryan—who, however reluctantly, still accepted Leo's view as the ideal norm, regardless of how unworkable it might be in the United States and other nations where Catholics were a minority. American Catholics remained vulnerable to accusations of disloyalty to the U.S. Constitutional principle of separation of church and state, and thus their capacity for genuine citizenship was open to question, so long as they adhered to Leo's teaching. They could only defend themselves with lame assurances that Leo's mandate, in fact, would not be implemented unless Catholicism became the creed of a majority of citizens, a prospect which, no doubt, had encouraged the nineteenth century's Know-Nothing movement and other anti-Catholic resistance, especially, to immigration.

Murray's critique of Leo's teaching was hardly a sell-out; but it did require—as J. Leon Hooper, among others, has shown—a massive theological reconstruction of the natural law tradition, along broadly historicist lines. Henceforth, the natural law could not be approached as if it were a set of Cartesian axioms, from which ethicists might deduce a chain of moral reasoning from clear and certain principles to universally valid applications. The principles of the natural law were emergent in history, and their interpretation was contingent upon a variety of cultural factors, including the ways in which these principles were historically embedded in a variety of religious traditions. Authentic development was possible within the church's understanding of the natural law. Such development would turn out to be in continuity with earlier authentic formulations, but it was not likely to be identical to them.

In reconstructing the natural law paradigm, Murray—an increasingly skillful interpreter of the church's own intellectual history—appealed to the writings of Thomas Aquinas, to the possibility of a Christian humanism relatively unscarred by the conceptual rigidities imposed by the modern Cartesian obsession with clear and distinct ideas. Such a rethinking of Catholic tradition may have been sufficient to catch his Scholastic adversaries off-guard; but by itself, it would hardly serve as a bridge to the mainstream of American life and thought. Here, too, the natural law provided the key, as Murray reinterpreted the works of Locke, Jefferson, and notably, James Madison, as authentic representatives of the natural law paradigm. A thread of continuity, he argued, linked Aquinas' principles with the philosophical arguments that had animated the authors of the U.S. Constitution. Murray thus regarded what he called "the American proposition," the nation's experiment in ordered liberty, as the model of a mature state, one that no longer required the anomalous moral supervision of the church.

In effect, Murray's embrace of the principles animating the U.S. Constitution amounted to a reversal of Pope Leo's priorities. In light of the historic changes that animated—and still animate—the American experiment in democracy, the papal norm had become the historical exception, and the American exception had become normative for Catholic social teaching. Religious freedom was no longer contingent upon prior assent to the church's view of the truth; it was the fundamental human right, which ultimately defines the limits which any government must respect, if it is to be considered morally legitimate. Given a recognition of these limits, the church cannot demand that the state transgress the boundaries of its own moral legitimacy, even in behalf of a good cause.

The practical consequences of Murray's rethinking of the natural law are scattered throughout his writings on various public policy questions over several decades. The substance of these writings—which focus on a number of issues ranging from aid to parochial schools, to the necessity of selective conscientious objection, to the quest for interracial justice, to the nature of religious education in a free society—effectively refute any glib dismissal of Murray's position, as if a reconstructed natural law paradigm must necessarily promote insensitivity to its own theological roots, or as if it must necessarily result in an unChristian acquiescence in the perduring social evils that continue to plague American society.

Some theologians today have taken, for example, John Murray Cuddihy's attack on the virtue of civility, as an excuse to liberate themselves from the kind of reasoned public discourse that John Courtney Murray identified with the natural law (Cuddihy, *No Offense*). But Murray's commitment to civility is not simply a reflection of his own intellectual superiority. It is—as a fair reading of his essays ought to suggest—the reflection of an authentically Catholic theological commitment to intercreedal cooperation that rests upon genuine insight into the nature of religious freedom. Public theology, in the manner of John Courtney Murray, need not be a betrayal of the church's prophetic mission in the world, but it does entail a degree of self-restraint in the way in which that mission is carried out. Respecting the religious freedom of others means engaging in public argument, in a search, if not always for moral consensus, at least for the kind of mutual understandings in which meaningful disagreement is no longer destructive of community and society. Murray is rightly acclaimed the most outstanding American Catholic theologian of his generation, because he explored with insight and originality the religious and moral conditions that make public theology both necessary and possible.

Suggested Readings

Writings of John Courtney Murray: *We Hold These Truths: Catholic Reflections on the American Proposition* (New York: Sheed and Ward, 1960); *The Problem of God, Yesterday and Today* (New Haven: Yale University Press, 1964); *Religious Liberty: Catholic Struggles with Pluralism,* ed. J. Leon Hooper (Louisville: Westminster/John Knox Press, 1993); *Bridging the Sacred and the Secular: Selected Writings of John Courtney Murray, S.J.,* ed. J. Leon Hooper (Washington, D.C.: Georgetown University Press, 1994).

John Murray Cuddihy, *No Offense: Civil Religion and Protestant Taste* (New York: Seabury Press, 1979).

Thomas P. Ferguson, *Catholic and American: The Political Theology of John Courtney Murray* (Kansas City: Sheed and Ward, 1993).

James Hennessey, "Murray, John Courtney (1904–1967)," in *The Modern Catholic Encyclopedia,* ed. Michael Glazier and Monika K. Hellwig (Collegeville, Minn.: Liturgical Press, A Michael Glazier Book, 1992).

George G. Higgins, "Some Personal Reflections," *America* 143 (November 30, 1985): 380-86.

J. Leon Hooper, *The Ethics of Discourse: The Social Philosophy of John Courtney Murray* (Georgetown: Georgetown University Press, 1986).

Thomas Hughson, *The Believer as Citizen: John Courtney Murray in a New Context* (New York: Paulist Press, 1993).

Robert P. Hunt and Kenneth L. Grasso, eds., *John Courtney Murray and the American Civil Conversation* (Grand Rapids: Wm. B. Eerdmans Publishing Co., 1992).

Dennis P. McCann, *New Experiment in Democracy: The Challenge for American Catholicism* (Kansas City: Sheed and Ward, 1987).

Robert W. McElroy, *The Search for an American Public Theology: The Contribution of John Courtney Murray* (New York: Paulist Press, 1989).

Donald E. Pelotte, *John Courtney Murray: Theologian in Conflict* (New York: Paulist Press, 1976).

Philip Scharper, "John Courtney Murray: Belated Hero," *Commonweal* 104 (March 4, 1977): 150-52.

PERIOD 5

RECENT TIMES

(Since 1965)

CHRISTIAN THEOLOGY SINCE 1965:
AN OVERVIEW

Martin E. Marty

Any effort to comprehend theological movement and movements over a period of a third of a century forces the one who is to do the surveying to make choices. The least useful approach would be to provide a bibliography in paragraph form, a book list crowded with as many names and book titles as possible. Such lists glaze the eye, enter but leave the mind, and serve more for reference than for reconnaissance.

A second approach, another one not especially promising, is to follow the theology of the previous century down the track on which the essays in this volume have begun to take the reader. There is a certain value, but a limited one, in pursuing questions such as: What happened to the legacy of Reinhold Niebuhr, Paul Tillich, and John Courtney Murray? Who were custodians of their reputations, and how did they fare? Or, who succeeded Edward J. Carnell and Carl F. H. Henry as shapers of evangelicalism? Did such figures as these inspire backlash and reaction? How do philosophical theology, process theology, and existentialist modes fare? To answer such questions in this limited space would not serve well the efforts to style and grasp the innovations of this very different period.

Having decided to neglect or reject such approaches, I have chosen instead to try to frame the endeavors of theologians in the recent century, and to place them on the horizon of inquiry. We shall ask what cultural changes impelled theologians to go about their work in different ways. What did theologians do to impinge on and shape elements of their culture? If we can learn something of the situation, the context, the place of theology and theologians, we shall be able to make more sense of the era than we shall if we only encounter lists and developments of previously established trends.

Setting the Late-Century Stage by Midcentury Reference

Things fall apart; the center cannot hold;
Mere anarchy is loosed upon the world.

Throw all aspiration to originality out the window: quoting William Butler Yeats' *The Second Coming* (1916) requires no reaching. It demonstrates no impulse to novelty. No English language poem challenges its place as the most frequently cited when people want to describe the main trends in culture, through the ending of the century near whose beginning the Irish poet wrote those lines.

The fact that something is frequently quoted does not mean that it has to be seen as a cliche or that it will turn trite. Thus certain lines in T. S. Eliot or Robert Frost remain fresh despite the fact they frequently get invoked because of their appropriateness. Yeats' epigraph, some would say also his epitaph on the century, teases his readers into doing their own fresh thinking.

"Things fall apart," or seem to have done so, in Christian theology after 1965 as have so many other cultural elements and products. At least, so they are portrayed and perceived by believers and other citizens who try to make sense of the final third of the century.

No doubt through the ages people have always looked around them and determined that meaning and plot were ever harder to find in the midst of cultural disintegration. After all, or at least before our times, John Donne was writing several centuries ago that "new philosophy calls all in doubt" and that " 'Tis all in pieces, all coherence gone." One can find similar claims in Ecclesiastes and Plato. The point is to ask what is special about one's own time of anarchy and incoherences. What is the nature of assaults on coherences? These questions involve recall of the period immediately before one's own—in this case, between 1918 and 1965—and then the seeking of some sort of "-archies" and "piecings together" in the midst of a time when perspective in an overview is admittedly hard to gain.

Ergo, first, the necessary backward glance. Near the end of the century most chroniclers of Christian theology look back, whether in nostalgia or disdain, at the midcentury years. They were a time when, surrounded by the falling apart of things (in two World Wars, economic Depression, cultural experimentation, ideological confusion), Christian theology still looked plotted.

For many, the prefix neo- helped provide landmarks and guidelines. Among Catholics, movements that can be called neoscholasticisms, beginning in the 1930s, helped them locate their new thinkers. Many of these, thinkers like Jacques Maritain and Etienne Gilson, were visitors to the United States. They appeared affirming much of the structure provided by a classic past, particularly the past marked by Thomism.

For Protestants in the same middle third of the century, neoorthodoxy dominated. The movement was given voice by Europeans like Karl Barth and was imported through the not fully neoorthodox Paul Tillich or home-grown in the gardens of the Niebuhr brothers and their kin and kind. It was a retrieval and revisiting of familiar and, now on Protestant Reformation grounds, classical theological motifs.

Of course, the neo- in both cases signaled change. Such change was apparent; one could not live in the mental furnished apartments [– *Welt anschaungen* or worldview] of the thirteenth or sixteenth centuries. But some of the figurative windows and doorways of that past mental abode were still in place, so the theological inhabitant was not so easily lost. Now, almost everyone agrees, these two "neo's" and their analogues have become items in the Christian museums and antique shops. They remain available for exploration, but they do not provide the matrix for the newer theological work.

There was a bridge-generation of thinkers who drew upon the motifs and approaches of the "neo-" generation, employing its models but engaging in fresh work as they faced the culture of pluralism. In the Protestant sphere, these included creative figures like John B. Cobb, Langdon Gilkey, Gordon Kaufman, and Schubert Ogden. Among Catholics, theologians such as Avery Dulles, ethicist Richard McCormick, and others, provided guidance in the tradition and produced some works of enduring value.

On Genius of Theologians and the Intactness of Culture

Coherences in theology are the result of the work of thinkers whose main themes and approaches cohere. Along with the notion that the movements in theology have lost their being-together, their coherence, one regularly hears the claim that "the giants are gone." In American theological circles, this proclamation usually appears along with the question about talent or genius: "Where are the John Courtney Murrays, or the Niebuhrs and the Tillichs, now at the end of the century, to match such towering figures at midcentury?"

This book, and especially its last two sections, provides some perspective to anyone who wishes to respond to such a question. The informed reader looks at the names of the Christian systematic theologians in the two sections. In the "Post–Civil War and New Intellectual Frontier (1866–1918)" section, she sees only one or two names of figures whose books are occasionally returned to print and who can be cited without much biographical referencing.

Look at the list: First strike from it Henry Ward Beecher as a clerical celebrity, Mary Baker Eddy and Ellen G. H. White as founders, Rufus Jones as a spiritual writer, Frances Willard as a reformer, and William James and Josiah Royce as philosophical "ringers" brought to the lineup because of their bearing on Christian theology. Then ask: Which *real* theologian on that list is read and readily available? Walter Rauschenbusch, a Social Gospel prophet and ethicist stands virtually alone.

More relevant is the question in respect to the cast of characters and candidates in the final section, "The Modern Era (1918–1965)." Only if one uses the broad definition of theology or theologian, are there some names that remain household words, names of authors whose writings still are attractive to publishers, marketers, and publics. In that company there are philosopher John Dewey, social philosopher W. E. B. DuBois, reformer Martin Luther King, Jr., and spiritual writers Dorothy Day and Thomas Merton. All of them would have been candidates for embarrassment were they to have appeared in a lineup of systematic theologians. Others are of historical importance as movement leaders, beginning with J. Gresham Machen and Edward Carnell or Carl Henry in fundamentalism and neoevangelicalism. Thus Henry was a theological force whose formal work has joined neoscholasticism and neoorthodoxy on the ash heap of post-contemporaneity. But who reads such writers today for intrinsic reasons? Further, philosopher Charles Hartshorne spans the century and stays in print, but he made his basic statement decades ago. For the rest, when historians recall their names, they inspire another question. It is now not, "Where are such figures today?" but "After you mention Murray, Tillich, and the Niebuhrs, who else towered at midcentury?" Did anyone tower? Were they not isolated geniuses who captured well their moment and basically drew upon past Christian thought to address their decades?

With all those questions posed, it is important to revisit them and the tentative answers given. Thereupon one can say: Because some are not in print, not read by any except specialists today, does not mean that they lacked or lack importance. If they did, this book would be beside the point, where actually it is much to many points. The unread but not unimportant figures of the recent past indicate something of the range of options. They still make available some treasures from the repository and repertory of such options in their time. Thus they become models and exemplars for our own moment, and as such have an extrinsic value atop the intrinsic worth of their lives and work for their own time. The point of all this, however, is to say that looking back in nostalgia provides little perspective.

The element that does survive such an inquiry, is one that reinforces the hunch that quoting Yeats in this context is relevant. Whoever reads the essays in these two foregoing sections and surrounds such reading with broader historical inquiry, will provide an insight. She can claim and then provide warrants and documentation for the claim that there was something we might call cultural *intactness* surrounding the churches and movements out of which they spoke and which they addressed. It is that intactness that no longer provides the penumbra around or the natural market for current theological work.

Leave aside for the moment the Eastern Orthodox represented here as often elsewhere only by the appearances of Georges Florovsky and John Meyendorff; Orthodoxy looked intact. But that leaves the two main cases of Roman Catholicism and Protestantism. Before 1965, John Courtney Murray, and slightly lesser figures like Gustave Weigel who do not show up here, could still count on the definable, disciplinable, boundaried Roman Catholicism of the pre–Vatican II and Vatican II era, before Catholicism in America as elsewhere began its protean sprawl. Of course, there was always, in the older Catholicism, variety—theological and cultural and personal. But the lines of authority were still clear; the canon laws were more easily invoked. The pope could crack the whip and have it sting, or close the door and have it barred. Dissenters quietly left instead of staying to stretch the boundaries of the church.

So in their prime at midcentury the Murrays and Weigels, by engaging in selective retrievals of themes from half-forgotten Catholic pasts, could be prophets. They had to be reckoned with by any who took seriously the status and vitality of the whole church. Such is not the case today. People like Avery Dulles, Rosemary Ruether, and David Tracy draw on Catholic classics, but they can rely on no automatic Catholic market. They may be read as much by non-Catholics who share something of their outlooks as by all the kinds of Catholicism, many of which do not. The intactness has disappeared.

Protestantism never advertised itself theologically as being so coherent, disciplined, or under the single pattern of authority represented as papal Catholicism. Protestantism had been born divided, ecclesiastically and theologically. All the ecumenical councils' horses and all the federations' men could not put it together again, or for the first time. Still, one can speak of a surviving cultural intactness in that period. Midcentury Protestantism, for all its division into moderate-liberal-modernist *versus* moderate-evangelical-fundamentalist zones and parties, found those who spoke for the parties addressing more or less the same things and themes. Whether or not the proverbial "person in the pew" or the average parson and lay leader read the Niebuhrs or Tillich or not, great numbers of them would recognize such figures on the cover of, say, *Time* magazine. The informed readers needed little explanation to understand why what was at issue was at issue.

Midcentury America, not only religiously but, insofar as religion impinged on culture, also culturally, was marked by a kind of Protestant intactness that was recognized by those who suffered from it or despised it as well as by those who made it up. Today the word "mainstream" is used to cover the company ecclesiastically. But at midcentury and until around 1965, that cohort's leaders were perceived or believed to have influence far beyond their ecclesial boundaries. In a sense, white male Protestants "ran the show" in the early 1960s. They alone were regularly called on by leading editors and broadcasters, or referred to by prime literary, intellectual, and academic leaders, when issues that brought theology and culture together were brought up. They could cast ripples, stir waters, create shock waves, and cause tremors in the ground beneath such Protestantism and its culture.

Their writings reached far into what was coming to be called "pluralist America." This was momentarily the proverbial *Protestant-Catholic-Jew* triad of cultural similarities described so well by Will Herberg in his book of that title in 1955. Women, African American, "marginal," and maverick or entrepreneurial voices were obscure or obscured. The Niebuhrs and Tillich could preach in cathedrals and speak in campus auditoriums to large crowds, many of whose members may have been uncomprehending but most of whom, when interviewed, showed they knew something was at stake in their lives when such speakers spoke or writers wrote.

That intactness is gone today. Traces of it remain within but not across theological traditions. My choice of an incident to illustrate the continuity: One prominent post-1965 theologian told me that he was "going home" to a denominational theological school after having been baffled or benumbed in a secular-pluralist private university setting. He was leaving for one reason. At that university, he had to wake up in the morning and spend it inventing a world to address, envisioning an audience that would find itself taken up with what my in-demand professor friend found important, and plotting a market for his product.

By afternoon each day, when he had accomplished just enough of such world-within-a-world construction to get to work, he was too wearied to do so. He preferred to be "at the far left end of improvisation" within an ecclesiastical tradition with its "world," its scaling of importances, its market. He probably oversimplified and homogenized life within such a tradition, but he was giving voice to a sense of the loss of cultural and communal intactness on which his predecessors had drawn.

If theological genius has always been rare, so that "Murray, the Niebuhrs, and Tillich" were isolated, or if they are to be seen not in isolation but in a cultural context of relative intactness, one more thing must be said during a last glance over the shoulder at figures who frame the picture of the current third of a century. That is, what replaces their world, one says while segueing, is not "mere anarchy," or not only mere anarchy, but instead a myriad of juxtaposed or competing "-archies." They deserve tracing.

A Period of New Particularisms

Her majesty Queen Elizabeth, after a horrible year in the career of the British royal family, bestirred herself to say in a formal speech that it had, indeed, been *annus horribilis,* not *annus mirabilis,* a year of wonders. Those who have welcomed the new freedoms and vitalities that came with theological endeavors in recent times would pronounce the 1960s a decade *mirabilis.* Those who mourned the loss of intactness and plot that surrounded theological enterprise in the preceding two periods, think of and speak of the time as *horribilis.* Many historians question whether it is proper or helpful to speak of historical changes and continuities in terms of decades at all. They stand little chance against other historians, journalists, and publics who will persist in doing so, even though they know that watersheds and landmarks do not occur and appear neatly at turns between "1950s and 1960s" or "1960s and 1970s."

So let there be, for present purposes, a "sixties," a period of significant shakings and turnings, in culture and theology alike. A conscientious chronicling would likely see the sixties arrive in 1965, not 1960 or 1961, and continue until around 1974 or 1975, not 1970 or 1971. Focusing on 1965 is more useful than fretting and fussing about the temporal boundaries of the decade. Politically, there were liberal continuities in the Kennedy and early Johnson years that connected them with the moderate impulses of the Eisenhower era that preceded them. The later Johnson years, ending in 1968, and the Nixonian follow-up saw a very different America bursting forth. And the liberalizing ethos of people who signed up for the Peace Corps and responded to Kennedyesque idealism was still buttoned down and orderly, in the spirit of the Affluent Society that preceded their commitments. But this continuity was disrupted by the dissidence and dissent of the succeeding half-generation on and off campuses. One can find parallels to such turnings in everything from fashion through music to religion.

Conventionally, I like to characterize the midsixties' turn of direction along the lines of a centripetal-centrifugal axis or a sudden counterspiraling. From Pearl Harbor, through World War II, the early cold war, and the Eisenhower to Kennedy-early-Johnson times in public life, the cultural direction was centripetal, a spiraling toward some sort of center. After 1965 this was reversed, and a centrifugal impulse and then explosion followed, with its spiraling outward to what Yeats-quoters would have called "mere anarchy."

In politics and culture, the centripetal pulsing is obvious. One thinks of the use of the letter "U" needed to categorize and catalog many of the main cultural inventions at midcentury: the United Nations, the Universal Declaration of Human Rights, The United Church of Christ, United Nations Educational, Scientific and Cultural Organization (UNESCO), United World Federalists, United Nations International Children's Emergency Fund (UNICEF), United Nations Relief and Works Agency (UNRWA). The World Council of Churches, the National Council of Churches, and the ecumenical Vatican Council II were typical inventions or elaborations in the score of years after World War II. These match notions such as "racial integration," "consensus history," "ecumenism and interfaith," and metaphors that included "global village" and "spaceship earth" or celebrations that won favor, such as Brotherhood Week.

A decade after 1965 it was a very different story. Now "racial separation," "conflict history," "the new denominationalism," "tribalism," "the new ethnicity," "multiculturalism," and the various "powers"—Black Power, "Sisterhood is Powerful," Chicano Power, and the like—became culturally more credible and more frequently voiced as slogans or ideals. Theology both gave some impetus to these changes and reflected them.

At the end of the period before the turn, conservative evangelicals were envisioning a unitive pattern of thinking in the National Association of Evangelicals orbit, as the thought of Carl F. H. Henry, described in this volume, envisioned. A decade or two later evangelicalism was rent into moderate-fundamentalist fissures in all the denominations, beginning with the largest, the Southern Baptist Convention. There was a Daughters of Sarah to reflect surrounding feminisms; an Evangelicals Concerned for gay and lesbian evangelicals; there were the Sojourners and any number of evangelical-left organizations. These were dwarfed by the much larger particularities, such as those that followed, for example, white-Reformed-scholastic lines in one direction and African American or Hispanic-Pentecostal flanks in others. They shared the name evangelical but not a single cohering and defining ethos.

In Catholicism, when John Courtney Murray experimented with new envisionings of church and state relations, he was scrutinized and even silenced for a time by colleagues, competitors, and authorities, so intact were Catholic authority patterns. Ten years after the Second Vatican Council the Vatican may have been in pursuit of dissident theologians, but successfully disciplined only a handful of them. Each disciplining greatly enhanced the marketability of such theologians within Catholicism. Most of them escaped with nothing but the sound of Vatican grumbling in their ears as they went their several ways. Vatican II was a fresh moment of ecclesiastical politics that followed the rule book. Post–Vatican II skirmishings went on with a rule book forgotten or even thrown away. Catholicism became in practice a congeries of constituencies, clienteles, convergences, and coalitions more than a congregation in simple communion.

Protestantisms of the (racially) largely white and European tradition, had always been divided, and also bore the signs of the centrifugal directing. For one thing, the Atlantic figuratively widened, causing a new chasm. Europe was less looked to than before for moorings, precedents, and reference points. Between 1945 and 1965 American theologians, Protestant and Catholic alike, had tended to trek to Oxford or Marburg or Rome for resource and formation. After that period, the American universities, private and secular or confessionally related but "open" like Notre Dame, became self-generators of theology. More than Europe, Latin America provided a resource for theologians during the years when liberation theology came into favor. But without Europe's beckoning, whether as locale or on printed pages, American theology ran many divergent ways and developed independent channels and courses.

We shall soon be documenting some of the movements of the new particularism. Here the point is only to paint the centripetal and centrifugal spirals with a broad brush and to point to points at which the turn came. Nothing stands out so much as a candidate for landmark status then as does the summer of 1965 in the United States. The spring of 1965 saw theologians progressively and optimistically endorsing Lyndon Johnson's Great Society, a welfare state that to them bore some marks of the kingdom of God. Theologians meanwhile had the luxury of naming and endorsing a movement called Secular Theology because so much of the secular order seemed to be in range of lining up as another match for the emergent Kingdom. Whites and blacks, Protestants and Catholics and Jews, marched together to the common drums of the civil rights movement, and that spring saw the most progressive welfare, civil rights, and education legislation in American history.

That summer of 1965 President Johnson committed United States troops to a land war in Vietnam. In Los Angeles, Watts burned at the hands of blacks who were anything but racial-integration-minded. They inspired white backlash and black power. Support for united international ventures turned to dissent; racial integration was replaced by racial separateness, as people after people (African-, Asian-, Native-, Hispanic-, and, hence and finally, European-Americans) dug up old hyphens to invent separatisms that oversimplified the actual situations of their peoplehood. The women's movement took shape—some date its vivid emergence after the preliminaries were over to Betty Friedan's publication of *The Feminine Mystique* already in 1963—and the homosexual movements that got together around 1969 disrupted another pattern of presumed coherence and, in the view of the antianarchy people, loosed mere anarchy upon their worlds. Yet the need for theological reflection merely continued to grow.

Not that all trends were toward nothing but the particular, the special, the self-enclosed. Ecumenism did survive in transformed forms, as did many social welfare expressions of religion. The presidency of Ronald Reagan after 1980 brought dramatic changes, however, and theologians who made proposals concerning social welfare were put on the defensive and have remained in that posture. New inventions brought the potential for cosmopolitanism to counter tribalism. Benjamin R. Barber came up with a lively metaphor for the two apparently contradictory but conjoined (and thus contributing to anarchy) strains: Jihad vs. McWorld (*Jihad vs. McWorld,* Times Books, 1965).

Barber spoke of the whole world, the international scene. But the United States matched his generalizations and was a place where the two trends competed intensely or coincided unnervingly. *McWorld* is the world of MacDonalds and, in the 1980s, Macintosh computers and networks, of international cinema and music styles and means to connect them. Such a world seems to imply centripetality, since the invention and deployment of the Internet, the Web, global communications, and the like, could bring the world toward homogeneity and coherence. But countering all that is the anarchy of the *Jihad,* the support of the particular cause of God, of disparate peoplehoods, of crusades and holy wars in the name of the tribe.

Theologically, *Jihad* seems to have had the world to itself more than did *McWorld*: hence, the "new particularism" of which we must speak.

Particularism poses itself against universalisms, and its localism contrasts with cosmopolitanism. Not that no universals were ever asserted or aspired to in theology. Theologians still spoke of God, of one God; if Christian, of God in Christ, or to God through Christ. They talked about the gathering of the people of God and their liberation from various oppressions; of the moral life; of the temporal and the eternal; sometimes, even of reconciliation among peoples including Christian people; of a universal beckoning love of God. But here and now, in history, most of them found it important to say that the way to the true universal was past the false universals and instead through the particularities of race, ethnicity, gender, age, class, taste, and more.

Sampling Some New Particularisms

1) *Issues of Gender*

The most far-reaching change in the theological enterprise in North America if not yet the world has been the rise of particularisms along the lines of gender, particularly through the voices of women. The theological authors in this book have been overwhelmingly men. The few women— Lydia Maria Child, Margaret Fuller, Phoebe Palmer, Harriet Beecher Stowe, Antoinette Brown Blackwell, Mary Baker Eddy, Ellen G. White, Frances Willard, and Dorothy Day—would not historically have been classified as theologians, nor would they have called themselves theologians. They would not have applied for or fit into slots as tenured professors in theological schools or universities, the customary modern abodes of formal theologians. The single exception is Georgia Harkness, the lone midcentury woman's voice in theological faculties.

Thirty years later, in mainstream Protestantism, in some evangelical circles, and in Catholicism (where the seminary world long was as much "all-male" as the priesthood remains at century's end), a significant minority of theological expressions come from women. We are not speaking here of those eloquent writers of novels, poetry, memoirs, devotional literature, or reflection who get smuggled into the theological tent in a time when its stakes are reaching ever more widely. Women are also prominent in the ranks of those called systematic or constructive theologians, who make their living by treating the classical texts, revisiting the traditional doctrines, and reworking the inherited expressions.

After Vatican II, Catholicism gave or allowed for (still unordained) new status to the roles of women, including women as teachers of theology. Many would say, better, that women won new status, because much of the leadership yielded dominance only grudgingly and gradually. Still, whoever takes the longer view of Christian history would have to note that the changes of this third of a century have been greater than those made in the rest of the two Christian millennia.

A few women in religious orders and in the laity had been welcomed as observers at the Vatican Council. Some of them spoke there of the frustration gifted Catholic women were experiencing. Not a few of the bishops went home chastened and with a new awareness of past repression and full of resolve to hear the emergent voices of women. Women saw their orders undergo fundamental change, and many seized the moment to be released of their vows and act as laywomen, while laywomen were no longer passive and patient.

Secular feminism also made its mark. As especially young Catholic women pursued graduate studies, they found themselves surrounded by assertive women who questioned the apparent contentment of Catholic women with structures that feminists saw to be unliberated and unliberating. Indeed, one of the main lines of attack against Catholic feminists by churchly opponents is that they were simply hitchhiking on secular bandwagons, or taking advantage of worldly opportunities for women in the professions. Catholic theologians, meanwhile, recovered traditions long obscured, such as the expression of women mystics in medieval times. Or they did some reinterpreting of biblical texts.

If in a decade or two the editors add another generation of theologians to an updated volume, they might well choose Rosemary Ruether as a decisive and representative figure. Trained in historical theology and a specialist on the early church, she remained within Catholicism, if often perceived by conservatives to be at its radical edges. From that posture and position she was able to get a hearing and to unsettle the complacent, as those who left the church and turned into antitheologians—Mary Daly would be representative there—could not do. The situation of Ruether illustrates a main theme in what we are calling particularist theological strands. That is, she did not work in isolation, as an elitist or entrepreneur who simply attracted an academic mandarin following. Tirelessly present at theological societies, academic gatherings, clerical and religious training centers, retreats, conferences, and the like, she and her colleagues chose to be attentive to Catholic texts and traditions and thus to move a people. That is the clue: particularist theology is grounded in the experience of particular peoples, whose life of faith and practice the theologian interprets in the light of a transcendent reference, in this case, of God.

Ruether and her contemporaries quickly perceived that they could not undertake their work without reaching to the center of theological expression, namely God-talk. And while respecting many attributes of God as seen through the ages, they chose not to speak of anything as static as divine attributes. Their God was not a static being, an "It" for theologians to describe. Instead, God was a "Thou," who addressed people in particular situations. The situation of being a woman, be she rich or poor, educated or not, giving birth to children and nurturing them or not, possessed of one set of characteristics or another, was seen as determinative of all the rest that was to be said in theology. This meant that sexual differentiation, usually seen as "gendered," which meant socially constructed, was a fundamental if not *the* fundamental element in the appropriation of faith.

Once the gender question came to be raised, the differentiation was no longer limited only to male-female or masculine-feminine. As various homosexual liberation movements developed in the 1970s, Christian theologians began to reflect on what it meant to be gay, lesbian, bisexual, or whatever. Thus feminist theologian Carter Heyward, a voice in and beyond the Episcopal Church, identified herself as lesbian and worked out frankly lesbian motifs and angles of vision for her Christian faith. Still, numerically and for what it meant for theological tradition, it was feminist gender particularly that attracted the most talent and attention.

Ruether and her compatriot sisters, among them notably Elizabeth Johnson, a highly regarded exemplar, found that one barrier to women's interpretation of Christian faith had been erected because of the almost exclusively male and masculine references and addresses to God. In 1992, Johnson published *She Who Is,* a much-honored book which may have been unsettling to traditionalists but which consistently stayed within the bounds of Catholic discourse and ecclesial boundaries (Johnson is a member of a religious order).

The code word for what was wrong with much of Christian theology was patriarchy. When God was seen in patriarchal terms, argued the feminists, there was little possibility for women to experience full and proper dimensions of liberation and potential. For almost all the feminist particularists, this meant that exclusively male pronouns for God had to be removed or complemented; God came to be seen as Mother as often as Father. There were even debates about the appropriateness of restricting the language of incarnation to Jesus Christ as a male human historic figure. With the change in pronouns and ascriptions, there also came many changes in perceptions of divine activity. For some Catholics this meant going to the roots in biblical texts, as did Elisabeth Schüssler Fiorenza, author of *In Memory of Her: A Feminist Reconstruction of Christian Origins* (1984), one of many feminist revisitations of biblical narrative. She unearthed many events and meanings whose richer nature had been obscured previously, back when questions about them had been asked only from men's points of view in monastery and seminary and then university alike.

Hermeneutics, the name given to technical modes of interpreting the Bible, modes that involved the preconceptions and situations of the interpreter in the tentative conclusions drawn, led many women to indulge in what they called "the hermeneutics of suspicion." They rendered suspect the meanings drawn from scriptures and classical texts by men of the past and present. Thus the Protestant Phyllis Trible dealt as early as 1978 with *God and the Rhetoric of Sexuality.* In respect to the Christian tradition itself, Ruether employed the hermeneutics of suspicion on early Christian texts, typically in *Sexism and God-Talk: Towards a Feminist Theology* (1984). Meanwhile, Sallie McFague, another Protestant—note that one's Catholicism or Protestantism is by no means the most important marker in feminist theology— dealt with the metaphoric character of God-talk, and that this understanding provided more liberty for varied and more meaningful expressions of relation to God.

"Relation" came to be a central term. Many of the women and gay theologians argued that to think of God as "Being," ineffable, objective, distant, "Wholly Other," as the neoorthodox had it, did not do justice to the biblical narratives and metaphors of a God who relates to the people. In this respect, they tended to favor the process theology and the metaphysic behind it that had become a main strand of theological endeavor also among men like John Cobb and Schubert Ogden, who provided leadership through the decades. Typical of this impulse and exposition was the work of Marjorie Hewitt Suchocki, as in her *God, Christ, Church: A Practical Guide to Process Theology* (1982). Here as so often, contributions from the particularisms of feminist theology flowed into theological streams that issued from men, and revealed a transcending of "mere" particularism. Another way to put it: In the earliest stages and among radicals, including some lesbian and some anti-male theologians, revenge against patriarchy and resentment of male hegemony—to use a word in fashion in this period—was often so profound that some feminists used their theology for exclusion, not enrichment. Second-generation feminism has tended to be more inclusive, more open to catholic and cosmopolitan expression, but never uncolored by the hermeneutics of suspicion or the call to revision of basic theological categories.

In sum: Women and homosexual theologians used their gender to explore how historical Christian teaching had often been enslaving, or at least demeaning, and that "the doctrine of man," as it had once been called, often assigned especially stigmatizing roles to women. Free of such stigmas, they turned to God-talk, seeing whether and in what ways the language of the Trinity, Father and Son and Holy Spirit, needed to be challenged. Then came the language of relation. Women's theology, more than much of the traditional theology, dealt with "embodiment," with concrete bodily existence. This is one reason that much of the front rank feminist theology took the form of ethics, especially bioethics, as in the work of Margaret Farley, Lisa Sowle Cahill, and Christine Gudorf, all three exemplars of Catholic reworkings.

Further, we have noted that God is seen as being "in relation" more than unchanging. The neoscholastics and neoorthodox had spoken of God as transcendent, as if God existed in awe-full aloofness from human affairs, but feminist theologies, like many of the liberalisms before them, stressed immanence, God's engagement with the world. Although many, including many women, criticized some feminist theology for downplaying Christology, refusing to see redemptiveness in the "redemptive violence" of Christ's cross, and overstressing self-esteem as a means of finding empowerment, the balance sheet would find women gaining power for self-understanding and relation to God in ways that backlash and reaction are not likely wholly to counter.

2) *Issues of Ethnicity and Race*

A second large cluster of particularisms in theology had to do with what we might call "peoplehood." A case can be made that the identification of theological inquiry with the expression of racial and ethnic experiences vies with the particularities of gendered understandings to make up the principal theological change of the last third of the century. Here the centrifugal and deuniversalizing nature of culture and theology were especially obvious. Like the gendered versions, some of the earliest and enduringly radical theologies of peoplehood, inspired sometimes by post-Holocaust Judaism but, in Christianity, by racial experiences, were exclusive.

Thus "early" James Cone, or Cone in radical moments, to take an example from perhaps the best known of the black or African American theologians, was of an exclusive sort. Not only could one not write theology for blacks unless one *were* black, Cone sometimes went on to imply and even say: Unless you are a black (or member of some other minority, such as Native American), you cannot write true Christian theology at all. Why? Because Christian theology is a theology of liberation, of release from oppression. And whites or majorities in North America were by definition and in the record enslavers, segregators, deprivers, and they had not experienced oppression of the sort from which Christ frees.

More than the feminists, many of whom were Catholic, the overwhelmingly Protestant cohort of black theologians in the first generation had been brought up in neoorthodoxy. Writers like Cone were often seen as being in the tradition of Karl Barth; they had just changed the "color" of his theology of transcendence. When feminists became assertive and found a corollary in what came to be called "womanist" (African American feminist) theology's challenge, Cone and others had to rethink their understandings of the power of God, who looked especially male and patriarchal as the liberator.

The racial and ethnic particularity that situated theology in the experience of peoples was part of a worldwide rejection of colonialism and the rise of new nationalisms (as in Africa) and "tribalisms"—no good word can be found for it—everywhere. Around the world people were moving beyond the domain of Soviet ideology and repression, beyond colonialism, beyond definition by prosperous people of the northern world. Resisting universal definitions, whether of human rights or politics, they withdrew into their own real or presumed tribal circles and experiences. Usually this meant negative and even hostile views of the "other," the neighboring tribe, or the heirs of the earlier exploiters. Theology that justified the various competing racial and ethnic groups rarely found itself adaptable to the need to address the whole "human family," the interests of all sorts of people. This, in the eyes of critics, was a challenge to catholic, universal, inclusive, and reconciling claims of Christian faith and theology. As with feminism, in the course of time the challenge to others was not to see itself as excluded but as potentially enriched, through encounter.

Some of the milder forms of ethnic reaction began to appear in the final third of the century in what was sometimes called "The Ethnic Revival." This had a bearing on, for instance, Catholicism in America. Long seen as homogeneous and stereotyped as monolithic by others, outsiders, and enemies (e.g., Protestants), Catholics did not seem free to acknowledge or expose to view what was a first fact of their life: that they were divided into ethnic groups—that it made a great difference whether one were a Catholic of Irish, Cuban, German, Mexican, Polish, or English descent. But the ethnic revival turned out to have more to do with the decor of life than its substance; to the luxury of cherishing one's own artifacts and inheritances; to "anti-defamation" efforts when one's ethnic group was demeaned. It had political force and cultural weight, but one is hard pressed to name a prominent theological work that reflected on white ethnicity.

In some ways, this form of particularism, therefore, had to do less with white-versus-white ethnicity and more with critiques of white supremacy over all ethnic casts. Theologians in the various racial traditions, while asserting the theological weight of their own experiences, tended to denigrate or reject all others. Native American Vine Deloria, Jr., for instance, came up with pithy and provocative book titles to jar the white supremacist world: *God Is Red* and *Custer Died for Your Sins,* were typical. But not many Native Americans followed in Deloria's train; Indian spirituality had more influence beyond its demographic circle than did Indian theology.

Racially particularist theology, à la James Cone, centered in the experience of the largest minority, African Americans. Here as elsewhere it would be misleading to overportray the role of theology in civil rights and then racial struggles and definitions. Instead, politics, organization, art and music, the charism of leaders apart from their faith, all had their roles. Yet if theology is the interpretation of the life of a people in the light of God, then it can be seen that such interpretation was urgent in the case of peoples being liberated but still suffering segregation and slights in church and world.

Black theology began, as did feminist versions, with a critique of the dominance, hegemony, and near monopoly of white men of European descent in the manufacture of theology. They had been privileged to establish and attend universities and seminaries, and to hold the prestigious chairs, acquire prominent names and reputations, and have access to publishers and communicators. They had spoken in terms of false universals, said their African American and other critics. They took their own privileged experiences and extrapolated on the basis of them in such ways that theology could never be appropriated or developed in the worlds of the poor and the oppressed.

Some of the more radical expressors gained names and were in the limelight as provokers, but did not stay long enough or summon theological energies to become systematic theologians. Here one thinks of the symbolic work of Detroit pastor Albert B. Cleage, Jr., who invented "the Shrine of the Black Madonna," and who developed the language of "God is Black" in the face of unconscious white efforts at monopolizing the color of God. He succeeded, as did the more moderate Joseph R. Washington, Jr., in his later stages, in focusing the black theological theme on the basics, the character of God.

535

James Cone made the earliest and enduring mark as a comprehensive black theologian with *A Black Theology of Liberation* in 1970. This was the book that turned neoorthodoxy against itself after the author had appropriated its themes. But while neoorthodoxy often talked about the liberation of the individual from personal sin, Cone made liberation the cornerstone of his theology. "Revelation" meant something other than expounding a book to black liberationists, with whom Cone sided. He answered no to his own question, one current in the sixties: "Must we Drop God-language?" Instead he advocated a radical hermeneutical reworking of the Christian stories and claims. So his chapter IV:4 had to be "God Is Black" and there must also be, then, a "Black Christ."

Cone's was matched by J. Deotis Roberts' rival work, *A Black Political Theology,* in 1974. It dealt typically with themes one comes to expect upon learning how consistently "black liberation" was seen as the code to the African American canon. Roberts had to be explicit about the way "Ethnicity and Theology" related. His God was a God of power, but also a God of pain and, as Professor Suchocki would have it, of relations. More than most, Roberts tried to show how particular liberation related to universal, if potential, "reconciliation."

At the heart of African American, then Native, Hispanic, and to some extent Asian American theology, is the call to liberation that follows upon the narratives of suffering. The "hermeneutics of suspicion" led the black theologians to question the West's commitment to human rights and equality. Though many of them turned out long and important books, much of the black experience was only immediately experienced, not reflected upon, at least in formal theology.

At present, there are explosions of interest, publications of histories and novels, and expoundings of Native American spirituality and rite, but in retrospect, only Vine Deloria became known in such a way that anthologists of theologians might include him. Similarly, though church leadership emerged in the Hispanic communities, no one gained a voice to represent the particularities of Mexican, Cuban, Puerto Rican, and other ethnic groups, to say nothing of Asian Americans in formal systematic or constructive theological work. Theology associated with the hyphenation of American groups was most regularly represented in the largest of them, African American.

3) *A Particular Species: Liberation, Imported and Native*

"Liberation!" was a key word in both feminist and racial and ethnic–oriented theological movements. But the term came to characterize one particular movement, not native to the United States but imported and influential—the theologies of Latin American provenance, born of the claim that God "has a preferential option for the poor." To most feminists, the God of liberation was a God of liberating power but possessing masculine attributes and being too readily identified with violence. (Many liberation theologies were nonviolent, but in Latin American nations where a prerevolutionary situation prevailed, some of the theologians felt impelled to write theologies legitimating violence.) Feminists withheld some of their judgment and identified with the liberationists, however, because this theology was said to grow up from or be relevant to "base communities" of laymen and laywomen.

To some observers, liberation theology was a movement that came and went within the half-century. By the 1990s, some apologists were writing on themes like "Whatever happened to liberation theology?" or to the effect that liberation theology was not dead—but these were signals that it did not occupy the spotlight it once had. To its critics, from Pope John Paul II to Americans on the political and ecclesiastical right, liberation theology had not been moved simply by biblical prophetic witness to the poor. The fatal taint had come because of its too-ready association with Marxism, a philosophy discredited through the decades and imploded as an ideology with the collapse of the Soviet Union. In reply to such charges, the Liberationists argued that they had used Marxian social views for analysis and critique but not for constructive programs. Such arguments over the content of this theology cannot be settled or even substantially addressed here, but mention must be made of Liberation, whatever its fate, for it is impossible to give an overview of North American theology without doing justice to the southern Americas' contributions to the career of theology.

Like feminist and ethnic or tribal theologies, liberation begins with particularity, with the notion that God relates to peoples, in this case to poor people, not in general or universal ways, but in particular ways. Although many of the theologians held chairs in universities, they contended that the personal involvement and commitment of the theologian to the struggle of the people was vital. Thus they contributed to the "practical theology" outlook of North American theologians who were discontented with mere "book theology." Second, as mentioned, the struggle meant identification with God's poor, who were the privileged in the Kingdom. As a political theology that expected and might exact total commitment and even ultimate sacrifice, it refused to see the poor mired in impotence and passivity. In this proclamation and vision, the poor and oppressed were, and could become even more, agents in the divine economy. This meant that they must be moved by hope. And, like the feminists, the liberationists stressed divine immanence, nearness, particular involvement in particular struggles; God was available and accessible.

Just as the other particular theologies were moved by a sense of release from oppression caused by the Other—the male, the white, the patriarch in power—so liberation had its vision of the enemy, beginning with Christopher Columbus and moving through a gallery and history of exploiters, down to the United States' economic venturers. Someone has said that to have a movement you do not need a God; you only need a devil. Liberation polarized peoples and movements and classes, and tended to demonize the one camp in the theological power equation. (Despite the quip, however, liberation emphatically has a God!)

Liberation theology called into question the churchly consequences of theology and ecclesiology determined by dominators. This meant that it intended to be antihierarchical, eager to establish the power of the hitherto powerless peasants and urban poor. It took some straining, not always without success, by North American theologians like Robert McAfee Brown to translate the word from the context of southern lands to the United States. This nation was not in a prerevolutionary situation in the 1970s. The masses were not sending out signals that they hungered for liberation in theological terms. But Brown and others kept pointing to the "underclass" and those economically deprived in the United States, to victims of an economy that served middle and upper classes well. Liberation influenced and was reproduced by feminists and black theologians, and in some respects is unable to be defined apart from them.

Liberation also provided theology with something it had lacked since the days of Dietrich Bonhoeffer's death for participating in the plots against Hitler: the image of heroism. Eventually on the walls of seminary and university professors there were pictures of Archbishop Oscar Romero, the Salvadoran who was murdered during mass in 1980; of Dom Helder Camara; of Olinda-Recife in Brazil, archbishop for the poor. Others turned to and translated the writings of Gustavo Gutiérrez. In these and other writings, seminary students saw models of activist theologians, interventionists in human struggles.

4) *The Particularity of Public Theology*

Liberation was also used to counter American civil religion, as defined by Robert N. Bellah in 1967 and as perverted, said theological critics, in superpatriotic American religiousness and by its apologists. Increasingly, the critics set out to generate a "public theology" to go with "public religion" in "the public church." Here "public" did not mean political, though it did not ignore the political scene. Rather it referred to the contention that Christian theology should not confine its speaking to the Christian community but should listen to the voices in the public order as well as within the church. Such theology demanded a somewhat different voice than did that directed to the needs and interests of the church and the academy.

Public theology was thus ecumenical and interfaith, having set out to transgress ecclesiastical boundaries and also the boundaries between religious and secular orders. So it seemed to be less particular and more nearly universal than the already mentioned movements and impulses. Critics, however, discerned and claimed that the scope of public theology in every case was limited to the particular experiences of particular nations. Most of American public theology was a reflection on the narratives, texts, and experiences of North Americans, and in the final instance, of the United States. Talk about the human family and human rights was not in conflict with American public theology, but it was not a prime theme. Particularity won again.

The Modes of Theology Congenial to Particularities

All the classical strands of theological inquiry and its varied philosophical backdrops, be they Platonic or Aristotelian, Hegelian or post-Kantian or Deweyite-pragmatic, continued into the period. Many theologians as always were properly to be thought of as philosophical theologians of classical sorts. But it is not to them that one turns when it is time to chronicle the work of a third of a century. Here we must speak of frontiers, horizons, and innovations. Philosophical theology aspires to the general and the universal by resorting to ideas, principles, theories, and contentions.

One school of theology, congenial to the particularisms already mentioned, grew out of their interests and reinforced them. It came to be called narrative theology. That is, in this third of a century there was a revival of interest in story and the meaning of story as a mode of interpreting theology. One reason for this reemphasis may have been inspired by the fact that storytellers were preempting the role systematic theologians had once played. Many believers got their interpretation of the Christian life through imaginative literature—by Flannery O'Connor, John Updike, J. F. Powers, John Cheever, and others—rather than from systematicians and preachers, of influence in midcentury times.

What could be more particular than a theology based on the careful telling of one's own story and the careful listening to that of others, be this in the singular or, more likely, in the plural as the experience of a people? Hence, narrative theology. In the theology that went with medical ethics, the thinkers were less ready to apply principles from Hippocrates or John Stuart Mill to the dying. Instead they listened carefully to the particularity, the unrepeatability and unduplicability of the life of a patient who had to make a decision. This they did by listening to the patient's story through ears sharpened by an awareness of its distinctiveness, even uniqueness.

Some philosophers were themselves inspirations to narrative theologians, among them Alasdair MacIntyre, who despaired of finding "commensurable" universes of discourse for theologians in their apparently anarchic pattern of particularities. He said that the important question was, "To what story do I belong?" Teacher of ethics Stanley Hauerwas was one of the more articulate proponents of narrative theology, as critic of theory, unsettler of ideologies, one who was suspicious of ideology. He believed that Christian systematic theology had to be born of the story of prophets and Jesus, people in the church present or past.

Narrative theology did not mean only spiritual autobiography. It might be effected through recall of narratives, for example biblical ones, that are not exhausted by the life of one reader, a single believer who lives out a life in isolation. The narrative may be someone else's, such as ancient Israel's, or it may be one's own, with full attention to the networks and nexuses of which it is a part. In these enlargements, many theologians paid attention to the way language shapes community. Thus George Lindbeck set forth some outlines of "cultural-linguistic" theology, which is congenial to narrative. Again, the particularizing and centrifugal force was obvious in such a framework. Lindbeck was attentive to the issue of the "language-games" one plays as being the only locales where theology made sense. Then theology is not a set of doctrinal truth claims, as universalists would have it be, but instead communally authoritative rules of discourse, attitude, and action. Lindbeck saw theology on this model as a stay against confusion, because it is not overambitious. His critics saw it as a retreat from universal and reconciling intents and the placing of theology into confinement.

Hermeneutics, Horizons, and Postmodernity

If the theologies that were applied to people in circumstances contributed to the appearance of "mere anarchy" at the outer reaches of centrifugal thrusts, some of the methods used to pursue theology of any sort reinforced the notion. The main strand of pioneering theology in much of the period could be classified as "hermeneutic" in intent. The fact that theologians asked so many questions about interpretation of texts and the problems of interpretation often alienated publics. They chose to get their theology from film and story, from poetry and art and experience, from spiritual adventure. They could not see why it was important to invent so many problems that seemed to have so little to do with their lives, or with God-talk—though the hermeneutical theologians often contended that lives and God-talk were precisely what they were about.

Hermes was the messenger of the gods; bridging from gods to humans always made heavy demands on the messenger or the interpreter. In the last third of this century many American theologians took up Hermes' problem in respect to sacred texts, to purported disclosures of the divine. They took up the problems of relativism, perspective, bias, and subjectivity, pondering why the same text meant so many different things to so many different people (and, in the mood of this chapter, peoples), and so many different things to the same people at different times. Gone, or at least questioned, was the older modern and Enlightenment notion that through fairness, impartiality, objectivity, and the use of reason people of goodwill could come to some agreement or at least to common understandings of their disagreements.

While hermeneutics had been isolated as a theological theme in the nineteenth century by German greats like Friedrich Schleiermacher and Wilhelm Dilthey, it was midcentury continental thinkers like Martin Heidegger and, more recently, Hans-Georg Gadamer, who posed the modern hermeneutical themes. They were taken up by constructive theologians, perhaps most notably by Catholic David Tracy. He was criticized by the narrative particularists for claiming that theology was a task of "critical correlation" between the interpreter who dealt with the classic texts of the Christian tradition and "ordinary" secular experience. But his intent was a large one: To locate the meanings of theology in the heart of the discourse where people fight about and pursue meanings. Tracy tried to teach a generation to be at home with and make the best of "plurality and ambiguity." Texts and symbols did not have and could never have a single set of meanings for all people and peoples. Anarchy and chaos prevailed, said those who saw a false universal aspiration in all this. Revisioning and reconstruction prevailed, said those who saw a positive witness to Christian faith, however tentatively and ambiguously made, in the rough and tumble of pluralism, where no exemptions are made for or privileges given to Christian theologians.

Tracy's kind of hermeneutical theology issued in a call for conversation

541

more than argument. Dogmatic, doctrinal, apodictic theology "argued"; that is, the theologians supporting it "knew" the answer and tried to defeat or persuade the other. Theologians who could live with ambiguity in the midst of pluralities chose conversation, which no one "wins." If argument is guided by the answer, conversation is guided by the question. One converses with the other and, Tracy ingeniously proposes, with the text, which also "speaks" and carries on the conversation. This was chaos, anarchy, said the doctrinaire or the devotee of "language-games" that are to provide order and clarity. Freedom, openness, respect—these are the marks seen by defenders of such a hermeneutical and revisionist approach.

Halfway through this period observers of theology began to speak of the "postmodern" situation. A never fully defined and not always appropriate designation, "postmodern" did point to what were regarded as inevitabilities in a time when centrifugal forces prevailed, cultures lost their center, and Christian theologians had to piece together clienteles and constituencies, rather than take them for granted. The postmodern world confronts all who are in it with a bewildering and yet promising array of options. They can and must pick and choose. Peter Berger wrote at length of "the heretical imperative," thinking of the Greek word *haeresis,* meaning "choice"—thus the theologians interpreted the believers and believing communities that made their way through a pluralist world. They saw them forming montages, collages, pastiches, of Christian and non-Christian options; of dealing with ad hoc instead of sustained patterns of ecumenism; of being unsystematic about systematic theology. Gone was the chaste, disciplined ordering of the modern, as exemplified in the steel skyscraper and the international style of skyscraper design at and after midcentury.

The postmodernist theologians were at home with chaos theory, and interpreted for people who had to live with chaos. Everything was in flux; the center, Yeats was right, did not hold. The patterns were seen to be evolutionary. Behind them was a God of process, not of progress, a God working toward a finished product such as the kingdom of God. Instead of offering clear plots and ensured answers, the postmodern theologian gamely invites the reader or audience to participate in the game.

One strand of postmodern theology has taken a radical, subversive—its friends and enemies alike would say—turn. Some of its roots extend back to figures like Friedrich Nietzsche, who pronounced "the death of God." A short-lived "death of God" theology drew notice in the late 1960s, but is remembered more today as a form of cultural comment than original theological inquiry. However, the "death of God" movement did provide an impetus for this strand of postmodernism, through the work of Thomas J. J. Altizer, Mark Taylor, and a circle of figures who moved from speaking of "the end of God" to "the end of the human" subject. They called into question the authority of all texts, seeing them and their words and concepts as arbitrary signs not firmly connected with any reality. Thus theology was "destabilized," and the critic became as inventive as the poet or prophet, the one who claimed the experience of God or who transmitted a written witness to a revelation.

Earlier theology (Gk.: *theos* + *logos,* language about God) was to have been "centered" in the transcendent subject or object, God. But in this version of postmodern theology there was a "deconstruction" of texts, meanings, significations, and realities in the form of a radical immanence that finds no focus, no center, no subject. To critics the result of this endeavor, which Taylor called "a/theology" was to leave readers or hearers with nothing but games, and religious studies more or less replaced constructive theology and took the form of "play" and arbitrariness. Needless to say, such postmodern theology did not become the language of the churches, to say nothing of the larger public. It stayed within the elite academy—where these articulators came to look like one more "identity-circle" of people who particularized theology in forms that appealed to them but communicated little to outsiders.

At the Horizons of the Particular

Of course, many kinds of theology were in continuity with those that had preceded this period. Philosophical theology, including the scholastic and orthodox styles, endured, though it belonged more in the classroom than in the public and ecclesiastical zones. Ecumenical theology remained, even after Vatican II disrupted the plot of Protestant denominational merger-mindedness. Evangelicalism generated theological systems of the styles that were invented during neoorthodoxy in the mainstream. But one enterprise showed a conscious effort to transcend "mere" particularism.

Here we refer to what is often called theology of dialogue or theology in dialogue. It deals with conversation not across the boundaries of Christian denominations but of the world religions: Judaism, Islam, Hinduism, Buddhism, and the rest. While the *Jihad* pole of *Jihad vs. McWorld* drew Christians into self-enclosed circles of privileged reading and interpretation, the *McWorld* side at least symbolized a world of interaction, as the religions of the world through their adherents bumped into one another, sometimes aggressively, sometimes passively while ignoring one another, and sometimes when setting out to realize their potential as contributors to reconciliation.

Pluralism impelled theologians to ask about the status and destiny of the other, under other Gods. John Cobb, John Hick, Paul Knitter, and their colleagues ventured in dialogue, one of whose rules was that one dare not set out to convert the other. The document *Nostra Aetate* from Vatican II legitimated forms of Catholic dialogue across such boundaries. To a few, usually dismissed as utopians (or dystopians!), the outcome should be a universal religion. The more dialogue continued and the more hermeneutics came into play, the fewer believed that such a "center" could or would or should form. At the opposite extreme were those whose theology was designed to dismiss or devastate the other. Not many could accept the notion that truth lay in a merger of religions, or half way between them.

So it was that more modest participants in dialogue professed to see value in their conversation, in their search for common ground. There were possibilities for reconciliation, they argued, if only people would go so deep in their own traditions that they could meet others in the depth of the exploration of their own. Because of this modesty, even these reachers toward the universal contributed to the postmodern sense that theological interpretation, though it may aspire to the universal, takes root in and strength from its reliance on the particular.

Theologians at the century's end, then, turn over to successors a more satisfying realization of what it means to deal with the other, to be faithful to the particular but not to be lost in an anarchy of private meanings, which could mean in a place where meanings and the search for them would be lost. They have found that their own explorations provide meaning for themselves and for some others. They have not yet worked through all the theological, social, cultural, and spiritual implications of this particularism—or envisioned where it might next go.

Suggested Readings

Thomas Altizer, *Total Presence: The Language of Jesus and the Language of Today* (New York: Seabury Press, 1980).

Rebecca S. Chopp, *The Power to Speak: Feminism, Language, and God* (New York: Crossroad, 1989).

Rebecca S. Chopp and Mark Lewis Taylor, eds., *Reconstructing Christian Theology* (Minneapolis: Fortress Press, 1994).

James H. Cone, *For My People: Black Theology and the Black Church* (Maryknoll, N.Y.: Orbis Books, 1984).

Langdon Gilkey, *Naming the Whirlwind: The Renewal of God-Language* (Indianapolis: Bobbs-Merrill, 1969).

Gustavo Gutiérrez, *A Theology of Liberation* (Maryknoll, N.Y.: Orbis Books, 1973).

Stanley Hauerwas and L. Gregory Jones, eds., *Why Narrative? Readings in Narrative Theology* (Grand Rapids: Wm. B. Eerdmans Publishing Co., 1989).

Carter Heyward, *The Redemption of God: A Theology of Mutual Relations* (Lanham, Md.: University Press of America, 1982).

John Hick and Paul Knitter, eds., *The Myth of Christian Uniqueness* (Maryknoll, N.Y.: Orbis Books, 1987).

Peter C. Hodgson and Robert H. King, *Christian Theology: An Introduction to Its Traditions and Tasks* (Minneapolis: Fortress Press, 1985).

Elizabeth Johnson, *She Who Is* (New York: Crossroad, 1992).

Sallie McFague, *Models of God: Theology for an Ecological, Nuclear Age* (Minneapolis: Fortress Press, 1987).

Rosemary Radford Ruether, *Woman Church: Theology and Practice* (New York: Harper & Row, 1985).

Elisabeth Schüssler Fiorenza, *In Memory of Her* (New York: Crossroad, 1983).

David Tracy, *The Analogical Imagination: Christian Theology and the Culture of Pluralism* (New York: Crossroad, 1981).

NOTES ON THE CONTRIBUTORS

Diane Apostolos-Cappadona is Research Associate, Center for Muslim-Christian Understanding, and Professorial Lecturer in Liberal Studies at Georgetown University, Washington, D.C.

R. Scott Appleby is Associate Professor of History and Director of the Cushwa Center for the Study of American Catholicism at the University of Notre Dame, Notre Dame, Indiana.

Donald S. Armentrout is Professor of Church History and Historical Theology at the School of Theology, University of the South, Sewanee, Tennessee.

William Baird is Professor Emeritus of New Testament at Brite Divinity School, Texas Christian University, Fort Worth, Texas.

William H. Berger is Copastor of the Historic Franklin Presbyterian Church (U.S.A.), Franklin, Tennessee.

Michael L. Birkel is Associate Professor of Religion at Earlham College, Richmond, Indiana.

Jerald C. Brauer is the Frederick W. Bateson Senior Professor in Residence and the Naomi Shenstone Donnelley Professor Emeritus, History of Christianity, at the Divinity School of the University of Chicago, Chicago, Illinois.

Dennis M. Campbell is Professor of Theology at The Divinity School, Duke University, Durham, North Carolina.

Richard L. Christensen is Assistant Professor of Church History at Phillips Theological Seminary, Tulsa, Oklahoma.

Milton J. Coalter is Library Director and Professor of Bibliography and Research at Louisville Presbyterian Theological Seminary, Louisville, Kentucky.

Will Coleman is Associate Professor of Theology and Hermeneutics at Columbia Theological Seminary, Decatur, Georgia.

James H. Cone is Charles Briggs Distinguished Professor of Systematic Theology at Union Theological Seminary, New York, New York.

Joseph Conforti is Professor and Director of American and New England Studies at the University of Southern Maine, Portland, Maine.

Donald A. Crosby is Professor of Philosophy at Colorado State University, Fort Collins, Colorado.

Lawrence S. Cunningham is Professor of Theology and Chair of the Department at the University of Notre Dame, Notre Dame, Indiana.

John Dillenberger is Professor Emeritus in Historical Theology at Graduate Theological Union, Berkeley, California.

Ruth Alden Doan is Associate Professor of History at Hollins College, Roanoke, Virginia.

James O. Duke is Professor of History of Christianity and History of Christian Thought at Brite Divinity School, Texas Christian University, Fort Worth, Texas.

John H. Erickson is Associate Professor of Canon Law and Church History at St. Vladimir's Orthodox Theological Seminary, Crestwood, New York.

John L. Farthing is Pastor of the Redfield United Methodist Church in Redfield, Arkansas, and Professor of Religion and Classical Languages at Hendrix College, Conway, Arkansas.

Ronald B. Flowers is Professor of Religion at Texas Christian University, Fort Worth, Texas.

Gerald P. Fogarty is the William R. Kenan, Jr., Professor of Religious Studies at the University of Virginia, Charlottesville, Virginia.

Albert H. Freundt, Jr., is Professor of Church History at Reformed Theological Seminary, Jackson, Mississippi.

W. Clark Gilpin is Dean of the Divinity School at the University of Chicago, Chicago, Illinois.

C. David Grant is Associate Professor of Religion at Texas Christian University, Fort Worth, Texas.

Arie J. Griffioen is Associate Professor of Religion and Theology at Calvin College, Grand Rapids, Michigan.

Allen Carl Guelzo is the Grace F. Kea Associate Professor of American History at Eastern College, St. David's, Pennsylvania.

Charles E. Hambrick-Stowe is Pastor of Church of the Apostles, United Church of Christ, in Lancaster, Pennsylvania, and Adjunct Professor of Church History at Lancaster Theological Seminary, Lancaster, Pennsylvania.

Robert T. Handy is Henry Sloane Coffin Professor Emeritus of Church History at Union Theological Seminary, New York, New York.

Nancy A. Hardesty is Associate Professor of Religion in the Department of Philosophy and Religion at Clemson University, Clemson, South Carolina.

S. Mark Heim is Professor of Christian Theology at Andover Newton Theological School, Newton Centre, Massachusetts.

John Newton Hewitt is a Tutor in the Political Science Department, The University of Melbourne, Parkville, Victoria, Australia.

Patricia R. Hill is Associate Professor of History and Director of American Studies at Wesleyan University, Middletown, Connecticut.

E. Glenn Hinson is John Loftis Professor of Church History, Baptist Theological Seminary at Richmond, Richmond, Virginia.

Alan D. Hodder is Associate Professor of The Comparative Study of Religion at Hampshire College, Amherst, Massachusetts.

W. Andrew Hoffecker is Professor of Church History at Reformed Theological Seminary, Jackson, Mississippi.

E. Brooks Holifield is the Charles Howard Candler Professor of American Church History at the Candler School of Theology, Emory University, Atlanta, Georgia.

Claude L. Howe, Jr., is Professor Emeritus of Church History at New Orleans Baptist Theological Seminary, New Orleans, Louisiana.

Tyron Inbody is Professor of Theology at United Theological Seminary, Dayton, Ohio.

Evelyn A. Kirkley is Assistant Professor of Theological and Religious Studies at the University of San Diego, San Diego, California.

Robert Kolb is Missions Professor of Systematic Theology and Director of the Institute for Mission Studies (I.M.S.) at Concordia Seminary, St. Louis, Missouri.

Bill J. Leonard is Dean of the Divinity School at Wake Forest University, Winston-Salem, North Carolina.

Charles H. Lippy is the LeRoy A. Martin Distinguished Professor of Religious Studies at the University of Tennessee at Chattanooga, Chattanooga, Tennessee.

Mark A. Lomax is Pastor of The First African Presbyterian Church of Lithonia, Georgia.

Bradley J. Longfield is Associate Professor of Church History at University of Dubuque Theological Seminary, Dubuque, Iowa.

Robin W. Lovin is Dean and Professor of Ethics at Perkins School of Theology, Southern Methodist University, Dallas, Texas.

Dennis P. McCann is Executive Director of the Society of Christian Ethics and Professor of Religious Studies at DePaul University, Chicago, Illinois.

Patricia McNeal is Associate Professor and Director of the Women's Studies Program at Indiana University South Bend, South Bend, Indiana.

George M. Marsden is Francis A. McAnaney Professor of History at the University of Notre Dame, Notre Dame, Indiana.

Martin E. Marty is the Fairfax M. Cone Distinguished Service Professor of the History of Modern Christianity at the University of Chicago, Chicago, Illinois.

Rebekah Miles is Assistant Professor of Christian Ethics at Brite Divinity School, Texas Christian University, Fort Worth, Texas.

Janet Nelson is a doctoral candidate in the Department of Religion at Syracuse University, Syracuse, New York.

Mark A. Noll is McManis Professor of Christian Thought, Wheaton College, Wheaton, Illinois.

Roger E. Olson is Professor of Theology at Bethel College and Seminary, St. Paul, Minnesota.

John B. Payne is Paul and Minnie Diefenderfer Professor of Mercersburg and Ecumenical Theology and Professor of Church History at Lancaster Theological Seminary, Lancaster, Pennsylvania.

Samuel C. Pearson is Professor of Historical Studies at Southern Illinois University at Edwardsville, Edwardsville, Illinois.

W. Creighton Peden is President of the Highlands Institute for American Religious Thought, Highlands, North Carolina, and Fuller E. Callaway Professor Emeritus of Philosophy, The University System of Georgia.

Klaus Penzel is Professor Emeritus of Church History at Perkins School of Theology, Southern Methodist University, Dallas, Texas.

Amanda Porterfield is Professor of Religious Studies and Director of Women's Studies at Indiana University-Purdue University at Indianapolis, Indianapolis, Indiana.

Russell E. Richey is Professor of Church History and Associate Dean for Academic Programs at The Divinity School, Duke University, Durham, North Carolina.

David M. Robinson is Oregon Professor of English and Distinguished Professor of American Literature, Department of English, at Oregon State University, Corvallis, Oregon.

Steven C. Rockefeller is Professor of Religion at Middlebury College, Middlebury, Vermont.

Delores J. Rogers is Associate Minister of Northfield Community Church and Part-Time Instructor in the Religion Department at De Paul University, Chicago, Illinois.

Jack Rogers is Vice President for Southern California and Professor of Theology at San Francisco Theological Seminary, Claremont, California.

John K. Roth is the Pitzer Professor of Philosophy at Claremont McKenna College, Claremont, California.

John Saillant is a Lecturer in the Department of History, Massachusetts Institute of Technology, and an Associate of the W. E. B. DuBois Institute for Afro-American Research, Harvard University, Cambridge, Massachusetts.

Jan Shipps is Professor Emeritus of History and Religious Studies at Indiana University-Purdue University, Indianapolis, Indiana.

James H. Smylie is E. T. Thompson Professor of Church History at Union Theological Seminary in Virginia, Richmond, Virginia.

Winton U. Solberg is Professor Emeritus of American Intellectual and Cultural History at the University of Illinois at Urbana-Champaign, Urbana-Champaign, Illinois.

Susie C. Stanley is Professor of Historical Theology at Messiah College, Grantham, Pennsylvania.

Stephen J. Stein is Chancellors' Professor of American Religious History and Chair of the Department of Religious Studies and Adjunct Professor of History at Indiana University, Bloomington, Indiana.

Bruce M. Stephens is Associate Professor of Religious Studies at the Delaware County Campus of Pennsylvania State University, Media, Pennsylvania.

Mark G. Toulouse is Professor of American Religious History and Associate Dean at Brite Divinity School, Texas Christian University, Fort Worth, Texas.

Darryl M. Trimiew is Associate Professor of Church in Society at Brite Divinity School, Texas Christian University, Fort Worth, Texas.

Kerry S. Walters is Johnson Distinguished Professor of Philosophy at Gettysburg College, Gettysburg, Pennsylvania.

Marilyn J. Westerkamp is Associate Professor of Early American History at the University of California, Santa Cruz, California.

Curtis W. Whiteman is Professor of Historical Theology at Westmont College, Santa Barbara, California.

INDEX